MITCHELL WAITE
Signature Series

OBJECT-ORIENTED PROGRAMMING IN JAVA™

Stephen Gilbert and Bill McCarty

Waite Group Press™
A Division of Sams Publishing
Corte Madera, CA

Publisher: Mitchell Waite
Associate Publisher: Charles Drucker
Acquisitions Manager: Susan Walton
Editorial Director: John Crudo
Project Editor: Andrea Rosenberg
Content Editor: Robert Lafore
Technical Reviewer: Chris Dent
Copy Editor: Jan Jue/Creative Solutions
Production Manager: Cecile Kaufman
Cover Designer: Sestina Quarequio, Karen Johnston, Sandra Schroeder
Interior Designer: Diana Jean Parks
Production Editor: Kelsey McGee
Illustrations: Diana Jean Parks and Iconomics/Margaret Tarleton
Production: Jenaffer Brandt, Michael Henry, Cheryl A. Jackson, Ayanna Lacey, Polly Lavrick, Lisa Pletka

Printed in the United States of America
  98 99 • 10 9 8 7 6 5 4 3 2

Gilbert, Stephen, 1950–
    Object oriented programming in Java / Stephen Gilbert, Bill McCarty.
        p. cm.
    Includes index.
    ISBN 1-57169-086-7
    1. Object-oriented programming (Computer science) 2. Java
(Computer program language) I. McCarty, Bill, 1953–   .
II. Title.
QA76.64.G55   1997
005.2'762—DC21

About the Authors

 Stephen Gilbert teaches computer science at Orange Coast College in Costa Mesa, California. Steve first saw a computer play tic-tac-toe in the summer of 1960 and wanted one of his own thereafter. When he purchased his first machine, a Vic-20 (which he subsequently trained to play an unbeatable game), his life took a sudden turn after years spent as a carpenter, chicken picker, and offset-press operator. Since then, he has been a programmer and systems designer for DRI Management Systems of Newport Beach, as well as for other clients in California, Oregon, and Washington. An advocate of life-long learning, Steve holds a B.S. degree in Business Computer Methods, an M.S. degree in Applied Computer Science and Technology, and is working—endlessly—on his Ph.D. at the Claremont Graduate School. Having long ago given up his ambition to become a professional surfer, he can be found sitting on the Newport Beach pier with his wife, Kathleen, or his children, Judah and Hosanna, whenever the surf's up.

 Bill McCarty teaches computer science at Azusa Pacific University. He holds a B.S. in Computer Science and a Ph.D. in Information Systems, the latter conferred by the Claremont Graduate School. Bill learned to write computer programs using the IBM 1130 while still a high school student back in the days of the IBM model 026 keypunch. Although on cold days he misses the warmth provided by the 026's vacuum tubes, he finds Southern California winters, for the most part, bearable. He survives them by reading and by writing software in the cheery solitude of his condo, which he shares with his wife, two children, three cats, and an unknown number of software bugs.

Contents

Table of Contents

Acknowledgments

Stephen Gilbert: It's certainly hard to acknowledge the people who helped make a book like this possible without sounding like the part of an Academy Awards acceptance speech where most people go into the kitchen for a snack or switch over to the Home Shopping Channel. Nevertheless, it's important that we, as authors, let those whose work, dedication, or inspiration brought about the current volume know that their efforts and influence did not go unnoticed.

First, I'd like to thank the people who offered me professional encouragement: Shin Karasuda, who taught me to program; Earl "Duke" Olrich, who continually offered me challenging assignments; and Eric Stewart, who (thankfully) never believed me when I said, "That can't be done."

Second, I'd like to thank those who believed that I could teach programming and who gave me the opportunity to try: Dr. Michael Godfrey, who first challenged me to become a teacher, and later asked why I didn't "write a book with all that object-oriented stuff in it;" Dr. Bill McCarty, who first recommended me for a teaching position at APU and who always has some crazy scheme in mind; and Professor Wendel Scarborough, who was both a mentor and a friend as I began my teaching career.

Finally, I'd like to thank those without whom programming or writing or teaching would have no meaning at all: my wife Kathleen, who held our family (and me) together during the endless writing and re-writing; my parents Dean and Jean Gilbert, who offered only encouragement to a son who could not decide what to do when he grew up; and to the Lord Jesus Christ, the true center of my life and family.

Bill McCarty: Finishing anything is an achievement and finishing a book is more than an achievement: It is a relief. Chief among those relieved by completion of this book are my wife, Jennifer, and my children, Patrick and Sara, who for over six months bore the real birth pangs of this work.

Many others have unknowingly lent a hand through their encouragement or assistance. My eighth-grade English teacher, Mr. Frisina, taught me things about language and writing about which no subsequent teacher, even in University, seemed aware. My dissertation committee, particularly Dr. Lorne Olfman and Dr. Paul Gray, helped me to see my writing through readers' eyes. My department chairman for more than five years, Wendel Scarbrough, demonstrated time after time how the enthusiastic pursuit of progress was both necessary and fun.

More thanks than I can express are due my co-author, Stephen Gilbert, who did all the really hard work, and with whom I look forward to writing many further, although shorter, books. Most significant in sustaining me now and in the future is my Advocate with the Father, the Lord Jesus Christ, who gave Himself that I might live and whom I serve unworthily but enthusiastically. To Him be all glory, forever and ever.

Stephen Gilbert and Bill McCarty: We're both grateful to the Waite Group family for capably shepherding two tenderfoots through the brambles of first authorship. Waite Group's former acquisition team members Joanne Miller and Jill Pisoni helped us put our book idea into a form that others could understand and contributed helpful ideas. Publisher Mitch Waite expressed confidence in our ability to do what we planned, leading us to think he might be right. Project Editor Andrea Rosenberg kept us on track, held the team together, and taught us much about the writing process. Technical Reviewer Chris Dent found both the obvious and the subtle problems in the text and examples. Any errors were added by us after his review.

Special thanks are due Content Editor Robert Lafore, who found the problems we knew about but hoped no one would notice, as well as other problems we somehow missed. Robert's gift for seeing what the reader sees is one we greatly envy. We are grateful for his contribution to this book but even more grateful to have had the opportunity to meet him and work with him.

Foreword

Difficult as it may be for some people to believe, there are computer languages that are just plain fun. Java is surely at the top of this list. On the one hand, it eliminates many of the things that make other languages less than amusing, such as pointers and the `printf()` function. On the other, it enables you to do powerful things simply and easily, such as writing full-scale Graphical User Interface (GUI) programs, complete with buttons and dialog boxes. Once you've worked with it for a while, it's hard not to feel affection for Java.

And yet, until recently it's been hard to find a beginner's programming book that captures this spirit of fun that's so much a part of Java. Textbook writers tend to forget that readers are people first and programmers second. Their typical "just the facts" approach can put even the most dedicated reader into a prolonged snooze.

With the book you hold in your hands, Steve Gilbert and Bill McCarty change that. *OOP in Java* is amusing, irreverent, and innovative. Where else could you follow the adventures of those lovable pachyderms, Jumbo and Brenda, as they try to turn their coffee shop, Jumbo's Jungle Java Joint, into a profitable business, using the latest in Java software? Their sometimes cooperative, sometimes acrimonious relationship is a saga in itself. There is also a wealth of imaginative descriptions. How is a computer program like and unlike an orange-juice squeezing machine? Why is ordering a pizza like invoking a method? What are the five fingers of death?

But *OOP in Java* is not merely fun to read. It systematically and authoritatively covers everything you need to know to become a full-scale Java programmer. Unlike many books, it starts from the beginning, explaining where Java fits into the history of programming. It explains object-oriented programming in a clear and convincing way, and in general keeps the reader oriented about how each topic fits into the big picture. The program examples are easy to follow, and there are plenty of figures.

Although it's aimed at people learning their first computer language, this book also works well for more experienced programmers. It answered many questions (such as the mysteries of user input in console mode) for which I had not been able to find answers in other books.

If you want to learn Java, and have a good time doing it, you've come to the right place.

Robert Lafore

Best-selling author
of such books as
C++ Interactive Course

Introduction

Why another book on Java? We wrote this book to teach beginning programmers the simple but powerful Java language as their first programming language. As programmers, we found the Java language not only useful, but fun. As teachers, we wanted to share this fun with our students. Unfortunately, most books on the Java language either assume the reader is already familiar with C++ or another object-oriented language, or don't present enough of the Java language to enable the reader to really learn how to program.

If you want to learn to program, either through self-study or classroom study, then this book is for you. Using Java, it teaches the basics of object-oriented programming without assuming any significant student preparation or background. We have used drafts of the book to successfully teach both introductory undergraduate courses and graduate courses. To assist the beginning reader, it introduces concepts gradually and with many figures and examples. However, the book also covers the Java language and its APIs (application programming interfaces) comprehensively and so can be profitably used as well by the more advanced reader, who can simply skip over familiar concepts and chapters. Questions and programming exercises at the end of each chapter give important feedback on progress and facilitate classroom use of the book.

What Does This Book Contain?

This book presents everything you need to know to develop network-aware Java programs. The book moves from simple material covering the basics of programming and object-oriented software to relatively advanced material on graphical user interfaces and networking. Beginning readers should read the chapters in sequence, but intermediate or advanced readers can begin at any appropriate chapter.

Chapter 1: What's All This Java Stuff?

This chapter explains why Java is important and introduces the history of computer programming and basic programming concepts. It also explains enough about HTML to enable you to create simple Web pages that contain Java applets.

Chapter 2: Programs: The Community of Objects

This chapter presents the basic concepts of object-oriented programming including classes, objects, and messages. By the time you've finished, you'll be able to create your own simple Java applets.

Chapter 3: The Atomic Theory of Objects: Working with Object Attributes

This chapter introduces Java's primitive (non-object) types and the operators that manipulate primitive values. It also explains literals, constants, and variables. When you've completed the chapter, you'll be able to use Java to perform simple calculations and conversions.

Chapter 4: Simply Methods: One Step at a Time

This chapter focuses on methods and messages. When you've finished it, you'll know how to create your own messages and the methods that handle them. You'll also be able to use a variety of Java's built-in objects to create simple graphical user interfaces.

Chapter 5: Making Choices: Teaching Your Objects About True and False

This chapter introduces the concepts of program flow of control and the selection statements `if`, `if-else`, and `switch`. It also teaches you about the boolean type and the conditional operators. Once you've mastered this chapter, your programs will be capable to make decisions, taking different actions based on input.

Chapter 6: Teaching Your Objects to Repeat Themselves

This chapter covers iteration and the looping statements `while`, `do-while`, and `for`. When you've finished, you'll be able to create programs that search or that process several batches of data, rather than a single batch.

Chapter 7: Testing and Debugging: When Things Go Wrong

This chapter gives techniques and hints for dealing with programs that don't work right. Once you've learned these, you should be able to cope with both compile-time and run-time errors.

Chapter 8: Flocking Objects: Arrays and Exceptions

This chapter covers arrays, which are used to group several variables into a single unit. The chapter also covers exceptions, a device used by Java to inform you that something unexpected has happened during program execution. When you've completed the chapter, you'll be able to use arrays to store program data for convenient access.

Chapter 9: Teams of Classes: Using Classes Together

This chapter introduces more advanced concepts of object-oriented programming, as multiple cooperating classes are used to create a single program. When you've finished, you'll know how to effectively organize larger programs.

Chapter 10: Inheritance: Object Families

This chapter focuses on the use of inheritance to create reusable classes. When you've completed this chapter, you'll be able to create software components that you can use again and again.

Chapter 11: Jumpin' Java: Menus, Graphics, Sound

Having learned the basics of object-oriented programming in Java, you're ready to learn more details about the many useful classes provided by Java's application programming interface. This chapter and the remaining chapters present the application programming interface, including the abstract window toolkit (AWT), the input-output classes, the data structure and utility classes, and the thread and network classes.

This chapter introduces the AWT, showing you how to create menus, how to draw lines and figures, and how to add sound to your programs. When you've finished, you'll be able to create attractive and dynamic Java applets and applications.

Chapter 12: The AWT: Containers, Components, and Layout Managers

This chapter continues the explication of the AWT begun in Chapter 11, presenting each of the AWT components and showing how to place them in containers and handle the events they generate. Java's layout managers are also presented in detail, enabling you to create powerful graphical user interfaces for your Java programs.

Chapter 13: Advanced AWT

This chapter presents additional object-oriented facilities of Java, including abstract classes and interfaces. These are used to support the advanced features and facilities of the AWT, including printing, advanced event handling, and component customization, which are also presented in this chapter. When you're finished with this chapter, you'll be able to extend the AWT to include essentially any needed capability.

Chapter 14: Streams and Files

This chapter presents Java's input-output classes, showing you how to read and write streams and files. When you've finished, you'll be able to store data from your Java programs on your computer's hard drive or diskettes.

Chapter 15: Data Structures and Utility Classes

This chapter presents the useful data structure and utility classes provided by Java, including stacks, vectors, and bitsets. It also covers the linked list data structure, which can be built without special library support. When you've completed this chapter, you'll be fluent in using collections to store program data.

Chapter 16: Advanced Topics: Threads and Networking

This chapter presents two of Java's most advanced capabilities: threading and networking. When you've finished with this chapter, you'll be able to create client-server programs that communicate between networked computers.

Appendix A

Appendix B

System and Software Requirements

Although Java runs on a wide variety of platforms, this book is geared to the needs of the MS Windows 95 user. This makes it possible to explain the operating system commands used to invoke the various Java tools and to give examples that closely match what readers can expect to see on their own systems.

The CD-ROM

The CD-ROM includes the Java Developer's Kit (JDK) versions 1.0.2 and 1.1.2, along with all the listings from the book. The CD-ROM is organized using a distinct directory for each chapter, to make it easy to locate a particular example. Separate directories on the CD-ROM contain a second version of each listing that uses only the Java 1.0 language and API features, allowing the examples to be run under either version 1.0 or 1.1. Note that the source code for the version 1.0 listings is generally different from that included in the text.

To install the JDK, simply follow the instructions on the CD-ROM. Be sure to check the read-me file for special information.

HTML Browsers

At the time this book was written, no HTML browser supported the 1.1 version of the Java language and API. Screen shots of HTML pages were prepared using Netscape Navigator version 3 or MS Internet Explorer version 3, executing the 1.0 version code included on the CD-ROM.

Browsers capable of supporting version 1.1 are expected to be available by the time of publication of this book or shortly thereafter. You should obtain the latest possible release of your browser (for example, Sun HotJava, Netscape Navigator, or MS Internet Explorer) in order to run the applets on the CD-ROM.

If you cannot yet obtain a browser that supports Java 1.1, you have two options. First, you can use the appletviewer program included on the CD-ROM with the JDK. However, appletviewer will not allow you to view the HTML text and graphics that surround Java applets in many examples in the text. Alternatively, you can use a browser that supports Java 1.0 and view the examples on the CD-ROM that use only the Java 1.0 language and API features. This will allow you to view all the text and graphics, but the program source code will be somewhat different than that presented in the text.

Java Versions

The text of this book was prepared using JDK 1.1 beta 2. Changes to the Java language and its APIs may have occurred subsequent to that version. The CD-ROM has been updated with program listings that conform to the latest language and API specifications available immediately prior to publication. The reader should consult the CD-ROM and the official Java Web site at `http://www.javasoft.com` for the latest possible information.

A Note to Teachers

Why should you consider teaching Java as a first programming language, rather than BASIC, Pascal, C++, or Scheme? While much of the excitement and interest surrounding Java focuses on its use as a language for programming Internet applications, we are exited about Java because we think it has several advantages over other languages for teaching programming.

First, Java is object-oriented from the ground-up. None of us teaching structured programming would first show students how to use the goto and only later teach selection and iteration. None of us teaching about functional decomposition would encourage students to first write huge monolithic, sequential programs before teaching them about procedural abstraction. All of us have shared the frustration of students who have been forced to unlearn the bad habits of their earlier training. In the same vein, we find it easier for students to learn object-oriented principles when they deal with the concepts of classes, objects, attributes, and methods as foundational principles rather than add-ons grafted onto a procedural framework.

A second advantage that Java offers over its competitors is the standardized, cross-platform, graphical-user-interface library, the Abstract Windowing Toolkit (AWT). Beginning programmers today have higher expectations than previous generations. If you doubt that, try handing your beginning students a stack of punched cards on which to write their first program. Today's novice expects to learn to write programs that look like the programs they work with every day. In this day and age, that means GUI programs.

Much of the criticism of Java has focused on the shortcomings of the AWT, especially when compared to the rich, platform-specific functionality provided in the native GUI libraries available. For teaching, however, we think that the AWT hits the spot:

- It is very easy to use and to grasp, even for beginning programmers, who can add `Buttons` and `Labels` to their programs with only a single line of code. Other native libraries such as the Win32 API, the Mac Toolbox, or versions of the X Window system are not really suitable for this purpose. More important, however, neither are the GUI frameworks, such as MFC, MacApp, or OWL, that provide wrappers around these APIs.

- Unlike proprietary GUI frameworks developed just for teaching, students can continue to use the AWT as they move into the real world.

- The binary cross-platform capabilities of the AWT allow students to see the practical advantages and limitations of writing portable programs from the beginning.

The third major advantage we see in Java is that it is a language that can be used throughout the computer science curriculum, in data-structures, telecommunications, and system programming classes. Java's inclusion of built-in networking, threads, and graphics capabilities mean that Java will not be a throw-away first language, one students will need to abandon once they move on to more advanced topics.

The final advantage Java offers is that it facilitates learning interface before implementation. When teaching students to drive, we don't first teach them how to do a tune-up. Instead, we teach them how to operate an automobile, using its interface: the steering-wheel, the accelerator, and the brake. In the same way, in this book students first learn to use existing classes such as `Label` and `Button` to create objects and to manipulate those objects by sending them messages. Only then do they peer inside and look at the actual implementation: data-types, sequence, and selection. Knowing how to create and use objects provides the necessary context for the lower-level construction details.

NOTE: Some of the software included on the bundled CD-ROM, including WinEdit and WinZip, is shareware, provided for your evaluation. If you find any of the shareware products useful, you are requested to register it as discussed in its documentation and/or in the About screen of the application. Waite Group Press has not paid the registration fee for this shareware.

1

What's All This Java Stuff?

Unless you have had the good fortune to spend the last year hidden away on some exotic south-seas isle, you've probably heard about Java. It has been written up in the *Wall Street Journal* and talked about on the TV network news. You may be wondering what Java is all about. In this chapter you'll find some answers, but here's a short version from the creators of Java:

Java is a simple, object-oriented, distributed, interpreted, robust, secure, architecture-neutral, portable, high-performance, multithreaded, and dynamic programming language.

If your response was "Huh?" don't feel bad. At the end of this chapter we'll talk briefly about what this techno-jargon means, but unless you are in the business of collecting cool and incomprehensible words, you just need to know that Java is a computer language you can use to write programs that will run on many different makes and models of computers.

One exciting aspect of Java is that you can use it to write programs that can then be distributed automatically over the World Wide Web. Users who want to run your SuperSpiffoDoItAll program no longer have to trot to ProgramLand to pick up a copy—they can run it directly from your Web page. And, when you come out with version 2—ReallySuperSpiffoDoItAllAndMore—you don't have to send out upgrade notices to all your customers. Every time they connect, they will automatically have the latest version.

If your response to all this is "Huh?" again, don't worry. You've come to the right place. This is the chapter where you'll get answers to these questions:

- What are the basic parts of a computer and how do they work?

- What are programming languages and where did they come from?

- What are object-oriented programming and structured programming, and how do they differ?

- What are the Internet and the World Wide Web?

- What is Java and how is it used to create programs that work anywhere?

But that's not all. In addition to learning the answers to these exciting questions, you will also gain an invaluable skill. In this chapter, as an added bonus, you will receive an extra programming language! Yes, that's right. In addition to learning Java, you will learn how to write programs in HTML (pronounced "H-T-M-L"—don't try doing this with your mouth full), the language used to create your own Web pages. You will learn

- How to create a Web page using HTML

- How to use tags to create headings and to emphasize your text

- How to add colorful pictures to your page

- How to make your pages come alive by adding a Java *applet*—a program that runs whenever someone views your page

Ready? Let's get started!

Programming: What's It All About?

Starting out, you'll need to know something about computers and programming. If you're already familiar with these concepts, you may wish to skip ahead to the section titled "OOP Versus Oops!" and read about the basic ideas of *object-oriented programming* (OOP). Of course, if you're already familiar with OOP, you may want to skip that section as well, moving ahead to the material on the World Wide Web and HTML. On the other hand, if this is your first exposure to programming, don't fret over the details. The first part of this chapter is simply an overview, the big picture.

IN THE BEGINNING...

Long ago, in a galaxy far away, there were no computer programs. Actually it wasn't that long ago or that far away. *Programming*—telling a computer what to do—is a very young art. From the invention of the modern digital computer in the late 1940s to now, the way that computers are programmed has changed considerably. These changes have occurred for one principal reason: Computer programs have continually gotten bigger, and bigger programs are harder to write, understand, and change.

Before computer languages, there was just the machine. It's not important which machine was first—ENIAC, the Mark-1, or even the Babbage/Lovelace Inference Engine. What is important is that people built machines that could follow instructions. Although these early machines were primitive, they all had three main pieces. The computers we use today still have the same three pieces:

Memory—This is a place to store the information you want to work on: the column of numbers to add or that note to your beloved. Unfortunately, your computer doesn't have any way to tell which is which. There are no little filing cabinets for tax receipts or love letters inside that box on your desk.

Memory inside a computer is composed entirely of a long line of electronic on-off switches. Each of these switches is called a *bit,* and each bit can "remember" exactly one piece of information: whether it's on or off. Each of these bits is located at a unique location, so you can give your computer commands such as "Turn off the bit at location 178395," or "Tell me whether bit 732834 is on." The sidebar "Bits, Bytes, and Hex" provides some insight into how these bits can be arranged and manipulated. The magic of digital computers is that, given such a simple memory scheme, they can be used to build spreadsheets and word processors and virtual-reality programs. This is largely the work of the CPU.

BITS, BYTES, AND HEX

Modern computers have a *lot* of memory. This memory is composed of a long line of transistors, each of which can be in either of two states. This means that computer memory can deal directly only with the numbers 0 and 1. That might not seem useful, but by combining many 0s and 1s, your computer is able to represent numbers, words, images, and sounds. How? The secret is the *binary* number system.

You probably remember from school that all numbers have a base. Or maybe you don't. In any case, the *base* of a number system is the number of digits that exist in the number system being used. Humans normally use a base 10 number system, which has 10 digits: 0 through 9. Many people believe that humans use the base 10 system because they have 10 fingers. On the other hand (pun intended), computers are built by use of binary memory elements that can hold only one of two possible values. Computers count using the base 2, or binary, number system.

When computer scientists first began programming computers, their programs were entered in binary, using 0s and 1s. Programming in binary involves writing a *lot* of 0s and 1s. It wasn't long before someone discovered that it was simpler to deal with *groups* of 0s and 1s. The most common grouping used today takes 8 bits and puts them together. These 8 bits are called a *byte.* (And believe it or not, half of a byte is called a *nybble.* Computing pioneers certainly had a sense of humor.) A byte is important

Continued...

BITS, BYTES, AND HEX Continued...

because most locations (*addresses*) inside the computer are specified by use of bytes rather than bits. If you were to address memory on a bit-by-bit basis, the numbers would simply be too large for you to deal with conveniently.

Another important grouping uses 3 bits. Because a group of 3 bits can represent a number from 0 to 8, this system resembles the base 8 number system. This is called the *octal* system, and it was the dominant number system used in computer programs for many years.

In recent years, a number system based on 4-bit groups has become more widely used. This number system, called *hexadecimal*, uses 16 *digits*—the numerals 0 through 9, and the letters *A* through *F* (or *a* through *f*). High-level languages such as Java allow you to ignore these alternate number systems, but as you learn the language, you might notice remnants of this earlier age. If so, you'll now have some idea of where they came from. Figure 1-1 shows the relationship between bits, bytes, octal, and hexadecimal numbers.

CPU—The second part of the hardware triad is the *central processing unit*, which is the unit that processes information stored in memory and carries out programming instructions. Today you would generally call it a *chip*, because most modern CPUs—such as Intel's Pentium or Motorola's PowerPC—are built by use of a single integrated circuit, which is manufactured on a single piece or chip of silicon. The CPU processes its information by using a set of built-in commands. These built-in commands, called the *instruction set*, are a

FIGURE 1-1

Bits, bytes, octal, and hex

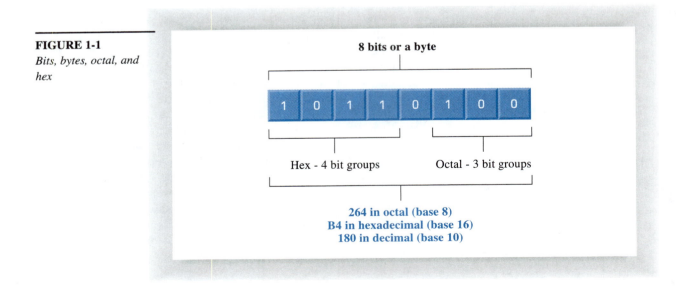

8 bits or a byte

| 1 | 0 | 1 | 1 | 0 | 1 | 0 | 0 |

Hex - 4 bit groups   Octal - 3 bit groups

264 in octal (base 8)
B4 in hexadecimal (base 16)
180 in decimal (base 10)

numerical language that is different for every CPU. The Pentium uses one instruction set, and Sun's SPARC CPU uses another. As a group, these numerical languages are called *machine languages*, because each is the native language of some computer.

I/O—The last part of your computer is a unit for getting information in and out of the computer. Your computer normally uses a video monitor and sometimes a printer to produce *output*. Output is how the computer speaks to you. To tell the computer to do something, you use your keyboard or mouse. This is called *input*, and input is how you speak to the computer.

The Stone Age

How do you tell your computer what to do? The first computers did not really have programs in the sense of today's programs. With these machines, the instructions for the CPU were entered into the computer by plugging a myriad of wires into carefully selected jacks on plug-boards—a difficult, time-consuming, and error-prone process. Setting up a program on the ENIAC, one of the first electronic computers, took a team of five people at least two days. You can almost hear them saying, "There has to be a better way." Well, there was.

John von Neumann realized that the instructions for solving a problem could be stored in the computer's memory along with the data that the instructions worked on. The instructions stored in memory were called *stored programs* and later just *programs*. This invention made it much simpler to set up the computer to solve a new problem. Rather than shifting hundreds or thousands of wires, the program could be entered into memory by use of a typewriter-like keyboard, or even loaded from paper tape or from the same kind of punched cards that were used for census tabulation.

Early computer programmers had to write instructions in the language that their machines understood—the native code usually known as machine language. These programs were composed of a long string of the 0s and 1s which made up—and still make up—the internal language of digital computers. To write a program in machine language, programmers had to go through three steps:

1. The programmer had to devise a strategy to solve the particular problem, such as sorting a collection of numbers or searching a collection of numbers for a given value. This strategy is called an *algorithm*. An algorithm simply gives the steps needed to solve a particular problem.

2. The programmer had to translate the logical steps necessary to solve the problem into precise instructions that the computer could carry out. These were very basic instructions, for example, loading a value into a certain location, multiplying that value by another, and storing the result at some other location.

3. These operations were translated into their numerical equivalents—*op-codes*. Only at this point could the program be keyed into the computer. Look at Figure 1-2 to get an idea of the process.

FIGURE 1-2

Programming in machine language: the programmer does all the translation

By modern standards, these programs were somewhat primitive. Though small, they quickly became complex. As the ambition of their creators soared, the limitations of machine language became apparent.

There were two major problems with machine language. First, the program instructions referred directly to the components of the computer. When a different CPU was used or memory was organized differently, the program would not work and needed to be rewritten. You may have experienced this if you ever purchased a new computer that uses a different CPU from your old computer—your old programs may not run on the new computer. Because a given machine language applies only to a specific CPU, we say that machine language is inherently *nonportable*.

The second problem with machine-language programs was they were tedious to write, incomprehensible to read, and, once the programs reached a certain size, too complex to be enhanced or extended.

The Second Generation

In the early 1950s, there were several attempts to solve these problems. The first attempts attacked the problem of incomprehensibility. "Why not," these early computer scientists thought, "put the computer itself to work doing all this repetitive stuff?" *Assembly languages* allowed programmers to refer to instructions and data by using descriptive names, making programs much easier to understand. However, each assembly-language instruction was translated into exactly one machine-language instruction, so the programmer still had to think like the computer to write a program in assembly language. Figure 1-3 shows how assembly languages took some of the drudgery out of programming.

The second failing of machine language, its nonportability, was also addressed during the early 1950s. With the development of *virtual machine languages* and program *interpreters*, programmers could write assembly-language instructions for an "ideal" machine. These pseudo-instructions would then be interpreted (expanded into machine language) by the computer when the program actually ran. While this code ran substantially slower—about 50 times slower than machine language—the programmers became much more productive, because they didn't have to rewrite their programs every time the hardware folks made a change to the CPU. Two famous interpreters were John Mauchly's Short-Code on the UNIVAC I (1950) and the Speedcoding system developed by John Backus for the IBM 701 (1953). Figure 1-4 shows how these virtual assembly languages worked.

These new languages weren't without their detractors. The old-timers (who had been writing computer programs for all of a year or two) said, "Short-Code is too slow. The best programs will *always* be written in machine language!" Grace Hopper took these complaints to heart. "Why can't we put the computer to work expanding our Short-Code programs into machine language *before* we let the computer run it?" she asked. Her invention became known as the program *compiler*. Using a compiler, programmers could have the productivity gain of writing Short-Code. The compiler program would translate the Short-Code into a machine language program. This *executable* program could then run at full speed, because the translation was already complete. Figure 1-5 illustrates the programming process using a pseudocode compiler.

FIGURE 1-3

Programming in assembly language

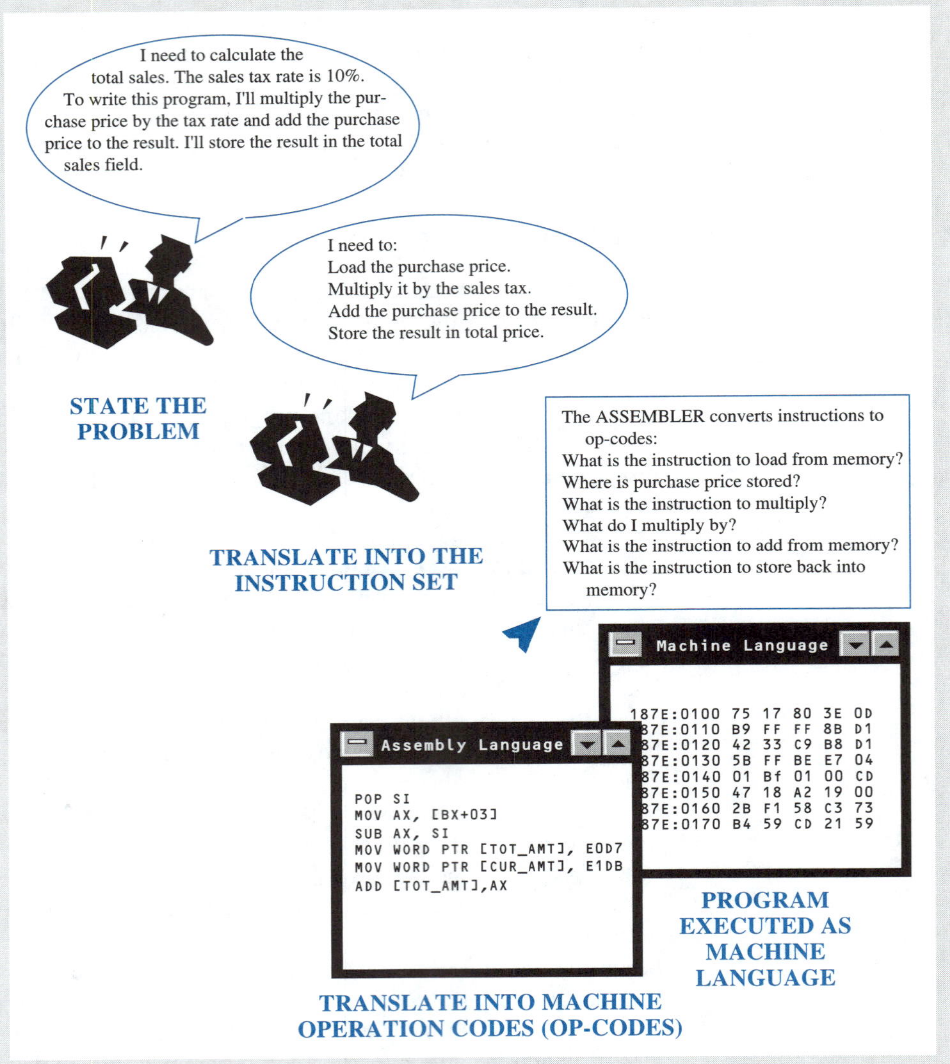

I need to calculate the total sales. The sales tax rate is 10%. To write this program, I'll multiply the purchase price by the tax rate and add the purchase price to the result. I'll store the result in the total sales field.

I need to:
Load the purchase price.
Multiply it by the sales tax.
Add the purchase price to the result.
Store the result in total price.

STATE THE PROBLEM

The ASSEMBLER converts instructions to op-codes:
What is the instruction to load from memory?
Where is purchase price stored?
What is the instruction to multiply?
What do I multiply by?
What is the instruction to add from memory?
What is the instruction to store back into memory?

TRANSLATE INTO THE INSTRUCTION SET

```
Machine Language

187E:0100 75 17 80 3E 0D
87E:0110 B9 FF FF 8B D1
87E:0120 42 33 C9 B8 D1
87E:0130 5B FF BE E7 04
87E:0140 01 Bf 01 00 CD
87E:0150 47 18 A2 19 00
87E:0160 2B F1 58 C3 73
87E:0170 B4 59 CD 21 59
```

```
Assembly Language

POP SI
MOV AX, [BX+03]
SUB AX, SI
MOV WORD PTR [TOT_AMT], E0D7
MOV WORD PTR [CUR_AMT], E1DB
ADD [TOT_AMT],AX
```

PROGRAM EXECUTED AS MACHINE LANGUAGE

TRANSLATE INTO MACHINE OPERATION CODES (OP-CODES)

FIGURE 1-4
*Virtual assembly-
language interpreters*

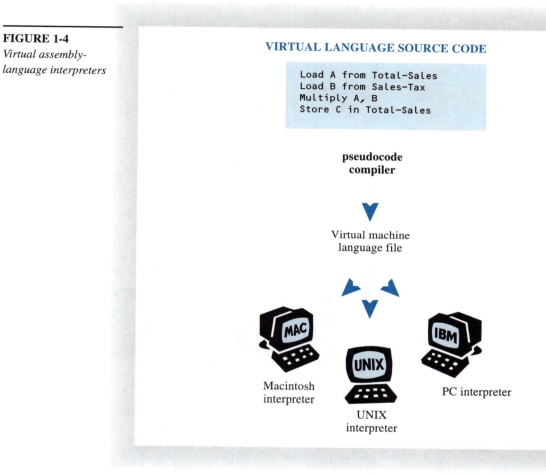

VIRTUAL LANGUAGE SOURCE CODE

```
Load A from Total-Sales
Load B from Sales-Tax
Multiply A, B
Store C in Total-Sales
```

**pseudocode
compiler**

Virtual machine
language file

Macintosh
interpreter

UNIX
interpreter

PC interpreter

FIGURE 1-5

*Virtual assembly-
language compilers*

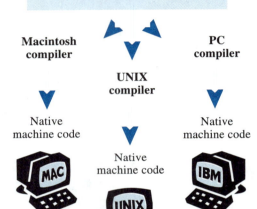

The Third Generation

Programmers used interpreters, compilers, and assemblers to develop programs that were larger and more complex than any before. As programs became larger and more complex, they also became harder to write, understand, fix, and change. Sound familiar? Programming had come full circle and was ripe for another change. That change came in the form of *high-level languages*.

   The idea of a high-level language is simple. If programs are too complex because humans don't think in computer language, let's break programming into two parts. Let's write programs in a language that is understandable, rather than in a language that looks like the computer's instruction set. Let's use a language that models the problem to be solved. Then another program can be used to translate the first program into the machine language the computer understands, just as with Speedcode and Short-Code.

Four major high-level languages were developed in the mid-to-late 1950s:

FORTRAN—the Formula Translator—was designed by John Backus at IBM, starting in 1954. This language let engineers and scientists write programs that looked a lot like the formulas they were used to dealing with.

COBOL—the Common Business Oriented Language—was developed beginning in 1959 by a consortium that included the U.S. Department of Defense (DOD). The developers of COBOL had two major goals. First, they wanted the language to look like English so programmers could easily describe common business operations. Second, they wanted the language to be *portable*. The DOD purchased computers from many vendors and wanted to make sure that the payroll system that ran on the computer at Fort Mead would also run on the machines at Fort Bragg, for example.

ALGOL—the Algorithmic Language—was a general-purpose language developed by a consortium in Europe, starting in 1958. At that time, IBM considered FORTRAN to be a proprietary language that could run only on IBM hardware. As a result, the Europeans decided to create an alternative language. ALGOL introduced many programming language features that are still being used today.

LISP—the List Processing language—was developed at MIT by John McCarthy in 1958. Based on lambda calculus rather than algebra as the other languages had been, LISP remains today the preferred language for artificial-intelligence programs.

The great benefit of these high-level languages is that they make little or no reference to the details of a particular computer. A program written in one of these languages can often be executed on a computer other than the one for which it was originally written, with relatively few changes (at least in comparison to the multitude of changes required to port an assembly language program from one computer to another). High-level languages are also easier to learn and use than assembly languages, and programmers who learn COBOL or FORTRAN have to think only about how to solve their problem, not about how the computer works inside. In Figure 1-6, you can see that in the use of a high-level language, most of the translation effort has been moved over to the computer. The programmer concentrates on the problem at hand.

These third-generation programming languages use a translation process similar to that used by assembly languages. The programmer writes a program, which is placed in a *source file*. The source file is processed by a compiler, which writes an equivalent machine language form of the program to an *object file*. Combining one or more object files with presupplied routines stored in *object-code* libraries is the task performed by a *linker*, which produces the final *executable*, or runnable program. Figure 1-7 shows the process of compiling, linking, and executing a program written in a third-generation language.

FIGURE 1-6

Using a high-level language

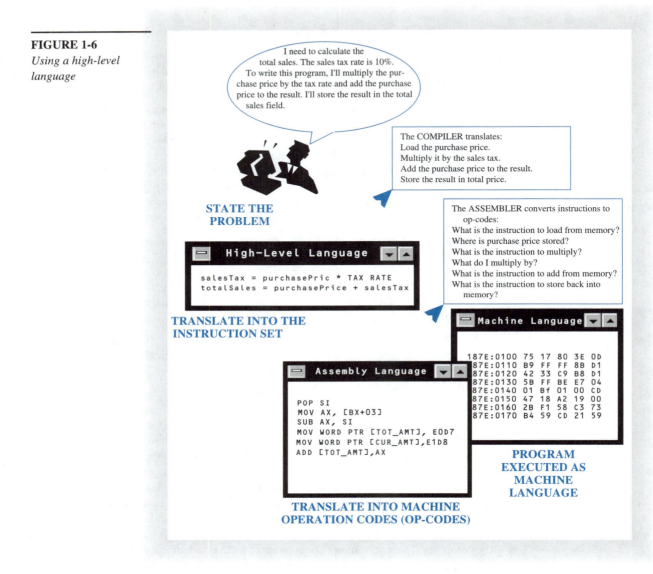

With these new languages, data-processing folks and engineers wrote programs larger and more complex than any they would have tried with machine or assembly language. And history repeated itself. As programs got larger, it became harder and harder to modify one part of these complex programs without breaking some other part. Software development bogged down.

In 1968, NATO asked, "Why is software so hard to write?" and "Why is it so unreliable?" The people who tried to answer those questions came up with a new way of

FIGURE 1-7

Compiling, linking, and executing a program

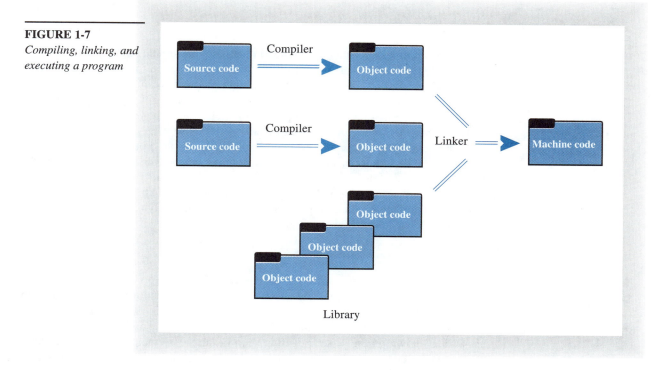

looking at programming. Their ideas became known as *structured programming*, or the *procedural programming paradigm*.

STRUCTURED PROGRAMMING

What were these new ways of organizing programs? A program is simply a series of steps that the computer takes to carry out some job, whether it be computing a trajectory or computing your taxes. Structured programming's contribution was to offer guidelines to help programmers avoid things that might cause their programs to behave unreliably. Some guidelines were rules of thumb that helped solve more difficult problems. Others had to do with how programmers arranged the instructions inside their programs. In a nutshell, these ideas revolved around the topics to be discussed next:

- Divide and conquer
- Single entrance, single exit
- Sequence, selection, and iteration
- Information hiding

Divide and Conquer

Since Roman times, warriors have relied in battle on the simple strategy of divide and conquer. Modern code warriors seized on this same principle to attack complex programs. Rather than writing one huge monolithic program, developers discovered that they could solve difficult problems more easily by breaking the problem down into chunks and then writing a separate program to solve each chunk. These chunks were called *subroutines*, *functions*, or *procedures*.

The process of dividing a big problem into little, solvable problems became known as *top-down design*, *stepwise refinement*, or *functional decomposition*. Despite the high-falutin' terminology, this method of organizing programs owes a lot to the technique you learned in junior high school when you had to write that report on the mythical Australian Tree Mollusk: Create an outline and continually refine it by adding new levels of detail. Look at Figure 1-8 for an example.

Single Entrance, Single Exit

In most computer languages, the `jump` or `goto` instruction tells the computer to stop running the current instruction and to start running the instructions at another location in the program. To understand a program with a lot of `goto` instructions, readers would use a pencil to connect the `goto` instruction with the next piece of code to run. Because these lines drawn on the program listing soon began to resemble a plate of spaghetti, this type of code became known as *spaghetti code*. In addition to organizing programs into procedures, the advocates of structured programming recommended generally that

FIGURE 1-8

Divide and conquer applied to grocery shopping

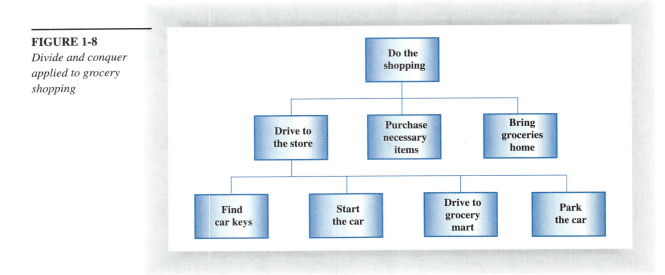

each procedure have only one entrance and one exit, thereby limiting the length of the spaghetti strands. Figure 1-9 shows an example of spaghetti code.

Sequence, Selection, and Iteration

Another way programmers avoided spaghetti code was to organize their programs using three fundamental principles—the building blocks of program flow:

Sequence: Perform the steps in a particular order.

Selection: Execute some instructions based upon some condition. This is the way that computer programs are able to make decisions. You will learn more about this in Chapter 5, "Making Choices: Teaching Your Objects About True and False."

Iteration: Repeat some instructions, based on a condition. This is how computer programs are able to keep doing things over and over. Things that are difficult for humans, such as successive approximations, are simple for the computer. Chapter 6, "Teaching Your Objects to Repeat Themselves," covers iteration.

These ideas now seem obvious to computer scientists, but in the late 1960s and early 1970s they were anything but. These principles can be applied to most programming languages, including Java, and can lead to clearer, more maintainable programs.

FIGURE 1-9
Spaghetti code

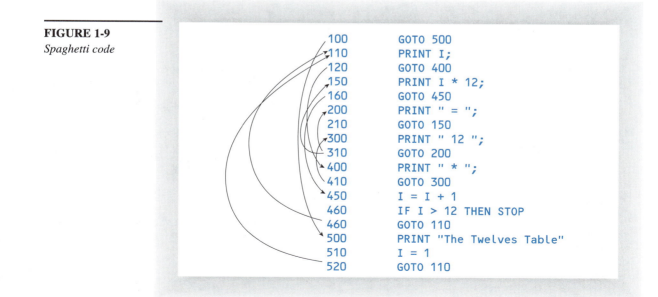

```
100        GOTO 500
110        PRINT I;
120        GOTO 400
150        PRINT I * 12;
160        GOTO 450
200        PRINT " = ";
210        GOTO 150
300        PRINT " 12 ";
310        GOTO 200
400        PRINT " * ";
410        GOTO 300
450        I = I + 1
460        IF I > 12 THEN STOP
460        GOTO 110
500        PRINT "The Twelves Table"
510        I = 1
520        GOTO 110
```

Information Hiding

Programs modeled after a plate of pasta were not the only problem these scientists discovered. Second only to errors resulting from spaghetti code were the many programming errors caused by the accidental manipulation of a piece of data in one procedure that was also used in another procedure. You're probably familiar with this problem in real life. That steak sandwich you were saving in the refrigerator for a late-night snack somehow gets modified when your teenager finds it after school. Giving everyone in the family his or her own refrigerator would be overkill for this situation, but that's exactly what's required to keep program A from stepping on the data that program B is using.

This new way of treating program data became known as *local variables*. A local variable is one that can only be changed—or even seen—inside the procedure that created it. Unlike the ideas about sequence, selection, and iteration, this concept required support in the programming language. Languages that support this idea—Pascal, C, and Java among them—are sometimes called *block-structured* languages. Figure 1-10 illustrates data hiding in the C programming language.

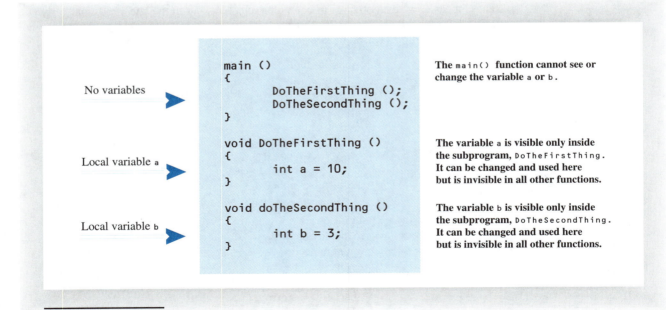

FIGURE 1-10
Local variables

OOP VERSUS OOPS!

"I thought that the tax rate was supposed to be 1.5 percent, not 15 percent. I guess no one will get a paycheck for the next few weeks. Oops!"

As long as programs have been written, "oops" has been a familiar word to programmers. One of the biggest changes in programming since the advent of structured programming shares this spelling: *OOP* or *object-oriented programming*. One of the aims of OOP is to help programmers banish "oops" from their vocabulary. Like structured programming, OOP is a set of guidelines and rules for organizing programs.

OOP is both evolutionary and revolutionary. It is evolutionary because it builds upon and expands the ideas of structured programming. OOP is revolutionary because it provides some features that are entirely new. These features provide a new way of organizing, designing, and even thinking about programs. And, just as the structured programming revolution spawned new programming language features and facilities, OOP is being incorporated into older programming languages. BASIC, Pascal, and yes, even COBOL, now offer object-oriented versions.

OOP History

Most object-oriented languages can trace at least part of their ancestry to a group of programmers working on a hospital simulation program in the late 1960s. A simulation program is used to ask questions such as "How often do the elevators have to run if the hospital holds 1,000 patients?" To do this, the simulation program has to create *variables* to hold the information about each of these 1,000 patients, as well as the doctors and nurses, inside the program. As the simulation program runs, the users watch what happens as patients, doctors, and nurses line up for the elevators. Set the elevator frequency too slow, and lines start to form in the hallways. Set it too fast, and the elevators go up and down too many times with only partial loads, resulting in early mechanical failure.

The programmers writing this code discovered one facet of the simulation that was very difficult to write. When it came time to display the lines of patients and doctors waiting in line for the elevator, they discovered that the instructions to draw a doctor were considerably different from the instructions to draw a nurse or a patient. Thus, they ended up with a whole lot of code just to find out what kind of person was waiting in the queue and then to display the person. But the real clincher came when someone decided that the programmers needed to add government inspectors and janitors to the simulation. By this time, there were thousands and thousands of places where the code would have to change. This rapidly became unmanageable.

The solution was discovered by looking at the problem from a different point of view. The complexity of the procedural solution is a result of the viewpoint selected.

Programmers reasoned, "If each of these variables 'knew' how to draw itself, our program would get a whole lot simpler."

The programmers considered whether they could just wrap up the instructions to display a doctor or a nurse along with all the other data about that particular doctor or nurse variable. Then they could just tell the variable to display itself. If it were a doctor, it would run the code that it contains, and presto—a doctor would appear on the screen. And if it were a nurse....

OOP Fundamentals

Object-oriented languages are languages that support this idea of bundling data and instructions into a variable—called an *object*—and then sending *messages* to the object telling it to perform certain operations. These days it seems as if every programming language claims to be object-oriented, but true object-oriented languages support at least these three "PIE" concepts:

Polymorphism means that different objects respond distinctively to the same message. For example, when you send the same message, "Speak!" to a Cat object, a Dog object, and a Cow object, each one responds appropriately. The Cat purrs, the Dog barks, and the Cow moos. Figure 1-11 illustrates this.

FIGURE 1-11
What is polymorphism?

Inheritance means that the language gives you the ability to extend or enhance existing objects. Using Java, you have a rich framework of predefined objects that you can readily add to and modify. Inheritance is the subject of Chapter 10, "Inheritance: Object Families." Figure 1-12 shows an example of how inheritance works.

Encapsulation means that the data and instructions for variables are wrapped up together and treated as a unit. The blueprints for these variables are called classes, and the units are called objects. In Chapter 2, "Programs: The Community of Objects," you will create your first object-oriented program, as well as learn more about the particular OOP vocabulary. Look at Figure 1-13 to see how encapsulation works.

FIGURE 1-12
What is inheritance?

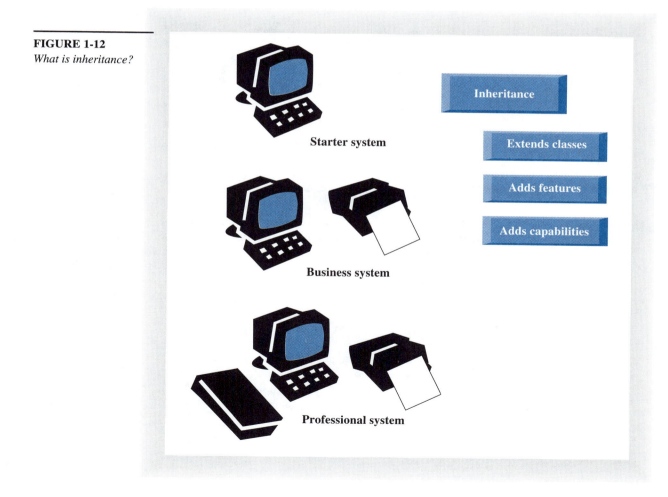

FIGURE 1-13

What is encapsulation?

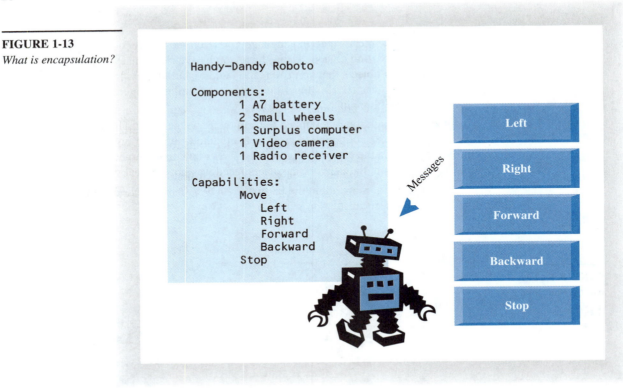

What's This Web Thing?

Now that you know something about the "what" and "how" of programming, it's time to learn about the "where." In the past, programs resided mainly inside a single computer. Recent developments have made it possible to connect computers on opposite sides of the globe and to run programs that move from one computer to another almost as easily as a bee moves from flower to flower, and *much* more quickly. The invention that makes this possible is known as the *World Wide Web* or simply the *Web*.

THE HISTORY OF THE WEB

If the 1980s go down in computer history as the object-oriented decade, the 1990s will surely be the Internet decade. Today you can't look at a billboard, listen to the radio, or watch a television commercial for Icelandic Jalapeño Milkshakes without seeing an address such as `http://www.hotncold.com` at the bottom of the screen. The World Wide Web is everywhere!

Just as modern programming languages have their roots in developments decades ago, the now-familiar World Wide Web had its beginnings in a 1960s U.S. Department of Defense project. The ARPANET, as it was then called, was designed to provide a robust and secure communications network for military use, one that could withstand the widespread devastation of nuclear attack. No one expected the telephones to continue working after an atomic war, so the military and defense-related research sites included in the initial project linked to form their own network. Through the 1970s and 1980s this network continued to grow as many universities not involved in the original project linked via the network. Figure 1-14 shows how the Internet is hooked together.

A major problem the network designers faced was how to deal with the wide variety of computer equipment that could be attached. Normally, different types of computers cannot communicate with each other, but if all of the computers had to be a certain make or model, much of the value of the Internet, as it came to be known, would be lost. In the universities especially, it was not uncommon to have whole computer labs where every computer was a different type. To solve this problem, the Internet adopted *communication protocols*. A protocol is simply an agreement among all of the computers connected to the Internet to transfer certain types of information in a standard way, regardless of the type of computer sending or receiving the information. These protocols evolved over time as the Internet community discovered new problems and solutions. They are in more widespread use today than ever: Every email message you send or receive via the Internet uses a variety of these protocols to navigate its way from sender to recipient. Table 1-1 shows some typical Internet protocols and their uses.

TABLE 1-1
TYPICAL INTERNET PROTOCOLS

PROTOCOL	USED TO
FTP	Transfer files from one system to another
HTTP	Request and send Web documents
ICMP	Establish routes for data movement from one system to another, by use of intermediate sites
SMTP	Transport email from one system to another
Telnet	Enable a user at a remote system to log on and use the resources of a server

FIGURE 1-14
How the Internet works

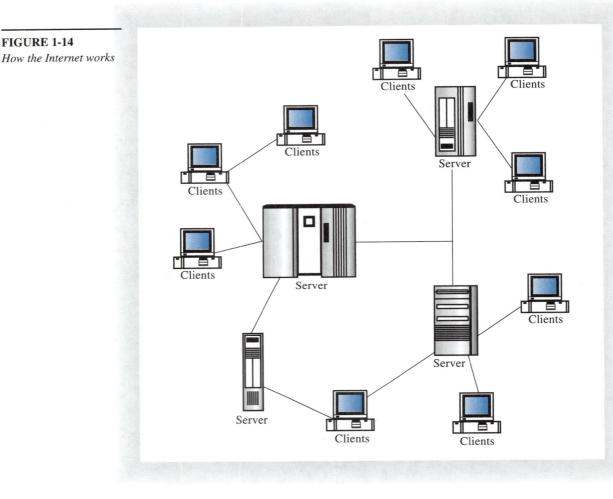

The Web Is Born

In 1989, Tim Berners-Lee of CERN, the European Laboratory for Particle Physics, proposed some new protocols for the delivery of *hypertext* documents. Hypertext documents are text documents that have references to other, external documents embedded. The reader of a hypertext document can read the information in a sequential manner just like email or a research paper. But, by activating a hypertext link, the reader can instantly retrieve any related document. A researcher browsing a journal article on stellar radiation could, with a single mouse click, instantly retrieve a referenced article—all without a trip to the library and without losing his or her train of thought. This ability to instantly access information marked the beginning the World Wide Web and Web surfing.

To implement this hypertext addition to the Internet, Berners-Lee's clever idea had two parts: a *client* program, called a *browser*, and a *server* program. The server program ran on an Internet host, responding to requests sent by clients. When a request was received, the server would transmit requested information to the client in a simple form. The client, or browser, would determine the appropriate way to display the data to its user. Placing this responsibility in the client made it easy to set up a server that you could use to gain access to information stored in many possible formats. Figure 1-15 shows how the server and client cooperate in this process. One ingredient essential to making this arrangement work was providing a unique address for every hypertext document anywhere in the world. This was accomplished through the adoption of URLs, or *uniform resource locators*. The unique address provided by a URL incorporates information that allows access to Web servers as well as to standard Internet servers, such as FTP or Telnet servers. Wishing to honor Berners-Lee for this notable achievement, some have urged his nomination for the royal title, "first Duke of URL."

As clever, interesting, and useful as the World Wide Web was, it was not until 1993, when Marc Andreessen conceived the first Web browser with a graphical user interface, that the Web became a household word. Andreessen's browser, Mosaic, was made available for free download via the Web. This led to an explosion of Web use, beginning in 1994 (now known as the "year of the Web"), when the general public

FIGURE 1-15
A Web client and server

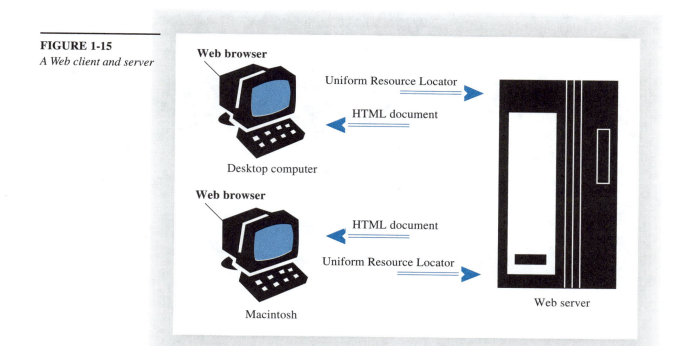

became aware of the existence of the Internet and the Web. Leading browsers such as Netscape Navigator and Microsoft Internet Explorer are still available free, as a struggle for commercial domination of the Web has ensued. Figure 1-16 shows a typical browser display, which includes a variety of text and graphics.

What Is HTML?

How are Web pages created? Like computer programs, Web pages are created by use of a computer language. This is a particularly simple language known as Hypertext Markup Language (HTML).

An HTML program is a simple text file. It doesn't have to be compiled or processed through a special interpreter. This makes it an easy language to learn. An HTML program includes a series of *tags* that are placed within the text that will appear on the Web page. These tags are instructions specifying that a particular block of text should be the title, another block should be displayed in a boldface font, and so forth. These tags are similar in purpose to the special symbols that printers used to mark up a document for printing before the advent of electronic publishing.

FIGURE 1-16

A browser display

Once a Web page is created, it is stored on a computer (server) that is constantly connected to the Internet. This computer continuously runs a special program, called a *Web server*, that waits until a user running a Web browser requests access to a page. When the Web server sees someone ask for a particular page, it jumps into action and sends the page over the Internet to the browser. When the browser sees the HTML tags inside the document, it uses them as instructions on how to format the document for display to the user.

The tags produce a richer, more interesting image than would otherwise be possible. Few today are impressed by a page that looks as though it were printed on a typewriter, no matter how neatly and accurately typed. Figure 1-17 shows how pages are stored, requested, sent, and displayed.

FIGURE 1-17

Accessing a Web page

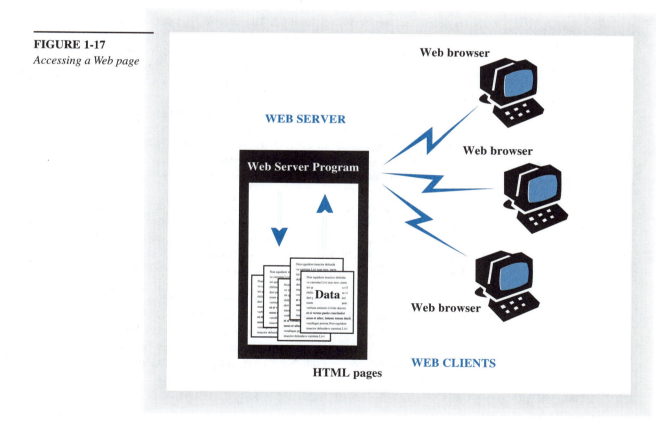

Looking into HTML

Most of the tags used in HTML specify the structure of a Web page, not its exact appearance. In an HTML program, you might say, "I want the title of this page to be 'Jumbo's Jungle Java Joint,'" but you can't give the browser instructions that say, "display the title in mauve type in the lower right-hand corner." Now, if you really have a hankering for mauve, you might find this limiting. Remember though, that the Web protocol allows people the world over to view your page—on all sorts of equipment. Each computer system has a different convention for displaying a title. So, by only specifying the structure of your document and not its appearance, you ensure that the Macintosh people will see the title where they expect it, as will the UNIX and Windows 95 folks. The browser itself decides exactly how a given tag should affect the appearance of a page. For example, there is a tag that defines a given block of text within a document as a top-level heading. The precise font that will be used and the size of the font are selected by the browser, not by the author of the page.

Although this makes the creation of Web pages much easier than it might otherwise be, it places a tremendous responsibility on the browser, because the browser determines the actual layout of the document. This means that no two browsers will display your pages quite the same. Two people using different browsers (or different versions of the same browser) may view the same Web page and come away with very different opinions of the visual quality of the page. One user may see a page with good layout, where the various components fit together nicely on the screen. Another might see a jumbled mess, where things just don't seem to fit right. Even the colors may look wrong, making it difficult to read the text because the background color and the text color are too similar.

This kind of mix-up usually occurs when the person who designed the page assumed that everyone in the world would be using the same video card and monitor. Additionally, if the designer of the page has used nonstandard tags supported only by a particular browser, it's likely that the page will appear broken under another browser or on a different machine. Figure 1-18 shows an example of this page portability problem.

Today the most popular browsers are Netscape Navigator and Microsoft Internet Explorer. Each is quite sophisticated and, as you'll see later, fully capable of running Java programs. Which browser you use is up to you, though savvy Web page designers tend to use both. By avoiding the use of browser-specific tags and by checking your Web page design efforts using both Navigator and Internet Explorer, you can ensure that most Web users will find your pages pleasing to the eye.

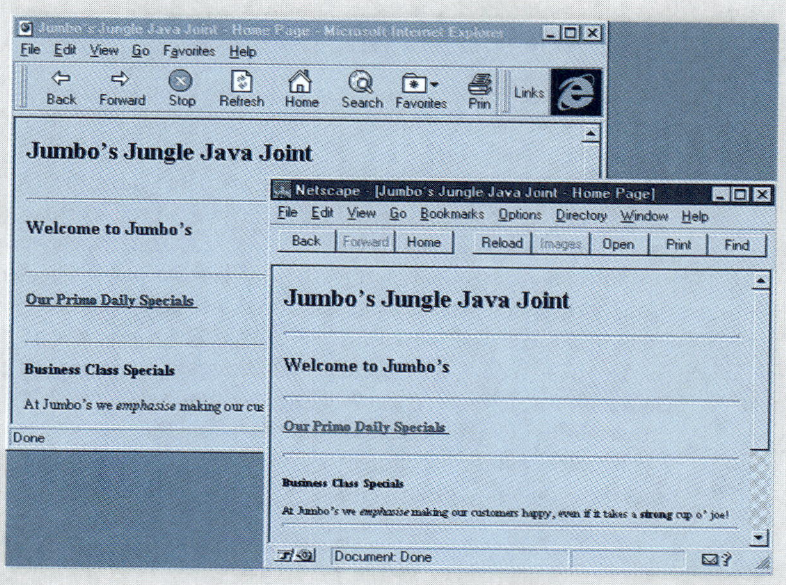

FIGURE 1-18
Dueling browsers

Choosing Your Tool: To WYSIWYG or Not to WYSIWYG

There are two ways of creating an HTML document. You can use an editor such as the Microsoft Windows Notepad to type text and tags directly into a file. Or, you can use a special HTML editor that supports what-you-see-is-what-you-get (WYSIWYG) editing. Among the popular HTML editors are Netscape Navigator Gold, which doubles as both an editor and a browser, and Microsoft Internet Assistant add-in for Microsoft Word. HTML editors are somewhat easier to use, but not all editors support the special applet tag used to include a Java applet in an HTML document.

In the examples that follow, you'll learn how to build a page using Notepad. Working directly with the HTML tags has the benefit that you'll more fully understand your document, not to mention HTML generally. However, by all means try HTML editors. If you find one that you like, use it. Once you understand tags, you'll find it easy to use Notepad to revise files produced by your favorite HTML editor to include any special tags not supported by that particular editor.

Building an HTML Page

As with most skills, the best way to learn how to build a Web page is to actually create one. Let's start with a simple example. Use Notepad to create a file containing the text shown in Listing 1-1. Save the file as `FirstPage.html` in any directory you choose. The Notepad program likes to create files that have the file extension `.txt`. Be sure you haven't erroneously saved the file as `FirstPage.html.txt`. To avoid this, you can put double quotes around the file name you type in the Save dialog box of Notepad.

While you are encouraged to personalize the pages you build, the examples in this book will feature a Web page for a fictional coffee shop—one that could only exist in the virtual world of the World Wide Web. The proprietor of Jumbo's Jungle Java Joint is, to put it baldly, an elephant. Once the star attraction at the circus, the "towering monarch of his mighty race" as the newspapers of the day called him, Jumbo retired after a little incident with a locomotive. Now the sole owner of his own little corner of Web space, Jumbo finds his new regime invigorating, and the air of cyberspace has worked wonders for his health.

Listing 1-1 FirstPage.html

```
<HTML>
<HEAD>
<TITLE>Jumbo's Jungle Java Joint - Home Page</TITLE>
</HEAD.
<BODY>
Welcome to Jumbo's
</BODY>
</HTML>
```

Note that the keywords, such as HTML, HEAD, and TITLE, occurring inside the HTML tags are not case sensitive. You can type **<HTML>** or **<html>** as you prefer; the browser will not differentiate. Using all uppercase letters within tags does help them stand out from the nearby text, making the structure of the document more obvious. Also, whitespace is generally ignored within an HTML document. You can freely include blanks, tabs, and returns within the text blocks of your HTML document. The browser will use the information contained in the tags to determine the layout of your document and will ignore the whitespace.

Once you've saved your file, start your favorite browser and open the file you created. Use the browser menu item for opening a *file*, not a *location*, because your file is not yet actually on the Web (unless, of course, you're working on a computer running a Web server program). The result should be similar to that shown in Figure 1-19. Congratulations: you've just created your first Web page!

FIGURE 1-19
Your first Web page

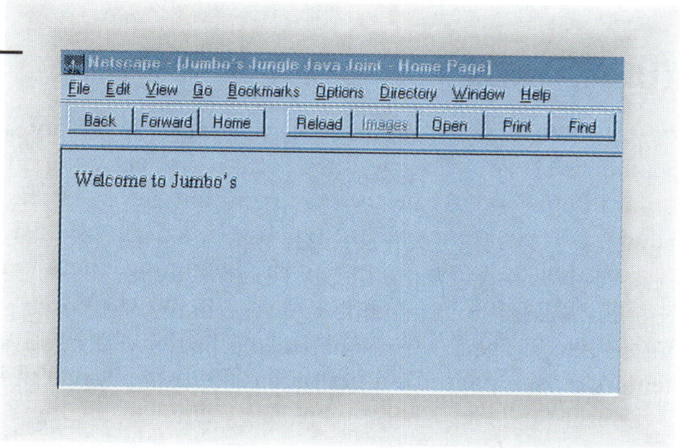

Basic HTML

Let's take a few minutes to look through the part of the page you just built before you make it fancy. But first, a word of caution. Although HTML is a simple language, its size and complexity are growing rapidly. Fortunately, the fastest area of HTML language growth is in browser-specific tags that you're advised to avoid anyway. Most of these tags merely allow you to do things that could be done more portably using Java. Because many Web designers are not Java programmers, they desperately need these tags. You, however, soon will not.

WHAT IS A TAG?

The frequent references to HTML tags in the preceding paragraphs have not described precisely what a tag is. A tag is simply a command to the browser. Here's an example of a tag:

```
<HTML>
```

This tag is placed at the beginning of every HTML document and tells the browser "Look out, what's coming next is an HTML document, so get ready." In fact, if you're looking at the contents of a file and notice that this tag appears as the first thing in the file, it's a safe bet you're looking at an HTML document.

As you can see, a tag is surrounded by angle brackets (< and >). These separate the tag from nearby text so the browser can easily distinguish text from the tags that specify how the text is to be formatted. The "word" between the angle brackets is the instruction or command. Of course, this word isn't likely to be found in a dictionary. It's a *keyword* that is part of the HTML language, and this particular keyword, HTML, simply tells the browser that any following text is to be considered an HTML document.

STRUCTURAL TAGS

Along with the `<HTML>` tag, there are several other tags that are found in almost every HTML document. These are sometimes called *structural tags*, because they identify certain standard items and divide the document into several parts, each with a specific purpose. The HTML program you just typed shows the most basic structural tags.

Notice that in addition to the `<HTML>` at the beginning, there is an `</HTML>` tag at the end. These tags define the beginning and end of the HTML document. Most HTML tags occur like this, in pairs. The first tag denotes the beginning of a block of text; the second tag, named like the first but with a leading slash, denotes the end. The pair is used like a set of bookends to enclose the text block.

Following the `<HTML>` tag is a `<HEAD>` tag, which identifies the heading portion of the document. HTML files are usually divided into two parts, a heading and a body. A number of items can be placed in the heading block, but the only one that is required is the `<TITLE>` item. Between the `<TITLE>` and `</TITLE>` tags is a block of text that will be used as the title of this HTML document. Most browsers display the title of an HTML document in the title bar of the browser window. Figure 1-19 shows how this most basic document appears using the Navigator browser. Notice how the window's title bar displays the words you typed between the `<TITLE>` and `</TITLE>` tags. The end of the heading portion is denoted, just as you might expect, by the `</HEAD>` tag.

After the heading of the HTML document comes the body, surrounded by the `<BODY>` and `</BODY>` tags. This is where you put the text and tags that you will see in the browser window. In your example page, the only text is the greeting, "Welcome to Jumbo's." And frankly, it looks puny. Jumbo is not going to attract any business this way. Let's spice it up a little. As we continue to make changes to Jumbo's page, update your own copy using Notepad, incorporating the changes as they're introduced. View the result of the changes with your browser.

HEADINGS

Let's start with some headings, which you can see in Listing 1-2.

```
Listing 1-2 Headings.html
<HTML>
<HEAD>
<TITLE>Jumbo's Jungle Java Joint - Home Page</TITLE>
</HEAD.
<BODY>
<H1> Jumbo's Jungle Java Joint     </H1>
<H2> Welcome to Jumbo's            </H2>
<H3> Our Primo Daily Specials      </H3>
<H4> Business Class Specials       </H4>
<H5> All-You-Can-Drink Specials    </H5>
<H6> Jumbo's Complaint Department  </H6>
If you wish to complain, go elsewhere!
Jumbo's is a negative-free zone!
</BODY>
</HTML>
```

HTML provides six levels of headings, from the largest, <H1>, to the smallest, <H6>. As with the tags you saw previously, the heading tags are paired with their "evil twins," the ending tags, </H1> through </H6>. Although the example program has lined up the ending tags so that they are easy to see, this formatting has absolutely no effect on the output. What does happen is that all of the text between each of the heading tag pairs is displayed in a slightly different size and/or style of text. On most systems, the quite small level-6 heading is truly difficult to read. Figure 1-20 shows the effect of the heading tags.

PARAGRAPHS

Titles do not a story make. You can add regular text to your page just by typing. Text that is not bracketed by some other type of tag is displayed as normal text. Jumbo wanted to use this feature to display a few sayings to ensure that the positive feelings keep on rolling. Unfortunately, he's not too positive about the results, which are shown in Figure 1-20. What went wrong? As you can see from the Listing, he put the two sentences on separate lines, but the browser crunched them together.

Remember, HTML doesn't describe how something will appear, but describes what kind of thing it is. By not putting a tag around his accumulated wisdom, Jumbo was telling the browser that this was just text and leaving it up to the browser to make do. Does that mean that you have to be content with text that just runs together? Not at all. One of the tags you can insert is the paragraph, or <P> tag. Unlike most of the other tags, the <P> tag has traditionally stood alone, not requiring a closing </P> tag. Because of this, some older browsers don't handle the </P> tag properly. Experiment to see how your favorite browser handles it, and choose whether to include it in your own documents. Listing 1-3 shows Jumbo's revised HTML page including <P> tags. Figure 1-21 shows the result of adding these paragraph tags to the page.

FIGURE 1-20

Web page with headings

Listing 1-3 Paragraphs.html

```
<HTML>
<HEAD>
<TITLE>Jumbo's Jungle Java Joint - Home Page</TITLE>
</HEAD.
<BODY>
<H1> Jumbo's Jungle Java Joint      </H1>
<H2> Welcome to Jumbo's            </H2>
<H3> Our Primo Daily Specials      </H3>
<H4> Business Class Specials       </H4>
<H5> All-You-Can-Drink Specials    </H5>
The all-you-can-drink specials
are especially attractive to those on a budget
or those who desire to make their income stretch
as far as possible.
<P>While not exactly premium blend, the
all-you-can-drink specials are as richly brown as
the finest Java.
<P>After a single cup, you'll agree you've had all
you can drink.
<H6> Jumbo's Complaint Department </H6>
If you wish to complain, go elsewhere! <P> Jumbo's is a
negative-free zone!
</BODY>
</HTML>
```

That's better. Notice that you can actually put the <P> tag anywhere, and the paragraph break will take place at that point. The only problem with this page is that there is a little too much space between the pithy sayings at the bottom of the page. Actually, all of the paragraphs have a lot of vertical space inserted whenever a paragraph starts. If you want to prevent the browser from wrapping text into a single line, but don't want the extra vertical space that comes with using the <P> tag, use the <BR> tag, explained next.

FIGURE 1-21

Web page with paragraphs

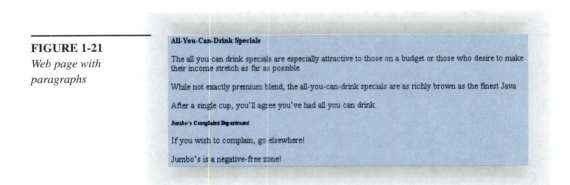

ENDING A LINE

The `<BR>` tag tells the browser to break the line at the indicated point. See Jumbo's HTML file in Listing 1-4 and its result in Figure 1-22.

```
Listing 1-4 Breaks.html
<HTML>
<HEAD>
<TITLE>Jumbo's Jungle Java Joint - Home Page</TITLE>
</HEAD.
<BODY>
<H1> Jumbo's Jungle Java Joint      </H1>
<H2> Welcome to Jumbo's            </H2>
<H3> Our Primo Daily Specials      </H3>
<H4> Business Class Specials       </H4>
<H5> All-You-Can-Drink Specials    </H5>
The all-you-can-drink specials
are especially attractive to those on a budget
or those who desire to make their income stretch
as far as possible. While not exactly premium blend,
the all-you-can-drink specials are as richly brown as
the finest Java. <BR>After a single cup, you'll
agree you've had all you can drink.
<H6> Jumbo's Complaint Department </H6>
If you wish to complain, go elsewhere! <BR>
Jumbo's is a negative-free zone!
</BODY>
</HTML>
```

ADDING A HORIZONTAL RULE

Now that the paragraphs stick together, the headings don't look as if they form units with the text. One easy fix for that is to use a horizontal *rule* to put each section into its own little unit. Separating sections of your document with a horizontal line, or rule, is easy. Just use the `<HR>` tag. Note that the `<HR>` tag, like the lone `<P>` tag, has no `</HR>` tag. Not only is a horizontal rule produced, but the line is broken at that point as well. Jumbo's new and improved HTML file is shown in Listing 1-5. The result is shown in Figure 1-23.

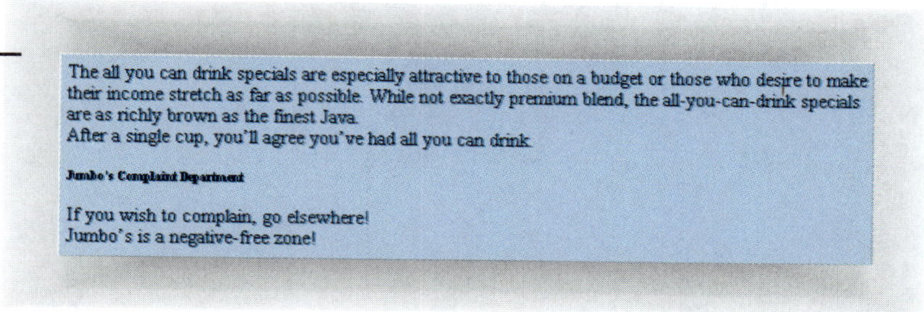

FIGURE 1-22

Web page with line break

The all you can drink specials are especially attractive to those on a budget or those who desire to make their income stretch as far as possible. While not exactly premium blend, the all-you-can-drink specials are as richly brown as the finest Java.
After a single cup, you'll agree you've had all you can drink.

Jumbo's Complaint Department

If you wish to complain, go elsewhere!
Jumbo's is a negative-free zone!

Listing 1-5 Rules.html

```
<HTML>
<HEAD>
<TITLE>Jumbo's Jungle Java Joint - Home Page</TITLE>
</HEAD.
<BODY>
<H1> Jumbo's Jungle Java Joint      </H1><HR>
<H2> Welcome to Jumbo's             </H2>
<HR>
<H3> Our Primo Daily Specials       </H3>
<HR>
<H4> Business Class Specials        </H4>
<HR>
<H5> All-You-Can-Drink Specials     </H5>
After a single cup, you'll agree,
you've had all you can drink.
<HR>
<H6> Jumbo's Complaint Department </H6>
If you wish to complain, go elsewhere! <BR>
Jumbo's is a negative-free zone!
</BODY>
</HTML>
```

BOLD, ITALIC, AND UNDERLINED TEXT

An easy way to add emphasis to a page is to use special fonts. One way to do that is to make some words bold, italic, or underlined. Unlike the other tags you have seen, these tags *do* deal with the appearance of the text. For that reason, some purist HTML authors eschew these tags in favor of the *strong* and *emphasized* tags, which hark back to structure—not appearance.

You make a word, paragraph, or section bold by placing it between the `<B>` `</B>` pair. Use of the strong tags, `<STRONG>` and `</STRONG>`, usually has the same effect. Italic, or

FIGURE 1-23
Web page with horizontal rule

slanted, text is created by use of the `<I> </I>` tag pair. You can usually substitute the emphasized tags, `<EM>` and `</EM>`, for italic. Finally, underlined text can sometimes be obtained by use of the `<U>` and `</U>` tags. Listing 1-6 shows Jumbo's improved HTML file, and Figure 1-24 shows the result of adding these tags to the page. Some browsers, such as older versions of Navigator, do not support underlined text. Don't be surprised if you don't see the underlines.

Listing 1-6 Styles.html

```
<HTML>
<HEAD>
<TITLE>Jumbo's Jungle Java Joint - Home Page</TITLE>
</HEAD.
<BODY>
<H1> Jumbo's Jungle Java Joint     </H1><HR>
<H2> Welcome to Jumbo's           </H2>
<HR>
<H3> Our Primo Daily Specials     </H3>
The special today is the <B>bold</B> Brazilian Roast<BR>
Or, you may prefer our <I>Italian</I> Espresso!<BR>
At least you'll never wait <U>on line</U>
<HR>
<H4> Business Class Specials      </H4>
At Jumbo's we <EM>emphasize</EM> making our customers
happy, even if it takes a <STRONG>strong</STRONG> cup o' joe!
<HR>
<H5> All-You-Can-Drink Specials   </H5>
After a single cup, you'll agree,
you've had all you can drink.
<HR>
<H6> Jumbo's Complaint Department </H6>
If you wish to complain, go elsewhere! <BR>
Jumbo's is a negative-free zone!
</BODY>
</HTML>
```

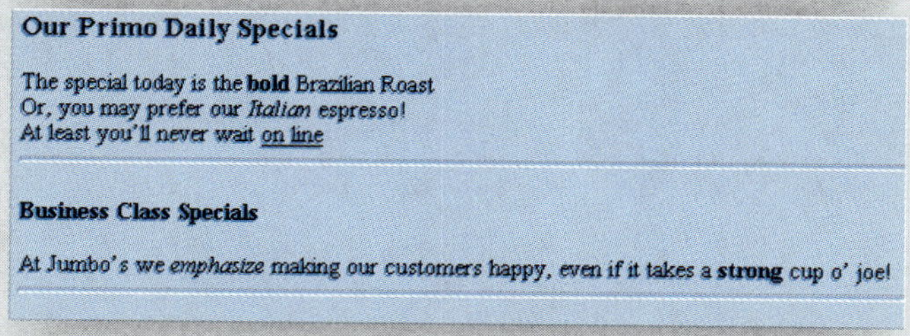

FIGURE 1-24

Web page with bold, italic, and underlined text

Our Primo Daily Specials

The special today is the **bold** Brazilian Roast
Or, you may prefer our *Italian* espresso!
At least you'll never wait <u>on line</u>

Business Class Specials

At Jumbo's we *emphasize* making our customers happy, even if it takes a **strong** cup o' joe!

COMMENTS

In addition to what shows up on screen, it's often helpful to include *comments*, that is, blocks of text that do not show up on the browser, in your HTML documents. Comments are a useful way of placing reminders in your documents, keeping a record of who created a particular document and when, recording changes to a document, or explaining why a particular document was written the way it was. Comments are identified by enclosing them in the <!-- and --> tags. These tags are unlike other tags you've seen, because the first tag lacks the ending angle bracket and the last tag lacks the beginning angle bracket. In a way, the entire comment can be considered a single tag. Listing 1-7 shows the revised page that includes some comments. Note that comments can span several lines.

Listing 1-7 Comments.html

```
<HTML>
<!-- *********************************
     This is a sample page:  don't use
     it for your own home page

     Created on January 31, 1885 by
     Hezekia Tinius McLanguage
-->
<HEAD>
<TITLE>Jumbo's Jungle Java Joint - Home Page</TITLE>
</HEAD.
<BODY>
<H1> Jumbo's Jungle Java Joint      </H1><HR>
<H2> Welcome to Jumbo's             </H2>
<HR>
<H3> Our Primo Daily Specials       </H3>
The special today is the <B>bold</B> Brazilian Roast<BR>
Or, you may prefer our <I>Italian</I> Espresso!<BR>
<!--The following line may NOT print in underline -->
At least you'll never wait <U>on line</U>
<HR>
<H4> Business Class Specials        </H4>
<!-- These are the preferred tags over <B> <I> and <U>    -->
At Jumbo's we <EM>emphasize</EM> making our customers
happy, even if it takes a <STRONG>strong</STRONG> cup o' joe!
<HR>
<H5> All-You-Can-Drink Specials     </H5>
After a single cup, you'll agree,
you've had all you can drink.
<HR>
<H6> Jumbo's Complaint Department </H6>
If you wish to complain, go elsewhere! <BR>
Jumbo's is a negative-free zone!
</BODY>
</HTML>
```

Table 1-2 summarizes the HTML formatting tags you've covered so far. Don't forget to use the structural tags (for example, <HTML>) in documents you build. The documents won't work without them. To speed your Web-building, you can build a simple template that includes the structural tags and store it for reuse in a file. To get some practice, use the information in Table 1-2 to build a page that tells people something about yourself. Use a variety of tags so you can become familiar with their function.

TABLE 1-2
HTML FORMATTING TAGS

TAG(S)	FUNCTION
`<Hn>, </Hn>`	Document heading (n=1, 2,..., 6)
`<P>`	Paragraph
` `	Line break
`<HR>`	Horizontal rule
`<B>, </B>`	Bold font
`<I>, </I>`	Italic font
`<U>, </U>`	Underlined font (not always supported)
`<STRONG>, </STRONG>`	Usually bold, but depends on browser
`<EM>, </EM>`	Usually italic, but depends on browser
`<!--...-->`	Comment (contents not processed by browser)

Images and Links

Putting formatted text on a Web page is cool, but two additional features will really make your pages come alive: *hyperlinks* and *images*. A hyperlink is a block of text that, when selected, loads a specified Web page in place of the current page. For most browsers, the user accomplishes this by simply clicking a mouse button while the mouse cursor is positioned over the hyperlink text block. Hyperlinks are what makes the Web a web: Hyperlinks allow the user to travel from one page to another in arbitrary, even circuitous, fashion. Imagine trying to surf the Web without hyperlinks! Figure 1-25 shows hyperlinks that form a web.

The ability to refer to external documents and images on a Web page easily and uniformly is part of the genius of the Web. As with text formatting, the real work that supports such references is done in the browser rather than in the server. To work its magic, the browser uses a device called a uniform resource locator (URL). URLs allow an HTML document anywhere on the Web to refer to any other document capable of being served by any Web server.

URLS

To find a particular file or document among all the gazillion (or thereabouts) documents on the World Wide Web, you need to know three things:

☕ How should the document be transferred? (What kind of document is it?)

☕ Where is it stored?

☕ What is its name?

FIGURE 1-25

A web of hyperlinks

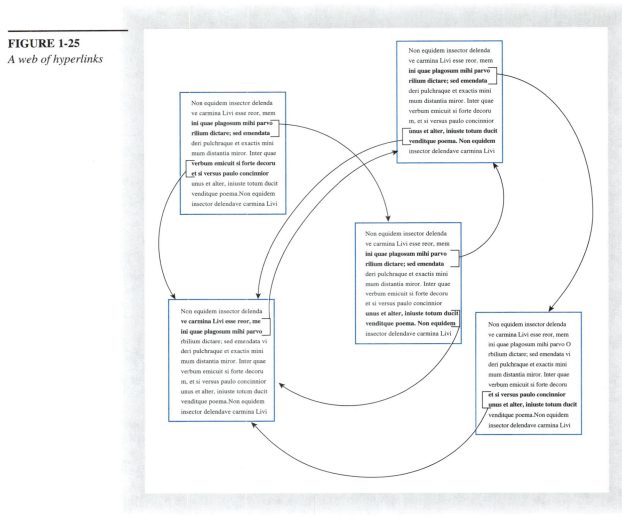

The URL is designed to answer these three questions. To understand how URLs work, let's start by taking one apart. Figure 1-26 shows a typical URL.

Animal, Vegetable, or Mineral

Documents on the Web are first classified by what language they speak. More accurately, you start searching for a document by specifying the protocol you want to use to get a particular document. A protocol, remember, is just an agreement between two computers or systems to treat certain types of files in certain ways—to speak the same language.

http://www.company.com/index.html

Protocol   Host name   File specifier

FIGURE 1-26
A URL

The URL in this example starts with *http,* which indicates that you want everything handled as a Web document. If you had begun your URL with *ftp* instead, you would have told the world that you wanted the documents transferred by use of File Transfer Protocol. In Table 1-1 you saw a list of common protocols that were used to transfer information over the Internet. When you use URLs, the list grows considerably. Some of the most popular are given in Table 1-3.

TABLE 1-3
SOME POPULAR INTERNET PROTOCOLS

PROTOCOL	PURPOSE
HTTP	Web documents, provided by Web server
FTP	Files, provided by FTP server
Telnet	Remote logins to server
File	Used to access files on the local system, that is, the same system on which the browser is running
Gopher	Files, provided by Gopher server (largely supplanted by HTTP protocol)
Mailto	Email transmission
News	Usenet newsgroup access

Where in the World?

Now that you have told the Web server how you want your document delivered, you need to tell it what document you want to get. That task breaks down into two parts. Unless you live alone, your home address does not uniquely identify you. Rather, it identifies the place where you reside. URLs are similar. The address part of a URL is not the address of a particular document, but is the address of a particular machine, or *host,* that contains the document.

Technically, every machine connected to the Internet has a unique address. Unfortunately, this address—called the *Internet Protocol* (IP) number—is not especially user-friendly. The IP number for a particular machine is a set of four 8-bit numbers separated by periods. That means you could have an IP address of `111.222.111.222`, but not an address of `111.222.333.444`, because the highest value an

8-bit number can hold is 255. In addition to the IP number for a specific machine, you can also include an optional TCP/IP (Transfer Control Protocol/Internet Prototcol) port number after the address.

Fortunately for those who don't memorize lists of 12-digit numbers for sport, there is an easier way. Instead of using an IP number, which is sort of like using latitude and longitude to locate your house, you can simply use what is called the *host name*. For the Waite Group, the host name for the Web site is `www.mcp.com`. Hmmm. That looks much easier, doesn't it!

Notice that the name, `www.mcp.com`, has two parts. This structure is similar to your home address. You not only have a street name and number, but you also have a city, state, and country part to your address. In the Internet world, addresses are broken up into two parts: the host name and the *domain name*. (One potential point of confusion is that this complete address is also sometimes just called a host name. Don't worry. This works just like your own address: You can refer to either the abbreviated form, 123 Main Street, or the fully qualified form with address, city, state, and ZIP code. Both are your address, but one is more detailed than the other.)

The domain name is the name assigned to an entire network. Just like the city, state, and country divisions for mail delivery, the Internet has been broken up into several broad domains that specify what type of organization or country a machine belongs to. Thus, commercial organizations belong to the `.com` domain, universities to the `.edu` domain, and government organizations to the `.gov` domain. In addition to specifying the "cybercountry" of a particular host, domains may also be divided into cities or counties. These are local network divisions within an institution or organization. For example, all the hosts on the Waite Group's network are in the `mcp.com` domain.

Nonetheless, the document you are looking for has to reside on a particular machine at a particular address, just as you live at a particular street address in a particular city, state, and country. This particular machine address is called the *host name*. The host name of the Waite Group's Web server is `www`, which is more fully known as `www.mcp.com`.

Location, Location, Location

Just specifying the host name is not enough to allow your documents to get delivered or retrieved, just as the street address "123 Main Street" is not enough information for the Postal Service to deliver that letter to your sweetheart. More information is needed. On your letter you would add the city and state and, preferably, the ZIP code. You need to do the same thing when specifying the location part of a URL.

The location part of a URL begins with two slashes (//). These slashes are an important part of the URL; leaving them off causes the browser to interpret the URL in an entirely different way, which you'll see shortly. For now, be sure you include them in any URL you write or otherwise use. After these slashes, you use the machine name and then additional domain qualifiers, separated by periods. This is best seen by use of an example.

Suppose you wanted to retrieve a document that was located on the host machine named `coolstuff`, located on the Big University network. The location part of the URL would begin with the slashes (//), followed by the host name (`coolstuff`), the university network name (`big`), and finally the general domain name (`edu`). Each of the domain name and host name portions would be separated from the others by periods, so that the fully qualified host name would be

```
//coolstuff.big.edu
```

What Do You Want?

Now that you've built a URL that specifies on what machine the file is located, you need to tell it, unambiguously, exactly which document you wish to retrieve. This is done by use of a *file specifier*. The file specifier follows the host name and is separated from it by a slash.

How do you write a file specifier? That can get a little complex, so let's take it piece by piece. The file specifier can include a *path*—that is, an optional series of directory names separated by slashes—followed by the file name. This is the simple case. In addition, most systems have special rules that map a file name given as part of a URL to a local file name. These rules are *not* standard from system to system and must be learned by the users of a system to use it effectively. For example, a common rule on UNIX systems is to allow a directory name of the form `~jumbo` as the first part of the URL's file specifier. This is shorthand for a directory named `public_html` that is located within the home directory of the user `jumbo`. These sorts of unwritten rules make for more convenient system use for those who know the rules, but are confusing to those unfamiliar with the system that supports them. Consult your system administrator to learn the rules of the system you use.

Often the file specifier is omitted, which causes a file designated by the administrator of the Web server to be loaded. Similarly, users often omit the file name portion of a file specifier that points into their `public_html` directory. Again, in this case a designated file will be loaded. Such a file is usually named `index.html` or `index.htm`, though the actual name is decided by the system administrator.

LINKS

The tag that creates a hyperlink, which lets you jump from one page to another, is a bit more complex than those you've seen so far. Here's an example:

```
<A HREF="http://www.mcp.com/waite">Select me to see the Waite
Group Home Page </A>
```

The tag used here, the `<A>` tag, specifies the address that is the destination of the hyperlink. The `HREF` attribute in the tag introduces the actual URL, which is placed within quotes so that the browser won't become confused by any special characters contained in the URL. The text between the `<A>` tag and the `</A>` tag will appear in the browser window in some way that distinguishes it to the user as a hyperlink. Several popular browsers give hyperlinks a special color and underline them so they're very apparent to the user.

Let's add a hyperlink to the example Web page from the previous section. If you don't have Web access, it won't do much good to add a hyperlink pointing to the home page of Waite Group Press. So, let's create a second page to which you can jump. Listing 1-8 shows the change you should make to the previous listing. Then save the result as `Links.html`. Listing 1-9 shows the new page, which you type and save as `MoreLinks.html`. Now, try the hyperlinks. Go to the menu page, and then go back to Jumbo's home page. Figures 1-27 and 1-28 show how you can surf your new miniweb by using the hyperlinks.

Listing 1-8 Links.html

```
<HTML>
<!-- Listing 1-8 Jumbo gets a menu    -->
<HEAD>
<TITLE>Jumbo's Jungle Java Joint - Home Page</TITLE>
</HEAD.
<BODY>
<H1> Jumbo's Jungle Java Joint      </H1><HR>
<H2> Welcome to Jumbo's             </H2>
<HR>
<A HREF="MoreLinks.html">
<H3> Our Primo Daily Specials       </H3>
</A>
<HR>
<H4> Business Class Specials        </H4>
<!-- These are the preferred tags over <B> <I> and <U>    -->
At Jumbo's we <EM>emphasize</EM> making our customers
happy, even if it takes a <STRONG>strong</STRONG> cup o' joe!
<HR>
<H5> All-You-Can-Drink Specials     </H5>
After a single cup, you'll agree,
you've had all you can drink.
<HR>
<H6> Jumbo's Complaint Department </H6>
If you wish to complain, go elsewhere! <BR>
Jumbo's is a negative-free zone!
</BODY>
</HTML>
```

Listing 1-9 MoreLinks.html

```
<HTML>
<!-- Listing 1.9 Jumbo gets a menu    -->
<HEAD>
<TITLE>Jumbo's Jungle Java Joint - Primo Menu Page</TITLE>
</HEAD>
<BODY>
<H1>The Place for Premium Java </H1>
<HR>
The special today is the <B>bold</B> Brazilian Roast<BR>
Or, you may prefer our <I>Italian</I> Espresso!<BR>
At least you'll never wait <U>on line</U>
```

```
<HR>
<A HREF="Listing1-08.html">Go back to Jumbo's home page </A>
</BODY>
</HTML>
```

RELATIVE URLS

The URLs you used in Jumbo's pages looked a little different from the ones you've seen so far. What's missing? If you look closely, you'll see that the URL used in Listing 1-9 has no protocol or host portion. This is what's called a *relative* URL. Relative URLs make it easier to build a web in two ways. First, they're shorter than full or *absolute* URLs. Second, they make it possible to move a web from one directory or system to another without having to change all the URLs to point to new locations.

When a browser encounters a relative URL, it simply supplies the missing portions of the URL by using the corresponding portions of the URL for the current page. Most browsers actually display the full URL as the current location, even when a relative URL was used to get there.

FIGURE 1-27
A hyperlink: going to Jumbo's menu

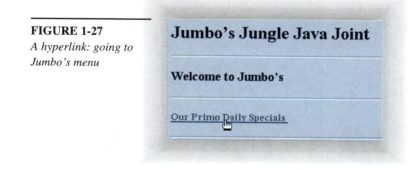

FIGURE 1-28
A hyperlink: returning to Jumbo's home page

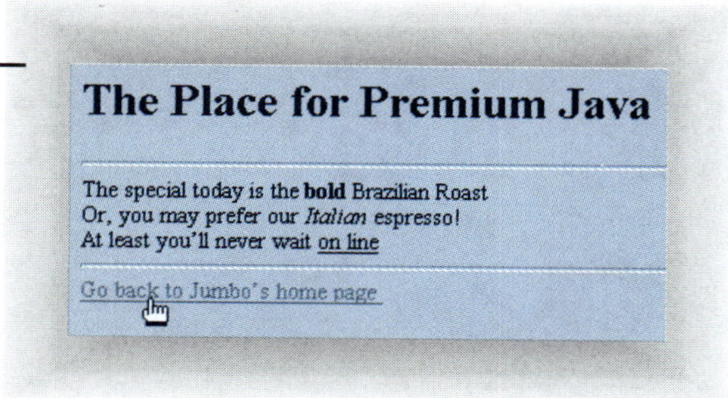

This is why moving a page to another part of your web is less likely to disrupt relative URLs than absolute URLs. Because relative URLs are understood relative to the location of the current page, moving the page that contains them won't mess them up, as long as they remain in the same relative position with respect to the referencing page. Figure 1-29 shows how this works.

FILE URLS

You may have noticed another unusual thing about the URL shown in Figure 1-28. Rather than starting with `http`, it starts with the word `file`. The File URL refers to a file on your local system, not one located on some server out on the Web. So, it's reasonable that the syntax would be somewhat different. Figure 1-30 shows the form of a File URL. Note the use of the colon and the three slashes after the protocol name, and note the use of `c|` to specify the drive, rather than `c:`, which might be expected for a PC system. This is a standard HTML practice. You can use your browser to discover the proper name for a file using the File protocol by simply opening the file and looking for the current location reported by the browser. Remember that File URLs refer to files on the client system. They're useful for testing your pages, but they should not normally be used in pages stored on a Web server.

FIGURE 1-29

Relative URLs allow pages to be moved

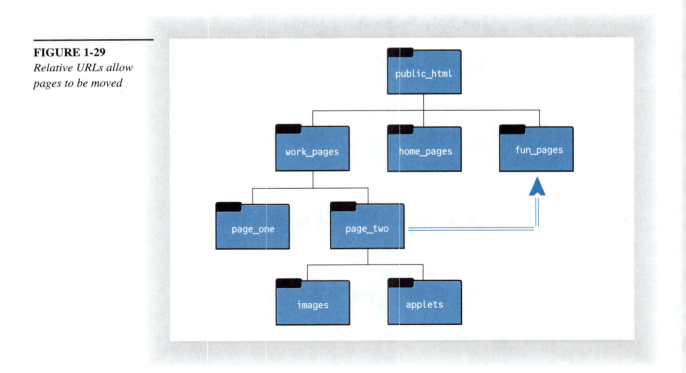

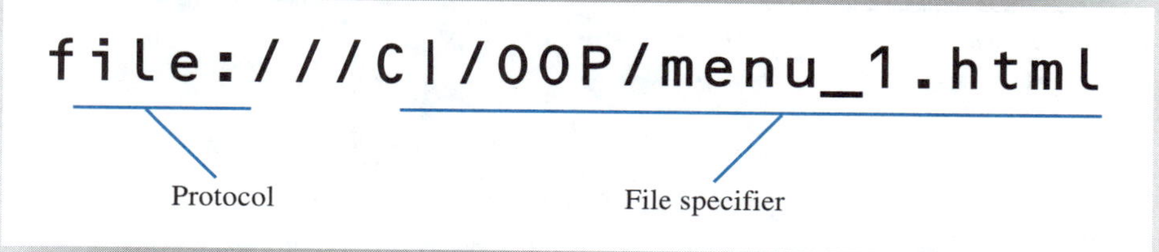

FIGURE 1-30
A file URL

`file:///C|/OOP/menu_1.html`

Protocol   File specifier

IMAGES

Like hyperlinks, images are an important part of visually appealing Web pages. You can add them to a page by using the `<IMG>` tag. Most browsers are capable of handling images stored in either GIF or JPEG format. Let's add an image to Jumbo's page, as shown in Listing 1-10. You can find the file `jumbo.gif` on the CD-ROM. In addition, you will want the file `T9.gif` from the directory `/java/demo/Animator/1.1/ images/Beans`. Make sure these files are in your working directory, and then revise `Links.html` to match the following listing, saving the result as `Logo.html`. Figure 1-31 shows the result.

Listing 1-10 Logo.html

```
<HTML>
<!-- Listing 1-10 Jumbo gets a logo     -->
<HEAD>
<TITLE>Jumbo's Jungle Java Joint - Home Page</TITLE>
</HEAD.
<BODY>
<H1> Jumbo's Jungle Java Joint      </H1>
<H2> Welcome to Jumbo's            </H2>
<IMG SRC="jumbo.gif">
<HR>
<A HREF="MoreLinks.html">
<H3> Our Primo Daily Specials      </H3>
<IMG SRC="T9.gif">
</A>
<HR>
<H4> Business Class Specials       </H4>
At Jumbo's we <EM>emphasize</EM> making our customers
happy, even if it takes a <STRONG>strong</STRONG> cup o' joe!
<HR>
<H5> All-You-Can-Drink Specials    </H5>
After a single cup, you'll agree,
you've had all you can drink.
<HR>
<H6> Jumbo's Complaint Department </H6>
If you wish to complain, go elsewhere! <BR>
Jumbo's is a negative-free zone!
</BODY>
</HTML>
```

FIGURE 1-31

Adding images

Note that the second image has a thin border around it. This means the image itself is a hyperlink. Click it and see what happens. It should send you to the menu page, just as the hyperlinked words "Our Primo Daily Specials" do. You've done this by putting the image tag between the pair of hyperlink anchor tags, `<A>` and `</A>`. Compare the two `<A>` tags in the listing to see how this was done. This is an example of the use of *nested* tags, that is, using one tag inside another.

More HTML

Don't you think it's about time that Jumbo's menu actually had a menu? Jumbo might not be the most astute marketer, so you may need to help him with his offerings.

For Jumbo's menu page you'd really like to have two kinds of lists. One list would let Jumbo highlight the unique qualities of his blends. This list would not have to be in any type of order. In HTML, this is called an *unordered list* and is created by use of the `<UL>` and `</UL>` tag pair. These define a bulleted list. Inside the list, you'll want to add some bulleted items. You do this by using the *list item* tags, `<LI>` and `</LI>`.

While this sort of list is fine for advertising bullets, some kind of numbered list would be better for the menu items. That way the customers can just tell Pierre the waiter that they would like two of the number 4 specials. To create a numbered list, called an *ordered list* in HTML-speak, you use the tags `<OL>` and `</OL>`. The individual list items use the same list item tags as the ordered list. Listing 1-11 adds one of each of these list types to the menu page. Figure 1-32 shows the result.

```
Listing 1-11 OrderedList.html
<HTML>
<!-- Listing 1-11 Jumbo's hyperlinked menu page          -->
<HEAD>
<TITLE>Jumbo's Jungle Java Joint - Primo Menu Page</TITLE>
</HEAD>
```

```
<BODY>
<H1>The Place for Premium Java </H1>
<HR>
<H2>Jumbo's quality ensures </H2>
<UL>
<LI>The Freshest Ingredients          </LI>
<LI>The Most Imaginative Concoctions </LI>
<LI>The Friendliest Atmosphere        </LI>
</UL>
<H2>Today's Specials </H2>
<OL>
<LI><B>bold</B> Brazilian Roast   </LI>
<LI><I>Italian</I> Espresso        </LI>
<LI><U>Luscious</U> Licorice-Lime</LI>
</OL>
<HR>
<A HREF="Logo.html">Go back to Jumbo's home page </A>
</BODY>
</HTML>
```

Lists can also be nested, that is, contained within other lists. Perhaps the Licorice-Lime was really not a good idea. On the other hand, maybe the customers only need some convincing. Listing 1-12 shows how nesting is done, and Figure 1-33 shows the result. Notice how indentation is used in the HTML file to clarify the structure of the list for a reader. Note also that the bullet symbols are different for first-level list items and second-level list items. The browser automatically selects bullets for you.

Listing 1-12 NestedList.html

```
<HTML>
<!-- Listing 1-12 Jumbo's menu gets nested        -->
<HEAD>
<TITLE>Jumbo's Jungle Java Joint - Primo Menu Page</TITLE>
</HEAD>
<BODY>
<H1>The Place for Premium Java </H1>
<HR>
<H2>Jumbo's quality ensures </H2>
<UL>
<LI>The Freshest Ingredients          </LI>
<LI>The Most Imaginative Concoctions </LI>
<LI>The Friendliest Atmosphere        </LI>
</UL>
<H2>Today's Specials </H2>
<OL>
<LI><B>bold</B> Brazilian Roast   </LI>
<LI><I>Italian</I> Espresso        </LI>
<LI><U>Luscious</U> Licorice-Lime</LI>
    <UL>
    <LI>Great for the whole family!!!    </LI>
    <LI>Add a topping of whipped cream!!! </LI>
    <LI>Try it ice-cold or piping hot!!!  </LI>
    </UL>
</OL>
<HR>
<A HREF="Logo.html">Go back to Jumbo's home page </A>
</BODY>
</HTML>
```

FIGURE 1-32

Lists

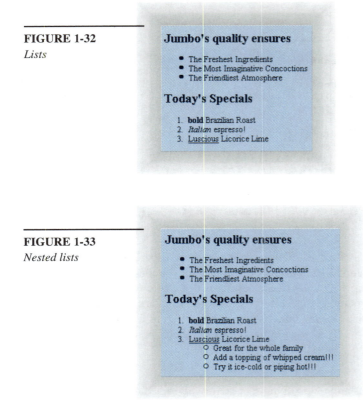

FIGURE 1-33

Nested lists

PREFORMATTED TEXT

Remember how the browser generally ignores whitespace (spaces, tabs, and returns) within the HTML document? This is usually a good and helpful thing, but occasionally you'll want to control the layout of a document, or a part of a document, so that the various elements line up precisely. The `<PRE> </PRE>` tag pair can be used for this purpose. The tags are useful for preformatted text. They cause the enclosed text to be displayed with a *monospaced* font, that is, one in which each letter occupies the same amount of space. Moreover, whitespace is displayed in the output just as it is placed in the input HTML file. This makes it possible to establish columns and so on and have them appear in the browser window.

As you can see if you type in the following listing, Jumbo is making one last attempt to get rid of that Luscious Licorice-Lime brew. In Listing 1-13 you can see the preformatted HTML text, and in Figure 1-34 you can see the result. Here's a revised listing of the menu page that uses the `<PRE>` tag, along with a figure that shows the result.

Listing 1-13 Preformat.html

```html
<HTML>
<!-- Listing 1-13 Jumbo's pricing strategy         -->
<HEAD>
<TITLE>Jumbo's Jungle Java Joint - Primo Menu Page</TITLE>
</HEAD>
<BODY>
<H1>The Place for Premium Java </H1>
<HR>
<H2>Today's Specials </H2>
<OL>
<LI><B>bold</B> Brazilian Roast  </LI>
<LI><I>Italian</I> Espresso!      </LI>
<LI><U>Luscious</U> Licorice-Lime</LI>
    <UL>
    <LI>Great for the whole family!!!    </LI>
    <LI>Add a topping of whipped cream!!! </LI>
    <LI>Try it ice-cold or piping hot!!!  </LI>
    </UL>
</OL>
<HR>
<H3>Today only pricing!!!</H3>
<PRE>
      1.   Brazilian Roast         1.25
      2.   Italian Espresso        1.75
      3.   Licorice-Lime            .25
</PRE>
<A HREF="Logo.html">Go back to Jumbo's home page </A>
</BODY>
</HTML>
```

FIGURE 1-34

Preformatted text retains its format in the browser

So, Where's the Java?

Now that you've learned a little HTML, you're ready to learn about Java itself. Later, when you've learned about Java applets, you'll see the HTML "incantations" necessary to add a Java applet to an HTML page.

WHO NEEDS JAVA, ANYWAY?

"Marvelous!" you think as you look down at the software package in your hands. Just what you've been looking for—the program that will solve all your problems, dry all your tears, fulfill all your dreams. Yes, life is truly good. And then you notice the fine print: "Runs on Macintosh only"; but your computer runs Windows. If your world does not exactly turn black and your blood does not quite run cold, at the very least you end up frustrated and annoyed. "Why can't every computer run the same programs?" you ask. Java may well be the solution to this problem.

Java is a computer language designed for programming on the Internet. At the moment, Java has the attention of the media and the public because of its ability to add action to otherwise lifeless Web pages. Most people accessing the Web do so using a modem and a dial-up connection. While full-motion images of the sort we've all grown to expect take too long to deliver over a modem, Java allows motion by sending still images over the Internet and then animating them locally, on the same computer that hosts the browser. This effectively overcomes the bandwidth bottleneck. However, the ultimate potential significance of Java extends far beyond such entertaining tricks.

Java's power comes from a new sort of portability known as *cross-platform binary portability*. Programs written in C or Pascal on one type of computer can often be ported to run on a different type of computer. The cost of doing this can sometimes be much less than the cost of rewriting the program from scratch. Nevertheless, such porting is often time-consuming and difficult, and frequently the results are less than ideal. For batch-oriented programs such as processing payroll or utility bills, such porting is often employed, but in these days of graphical user interfaces, moving a program from Windows to the Macintosh or UNIX is often a Herculean task. And, even if the program is intentionally written to be portable, what is actually portable is the source code—the high-level-language instructions—not the actual executable code. What if you could put that Windows 95 program disk in your X Window UNIX machine (and vice versa) and just have it work?

This is the portability provided by Java. A Java executable written for one computer can be run, without modification, on another computer supporting Java. The other computer does not need the corresponding source code to accomplish this feat; porting is automatic and virtually instantaneous. This means that users owning entirely different types of computers can download a Java executable from a server and run that executable on their systems and expect an identical result. Figure 1-35 shows this process. The capability of downloading a program and executing it on a variety of computers is expected to lead to entirely new kinds of application programs. This is the true magic of Java.

FIGURE 1-35

Downloading and exe-cuting a Java program

JAVA SOURCE CODE

```
public myApplet extends Applet {
    public void init() {
        Label myLabel = new Label("Hi");
        add(myLabel);
    }
}
```

**Javac
pseudocode
compiler**

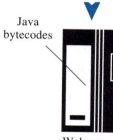

Java
bytecodes

Web server

Macintosh
Java virtual
machine

Win 32 PC
Java virtual
machine

UNIX X Window
Java virtual
machine

THE HISTORY OF JAVA

Java began life in 1991 as a programming language for consumer electronics devices at Sun Microsystems, Inc. At the time, Sun was seeking to diversify its business beyond the very popular UNIX-based workstations for which the company is still noted. Sun engineers seeking to build an intelligent remote control for multihundred-channel cable TV needed a simple programming language capable of hosting highly reliable software, because nothing is guaranteed to generate complaints like customers having their cable TV go down in the midst of a movie.

The Sun folks looked at several alternatives. Building a compiler for an existing language such as C++ seemed to require too much effort, because the hardware components of the system changed so frequently. Use of assembly language was rejected because of the difficulty of producing reliable software. In the end, the engineers decided to create a new language called *Oak,* built specifically for their task. Oak was based on C++ but lacked certain C++ features known to be a common source of programming errors. It also had additional features not found in C++.

Unfortunately for Sun, but fortunately for the rest of us, the anticipated market for intelligent remote controls failed to appear. This looked like the end of Oak. But the engineers working on the project took a step back and asked themselves, "What can we possibly use this thing for?" Some of them looked at the Internet and saw a unique fit. In a short period of intense coding they crafted a Web browser called *HotJava,* using Oak, which they rechristened *Java.* HotJava introduced the idea of an applet, a small program that could be downloaded from a Web server and executed within an environment provided by a browser. This early demonstration of the capability for animation of Web pages captured the attention of Sun executives, who decided to sponsor the Java project.

A preliminary (alpha) version of Java and HotJava was made widely available over the Internet as part of a free Java Developer's Kit (JDK). Sun reasoned that the only way to achieve wide-scale acceptance of Java as a universal standard was to make it available to everyone. The experiences of users and developers who experimented with Java were helpful to Sun engineers, who released a second (beta) version of the JDK that incorporated suggested improvements and corrections. In 1996, Netscape Communications Corp. announced that support for Java applets would be included in version 2.0 of its Navigator browser. Later that year Microsoft followed suit by announcing Java support for its Internet Explorer version 3.0. The Java revolution was on!

THE FEATURES OF JAVA

One of the first lessons children learn is to differentiate between types of advertising. Toys that are advertised as "new, exciting, fun, and thrilling" may pique our interest, but the words don't actually tell us much. When the box we carry home says, "Batteries not included," "Some assembly required," or "Illustration is 3× actual size," we quickly and painfully learn that these words convey real meaning. We normally call the former category "buzzwords" because of the emotional reaction they elicit despite their limited semantic content.

The features of Java were described in an early paper written by Sun engineers, "The Java Language: A White Paper." This paper defined Java as "a simple, object-oriented, distributed, interpreted, robust, secure, architecture neutral, portable, high-performance, multithreaded, and dynamic language." Although this torrent of computer-speak jargon has often been labeled the "buzzword description" and was doubtless intended with tongue in cheek, it nevertheless accurately identifies many of the features of Java that make it so well-suited for programming Internet applications. Let's briefly examine each of these words, with a view to better understanding what makes Java tick.

Simple

Let's face it, using a phone is simple, but programming a computer is not. So, when the designers of Java describe it as a simple language, you really have to ask, "Compared with what?"

Today, one of the most popular computer languages is C++ (pronounced "Sea-plus-plus"). This language was developed by AT&T's Bell Labs to bring object-oriented features to its popular C language. Despite its success, C++ has been widely criticized for being too complex.

Java, though adopting much of the look and feel of C++, is a much simpler language than C++. It has fewer and less-complex constructs, so it is easier to learn.

Object-Oriented

Like C++, Java is an object-oriented language. Object-oriented languages allow the programmer to organize a program so that it closely models the real world in structure and in the interactions among its components. This is particularly valuable in implementing applications using the graphical user interfaces popularized in the PC world by the various versions of Microsoft Windows. Writing an application using a graphical user interface tends to be much easier by use of an object-oriented language than otherwise.

Distributed

Java was built with the Internet and Web in mind. As do most other languages, Java includes prebuilt components or *libraries* that provide important additional capabilities beyond the language itself. However, Java's standard libraries specifically include network-aware units that greatly facilitate writing Internet applications. Additionally, the building blocks of a particular Java application do not have to reside locally, on your desktop machine, as they do with traditional programming languages.

Interpreted

Remember the second generation of programming languages? One of the first advances, after the invention of the program itself, was the invention of the program interpreter. Like the early Short-Code and Speedcode systems, Java is an interpreted language.

This means that Java's executable files are composed of so-called *bytecodes* that are instructions and data relating to a hypothetical computer called the *Java virtual machine.* Each machine that runs a Java program uses a small program, known as the *Java run-time system,* to execute the Java bytecodes in your program. This design is what makes it possible to run the same program on a Macintosh, a Sun, and a PC.

Robust

A robust program is one that does not fail (at least in a catastrophic way). If you've used a computer for any length of time, you're obviously aware that much modern software lacks this property. One cause of this is the complexity of modern software systems.

Java contains features that make the task of writing robust software easier. The designers did this by first omitting features (found in other languages) that are known to cause errors. They then added features (such as strong typing) that allow the developer to discover errors early, rather than after the product is in the customer's hands.

Other features in this same vein include automatic memory allocation, garbage collection, and exception handling. In Java programs, exceptions can be detected and handled according to instructions written by the programmer, often allowing software to keep working in the face of unexpected problems.

Secure

One of the potential terrors of the Internet is the possibility of security breaches—viruses that infect your computer, or hackers who take advantage of a software glitch to invade your personal cyberspace and make off with confidential information. Java has a multitude of ways for dealing with evildoers who would try to compromise your system using a Java program.

Applets, which are Java programs automatically downloaded when a Web page is displayed, are subject to a number of limitations that are designed to reduce the chance that simply viewing someone's page might result in harm to your system or data. No such system is absolutely reliable and none will ever be; but Java represents the state of the art in reducing the chances of a disaster.

Architecture Neutral

This means, of course, that your Java program will work identically whether you run it in a Quonset hut or in a Georgetown townhouse. No, wait! That's not what it means at all.

The word *architecture* in this phrase does not refer to the building in which you live, but to the home in which your computer program lives—in other words, the computer system. Java's bytecodes are designed to be read and interpreted—in exactly the same manner—on any computer hardware or operating system that supports a Java runtime. No translation or conversion is necessary.

Portable

An early form of portability involved carrying media, for example, floppy disks, from one system to another. Portability became a much larger problem once different sorts of computers were interconnected to form the Internet.

Java programs contain no implementation-dependent aspects, so the result of executing a series of Java bytecodes should always be the same, no matter on what system they are executed. Moreover, the Java run-time system itself, though it is written in C, is written in a way that simplifies porting the Java run-time to a new computer system.

High Performance

A typical problem with interpreted languages is that they are somewhat less efficient than compiled languages. A program written by use of an interpreted language may run 20 to 100 times slower than the same program written by use of a compiled language.

Java aims at overcoming this problem through the use of a technique known as *just-in-time compilation.* A just-in-time compiler is an interpreter that remembers the machine code sequences it executes corresponding to the input bytecodes. Having figured out the proper machine code sequence once, it doesn't have to figure it out again if the same code is reexecuted. Instead, it retrieves the memorized sequences and executes them straight away. Studies have suggested that just-in-time compilation may make interpretation of Java bytecodes almost as efficient as native execution of machine-language code.

Multithreaded

Most of us can walk and chew gum at the same time. All of us do many other things simultaneously. Computers are no different. If they are able to perform activities in parallel, the performance of the entire system can be improved. This technology is known as *multithreading.* A multithreaded system can, for example, format a floppy disk while a user surfs the Web using a browser. Multithreaded applications allow you to complete more tasks in a given time and to use a system's resources more efficiently.

However, developing multithreaded applications in C or C++ can be agony, because these languages lack standard support for operations necessary to create and control threads. Java includes support for multithreaded applications as part of its basic library.

Dynamic

Java's program units, *classes*, are loaded dynamically (when needed) by the Java run-time system. Loaded classes are then dynamically linked with existing classes to form an integrated unit. The lengthy link-and-load step required by third-generation programming languages is eliminated.

Thus, when parts of an application you use are updated, you don't have to buy the latest copy. The dynamic nature of Java allows you as a developer to always have the most up-to-date version of your software available to your users.

Using Java with HTML: Applets

Of course, the whole point of the minicourse in HTML earlier in this chapter was to show you how to add Java applets to your Web pages. Well, you're finally ready to do exactly that!

The tags used for this purpose are <APPLET> and </APPLET>. Several attributes should appear within the <APPLET> tag. The first is a CODE attribute that specifies the Java class file that contains the applet, using a URL. Usually the applet will be stored in the same directory as the page that uses it, so the URL is normally a relative URL. When this is not the case, the CODEBASE attribute can be used. It specifies the base directory containing files used by the applet, such as images and sound files. The CODE attribute then specifies only the file name, omitting the path.

Two other tags are generally included as well, the <WIDTH> tag and the <HEIGHT> tag. Each can specify the size of the window in which the applet will run, measured in *pixels*. Pixels are the tiny dots that make up the image on a video monitor. Most popular monitors display about 72 pixels to the inch, so using a width of about 200 and a height of about 150 is reasonable for a small applet. This could be done by specifying **HEIGHT=200 WIDTH=150** in the <APPLET> tag. Of course, the size of your applet is limited by the capabilities of your video card and monitor. For example, VGA provides a screen 640 pixels in width and 480 pixels in height. Of course, your browser will use some of this space—your applet can't have it all! Using a Super VGA video card and monitor that allow 1024×768 pixels or more is a real advantage.

Another way to specify the size of the applet window is by assigning the applet a percentage of the available space. This could be done, for example, by specifying **HEIGHT="75%"** within the <APPLET> tag. However, this method works only with browsers, such as Navigator or Internet Explorer. It won't work with the Appletviewer program you'll meet in Chapter 2.

The following listing shows how an applet can be included in an HTML page. Type the listing, changing the reference to the applet to match the directory where you installed the JDK files, and save it as Applet.html. Then load it into your browser and watch it run. Can you find the winning strategy? Listing 1-14 shows the HTML file, and Figure 1-36 shows a winning game.

FIGURE 1-36

A winning game

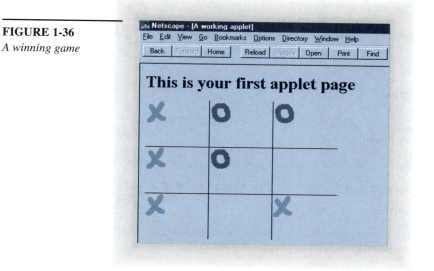

```
<HTML>
<HEAD>
<TITLE>A working applet </TITLE>
</HEAD>
<BODY>
<H1>This is your first applet page </H1>
<APPLET CODEBASE="/Java/demo/TicTacToe/1.1" ⇐
  CODE="TicTacToe.class"
  WIDTH="320" HEIGHT="240">
</APPLET>
</BODY>
</HTML>
```

Several other attributes can be used within the APPLET tag. The first is ALIGN, which can be either LEFT, RIGHT, or CENTER. This controls whether the applet's window is at the left margin, the right margin, or the center of the browser window. For example, to place the applet in the center of the browser window, include ALIGN=CENTER within the APPLET tag.

The VSPACE and HSPACE attributes can be used to include a margin around the applet's window. Specify a number measured in pixels. For example, including VSPACE=25 HSPACE=35 causes a 35-pixel horizontal margin and a 25-pixel vertical margin to surround your applet. Another useful attribute is ALT, which specifies a string to be displayed in place of the applet by browsers that don't support Java. For example, you might include the following within the APPLET tag:

```
ALT="This is a Java applet. You're really missing something
great!"
```

It seems that this string should also be displayed when the user has disabled Java support in the browser configuration. Unfortunately, some browsers fail to display the ALT text when this is the case.

Try these tags by adding an additional applet to the Listing 1-14 HTML file and viewing the result using your browser.

Summary

- Programming advances have occurred as programmers struggle to write larger and more complex programs.

- Computers have three main components: memory, CPU, and input/output.

- Computer memory consists of bits, which can be in an on or off state.

- A byte consists of 8 bits.

- In machine-language programming, the programmer writes numbers that represent the op-codes and data of the program.

- In assembly-language programming, the programmer refers to instruction op-codes and data by name.

- Virtual machine languages and interpreters allow programmers to write instructions for an "ideal" machine, but such programs generally execute slower than those written in assembly language.

- Compilers translate a high-level source language into native machine language and generally produce more efficient code than interpreters.

- Structured programming stressed the benefits of a divide-and-conquer approach to program construction, along with certain elements of programming style. These elements include single entrance and exit; sequence, selection, and iteration as primary control structures; and information hiding.

- Object-oriented programming extends structured programming by adding polymorphism, inheritance, and encapsulation.

- Polymorphism is the ability of different objects to respond distinctively to the same message.

- Inheritance is the ability to extend or expand existing objects.

- Encapsulation means that related data and instructions are treated as a unit.

- The Internet is based on protocols, which are standard ways of exchanging information between computers.

- The Web uses the Internet to create a vast hypertext document.

- Hypertext allows a reader to jump from topic to topic, rather than reading serially.

☕ Web servers store and provide access to hypertext and other documents.

☕ Web browsers control the formatting of Web documents.

☕ HTML is a simple language for specifying the format, and secondarily the appearance, of Web documents.

☕ HTML is based on the use of text files, which are "marked up" by use of special structural and formatting tags.

☕ HTML files can include images, hyperlinks, and executable Java programs called applets.

☕ URLs are used to specify the location and identity of every document on the Web.

☕ Java was created by Sun Microsystems, Inc. as a language for programming electronic appliances and was later adapted for use as an Internet programming language.

☕ Java is based on C++, but lacks certain problematical C++ constructs and adds certain useful constructs.

☕ Java is designed for producing reliable, portable software that is network aware.

Quiz

1. The modern digital computer was invented in the late _____.

2. Computers have three main components: _____, _____, and _____.

3. The on-off switches that make up a computer's memory are called _____, and each can store one piece of information.

4. A byte consists of _____ bits.

5. Instructions stored in the memory of a computer are called stored _____.

6. The numbers that represent machine-language operations are called _____.

7. Because machine-language programs work on only a specific CPU, such programs are not _____.

8. Low-level languages that allow the programmer to refer to instructions and data by name are called _____ languages.

9. By using program _____, programmers can write instructions for an ideal machine and expand their code into machine instructions a line at a time.

10. Program interpreters were disliked by some, who felt they executed programs too _____.

11. A program that translates an entire source program into machine language for efficient execution is called a _____.

12. High-level languages allow programmers to focus on the _____, rather than on how the computer works inside.

13. The structured programming technique of attacking a problem a piece at a time is known as _____.

14. Structured programming holds that each procedure within a program should have a(n) _____ entry and exit.

15. Structured programming recommends that programmers use only three control structures in their programs: sequence, _____, and _____.

16. Information hiding involves the use of _____ variables.

17. Polymorphism means that different objects respond distinctively to the _____ message.

18. Inheritance allows the ability to _____ existing objects.

19. Encapsulation involves treating related data and instructions as a(n) _____.

20. The Internet began as a communications network for _____ use, known as the ARPANET.

21. The Internet is based on the use of _____, standard ways of exchanging data between computers.

22. Hypertext documents allow a user to _____ from one document or topic to another, rather than reading serially.

23. The two programs involved in Web transactions are the _____, which runs continuously on a host, and the _____.

24. The _____ program decides how to format a Web document for display to the user.

25. HTML is a simple language for specifying the _____ of Web pages, not their appearance.

26. HTML embeds structural and formatting commands known as _____ in a text file.

27. The HTML tag used to specify an applet is the _____ tag.

28. The device used to specify the format, location, and identity of every Web document is known as a(n) _____.

29. An executable Java program embedded in a Web page is called a(n) _____.

Exercises

1. Using HTML, create your own home page. Use at least one list, one image, and several hyperlinks. If you have access to a Web server, post your page so others can admire it.

2. Add the `Clock` applet or another applet from the Sun JDK to an HTML page. You'll find these applets in distinct directories below `c:\Java\demo` (assuming you installed the JDK in `c:\Java`).

3. Create an HTML page that contains a list of different pizzas with suitably appetizing names. Under the name of each pizza, list its ingredients. Use a list of lists to do this.

4. Create a web of HTML pages that simulate the place where you live or work. Each page should represent a single location, such as your living room or your dining room. Hyperlinks should lead from each location to the immediately adjacent locations. For example, a hyperlink might lead from your kitchen to your dining room, but you probably wouldn't need a link joining your living room to the laundry room. Decorate each room with text and graphics that make it feel like home. If you own or can borrow a digital camera, you can use actual photos of each location on its page.

5. Create an HTML map that you can use to help visitors find your office or school. Make a page for each freeway junction or intersection that describes the location and has hyperlinks that trace the route there and back. Try out the map on a willing visitor. Buy the visitor lunch if he or she gets lost.

6. (Requires Web access) Visit the following Web sites for more information on Java. Use links found there and your favorite search engine to locate more sites. Summarize your findings in an HTML jump page that contains hyperlinks to the most useful and interesting sites.

URL	Description
`http://www.javasoft.com`	JavaSoft's (a Sun subsidiary) home page
`http://sunsite.unc.edu/javafaq`	Sunsite's Java page
`http://www.gamelan.com`	Gamelan's Java page
`news:comp.lang.java`	The `comp.lang.java` Usenet newsgroup

2

Programs: The Community of Objects

"You can't tell the players without a program!" goes the old saw designed to separate you from your dollars when you visit the ballpark. In a sense it's true, especially if you find yourself stuck on the top row of the bleachers. In this chapter, you'll learn the numbers, positions, and stats of the major players in OOP, see the view from the top of the stands, and finish in the dugouts with a front-row view of the action.

In Chapter 1, "What's All This Java Stuff?," you learned about the history of writing computer programs. This chapter will give you an overview—the view from the heights—of object-oriented programming in Java. After spending a little time building an object-oriented foundation, you will start building your own classes and objects. Every building needs an inspector, so you will spend some time taking programs apart, line by line, until you have a good understanding of the basic structure of a Java program, and of the rules and regulations you'll need to follow for every applet you build. Last, you'll get a preview of some of the chapters ahead, as you enhance and extend the programs you've built, putting some of those object-oriented principles to work. In this chapter you will learn

- How object-oriented programs are organized

- How classes are defined and objects created

- The meanings of state, behavior, methods, and messages

- How to use the tools required to build a Java applet

- The basic structure and rules required for every Java program

- How to populate your programs with a cast of objects, including `Label` and `Font`

- How to send a variety of messages to your objects, causing them to perform useful and entertaining tasks

- How to train your objects to respond to events in the real world

- How inheritance allows you to reuse and extend the objects you build today

The Way of OOP

In Java, programs are communities of objects. Each object in your program has its own attributes and behavior, and the program runs by the interaction among these objects. In this sense a Java program resembles your high school play, with the objects taking the part of the characters: the simple, yet straightforward `Label` family; those impulsive, action-oriented `Buttons`; and that fascinating, artistic `Graphics` fellow. In your program, each object has a personality that is displayed in its behavior "on stage." Unlike human actors, though, Java objects know how to take direction. When you tell Jacques the `Graphics` guy to draw a circle, he won't stand around asking you what his motivation is.

In this section, you'll learn a bit more about object-oriented programming. In the next section, you'll use your newfound expertise to construct your first Java applet.

MODELS AND THE REAL WORLD

Are programs real? Just what is a program? Fred Brooks, one of the luminaries of computer science, dealt with the ephemeral nature of computer programs when he wrote *The Mythical Man-Month* over 25 years ago.

The programmer, like the poet, works only slightly removed from pure thought-stuff. He builds his castles in the air, from air, creating by exertion of the imagination.... Yet, the program construct, unlike the poet's words, is real in the sense that it moves and works, producing visible outputs separate from the construct itself. It prints

Continued...

Continued...

results, draws pictures, produces sounds, moves arms. The magic of myth and legend has come true in our time. One types the correct incantation on a keyboard, and a display screen comes to life, showing things that never were nor could be.

Computer programs are information-processing systems. Like the juice maker in your kitchen, a computer program is a machine. You put oranges in one end of your juicer, turn on the electricity, and get orange juice out the other. Your computer program works similarly, except that it is more versatile. A juice-making machine—even the fanciest—does basically one thing. A computer program, on the other hand, can be designed to model or represent not only things in the real world, but things that never were nor could be.

Like most machines, a computer program is made of various parts or components that interact in precisely defined ways. Such a collection of interacting components is called a *system*—thus, computer programs are sometimes called information systems. Traditionally, when building one of these information-processing systems—a computer program—the builder concentrated on what the program needed to do. For complex programs, the main task would be broken up into subtasks. Each component in a traditional, procedural program thus ended up being a task or subprogram. In some programming languages these were called *procedures* or functions. A procedural program was designed so that information or data was passed from one station on a "data assembly line" to the next station until the data was fully processed, so to speak. Picture the conveyor belt of Figure 2-1, and you'll have a good idea of the organization of a traditional computer program.

OOP programs are organized somewhat differently. True, they are still systems of cooperating components, but the components are not divided according to tasks. Rather, the components are units that combine data with the procedures that operate on the data. These components are called objects. As you learned in Chapter 1, this process of combining data and procedures is called encapsulation, and it is one of the three major organizing principles of an object-oriented program. An object-oriented

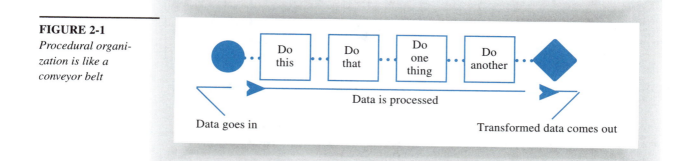

FIGURE 2-1

Procedural organization is like a conveyor belt

program acts more like the modern workgroup of Figure 2-2 than like the old-fashioned assembly line.

Remember

An OOP program is a system of cooperating objects.

WHAT ARE OBJECTS?

Objects are the building blocks of OOP software, just as subroutines were the building blocks of an earlier generation of software. Objects are the chunks in a computer program, where each chunk represents a part of the system modeled by the program. These things may be real things, such as students or library books, or they may represent more abstract concepts such as times or numbers.

All objects have three characteristics:

Identity: "Who" the object is

State: The object's components and their current characteristics

Behavior: What the object can do

What Is Identity?

Identity is how you tell one object from a similar object. Identity doesn't mean that every object has an ID number or some such thing. Identity can be as simple as giving

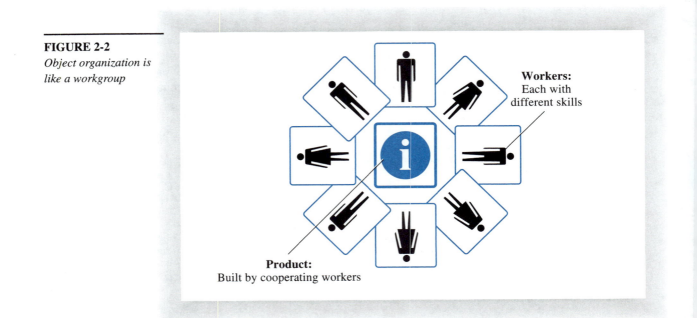

FIGURE 2-2

Object organization is like a workgroup

an object a name. Given identical twin `PizzaDeliveryPerson` objects, you can tell Fred from his brother Ned by their names. Even if their parents had named both of them the same, Fred and Ned would have two separate identities—it would just be much more confusing for the rest of us.

What Is State?

Saying that an object has *state* means that a particular object has properties that can change over its lifetime. The gas tank in your car can fluctuate between the full and empty states. Your hair color can fluctuate between the blond state last week, the auburn state this week, and possibly the mauve state next week.

What Is Behavior?

Finally, every object knows how to do something. Different objects may have different capabilities. The airplane object that took you to Hawaii knows how to fly. The caterpillar object on the sidewalk knows how to crawl.

 Remember

Every object has three characteristics: identity, state, and behavior.

WHAT ARE CLASSES?

When your child brings home a cardboard box, opens the lid, points inside, and asks you, "What's that?" what do you do? Providing the creature is not obviously dangerous, you try to classify it.

"Hmmm," you say, "It's got six legs. Must be an insect of some sort."

We call things that share the same general characteristics a *class* in the natural world. The same terminology has spilled over into OOP. A class, then, is a blueprint or pattern that defines the common elements of a group of objects. Just as creatures with certain attributes are classified as insects and not birds, your `PizzaDeliveryPerson` objects, Fred and Ned, belong to the `PizzaDeliveryPerson` class. Conversely, every object is an instance of some class; that is, Fred and Ned are instances of the `PizzaDeliveryPerson` class. Like objects, classes also have identity—that is, they are named to differentiate them from similar classes. Unlike objects, every class *must* have a name. See Figure 2-3 for an example.

 Remember

A class is a blueprint or pattern that can represent many objects. Every object is an instance of some class.

What Are Methods and Messages?

Earlier you saw that objects know how to do things. How do they know? The short-and-sweet version is that every class defines *methods* for performing certain operations.

FIGURE 2-3
Classes and objects

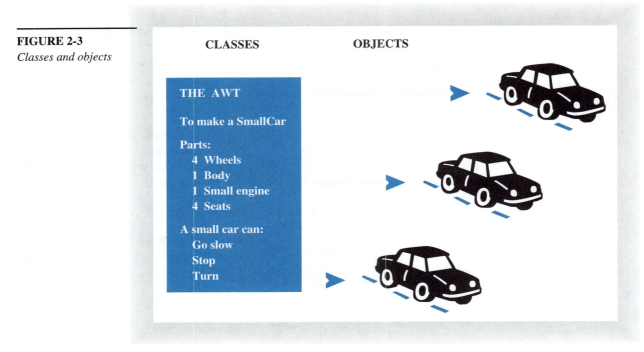

Every object that is a member of the class knows how to perform all of its behavior by virtue of the methods defined in its class. Thus, Fred is able to drive fast because he is a `PizzaDeliveryPerson`, and the `PizzaDeliveryPerson` class defines a method for driving fast.

"OK," you say, "Fred has the ability to drive fast because he's a `PizzaDeliveryPerson`. Does that mean he has to drive fast? What sets him off?"

Well, in the real world, which, after all, your computer program is intended to model, Fred drives fast because Bill out on Mountain Drive ordered a double pepperoni and told Fred, "Make it speedy if you want a tip." Bill thus sent a message to Fred that he wants his pizza right away. Bill couldn't care less how Fred accomplishes that. He may or may not know that all `PizzaDeliveryPerson` objects have the ability to drive fast—an ability they received just from being `PizzaDeliveryPerson`s. By sending the "make it speedy if you want a tip" message to Fred, he causes Fred to display certain behavior. Figure 2-4 illustrates the interaction between Bill and Fred.

Remember

Classes give objects the ability to perform actions through methods. Objects invoke methods upon receiving a message.

FIGURE 2-4
Bill sends Fred a message

What Are Properties and Attributes?

Properties and *attributes* are two words that mean the same thing—a storage area defined inside a class to hold the state of any objects it creates. Let's look at a `Pizza` object. Suppose, while modeling your pizzeria, you felt it was important to find out if customers were receiving their `Pizza` objects hot, because, in your experience, this is a critical factor in the success of a pizzeria. Each `Pizza` object would then have to be capable to change states from "piping hot" to "ice cold" and various temperatures in between. For any `Pizza` object to know what its state is, it would have to have some place to hold these different states.

To do this, the `Pizza` class defines a property or attribute called, for example, `temperature`. Every `Pizza` object created using the `Pizza` class thus receives the capability to record its temperature. A class, then, is a definition of methods and attributes that can be used to create objects of a certain sort. A `Car` class, for example, would contain attributes such as `color` and `body style`, and would define methods such as `start( )`, `stop( )`, and `turn( )`. Figure 2-5 shows a graphical representation of such a class definition.

Remember

Classes give objects the capability to store state by defining attributes.

WHAT IS INHERITANCE?

"Don't reinvent the wheel."

How often have you heard that? It's good advice. When building a computer program, why put all your energy into solving the same problem that thousands of programmers before you have already solved? There is no good reason.

FIGURE 2-5

A class definition

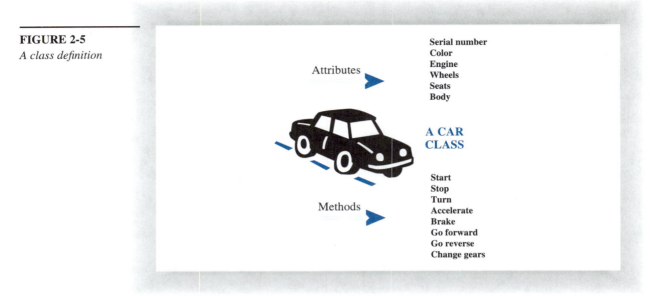

Attributes

- Serial number
- Color
- Engine
- Wheels
- Seats
- Body

A CAR CLASS

Methods

- Start
- Stop
- Turn
- Accelerate
- Brake
- Go forward
- Go reverse
- Change gears

Ways to avoid the programming equivalent of reinventing the wheel have been around since the beginning of computing. Function libraries, for example, are collections of subroutines that can be reused on demand and are arguably the most successful and accepted form of reuse in computer programs. Nevertheless, function libraries have several limitations. First, function libraries are organized around, naturally, functions—not objects—which hampers the use of function libraries in support of OOP. Second, function libraries offer no built-in way to extend the power of their components. If a programmer purchases a commercial library that doesn't do exactly what is desired, the only solution is to modify the original language instructions—the source code—if they are available.

OOP provides a revolutionary and elegant solution to both problems: *inheritance*. Rather than marketing libraries of functions, companies that develop software using OOP can market libraries of classes. Class libraries differ from function libraries in one important respect—they are extensible without modification of or even access to their source code. Class library vendors need not publish their source code, yet purchasers know that they can use the class library to meet their specific needs.

Recall that classes are used to create objects. This process is called *instantiation*, because an object is an instance of the class. But classes can also be used as a basis for creating new classes that can include new properties and methods. Such a new class is called a *subclass*, not because it has fewer capabilities, but because it appears below its superclass in a typical class hierarchy diagram. You might find it easier just to call the new class a *child* class and the original class a *parent* class. Figure 2-6 shows an illustration of a superclass and a subclass.

FIGURE 2-6

Inheritance, superclass, and subclass

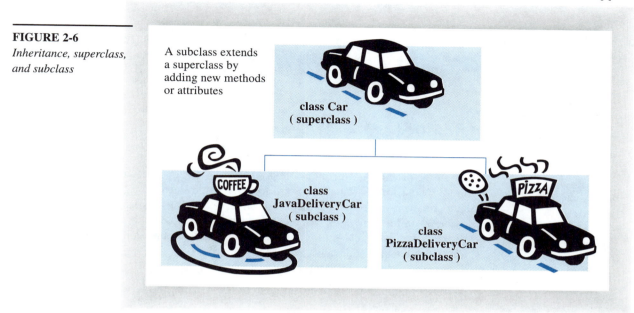

A subclass extends a superclass by adding new methods or attributes

class Car
(superclass)

class
JavaDeliveryCar
(subclass)

class
PizzaDeliveryCar
(subclass)

Remember

Inheritance is the ability of a class to create a new class. The newly created class, or child, is called a subclass. The creating class, or parent, is called a superclass. The subclass may have new properties and/or methods.

Putting OOP to Work: Building Objects

In the last chapter, you spiced up Jumbo's Jungle Java Joint by adding the `Tictactoe` applet. This applet, along with a host of others, has been supplied by Sun as part of the Java Developer's Kit (JDK). While `Tictactoe` is cool, the purpose of the JDK is not to supply you with neat applets. The JDK provides you with the tools needed to build your own applets and with some samples to study and learn from. The JDK provides several tools, but to get started, you'll need these:

- A text editor to write the Java instructions your applet will use. The JDK does not include a text editor, but you can use the MS-DOS Edit program.

- The Javac compiler to turn your source code into the object code that can be run on screen. This comes with the JDK.

> *" Different objects have different capabilities: An airplane object can fly, and a caterpillar object can crawl. "*

☕ The Appletviewer application, which also comes with the JDK. Appletviewer allows you to test your applets as you work. You may also want to have your Web browser running so you can see your applets in the context of the Web page.

CREATING YOUR JAVA PROGRAM: JUMBO'S JUNGLE JAVA JOINT STARTS JUMPIN'

One of the problems of being a sole proprietor, as Jumbo is about to find out, is keeping all the customers happy. The walls of the Jungle Java Joint look a little bare, and there are always a few bad apples who see an undecorated expanse as an invitation to senseless graffiti. One night that old herd instinct gets hold of some young pachyderms and they...well, you'll just have to recreate their applet to find out.

Creating an applet in Java is a four-step process:

1. Create the source code by using a text editor to write Java instructions.

2. Compile those instructions into bytecodes by using the Java compiler, Javac.

3. Create an HTML document to act as a host for your applet. This can be a full-fledged Web page, but most programmers just write a simple test file, which is easily edited and changed.

4. Execute, or run, your applet by loading the HTML file that references it, using either the standalone Appletviewer or your Web browser.

Look at Figure 2-7 to fix the Java development process in your mind, then break out your computer, and let's get started.

Creating Source Code

Java source code consists of Java instructions created in a text editor. Your Java source code files will always have the extension `.java`. Notice that the extension is four characters long. This is one of the reasons Java does not (yet) work on Windows 3.1; in Windows 3.1, file extensions can be only three characters long. If you use the JDK with Windows 95, the easiest way to create these text files is to use the Edit program in an MS-DOS window. (The Windows 95 version of Edit is a character-mode application, but it has changed considerably from the version of Edit supplied with Windows 3.1. The new version of Edit enables you to have multiple files open simultaneously and supports long file names.) Follow these step-by-step instructions to create the Java source code for your first applet, `GraffitiOne`.

Step 1: Open an MS-DOS Window   Open an MS-DOS window by first selecting Programs on the Windows 95 taskbar and then selecting MS-DOS Prompt from the Programs menu (see Figure 2-8).

FIGURE 2-7
*The Java development
process*

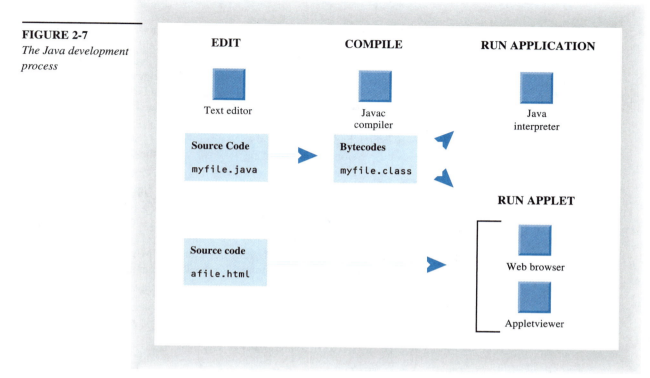

FIGURE 2-8
*Starting an MS-DOS
window from the
Windows 95 Programs
menu*

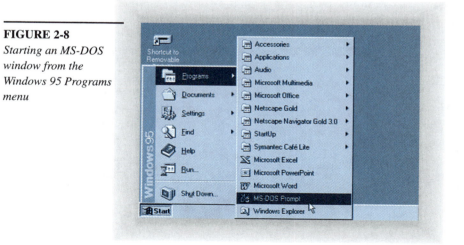

When the MS-DOS window opens, you can customize your working environment to your taste. By right-clicking on the menu bar, you can modify a list of properties. Under Windows 95, MS-DOS windows can have a toolbar that enables you to gain quick access to the various options. The property that will be most important to you is the ability to set the font so it is easily readable. You will spend a lot of time looking at your text in Java. Make it easy on yourself. Figure 2-9 shows an MS-DOS property sheet.

You can easily switch back and forth between a full-screen MS-DOS session and the smaller windowed version by pressing ALT-ENTER when the MS-DOS window is selected.

Step 2: Open a New Source File When you open an MS-DOS window, you are normally placed inside the Windows directory. Generally, it's not a good idea to save your JAVA files in this directory. For larger projects, you may want to keep a separate directory for each Java project. That means the first thing you will usually do is switch to the directory when you want to store your JAVA and HTML files. You do this by using the CD (Change Directory) command, like this (assuming you have already created the Examples directory):

```
C:\Windows > CD \OOP\Examples
```

Start to edit your program by typing

```
C:\OOP\Examples > edit GraffitiOne.java
```

and then pressing ENTER. Be sure that you type the extension in lowercase. The Java language is case sensitive, and this sensitivity extends to file names (unlike C or

FIGURE 2-9

An MS-DOS property sheet

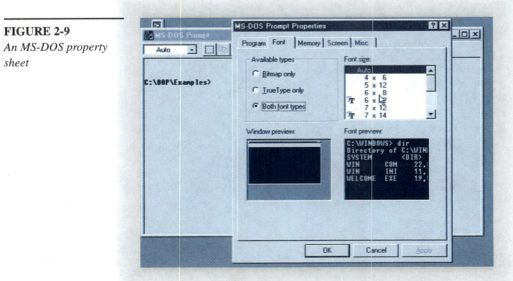

Pascal, for example). You should see a window that looks like Figure 2-10. Make sure that the title bar displays the title `GraffitiOne.java`. If you see anything else, select the Save As option from the File menu and change the name so that it exactly matches.

Step 3: Enter the Source Code Type in the source code from Listing 2-1. When you are done, save your changes. Make sure you pay special attention to

Capitalization: Java considers *Cat* and *cat* to be two different things.

Punctuation: It is easy to confuse the braces (`{ }`) that enclose a section of code with the parentheses (`( )`) that enclose arguments and expressions. You might also notice that most lines end with the semicolon (`;`) character. While the Javac compiler will tell you when you make a mistake, it's certainly advisable to avoid making one in the first place.

Listing 2-1 GraffitiOne.java -- your first Java applet

```
// What happens when adolescent elephants are left ⇐
unsupervised?
//
import java.applet.*;
import java.awt.*;

public class GraffitiOne extends Applet
{
    Label senselessScrawl = new Label("Elephants Rule!!!");

    public void init()
    {
        add( senselessScrawl );
    }
}
```

FIGURE 2-10

Editing your first source file

HTML Spells Home

Step 4: Create the HTML File   Java applets, the type of Java program you are creating, run inside a Web page or HTML document. You already saw how this works when you added the `Tictactoe` applet to Jumbo's home page. To run the `GraffitiOne` applet you just created, you need to create a place for it to live. You can do that by creating a new file from inside Edit. This is a three-step process:

1. Select New from the File menu. Edit will create a file called `UNTITLED1`.

2. Next, type in the information that will go into the HTML file. You will need to create an `<APPLET>` tag, remembering to set the `CODE` parameter to point to `GraffitiOne.class`. As in Chapter 1, you may dispense with the quotation marks, provided that the name of the applet contains no spaces or other unusual characters. Remember, though, that the `CODE` parameter is case sensitive. That means you must enter the code with exactly the same spelling and capitalization as the file appears in the directory. While you can create just a minimal test file (one that includes only the `<APPLET>` and `</APPLET>` tags), by typing in the full HTML text in Listing 2-2, you can give viewers of your page some idea of what they are observing.

Listing 2-2 ElephantsRule1.html

```
<HTML>
<HEAD>
<TITLE>Elephants Rule!!!  [1.0]</TITLE>
</HEAD>
<BODY>
<IMG SRC="Jumbo.gif" ALIGN=RIGHT>
<H1>Jumbo's Jungle Java Joint</H1>
<HR>
<H2>The Night the Lights Went Out at Jumbo's</H2>
Kept perhaps too long under the discipline of their elders, a
group of the younger pachyderms express themselves by ⇐
plastering
the side of Jumbo's Jungle Java Joint with an applet ⇐
expressing
their natural pride in the herd.
<HR>
<APPLET CODE=GraffitiOne.class HEIGHT=100 WIDTH=300>
</APPLET>
</BODY>
</HTML>
```

3. Finally, select Save As from the File menu to give your new file a name. The HTML file does not have to have the same name as the JAVA source code file—one Web page can hold several applets. Because you are displaying the `GraffitiOne` applet inside your page, why don't you name it `ElephantsRule1.html`? Figure 2-11 shows an example.

All right! The first leg of your journey is finished. The rest goes quite a bit more quickly, so take a breath and get ready to compile and run.

Compiling Your Code

As you recall, compiling your program is the process of turning the source code statements you typed in `GraffitiOne.java` into a runnable program—what is known as object code. Because compiled Java programs can run unchanged on any computer that supports Java, the output from the Java compiler is a device-independent form of object code called bytecodes. The program that converts your source code into bytecodes is called Javac, which is just shorthand for "Java compiler."

One of the advantages of working on a multitasking operating system such as Windows 95 is that you don't have to close one window to work in another. By opening another MS-DOS window, rather than shutting down your editing window, you can fix any mistakes in your source code without having to restart the Edit program and find your file again. The Edit program will let you keep several files open at the same time, and you can switch between them by selecting the appropriate window from the View menu.

Step 5: Compile Your Java Source Code   Once you have started a new MS-DOS window, set your working directory to the directory where you stored the JAVA and HTML files you just created. Refer to "Step 1: Open an MS-DOS Window" for instructions on how to do this. Once you are in the correct directory, you compile your Java program by typing

```
javac GraffitiOne.java
```

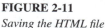

FIGURE 2-11

Saving the HTML file

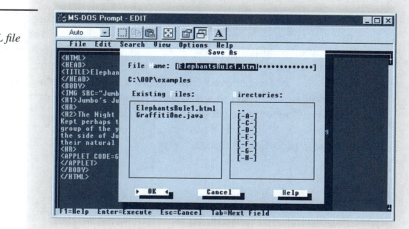

If all goes well, your computer will trundle along for a while, and eventually you will get a new prompt. If that happens, congratulations! Quite possibly, though, you will see some additional information printed on screen, usually with the word *error* prominently displayed.

When Bad Things Happen

Sometimes the messages that Javac prints to the screen are useful. At other times, they can seem inscrutable. Soon you'll be an expert at deciphering these strange sayings, but for now, here's a little introduction to get you started. The most common problems you're likely to encounter are discussed next.

Misspelling the Name of Your Source File   Here is an example of misspelling the source file name:

```
C:\OOP\Chap01>javac Graffitione.java
error: Can't read: Graffitione.java
1 error
```

Remember folks, spelling counts! If you make this mistake, Javac will respond that it cannot read the file. Actually, it will say that if it cannot read the file for a variety of reasons, but the most common reason is misspelling the input file name. In this example, the name is spelled `Graffitione.java` instead of `GraffitiOne.java`.

Forgetting or Mismatching the Number of Braces   Here is an example of a missing curly brace:

```
C:\OOP\Chap01>javac GraffitiOne.java
GraffitiOne.java:17: '}' expected.
}
 ^
1 error
```

Curly braces in a Java program come in pairs. For every opening brace, (`{`), there must be a matching closing brace, (`}`). The line that says `GraffitiOne.java:17` is the Java compiler's attempt to tell you where the error occurred. Unfortunately, what it really tells you is where the compiler first noticed that a required brace was missing. Frequently this is far removed from where the actual brace is missing. Your best defense against committing this error, and being forced to hunt down the errant brace, is to rigorously adhere to a set of coding standards for the placement and indentation of code blocks and braces. For now, carefully count the number and direction of each brace if you get this error message.

Mistaking Parentheses for Braces   Here is an example of incorrectly using braces instead of parentheses:

```
C:\OOP\Chap01>javac GraffitiOne.java
GraffitiOne.java:13: Instance variables can't be void: init
    public void init{ }
                   ^
GraffitiOne.java:13: ';' expected.
    public void init{ }
                   ^
2 errors
```

Most character sets have three sets of matching delimiters: parentheses, braces, and brackets. We often differentiate between braces and brackets by describing their shape. We say "square brackets" and "curly braces." This helps considerably, but, let's face it, even with the advent of high-resolution monitors, it is awfully hard to tell the difference between a brace and a parenthesis. The compiler is telling you that there are two errors here. In fact, there is only one—a set of braces appears where a set of parentheses should go. As you gain some familiarity with Java, you will make this mistake less frequently, but for now, you'll just have to double-check this item if you see a message like this.

Misspelling the Name of a Variable   Here is an example of a misspelled variable:

```
C:\OOP\Chap01>javac GraffitiOne.java
GraffitiOne.java:15: Undefined variable: senslessScrawl
        add( senselessScrawl );
             ^
1 error.
```

This is the last of the common compiler errors you are likely to encounter, and unlike the others, this is one you will probably encounter all of your programming life. What makes this especially difficult to understand is the error message that Javac spits out. "How can it tell me that `senselessScrawl` is an undefined variable when I've defined it just a few lines above? What's the matter with this compiler?" you will find yourself repeating. For your peace of mind, you need to quickly learn to interpret "undefined variable" to mean "misspelled word." While you happily created a `senseLessScrawl` variable inside your program, the `senselessScrawl` is nowhere to be found. As has been said before, Java is a case-sensitive language. This means that Javac would also see the two names `senselessScrawl` and `senseLessScrawl` as referring to different variables.

Recompiling   Fix any errors and recompile. If all went well, your Java source code file has now been transformed into a set of bytecodes. These bytecodes will have the same name as your source file, but the extension will be .class. Remember, that is the name you used in the <APPLET> tag inside your HTML file. At this point, you may want to double-check using the DIR command. Figure 2-12 shows a sample directory.

Compiler Switches

Maybe you find it disconcerting to sit and wait while the Javac compiler crunches away on your source code. If so, Javac has several switches or auxiliary commands that can be given to change the way it works. One of those is the verbose switch, which causes Javac to report every single thing it is doing while it works on your source code. These switches are given before the source file name and are preceded by the hyphen (-) character. To compile the GraffitiOne.java program with verbose output, you would use the command line:

```
C:\OOP\Chap01>javac -verbose GraffitiOne.java
```

The output from running this command can be seen in Figure 2-13. Other switches recognized by Javac can be found in Table 2-1.

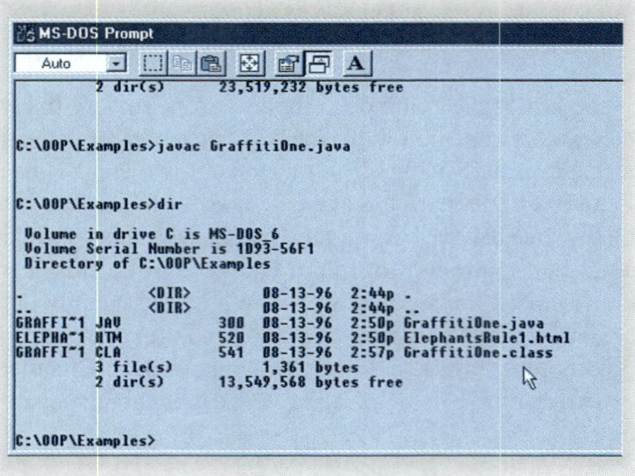

FIGURE 2-12

A directory showing Java source code, object code, and the HTML file

FIGURE 2-13

Compiling with the
−verbose switch

TABLE 2-1
COMMAND-LINE SWITCHES FOR JAVAC

SWITCH	MEANING
−classpath *path*	Allows Javac to search an alternate path for CLASS files, rather than just relying on the **CLASSPATH** environmental variable.
−d *directory*	Causes Javac to put the output into the named directory, rather than into the same directory as the JAVA source code files. Any directory specified that does not exist will be automatically created. If the file being compiled contains a package statement, the CLASS file created will treat this directory as the root directory for purposes of placement.
−g	Adds line number and debugging information to the object code that is generated. This option will not work if the −O option is selected.
−nowarn	Turns off warning messages, but still displays error messages.
−O	Turns on optimization, which makes object code that executes as quickly as possible. Note that this is a capital *O,* not a zero. This option does not work when debugging information is included (−g).
−verbose	Causes Javac to print a file-by-file display of its activity.

LOOKING AT YOUR PROGRAM

Now that you've compiled your applet, suffering the slings and arrows of Javac, it's about time you were rewarded for your labors and got a look at your work. If you have your Web browser running, you can tell it to open a file (not a URL) and point it to the ElephantsRule1.html file you created earlier. If you try to open the CLASS or JAVA files, that will not work.

Alternatively, you may want to use the Appletviewer application from the JDK. One of the disadvantages of using a browser is that you may have to quit the browser and restart it to persuade it to load a revised version of your Java program. If you're making lots of program changes, as when you're first trying to get a program to work, this can be quite annoying. Appletviewer, by contrast, performs this service cheerfully and without need of coercion. Most of the time, development using the `Appletviewer` is a little simpler, but you get to see only the applet itself, not the surrounding HTML file.

Because the Appletviewer doesn't display the context of the applet, it seems logical that you would start it by using the CLASS file. That's logical, but wrong. The Appletviewer application wants, as a command-line parameter, the name of the HTML file you created. It won't show you any of the HTML instructions, ignoring all but the `<APPLET>` tag. Nevertheless, that's what it wants. To start your applet with Appletviewer, use the incantation

```
appletviewer ElephantsRule1.html
```

Congratulations! You're a programmer. Figures 2-14 and 2-15 show the results of running the `GraffitiOne` applet inside the `ElephantsRule1.html` file.

FIGURE 2-14
The `GraffitiOne`
applet displayed by use
of Netscape Navigator

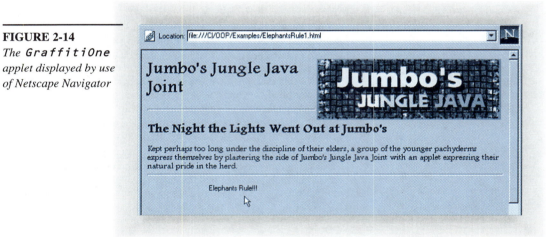

FIGURE 2-15
The GraffitiOne applet displayed by use of the Appletviewer application

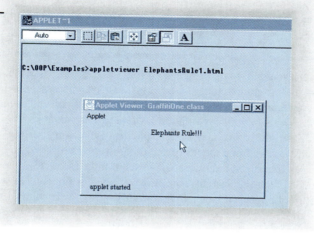

Building Inspector: Checking Out the Details

Let's face it, GraffitiOne is not going to set the world on fire, as far as nifty applets go. It's got no splash, no razzle or dazzle—it just sits there doing nothing. You could do better than that with plain old HTML! Well, that's true, but GraffitiOne is valuable, nonetheless, as an illustration of a minimal Java program. To understand a new subject, you always want to get to the heart of the matter, and the easiest way to do that is to strip away the extraneous. As *Dragnet*'s Sergeant Friday used to say, "Just the facts, Ma'am."

JAVA PROGRAMS: ORGANIZED LABOR

Java can create three types of programs (see the "Applet Versus Application" sidebar). This program is an applet, a program meant to be hosted by a Web browser, which provides a home for the applet. While there are some differences between applications and applets, the basics of writing a Java program remain the same, whether application or applet.

" Inheritance in OOP provides a revolutionary and elegant solution to the problems of code reuse. "

APPLET VERSUS APPLICATION

Java can create three main types of programs. *Applets,* like the `GraffitiOne` program, are programs that are hosted inside a Web browser or viewed by use of the Appletviewer application. *Applications,* by contrast, are run as standalone programs. You run an application by using the Java interpreter, named, reasonably, Java. These standalone applications have more capabilities than applets. They can read and write files, for instance, or do anything any other programming language such as C or Pascal can do. Applets are not allowed to do such things: Because applets are automatically downloaded over the Web by your browser, the designers of Java wanted to avoid the possibility of applet viruses. In addition to reading or writing files, applets are generally prohibited from making arbitrary network connections or running other programs on your machine.

So, if Java can make applets and applications, what's the third type of Java program? Applications come in two flavors: *console-mode* applications and *GUI* applications.

Console-mode applications use the traditional "glass teletype" to interact with the user. This type of interface, which was all that existed 20 years ago, is also sometimes called a command-line interface. Users interact with your console-mode application by typing in commands and responding to prompts in a command window. If you normally work in Windows, you might consider a console-mode application to be a "DOS" program.

The second type of Java application, GUI (graphical user interface), looks and acts like a familiar Windows, Mac, or UNIX X Window program. A Java GUI application is built around a bitmapped or graphical display and has four main components:

- *Windows,* which are rectangular regions of the screen that can display data or act as input areas for getting responses from your users.

- *Icons,* or pictorial representations of various actions that your program can perform. The most common iconic device in modern GUIs is the graphical control. A control graphically represents an input device that the user can use intuitively. Thus, rather than typing in commands to move through a file, the user can drag in a scroll bar. Rather than typing in a command to save the file, the user can click on a button or choose a menu item.

- A *mouse* or other type of input device that allows the user to directly manipulate these controls, mark documents for actions, and choose menu items. This reliance on alternate input devices leads to the last characteristic of a GUI interface, which is...

- *Point and click.* Most students find multiple-choice tests easier than fill-in-the-blank exams. Why? Because humans usually find recall more difficult than recognition. If asked to name our classmates in the fourth grade, most of us would be lucky to remember two or three. On the other hand, if we were given the class picture, even years later, names and incidents would come flooding back.

Every Java program is organized as a class definition and looks like this:

```
... some stuff
public class SomeClassName
{
    ... some more stuff
}
```

You'll look at the lines that start with `...` in a few moments, but now let's concentrate on the single line of text and the lines with the curly braces. We call the single line of text, `public class SomeClassName`, the class header. The curly braces act as delimiters that enclose the definition of the class. All of this is put into a text file that *must* have the name

```
SomeClassName.java
```

You recall that a class is simply the blueprint to make an object. Suppose you obtained a set of blueprints for the Porsche 928. Could you get into the blueprint and drive it to work, impressing your friends and coworkers? No. If you were skillful (and rich), you might be able to follow the instructions on the blueprint to build a real Porsche that you could drive. If you were very rich, you could build a factory to build lots of Porsches. You wouldn't need to have a separate set of blueprints for each car you made; the one set of instructions would be enough to build as many 928s as you wanted. The blueprints wouldn't help you at all, though, if you decided you wanted to build a 1962 Chevy Impala.

A class acts the same way as the blueprint does. It provides the information necessary to build an object. And, if you wish, you can build several objects from the same class definition. Let's look more closely at the header for your first applet.

THE HEAD OF THE CLASS

The header for the applet you just wrote says

```
public class GraffitiOne extends Applet
```

What does each word mean? You can break this line into three phrases. The first phrase, `public class`, is an example of a *declaration*. A declaration simply tells the compiler what you are doing. Writing `public class` at the beginning of your program is just like writing "History Term Paper" at the beginning of an assignment. When the professor picks up your paper, he or she knows what is coming next, because you have declared your intentions. In the same way, when the Java compiler sees `public class`, the compiler expects to see a class definition coming right on its heels. (While you may sometimes create a class that is not `public`, that will occur only in advanced situations.)

WHAT ARE KEYWORDS?

The words `public` and `class` are language keywords. A keyword is a word that has special meaning to Java—the built-in Java vocabulary, so to speak. These words are also sometimes called reserved words, because Java has reserved them for its own use.

That is important to you for two reasons: First, it means you cannot name your classes, variables, or methods the same as any of Java's keywords. Second, if you want to communicate with Java, you must use the vocabulary it understands.

Note that Java understands these keywords only in the most literal and pedantic manner. Dr. Fred Brooks, author of *The Mythical Man-Month*, likens this process to that of discovering just the right incantation to loose the genie from the bottle. With Java, not only do you have to use exactly the right words, spelled in exactly the right way, but you even have to make sure that the case of the letters is correct. Fortunately, in the case of the keywords, that is simple, because all the keywords use lowercase letters exclusively. Still, after spending an hour trying to figure out why the compiler doesn't understand `Public Class MyClass`, you might start wondering just how smart your computer is. The entire list of keywords is shown in Table 2-2. (Actually, `true` and `false` are not really keywords, but literals, which you'll learn about in Chapter 3, "The Atomic Theory of Objects: Working with Object Attributes.")

TABLE 2-2
THE JAVA KEYWORDS

abstract	default	goto	null	synchronized
boolean	do	if	package	this
break	double	implements	private	throw
byte	else	import	protected	throws
case	extends	instanceof	public	transient
catch	false	int	return	true
char	final	interface	short	try
class	finally	long	static	void
const	float	native	super	volatile
continue	for	new	switch	while

WHAT ARE IDENTIFIERS?

The next part of your class header (shown next) is the class name, `GraffitiOne`.

```
public class GraffitiOne extends Applet
```

`GraffitiOne` is not part of Java's built-in vocabulary, it is a name that you have chosen to call your class. While your school assignment might begin with "History Term Paper," the name of your paper might be "The Effect of Inflation on Third Century Roman Farmers." When selecting a name for your paper, you would try to create a name that reflected its content. You should do the same thing when you name your classes. The name of a class should give some insight into the nature or purpose of the class.

Not only will you provide your own names for the classes you create, but you will also be making up your own names for objects, attributes, and methods. These names that you make up—as opposed to the built-in vocabulary of Java—are called *identifiers*. Unlike the Java keywords, identifiers are not restricted to lowercase letters. They are still, however, case sensitive. That means if you were to create a class named `SpellChecker`, you could not later refer to the same class as `Spellchecker`. You could, though, make a new class called `Spellchecker`, and the compiler would know that these were two entirely different classes.

Besides being case sensitive, Java imposes a few other restrictions on how you create your identifiers. Identifiers must start with either a letter, the underscore (`_`), or the dollar sign (`$`), and all of the rest of the characters must be letters, digits, the dollar sign, or the underscore. There is no (defined) maximum length on the name of an identifier in Java as there is in some other languages. In practical terms, that means it's often easier to remember what you can't put in a Java name. Identifiers may *not*

☕ Start with a digit. *2Bad* and *4Rent* are both illegal identifiers.

☕ Contain spaces or special characters other than the underscore and dollar sign. Thus *Object-Oriented* is not allowed (hyphen) nor is *Big Ben* (space). In those instances where putting in a hyphen seems irresistible, you'll have to settle for an underscore.

INTENTIONS AND CONVENTIONS

If you can use almost any names you wish, what types of names should you use? There are two rules you should always follow when creating identifiers:

☕ Be understandable

☕ Be truthful

As you saw in Chapter 1, one of the first advances in programming languages occurred when programmers were allowed to use names to refer to memory locations. Rather than saying "Add the value in location 103732 to the value stored in location 372345, and put the result in location 732345," the programmer could say "Add MonthlySales to QuarterlySales and store the result in YearToDateSales." The incomprehensible became meaningful. But with this power comes responsibility. No programming language will force you to use understandable names. The programmer who writes

```
X1 = X2 + X3
```

fails to use the power that long identifiers bring to understandability.

Not only should your names be understandable, but they should also be truthful—an identifier name should accurately describe what the identifier stands for or does. Its name should honestly proclaim your intentions.

The Java community has (generally) agreed on a helpful set of naming conventions for program identifiers. Naming conventions are a little like social conventions. No one goes to jail for talking loudly in a movie theater or wearing Bermuda shorts to a formal dinner, but if you want to win friends and be accepted, you will refrain from doing so. The Java naming conventions were developed to enhance readability and understandability. Most identifiers use mixed case to improve readability. Different types of capitalization differentiate between different types of names in a Java program. Table 2-3 has a list of the naming conventions generally accepted among Java programmers. (You'll learn about methods, fields, and constants in Chapter 3 and in Chapter 4, "Simply Methods: One Step at a Time.")

TABLE 2-3
JAVA NAMING CONVENTIONS

Type of Name	Convention
Class names	`CapitalizeEveryWord`
Constants	`CAPITALIZE_WITH_UNDERSCORES`
Method and field names	`startWithLowercaseAndCapitalizeOtherWords`

WHAT DOES extends MEAN?

You're almost finished looking at the header for the `GraffitiOne` class. The last part is the line that says `extends Applet`. What does that mean? The word `extends` is a keyword that tells the Java compiler that the class you're defining is actually a child or descendent of another class, in this case the `Applet` class. Using the `extends` keyword tells the compiler you want to use the object-oriented feature called inheritance. Inheritance allows you to add features to an existing class. (You'll learn about it in detail in Chapter 10, "Inheritance: Object Families.")

Where Does Applet Come From?

So far so good. We know that you have created a `public` class named `GraffitiOne` that adds a little something to, or `extends`, the `Applet` class. Where, you wonder, is the `Applet` class? Is that one of those keywords? No, it couldn't be a keyword, you reason, because all keywords are written in lowercase, and anyway, keywords are like instructions or commands, while `Applet` is a class.

`Applet` is a library, or built-in, class. In some languages, such as BASIC or Pascal, certain facilities are built into the language. Both these languages know how to do output—for instance, using `PRINT` in the case of BASIC, and `Writeln` in the case of Pascal. Other languages, such as C, have no facility for output defined in the language. Instead they rely on a standard library of input/output procedures available to the programmer. Java has followed the lead of C and C++ in this regard and even gone them one better. Java not only includes libraries (in the form of classes) to do input and output, but it also provides an entire user interface library called the *Abstract Window Toolkit* (AWT). Java even provides classes that allow you to do things on the Web. One of these classes is called `java.applet.Applet`.

Building on the Work of Others

"So why didn't you say that `GraffitiOne` extends `java.applet.Applet`, instead of just `Applet`?" you wonder. "And didn't you say that identifiers could have no 'special' characters in them? Surely the period is a special character. Well, you're right on all counts.

First, you could, indeed, have used `extends java.applet.Applet` in your code, and everything would have worked just fine. The only drawback would be a little more typing. So, what of the special character—the period—in the class name? Actually, `java.applet.Applet` is not merely a class name, although it identifies a specific class. It's actually a multipart name. When humans first started identifying themselves, how did they handle the problem of two people with the same name? A common solution was to add some additional information to differentiate between them. Thus, Terry from York would not be confused with Terry from Lancaster, and John the Butler was kept separate from John the Baker. Eventually these naming conventions became regularized, and Baker and Butler became the two Johns' surnames. Java uses a similar technique. `Applet` is a class that belongs to the family `java.applet`. In Java, this type of family is called a *package*.

Creating packages is a fairly advanced topic that you will cover in Chapter 10, but using classes from the packages supplied by Java will be an everyday occurrence. All applets and all but the rarest application will use some of the presupplied classes. You tell the Java compiler that you want to use a package by using the `import` statement.

Statements and `import` Rules

The applet `GraffitiOne` has the following `import` statements:

```
import java.applet.*;
import java.awt.*;
```

These lines tell the compiler that you want access to all of the classes in the `java.applet` package and all of the classes in the `java.awt` package. The `java.awt` package supplies some graphics and component classes you will use in building your applets. Let's return to that in a few moments. Now just look at the line that imports the `java.applet` package. First, notice that the line ends in a semicolon. Lines that end in semicolons are called *statements*. A statement in a programming language is a complete sentence—it contains a complete instruction. Some statements may be longer and more complex than others, just as some sentences can be longer than others. But every statement ends in a semicolon, and no statement is finished until it reaches a semicolon. You'll take a closer look at statements in Chapter 3.

Next, notice the star (*) right before the semicolon. This acts a little like the wildcard character under DOS and UNIX; that is, it tells the compiler you want to have access to all the classes in that package. Because the only class used in `java.applet` was the `Applet` class, you could just as easily have said: `import java.applet.Applet`. You're probably getting excited, thinking, "Why don't I just write `import java.*` and get all the packages?" Unfortunately, that doesn't work. The star character is only somewhat similar to the DOS/UNIX wildcard character. It can be used to stand for all *classes*, but not for all *packages*.

THE CLASS BODY

Whew! You've finally gotten the class header out of the way and thrown in a few `import` lines as well. Now it's time to tackle the *body* of the class. The class body is where you will define *attributes* and *methods*. Attributes are pieces of information that you want each object to carry around. Attributes will be used to hold the object's state. Some examples of attributes you carry around are your age, your eye color, and your favorite food. Your Porsche class might carry around body color, serial number, and year built. Methods are where you define the actions your objects can perform. These are similar to procedures or functions in other languages. You might want your Porsche class to have methods called `start( )`, `go( )`, and `stop( )`.

Braces, Whitespace, and Semicolons

Every class header must end with an opening brace (`{`) that begins the class definition. The class definition ends with a closing brace (`}`). These two symbols are used to show where Java code starts and ends. Some languages, such as Pascal, use the words *begin* and *end* to mean the same thing. The Java code between the two braces is called a *code block* or, more commonly, just a block. The block that starts right after the class header and ends after the last method or attribute is called the *class body*. See Figure 2-16 for an illustration.

In the last chapter, when you added the `Tictactoe` applet to Jumbo's Web page, you might have taken a look at the JAVA files and noticed that they looked a little different from the code you've typed here. Most likely, the opening brace of the class body appeared on the same line as the class header, like this:

FIGURE 2-16

The class header, braces, and body

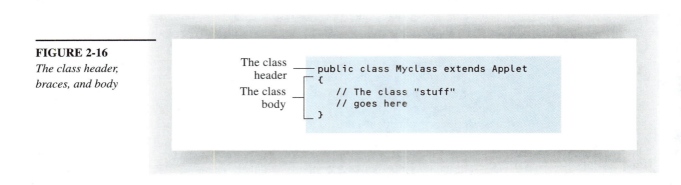

```
public class Myclass extends Applet
{
    // The class "stuff"
    // goes here
}
```

```
public class GraffitiOne extends Applet {
    //    class body stuff
}
```

You wonder, "Doesn't it make a difference that the braces are in two different places?"

No and yes. Java, like C and Pascal, is a freeform language. Java uses punctuation, not the position of the characters on the page, to interpret your source code. Early languages, such as FORTRAN or COBOL, were written by use of punched tabulation cards. In these languages, each element had to fit in a particular position so that it could easily be read by the card reader. Thus, the end of a line acted as the end of a statement. This isn't true in Java.

What kind of punctuation does Java use? You've already seen two examples. When you looked at the `import` statement, you saw that it ended with a semicolon. In Java, the semicolon acts a little as the period does in English—it ends a statement, which you can think of as roughly analogous to a sentence. The second punctuation character you've encountered is the brace. Braces are used to enclose a section of Java code and are thus similar to the way you use parentheses in English—to set off or enclose a parenthetical thought or remark.

If spacing really doesn't matter, does that mean you can write your whole program as one big line of text? Yes, you can. Or, you can write it out one word at a time. Listings 2-3 and 2-4 are both legal class definitions. To the Javac compiler, they appear identical.

Listing 2-3 Scrunched-up class definition

```
public class GraffitiOne extends Applet { Label
senselessScrawl = new Label("Elephants Rule!!!"); public void
init(){ add( senselessScrawl ); }}
```

Listing 2-4 Spread-out class definition

```
public
class
GraffitiOne
extends
Applet
{
Label
senselessScrawl
=
new Label
(
"Elephants Rule!!!"
)
;
public
void
init
(
)
{
add
```

continued on next page

continued from previous page

```
(
senselessScrawl
)
;
}
}
```

The obvious question is, "Which of these would *you* rather read?" The answer is equally obvious, "Neither!" Formatting source code is not for the benefit of the computer, but for the benefit of you, the human reader. If we were concerned only about the computer's understanding, we would write in machine language and avoid the translation step altogether.

This book will generally use a style that lines up the opening and closing braces in a block and then indents the stuff inside the block. Each beginning and ending brace will generally be on a line by itself. This makes it easy to separate the inside of the block from the outside, and lining up the braces makes it easy to see whether you've missed a brace. The style you saw in the `Tictactoe` example, where the opening brace is on the same line as the class definition, is the traditional style of laying out code in UNIX and C. The chief advantage of this style of coding is that you can see more lines displayed on your video terminal, because the opening brace is not taking up a line of its own.

It's not really important which layout style you adopt. It *is* important that you are consistent in using a style.

State and Behavior

Finally, you're ready to start looking at that other stuff—the actual Java code in your program. Recall that any class consists of its attributes and its methods. Your class consists of one attribute (a `Label` that contains the text "Elephants Rule!!!") and one method (`init( )`) that adds the `Label` to the surface of your applet where it can be proudly displayed. Let's take an in-depth look at these two pieces.

THE PROPERTIES OF ATTRIBUTES

The single attribute for this class, the `Label` object named `senselessScrawl`, is defined and created in the line

```
Label senselessScrawl = new Label( "Elephants Rule!!!");
```

In Java, the attributes of a class are stored in *instance variables*, or *fields*. A variable can be thought of as a bucket or a mailbox or a slot; a variable is a place in memory where you store information. You might think of it as similar to the form you have to fill out if you hope to win the Publisher's Clearing House sweepstakes and find Ed McMahon on your front lawn with a check for $10,000,000. When you fill out the form, there are lots of slots or boxes that can be filled with information. There's a box to hold your name; there's a box to hold your address. There's even a box to hold the name of the magazine you want to subscribe to. Each of those slots or boxes or fields

" A class, like a blueprint, provides the information needed to build an object. "

acts as a variable. PCH sends out thousands of forms, and each form they get back has a different value filled in for the name or address field.

An instance variable, or field, is a place you've reserved inside your class to store information. For your Porsche 928 class, you create a slot to hold the color of each automobile that comes off the line. You might also want to store the serial number and how much it cost you to build each car. Each car—each instance or object—could have a different value stored in that slot: One might store red, while another might store blue.

One more thing to know about class fields: You must tell the Java compiler what type of thing you are going to store inside the slot. If you go home and take a look through your cupboards and browse through your refrigerator, you'll notice a wide variety of packaging. Milk comes in cartons, soda comes in cans and bottles, cereal comes in cardboard boxes. Why don't we use one sort of container to store everything? Partly because when you store the milk inside the cereal box, the box disintegrates and leaks milk all over the inside of your cupboard! We package things in containers that are adapted to the types of things they are going to hold: wet things in waterproof containers, big things in big containers, little things in little containers. Most of us don't purchase our Tabasco sauce in 50-gallon drums or our heating oil in table-size decanters.

Instance variables work in a similar manner. For every attribute you define in a class, you need to tell Java what type of thing it is. For your first applet, the `GraffitiOne`, you're going to define a field that is a `Label`.

Making a New `Label`

`Label` is a built-in class supplied with Java. A `Label` can do several things. First and foremost, as you might suspect, a `Label` can hold some text. A `Label` that couldn't label anything wouldn't be of much use. In addition to holding text, a `Label` can display itself or move itself around the screen. A `Label` object also holds information about its appearance: what typeface or font it should use to display itself, as well as whether it should display its text left-aligned or right-aligned.

Defining Property Rules

All fields are defined in essentially the same way. You perform these three tasks to define a field:

1. Tell Java what kind or type of thing you are going to store.

2. Provide a name for the field.

3. Give the field a value.

Start with Some Class   To tell Java what kind of thing you're going to store, you name the class that the attribute belongs to. You want to store a `Label` object, so your definition starts with `Label`:

```
Label senselessScrawl = new Label( "Elephants Rule!!!");
```

If you wanted to store the color of each Porsche 928 that came off your assembly line, you would create a field that could hold `Color` values (another supplied object type in Java). Your definition of that attribute would then start with `Color`:

```
Color . . . ;
```

Give Your Field a Name   The next step is to provide an identifier, or name, for your field. The class type is not enough to uniquely identify each field. In the `GraffitiOne` applet, you've named your field `senselessScrawl`:

```
Label senslessScrawl = new Label( "Elephants Rule!!!");
```

When you name a field, you can create a separate definition for each field, or you can use commas to separate definitions. If you, for some reason, felt that all of your Porsches should have doors that were different colors from the bodies, you could create those definitions like this:

```
Color bodyColor;
Color doorColor;
```

or like this:

```
Color bodyColor, doorColor;
```

In this example, both `doorColor` and `bodyColor` are different fields, even though both can refer to `Color` objects. Now, looking at this line of code, quickly tell what color `bodyColor` will have if you create a new Porsche object. Give up? The answer is, "none." While you have created a field or slot that can refer to a `Color` object, you haven't yet put a reference to a `Color` object into that slot. When fields are not given a value, Java provides them with a special value so that you will know they don't have a value yet. That special value is called `null`.

It's easy to give each of your attributes a value. For your `Label` object, just make a new `Label` object and assign its reference to the slot you've created: `senselessScrawl`. You say you don't know how to make a `Label` object? Never fear. The `Label` class itself, like all other classes, has a built-in method to create or construct a new `Label` object for you. Even if you don't know how to create a `Label`, the `Label` class does. All you need to do is say the word.

Assigning Values   "Wait," you say, "What do you mean, 'assign its reference to the slot'? How do I do that? And what does that mean?"

Assignment means, simply, to store a value in a variable or field. To store a value, you use the assignment operator, =. While this might look like the equal sign you learned about in algebra, it's not exactly the same. In algebra, you used this symbol to say something like

```
13 = x + 7
```

Because in an equation, both sides are—by definition—equal, you know that x has to have the value 6 for the equality to hold. This equation, which makes perfect sense in algebra, is complete nonsense in Java (and most other programming languages).

When you use the assignment operator, you are telling Java to copy the value that is on the right-hand side, and store it in the location on the left-hand side. Thus, any time you use the assignment operator, the left-hand side must be a field or variable; it has to be a place where you can store something. So, with that out of the way, let's look at asking the `Label` class to construct a `Label` for us.

Building new ***Objects with Constructors***   Earlier you learned that classes act like blueprints to build objects. How do you build an object if you have one of those blueprints? Easy—each class has a special method that acts like a factory. If you tell the class you want a new object, it will churn one out for you. To use this special method, you need to do two things:

☕ Use the keyword `new` to alert the class that you want it to build you a new object. (Intuitive, huh?)

☕ Use the name of the special method that the class provides, sending it any additional information it might require to customize the created object to your specifications.

When you have done that, Java will provide you with a value you can store in your field. This value will be a reference to the new object you just asked it to create. You can think of this reference as a remote controller that will allow you to tell the object to do your bidding.

How do you know what the name of that special "factory" method is? Well, that's the easiest part of all. These special methods, called *constructors*, always have the same name as the class for which they construct objects. Thus, the name of the constructor method for `Label` objects is `Label( )`, and the constructor for `Color` objects is `Color( )`.

Parentheses and Arguments   Did you notice the parentheses after the name of each of these constructors? When Java sees the parentheses, it knows that you want it to run one of these special constructor methods and to give you back an object. If you leave the parentheses off, Java is confused, thinking you are trying to define a new field variable. You will always use the parentheses when using `new` to create an object. You will never use the parentheses when using a class name as the first word in a field definition.

The parentheses serve an important purpose. They let you customize the way that Java constructs your objects. By putting values inside the parentheses, you tell Java that you want to send some information to the constructor method that it will need to make an object to your liking. You might want to make sure that your Porsche is painted red when it's built, rather than having it repainted after you get it. The `GraffitiOne` applet wants to make sure that its `Label`, `senselessScrawl`, refers to the value `"Elephants Rule !!!"`. Putting these values inside the parentheses when using a method is called sending an *argument* to the method. In this case the text, `"Elephants Rule !!!"`, is the single argument to the `Label` constructor.

Attribute Recap

Before you finish your tour of `GraffitiOne`, you'll want to make sure you understand how to define an attribute for a class. The field definition

```
Label senselessScrawl = new Label( "Elephants Rule!!!" );
```

Begins with a class name. This field is going to be a `Label`.

Names this field `senselessScrawl`. You will decide what name should go here, subject to Java's naming rules and restrictions.

Creates a new `Label` that stores the initial value `"Elephants Rule!!!"`. A reference to this new `Label` is then assigned (or stored) in the field `senselessScrawl`.

Technically, the acts of defining the new `Label` field and creating a new `Label` object could be done separately. However, the code to construct the new `Label` would then need to go inside a method that might be somewhat removed from where you defined the original field. There is a chance—a very good chance—that you would forget to provide an object at all, which is a quick way to have your applet crash and burn (at least figuratively).

THE BEHAVIORAL METHOD

Where and when do objects begin life? How do Java programs run? Why do trees exist?

Hard questions, all. And as with all hard questions, the answer is usually "that depends." In the case of how Java programs run, it depends on what kind of programs they are. Java applications, both console and GUI, start running when the Java interpreter—appropriately named *Java*—loads them and attempts to find a method with the special name `main( )`. Java applets, on the other hand, start to run either when they are loaded by a Web browser, such as Netscape Navigator or Microsoft Internet Explorer, or when they are run using the JDK Appletviewer utility. As you saw when you ran `GraffitiOne` for the first time, your Web browser will display your applet in the context of the HTML page you create, while Appletviewer shows only the applet itself. In both cases, though, you refer to the compiled CLASS file by using the `<APPLET>` tag in an HTML document.

When an applet is loaded, the browser or Appletviewer will do three things. First, it will set aside the space that has been reserved for your applet when you wrote the `HEIGHT` and `WIDTH` parameters inside your applet tag. Next the Appletviewer—or more precisely, its run-time Java Virtual Machine (VM)—will construct any objects that you specified as fields when you defined your class. In our case, the VM would construct the `Label` object, `senselessScrawl`. Finally, the Appletviewer will invoke or run a set of five specific methods. Those methods are init( ), which runs when the applet is first loaded

start( ), which runs after init( ) is done or whenever a user returns to your page after leaving it

stop( ), which runs when the user leaves your page

paint( ), which runs when Java displays the surface of your applet

destroy( ), which runs when the applet is discarded

You do not have to write code for any of these methods: If you don't, Java will write it for you. What does the code that Java writes do? Nothing. Or at least nothing interesting. To make your applet do anything at all, you will need to write at least one of these methods yourself. In GraffitiOne, you've written some code for the init( ) method.

Defining Behavior

How do you write a method? Good question! Like a class definition, a method definition has two parts: a header and a body. Also like a class definition, the body of the method is enclosed in braces. The entire body of a method lives inside the class that it is part of. Figure 2-17 illustrates this graphically. The body of a method definition provides a list of steps—written in Java code—that an object created from the class will follow to perform some operation.

A Method Header's Five Easy Pieces

The header for the init( ) method looks like this:

```
public void init( )
```

FIGURE 2-17

A class and its methods

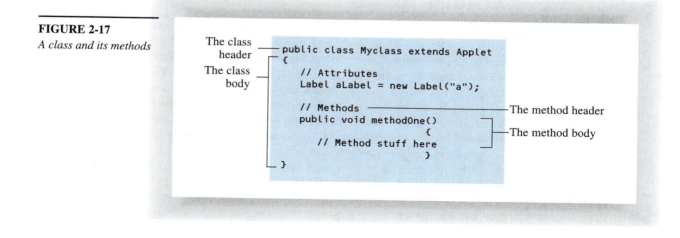

This method header has five parts. First is the keyword `public`. A `public` method is one that can be seen and used by other classes. So, making the `init()` method `public` allows its use by classes other than the `GraffitiOne` class. This is an important issue when you create large programs. For the moment, creating large programs is among the least of your concerns, so let's defer a thorough explanation of this point until Chapter 10.

The second part of the header is another keyword, `void`. Does that mean that this is a meaningless method? No. Generally, methods come in two basic types: those that tell you something you want to know, and those that perform some action for you. The job of the `init()` method is to perform an action, not provide information. When you write a method that returns no value, you should declare it to return type `void`, but if the method does produce some information, the kind of information it produces would go here.

The third piece is the name of the method, `init`. This is followed immediately by the fourth piece, the paired parentheses, which always appears in a method header. The Java compiler will not accept a method header that lacks these parentheses. Outside a program, as in the text of this book, it's customary when writing the name of a method to include the parentheses along with the method name itself. Including the parentheses makes it clear that we're referring to a method, rather than to a similarly named program variable. From now on, we'll follow that convention diligently.

The parentheses are used to enclose the fifth and final part of the method header, the arguments. If there *were* any arguments, this is where they'd be placed. Remember that Java arguments have nothing to do with disputes; they are values provided to a method that cause it to adjust its behavior to accommodate some special situation. In effect, they "customize" the method, and you'll learn more about them in Chapter 4. You know from looking at the method header that the browser provides no arguments when it invokes the `init()` method. If there were any, they'd be shown in the method header.

A CLOSING COMMENT

The lines in Figure 2-17 that begin with `//` are comments. Helpful as they can be to a human reader of a program, they are entirely ignored by the Java compiler. Thus, you can write comments in any form you please, without worrying about rules.

Even though the computer doesn't need them, you should include comments in every program you write. While the computer is content with a machine-language program of 0s and 1s, the whole point of writing programs in a high-level language is to make them clearer and more understandable to humans. Comments are indispensable in this regard. They don't cause your program to run slower or to use more memory, so include them freely in your programs.

Java has three kinds of comments. The first begins with a pair of slashes with no space between them (`//`). When the Java compiler finds these paired slashes, it simply ignores the remainder of the line. If the slashes are at the beginning of the line, the entire line is ignored.

The second kind of comment is useful because it can span multiple lines. When the Java compiler finds /*, it ignores all subsequent text until it finds */, even if the text occupies several lines. Here is an example of a multiline comment:

```
/* This is
a
longer
comment that spans several lines */
```

The multiline comment is useful for including longer comments in your program, because it's not necessary to include // on every line. You merely tell the Java compiler that a comment has begun and subsequently tell it that the comment has ended.

The third kind of comment begins with /**. It ends with the same */ as the multiline comment. These so-called *doc* comments are used by the Javadoc utility included in the JDK. Like other comments, they are ignored by the Java compiler. The Javadoc utility rummages through JAVA source files, looking for classes, methods, and doc comments. From these, Javadoc builds a database containing information about the source files, which it ultimately converts into program documentation in HTML format. Although the Javadoc utility can help document your Java programs, we won't deal with it in this book, because our emphasis is on writing Java programs. The Javadoc utility is most useful when you're writing programs of more than 1,000 lines. Consult the documentation that comes with the JDK for more information on how to use the Javadoc utility.

Messages

The useful thing about objects is that they can do things. You ask an object to do something by sending it a message. Methods contain the steps used by an object to carry out your request. Because the Label object in GraffitiOne doesn't seem to be doing anything, let's send it a message. Perhaps you could tell it to use really big type to display itself. In Listing 2-5 you'll add a new field to the GraffitiTwo class and extend the init( ) method of the class.

INTRODUCING A NEW OBJECT: THE FONT

The new field you'll need is a Font object. Font objects are used to hold the typeface, size, and other information about a text font. The particular Font object in the revised class is named realBigFont. As you'll see, this is an appropriate name. The new operator is used with a constructor for the Font class, Font( ), to create the Font object. In the GraffitiOne program, you created your Label object like this:

```
Label myLabel = new Label("Elephants Rule!!!");
```

The Label class used the text "Elephants Rule!!!" to change the state of your Label object. You create a new Font object in exactly the same way, except that the Font class needs three pieces of information to make a Font, not merely one.

Listing 2-5 GraffitiTwo.java--sending messages to objects

```
// The "kids" give their label some orders
//
import java.applet.*;
import java.awt.*;

public class GraffitiTwo extends Applet
{
    Label senselessScrawl = new Label("Elephants Rule!!!");
    Font   realBigFont = new Font("Helvetica", Font.BOLD, 36);

    public void init()
    {
        senselessScrawl.setFont( realBigFont );
        add( senselessScrawl );
    }
}
```

The first argument (piece of information) the `Font` class needs is the name of the typeface you want your `Font` object to use. While you can use any typeface name you like here, the only typefaces Java is guaranteed to recognize are `"Helvetica"`, `"TimesRoman"`, `"Courier"`, `"Dialog"`, and `"Symbol"`. In addition to the typeface, you'll need to specify in what style the type should be rendered. The `Font` class gives you three choices: `BOLD`, `PLAIN`, and `ITALIC`. To choose one of these, you have to use the class name, `Font`, along with the style you want. A period separates the class from the style, like this: `Font.BOLD`.

Finally, you need to tell the `Font` class how big to make the text, which you've specified here as `36`. What does `36` mean? Type is usually measured in something called *points,* which are about 1/72 inch. However, your browser's capability to resize and rescale images makes this result rather unreliable. A better way to look at things is to assume that standard text is printed in a 12-point font. Thus, whatever the actual size of a 36-point font, it's about three times the size of standard text. In other words, it's big. Table 2-4 summarizes the arguments of the `Font` constructor.

TABLE 2-4
Font CONSTRUCTOR ARGUMENTS

ARGUMENT NUMBER	MEANING
1	Font family (for example, `"Helvetica"`, `"Courier"`, and so on)
2	Font style (`Font.PLAIN`, `Font.BOLD`, or `Font.ITALIC`)
3	Font size (in points)

GIVING YOUR LABEL SOME INSTRUCTIONS

Now let's focus on the changes made to the `init( )` method. Previously, the body of the method contained a single statement. It's still there, but now it has a companion preceding it. The companion statement looks like this:

```
senselessScrawl.setFont( realBigFont );
```

This statement sends a message to the `senselessScrawl` object. The message is called `setFont`, and there is a piece of information associated with the message, contained in the field `realBigFont`. Another way of expressing this idea is to say that the statement invokes the `setFont( )` method of the `senselessScrawl` object with the argument `realBigFont`. The two expressions are equivalent, because it is the `setFont( )` method that the `senselessScrawl` object uses whenever it receives a `setFont` message. Messages and methods *always* exist in this complementary fashion. Methods define behavior and messages trigger the behavior. Figure 2-18 shows the form of a statement invoking a method, or sending a message, if you prefer the alternate way of expressing this idea.

What does the `senselessScrawl` object do when it receives the `setFont` message? To find out, you must know what sort of object `senselessScrawl` is. Looking back at the class definition, you see that `senselessScrawl` is a `Label` object. So, what does a `Label` object do when it receives a `setFont` message? It simply remembers the `Font` it receives along with the message and draws itself using that `Font` in response to any subsequent commands that it draw itself. So, the `setFont` message is simply a way of telling a `Label` what `Font` it should use.

What about the following statement, the one that's been there all along?

```
add( senselessScrawl );
```

It, too, is a method invocation. It invokes the `add( )` method, supplying the `senselessScrawl` object as an argument. The object to which it sends the message is not specified. When this is the case, the message is sent to the current object. In this case, that will be the applet itself. An applet's response to an `add` message is to add the specified object to the display window. In this case, the `Label` object known as

FIGURE 2-18

Sending a message

senselessScrawl is added to the applet window. Listing 2-6 shows the HTML used to run the GraffitiTwo class, and Figure 2-19 shows the new output. Give it a try and see how big the 36-point Label is on your monitor.

Listing 2-6 ElephantsRule2.html

```
<HTML>
<HEAD>
<TITLE>Elephants Rule!!!   [2.0]</TITLE>
</HEAD>
<BODY>
<IMG SRC="Jumbo.gif" ALIGN=LEFT>
<H1>Jumbo's Jungle Java Joint</H1>
<HR>
<H2>The "Graffiti Wars" Start to Escalate</H2>
"There are no bad elephants," Jumbo thought to himself.
"I'll just clean this off, and hope none of the other
customers take offense. Especially those army ants!"
<P>
It looks like Jumbo badly misjudged the situation,
however. That night the "kids" returned, and made sure
that all and sundry knew who was the real "King of the
Jungle."
<HR>
<APPLET CODE=GraffitiTwo.class HEIGHT=75 WIDTH=400>
</APPLET>
<HR>
</BODY>
</HTML>
```

Events

It's nice to see that an applet can display text in various fonts, styles, and sizes. But HTML can do that. The unique thing about applets is their capability to respond dynamically. Let's add some dynamic behavior to the Graffiti applet. Listing 2-7 shows an improved GraffitiThree class.

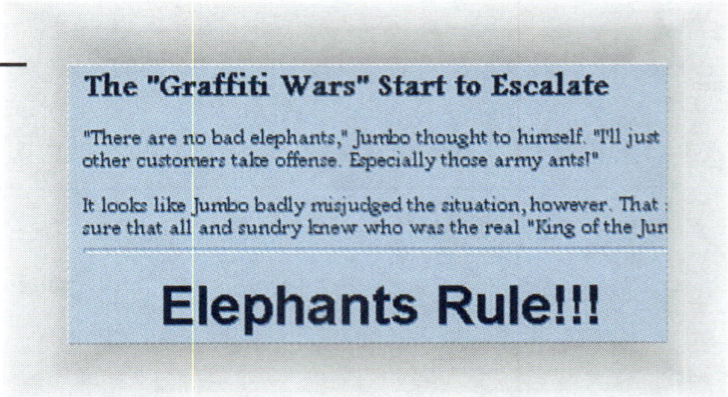

FIGURE 2-19
The Label gets big

```
Listing 2-7 GraffitiThree.java
// The kids start to scare the customers
// The day becomes eventful at Jumbo's
//
import java.applet.*;
import java.awt.*;
import java.awt.event.*;

public class GraffitiThree extends Applet implements ⇐
  MouseMotionListener
{
    Label senselessScrawl = new Label("Elephants Rule!!!");
    Font  realBigFont = new Font("Helvetica", Font.BOLD, 36);

    public void init()
    {
        senselessScrawl.setFont( realBigFont );
        add( senselessScrawl );
        addMouseMotionListener(this);
    }

    public void mouseMoved( MouseEvent event )
    {
        senselessScrawl.setLocation( event.getX( ), ⇐
          event.getY( ) );
    }

    public void mouseDragged( MouseEvent event )  { }
}
```

"Most of us don't purchase our Tabasco sauce in 50-gallon drums, or our heating oil in table-size decanters."

EVENTS: JAVA TALKS BACK

Not only can you send messages to an object, as you did when you sent the `senselessScrawl` the `setFont` message, but things in the outside world can also send messages to your applet, provided that your objects are prepared to listen. You can tell your applet to listen for all sorts of outside events. Every time you move your mouse over your applet, your Web browser sends a message to your applet saying, "Somebody moved a mouse over you." The name of this message is `mouseMoved`, and by writing a `mouseMoved( )` method, you can respond when that happens. This type of message is called an *event*, and by writing a method, you can arrange to do something when the event occurs. Let's take a closer look at the steps you'd need to handle this event. If some of this seems strange, don't worry. You will be coming back to writing methods in depth in Chapter 4. Now you'll get an overview.

Making Hay While Your Mouse Moves

To make your applet take some action when an event occurs

1. Prepare to accept event messages.

2. Start listening for events.

3. Respond to the event messages.

Preparation   The first step in listening for events is to import the package `java.awt.event`. The classes in `java.awt.event` give your applet the power to receive and handle messages, such as those sent by the mouse when it moves. To prepare to receive the messages from the mouse, the applet must also declare its willingness to receive those messages. It does this by including a new phrase in its class header: `implements MouseMotionListener`.

Listening   Once that's accomplished, all that's left is to throw the switch saying "Give me the messages." Invoke the method `addMouseMotionListener( )` inside `init( )`:

```
addMouseMotionListener(this);
```

When you call this method, you pass an argument, the keyword `this`, which works like the word "me" in English. It refers to the applet itself. The message says, in effect, "Send *me* a message whenever the mouse moves: I'm listening!"

How, exactly, does an applet listen? Because listening is a behavior, you might guess that listening involves a method, and you'd be right. In fact, the `GraffitiThree` applet includes two new methods, each one listening for a different sort of message from the mouse. You determine what happens when the mouse is moved by writing statements that go inside each of these methods. Let's look at the first new method, `mouseMoved( )`.

Responding   The `mouseMoved( )` method is called whenever the user moves the mouse across the surface of the applet window. Each time the message is sent, Java sends along an argument containing useful information about the event, such as the position of the mouse. To handle this argument, the method header of `mouseMoved( )` looks a bit different from others you've seen, such as `init( )`. Even though you've *called* methods such as `setFont( )` using arguments, you've not previously seen a method that handles one.

In a method header, an argument has two parts: a *data type* and a *name*. The data type of the argument to `mouseMoved( )` is `MouseEvent`, which seems appropriate enough. You'll learn more about events in Chapter 8, "Flocking Objects: Arrays and Exceptions," so for the moment let's simply say that a `MouseEvent` object is used to describe something that's happened involving the mouse. You can give the argument a name of your choice, here `event`. This is the name by which the argument is known inside the `mouseMoved( )` method. The name was chosen so that its association with the `MouseEvent` object could be easily remembered.

What the applet does in response to the movement of the mouse is determined by the statements that you write within the body of the `mouseMoved( )` message. In `GraffitiThree`, a message named `setLocation( )` is sent to the `Label` object known as `senselessScrawl`. The `setLocation( )` method causes the `Label` object to move itself to a new position. The new position it is moved to is determined by asking the

MouseEvent argument for the location of the mouse, via the getX( ) and getY( ) methods. Figure 2-20 shows how this works: An X value and a Y value are used to specify the position of the mouse in pixels. By causing the Label to move to the same position on the screen as the mouse, you cause the Label to track the movements of the mouse.

What about the second new method, mouseDragged( )? This message is sent to the applet whenever the mouse is moved while the mouse button is held down. You'll notice that there are no statements in the body of this method, which consists only of the curly braces ({}). What does the applet do when it receives a mouseDragged( ) message? Nothing. So, why bother to define the mouseDragged( ) method at all? It's required. When the applet declares it knows how to handle mouse movement messages (by including implements MouseMotionListener in its class header), it is promising that it will define a method to handle each type of message relating to mouse movement. There are exactly two of these methods, mouseMoved( ) and mouseDragged( ); if you omit either, the applet will not compile.

Type in the JAVA source file and the HTML file, and give this applet a try. Can you cause any odd behavior by moving the mouse quickly or to unusual positions? Try moving the mouse to the extreme limits of the applet's window. Figure 2-21 shows the applet running under Netscape Navigator.

FIGURE 2-20

The user interface coordinate system

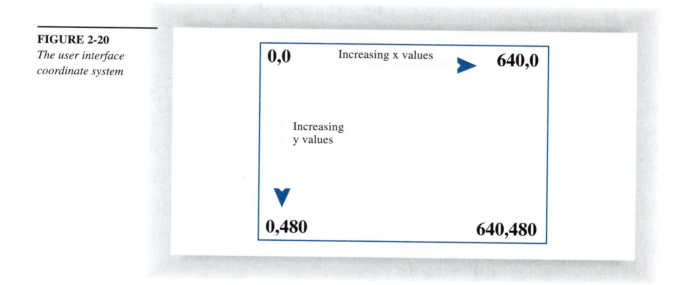

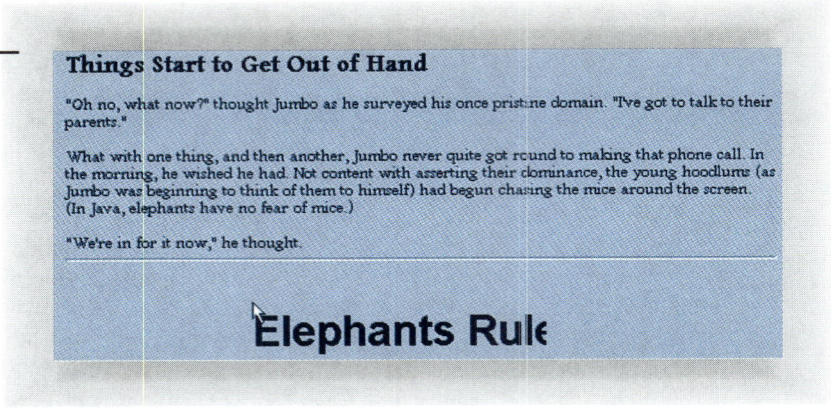

FIGURE 2-21

*The elephants chase
the mice*

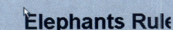

Things Start to Get Out of Hand

"Oh no, what now?" thought Jumbo as he surveyed his once pristine domain. "I've got to talk to their parents."

What with one thing, and then another, Jumbo never quite got round to making that phone call. In the morning, he wished he had. Not content with asserting their dominance, the young hoodlums (as Jumbo was beginning to think of them to himself) had begun chasing the mice around the screen. (In Java, elephants have no fear of mice.)

"We're in for it now," he thought.

Elephants Rule

Listing 2-8 ElephantsRule3.html

```
<HTML>
<HEAD>
<TITLE>Elephants Rule!!!  [3.0]</TITLE>
</HEAD>
<BODY>
<IMG SRC="Jumbo.gif" ALIGN=RIGHT>
<H1>Jumbo's Jungle Java Joint</H1>
<HR>
<H2>Things Start to Get Out of Hand</H2>
"Oh no, what now?" thought Jumbo as he surveyed his once
pristine domain. "I've got to talk to their parents."
<P>
What with one thing, and then another, Jumbo never quite got
round to making that phone call. In the morning, he wished
he had. Not content with asserting their dominance, the
young hoodlums (as Jumbo was beginning to think of them to
himself) had begun chasing the mice around the screen. (In
Java, elephants have no fear of mice.)
<P>
"We're in for it now," he thought.
<HR>
<APPLET CODE=GraffitiThree.class HEIGHT=100 WIDTH=400>
</APPLET>
</BODY>
</HTML>
```

Inheritance

One of the advantages of object-oriented software is that, with proper planning and design, it can be reused or extended to handle new problems and situations by simply adding new methods.

Reuse is achieved primarily through a device known as inheritance. You've been the beneficiary of the power of inheritance throughout this chapter. The GraffitiThree class contains no instructions telling it how to draw itself, yet it can do so. How?

THE ANTS STRIKE BACK

The secret lies in the extends keyword that appears in the class header. The GraffitiThree class header says it extends Applet. This means that a GraffitiThree is a special sort, or subtype, of Applet. In a stroke, this gives GraffitiThree all the power of the built-in class Applet. Applet classes already know, among other things, how to draw themselves. The fact that GraffitiThree is an Applet means that it inherits all the fields and methods of its parent class, Applet.

To better illustrate this phenomenon, let's extend a class you're familiar with, the GraffitiThree class. Listing 2-9 shows the result.

Listing 2-9 AntsAreCool.java

```
// The customers rise up
// The ants turn the elephants' applet against them
//
import java.applet.*;
import java.awt.*;

public class AntsAreCool extends GraffitiThree
{
    Label antLabel = new Label("Ants are Cool!!!");
    Font  antFont  = new Font("Times Roman", Font.ITALIC, 48);

    public void init( )
    {
        super.init( );
        antLabel.setFont( antFont );
        add( antLabel );

        senselessScrawl.setText("Elephants dRule!!!");
    }
}
```

AntsAreCool is a new class that extends GraffitiThree. That is, an AntsAreCool object is also a special sort of GraffitiThree object, capable to do anything a GraffitiThree object can do, and more. You notice the AntsAreCool class has two new fields, antLabel and antFont. What might not be immediately obvious is that every AntsAreCool object also has senselessScrawl and realBigFont objects. The latter are present, though unseen, by virtue of inheritance.

AntsAreCool has also changed the init( ) method a little. Because there is already a method by this same name in the parent class, GraffitiThree, this version of the init( ) method replaces the earlier version, but only for AntsAreCool objects.

The AntsAreCool version of the init( ) method begins by sending an init message to an object know as super. This is a shorthand way of sending an init message to the GraffitiThree object, which will interpret the init message using its own init( ) method. This gives you the best of both worlds: You can add behavior unique to the AntsAreCool object to its init( ) method, but you can cause the statements of the init( ) method of the component GraffitiThree object to be executed as well.

The init( ) method of the GraffitiThree object will set the Font of the senselessScrawl Label and add the Label to the output window. The new init( ) statements in the AntsAreCool object set the Font of the antLabel object and add it to the window, which should therefore contain both Labels. Note that the AntsAreCool object also inherits the mouseMoved( ) method of GraffitiThree, causing the senselessScrawl Label to track mouse movements as before. The related HTML file is shown in Listing 2-10. Type in the source code and the HTML file, and see the power of object-oriented programming at work. Remember

> Put AntsAreCool.java and GraffitiThree.java in the same directory.

> Separately compile each JAVA file by use of Javac, to obtain a CLASS file for each source file.

> Put AntsAreCool.html in the same directory as the CLASS files.

Once you've checked that the HTML file and the two CLASS files are present in the same directory, you can view the applet using Appletviewer or a browser. Figure 2-22 shows the ants' revenge.

Listing 2-10 AntsAreCool.html

```
<HTML>
<HEAD>
<TITLE>Ants Are Cool! Elephants dRule!</TITLE>
</HEAD>
<BODY>
<H1>Jumbo's Jungle Java Joint</H1>
<HR>
<H2>The Ants Fight Back</H2>
"We're big, we're bad, elephants are rad." Jumbo could hear
the commotion before he reached the door. What he didn't
expect to hear, though, was the laughter. "At least I won't
have to break up a fight," he thought.
<P>
Just as he feared, the ants had fought back, and turned
the "young turks'" applet back on themselves.
<P>
"I've got to find some way to put a stop to this," he
muttered under his breath, as he turned his key in the door,
and let the surging tide flow past him and settle in at the
tables. "At least business is up. I wonder if there's an
angle here," he thought as he began his daily ritual,
crushing the morning's Java beans.
<HR>
<APPLET CODE=AntsAreCool.class HEIGHT=300 WIDTH=400>
</APPLET>
</BODY>
</HTML>
```

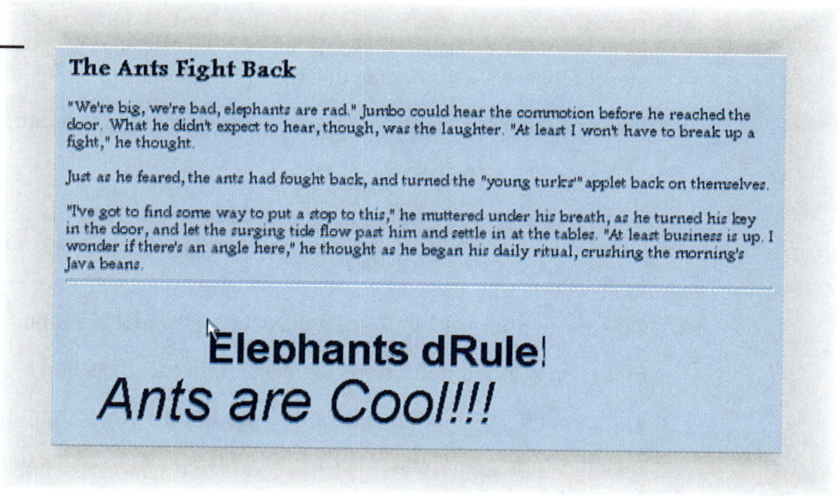

FIGURE 2-22
The `AntsAreCool`
applet

The Ants Fight Back

"We're big, we're bad, elephants are rad." Jumbo could hear the commotion before he reached the door. What he didn't expect to hear, though, was the laughter. "At least I won't have to break up a fight," he thought.

Just as he feared, the ants had fought back, and turned the "young turks" applet back on themselves.

"I've got to find some way to put a stop to this," he muttered under his breath, as he turned his key in the door, and let the surging tide flow past him and settle in at the tables. "At least business is up. I wonder if there's an angle here," he thought as he began his daily ritual, crushing the morning's Java beans.

Elephants dRule!
Ants are Cool!!!

Summary

☕ Computer programs are information-processing systems.

☕ Unlike procedurally oriented programs, which resemble a conveyor belt in structure, object-oriented programs consist of a system of cooperating objects with a structure that resembles the modern workgroup.

☕ Objects have identity, state, and behavior.

☕ A class is a blueprint or pattern that can represent many objects.

☕ Every object is an instance of some class.

☕ Objects have the capability to perform actions using methods.

☕ Objects invoke methods upon receiving a message.

☕ Classes give objects the capability to store state by defining object attributes.

☕ Inheritance is the capability of a class to create a new class.

☕ A newly created class that's derived from a previous class is called a child, or subclass.

☕ The class from which a child class is derived is called a parent, or superclass.

☕ A child class may have new properties and methods.

☕ There are three types of Java programs: applets, console applications, and GUI applications.

☕ Identifiers are used to name classes and variables.

☕ Java's keywords may not be used by programmers as identifiers.

☕ Java is a case-sensitive language.

☕ Conventions govern capitalization of identifiers. These conventions, though ignored by the compiler, help programmers know what kind of thing a name refers to.

☕ Classes are defined by use of a class header and a class body.

☕ Field and method definitions appear within the class body.

☕ The `import` statement is used to access library classes and packages.

☕ Java depends upon punctuation, not whitespace, in understanding a source program.

☕ `Applet`, `Label`, and `Font` are useful built-in JAVA classes.

☕ Objects are created by use of the `new` operator.

☕ Objects are given values by use of the = operator.

☕ Methods define behavior and messages trigger behavior.

☕ Methods are defined by use of a method header and a method body.

☕ Some methods return a value, others simply perform processing.

☕ Arguments are used to customize the behavior specified within a method.

☕ Comments can be included in a Java program to help the reader understand and use the program.

☕ Java informs programs of events by invoking defined methods and providing descriptive arguments.

Quiz

1. In Java, programs are communities of _____.
2. A collection of interacting components of any sort is called a(n) _____.
3. Object-oriented programs are organized more like the modern _____ than like the old-fashioned assembly line.
4. All objects have three characteristics: identity, _____, and _____.
5. You tell one object from another using its _____.

6. Because an object has a(n) _____ stored by its fields, its properties can change over its lifetime.

7. Every object has _____ defined by its methods and knows how to respond to messages.

8. A class is a(n) _____ that can be used to instantiate many objects.

9. Every object is a(n) _____ of some class.

10. Classes give objects the capability to perform actions through _____.

11. Objects _____ methods upon receiving a(n) _____.

12. Classes give objects the capability to store state by defining object _____.

13. The capability to create a new class based on a old one is called _____.

14. A newly created class is called a(n) _____.

15. The creating class is called a(n) _____.

16. The created class may have new _____ and _____ not found in the old class.

17. The three types of programs that can be created by use of Java are _____, _____, and _____.

18. A class definition includes a class _____ and a class body.

19. Language keywords are sometimes called _____ because they cannot be used to name classes, variables, or methods.

20. Identifiers may not start with a(n) _____ or contain _____ characters, other than the underscore (**_**) or the dollar sign (**$**).

21. In class names, every word should start with a(n) _____ letter.

22. Method and field names should start with a(n) _____ letter.

23. The keyword `extends` denotes _____.

24. The _____ statement is used to access library classes and packages.

25. A built-in Java object that can be used in an applet to hold text, display itself, and move around the screen is the _____.

26. The _____ operator is used to create a new object.

27. The _____ operator is used to store a value in an object.

28. The _____ method is run when an applet is first loaded.

29. Program readability can be improved by good use of whitespace and by _____, which are ignored by the compiler.

30. Methods _____ behavior and messages _____ the behavior.

31. When the mouse is moved over the applet window, Java sends a(n) _____ message called `mouseMoved( )` to the applet.

Exercises

1. Delete the `import` statements from the `GraffitiThree` applet. What happens when you try to compile and run the applet?

2. Delete the phrase `extends Applet` from the `GraffitiThree` applet. What happens when you try to compile and run the applet?

3. Delete the semicolon at the end of the line `import java.applet.*;` in the `GraffitiThree` applet. What happens when you try to compile and run the applet?

4. Delete an opening curly brace (`{`) from the `GraffitiThree` applet. What happens when you try to compile and run the applet? Delete a closing curly brace (`}`) and repeat the experiment.

5. Change the name of the `init( )` method in the `GraffitiThree` applet to `Init( )`. What happens when you run the applet?

6. Delete the statement `add(senselessScrawl);` from the `GraffitiThree` applet. What happens when you run the applet?

7. Change the text string `"Elephants Rule!!!"` in `GraffitiThree` to some new string. Be sure to retain the beginning and ending double quotes. What happens when you run the applet?

8. Change the parameters of the `Font` constructor in `GraffitiThree` to new values. What happens when you run the applet?

9. Experiment with the `AntsAreCool` applet by removing each occurrence of the keyword `public`. What happens when you try to compile and run the applet?

10. Delete the line `super.init( );` from the `AntsAreCool` applet, and then recompile and run it. What happens when you run the applet?

11. Create an applet that shows various fonts available on your system, in plain, bold, and italic faces. Choose a font size large enough to facilitate comparison of the fonts.

12. Create a new child class based on the `GraffitiThree` class. Your child class should include a `mouseMoved( )` method that shifts the position of a `Label` you create, rather than the `Label` in the `GraffitiThree` class.

3

The Atomic Theory of Objects:
Working with Object Attributes

At one time, the ancient Greeks believed that everything in the world was made up of four simple elements: earth, air, fire, and water. About 400 B.C., two Greek philosophers developed an alternative explanation, one that we still accept today. They proclaimed that the world was not made of earth, wind, and fire; instead, they said, the world was made out of atoms—indivisible particles composed of a single substance, but differing in size and shape. What are Java's objects made of? Are `Labels`, `Buttons`, and `Strings` made of earth, air, fire, and water? Or is there some atomic theory of objects to be discovered and mastered?

If you take apart your favorite applet, you'll find objects. `Buttons`, `Labels`, `Strings`—all these are objects. But what do you find if you take apart an object itself? As you saw in Chapter 2, "Programs: The Community of Objects," objects are composed of two parts: attributes and methods. Attributes define the state of an object—the current speed of a particular car, for instance—while methods define the behavior of the object—accelerating or turning.

> *" Programs are made from objects, and objects are made from attributes and methods. Then what are attributes and methods made from? "*

"So," you're wondering, "if programs are made out of objects, and objects are made out of attributes and methods, then what are attributes and methods made from?" This chapter and Chapter 4, "Simply Methods: One Step at a Time," will answer those questions for you. In the next chapter you will learn all about methods. In this chapter you will learn

- The differences and similarities between primitive types and objects

- The characteristics of specific primitive types including integers, floating-point numbers, and characters

- How to define and use literals, variables, and constants

- How to use operators to manipulate primitives

- How to use some new objects, `Button` and `TextField`, to create useful applets

The Great Divide: Atoms, Elements, Ants, and Elephants

What are attributes made of? Let's take a look. Do you remember the first Java program you looked at, `GraffitiOne`? This applet had a single attribute, the `Label` object `senselessScrawl`. From that you might correctly deduce that one thing an attribute can be made from is...another object. You might think that this begs the question. You ask what objects are made from and receive the answer: "attributes and methods." You ask what attributes are made from and you hear "objects." "Surely that can't be the whole story," you think. You're right.

Objects are the building blocks of Java programs—they are the main things you will see and use as you write your applets and applications. In this sense, they are like chemical compounds. Most of the things you see and use in the real world are compounds—composed of multiple elements. The elements that make up these compounds are themselves composed of smaller units called atoms. Water, for instance, is composed of two hydrogen atoms along with one oxygen atom—the familiar $H2O$.

Java programs have a hierarchy that is roughly analogous to the real world. At the lowest level, everything in a Java program is composed of bits. You might think of this as Java's subatomic level. As you saw in Chapter 1, "What's All This Java Stuff?" computer memory—where data and instructions are stored—is really just a featureless series of locations that can hold on/off values. In Java programs—as in real life—most of us never deal directly with these subatomic values.

When subatomic particles such as protons, neutrons, and electrons are combined, they form atoms, which, depending on the number of particles in each atom, constitute the different elements. Thus, the protons in a hydrogen atom are identical to those in an oxygen atom. In high school chemistry you learned the periodic table, a list showing the number of protons in each of the primitive elements that make up the physical world.

In a similar way, Java's "subatomic" bits can be combined in various ways to make "elements." Java has several simple, "pure" values, which are known as primitive types or values, or simply *primitives*. All object attributes eventually are composed of these primitive values. Figure 3-1 illustrates how programs, objects, types, and bits are related to each other.

FIGURE 3-1

Programs, objects, types, and bits

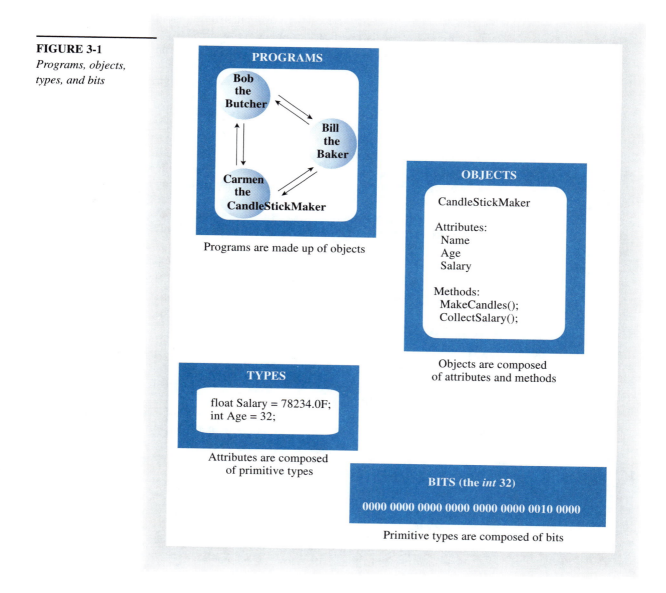

PROGRAMS

Bob the Butcher

Bill the Baker

Carmen the CandleStickMaker

Programs are made up of objects

OBJECTS

CandleStickMaker

Attributes:
 Name
 Age
 Salary

Methods:
 MakeCandles();
 CollectSalary();

Objects are composed of attributes and methods

TYPES

float Salary = 78234.0F;
int Age = 32;

Attributes are composed of primitive types

BITS (the *int* 32)

0000 0000 0000 0000 0000 0000 0010 0000

Primitive types are composed of bits

PRIMITIVES

Like objects, primitives have state and behavior. Knowing that, you may want to think of them as very simple objects—some sort of single-celled creature in the object world. But that's not the whole picture.

Primitives are different from true objects in several ways. First, objects can be composed of many different attributes, but primitives hold only a single value. Second, objects have a variety of methods and are manipulated by sending them messages that invoke those methods. By contrast, primitives are manipulated by *operators,* as you'll see. Finally, the range of available primitives is fixed. It's impossible to extend the state or behavior of primitives, however much you might wish to do so. These are all important differences you'll need to keep in mind as you program using primitives.

WHY PRIMITIVES?

Why does Java have both objects and primitives? Some object-oriented languages, notably Smalltalk, have only objects. This makes the language more internally consistent, or "cleaner." Languages like this are called "pure" object-oriented languages because everything *must* be done by creating objects and sending messages.

Why didn't Java require that? Primitives have two advantages over objects: simplicity and efficiency. There is more overhead involved in creating and storing objects than there is in creating and storing primitives. Because, as the saying goes, "you can never be too rich, too thin, or have too much CPU power," the designers of Java sacrificed some object-oriented "purity" for the sake of efficiency. While primitives are certainly more efficient, objects are much more powerful—because of the variety of methods they contain and because of their extensibility.

WHAT PRIMITIVES?

Java provides four main families of primitives: the integer types, the floating-point types, the char type (used to store characters), and the boolean type. In the sections that follow, you'll examine each of these families and the members of each family, except for the boolean family, which you'll meet in Chapter 5, "Making Choices: Teaching Your Objects About True and False." You'll also be introduced to the String data type, which shares some characteristics of both object and primitive data types.

Meet the Integers

What are integers? Integers are whole, or counting, numbers—that is, numbers without any decimal points or fractional parts. Java's integer family is prolific, indeed, with four varieties: byte, short, int, and long. All of Java's integers are signed. That doesn't mean they have some label attached, but rather that they can all hold negative as well as positive values (in addition to zero, of course).

How then do the integer types differ? They differ mainly in the range of numbers they can represent—all the way from the small personal size (`byte`) on up to the jumbo model (`long`). Of course, the designers of Java could have provided a single integer type, the `long`, but they provided the others for the same reason your grocery store sells different-sized boxes of breakfast cereal: cost. `long`s require more storage space than other integer types, and manipulating `long`s takes more time than manipulating some of the smaller types.

MAKING A CHOICE

With this virtual cornucopia of integral types, which should you choose to meet a given need? A good guideline is to use the smallest type that will still be large enough to hold all the values you can reasonably anticipate your data may assume.

You might reasonably use a `byte` type (having maximum value of 127) to hold the number of dependents on an insurance policy, but you certainly wouldn't use a `byte` to represent the population of even a small town. It doesn't hurt to be generous. You may pay a small performance penalty for using a larger integer than required, but choosing a type that's too small can cause your program to fail. Table 3-1 summarizes the integer types and the range of values that each accommodates.

TABLE 3-1
THE INTEGER DATA TYPES

TYPE	STORAGE REQUIRED	SMALLEST VALUE	LARGEST VALUE
`byte`	1 byte	-128	127
`short`	2 bytes	-32,768	32,767
`int`	4 bytes	-2,147,483,648	2,147,483,647
`long`	8 bytes	-9,223,372,036,854,775,808	9,223,372,036,854,775,807

THE LITERAL TRUTH

How do you create integer values in your programs? There are two kinds of integer values you can create. One kind, integer *literals,* is used to store values you know at the time you write the program, and which will not change as the program runs. For example, the number *3* is a legal integer literal in Java. The value of a literal is given *literally* by the way you write it. To create an integer literal, all you need do is write the number, making sure you don't use commas, spaces, or decimal points. In fact, if you looked at a Java literal, you'd probably call it a numeral.

The second kind of integer value you can create is called a *variable.* As the name suggests, you create variables to store values you don't know when you write the program (but which will be known when the program runs), and values that may change during program execution. Each integer variable is given a name to allow you to access and change its value. For example, an integer variable might be named `ageInYears`. Another difference between literals and variables is that you can't simply look at a variable and determine its value.

INTEGER STORAGE SPECIFICS

When writing an integer literal, you're not required to tell the Java compiler which of the four integer types you are trying to create. How much storage does an integer literal use then? At first glance, you may think, "As much as necessary." But that's not entirely correct. Rather than trying to fit your literals into the smallest space possible—using `byte` for the literal *110,* for instance—Java simply stores all integer literals as type `int`, unless the literal is too large to be stored as an `int`, in which case it's stored as a `long`.

Sometimes you might want Java to store an integer literal as a `long`, even though the value is small enough to fit into an `int`. In such a case, you can simply follow the numerical value with the letter `L`. You can also use the lowercase `l`, but its similarity to the digit *1* makes it easy for someone, including you, to misread your code. If you want to avoid this problem, you'll adopt the *convention* (a self-imposed rule) of only using `L` to specify `long` storage. Table 3-2 shows some examples of valid and invalid integer literals.

TABLE 3-2
INTEGER LITERALS

INTEGER LITERAL	VALID?
12	Yes
12.5	No: contains fraction
12a	No: contains nondigit *a*
12L	Yes: stored as a `long`
1,212	No: contains comma

LITERAL ALCHEMY: BASE INTEGERS

So far, the integer values you've worked with have all been ordinary, base 10 numbers. Java also allows you to write integer literals in octal (base 8) and hexadecimal (base 16). Since you tell Java that you want a literal to be stored as a `long` by appending an `L` to it, you might expect that literals in other bases would similarly have an *O* or an *H* appended to them. Unfortunately, for historical reasons, this is not the case.

To write a literal value using octal notation, simply start the number with a zero. To specify a number using hexadecimal notation, start the literal with the prefix *0x*. Notice that this is the digit *0* and the letter *x*. One unfortunate side effect of this scheme is that while the numeric literal `10` is the decimal value `10`, the numeric literal

010 represents the decimal value 8, because the literal starts with zero, and is interpreted as an octal number.

The MoreInts applet, shown in Listing 3-1 and Listing 3-2, demonstrates how integer literal values in base 10, base 8, and base 16 are specified in Java. The output of the applet is shown in Figure 3-2. Remember that your applet output may not look exactly like that shown in the figure, owing to variations in video monitor resolution and other factors. While the input values in the MoreInts applet are specified by use of decimal, octal, and hexadecimal, the output is always decimal.

Listing 3-1 MoreInts.java

```
//   MoreInts.java
// More Intsteresting (really big groan) properties of
// integers.
//
import java.awt.*;
import java.applet.*;

public class MoreInts extends Applet
{
    // Attributes
    Label theResult = new Label("");   //  Store the answer

    int decInt  = 77;    //  Initialized with decimal value
    int octInt  = 077;   //  Initialized with octal value
    int hexInt  = 0x77;  //  Initialized with hex value

    // Methods
    public void init( )
    {
        theResult.setText( "The decInt = "   + decInt +
                   ", the octInt = "         + octInt +
                   ", while the hexInt = "   + hexInt );
        add( theResult );
    }
}
```

Listing 3-2 MoreInts.html

```
<HTML>
<HEAD>
<TITLE>MoreInts.java</TITLE>
</HEAD>
<BODY>
<APPLET CODE=MoreInts.class HEIGHT=300 WIDTH=300>
</APPLET>
</BODY>
</HTML>
```

FIGURE 3-2
Output of the
MoreInts applet

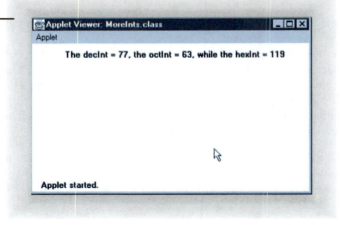

More than Whole: Floating-Point Types

Sometimes a whole number isn't, well, whole enough. That's when you really need a number that can hold a fraction. Java provides a family of primitive data types that can store such *floating-point* numbers.

Just as there are several varieties of Java integers, there are two varieties of Java floating-point values: floats and doubles. As with the integer family, the big difference between the types is in the amount of space set aside to store each number. The double primitive type uses 64 bits of storage, while the float type uses only half that much, 32 bits. Unlike the integers, though, this additional size affects not only the range of numbers that can be represented, but the precision of that representation as well.

FLOATING LITERALS

Floating-point literal values, like integers, are written without commas. Then how is Java supposed to know that you want a floating-point value instead of an integer? There are actually two ways you can write a floating-point value so that Java can tell that's what you want. In most situations, the easiest way is just to include a decimal point. These are all acceptable floating-point literal values:

```
3.54
.7653
2.0
```

You also can write floating-point literals using *exponential*—sometimes called *scientific*—notation. Exponential notation makes it easier to write very large or very small numbers, especially because Java numeric literals cannot have commas. By use of exponential notation, floating-point literals are written in two parts: a decimal number with one digit to the left of the decimal point, followed by an exponent. The number and the exponent are separated from each other by the letter E, which can appear as either uppercase or lowercase.

What does the exponent represent? It signifies that the number should be increased or decreased by the indicated power of 10. A simple way to think of it is to realize that the decimal point is just shifted left or right the number of places that the exponent signifies. If the exponent is negative, the decimal is shifted left, making the number smaller. If the exponent is positive, the decimal point is shifted right.

Consider writing the number "1 million." Without using commas, you have to count carefully to make sure that "1000000" represents 1 million, and not 10 million. Using exponential notation, you could write this number as 1.0E6 and you would know immediately.

FLOATING STORAGE

Remember that Java stores integer literals as ints unless they happen to be too large, or you specifically request long storage by appending an L. A similar syntax is used with the floating-point types. Unless you say otherwise, Java will store floating-point literals as doubles. You can explicitly tell the compiler to use double storage by appending a d or D to the literal number, but there is little purpose in doing so, save for documentation.

In a similar manner, you can tell Java to store floating-point literals as floats by appending an F or f to the number. This means that a number written as 5.0E2 would be stored as a double, while 5.0E2F would be stored as a float. Table 3-3 summarizes the differences between floats and doubles. Both types observe the IEEE 754-1985 standard for storing floating-point numbers and so function properly across a wide range of computing platforms.

The Floats applet, shown in Listing 3-3 and Listing 3-4, demonstrates how floating-point values are specified in Java. The output can be seen in Figure 3-3.

TABLE 3-3
floatS AND doubleS

TYPE	SIZE	APPROX. PRECISION	APPROX. MIN. VALUE	APPROX. MAX. VALUE
float	4 bytes	7 digits	±1.40E -45	±3.40E+38
double	8 bytes	15 digits	±4.94E -324	±1.79E+308

Listing 3-3 Floats.java

```java
import java.awt.*;
import java.applet.*;

public class Floats extends Applet
{
    // Attributes
    Label thePrice          = new Label(".....................");
    Label theWeight         = new Label(".....................");
    Label thePricePerOunce  = new Label(".....................");

    float  price = 2.95F;
    double weight = 12.0;
    double unitPrice;

    // Methods
    public void init( )
    {
        thePrice.setText("Price: " + price);
        theWeight.setText("Weight: " + weight);
        unitPrice = price / weight;
        thePricePerOunce.setText("Unit price: " + unitPrice);
        add(thePrice);
        add(theWeight);
        add(thePricePerOunce);
    }
}
```

FIGURE 3-3

Output of the **Floats** *applet*

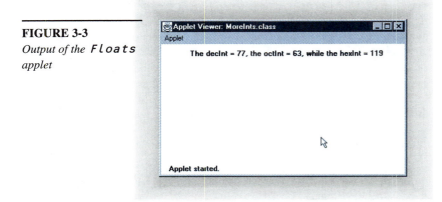

The decInt = 77, the octInt = 63, while the hexInt = 119

Listing 3-4 Floats.html

```
<HTML>
<HEAD>
<TITLE>Floats.html </TITLE>
</HEAD>
<BODY>
<APPLET CODE="Floats.class" WIDTH=400 HEIGHT=300>
</APPLET>
</BODY>
</HTML>
```

Interesting Characters: The `char` Type

The third family of primitives provided by Java consists of only a single type, but a host of characters. This is the type `char`, which is used to store individual characters including letters, punctuation, and digits.

How does Java do this? Remember from Chapter 1 that computers can store only the values 0 and 1. If you group a bunch of 0s and 1s together, however, you can use them to represent whole numbers. If you interpret the 1s and 0s properly, you can even use them to represent floating-point numbers. But how can you store letters—as opposed to numbers—in a digital computer? You can't. Instead, if you want to store letters in your computer, you can store numbers, and then use those numbers to represent certain letters. This is how the `char` data type works.

ASK ME, ASK YOU, ASCII

Have you ever invented a secret code? One of the simplest is to give each letter an ID number. You could give *A* the value 1, *B* the value 2, and so on. You could translate the message "HI MOM" as 8-9-13-15-13, and the message 10-21-13-2-15 as...well, you figure it out.

This type of code works only if the sender and the receiver both agree on how the translation should be done—that is, what character each number stands for. This agreement is called the *key*. The most widespread example of this kind of agreement is ASCII, the American Standard Code for Information Interchange. ASCII is a 7-bit code that was originally designed for byte-at-a-time transfer over communication equipment. Only 7 bits out of each byte are used, which provides enough codes for the English alphabet, the digits, and some punctuation. A later version, extended ASCII, uses all 8 bits. While ASCII is a widely accepted scheme for character-numeric conversion, it is not the only one. In the IBM mainframe world, a character-encoding method called EBCDIC (Extended Binary Coded Decimal Interchange Code) long reigned supreme. But, just as EBCDIC gradually gave way to ASCII in popularity, so now ASCII itself is slowly losing ground to a new translation standard called *Unicode*. Figure 3-4 illustrates the way that Unicode characters are translated to numbers.

FIGURE 3-4

Characters and binary numbers

characters	decimal	unicode	binary
A	65	'\u0040'	00000000 01000000
B	66	'\u0041'	00000000 01000001
C	67	'\u0042'	00000000 01000010
D	68	'\u0043'	00000000 01000011
E	69	'\u0044'	00000000 01000100

UNICODE

Unicode is an international standard that accommodates characters from many of the world's languages, unlike ASCII, which is suitable only for English and a few Western European languages. Unicode supports such languages as Greek, Hebrew, Cyrillic, Arabic, and Thai, as well as several systems for writing Japanese. To support these extra character sets, Java uses two bytes of storage for each `char`, unlike the one byte that would be required for ASCII storage.

Unfortunately, at the current time, Java environments generally do not provide fonts and other support necessary for entering and displaying Unicode characters. The fault lies not with Java, but with the underlying operating systems—Windows 95, for example, lacks Unicode support. However, as worldwide demand for Java continues to grow, it seems likely that Unicode support will be included in future software releases. Meanwhile, the first 128 Unicode characters have values identical to their extended ASCII counterparts, so on a system that does not support Unicode, Java's Unicode characters behave identically to their extended ASCII cousins.

LITERAL charS

How do you write char literals in your programs? There are several ways but—unlike writing both integers and floating-point numbers—you cannot simply write char literals as the characters they represent; you need to use some punctuation.

The most common way to write a char is to enclose a character in single quotes (the apostrophe character). For example, 'x' is the way that you write the char literal containing the lowercase character *x*. You can do this for any character you type in, but only a single character can appear between the single quotes; if you write 'OK', the compiler will definitely tell you things are not OK. You've tried to stick two chars where only one can go.

Sometimes you'll need to specify characters that don't appear on your keyboard. To do that, you'll have to learn about *escape sequences.*

THE GREAT ESCAPE

Despite the way it sounds, an escape sequence is not a scene from a World War II movie. Instead, it's a way of representing characters that cannot be typed from the keyboard. An escape sequence consists of two parts: the *escape character* and a *translation value.* The escape character is some agreed-upon symbol that tells the Java compiler, "Look out! You need to translate the next character in a special way!" In Java, as in the C language, this special escape character is the backslash (\).

If the backslash marks the beginning of an escape sequence, what can be used for the translation value, the part of the escape sequence that follows the escape character? Perhaps the easiest translation value to use is an actual Unicode character code. Unicode values must be specified as a four-digit hexadecimal number, preceded by a lowercase u. The whole thing, like all Java char literals, should be enclosed in single quotes.

This might seem complex, yet a simple example should make everything fairly clear. Suppose you want to use the trademark symbol (™), as a literal char in your Java program. The hexadecimal Unicode value for this character is 2122. To write this value as a literal by using escape sequences, you would write '\u2122'. Note the single quotes surrounding the whole expression, which consists of the escape character (\), followed by the letter u and the Unicode character value. In your Java programs, you can use these Unicode escape sequences anywhere that another sort of character might appear: in char literals (as you've just seen), in String literals (which you'll meet in a moment), or even in identifiers. You can find the codes for other Unicode characters on the Web at http://unicode.org, the home page of the Unicode consortium.

In addition to these Unicode escape sequences, Java allows you to use the escape character to specify other types of special characters. These include some of the "invisible" characters that have traditionally been used to control computer operation—thus the sobriquet "control characters"—as well as single quotes, double quotes, and the escape character itself. A literal specifying one of these last few characters is cumbersome to write because of the characters' special role as punctuation for character and String data types. To write the single quote as a char literal, you write '\''. Table 3-4 gives the escape sequences that Java recognizes for this purpose.

FIGURE 3-5

Output of the `Chars`
applet

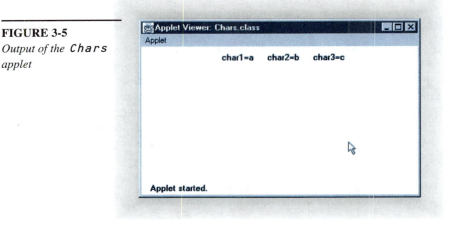

Listing 3-5 and Listing 3-6 show the `Chars` applet, which demonstrates the use of Java's `char` literals by creating and initializing three `char` variables: `char1`, `char2`, and `char3`. The output can be seen in Figure 3-5.

TABLE 3-4
ESCAPE SEQUENCES FOR `char` LITERALS

SEQUENCE	MEANING
\b	Backspace (\u0008)
\t	Tab (\u0009)
\n	Newline (\u000A)
\f	Form feed (\u000C)
\r	Return (\u000D)
\"	Double quote (\u0022)
\'	Single quote (\u0027)
\\	Backslash (\u005C)
\ddd	Any character, specified by octal digits *ddd*

N E W L I N E   A N D   E N T E R

You may not be thoroughly familiar with the *return* and *newline* characters. Under MS-DOS, these generally occur as a pair, return-newline, to mark the end of a line in a text file. On some systems, such as UNIX, the newline alone is used for this purpose, while others, like the Macintosh, use the return character alone. To help preserve cross-platform capability, your Java programs should ignore MS-DOS conventions

Continued...

NEWLINE AND ENTER Continued...

and place a newline at the end of a line of text. Java will supply the return, when and if it is needed, based on the requirements of the local operating system.

Listing 3-5 Chars.java

```java
import java.awt.*;
import java.applet.*;

public class Chars extends Applet
{
    // Attributes
    Label label1 = new Label("");
    Label label2 = new Label("");
    Label label3 = new Label("");

    char char1 = 'a';
    char char2 = 98;
    char char3 = '\143';

    // Methods
    public void init( )
    {
        label1.setText("char1=" + char1);
        label2.setText("char2=" + char2);
        label3.setText("char3=" + char3);

        add(label1);
        add(label2);
        add(label3);
    }
}
```

Listing 3-6 Chars.html

```html
<HTML>
<HEAD>
<TITLE>Chars.html </TITLE>
</HEAD>
<BODY>
<APPLET CODE="Chars.class" WIDTH=400 HEIGHT=300>
</APPLET>
</BODY>
</HTML>
```

Stringing Along with Strings

One of the most important forms of computer input and output is text. Inside a Java program, text is stored in String objects. Strings are not really primitive data types. They are true objects. But because text data is so common and important, Java provides some special ways of working with String objects that sometimes make Strings seem as if they're one of the basic types.

What can `Strings` be used for? Information typed by the user on the keyboard can be loaded into a `String` variable and processed by your program. Output from your program can be stored in a `String` variable, which can be displayed on your video monitor. `Strings` are a convenient form for storing and processing information because Java provides a comprehensive set of methods for working with `Strings`, as well as some interesting `String` operators.

STRING LITERALS

You've seen how literals of type `char` are used to store individual characters. `String` literals, by contrast, store a variable number of characters: anything from zero to some undefined, but very large, upper limit. A `String` literal is formed by simply placing text inside double quotes: `"this is a String literal"`. The characters within the quotes can include ordinary letters, digits, and punctuation, as well as Unicode characters and the escape sequences shown in Table 3-4.

This ability to embed escape sequences is an important part of learning to use `Strings`. For example, the following `String`

```
"The line\n"
```

contains the text `"The line"` followed by a newline character.

Suppose you wanted to create a `String` that contained two characters: a backslash followed by a double quote. How would you go about it? You'd write `"\\\""`. Let's analyze this "monster"; you'll discover that it's really quite straightforward, as Figure 3-6 demonstrates.

The surrounding double quotes tell you that this is a `String` literal. Since the first character inside the double quotes is a backslash, you know that the literal begins with an escape sequence, and the next character tells you it's the escape sequence that stands for a backslash. The next character, the third one, is also a backslash—telling you that yet another escape sequence is starting. This escape sequence stands for a double quote, so the second character of the literal is just that, a double quote. The

FIGURE 3-6

Using escape characters inside string literals

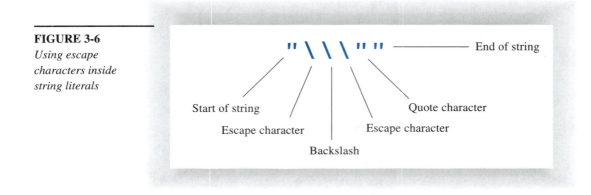

> *Using a larger integer than required may cost a small performance penalty, but choosing a type that's too small can cause program failure.*

next, and final, character is a double quote, which tells you the `String` literal is finished. So, as promised, you have two characters in the literal: a backslash, followed by a double quote. Nifty, huh? Okay, now, how would you create a `String` literal containing a single quote, followed by two backspaces, a return...?

Variables: Something to Declare

Now that you know how to create literals, it's time to learn how to create variables. Programs would be pretty boring, not to mention useless, if all the values in the programs stayed the same forever!

Creating a variable is called *defining* or *declaring* the variable. You have to declare variables in Java so that when the compiler sees the word `daysInYears`, it knows whether it is a method, a class, an integer, or whatever. Variables can be defined inside classes, in which case they're called *fields* (or sometimes *instance variables*), or defined inside methods, in which case they're called *local variables,* or simply *variables*. This usage is somewhat confusing at times. When someone says "variable," you don't know whether he or she means a local variable or just any sort of variable. But, as is usually the case with such poor usage, it's part of the programming idiom and you're stuck with it.

SIMPLE DEFINITION

To define a variable, you write a declaration statement like this:

```
type var;
```

where `type` specifies `int`, `Long`, `String`, or another type and `var` gives your variable a name. Recall the rules for creating Java identifiers given in Chapter 2. The name you specify must observe these rules, just like other Java identifiers. Here are some examples that may make things more concrete:

```
String   fullName;
char     middleInitial;
byte     numberOfKids;
short    ageInYears;
int      javaConsumption;
long     weightInGrains;
double   mortgageAmount;
float    bankBalance;
boolean  isMarried;
```

When you want to declare several variables of the same type, you can combine them into a single declaration statement like this:

```
type var1, var2, var3;
```

THE VALUE OF INITIALIZATION

A variable is just a storage location that can hold a value of a specified type. You can think of it as a mailbox, a bin, or a bathtub, but no matter how you think of it, a variable without a value has no, well, value. Unless you store something in a variable, it cannot be used. Variables are unlike literals, where the name of a literal *is* its value.

Java will automatically give fields—object attributes—a value if you don't provide one. These automatic values are called *default* values. Numeric fields and `char` fields are initialized to zero, but object fields receive a special `null` value that you'll meet later in this chapter. If a variable is a *local* variable—defined inside a method—Java does not provide a default value; you must provide a value before it is used. For both fields and local variables you can choose to provide your own initial value for a variable when it is created. This process is called *initialization*.

To create a variable and give it an initial value, you add an *initializer* to the declaration. An initializer has two parts. The first part is the assignment operator (=). The second part is an expression that provides the initial, or starting, value for your variable when the program runs. Figure 3-7 shows the syntax for a variable declaration with an initializer.

Don't be concerned if you find yourself asking, "What is an expression?" You'll return to that in the second half of this chapter. You've already met the simplest form of an expression, though: the literal. The easiest way to initialize a variable is to use a literal value with an initializer. Here are the some examples:

```
String   fullName       = "Jumbala \"Jumbo\" Gumbola";
char     middleInitial   = 'M';  //  Middle name, Mambala
byte     numberOfKids    = 7;    //  Not including grandchildren
short    ageInYears      = 152;  //  Not confirmed
int      javaConsumption = 72335;//Avg annual consumption in cups
long     weightInGrains  = 102198735L;  //  As of last checkup
double   mortgageAmount  = 343572.76;
float    bankBalance     = -7.54;
boolean  isMarried       = true;
```

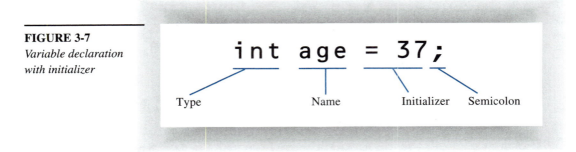

FIGURE 3-7
Variable declaration with initializer

Listing 3-7 and Listing 3-8 show the Medley application, which includes a medley of declarations of variables of various types. The output of the application is shown in Figure 3-8.

Listing 3-7 Medley.java

```java
import java.awt.*;
import java.applet.*;

public class Medley extends Applet
{
    // Attributes
    Label label1 = new Label("");
    Label label2 = new Label("");
    Label label3 = new Label("");
    Label label4 = new Label("");
    Label label5 = new Label("");
    Label label6 = new Label("");
    Label label7 = new Label("");
    Label label8 = new Label("");
    Label label9 = new Label("");

    String   fullName       = "Jumbala \"Jumbo\" Gumbola";
    char     middleInitial   = 'M';          // Middle name, ⇐
        Mambala
    byte     numberOfKids    = 7;            // Not ⇐
        including grandchildren
    short    ageInYears      = 152;          // Not confirmed
    int      javaConsumption = 72335;        // Average ⇐
        annual consumption
                                             // in cups
    long     weightInGrains  = 102198735L;   // As of last ⇐
        checkup
    double   mortgageAmount  = 343572.76;
    float    bankBalance     = -7.54F;
    boolean  isMarried       = true;


    // Methods
    public void init( )
    {
        label1.setText("fullName=" + fullName);
        label2.setText("middleInitial=" + middleInitial);
        label3.setText("numberOfKids=" + numberOfKids);
        label4.setText("ageInYears=" + ageInYears);
        label5.setText("javaConsumption=" + javaConsumption);
        label6.setText("weightInGrains=" + weightInGrains);
        label7.setText("mortgageAmount=" + mortgageAmount);
        label8.setText("bankBalance=" + bankBalance);
        label9.setText("isMarried=" + isMarried);

        add(label1);
        add(label2);
        add(label3);
        add(label4);
        add(label5);
```

continued on next page

continued from previous page

```
            add(label6);
            add(label7);
            add(label8);
            add(label9);

    }
}
```

Listing 3-8 Medley.html

```
<HTML>
<HEAD>
<TITLE>Medley.html </TITLE>
</HEAD>
<BODY>
<APPLET CODE="Medley.class" WIDTH=400 HEIGHT=300></APPLET>
</BODY>
</HTML>
```

INITIALIZATION VARIATIONS

Just as you can declare multiple variables on a single line, you can also initialize multiple variables. Thus, you can write

```
int ageInYears = 152, numberOfKids = 7, IQ;
```

This creates three integer variables: `ageInYears`, `numberOfKids`, and `IQ`. There are two important things to notice about this example. First, you only need to write the type—`int`—once. If you wrote

```
int ageInYears = 152, int numberOfKids = 7, int IQ;   // Wrong!!!
```

FIGURE 3-8

Output of the Medley application

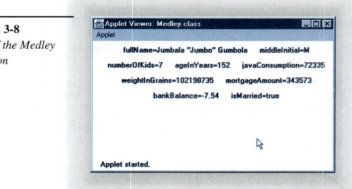

the Java compiler would let you know you had done a bad thing and would refuse to finish compiling your program. The second thing you should notice is that only the variables `ageInYears` and `numberOfKids` have been given an initial value. `IQ` is an uninitialized variable and will need to be given a value by some method before it is used in your program.

While Java allows you to create many variables on a single line, you'll probably find your programs clearer and easier to read if you put each variable on its own line, and if you initialize each variable when you create it.

COMPATIBILITY COUNTS

Here are two variable declarations you might find confusing. One of them compiles and runs without any warnings or errors, even though it might seem incorrect. The second won't even compile. Can you find the problem with each declaration?

```
long     netWorthInCents = 27;      // Why does this work?
float    gradePointAverage = 2.75;  // Why doesn't this work?
```

The first example stores the integer literal value, 27, in the `long` variable, `netWorthInCents`. Why doesn't Java require you to write `27L` instead? It seems like the original declaration would be filling only half of `netWorthInCents`. This example works because every integer value is also a valid `long` value; the valid range of `int`s is subsumed within the valid range of `long`s. Thus, Java will accept an `int` used to initialize a `long`. The initialization is said to be *compatible.*

"Makes sense," you think. "So why doesn't the second one work? It seems like the value `2.75` should fit inside a `float`, even though floating-point literals default to `double`s." That's true. The value `2.75` would fit handily inside a `float`. But the Java compiler does not look at the value you are trying to store; it looks at the type to see what the *potential* value is. Earlier, Java let you initialize a `long` variable with an `int` value, because all possible `int`s are also valid `long`s. Recall that floating-point literals are `double` by default. You *can't* initialize a `float` variable with a `double` value, because not all possible `double` values are valid `float` values—they are incompatible. Oversimplified a bit, the idea of compatibility is this: You can go from fewer bytes to more bytes, but not the other way. A `double` literal that occupies 64 bits will not fit into a `float` variable that has room for only 32.

To give `gradePointAverage` a valid value, you must provide a `float` value, rather than a `double`. This is easily accomplished by writing

```
float   gradePointAverage = 2.75F;  // Value and variable now compatible
```

OBJECTS, STRINGS, PRIMITIVES, AND REFERENCES

If you recall your first program, `GraffitiOne`, you had to do something very similar to initialization when you created your first object, the `Label senselessScrawl`. The declaration for that object was written as

```
Label senselessScrawl = new Label("Elephants Rule!!!");
```

Even though this looks similar to initializing a primitive variable—and it performs the same function—there are major differences between primitives and objects when it comes to initialization. The first difference is both subtle and important: Object variables—such as `senselessScrawl`—do not hold or contain objects; they refer to objects. It may help to think of object variables as similar to the remote control for your garage door. The remote control does not contain the door itself, but it does allow you to open and shut your garage. The kind of reference held by a Java object variable is called a *handle,* because you can use it to obtain, or change, the value of the variable.

The most important consequence of the difference between values and handles is that you can have two (or more) object variables that refer to the same (actual) object, just as you could have two garage-door openers that open the same garage door. Primitive variables *don't* act this way. Two integer variables may hold identical values, but they don't refer to the same number in memory. Figure 3-9 illustrates the difference between primitive values and object references.

Earlier, you learned that `String` objects acted like primitive values in some ways, and object types in others. One way that `String` objects act like primitive values is that you can initialize them with a literal `String` instead of using `new` like you do with other objects. Here are some `String` declarations:

```
String  fullName        = "Jumbala \"Jumbo\" Gumbola";
String  DBA             = "Jumbo's Jungle Java Joint";
String  mailingAddress  = "";
String  politicalParty;
```

FIGURE 3-9

Primitive values and object references

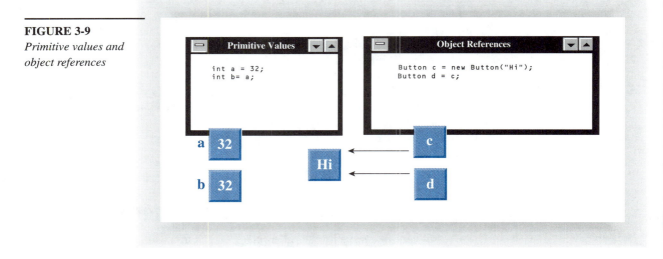

These don't look a whole lot different from the initialization of an `int` or a `char`, and unlike `Labels`, they don't use `new`. There are a couple of ways in which `Strings` act differently than either primitives or other objects. Notice the initialization for `mailingAddress`: The literal `String` is just a pair of double quotes with no intervening space. What does that mean? `Strings` can hold a variable number of characters, including none. This means that `mailingAddress` is a `String` with no characters inside it—sometimes called an *empty* string. By contrast, `politicalParty` is uninitialized. `Strings`, like objects, hold a special value, named `null`, when they don't refer to any real value. In this sense, `Strings` act like objects: They hold references, not values.

`Strings` are also like objects in other ways. First, they contain methods that give them useful and powerful capabilities. You can find the number of characters contained in a string by invoking the `length( )` method on it. Similarly, the `charAt( )` method can be used to ask a `String` for the `char` at a specific position within it. You'll use these methods extensively in Chapter 8, "Flocking Objects: Arrays and Exceptions," when you take an in-depth look at the `String` class.

Primitives do not have methods, nor do they respond to messages. In contrast to objects, primitives are manipulated by operators such as the addition operator (`+`). Again, `String` objects have some attributes of primitives, in that Java provides the concatenation operator to manipulate `Strings` along with the `String` methods.

WHEN VARIABLES DON'T: `static final`

Up to this point, you've seen literals and variables. It's time now to meet the third kind of value, *constants*. Sometimes it's useful to give a name to a value, even though the value doesn't change during the execution of the program. Often this can make a program easier to read, or as you'll see later, a class easier to use. Specifying that a field is constant can also make your program operate somewhat more efficiently.

By prefixing the declaration of a field (not a local variable) with the keywords `static final`, you can tell the Java compiler that the value of the field will not change. The compiler will tell you, by refusing to compile your program, if any statements violate this declaration. For example:

```
static final float PI = 3.14159F;
```

defines a constant called `PI` which contains the approximate value of π.

Conventionally, Java programmers capitalize the names of `static final` fields and use underscores to separate distinct words within their names. The compiler is not aware of this convention and relies solely upon the presence or absence of the keywords to determine if a field is constant or not. However, human readers of your program will appreciate it if you observe this social grace by properly naming your constant fields.

Dr. Data: Operators and Operations

The whole point of getting information into a computer is to be able to manipulate it. *Operators* are Java's way of manipulating primitives, while methods are used for manipulating objects. You'll learn about operators in this chapter, shifting the focus to methods in Chapter 4.

Operators are special symbols that are used to "operate on" values—thus the name. The values that operators operate on are called *operands*. Operands can be literals or variables. When operands are combined with operators, the operation produces a new value. This value is called a *result*. Most operators are binary operators, which combine two operands to form a result. Java also has several unary operators (which require only a single operand) and a special ternary operator (which requires three operands). You'll meet some unaries and binaries in this chapter; Java's ternary operator is presented in Chapter 5.

NUMERIC OPERATORS

Since most of Java's primitive types are numeric, it's natural that Java provides numeric operators to manipulate primitive values. The principal numeric operators are given in Table 3-5. These operators are capable of operating on both integer and floating-point types. As you'll see in a moment, they're also capable of operating on `chars`.

TABLE 3-5
NUMERIC OPERATORS

OPERATOR	MEANING
+	Addition
−	Subtraction
*	Multiplication
/	Division
%	Remainder or modulus

Java's addition and subtraction operators work the same as they did when you first learned them in grammar school. Writing `2 + 2` uses the addition operator to operate on the two operands—the literal values `2`—and produces a result: `4`. The multiplication operator also works as you'd expect, although the multiplication symbol (`*`) may be different from what you've seen. The `*` is used because `x` can be the name of a variable, and would be confusing to the compiler and the reader.

Java's division, like that in most computer languages, has some special features. Division performed on integer operands always results in a whole number—any fractional part of the result is discarded. So, in integer division, 99/100 is zero. It's a good thing most teachers don't use Java's integer division in assigning grades to students! You might also find the remainder operator unfamiliar. While the division operator returns a quotient, the remainder operator—also known as the modulus operator—returns a remainder. For example, given the expression 5%3 Java will divide 5 by 3, obtaining the quotient 1 and the remainder 2. It is the remainder, 2, which is returned as the result of the modulus operator. Unlike some other programming languages, Java's remainder operator also works on floating-point numbers, even though, in principle, division with floating-point numbers should not produce any remainder. In this case, the remainder is the amount left when the quotient is restricted to whole numbers. For example, 100.0%3.0 has the value 1.0, because 3.0 evenly divides 100.0 a total of 33 times, with 1 as the remainder.

EXPRESS YOURSELF

Operators and operands can be combined to build expressions. The result of one operation may then become an operand of a subsequent operation. For example, in the expression

```
3 + 2 - 1
```

the operands of the addition operator are combined to produce a result, namely 5. This is an invisible or temporary value that Java stores internally until it is finished evaluating this whole statement. This temporary result is then combined by use of the subtraction operator with the operand 1, giving the final result of 4.

An expression can be used as an expression statement by following it with a semicolon. Expression statements simply evaluate the specified expression, then throw the result away. This doesn't sound very useful, and it generally isn't. But many method calls actually take the form of an expression statement. Unless the result of evaluating an expression statement is explicitly saved, it is lost. The good news is that, in a moment, you'll learn some operators that make it possible to save the result of an expression by storing it in a program variable.

USING THE ASSIGNMENT OPERATOR

Rather than throwing away all the hard work your arithmetic operators have been doing, you can use the assignment operator to store the result of an expression in a variable. The symbol for assignment in Java, and in many other program languages, is the equal sign (=). This is an unfortunate choice, because the symbol is the same as that used in algebra to represent the idea of equality. To avoid confusion, some programming languages use a special symbol, or combination of symbols, to denote assignment (:=, for example). Assignment and equality are quite different things. For one thing, assignment is not symmetric. The assignment

```
a = b + 1;
```

cannot be reversed as

```
b + 1 = a; // illegal
```

Assignments store a value in a variable, which must appear to the left of the assignment operator. The second of the two previous equations places an expression to the left of the assignment operator, which is not allowed. Similarly, the following assignment is perfectly legal, though it is algebraic nonsense:

```
a = a + 1;
```

This assignment computes the value of the expression a + 1, and assigns this value to the variable a. The result is that the value of a has been increased by one.

Assignments can be specified in a cascading arrangement like this:

```
a = b = c = 0;
```

Such an expression involving multiple assignments is evaluated right to left (that is, assignment is "right associative"), so the first subexpression evaluated is c = 0. This stores the value zero in c but, being an expression, it also returns a result, namely zero. This result becomes an operand of the next operator, so we have b = 0. This stores zero in b, and produces a result that is finally stored in a by the leftmost assignment operator. You could have written

```
a = (b = (c = 0)));
```

but the parentheses make this expression more complex than the first, and the rules of Java make it clear that the two expressions are evaluated identically.

Listing 3-9 and Listing 3-10 show the Arithmetic applet, which demonstrates the use of Java's arithmetic operators. The output of the applet is shown in Figure 3-10.

Listing 3-9 Arithmetic.java

```java
import java.awt.*;
import java.applet.*;

public class Arithmetic extends Applet
{
    // Attributes
    Label label1 = new Label("");
    Label label2 = new Label("");
    Label label3 = new Label("");
    Label label4 = new Label("");

    float radius = 2.0F;
    float pi       = 3.14159F;
    float circleArea;

    double triangleBase = 25.0;
    double triangleHeight = 15.0;
    double triangleArea;

    float monthlyRent = 800.0F;
    int    monthsDue = 2;
    float depositAmount = 1000.0F;
    float amountDue;
```

```
double  interestAmount = 19270.0;
double  principalAmount = 125000.0;
int     months = 24;
double  interestRate;

// Methods
public void init( )
{
    circleArea = pi * radius * radius;
    triangleArea = 0.5 * triangleBase * triangleHeight;
    amountDue = depositAmount + monthsDue * monthlyRent;
    interestRate = (100.0 * interestAmount) /
                        (principalAmount / (months / 12.0));

    label1.setText("circleArea=" + circleArea);
    label2.setText("triangleArea=" + triangleArea);
    label3.setText("amountDue=" + amountDue);
    label4.setText("interestRate=" + interestRate);

    add(label1);
    add(label2);
    add(label3);
    add(label4);

}
}
```

Listing 3-10 Arithmetic.html

```
<HTML>
<HEAD>
<TITLE>Arithmetic.html </TITLE>
</HEAD>
<BODY>
<APPLET CODE="Arithmetic.class" WIDTH=400 HEIGHT=300></APPLET>
</BODY>
</HTML>
```

FIGURE 3-10

Output of the
Arithmetic applet

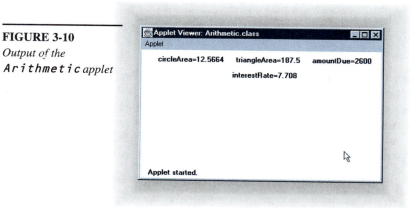

UPS AND DOWNS: INCREMENT AND DECREMENT OPERATORS

You might have noticed a difference between the arithmetic operators and the assignment operator. The assignment operator does more than simply compute a value as the arithmetic operators do: It affects the state of the program by changing a program variable. This kind of behavior is known as a *side effect*. The side effect may be the most important thing the assignment operator does, but like all operators, the assignment operator also produces a result. With the assignment operator, that result is the new value of the variable that was changed. The difference between a side effect and a result is that a result must be stored in a program variable or it is lost. A side effect changes the value of a program variable, whether or not the result of the expression is explicitly saved.

Java has several other operators besides the assignment operator that have side effects. The most used of these are the increment operator (++) and the decrement operator (--). Each of these operators is represented by a two-character token; do not put a space between the individual characters when entering them. The increment operator adds 1 to a variable, while the decrement operator subtracts 1 from a variable. You cannot use these operators with literals. While you could easily add 1 to the variable i by writing

```
i = i + 1;
```

these special operators simply allow you to specify the common operations of incrementing and decrementing more compactly.

Both operators are unary operators; unlike the more common binary operators that operate on two values, these operators operate on a single value. For example:

```
a++;
```

increments the value of a and

```
b--;
```

decrements the value of b.

BEFORE AND AFTER

The increment and decrement operators not only change the variable they operate on, but like all operators, they also produce a value. The value of an increment or decrement can be saved to another variable by use of the assignment operator. The value that is produced by an increment or decrement operator depends on how (that is, where) it is used. Each can be used in either of two ways: before a variable or after a variable. For example, it's possible to use the increment operator and write

```
a = ++b;
```

or

```
a = b++;
```

The former is called the *prefix* increment form and the latter is called the *postfix* increment form. In each case the value of b is incremented, but the result produced by each expression is different; thus, a ends up with different values. When used with a prefix operator, a receives the new value of b, the one it holds after being incremented. In the postfix increment form, a receives the old value of b, the one it held before being incremented. Table 3-6 gives equivalent statements for each operator to help make this clear.

TABLE 3-6
MEANING OF INCREMENT AND DECREMENT OPERATORS

EXPRESSION	MEANING
a = b++;	a = b; b = b + 1;
a = ++b;	b = b + 1; a = b;
a = b--;	a = b; b = b − 1;
a = --b;	b = b − 1; a = b;

The decrement operator works in a similar fashion. Using increment and decrement operators within assignments can get confusing, and your code may be clearer if you avoid them. These kinds of assignments are likely to be found in code that others have written, however, so it's important to understand how they work even if you choose to avoid them in code you write. Table 3-7 gives some examples you can use to check your understanding.

TABLE 3-7
INCREMENT AND DECREMENT OPERATORS

INT A = 1, B = 2, C ;	// INITIALIZATION
a++;	// a is now 2
++a;	// a is now 3
c = a++;	// a is now 4, c is now 3
c = ++b;	// b is now 3, c is now 3
c = a++ + b++;	// a is now 5, b is now 4, c is now 7
c = ++ a + b ++;	// a is now 6, b is now 5, c is now 10

FIRST THINGS FIRST: PRECEDENCE

Remember from grade school arithmetic the "my dear Aunt Sally rule," which says that multiplication and division are to be done before addition and subtraction? It's this rule that says that the result of 1 + 2 * 3 is 7, and not 9. The expression is evaluated as though it had been written 1 + (2 * 3). The parentheses around the multiplication are implicit, because multiplication and division have a higher *precedence* than addition and subtraction. Precedence is the order in which operations should be performed. The Java compiler is aware of precedence and uses it to decide how to evaluate complex expressions that lack parentheses. The precedence of Java's arithmetic operators is shown in Figure 3-11.

In the absence of parentheses, operations with higher precedence will be performed before operations with lower precedence. What happens when operators at the same level of precedence are used in an expression? Given the expression

```
a = 7 * 5 / 9;
```

should Java treat this as

```
a = (7 * 5) / 9;
```

in which case the result would be 3, or should it evaluate the expression as

```
a = 7 * (5 / 9);
```

FIGURE 3-11

Precedence of arith-metic operators

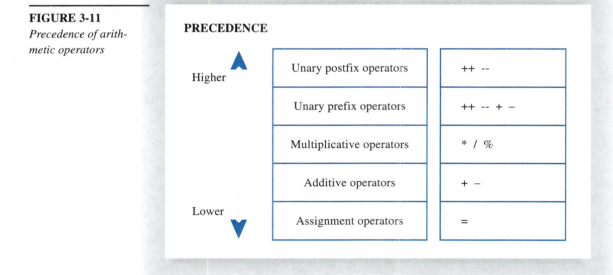

PRECEDENCE		
Higher ▲	Unary postfix operators	++ --
	Unary prefix operators	++ -- + −
	Multiplicative operators	* / %
	Additive operators	+ −
Lower ▼	Assignment operators	=

in which case the result would be 0? To decide this question, Java looks to an operator's associativity, which can be right or left. You've already seen that the assignment
operator is right-associative, meaning that its operations occur from right to left. What
about the other operators? All of the other operators are left-associative, which means
that operations within those rows are performed left to right in the order in which they
appear in the expression.

Good practice calls for using parentheses to make clear how a complex expression is
to be evaluated. Some programmers also use whitespace around operators that will be
evaluated later. Writing something like

```
a = c + d*e;
```

can help a human reader understand your program more quickly. This is especially
useful in complex expressions that are already cluttered with numerous sets of parentheses.

Note the presence in Figure 3-11 of the unary operators + and –. These allow writing
expressions such as

```
a = -b;
```

or

```
a = +2.0;
```

Listings 3-11 and 3-12 show the `Increment` applet, which demonstrates the use of
Java's increment and decrement operators. Figure 3-12 shows the output of the applet.

Listing 3-11 Increment.java

```java
import java.awt.*;
import java.applet.*;

public class Increment extends Applet
{
    // Attributes
    Label label1 = new Label("");
    Label label2 = new Label("");
    Label label3 = new Label("");
    Label label4 = new Label("");
    Label label5 = new Label("");
    Label label6 = new Label("");

    int a = 1;
    int b = a++;
    int c = 1;
    int d = ++c;
    int e = 0;
    int f = 1 + 2 * 3 + 4 * ++e;

    // Methods
    public void init( )
    {
        label1.setText("a=" + a);
        label2.setText("b=" + b);
```

continued on next page

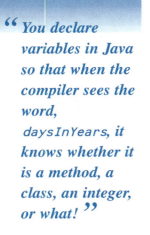

continued from previous page

```
                label3.setText("c=" + c);
                label4.setText("d=" + d);
                label5.setText("e=" + e);
                label6.setText("f=" + f);

                add(label1);
                add(label2);
                add(label3);
                add(label4);
                add(label5);
                add(label6);

        }
}
```

" *You declare variables in Java so that when the compiler sees the word,* `daysInYears`, *it knows whether it is a method, a class, an integer, or what!* "

Listing 3-12 Increment.html

```
<HTML>
<HEAD>
<TITLE>Increment.html </TITLE>
</HEAD>
<BODY>
<APPLET CODE="Increment.class" WIDTH=400
HEIGHT=300></APPLET></BODY>

</HTML>
```

FIGURE 3-12

Output of the `Increment` *applet*

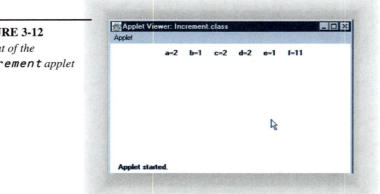

String **ARITHMETIC, SURGERY, AND RECONSTRUCTION:** String **OPERATORS**

In addition to its numeric operators, Java provides operators and methods for working with `String`s. String arithmetic allows the joining or concatenation of `String`s, and `length( )`, `charAt( )`, and other methods make it possible to teach your `String`s to do tricks.

String **Arithmetic**

When used with `String` operands, the + operator does not mean addition. Instead it indicates that the text contained in the `String`s is to be joined or *concatenated*. For example, in

```
String firstName = "Jumbala";
String lastName  = "Gumbola";
String fullName  = firstName + lastName;
```

the contents of the `String`s `firstName` and `lastName` are joined and stored in `fullName`, which now has the value `"JumbalaGumbola"`.

This is an instance of what object-oriented theoreticians call *operator overloading*. When the same operator has different meanings from one context to another, the operator is said to be overloaded.

Notice that there is no space between the first and last name when they are joined. To add space, you could change the assignment to read

```
String fullName  = firstName + " " + lastName;
```

by using the concatenation operator to concatenate a literal string (consisting of only one character, a space) with the variables `firstName` and `lastName`. Joining `String` variables and literals together is not the full extent of the concatenation operator's power. It can also magically turn any of the basic types into `String` objects so you can see the output of all your operations. To get a `String` that displays Jumbo's net worth, write

```
long   netWorthInCents   = 27;
String financialPosition = fullName + " has a net worth of "
                              + netWorthInCents;
```

Some String **Methods**

In addition to operators, `String`s also have methods, because they are really objects. As a sample of what can be done by use of `String`s, let's look at some messages handled by `String` objects. You'll see more of these `String` methods in Chapter 8—this is just a sample of what's possible. Every `String` includes methods that respond to these useful messages.

```
String   firstName    = "Jumbala";
int      firstLen     = firstName.length( );  ⇐
   //  How long it is
String   firstCaps    = firstName.toUpperCase( );  ⇐
   //  An uppercase copy
char     lastLetter   = firstName.charAt(firstLen-1);  ⇐
   //  The last letter
```

Before you can use any methods, you need to have a `String` object to send the messages to. Here, the `String` variable called `firstName` is created and initialized to refer to the text "Jumbala." You can find out the length of any `String` object by using the `length( )` method. In this example, the length is stored in an integer variable called `firstLen`. Can you correctly predict this length? The correct answer is 7, one for each letter of the text "Jumbala."

Another method of the `String` class is `toUpperCase( )`, which here makes a copy of the `String` `firstName`, while converting all the alphabetic characters to uppercase. The result is stored in the `String` `firstCaps`. In Java you cannot change the value of a `String`: They are said to be immutable. However, you can easily create a new `String` from another `String` or `String` expression. In this way, the `toUpperCase( )` method does not change the value of the `String` `firstName`, but returns a new `String` that has all uppercase letters.

The third line uses the `charAt( )` method to obtain the individual character at a designated position in the `String`. Characters within a `String` are numbered from left to right, starting with zero. So, the characters of a `String` containing 7 characters will be designated 0, 1, 2,..., 6, as shown in Figure 3-13. The last character is always designated by a number one less than the length of the `String`. Here, the `charAt( )` method's argument will cause it to return the last character of the `firstName`, which will be stored in the appropriately named field `lastLetter`. What do you expect to see printed? If you said the lowercase *a,* you are correct. Remember that the `toUpperCase` method did not change the value of the `String` `firstName`. Note also that the type of `lastLetter` is `char`, the type used for holding individual characters.

Listings 3-13 and 3-14 show the `Strings` applet, which demonstrates how Java's `Strings` work. Figure 3-14 shows the output of the applet.

FIGURE 3-13
Numbering the characters of a String

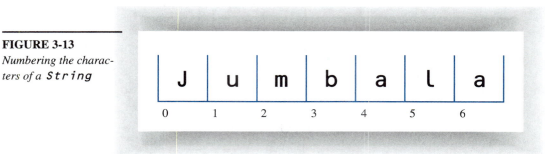

Listing 3-13 Strings.java

```java
import java.awt.*;
import java.applet.*;

public class Strings extends Applet
{
    // Attributes
    Label label1 = new Label("");
    Label label2 = new Label("");
    Label label3 = new Label("");

    String firstName = "Jumbala";
    String middleName = "Mambala";
    String lastName = "Gumbola";
    String fullName;
    char    middleInitial;
    int     nameLength;

    // Methods
    public void init( )
    {
        fullName = "\"" + firstName + " " + middleName + ⇐
            " " + lastName + "\"";
        middleInitial = middleName.charAt(0);
        nameLength = fullName.length() - 2;

        label1.setText("fullName=" + fullName);
        label2.setText("middleInitial=" + middleInitial);
        label3.setText("nameLength=" + nameLength);

        add(label1);
        add(label2);
        add(label3);

    }
}
```

Listing 3-14 Strings.html

```html
<HTML>
<HEAD>
<TITLE>Strings.html </TITLE>
</HEAD>
<BODY>
<APPLET CODE="Strings.class" WIDTH=400
HEIGHT=300></APPLET></BODY>
</HTML>
```

FIGURE 3-14

Output of the
Strings applet

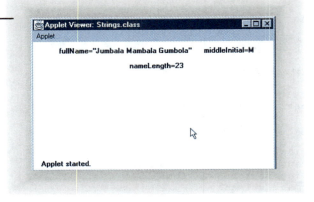

MUTANTS AT WORK: MORE ASSIGNMENT OPERATORS

One of the main reasons that people use computers is that people are lazy. If humans were not lazy, the wheel would doubtless never have been invented. In this sense laziness is a virtue. Many programmers possess a surfeit of this virtue, and those who do, find writing code like this

```
totalDollarsEarned = totalDollarsEarned + 2.33;
```

insufferable. "Why," such programmers wonder, "should we have to type the variable name twice—once on each side of the assignment operator—when all we want to do is add some value to another value, and store the result?" If necessity isn't the mother of invention, then the desire to save unnecessary keystrokes certainly is, so these programmers decided to wed the assignment operator to the arithmetic operators in what can only be described as a marriage of convenience.

Imagine what would happen if the assignment operator married the addition operator:

```
totalDollarsEarned += 2.33;
```

Java provides this, and several other, shorthand assignment operators. Each, like its assignment operator parent, is a side-effect operator that stores a value in a program variable. Table 3-8 gives an example of each of these assignment operators, along with equivalent expression statements that specify their operation.

Listing 3-15 and Listing 3-16 show the `Assignments` applet, which demonstrates Java's assignment operators. Figure 3-15 shows the output of the `Assignments` applet.

TABLE 3-8
THE SHORTHAND ASSIGNMENT OPERATORS

EXPRESSION	MEANING
a += b	a = a + b
a -= b	a = a - b
a *= b	a = a * b
a /= b	a = a / b
a %= b	a = a % b

Listing 3-15 Assignments.java

```java
import java.awt.*;
import java.applet.*;

public class Assignments extends Applet
{
    // Attributes
    Label label1 = new Label("");
    Label label2 = new Label("");
    Label label3 = new Label("");
    Label label4 = new Label("");
    Label label5 = new Label("");

    int a = 1;
    int b = 1;
    int c = 1;
    int d = 12;
    int e = 16;

    // Methods
    public void init( )
    {
        a += 1;
        b -= 2;
        c *= 3;
        d /= 4;
        e %= 5;

        label1.setText("a=" + a);
        label2.setText("b=" + b);
        label3.setText("c=" + c);
        label4.setText("d=" + d);
        label5.setText("e=" + e);

        add(label1);
        add(label2);
        add(label3);
        add(label4);
        add(label5);
    }
}
```

Listing 3-16 Assignments.html

```
<HTML>
<HEAD>
<TITLE>Assignments.html </TITLE>
</HEAD>
<BODY>
<APPLET CODE="Assignments.class" WIDTH=400 ⇐
   HEIGHT=300></APPLET></BODY>
</HTML>
```

HOLLYWOOD RELIGION: CASTS AND CONVERSIONS

Although all bytes, shorts, ints, and longs are integers, it's not always possible to directly assign the value of one integer variable to another. Assume you have an int variable containing the value 1024 and you want to assign its value to a byte variable. The largest possible value a byte variable can hold is 127, so the value 1024 just won't fit. Java prohibits such assignments by issuing an error message when programs containing them are compiled. Of course, things work more smoothly the other way around. There's never a problem assigning the value of a byte variable to an int, or to a short or a long for that matter. As you saw with initialization, these are compatible expressions because you can easily go from fewer bytes to more bytes.

A Cast of Thousands

For integer literals, Java will allow you to directly assign a value to a variable as long as the result of the assignment does not exceed the storage capacity of the variable. Occasionally, however, you may wish to transfer a value stored in a large-capacity

FIGURE 3-15

Output of the Assignments applet

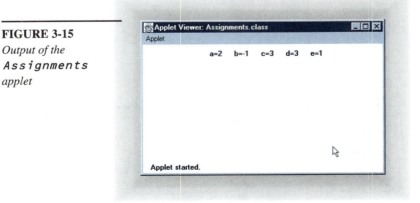

variable into a variable of smaller capacity. This can be done by use of a *cast,* which "coerces" the type of its operand to the specified type like this:

```
byte b;
int i;
// ...
// assign some value to i
// ...
b = (byte) i;
```

Here, the value stored in the variable i is cast to a byte value, which is then stored in the variable b. A cast is specified by giving the name of the desired type, enclosed in parentheses, to the left of the quantity that is to be cast to a new type. It's possible to cast values to type byte, short, int, or long as well as to noninteger types. One potential source of confusion is the effect of the cast on the variable i. A cast always creates a new, temporary value. It never changes the type of a variable. No matter what you do, the variable i will always be an int.

A cast is a way of telling Java, "I know this operation may cause problems, but let me do it anyway." You saw that the Java compiler prevented your putting the value 1024 inside the byte b. In this example, so long as the value stored in i is small enough to fit in b, all is well. If, however, the value stored in i exceeds 127, b cannot accurately represent the value. In such a case Java simply sticks the parts that fit into the variable and throws away the rest. As a consequence of this, using a cast to stick a big value in a small variable has some risk. It is like trying to stuff an entire side of beef into a freezer. Only the parts that fit end up inside. In the preceding example, if i had the value 250, after the assignment, b would have the value –6. (The variable i, of course, would still contain 250.) Figure 3-16 shows why this is so.

FIGURE 3-16

A numeric cast

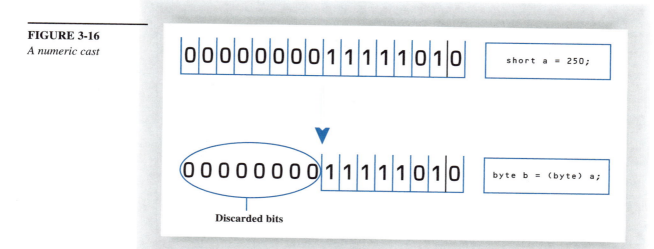

Discarded bits

In most cases this is not the sort of behavior you want. It's usually better to go back and reorganize the program to avoid the need for a cast, or to check the value of i to make sure that b can accommodate it, before performing the cast.

Casting can also involve values from the different numeric families: integers and floating points. Java considers a cast from an integer type to a floating-point type to be a compatible conversion and will automatically perform such a conversion without requiring a cast. However, the reverse situation is not compatible. Java will not automatically convert a floating-point value to an integer. When a cast is used to coerce Java into making the conversion, the fractional part of the floating-point number is not converted. No rounding is done; the floating-point value 0.99 will, when cast to an integer value, become zero.

Listing 3-17 and Listing 3-18 show the Casts applet, which demonstrates casting. Figure 3-17 shows the output of the Casts applet.

Listing 3-17 Casts.java

```java
import java.awt.*;
import java.applet.*;

public class Casts extends Applet
{
    // Attributes
    Label label1 = new Label("");
    Label label2 = new Label("");

    long bigOne = 1;
    int smallOne;

    long veryBig = 4000000000L;
    int   notBigEnough;

    // Methods
    public void init( )
    {

        smallOne = (int) bigOne;
        notBigEnough = (int) veryBig;

        label1.setText("smallOne=" + smallOne);
        label2.setText("notBigEnough=" + notBigEnough);

        add(label1);
        add(label2);
    }
}
```

Listing 3-18 Casts.html

```
<HTML>
<HEAD>
<TITLE>Casts.html </TITLE>
</HEAD>
<BODY>
<APPLET CODE="Casts.class" WIDTH=400 ⇐
   HEIGHT=300></APPLET></BODY>
</HTML>
```

Casting Character Roles: char Conversion

When used with integer values, chars act like ints with values from 0 to 65535. A char can be cast to a byte or a short, but the result may be negative if the char value is too large to fit in the smaller data type. You can also go the other way, and cast a byte, short, or int to a char. Table 3-9 shows some character conversions. Remember that the numerical value of a char is determined by its position within the Unicode character set, which is identical to the ASCII character set in the first 256 positions.

TABLE 3-9
CHARACTER-INTEGER CONVERSION

CAST	RESULT
(byte) 'A'	65
(char) 65	'A'

FIGURE 3-17
Output of the Casts applet

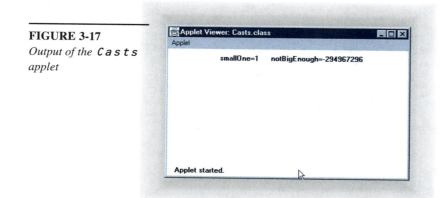

" Java operators manipulate primitives; methods manipulate objects. "

Later in this chapter you will learn about `TextField` and `Button` objects, along with the `actionPerformed( )` method. For now, the `CharInt` applet, in Listings 3-19 and 3-20, will give you an interactive example of the way `chars` behave. Type a single character into the `TextField` and press ENTER, or click the Add 1 button. The `Label` will display the character you typed, along with its integer value. It also will display the next character in the Unicode sequence, along with its integer value. Notice the cast used to convert `oldValue` (an `int`) to `newChar` (a `char`). Also notice that you don't need any cast to assign a `char` to an `int`. Figure 3-18 shows the `CharInt` applet at work.

Listing 3-19 CharInt.java

```java
//   CharInt.java
//   Working with chars
//
import java.applet.*;
import java.awt.*;
import java.awt.event.*;

public class CharInt extends Applet implements ActionListener
{
    TextField inputField = new TextField("", 1);
    Label theOutput = ⇐
      new Label("The result goes here...................");
    Button     addOne     = new Button("Add 1");

    public void init()
    {
        add(inputField);
        add(theOutput);
        add(addOne);
        addOne.addActionListener(this);
    }

    public void actionPerformed(ActionEvent event)
    {
        String inputString = inputField.getText();
        char    oldChar    = inputString.charAt(0);
        int     oldValue   = oldChar; // No cast required
        int     newValue   = oldValue + 1;
        char    newChar    = (char) newValue;
        theOutput.setText( "oldChar = " + oldChar + ⇐
          "(" + oldValue + ")" +
                            "; oldChar + 1 = " + newChar +
                            "(" + newValue + ")");
    }
}
```

Listing 3-20 CharInt.html

```html
<HTML>
<HEAD>
<TITLE>CharInt.java</TITLE>
</HEAD>
<BODY>
```

```
<H1>Working with chars</H1>
<HR>
The CharInt applet gives some examples of working
with chars. <P>
<UL>To use this applet:
<LI>Type a single character into the TextField
<LI>Press ENTER or click the Add 1 Button
</UL>
The applet will display the character pressed along
with its integer value. It will also display the next
character in the Unicode sequence along with its
integer value.
<HR>
<APPLET CODE=CharInt.class HEIGHT=150 WIDTH=300>
</APPLET>
</BODY>
</HTML>
```

OVERFLOW, UNDERFLOW, AND LOSS OF PRECISION

What happens when you add 1 to the variable a? Well, that all depends. If you are old enough to remember when automobile manufacturers made odometers that had only five digits, you may understand where this is going. On such a car, when you reached 99,999 miles, all you had to do was drive one more mile to get a brand-new car. The odometer would roll over, and you would have a car that had zero miles on it. The problem, of course, is that what the odometer reported and the reality of your worn-out car were completely at odds.

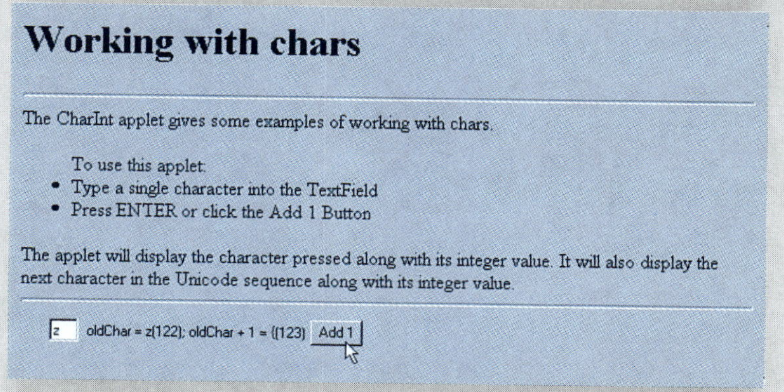

FIGURE 3-18
Output of the
CharInt applet

Working with chars

The CharInt applet gives some examples of working with chars.

To use this applet:
* Type a single character into the TextField
* Press ENTER or click the Add 1 Button

The applet will display the character pressed along with its integer value. It will also display the next character in the Unicode sequence along with its integer value.

z   oldChar = z(122); oldChar + 1 = {(123) [Add 1]

A similar situation can occur when you are writing computer programs: Your computations can overflow. This means you have created an expression that is too large to be stored in the variable you are trying to store it in. For example, adding 1 to an int variable containing 21474834647 causes an overflow to occur, because the latter is the largest possible int value. Unlike your automobile, the result will not be zero, but −21474834648. That is because the bits that are left after throwing away those that don't fit happen to represent the value −21474834648.

This is why it's important to make sure that all your variables have a type that can accommodate the maximum reasonable value the associated variable can assume. If the type is chosen inappropriately, the results may be more nonsense than sense—just like that '53 Pontiac with 1,000 miles on the odometer.

Floating-point variables do not overflow in quite the same way as integers. Floating-point arithmetic can only represent a limited number of digits accurately. The number of digits represented is termed the *precision* of a floating-point type. If you look back at Table 3-3, you'll see that the float data type accommodates about 7 digits, while the double accommodates about 15. When a computation is performed, any resulting low-order digits that do not fit in the result variable are simply lost. The applet FirstFloat, shown in Listings 3-21 and 3-22, demonstrates this behavior. Notice in the output that result1 has the expected value, but result2 is displayed as simply 1, as you can see in Figure 3-19.

Listing 3-21 FirstFloat.java

```java
//   FirstFloat.java
//   Working with floats
//
import java.applet.*;
import java.awt.*;

public class FirstFloat extends Applet
{
    float whole;
    float fraction1, fraction2;
    float result1, result2;
    Label theOutput1 = new Label("The result goes here.");
    Label theOutput2 = new Label("The result goes here.");

    public void init()
    {
        whole = 1.0f;
        fraction1 = 1.0E-5f;
        fraction2 = 1.0E-7f;

        result1 = whole + fraction1;
        result2 = whole + fraction2;

        theOutput1.setText("Result1=" + result1);
        theOutput2.setText("Result2=" + result2);

        add(theOutput1);
        add(theOutput2);
    }
}
```

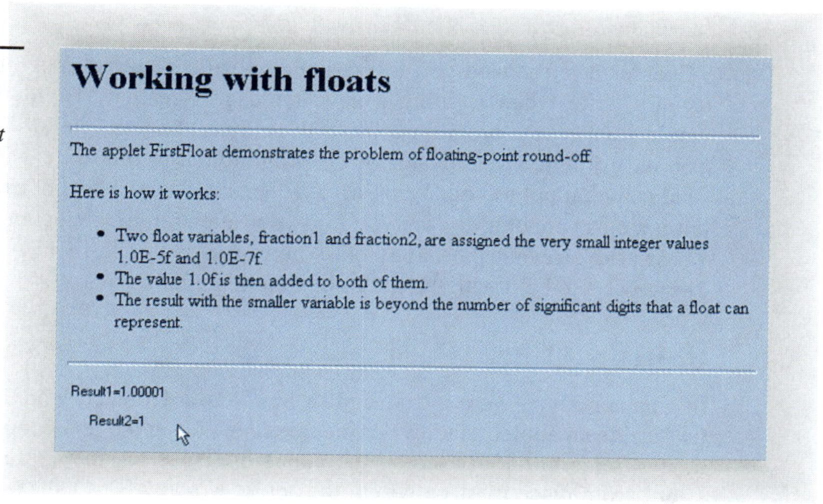

FIGURE 3-19
Output of the
FirstFloat applet

Working with floats

The applet FirstFloat demonstrates the problem of floating-point round-off

Here is how it works:

- Two float variables, fraction1 and fraction2, are assigned the very small integer values 1.0E-5f and 1.0E-7f.
- The value 1.0f is then added to both of them.
- The result with the smaller variable is beyond the number of significant digits that a float can represent.

Result1=1.00001

Result2=1

Listing 3-22 FirstFloat.html

```
</HEAD>
<BODY>
<H1>Working with floats</H1>
<HR>
The applet FirstFloat demonstrates the problem of
floating-point round-off.<P>
Here is how it works:
<UL>
<LI>Two float variables, fraction1 and fraction2 are assigned
the very small integer values 1.0E-5f and 1.0E-7f.
<LI>The value 1.0f is then added to both of them.
<LI>The result with the smaller variable is beyond the
number of significant digits that a float can represent.
</UL>
<HR>
<APPLET CODE=FirstFloat.class HEIGHT=150 WIDTH=100>
</APPLET>
</BODY>
</HTML>
```

Putting Primitives to Work

By building more applets, you can see how all of these parts work. Jumbo's Jungle Java Joint is in a bit of financial trouble, no doubt in part because of the owner's fondness for his own product. Having seen the promise of Java, Jumbo is determined to see if he can put this new technology to work. In the following section, you'll see how objects can be bolted together as you create a calculator you can use to explore some of the finer points of Java's support for floating-point arithmetic. The calculator will provide some assistance to Jumbo's quest for a positive net worth.

Chapter 2 introduced you to the `Label` object. The first program that programmers usually write when learning a new language is called "Hello World." As its name would suggest, the program consists of printing the text "Hello World" to the console. You have fulfilled the dictates of the programmer's culture by using a `Label` object to send some output to your Web page. "Elephants Rule!!!" is not exactly "Hello World," but it's close enough. Before you turn your attention to slicing and dicing integers and `float`s, let's revisit the `Label` class and meet a couple of new objects, `Button` and `TextField`, to help with the job of input and output.

USING Label**s**

In Chapter 2 you were introduced to Java's `Label` object, which was used to display text inside an applet window. You learned how to set the text contained within a `Label`, how to select the font used by the `Label` in displaying the text, and how to move the `Label` from place to place within the applet window. The `Label` does have some idiosyncratic behavior, though, that you'll want to be on the lookout for.

Label **Caveats**

If you want to use a different font for your `Label` objects, you should use the `setFont( )` method *before* you add the `Label` to the applet window. Once a `Label` has been added to the applet, Java "freezes" certain aspects of the `Label`'s appearance, among them the font. There are methods you can use to "unfreeze" the `Label`, but it's simpler to avoid this problem in the first place.

Similarly, it's important to add all the desired components (`Label`s, `Button`s, and so on) to the applet window in the `init( )` method. You might prefer to have a `Label` appear when a button is pressed; however, the window's appearance has long since been frozen by the time this happens. Java will create your `Label`, but it will exist in a state of limbo outside the applet window, where it cannot be seen. (If you really object to these constraints, don't fret. Later, in Chapter 12, "The AWT: Containers, Components, and Layout Managers," you'll learn how to relax them.)

Label **Alternatives**

`Label` objects are not always the most convenient way to present output data to the user, especially if you want to display lots of text. The biggest problem is that `Label`s are limited to a single line of text. Although you can create a series of `Label`s, each containing one line of a multiline message, this approach can be quite unwieldy. Fortunately, it's also unnecessary, because multiline text messages are handled very nicely by the `TextArea` component, which you'll meet in Chapter 5.

Another alternative to using `Label` objects is to print your text right on the surface of the applet itself by using the `drawString( )` method of the `Graphics` class, which you'll meet in the next chapter. If you have been doing a lot of experimentation and find yourself getting frustrated with the limitations of the `Label` object, just realize that there are alternatives coming up, but you can't learn everything at once. Use `Label`s where you want to display small amounts of text. This is a job for which they're well suited.

ACTION: THE `Button` OBJECT

One of the best things about Java is the ease with which it's possible to create programs that include `Label`s, `Button`s, and other components. Components are the user-interface objects that make Java programs active. The user clicks a component with the mouse and the component responds. The `Label` component is mostly static. Most programs do not encourage the user to click on a `Label`, and clicking on a `Label` in Java brings the user few rewards. The `Button` component, however, invites the user to click and cheerfully responds when clicked.

What Is a `Button`?

Listings 3-23 and 3-24 show the `FirstButton` applet, and Figure 3-20 shows how the applet appears on the screen. Notice the `Button` marked "Press Me." `Button`s are components that contain text, like `Label`s. However, `Button`s have an outline that sets them apart from the surrounding space. Clicking the mouse button while the mouse cursor is over the `Button`'s outline causes the `Button` to momentarily change shape, in a way that reminds the user of a real push button. The most important thing about pushing a `Button` is that the action causes the Java run-time system to create an event and send it to your program. Your program can detect this event and respond in a way you deem appropriate. You'll learn more about events in Chapter 13, "Advanced AWT."

Listing 3-23 FirstButton.java

```
//   FirstButton.java
//   Getting simple input
//
import java.applet.*;
import java.awt.*;
import java.awt.event.*;

public class FirstButton extends Applet ⇐
    implements ActionListener
{
    Button pressMe    = new Button( "Press Me" );
    Label theOutput   = new Label("This is where the output ⇐
      will appear");
    Label moreOutput = new Label("And more output will ⇐
      appear here!!!!");

    public void init()
    {
        add( theOutput );
        add( moreOutput );
        add( pressMe );
        pressMe.addActionListener(this);
    }
```

continued on next page

continued from previous page

```
    public void actionPerformed(ActionEvent thisEvent)
    {
        theOutput.setText("Thank you for visiting Jumbo's");
        moreOutput.setText(⇐
            "The finest Java Joint in the
            Jungle");
    }
}
```

Listing 3-24 FirstButton.html

```
<HTML>
<HEAD>
<TITLE>A Hearty Jumbo's Welcome for All</TITLE>
</HEAD>
<BODY>
<IMG SRC="Jumbo.gif" ALIGN=RIGHT>
<H1>Jumbo Rebuilds <BR>
His Business</H1>
<HR>
"Idle hands are the devil's workbench," thought Jumbo
as he cleaned the last remnants of "Elephants dRule" off the
bamboo facade. "Still, this shows a lot of creativity. I
wonder if I could harness that?"<P>
Later that day he approached Brenda, the smartest of the
youngsters, to gauge her reaction to his proposal. "No probs,"
said Brenda. "What you want is something that will make
everyone feel welcome.
We can knock that out in no time." And true to her word, she
did.
<HR>
<APPLET CODE=FirstButton.class HEIGHT=100 WIDTH=200>
</APPLET>
</BODY>
</HTML>
```

Creating and Placing a Button

Creating a Button is done almost the same way as creating a Label. Of course, the program must call the Button( ) constructor, rather than the Label( ) constructor, and must store the returned Button reference in a field of type Button. Here's the statement in FirstButton that creates the applet's Button:

```
Button pressMe = new Button( "Press Me" );
```

FIGURE 3-20
Output of the
FirstButton
applet

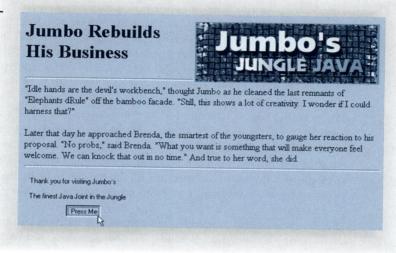

FIGURE 3-20
Output of the
FirstButton
applet

When you create a new Button, one of the things you want to do is to specify what text should appear when the Button is displayed. Just as you had to provide the `Label` constructor with the text you wanted to display, so too you provide the `Button` constructor with the text that should appear on its face. As with `Labels`, you can change the text by sending a `Button` object the `setText` message, or read the contents of a `Button` by using the `getText` message. Also as with `Labels`, `Buttons` must be added to the applet window by use of the `add( )` method. The `FirstButton` applet includes the appropriate call in the `init( )` method.

That's really all you need to add a `Button` object to your applet. Java takes care of all the details of positioning, sizing, and operating your button. If you simply add a `Button` to your applet, you can click on it and see that it does, indeed, move up and down. Most of the time, though, a Button that moves up and down is not of much utility. You really want something to happen when a Button is pressed. You want to take some action.

Where the Action Is Performed: `actionPerformed( )`

To make your applet actually do something when the Button is pressed, you will need to make your applet listen for an `ActionEvent`, just like you did for the `MouseMotionEvent` in the `GraffitiThree` applet of the previous chapter. As with `GraffitiThree`, listening for an event is a three-step process: preparation, listening, and responding.

To prepare an applet to listen for an action event, you have to do two things. First, you import the classes in `java.awt.event`, just as you did in the `GraffitiThree` applet. Second, you'll also need to modify the class header, though this time the phrase you need is `implements ActionListener`. This advertises that your class is interested in `ActionEvents`, the kind that originate with `Buttons` being clicked, instead of `MouseMotionEvents`.

To actually begin listening for `ActionEvents`, you need to make a connection between the `Button`, which is the source of the `ActionEvents`, and the applet, which will handle them. This is done by sending the `Button` the `addActionListener( )` message just after the `Button` is added to the applet surface. The message will cause `ActionEvent` messages originating with the `Button` to be forwarded to the applet. The `this` argument means "me" and refers to the applet, because it is the object sending the message.

Finally, you need to respond when your applet receives an action event. You do this by writing a specific method. To handle the `ActionEvent` messages, an `actionPerformed( )` method is needed. The order in which methods appear in a class does not matter. You can put `actionPerformed( )` before `init( )` or after it. The `actionPerformed( )` method will be invoked whenever the user clicks the `Button`, and the statements in its method body will be executed.

In the `FirstButton` applet, the `actionPerformed( )` method begins by sending the `setText( )` message to the `Label` object known as `theOutput`. The argument of the `setText( )` message is the `String` "Thank you for visiting Jumbo's". In response to the message, the `setText( )` method within the `Label` object replaces the text contained within the `Label` object with the value of the argument sent along with the message. The `actionPerformed( )` method then sends a second `setText( )` message, this one going to the second `Label` known as `moreOutput`.

That's all there is to it! Fire up your editor, type in the source code for `FirstButton`, and give it a try.

INTRODUCING THE `TextField` OBJECT

Let's see. You've got the `Label` object to do some output. You've got the `Button` object to start things rolling. All you really need is some way to get some input from the user. One of the main ways that this is done in Java is through the use of the `TextField` object.

A somewhat more sophisticated control than the `Button`, the `TextField` can be used to obtain text typed by the user on the keyboard. Listings 3-25 and 3-26 show the `FirstTextField` applet, which demonstrates how to create and use a `TextField` object. Figure 3-21 shows the applet as it runs.

Listing 3-25 FirstTextField.java

```
//   FirstTextField.java
//   Getting simple text input
//
import java.applet.*;
import java.awt.*;
```

```
import java.awt.event.*;

public class FirstTextField extends Applet ⇐
                            implements ActionListener
{
    TextField yourName = ⇐
        new TextField("Type your name in here", 25);
    Button pressMe    = new Button( "Press Me" );
    Label theOutput   = ⇐
        new Label("This is where the output will appear");

    public void init()
    {
        add( yourName );
        add( pressMe );
        add( theOutput );
        yourName.addActionListener(this);
        pressMe.addActionListener(this);
    }

    public void actionPerformed(ActionEvent thisEvent)
    {
        String message = yourName.getText();
        theOutput.setText("Hello, " + message + ". ⇐
            Welcome to Jumbo's");
    }
}
```

Listing 3-26 FirstTextField.html

```
<HTML>
<HEAD>
<TITLE>Jumbo's -- Where Everybody Asks Your Name</TITLE>
</HEAD>
<BODY>
<IMG SRC="Jumbo.gif" ALIGN=RIGHT>
<H1>Jumbo Expands</H1>
<HR>
"You know what?" Jumbo drawled to Brenda as they sat on the
terrace sipping two Espresso-Surprises. "That's really not a
welcome sign. It's a thank-you sign. We really need something
to hook folks as they walk by." <P>
Brenda's last applet was a hit, and she knew it. Business was
up, and harmony had replaced conflict at Jumbo's: even with
the ants.
"Got just the thing, JG. Look at this," she said as she
showed him the latest applet. But inside she was thinking,
"I'm not gonna keep working for peanuts."
<HR>
<APPLET CODE=FirstTextField.class HEIGHT=100 WIDTH=250>
</APPLET>
</BODY>
</HTML>
```

FIGURE 3-21

Output of the
FirstTextField
applet

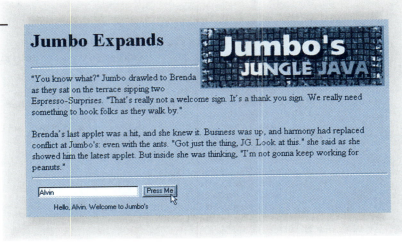

Creating a `TextField`

Creating a `TextField` is done much the same way as creating a `Label` or a `Button`, except that the constructor for the `TextField` is usually called with two arguments. The first, like the argument passed to the `Label` or `Button` constructor, provides the initial value of the `TextField`. The second argument specifies the desired width of the `TextField`, in columns.

The width of a `TextField` is something of an approximation, because the letters of many fonts are of unequal sizes. For example, the capital letter *W* is usually wider than the lowercase letter *i*. When specifying a width, it's a good idea to specify a value a little larger than needed, just to accommodate the possibility that your `String` contains some wide letters. If you want a blank `TextField`, you can specify an empty string like this:

```
TextField emptyField = new TextField("", 40);
```

This text field can contain approximately 40 characters, but initially it will be empty.

Getting Text Input

In the `FirstTextField` applet, whenever the `pressMe Button` is clicked, the `actionPerformed( )` method will be invoked, just like it was for the `FirstButton` applet. The `actionPerformed( )` method is also invoked whenever the user presses ENTER inside the `TextField`. By sending the `addActionListener( )` message to the `TextField`, the applet is notified by an event whenever ENTER is pressed inside the `TextField`. This is a special capability of `TextField` objects. Prove to yourself that this works by giving it a try.

The whole *raison d'être* for the `TextField` object is to retrieve some text from the user. Java takes care of all of the messy details of moving the cursor, displaying the characters, and so on. All you, the programmer, have to do is get the text when the user cries "Action!" Not surprisingly, the `TextField` class has a `getText( )` method that gives you back the current contents of the `TextField` as a `String` object. The first statement in the `actionPerformed( )` method is used to obtain the value typed into the `TextField yourName` by the user, and store that value in the `String` object `message`:

```
String message = yourName.getText();
```

After retrieving the user's name, all that's left to do is to use the `String` concatenation operator to make a nice, friendly message—just like one of those direct-mail places. The second statement

```
theOutput.setText("Hello, " + message + ". Welcome to Jumbo's");
```

concatenates the input `String` with some `String` literals and replaces the contents of the `TextField` with the result.

GETTING INTEGER INPUT

You know how to get a `String` from the user, but suppose you want to get a number, like the user's age or income? Because the `TextField` does such a nice job of allowing the user to type in text, and because it makes it so easy for you to retrieve it, you're probably thinking, "This is a breeze. Just show me how to create an `IntField` object and a `DoubleField` object, and I'll be on my way." Well, there's some good news and some bad news; first the bad news:

Java doesn't have an `IntField` or a `DoubleField` object or any other object that reads numbers. The only (straightforward) way to get numeric input is to first get text input, and then convert that text to a number. And, in the current implementation of Java, there is no built-in way to restrict the user input to only digits or to restrict the number of digits before or after the decimal place. Those capabilities have to be built by you, the programmer. You will need to build more complex components such as the `Keypad` class, which you'll construct in Chapter 8.

That's the bad news. The good news is that it is fairly easy to convert text input, captured through a `TextField` object, into numeric input. Type in, compile, and run the `FirstIntField` applet shown in Listings 3-27 and 3-28. When you're finished, let's look at it more closely.

Listing 3-27 FirstIntField.java

```
//   FirstIntField.java
//   Getting simple numeric input
//
import java.applet.*;
import java.awt.*;
import java.awt.event.*;
```

continued on next page

continued from previous page

```
public class FirstIntField extends Applet ⇐
  implements ActionListener
{
    TextField startInt   = new TextField( 10 );
    Button    pressMe    = new Button( "Press Me" );
    Label     theTitle   = ⇐
      new Label("Brenda and Associates - " +
                "Applets Starting at Pennies a Day");
    Label     theOutput =
      new Label("Enter starting price " +
                " (in pennies), and press the button");
    long      totalDue = 0;
    int       dayNo    = 0;

    public void init()
    {
        add( theTitle );
        add( theOutput );
        add( startInt );
        add( pressMe );
        startInt.addActionListener(this);
        pressMe.addActionListener(this);
    }

    public void actionPerformed(ActionEvent thisEvent)
    {
        int curAmt = Integer.parseInt( startInt.getText( ) );
        startInt.setEditable(false);

        totalDue += curAmt;
        curAmt   *= 2;
        dayNo++;

        startInt.setText( "" + curAmt );
        theTitle.setText( "Day number "+ dayNo + ⇐
          ". Amount owed is " + totalDue + " cents" );
        theOutput.setText("Your next applet will cost " + ⇐
          curAmt/100 + " dollars, and " + ⇐
          curAmt % 100 + " cents");
    }
}
```

Listing 3-28 FirstIntField.html

```
<HTML>
<HEAD>
<TITLE>Jumbo Gets An Education</TITLE>
</HEAD>
<BODY>
<IMG SRC="Jumbo.gif" ALIGN=RIGHT>
"What do you mean you won't work for peanuts?" Jumbo
bellowed, as he was wont to do when surprised. "What do I
look like, some kind of King of the Jungle?" <P>
```

```
Brenda planned her answer carefully. "Easy, JG," she said
softly. "All the guys want is a guarantee that we'll have a
job tomorrow. If you agree to buy an applet every day, we'll
let you set the price for the first one--as low as a penny.
Of course the price for every additional applet will double,
but after thirty days you can quit. You'd spend more than
that on peanuts. We'll even throw in a metering applet for
free, and every day you can press the button to see how much
you owe us." <P>
"You don't have to do that," said Jumbo, mollified and
signing on the dotted line. "Let's make it 32 days to make up
for the applets you've already given me."
<HR>
<APPLET CODE=FirstIntField.class HEIGHT=100 WIDTH=300>
</APPLET>
</BODY>
</HTML>
```

Figure 3-22 shows the output of the `FirstIntField` applet. Does Jumbo really get a deal, or does Brenda take him for a ride? Try to figure out what Jumbo's total bill will be and then run the applet to find out if you were right. You'll need to press the button day-by-day to see Jumbo's bill accumulate.

FIGURE 3-22

Output of the
FirstIntField
applet

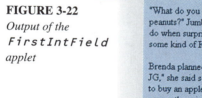 

Fields and Local Variables

So far, you've been working mainly with fields, which are variables declared inside a class, but you've read that Java supports another kind of variable, the local variable. The `FirstIntField` applet demonstrates the use of local variables as well as a method of getting integer input. Near the top of the listing, six fields are defined: `startInt`, `pressMe`, `theTitle`, `theOutput`, `totalDue`, and `dayNo`. Inside the `actionPerformed( )` mainly method, another variable is declared, the `int curAmt`. This integer is a local variable. Unlike fields, which are created when the applet is created, this local variable is created when the `actionPerformed( )` method is invoked. The variable `curAmt` can only be used within the `actionPerformed( )` method. When the `actionPerformed( )` method terminates, `curAmt` is destroyed and the memory it used is recycled. Each time the method is reentered, this variable is re-created. It does not retain the value it held at the end of the previous invocation.

Local variables can be initialized by use of initializer expressions, but they need not be. However, a local variable lacking an initializer is not automatically initialized to zero or any other value. It must be given a value before being used. The Java compiler is clever enough to examine every use of a local variable and determine whether the local variable will have an appropriate value at run-time. If not, the compiler will issue an error message and refuse to compile the program. Remember: Local variables *must* be initialized before use.

Converting `Strings` to `Integers`

How then does the applet `FirstIntField` initialize the local variable `curAmt`? Look at the line of code where `curAmt` is given a value:

```
int curAmt = Integer.parseInt( startInt.getText( ) );
```

This statement defines the local `int` variable, `curAmt`, and then initializes it by using the `parseInt( )` method of the `Integer` class. The `Integer` class is a special built-in Java class that has useful methods for working with integers. Its `parseInt( )` method is capable of converting a `String` value containing digits into an `int` value. In the `FirstIntField` applet, `parseInt( )` is given a value from the `TextField` object `startInt` into which the user has entered digits representing whole numbers.

Of course, it's altogether possible that the user will enter something other than digits into `startInt`. This, of course, means that `parseInt( )` will not find a valid integer in the field. When this occurs, the applet will attempt to print a message to its "output stream," which you will see at the DOS prompt if you run the applet using `Appletviewer`. You can look at the error message and see the faulty input value. This can be helpful in tracking down the cause of a program malfunction. Certainly it's better practice to deal explicitly with the possibility of bad input by the user; you'll see how to do this in Chapter 8.

Other `FirstIntField` Features

Once the applet retrieves the value entered by the user into the `TextField startInt`, the `actionPerformed( )` method proceeds to use many of the numeric operators you have studied in this chapter. Can you tell what will happen by looking at the code? Here's a step-by-step description:

☕ After retrieving the value typed in by the user, the `setEditable(false)` message is sent to the `TextField startInt`. This prevents Jumbo from typing in another number if he doesn't like where things are heading.

☕ The current applet price, `curAmt`, is added to the total amount due Brenda's company, by use of the shorthand arithmetic assignment operator: `totalDue += curAmt;`

☕ The multiplication shorthand assignment operator is then used to double the price for the next applet to be sold: `curAmt *= 2;`

☕ The increment operator is then used to increase the field `dayNo`, which holds the current day of the contract, `dayNo++;`

☕ The current applet price, `curAmt`, is converted back into a text `String`, where it is stored back in the `startInt TextField` by use of the `setText( )` method: `startInt.setText( "" + curAmt );`. Remember, because `curAmt` is a local variable, it will not hold its value between invocations of the `actionPerformed( )` method.

☕ *String* arithmetic is used to create a `String` showing the number of days and the total amount owed by Jumbo. This `String` is used to replace the text in the `Label` variable, `theTitle`.

☕ Similarly, the `Label` variable, `theOutput`, uses a `String` to display the cost, in dollars and cents, of the next applet Jumbo purchases. To compute the dollars and cents, the special properties of integer division and the remainder operator are employed. For example, if the amount is 20025 cents, you can use integer division to divide that amount by 100, giving the quotient 200, which is the dollar amount. Similarly, you can use the remainder operator to compute the remainder of dividing the amount by 100, giving the result 25, which is the number of cents.

GETTING FLOATING-POINT INPUT

Converting a `String` containing a floating-point number into a floating-point value is done a little differently from what was done to get an `int` value. The process involves two steps. First, the `valueOf( )` method of the `Double` class is used to create a `Double` object. A `Double` object is a special Java object used for working with `doubles`. A `Double` actually contains a `double` (note the different spellings for the primitive type and for the class; the class starts with an uppercase *D*), along with some other fields and methods. In object-oriented terms, a class or object like `Double` is called a *wrapper* because it is wrapped around a simpler thing of similar type. Figure 3-23 shows how this wrapper class works.

The second step is to get the `double` out of the `Double` wrapper. The `double` within the `Double` can be accessed by use of the `doubleValue( )` method. The `double` value can then be stored in an ordinary `double` variable, displayed as output, or used in any other way that a `double` value can be used. Listings 3-29 and 3-30 show a simple applet, `FirstDoubleField`, that illustrates the process of converting a `String` to a `double`. Figure 3-24 shows the `FirstDoubleField` applet running under Netscape Navigator. Note that in `FirstDoubleField`, we don't want to take any action when ENTER is pressed inside either of the `TextField`s; we want to wait until the button is pressed. To accomplish this, we send the `addActionListener( )` to only the button. Because the `TextField`s are never instructed to forward their `ActionEvent`s to the applet, the applet never sees them. The only way to compute the sum is by pressing the button.

Listing 3-29 FirstDoubleField.java

```java
//   FirstDoubleField.java
//   Getting floating point numeric input
//
import java.applet.*;
import java.awt.*;
import java.awt.event.*;

public class FirstDoubleField extends Applet ⇐
   implements ActionListener
{
    TextField firstDouble  = new TextField( 20 );
    TextField secondDouble = new TextField( 20 );
    Button addMe           = new Button( "Add Me" );
    Label  theOutput       = ⇐
      new Label("The sum of both numbers appears here");

    public void init()
    {
        add( new Label("Enter two floating point numbers" ⇐
          "and press 'Add Me'"));
        add( firstDouble );
        add( secondDouble );
        add( theOutput );
        add( addMe );
        addMe.addActionListener(this);
    }

    public void actionPerformed(ActionEvent thisEvent)
    {
        Double first = Double.valueOf( ⇐
          firstDouble.getText( ) );
        Double second = Double.valueOf( ⇐
          secondDouble.getText( ) );
        double result = first.doubleValue() + ⇐
          second.doubleValue();
        theOutput.setText( first + " + " + second + ⇐
          " = " + result );
    }
}
```

FIGURE 3-23

A wrapper class

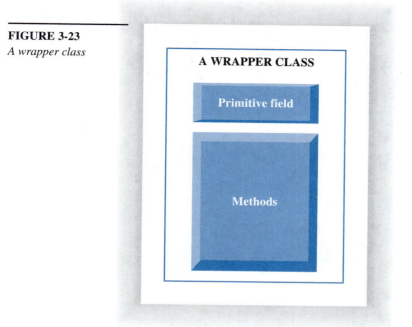

A WRAPPER CLASS

Primitive field

Methods

Listing 3–30 FirstDoubleField.html

```
<HTML>
<HEAD>
<TITLE>Jumbo Adds Two Doubles</TITLE>
</HEAD>
<BODY>
<IMG SRC="Jumbo.gif" ALIGN=RIGHT>
<H1>Jumbo's Luck Holds</H1>
<HR>
"That was close," thought Jumbo as he looked at Brenda's
applet meter and the final amount he owed on day 32.
"About this contract." Jumbo turned and said, "It doesn't say
I have to quit after 32 days. It just says I can."<P>
Despite her chagrin, Brenda couldn't keep a note of grudging
respect out of her voice. Maybe there was something to be
said for age and experience after all. "OK," she said, "No
more tricks. What do you want?" Jumbo scratched behind his
ear with his trunk. "I'd just like some help adding up the
receipts," he said.
<HR>
<APPLET CODE=FirstDoubleField.class HEIGHT=150 WIDTH=300>
</APPLET>
</BODY>
</HTML>
```

FIGURE 3-24

Output of the
FirstDoubleField
applet

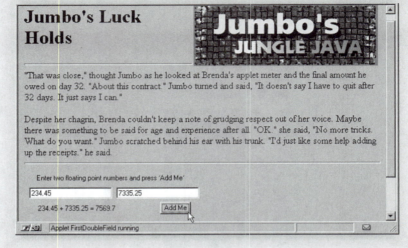

SimpleCalc

The SimpleCalc program, shown in Listings 3-31 through 3-35, uses four applets that can add, subtract, multiply, and divide double quantities. There's nothing new in SimpleCalc, but it's the largest program you've been shown so far, so it's worth studying. Notice how the HTML file accesses the four applets. Each works independently of the other three, though all four are present on the same page, if you view the page using a browser. The JDK Appletviewer obligingly starts four separate applets.

Experiment with SimpleCalc to learn more about how Java handles floating-point arithmetic. For example, divide a number by zero and watch what happens. Enter some very large values, some values using exponents, and some very small values. When you enter values that produce numbers outside the set of valid floating-point values, Java will display something like -1.#IND, which is Java's way of telling you the result isn't good. Internally, Java's floating-point numbers can assume any one of three values that represent an error condition: infinity, negative infinity, and NaN (not a number). The NaN value results from operations like division by zero. Infinity and negative infinity result from positive or negative values that are too large to be represented. For example, a double result of 1.0E309 would be represented as infinity, because the largest possible value for a double is approximately 1.7E308. Of course, this is a very large number indeed.

Listing 3-31 SimpleCalc.html

```
<HTML>
<HEAD>
<TITLE>SimpleCalc.java</TITLE>
</HEAD>
<BODY>
<APPLET CODE=AddDoubles.class   HEIGHT=50 WIDTH=400></APPLET>
<APPLET CODE=SubDoubles.class   HEIGHT=50 WIDTH=400></APPLET>
<APPLET CODE=MultDoubles.class  HEIGHT=50 WIDTH=400></APPLET>
<APPLET CODE=DivDoubles.class   HEIGHT=50 WIDTH=400></APPLET>
</BODY>
</HTML>
```

Listing 3-32 AddDoubles.java

```java
//  AddDoubles.java
//  Add two doubles and display the result
//
import java.applet.*;
import java.awt.*;
import java.awt.event.*;

public class AddDoubles extends Applet implements ActionListener
{
    TextField firstDouble  = new TextField( 10 );
    Button addButton       = new Button("+");
    TextField secondDouble = new TextField( 10 );
    Label theOutput        = new Label("999,999,999.99");

    public void init()
    {
        add( firstDouble );
        add( addButton );
        add( secondDouble );
        add( theOutput );
        addButton.addActionListener(this);
    }

    public void actionPerformed(ActionEvent thisEvent)
    {
        Double first = Double.valueOf( ⇐
          firstDouble.getText( ) );
        Double second = Double.valueOf( ⇐
          secondDouble.getText( ) );
        double result = first.doubleValue() + ⇐
          second.doubleValue();
        theOutput.setText( " = " + result );
    }
}
```

Listing 3-33 SubDoubles.java

```java
//   SubDoubles.java
//   Subtract two doubles and display the result
//
import java.applet.*;
import java.awt.*;
import java.awt.event.*;

public class SubDoubles extends Applet implements ActionListener
{
    TextField firstDouble   = new TextField( 10 );
    Button subButton        = new Button("-");
    TextField secondDouble  = new TextField( 10 );
    Label theOutput         = new Label("999,999,999.99");

    public void init()
    {
        add( firstDouble );
        add( subButton );
        add( secondDouble );
        add( theOutput );
        subButton.addActionListener(this);
    }

    public void actionPerformed(ActionEvent thisEvent)
    {
        Double first = Double.valueOf( ⇐
          firstDouble.getText( ) );
        Double second = Double.valueOf( ⇐
          secondDouble.getText( ) );
        double result = first.doubleValue() - ⇐
          second.doubleValue();
        theOutput.setText( " = " + result );
    }
}
```

Listing 3-34 MultDoubles.java

```java
//   MultDoubles.java
//   Multiply two doubles and display the result
//
import java.applet.*;
import java.awt.*;
import java.awt.event.*;

public class MultDoubles extends Applet ⇐
                      implements ActionListener
{
    TextField firstDouble   = new TextField( 10 );
    Button multButton       = new Button("*");
    TextField secondDouble  = new TextField( 10 );
    Label theOutput         = new Label("999,999,999.99");

    public void init()
    {
        add( firstDouble );
        add( multButton );
```

```
                add( secondDouble );
                add( theOutput );
                multButton.addActionListener(this);
        }

        public void actionPerformed(ActionEvent thisEvent)
        {
                Double first = Double.valueOf( ⇐
                  firstDouble.getText( ) );
                Double second = Double.valueOf( ⇐
                  secondDouble.getText( ) );
                double result = first.doubleValue() * ⇐
                  second.doubleValue();
                theOutput.setText( " = " + result );
        }
}
```

Listing 3-35 DivDoubles.java

```
//   DivDoubles.java
//   Divide two doubles and display the result
//
import java.applet.*;
import java.awt.*;
import java.awt.event.*;

public class DivDoubles extends Applet ⇐
                         implements ActionListener
{
    TextField firstDouble  = new TextField( 10 );
    Button divButton       = new Button("/");
    TextField secondDouble = new TextField( 10 );
    Label theOutput        = new Label("999,999,999.99");

    public void init()
    {
            add( firstDouble );
            add( divButton );
            add( secondDouble );
            add( theOutput );
            divButton.addActionListener(this);
    }

    public void actionPerformed(ActionEvent thisEvent)
    {
            Double first = Double.valueOf( ⇐
              firstDouble.getText( ) );
            Double second = Double.valueOf( ⇐
              secondDouble.getText( ) );
            double result = first.doubleValue() / ⇐
              second.doubleValue();
            theOutput.setText( " = " + result );
    }
}
```

Summary

- Objects have state, behavior, and identity.

- Java's values are of two types: objects and primitives.

- Primitive values cannot be decomposed into simpler parts.

- The four families of primitive types are integer, floating-point, character, and Boolean.

- The `String` type shares characteristics of both primitive and object types.

- Java has four integer types: `byte`, `short`, `int`, and `long`.

- `long` values can store larger quantities than the other types, but occupy more space and require more time to manipulate.

- Literals contain values that are known when the program is written and that cannot change during program execution.

- Variables contain values that can change during program execution.

- Java stores small integer literals as `int`s and larger ones as `long`s.

- Java has special notations that make it easy to specify octal and hexadecimal literals.

- Floating-point numbers include a fractional part and a whole part.

- `char` values represent individual characters, using the Unicode standard encoding.

- Unicode allows specification of characters from a variety of languages.

- Text data can be stored in `String` objects.

- Declaration statements are used to create and initialize variables.

- The type of a variable and the type of its initializer must be compatible.

- Object types other than `String`s use the `new` operator to create new objects.

- Object variables store an object's name, which allows reference to the object, rather than the object itself.

- Primitive variables store the primitive itself.

- `static final` variables, like literals, do not change value, but, unlike literals, they have a name.

- Operators are used to manipulate the values stored in literals and variables.

- Java's numeric operators include addition (+), subtraction (−), multiplication (*), division (/), modulus (%), increment (++), and decrement (−−).

⫸ Expressions consist of operators and their operands.

⫸ A simple Java statement is the expression statement, which consists of an expression followed by a semicolon.

⫸ Java evaluates an expression statement and discards its result.

⫸ Assignment operators can be used within expressions to change the state of variables.

⫸ Java's increment and decrement operators can be used in prefix and postfix form.

⫸ String "arithmetic" using the + operator allows concatenation of `String`s.

⫸ Casts can be used to coerce the type of an expression, though loss of data is possible.

⫸ `Label`s, `Button`s, and `TextField`s are useful user interface objects.

⫸ Fields are defined outside of methods and are part of an object's state.

⫸ Local variables are defined within methods and are not part of an object's state.

Quiz

1. Java's objects have identity, state, and _____.

2. Java's values are of two types: objects and _____.

3. It's possible to extend the state and behavior of _____ values.

4. Java has four integer types: `byte`, `short`, _____, and _____.

5. Java's family of numeric types whose members have values that include fractional parts are the _____ types, `float` and `double`.

6. `long` values can store large numbers, but require extra _____ and _____.

7. Values that are unnamed and that do not change value during program execution are known as _____.

8. Named values that can change during program execution are known as _____.

9. Java stores small integers as _____ and longer ones as _____.

10. Numbers specified in base 8 are called _____ numbers, and numbers specified in base _____ are called hexadecimal numbers.

11. `char` values represent individual _____.

12. `char` values use the standard encoding known as _____, rather than the more familiar ASCII.

13. Text data can be stored in _____ objects.

14. _____ statements are used to create and optionally initialize variables.

15. The type of a variable and the type of its initializer need not be the same, only _____.

16. Object types usually use the _____ operator to create new objects.

17. Object variables actually store the _____ to an object rather than the value of an object.

18. `static final` variables do not change _____ during program execution.

19. Operators are used to manipulate the values stored in _____ and _____.

20. Binary operators require two _____, while unary operators require only one.

21. Java's numeric operators include addition, subtraction, multiplication, division, and _____.

22. Expressions consist of _____ and their _____.

23. An expression statement is evaluated by computing its result and then _____ the result.

24. Assignment operators can be used to change the _____ of variables.

25. Casts are used to change the _____ of a value.

26. The _____ component can be used to display text.

27. The _____ component can be used to trigger program actions.

28. The _____ component can be used to allow the user to enter text.

29. Fields are defined _____ methods, while _____ variables are defined inside them.

Exercises

1. Give some examples of things in the real world that are composed of other things. How does the fact that Java's objects have "structure" make them more useful?

2. Objects typically require significantly more storage space than `long`s. What is the wisdom of having both object and primitive types?

3. Give three reasons why you shouldn't simply declare every variable in your program as a `long`.

4. Why do you suppose the designers of Java decided to follow the IEEE 754 standard for the structure of floating-point numbers?

5. What are "special" characters and why are they needed?

6. Why shouldn't we simply store all computer data as text?

7. Why are the rules of Java, like those of other programming languages, so detailed and strict?

8. Explain the difference between assignment and equality.

9. Give two reasons why parentheses are useful in writing expressions.

10. What would be the result if every operator in the Java language had the same precedence? How would expressions be "different"?

11. Since local variables are not part of the state of an object, why are they useful?

12. The area of a rectangle is the product of the length of its base and the length of its height. Write an applet, based on `MultDoubles.java`, that computes and displays the area of a rectangle given the length of its sides.

13. The area of a circle is π times the square of its radius, which is one-half the diameter of the circle. Write an applet, based on `MultDoubles.java`, that computes the area of a circle given its diameter. You may use the approximate value of 3.14159 for π.

14. There are 454 grams to one pound. Write an applet, based on `MultDoubles.java`, that allows the user to enter a number. Pressing a button marked "Convert" will display two values: (1) the weight in pounds corresponding to the input value, taken to be in grams; and (2) the weight in grams corresponding to the input value, taken to be in pounds.

15. Given two linear equations of the form

```
ax + by = c
dx + ey = f
```

It's possible to solve for their simultaneous solution, given by

```
x = (ce - bf) / (ae - bd)
y = (af - cd) / (ae - bd)
```

Write an applet, based on `MultDoubles.java`, that solves such an equation, given values for a, b, c, d, e, and f. Don't worry about the possibility of division by zero; let Java handle this as it deems appropriate.

4

Simply Methods: One Step at a Time

Pet rocks: Why would anyone purchase a pet rock? They don't *do* anything! In Chapter 3, "The Atomic Theory of Objects: Working with Object Attributes," you learned about the attributes of objects—about the different types of data that Java provides, the differences between primitive types and object types, and about what it takes to declare and define data objects—fields and variables—in a Java program. Yet no matter how well you studied and learned, the objects you can build using only data act just like that pet rock—a quaint curio, but not a useful artifact. It's the methods of an object that bring it to life.

In this chapter you will learn

- How messages and methods really work. You will look at the theory and structure of messages, and the relationship between messages and methods.

- How to write your own methods, and send your own messages.

- How to use the methods of classes such as `Applet`, `Math`, and Java's utility classes.

- How to use the `paint( )` method and get your first introduction to `Graphics` objects.

- How to design families of classes to create programs.

Writing Class Methods

Sending messages is nothing new to you. You've been sending messages to objects almost from the very first, confidently expecting that each object would know what to do when you told it to `setText( )`, `setFont( )`, or `add( )`. Objects understand messages because objects have methods that define the behavior that corresponds to each message. A *method* is a small software program that tells the object what to do when it receives a given message, just as a recipe guides a cook. However, computers lack imagination and creativity; they follow their "recipes" precisely and without variation. Thus, methods for computers must be extremely detailed and precise.

Messages and methods are paired up: Each message must have a corresponding method. There's no point having a method for a message that will never be sent. We reflect this in the way we speak about messages and methods. One way to send a message to Jumbo's new Pizza Emporium is to pick up the phone and give him a call. Sometimes you talk about sending a message, other times you talk about calling or invoking a method. These, in fact, are the same act. Because of the close relationship between messages and methods, you will see the terms used interchangeably. Figure 4-1 shows how method calls and declarations work together. Notice how a method declaration starts with a return type and is followed by the instructions that the method performs, enclosed in braces. In contrast, when you call a method, you don't start with the return type, and you end the method call with a semicolon instead of a set of instructions. You'll learn more about defining and calling methods as you read through this chapter.

INTERFACE AND IMPLEMENTATION

The last time you ordered a pizza over the phone, most likely the conversation went something like this:

Hello, is this Jumbo's Pizza Emporium? Good. This is Carol Coder at 123 Maple Drive. I'd like to order a medium Rain-Forest Special™ on a thin crust. Hold the tofu. Can I get a rush on that? Twenty minutes? Fine. Thank you!

Remember from Chapter 1, "What's All This Java Stuff?" and Chapter 2, "Programs: The Community of Objects," that this is an example of sending a message. In OOP terms, you told the `PizzaDeliveryDude` object what you wanted done. You could say that you called the `makeMeAPizza( )` method and the `deliverIt( )` method. Additional information was required for each of these messages. This additional information allowed the `PizzaDeliveryDude` object to modify his behavior to suit your needs. For the `makeMeAPizza` message you had to include arguments that specified:

☞ Medium size

☞ Rain-Forest Special™

FIGURE 4-1

Method calls and declarations

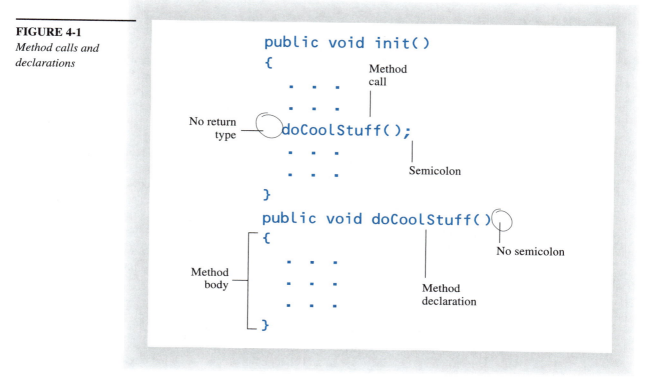

🍵 Thin crust

🍵 No tofu

When you asked that it be delivered, you had to include information on where (123 Maple Drive) and when (a rush order).

In all this message sending and method calling, though, it's easy to overlook one thing. Notice how many things you *didn't* have to tell the `PizzaDeliveryDude`. You didn't have to specify

🍵 Every ingredient in the pizza

🍵 How to cook the pizza

🍵 What vehicle to deliver the pizza in

and a whole slew of other details. In computer terms, we call these details the *implementation*, while messages such as `makeMeAPizza` are called the *interface*. You need both parts to make a computer program, as well as to operate a successful Pizza Emporium. If folks could order pizzas, but you had no way of making them, you'd be in deep, deep trouble with your (ex-) customers. On the other hand, the best pizzas in the world are of no use without a mechanism for ordering them.

The interface of a Pizza Emporium, as well as a computer program, is its face to the world. The interface is *what* the program does—the services it offers. In an OOP program, the interface is represented by the messages your program responds to. How do you decide what messages your objects should have? Creating the interface for a class is done through a process called *object-oriented design* (OOD). In many ways this is the most important as well as the most difficult part of creating a good object-oriented program. At the end of this chapter, you'll learn about some of the basics of OOD and you'll be returning to them throughout the remainder of the book.

The *how* part of an OOP program—its implementation—is represented by methods: the code that implements the step-by-step instructions to carry out a service. Separating the *what* from the *how*—the interface from the implementation—is one way that OOP programs become more robust and reusable. Think back to the `PizzaDeliveryDude` object. Do you care what steps he goes through to create your pizza? No! You don't care if he stands on his head while he makes it. You care only about two things:

☕ How you order a pizza: the input and messages the `PizzaDeliveryDude` object responds to

☕ What the pizza is like: Is it tasty, tofu-free, and delivered quickly?

You care only about the interface. The advantage to this is that if Jumbo discovers that pizzas can be made more efficiently by workers' standing on their heads or swinging from vines, he can go ahead and change his procedures—his implementation—without affecting you.

In this section, we'll open up the "cookbook" and look at the "recipes," or methods, that objects use to govern their behavior. Then we'll revisit the way that messages are sent, drawing on new knowledge about the "internals" of methods.

SIMPLE METHODS

If you hearken back to the applet `FirstButton` in Chapter 2, you'll recall that it displayed a greeting on the screen by sending a `setText` message to a `Label` object when the button was pressed. The first applet in this chapter, aptly named `FirstMethod`, performs a similar function, but to set the text, it uses a method that you will write, `showMessage( )`, rather than directly manipulating a `Label` object. Take a few minutes to enter, compile, and run the applet in Listings 4-1 and 4-2. Figure 4-2 shows what the applet looks like when it runs. When you're done, we'll take a closer look at writing simple methods.

Listing 4-1 FirstMethod.java

```
// FirstMethod.java
import java.applet.*;
import java.awt.*;
import java.awt.event.*;
```

```
public class FirstMethod extends Applet implements
ActionListener
{
    // Attributes
    Label theLabel = new Label ("Press the button, please.");
    Button pressMe = new Button ("Ok");

    // Methods
    public void init( )
    {
        add(theLabel);
        add(pressMe);
        pressMe.addActionListener(this);
    }

    public void actionPerformed(ActionEvent theEvent)
    {
        showGreeting( );
    }

    public void showGreeting( )
    {
        theLabel.setText("Hi, Sam!");
    }

}
```

Listing 4-2 FirstMethod.html

```
<HTML>
<HEAD>
<TITLE>Jumbo Learns Methods</TITLE>
</HEAD>
<BODY>
<IMG SRC="Jumbo.gif" ALIGN=RIGHT>
<APPLET CODE=FirstMethod.class HEIGHT=100 WIDTH=200>
</APPLET>
<HR>
"Part of the problem," said Brenda as she bent over the
code listing printed out on the table, "is that I really
didn't have a plan when we started working on this. We
need some methods to this madness--a little pun JG--so
I've started writing methods to organize your applets.
You just wait. This'll be so cool!"<P>
"I like the enthusiasm." Jumbo thought to himself. To
Brenda he said, "Who's Sam?"
</BODY>
</HTML>
```

WHAT'S COOKING: INSIDE A METHOD

The applet FirstMethod patiently waits for someone to press the solitary button on the applet window. When the button is pushed, the applet responds with a greeting. The applet includes three methods: init( ), actionPerformed( ), and showGreeting( ).

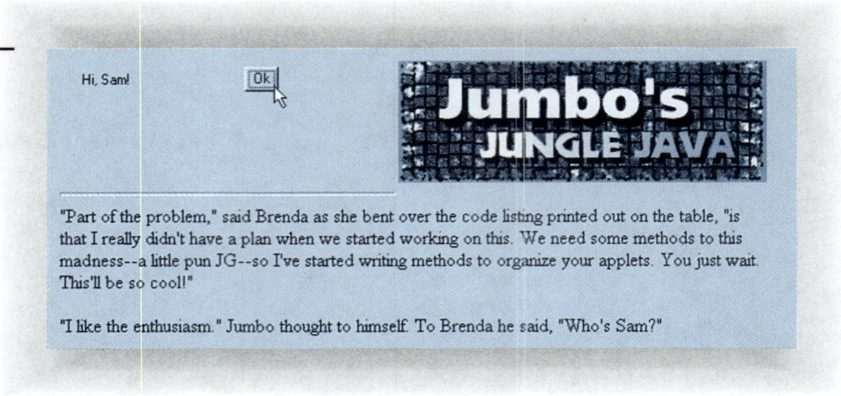

FIGURE 4-2
Running the
FirstMethod
applet

"Part of the problem," said Brenda as she bent over the code listing printed out on the table, "is that I really didn't have a plan when we started working on this. We need some methods to this madness--a little pun JG--so I've started writing methods to organize your applets. You just wait. This'll be so cool!"

"I like the enthusiasm." Jumbo thought to himself. To Brenda he said, "Who's Sam?"

You can't see exactly how the `init` message and the `actionPerformed` message are sent, because they are sent by the browser. The `showGreeting( )` method, however, is one we've written, and it's called by a statement within the `actionPerformed( )` method. Let's look at the method declaration first, and then we'll examine the method call.

THE FIVE FINGERS OF DEATH: METHOD DECLARATIONS

This section really doesn't have anything to do with old kung fu movies, but the subtitle serves as a handy reminder that there are five parts to the method declaration for `showGreeting( )`. A method declaration, like the declaration for a variable, is the way you tell the Java compiler just what it should do when it sees the word *showGreeting*. Just as a variable declaration tells the Java compiler what type of values are valid for that variable, the method declaration tells the compiler what kinds of arguments the method can accept, who is authorized to send messages, and what type of output the method produces. You have to follow a recipe to write a method declaration. Take a quick look at Figure 4-3, which shows the ingredients, before you move into the details.

The first part of a method declaration is the *access specifier*. In the case of the `showGreeting( )` method in the `FirstMethod` applet (shown in Listing 4-1), this is the keyword `public`. For now, every method you write will include this keyword. You'll see why this is important in Chapter 9, "Teams of Classes: Using Classes Together," when you look at keywords that are sometimes more appropriate. The simple result of including this keyword is that access to this method is available to the public: Any other method of any other class within your program can call the `showGreeting( )` method. If you fail to include the `public` keyword, you might be barred from using the `showGreeting( )` method, a most awkward situation indeed!

The second part of the method declaration is called the *return type*. This is where you identify what kind of output the method is going to produce. This is used for methods

FIGURE 4-3

The five parts of a method declaration

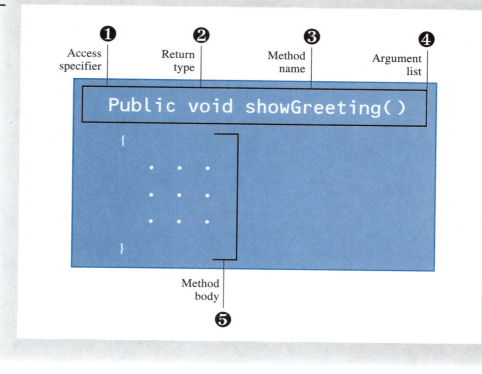

that provide you with some information. The `showGreeting( )` method does not return a value, so its return value is specified as `void`.

The third part of the method declaration is the *method name*. Every method must have a name, which *must* follow Java's rules for identifiers. Identifiers, as you recall, must begin with a letter, underscore, or dollar sign, and can be followed by letters or digits or both. Names can be any length. The name of this method is, of course, `showGreeting`.

The fourth part of the method declaration is the *argument list*. The `showGreeting( )` method has no arguments, so its argument list consists simply of a pair of parentheses. You have to include the parentheses, even when there are no arguments, because that is one of the ways that the Java compiler knows that `showGreeting` is a method, and not something else.

The fifth and final part of the method declaration is the most interesting: the *method body*. It consists of a series of Java statements enclosed in curly braces (`{}`). The method body includes statements that define local variables, statements that access and modify fields and local variables, and statements that do other kinds of processing and manipulation. The real work of the method is done inside its body. Chapter 5, "Making Choices: Teaching Your Objects About True and False," and Chapter 6, "Teaching Your

Objects to Repeat Themselves," focus on the statements used within method bodies. The body of the `showGreeting( )` method is quite simple, consisting of a single statement. This statement sends the `setText` message to the object known as `theLabel`, providing it with the text `String` `"Hi, Sam!"`.

METHOD CALL

How is the `showGreeting( )` method used inside your applet? That is, how do you call methods that you write? You call them exactly as you call methods that you don't write. The `actionPerformed( )` method of `FirstMethod` contains a call to your `showGreeting( )` method. You can call a method within your program as many times as needed. When you make a method call, the instructions within the method are executed. When the last instruction is finished, the program resumes execution where it left off, on the next line of code after the method call. Figure 4-4 illustrates how control is transferred to methods.

FIGURE 4-4

Flow of control between methods

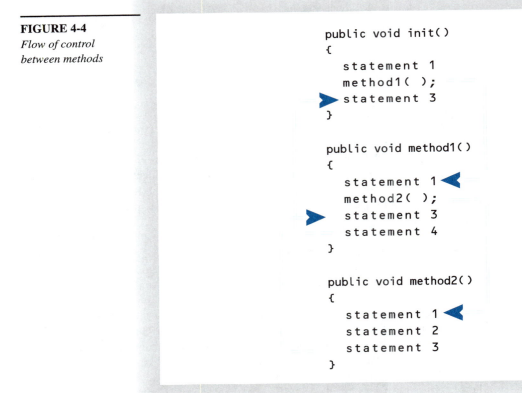

```
public void init()
{
    statement 1
    method1( );
    statement 3
}

public void method1()
{
    statement 1
    method2( );
    statement 3
    statement 4
}

public void method2()
{
    statement 1
    statement 2
    statement 3
}
```

In the `FirstMethod` applet you want to change the text within the `Label` control only once, so the program contains a single call to the `showGreeting( )` method. How does the `showGreeting( )` method accomplish its task? Surprise! It passes the buck—sending a message to the `Label` object, `theLabel`. The first part of this method call gives the name of the object to which the message will be sent, namely `theLabel`. The object name is followed by a dot and then the name of the message, `setText( )`. The name of the message is followed in its turn by the paired parentheses enclosing the `String`, `"Hi Sam!"`, that you want to set the `Label`'s text to. That's all there is to it.

You've probably noticed one major difference between calling the `showGreeting( )` method and calling the `setText( )` method. When you called `setText( )`, you had to put an object name, `theLabel`, in front of the message name. But when you called `showGreeting( )`, you didn't. Is that because `showGreeting( )` is written by you, while `setText( )` is built-in? No, that's not it at all. While the details will have to wait until later in this chapter when you learn about the special `this` object, you should know that you don't need a special object name to call methods within the same class. If you don't provide an object name, the object you're already "in" is assumed.

METHODS WITH RETURN VALUES

The `showMessage( )` method performs an action, but it doesn't have any output—it doesn't return any information to the caller. When a method has completed processing a message, it can return a value to the sender of the message. Often this value is the result of a process, or an answer to a problem solved by the method. The applet `SecondMethod`, in Listings 4-3 and 4-4, shows you how to write a method, `getGreeting( )`, that returns a value. Figure 4-5 shows the `SecondMethod` applet as it runs.

Listing 4-3 SecondMethod.java

```
//   SecondMethod.java
import java.applet.*;
import java.awt.*;
import java.awt.event.*;

public class SecondMethod extends Applet implements
ActionListener
{
    // Attributes
    Label theLabel = new Label ("Press the button, please.");
    Button pressMe = new Button ("Ok");

    // Methods
    public void init( )
    {
        add(theLabel);
        add(pressMe);
        pressMe.addActionListener(this);
    }
```

continued on next page

continued from previous page

```
public void actionPerformed(ActionEvent theEvent)
{
    String greeting = getGreeting( );
    theLabel.setText(greeting);
}

public String getGreeting( )
{
    return "Hi, Sam!";
}
}
```

Listing 4-4 SecondMethod.html

```
<HTML>
<HEAD>
<TITLE>Jumbo Learns Methods</TITLE>
</HEAD>
<BODY>
<IMG SRC="Jumbo.gif" ALIGN=RIGHT>
<APPLET CODE=SecondMethod.class HEIGHT=100 WIDTH=200>
</APPLET>
<HR>
<H1>Jumbo Tries Another Method</H1>
"JG! Come here, quick!" Brenda hollered down from the
veranda. Huffing and puffing, Jumbo shimmied up the
"vineway." "What I need is an escalator," he thought to
himself. "I told you this was cool, JG!" Brenda went on.
"Look at this applet. It returns a value. This is way cool."
<P>
The display looked the same as before. Although Jumbo
had plenty to say, lack of breath spared Brenda his
reflections on her new applet. All he managed to get out
between wheezes was, "Really, who IS Sam???"
</BODY>
</HTML>
```

FIGURE 4-5

Running the
SecondMethod
applet

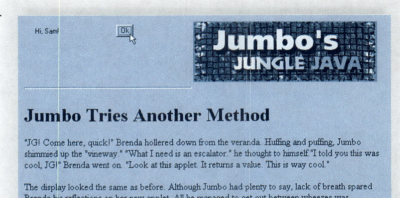

A New Declaration

Despite Jumbo's skepticism, the `getGreeting( )` method is different from the `showGreeting( )` method that came before it. Let's see how. Notice how the first line of the method declaration has changed. Instead of `void`, it now has the word `String`, which tells us that the `getGreeting( )` method will return a result of type `String`. The return type of a method can be either a primitive type or an object type.

A Different Body

The body of the method has changed somewhat as well. In the previous applet, the job of the `showGreeting( )` method was to change the text within the `Label`. In this applet, the job of the `getGreeting( )` method is simply to provide the text. The `actionPerformed( )` method uses the provided text to send the `setText` message to the `Label`. To return the appropriate text back to the calling statement, the `getGreeting( )` method uses the `return` statement. The `return` statement consists of simply the keyword `return` followed by an expression that gives the value to be returned. Here, this is the `String` literal `"Hi, Sam!"`.

The `getGreeting( )` method is what computer scientists call a *procedural abstraction*. Creating a method just to return a literal value is a rather silly way of making a simple task more complex. But the point is that the `getGreeting( )` method could be much more complex than it is. The beauty of procedural abstraction is that we can make the `getGreeting( )` method as complex as we wish without having to change the way the method is used: The sender of the `getGreeting` message is isolated from the bad effects of such changes and doesn't have to know what's inside the `getGreeting( )` method to use it. All that must be known is the return type of the method.

Sometimes, procedural abstraction is called "black box" design. When you go to the store and purchase a CD player for your stereo system, you have a wide variety to choose from. You can choose a relatively complex and expensive unit that, no doubt, produces exquisite sound, or you can spring for one of Jumbo's $19.95 specials, a simpler unit that goes well with Rain-Forest™ pizza and a cup o' joe. No matter which choice you make, you don't have to make any changes to the rest of your stereo system: You just plug it in and it works. This is the real power behind object methods—complexity can be hidden behind an interface. For the user of the `getGreeting( )` method, it makes no difference whether the method contains a single line of code or a million.

METHODS WITH ARGUMENTS

Unless your name is Sam, there's still a small problem with this applet: It greets everyone as "Sam." To remedy this, you need to learn how to pass an argument to the method, so you can tell it who you are. When the applet knows you by name, it can provide a more personal greeting. The applet `ThirdMethod` shows how to modify the getGreeting( ) method to handle a single argument. The code is presented in Listings 4-5 and 4-6, and Figure 4-6 shows what ThirdMethod looks like as it runs.

Listing 4-5 ThirdMethod.java

```
//   ThirdMethod.java
import java.applet.*;
import java.awt.*;
import java.awt.event.*;

public class ThirdMethod extends Applet implements
ActionListener
{
    // Attributes
    Label theLabel =⇐
          new Label ("Please enter your first name.");
    TextField theName = new TextField(20);
    Button pressMe = new Button ("Ok");

    // Methods
    public void init( )
    {
        add(theLabel);
        add(theName);
        add(pressMe);
        pressMe.addActionListener(this);
    }

    public void actionPerformed(ActionEvent theEvent)
    {
        String newText;
        String usersName;
        usersName = theName.getText( );
        newText = getGreeting(usersName);
        theLabel.setText(newText);
    }

    public String getGreeting(String name)
    {
        String greeting;
        greeting = "Hi, " + name + "!";
        return greeting;
    }
}
```

Listing 4-6 ThirdMethod.html

```
<HTML>
<HEAD>
<TITLE>Jumbo Learns Methods</TITLE>
</HEAD>
<BODY>
<IMG SRC="Jumbo.gif" ALIGN=RIGHT>
<APPLET CODE=ThirdMethod.class HEIGHT=100 WIDTH=200>
</APPLET>
<HR>
<H1>An Argument Ensues</H1>
```

```
"Alright, alright! Would you stop going on about Sam?
You're not my father! Anyway, we haven't seen each
other for over a month." <BR>
Brenda paused to catch her breath and Jumbo used the
respite to express his concern. "Argument?" he enquired
solicitously. <P>
"Yeah," replied Brenda after a momentary pause, "that's
how I fixed it. Once I learned how to pass arguments to
methods, that was all it took. At least you won't have
Sam to kick around anymore"
</BODY>
</HTML>
```

All About Arguments

How has the method `getGreeting( )` changed? The first thing you'll notice is the argument list added between the paired parentheses following the method name. Of course, it's not much of a list, consisting of a single formal argument of type `String`, that will be known as `name` within the body of the method.

What exactly is an argument list, and what are formal arguments or, as they're sometimes called, *parameters?* It's really pretty simple: formal arguments are similar to the local variables that you saw back in Chapter 3. What were the two things you needed to create a local variable? You needed a type and a name. To create a variable to hold the cost of Rain-Forest™ pizza topping mix, you would write something similar to

```
double rainForestPizzaToppingCost;
```

Formal arguments work the same way. In the declaration of `getGreeting( )`, the argument `name` is given the type `String`.

```
public String getGreeting(String name)
```

FIGURE 4-6

Running the
`ThirdMethod`
applet

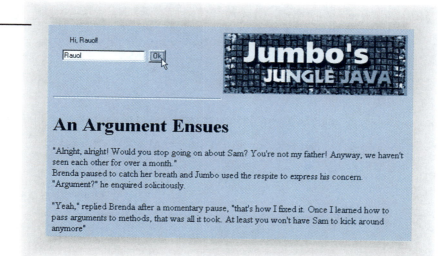

As you remember, to use the variable `rainForestPizzaToppingCost`, you have to give it a value—either through assignment or through some type of input/output operation. Formal arguments also have to be given a value before they can be used, but this is where arguments differ from other types of local variables. A formal argument doesn't get its value through an assignment, but through a value passed as an *actual* argument when the method is invoked. Take a look at the `actionPerformed( )` method of the `ThirdMethod` applet, and find the line where `getGreeting( )` is being called:

```
newText = getGreeting(usersName);
```

The actual argument to the `getGreeting( )` method is a `String` called `usersName`. Because the `getGreeting( )` method declares a formal argument of type `String`, you would expect that each place the `getGreeting` message is sent, a `String` would be passed along with the message. Examining the `actionPerformed( )` method, where the `getGreeting` message is sent, you can see that is indeed the case. The contents of the `TextField` known as `theName` are first retrieved and stored in the local variable `usersName` before being sent along with the `getGreeting` message. Figure 4-7 shows how formal and actual arguments work.

Good Arguments, Bad Arguments, and Shorthand

Whenever a method is called, the type of each actual argument must be compatible with the type of each formal argument (parameter). Usually the types should be identical, because this ensures compatibility. If you try to use a method with the wrong type or number of arguments—calling the new `getGreeting( )` method with no arguments,

FIGURE 4-7

Actual and formal arguments of a method

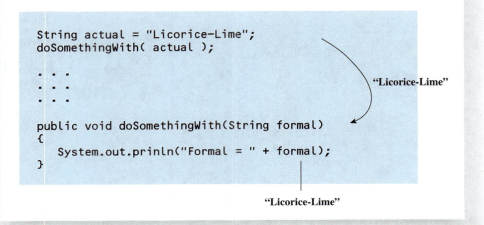

```
String actual = "Licorice-Lime";
doSomethingWith( actual );

. . .
. . .
. . .

public void doSomethingWith(String formal)
{
    System.out.println("Formal = " + formal);
}
```

"Licorice-Lime"

"Licorice-Lime"

for instance—Java will do its darnedest to stop you. As usual, it will refuse to compile your application.

The actual parameters—the values you use when you invoke a method—can be variables, constants, or even expressions. Each formal argument is, in effect, a local variable, and Java initializes these local variables with the values passed along with the message. So, even if you send a constant, the formal argument that receives it will always act similar to a variable, the value of which can be changed by assignment.

If you examined the `ThirdMethod` applet closely, you may have noticed that the `getGreeting( )` method was rather wordy. It's possible to write the body of this method as a single Java statement. The `actionPerformed( )` method, too, can be expressed more compactly. Here are shorter, equivalent versions of the two methods. The longer, original versions are somewhat easier to understand at first, but after you've had further experience with Java, you'll probably prefer the more concise style.

```
public void actionPerformed(ActionEvent theEvent)
{
        theLabel.setText(getGreeting(theName.getText( )));
}

public String getGreeting(String name)
{
    return "Hi, " + name + "!";
}
```

Why do these methods work? After all, previously you had to declare a variable name and type for each value, didn't you? Well, almost. You remember that there was one case where you didn't have to do either: when writing literal values. Expressions can frequently be used in a similar manner. Rather than creating a `String` variable, storing the result of an expression in the variable, and then returning the variable, you can just return the expression itself. Java will make a temporary place to store the value, and then return that value. Likewise, when the only purpose for a variable is to hold the value of an expression before it is passed to a method, you can simply use the expression in place of the variable.

Passing Arguments by Value

What happens if, within a method, you assign a value to a formal argument? What would happen if, inside the method `getGreeting( )`, the `name` argument was set to `"Mud"`? Would the actual arguments be changed at all? No. When the `getGreeting( )` method receives a message, the first thing it does is to copy the values of its actual arguments. It then works with these copies, which it can change in as many ways and as many times as the programmer chooses. Because the method is working with copies of the actual arguments, the real arguments never change. Figure 4-8 illustrates this.

This isn't to say that a method can't produce side effects. A method can change the values of any fields within the object that encloses it. Unlike arguments, fields are not copied when the method is entered. The method can directly access them. Also, as you'll learn in Chapter 8, "Flocking Objects: Arrays and Exceptions," when an object is passed as a formal argument, it's possible to change the value of the object's fields.

FIGURE 4-8

Passing by value

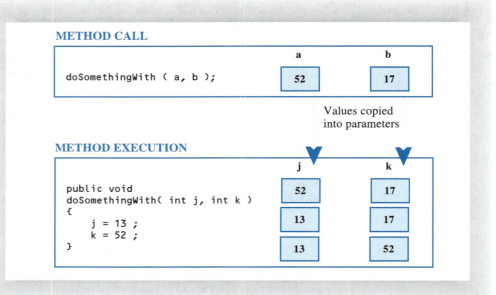

FOCUS ON METHOD BODIES

Method bodies consist of a series of Java statements, surrounded by curly braces. You learned about declaration statements and expression statements in Chapter 3. Each can appear within a method body. Two more types of statements that can appear inside a method are the *compound* statement and the *return* statement.

Compound Statements and Scope

A compound statement consists of a set of curly braces that surround a series of statements. Sound familiar? You're right: A method body is itself a compound statement, and it can contain other compound statements. These are called *nested* compound statements.

Each compound statement establishes a scope for variable names. Think of a scope as analogous to a neighborhood. There can be a Tom in one neighborhood and a Tom in another neighborhood. If you live in the first neighborhood and you mention Tom to your neighbors, everybody knows you mean the Tom from your neighborhood, not the one from the other neighborhood. Figure 4-9 shows how this works in Java.

When a Java statement references a variable, the Java compiler (Javac) first looks for the variable's declaration within the immediate compound statement, the one that contains the statement that references the variable. If the declaration is not found, the compiler will continue its search by looking inside the compound statement that contains the immediate compound statement. Eventually, when every enclosing compound statement has been searched, Java looks for a field declaration. If the sought-for variable has still not been found, the compiler will print an error message and halt.

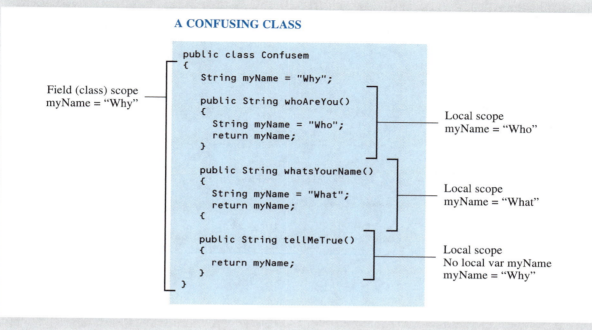

FIGURE 4-9

Local scope and class scope

Local variables have a limited lifetime, existing only for the duration of a method call. They are created when their declaration is encountered, and destroyed when the method completes its work. They do not retain their value from one method call to the next. Similarly, local variables defined inside a compound statement are destroyed when the compound statement is exited. Fields, by contrast, are created when the containing object is created and continue to exist until the object is destroyed.

What better way to see how this works than to create an applet? The applet `Scope`, shown next in Listings 4-7 and 4-8, and in Figure 4-10, creates three distinct variables named `dollar`: one is a field, one is a local variable of a method called `inJungle( )`, and the other is a local variable of a method called `inVeldt( )`. When you run the applet, each of the variables is shown to have a different value. Note that the `actionPerformed( )` method does not define a local variable named `dollar`, so referencing `dollar` in the `actionPerformed( )` method yields the value of the field named `dollar`.

Listing 4-7 Scope.java

```
//   Scope.java
import java.applet.*;
import java.awt.*;
import java.awt.event.*;
```

continued on next page

continued from previous page

> *It makes no difference to the user whether the method contains a single line of code or a million.*

```java
public class Scope extends Applet implements ActionListener
{
    // Attributes
    int dollar = 1;
    Button goButton = new Button ("Go!");

    // Methods
    public void init( )
    {
        add(goButton);
        goButton.addActionListener(this);
    }

    public void actionPerformed(ActionEvent theEvent)
    {
        remove(goButton);

        add(new Label ("In Field:         " + dollar));
        add(new Label ("In theVeldt( ): " + theVeldt( )));
        add(new Label ("In theJungle( ):" + theJungle( )));

        invalidate( );
        validate( );
    }

    public int theVeldt( )
    {
        int dollar = 2;
        return dollar;
    }

    public int theJungle( )
    {
        int dollar = 3;
        return dollar;
    }
}
```

Listing 4-8 Scope.html

```html
<HTML>
<HEAD>
<TITLE>Jumbo Learns Scope</TITLE>
</HEAD>
<BODY>
<IMG SRC="Jumbo.gif" ALIGN=RIGHT>
<APPLET CODE=Scope.class HEIGHT=100 WIDTH=150>
</APPLET>
<HR>
<H1>How Much Is That Rain-Forest Special?</H1>
"Listen Brenda, it's really simple. I finally understand
this thing about methods. We want to expand our delivery,
right? And it costs more to deliver outside the jungle,
right? So you just come up with an applet that converts
dollars to pizzas. In the jungle we'll use one value,
in the veldt and in the fields another. You can use
that scope trick." <P>
```

```
Jumbo was excited. Brenda was only half listening as
she thought about the mounting piles of Rain-Forest
pizza topping mix.
</BODY>
</HTML>
```

Applet Tidbits

The `Scope` applet uses three new methods: You've not previously seen `remove( )`, `invalidate( )`, and `validate( )`. The `remove( )` method removes a component from the applet window. In `Scope`, it's used to remove the `Button` once it has been pressed and is no longer needed.

The `invalidate` and `validate` messages are used because you're adding new components to the applet inside the `actionPerformed( )` method. Until now, all of the components have been added in the `init( )` method. Without the `invalidate( )` and `validate( )` methods, calling `remove( )` or `add( )` would have no obvious effect. Because the applet window has already been laid out and displayed, it's too late to add or remove window components. Use of `invalidate( )` and `validate( )` overcomes this difficulty. The `invalidate( )` method tells the applet that the window has been

FIGURE 4-10

Running the ***Scope***
applet

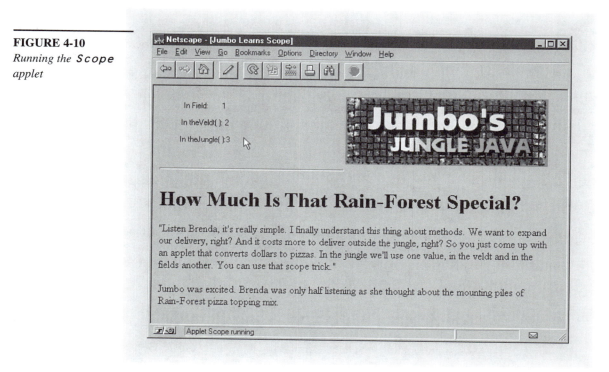

updated in a way that leaves the display invalid. Invoking `validate( )` tells the applet to take all its components and lay them out again. The applet normally won't respond to a `validate( )` unless the `invalidate( )` message has been sent: Why should it lay out all its components a second time when everything's okay? Using `invalidate( )` and `validate( )` lets you build applets that change their appearance as the user interacts with your program.

A good way to understand this is to hack the `Scope` applet by removing one or both of the `invalidate( )` and `validate( )` messages, and running the applet. Pressing the button won't seem to do anything. However, you can force Java to lay out the applet window by minimizing it and restoring it, using the buttons in the upper-right corner of the window's title bar. When you do this after pressing the button, the button will disappear and the labels will appear.

`return` Statements

Another type of statement that can be used within a method body is the `return` statement. You've been using the `return` statement almost from the very beginning, but without looking at it formally. The `return` statement consists simply of the keyword `return` followed by an expression and a semicolon:

```
return expression;
```

The expression need not be wrapped in parentheses, but often this gives the statement a more finished look, so many programmers include them. The type of the expression must, of course, match the type of the value returned by the method. There *can* be multiple `return` statements within a method, but this won't be a very useful bit of knowledge until you've learned how to use conditional statements, which are presented in Chapter 5. Without such conditionals, the `return` statement must be the last statement in the method. A method that has the return type of `void` can include the `return` statement, but it cannot return a value, so its `return` statement cannot include an expression.

The `return` statement does more than simply supply output for the method. The first `return` statement your method encounters will send the computer racing back to the statement that originally sent the message being handled, so any other `return` statements in the method will have to await some future invocation for their chance at execution. When a `return` statement is executed, the current method ends at that point. If you have code that can never be reached because of this, Java will refuse to compile your program. You might want to try this by moving the `return` statement in the `actionPerformed( )` method to a place above the call to `invalidate( )`.

Send Me a Message, Send It by Mail

Message sending should be familiar to you by now. However, there are a couple of fine points we've glossed over up to this point. Let's look at the default receiver of a message, at overloaded and overridden methods, and then at static methods.

"WHO" GETS THE MESSAGE? NO, `this` GETS THE MESSAGE

Java's handling of the default receiver of a message might remind you of the classic comedy sketch by Bud Abbott and Lou Costello, "Who's on First?" about a baseball team with a player named "Who." If you've not heard this bit, you can at least imagine what ensues during Abbott and Costello's description of a triple play, given the names of the other players, such as "What" and "I don't know."

The statement used to send a message looks like this:

```
receiver.message(argument1, argument2);
```

This is actually nothing more than your old friend the expression statement, in disguise. When Java encounters an expression statement, what does it do? First it evaluates the expression and then, barring assignment, it discards the result. When you send a message, evaluation consists of nothing more than performing the method that corresponds to the message being sent.

But, you may have noticed that sometimes a message is sent seemingly to no one:

```
message(argument1, argument2);
```

Whose method handles this sort of message? Every object has a field named `this`, which does not have to be explicitly defined. The keyword `this` always refers to the current object, that is, the one that contains the method being executed. You might want to think of the object "talking to itself." When no receiving object is specified for a message, the message goes to the `this` object, just as if we had written:

```
this.message(argument1, argument2);
```

In fact, this statement is perfectly fine, and some programmers write such statements in this way, just to remind themselves that they are sending a message to the current object. However the statement is written, Java will look at the current object to see if it has a method to handle that message. If it does, then Java will tell the current object to execute the method.

METHOD SIGNATURES AND OVERLOADED METHODS

As it happens, deciding what object is to receive a message is just the first step in a series of steps culminating in the execution of an appropriate method. The complication arises because it is possible for an object to contain multiple methods having the same name, termed *overloaded* methods. Of course, such overloaded methods are not identical, otherwise there would be no point in having more than one of them. Overloaded methods always differ in their *signature*. The signature includes not only the method name (which doesn't help distinguish overloaded methods, but is helpful in other cases), but also the number and type of the arguments (if any) of the method.

" If getting your labels to line up has been driving you crazy, then never fear, ultimate power is within your grasp. "

This information, along with the return type (which is *not* part of the method signature), appears conveniently in the header of every method. Take, for example, the following method headers:

```
public boolean myMethod(int theArg)
{
    // body omitted
}

public boolean myMethod(int theFirstArg, long theSecondArg)
{
    // body omitted
}

public boolean myMethod(int theFirstArg, float theSecondArg)
{
    // body omitted
}
```

The method `myMethod( )` is overloaded, because there are three method declarations that have this name. The signature for the first method declaration is its name, `myMethod( )`, along with its argument type: `int`. The signature for the second method declaration is its name, again, `myMethod( )`, along with its argument types: `int` and `long`. The signature for the third method declaration is `myMethod(int, float)`, as written in the compact form often used to describe a method signature. Because the three signatures are distinct, the Java compiler does not object to this overloading of the method.

How does Java decide which method body to execute when a message is sent? Recall that when a method is invoked, the formal arguments of the method take the values of the actual arguments appearing in the method call. It makes sense, then, that the number and types of the arguments of a method must agree with those used in the invocation (that is, in the message). More precisely, the types of the actual arguments must be *compatible* with those of the formal arguments. For example, there's no problem in passing an `int` to a method that expects a `long`. Java will happily convert the `int` to a `long`, because no loss of data can occur.

If you were to send the message `myMethod(1)`, then the first method body would be executed, because the header of only the first declaration matches the number of actual arguments (one) provided with the message. If you were to send the message `myMethod(1, 2L)` or the message `myMethod(1, 2)`, then the second method body would be executed. Both the second and the third method bodies have the same number of arguments, but the second method body is a closer match to the actual arguments provided with the message. Although the third method body *could* be used to process this message, Java is reluctant to unnecessarily convert a `long` or an `int` to a `float` and therefore prefers the second method header.

Just as it may sometimes be difficult for you to decide which method body should be used to handle a given message, the Java compiler may fail to make up its mind. When this occurs, it will print an error message and terminate the compilation. It's best to avoid this possibility by overloading methods sparingly. Allowing a variety of argument types makes a method more convenient to use, but can also contribute to program complexity. Remember that discretion is the better part of a programmer's valor.

INHERITED AND OVERRIDDEN METHODS

You've seen what happens when an object includes multiple declarations of a given method. What happens, though, when the current object doesn't declare a given method at all? How does Java route the related message?

Inherited Methods

In such a case, Java applies the object-oriented principle of inheritance. Java looks at the object's parent class, the one named by the `extends` keyword in the `class` declaration. If it finds an appropriate method there, all is well and the method is executed. If not, Java continues up the family tree of objects until the method is found, or until the topmost class, `Object`, has been searched. (Even classes that do not explicitly *extend* a class are understood as *extending* the class `Object`, the "universal parent class.") If even this last class fails to provide a definition for the errant method, the Java compiler will print an error message and terminate compilation of your program. Figure 4-11 shows how Java searches the inheritance tree for a called method.

FIGURE 4-11

Searching for a called method

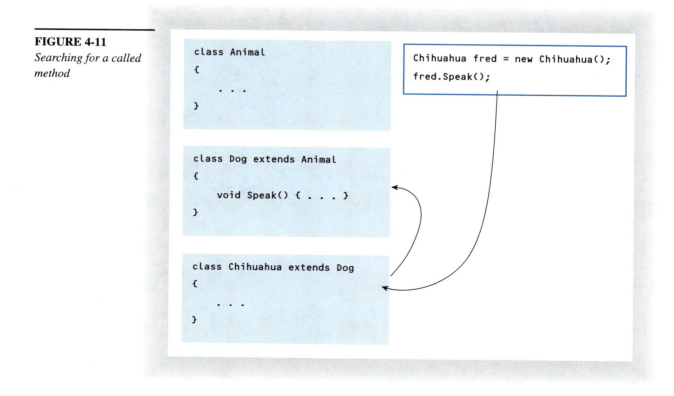

```
class Animal
{
    . . .
}
```

```
class Dog extends Animal
{
    void Speak() { . . . }
}
```

```
class Chihuahua extends Dog
{
    . . .
}
```

```
Chihuahua fred = new Chihuahua();
fred.Speak();
```

Overridden Methods

It is possible for a method to be defined both in an object and in that object's parent. When this happens, the method in the object will respond to the corresponding message—the parent's method will not be invoked at all. Such a method in a parent class is called an *overridden* method. The ability to override a parent's methods is what allows child objects to respond distinctively, in ways their parents never dreamed of. This is perhaps every real parent's nightmare, but it is the source of much of the power of object-oriented programming, because it allows the behaviors of a parent object to be extended or expanded. Figure 4-12 shows how one method can override another.

SOME THINGS ARE ALWAYS THE SAME: static FIELDS AND METHODS

Because every message of the sort you've seen so far refers to an object, explicitly or implicitly, it would seem that you can't have methods without objects. Sometimes, though, it's convenient to have methods that don't have associated objects. For instance, such methods are often used to create objects and wouldn't be nearly as useful if you were required to already have an object in order to use them. Methods that

FIGURE 4-12

An overridden method

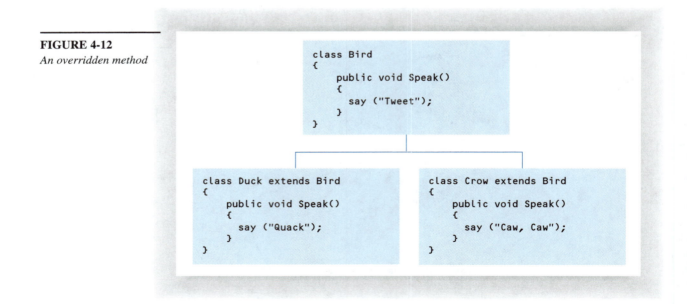

```
class Bird
{
    public void Speak()
    {
      say ("Tweet");
    }
}
```

```
class Duck extends Bird
{
    public void Speak()
    {
      say ("Quack");
    }
}
```

```
class Crow extends Bird
{
    public void Speak()
    {
      say ("Caw, Caw");
    }
}
```

don't have associated objects are called *static methods* and are defined by simply following the keyword `public` in the definition of the method with the keyword `static`. `static` methods, along with `static` fields, are associated with a class as a whole, rather than with any individual instance of the class. As such, they exist and can be used even before an instance of the class has been created.

`static` Fields

`static` fields are closely related to the `static final` fields you met in Chapter 3. Like `static final` fields, they are part of the class, rather than part of any instance (object) of the class. So, they can be accessed even before the first instance has been created. Also like `static final` fields, they are stored in the class, and so consume less memory than if each object were to hold its own copy of their value. An important implication of being stored in the class is that each `static` field represents a single value, shared by all instances of the class.

However, `static` fields are different from `static final` fields in one important way: They are allowed to change in value. You may find this confusing, because "static" in ordinary speech normally means "unchanging." To avoid this, think of the keyword `static` in a Java program as really meaning "class." Both `static` and `static final` fields are really class fields associated with a class, rather than with instances of the class.

`static` Methods

Sending a message that is handled by a `static` method is a little different from sending a message to a non-`static` method. Because there's no obvious object involved, just *who* are you supposed to send the message to? You might be tempted to simply omit the name of the receiving object, but recall that this means you are sending the message to the `this` object. Because it's possible that no instances of the related class exist, there may be no `this` object. Happily, Java's designers were well aware of this dilemma. When sending a message to a `static` method, you simply use the class name where you would otherwise use an object name. For example, to send a message to the `static` method `sqrt( )` in the class `Math`, simply write

```
y = Math.sqrt(x);
```

where x is the value whose square root is to be extracted and y is the result variable.

If this looks as if you're sending the message to an object with the same name as the class, you're right. Every Java class has an associated object that shares the name of the class. `static` fields and methods are, in effect, fields and methods of this "class object." Figure 4-13 shows `static` fields and methods at work.

FIGURE 4-13
static fields and methods

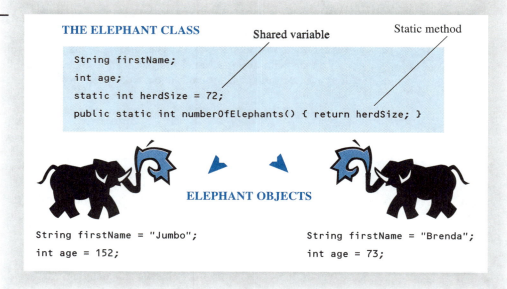

THE ELEPHANT CLASS   Shared variable   Static method

```
String firstName;
int age;
static int herdSize = 72;
public static int numberOfElephants() { return herdSize; }
```

ELEPHANT OBJECTS

```
String firstName = "Jumbo";
int age = 152;
```

```
String firstName = "Brenda";
int age = 73;
```

More, More, More Applet Methods

Your knowledge of applet behavior is growing fast, but it's nowhere near complete. Applets are truly amazing objects, with a few more tricks up their sleeves that you'll want to master. In this section you'll learn how to write text on an applet window any place you desire, without using a `Label` object. Then you'll learn more about the messages the browser sends to applets, messages you will intercept and act on with increasing frequency and sophistication throughout the remainder of the book.

LEARNING TO USE drawString( )

To circumvent some of the limitations of the `Label` object, Java provides you with the `drawString( )` method, which lets you place text anywhere within an applet window. If getting your labels to line up and your displays to look good has been driving you crazy, then never fear—ultimate power is within your grasp...more or less.

To send the `drawString` message, you need to send along three pieces of information, or arguments. First, you have to tell the method exactly what you want to draw. As you might infer from the method name, this first argument is a `String` object containing the text to be drawn. The next two arguments tell Java where you want to place the text inside the applet window. The first of these specifies the horizontal or x coordinate, and the second specifies the vertical or y coordinate. Both coordinates are integers and represent pixels (the individual tiny dots that make up the display surface), rather than character columns or rows. The coordinates for both the horizontal and the vertical dimensions start at zero, which represents the upper-left corner of the display. If you recall using the `setLocation( )` method to send your `Label` scurrying across the screen in Chapter 2, you've got the idea. There is one difference between using the `x,y` coordinate with a `Label` object and with `drawString( )`, though. When a `Label` object is moved, the coordinate represents the upper-left corner of the `Label` object. With the `drawString( )` method, the `x,y` coordinate represents the position where the baseline of the letters will be displayed. Figure 4-14 illustrates the difference between `Label` coordinates and `drawString( )` coordinates.

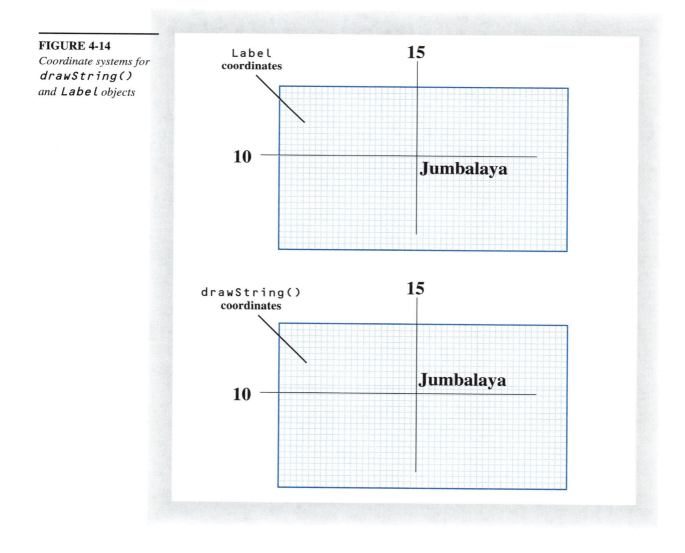

FIGURE 4-14

Coordinate systems for **drawString()** *and* **Label** *objects*

Meet Jacques the Graphics Guy

So far, using `drawString( )` seems as if it should be pretty straightforward. "Let's see," you think, "who should I send the message to? The `String` class looks like a likely candidate. Hmmm. Nope, it doesn't know how to draw on the screen. Well then, *surely* the `Applet` class can do it." Sorry, you're still out of luck. "Then who?" you wonder.

Java has a special artistic class that knows how to draw things on the screen: the `Graphics` class. To draw a circle on the screen, all you have to do is create one of these `Graphics` objects—call it `jacques` if you like—and then tell it to do your bidding. Tell `jacques` to draw a circle: *Voilà*, you have a circle. Tell him to draw some text: *Presto*, the text appears. Your every wish is his command.

You can tell your applet that you want one of these `Graphics` characters by sending it the `getGraphics` message like this:

```
Graphics jacques = getGraphics( );
```

When you get the `Graphics` object back, you'll find it brings a whole toolbox of artistic gizmos along with it. If you want to change the font, your `Graphics` guy has a `setFont( )` method. Want to change the color (something the `Label` class didn't allow you to do)? Your personal artist has a `setColor( )` method. But enough talking. Take a look at the `BadPaint` applet in Listings 4-9 and 4-10. Figure 4-15 shows the applet running, but you really need to compile and try it on your own monitor to get the full effect.

Listing 4-9 BadPaint.java

```java
//  BadPaint.java
import java.applet.*;
import java.awt.*;
import java.awt.event.*;


public class BadPaint extends Applet implements ActionListener
{
    // Attributes
    String theNewSlogan = "Pizza's cool 'n' Java too!!!";
    Font bigFont = ⇐
       new Font("Helvetica", Font.BOLD + Font.ITALIC, 36);
    Button theButton = new Button("Shazam");

    // Methods
    public void init( )
    {
        add(new⇐
           Label("Jumbo's Jungle Java and Pizza Emporium"));
        add(theButton);
        theButton.addActionListener(this);
    }
```

```
    public void actionPerformed(ActionEvent theEvent)
    {
        Graphics jacques = getGraphics( );
        jacques.setFont( bigFont );
        jacques.setColor( Color.blue );
        jacques.drawString( theNewSlogan,  25,  75 );
        jacques.drawString( theNewSlogan, 100, 125 );
        jacques.drawString( theNewSlogan, 175, 175 );
    }
}
```

Listing 4-10 BadPaint.html

```
<HTML>
<HEAD>
<TITLE>Jumbo's Gets Graphic</TITLE>
</HEAD>
<BODY>
<IMG SRC="Jumbo.gif" ALIGN=RIGHT>
<H1>Check Out What's New at Jumbo's!!!</H1>
<HR>
"I hope you know what you're doing," fretted Jumbo.  <BR>
Brenda assured him, "No probs, JG," but to herself she
thought, "I sure hope nobody moves this applet around."
<APPLET CODE=BadPaint.class HEIGHT=300 WIDTH=600>
</APPLET>
</BODY>
</HTML>
```

FIGURE 4-15

Running the
BadPaint applet

Looking at `BadPaint`

The `BadPaint` applet illustrates all the major points you'll need to remember to start using the `Graphics` object and its `drawString( )` method. (You'll get fully acquainted with using `Graphics` objects in Chapter 11, "Jumpin' Java: Menus, Graphics, Sound.") Take a look at the `actionPerformed( )` method, which is called when anyone presses the `Shazam` button. First, your applet is asked to lend you a `Graphics` object—which you name `jacques`—by invoking its `getGraphics( )` method, like so:

```
Graphics jacques = getGraphics( );
```

You can tell that the `Graphics` object comes from your applet, because there is no object in front of the `getGraphics` message, which means you might as well have written `this.getGraphics( )`. And `this`, of course, is the current `BadPaint` applet. Now that you have a `Graphics` object, you can tell it to do things. The next two lines tell it to use a big font and to use the color blue.

```
jacques.setFont( bigFont );
jacques.setColor( Color.blue );
```

Both of those probably make sense, but you may be wondering where the `Color.blue` came from. `Color.blue` is a `static final` field of the `Color` class, which includes names for several other familiar colors. Contrary to Java conventions, the authors of the `Color` class did not use uppercase characters for these static identifiers, as you saw with `Font.BOLD`, for instance. (Not everybody's perfect, including Sun's Java team.) Speaking of fonts, take a look near the top of Listing 4-9, where the object `bigFont` is defined. Notice that the font style is given as `Font.BOLD + Font.ITALIC`, to include both bold and italic characteristics. (The ability to easily combine these characteristics using addition is a handy feature, resulting from clever choices by the designers of the `Font` class.) Finally, `jacques` is told to draw the `String theNewSlogan`, three times at different locations by changing the `x,y` arguments to the `drawString( )` method:

```
jacques.drawString( theNewSlogan,  25,  75 );
jacques.drawString( theNewSlogan, 100, 125 );
jacques.drawString( theNewSlogan, 175, 175 );
```

Using `paint( )` Inside the Lines

However, there's a subtle problem with the applet. Press the button and then minimize and restore the applet, or resize it. Surprise: the text has disappeared. One of the advantages of using a `Label` for text output is that `Label`s are automatically redrawn when the applet window is redrawn. There is no such provision for text you've drawn yourself. Once it's gone, you have to redraw it if you want it to be seen. One possible solution is for the `Graphics` object to remember everything that is drawn on a window, much as the `Label` does. The problem with that is cost: It is too expensive (in terms of the computer memory and processing time required) to do that.

Instead, the designers of Java came up with another method: a special method called `paint( )`, which is called by the browser whenever the applet window is repainted. If you place all your `drawString` messages within the `paint( )` method, they'll be redrawn along with the rest of the window and will look good as new. The applet `SecondPaint`, in Listings 4-11 and 4-12, and illustrated in Figure 4-16, shows how this is done.

Listing 4-11 SecondPaint.java

```
//   SecondPaint.java
//   Illustrates changing the font and color for the paint( )
method
import java.applet.*;
import java.awt.*;

public class SecondPaint extends Applet
{
    // Attributes
    String theNewSlogan = "Pizza's cool 'n' Java too!!!";

    // Methods
    public void init( )
    {
        add(new⇐
            Label("Jumbo's Jungle Java and Pizza Emporium"));
    }

    public void paint( Graphics jacques )
    {
        jacques.setFont(new Font("TimesRoman",⇐
            Font.BOLD, 36));
        jacques.setColor( Color.red );

        jacques.drawString( theNewSlogan, 175,  50 );
        jacques.drawString( theNewSlogan, 100, 100);
        jacques.drawString( theNewSlogan,  25, 150);
    }
}
```

Listing 4-12 SecondPaint.html

```
<HTML>
<HEAD>
<TITLE>Jumbo's Gets More Graphic</TITLE>
</HEAD>
<BODY>
<IMG SRC="Jumbo.gif" ALIGN=LEFT>
<H1>Jumbo's New Resizable Applet</H1>
<HR>
"I admit, that was a little awkward, but it's all
fixed now," said Brenda, trying to soothe Jumbo's ruffled
hide. "You don't even need to press that silly button. It's
all automatic."<P>
```

continued on next page

continued from previous page

```
"Are you sure that this will bring the customers? We seem
to have an awful lot of that Rain-forest topping mix lying
around."<BR>
Brenda looked away and didn't answer.
<APPLET CODE=SecondPaint.class HEIGHT=300 WIDTH=600>
</APPLET>
</BODY>
</HTML>
```

Major Changes

Look at the code inside the `paint( )` method of `SecondPaint`, and compare it with the code in the `actionPerformed( )` method of `BadPaint`. What things have changed? The biggest change is that you no longer have to ask your applet for a `Graphics` object. Whenever the `paint( )` method is called, which the browser will do whenever the applet has been obscured or resized, it will automatically pass a brand-new `Graphics` object along to you as an argument. Because the purpose of `paint( )` is to paint, Java wants to make it easy for you.

The rest of the changes are cosmetic. Rather than creating a `Font` object as a field, a temporary `Font` object is created every time the applet needs to be repainted. Instead of painting with blue, the text is painted in red. Rather than traveling from left to right, the text is offset from right to left as you read down the screen. Finally, because the `paint( )` method is called automatically every time the wall, er...applet gets obscured, there's no need for a `Button` object. So, Jumbo won't need to waste his time checking to see if the applet's been resized.

FIGURE 4-16

Running the
`SecondPaint`
applet

APPLET METHODS

You've now met several applet methods that are invoked by the browser, rather than by you, the programmer. Let's get better acquainted with them. Four of these are known as the applet life-cycle methods: `init( )`, `start( )`, `stop( )`, and `destroy( )`. The `init( )` method is called the first time the user directs the browser to a page containing the applet. The `init( )` method is a handy place to create components and place them on the applet window, just as you've been doing.

The Applet Life Cycle: `start( )`, `stop( )`, and `destroy( )`

The `start( )` method is similar to the `init( )` method, with a subtle, but important difference. The `start( )` method is called every time a page containing an applet is loaded—not just the first time, but every time. This could happen when a user leaves the page with your applet and then returns to it. In this case the `init( )` method would only be called the first time your applet was accessed, but the `start( )` method would be called again whenever the user returned to your page. The `start( )` method is sometimes needed to restart an applet that is supposed to return to a given state each time its page is viewed. If you define a `start( )` method in your applet, its statements will be performed each time the page containing the applet is entered.

Similarly, the `stop( )` method is called whenever the user leaves the page containing the applet. If the `stop( )` method is not written, the applet continues running even though the user has moved on. Sometimes, this is exactly what you want, but for applets that use a lot of CPU cycles, this can be unacceptable. The `stop( )` method gives your applet the opportunity to "turn itself off" so that it won't interfere with other things the user wants to do. None of the applets we've looked at so far requires a `stop( )` method. Without program loops—which you'll meet in Chapter 6—it's difficult to use many CPU cycles.

After the user has left a page, the browser may decide that a stopped applet will probably not be needed again, at least for a while, and that keeping it around is creating an unnecessary drain on system resources. Before the browser dumps the applet overboard, it calls the `destroy( )` method, which gives the applet a chance to clean up any messes it's made, making peace with its creator before the final hour of its destruction. Applets that allocate system resources, such as threads, commonly use the `destroy( )` method to explicitly return these resources to the operating system. This is at least polite, and sometimes necessary, because some operating systems are more helpful than others in tidying up after a terminated program.

The applet life-cycle methods are summarized in Table 4-1. Figure 4-17 shows how, during the life of an applet, the various methods are invoked.

FIGURE 4-17

The applet life cycle

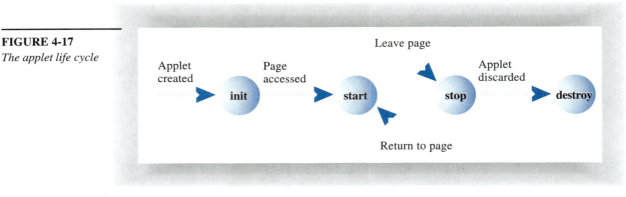

TABLE 4-1
APPLET LIFE-CYCLE METHODS

MESSAGE	SENT BY	MEANING
init( )	Browser	Applet is being loaded by the browser.
start( )	Browser	Browser has entered the page containing the applet.
stop( )	Browser	Browser is leaving the page containing the applet.
destroy( )	Browser	Applet is being discarded by the browser.

Looking at the Time of Your Life

A picture may be worth a thousand words, but a good applet is worth, well, at least a picture and a half. To see how, and when, the applet lifetime methods are called, what better place to look than the applet LifeTime, which you can see in Listing 4-13? This applet can be used to demonstrate the operation of these methods, along with that of the paint( ) method. The applet simply counts and displays the number of times each method has been invoked by the browser. Of course, when running the applet in a browser, you shouldn't expect to see a nonzero count for the destroy( ) method, because it won't be invoked until the applet has disappeared from view.

Listing 4-13 LifeTime.java

```
//   LifeTime.java
//   Illustrates messages sent from the browser to the applet
import java.awt.*;
import java.applet.*;

public class LifeTime extends Applet
{
    // Attributes
    int initRcvd, startRcvd, stopRcvd, destroyRcvd, paintRcvd;

    // Methods
    public void init( )
    {
```

```
        add( new Label(⇐
             "Messages recieved in an applet's lifetime"));
        initRcvd++;
    }
    public void start( )   { startRcvd++;    repaint( );      }
    public void stop( )    { stopRcvd++;     repaint( );      }
    public void destroy( ) { destroyRcvd++; repaint( );      }

    public void paint( Graphics jacques )
    {
        paintRcvd++;

        jacques.drawString( "init( )      : " + initRcvd,⇐
                    10,  40 );
        jacques.drawString( "start( )     : " + startRcvd,⇐
                    10,  55 );
        jacques.drawString( "stop( )      : " + stopRcvd,⇐
                    10,  70 );
        jacques.drawString( "destroy( )   : " + destroyRcvd,⇐
                    10,  85 );
        jacques.drawString( "paint( )     : " + paintRcvd,⇐
                    10, 100 );
    }
}
```

OTHER APPLET METHODS

In addition to the lifetime methods, applets have several other methods that you have already met. Before you head off into some new and uncharted areas of the Java Jungle, take a look at Table 4-2, and make sure you're familiar with these commonly used methods. You'll meet each of these again and again, and time spent now in getting familiar with them will speed your journey later.

TABLE 4-2
SUMMARY OF NON–LIFE-CYCLE APPLET MESSAGES

MESSAGE	SENT BY	MEANING
add( )	Programmer	Add a component to the applet window.
remove( )	Programmer	Remove a component from the applet window.
actionPerformed( )	Component	Signal the applet that a component has sustained an action event.
invalidate( )	Programmer	Mark the currently displayed window as invalid, that is, not in sync with recent changes.
validate( )	Programmer	Cause an invalidated window to be reformatted, synching it with any changes.

A Trip to the Library

The most marvelous thing about the advent of the Internet and the World Wide Web is the way they put a whole world of information at your fingertips. It's almost like having all the libraries of the world right there in your living room. Think about that for a second. What are the advantages of libraries? For one thing, you don't have to have a copy of every book ever written stuffed inside your house. Libraries, like the Internet, are resources that allow all of us to share our common heritage, to learn from those who came before us, and to build upon their knowledge.

Programming-language libraries are something like that. Programming libraries are collections of methods and objects that you can "check out" when you need some specialized information or capabilities. Like other modern languages, Java is a relatively sparse language. It depends upon its extensive library of objects to provide such necessary and fundamental capabilities as input and output. The benefit of this arrangement is that Java's capabilities can be readily extended by creation of additional library objects. This is an important consideration given the rapid rate of change of software technology. A language lacking the ability to adapt to a changing technical environment would soon find itself on the scrap heap.

PACKAGES

Many of Java's useful objects are defined in a package called `java.lang`. A package is simply a set of classes stored together in a single directory. All the classes contained in `java.lang` are automatically available to every Java program: They are *fundamental* classes. Other packages and classes are *optional* and can be included at the whim of the programmer, by simply referencing them by name.

The full names of these packages and classes, however, are long, and writing them over and over quickly becomes tedious. One of the statements you've already seen, the `import` statement, was included in the language to make it easier for you to reference these optional packages and classes. One the most useful optional packages is the `java.util` package. If you wish to use a particular class within `java.util`, such as the popular `Date` class, you simply refer to the class as `java.util.Date`, and Java will know which one you mean. However, you can instead include this statement at the top of your program:

```
import java.util.Date;
```

Thereafter, you can simply refer to the `Date` class, and Java will know you mean `java.util.Date`. The `import` statement simply lets you abbreviate long class names.

If you wanted to use more than one class from `java.util`, say `Date` and `Random`, you could begin your program with two `import` statements:

```
import java.util.Date;
import java.util.Random;
```

Alternatively, you could write the `import` statement

```
import java.util.*;
```

> **Programming libraries are collections of methods and objects: You can check them out when you need specialized information.**

which would allow you to make abbreviated reference to any class within the `java.util` package. Note that the `import` statement does not actually insert the classes into your program, it merely facilitates naming. There is no significant performance penalty for using the `import` statement.

DOING YOUR MATH HOMEWORK:
THE `java.lang.Math` CLASS

The Java class `java.lang.Math` includes a host of useful fields and methods for arithmetic and mathematics—so you don't have to write them yourself. The `java.lang.Math` class is quite a bit different from the other library classes you've met so far. Unlike `Button`, `Label`, or `Applet`, the primary fields and methods in `java.lang.Math` are `static`. That means it is not necessary to create a `Math` object in order to use them. For example, the class contains `static final` constants named `E` and `PI`, having the value of the base of natural logarithms (*E*) and the ratio of the circumference to the diameter of a circle (*PI*). You can use these without any further ado by referring to `java.lang.Math.E` and `java.lang.Math.PI`. Or, you can simply reference `Math.E` and `Math.PI`, because the `java.lang` package is automatically available.

The most useful methods of the `Math` class are described in Table 4-3.

TABLE 4-3
USEFUL METHODS OF THE `java.lang.Math` CLASS

METHOD	PERMISSIBLE ARGUMENT TYPES	MEANING
`abs(x)`	`int, long, float, double`	Absolute value of `x`
`acos(x)`	`double`	Arccosine of `x`
`asin(x)`	`double`	Arcsine of `x`
`atan(x)`	`double`	Arctangent of `x`
`atan2(x, y)`	`double`	Theta component of the polar coordinate (`r, theta`) that corresponds to the Cartesian coordinate (`x,y`)
`ceil(x)`	`double`	Smallest integral value not less than `x` (ceiling)
`cos(x)`	`double`	Cosine of `x`
`exp(x)`	`double`	`e`^{x}, where `e` is the base of the natural logarithms
`floor(x)`	`double`	Largest integral value not greater than `x`
`log(x)`	`double`	Natural logarithm of `x`
`max(x, y)`	`int, long, float, double`	The larger of `x` and `y`
`min(x, y)`	`int, long, float, double`	The smaller of `x` and `y`
`pow(x, y)`	`double`	`x`^{y}

Table continued…

TABLE 4-3 USEFUL METHODS OF THE `java.lang.Math` CLASS CONTINUED…

METHOD	PERMISSIBLE ARGUMENT TYPES	MEANING
random( )	Not applicable	A pseudorandom **double** between 0.0 and 1.0
rint(x)	double	Closest integer to x (returns a **double**)
round(x)	float, double	Closest integer to x (returns an **int** or **long**)
sin(x)	double	Sine of x
sqrt(x)	double	Square root of x
tan(x)	double	Tangent of x

Be careful if you use the method `Math.log( )`, `Math.pow( )`, or `Math.sqrt( )`. These methods expect their arguments to be within established ranges, like the actual mathematical functions. For example, the `Math.sqrt( )` function is intended for nonnegative numbers. Invoking these methods with out-of-range arguments will cause a program exception, which is Java's way of telling you that a bad thing has happened.

A GREAT UTILITY VEHICLE:
THE `java.util` PACKAGE

Unlike `java.lang`, the `java.util` package is not an automatic package; you must name its classes by their full names or use an `import` statement to access them. However, its useful contents more than compensate for this minor inconvenience. The `java.util` package's main classes are some very useful data structure classes that you'll study in Chapter 8 and Chapter 15, "Data Structures and Utility Classes." But it also includes two very useful classes for working with dates, and another for working with random numbers.

Creating and Using `Date` and `Calendar` Objects

The class `java.util.Date` allows you to store a date and time with millisecond precision. The most common use for the class is obtaining the current date and time. Writing

```
Date theNow = new Date( );
```

creates a new `Date` object and initializes it with the current date and time.

To manipulate dates, you use the `java.util.GregorianCalendar` class. `GregorianCalendar` objects hold a date and time, just like `Date` objects, but they have more (and more powerful) methods for working with dates and times. You can create a `GregorianCalendar` like this:

```
GregorianCalendar thePresent = new GregorianCalendar( );
GregorianCalendar theFuture = new GregorianCalendar(2099, 12,⇐
   31);
```

The first statement creates a `GregorianCalendar` object initialized to the current time. The second statement creates a `GregorianCalendar` object initialized to a date in the distant future. Some of the handiest methods for working with `GregorianCalendars` are summarized in Table 4-4.

TABLE 4-4
KEY METHODS OF THE `GregorianCalendar` CLASS

METHOD	MEANING
`boolean isLeapYear( )`	Determine if the stored date falls in a leap year.
`Date getTime( )`	Return a date object corresponding to the stored date.
`boolean equals(Calendar when)`	Determine whether the stored data is the same as that specified.
`boolean before(Calendar when)`	Determine whether the stored date is before the specified date.
`boolean after(Calendar when)`	Determine whether the stored date is after the specified date.
`void add(int interval, amount)`	Add an interval of time to the stored date. Codes for intervals are given in Table 4-5. The `amount` parameter is used to specify multiples of the specified interval.

TABLE 4-5
CONSTANTS USED TO SPECIFY `GregorianCalendar` TIME INTERVALS

CONSTANT	MEANING
`YEAR`	One year
`MONTH`	One month
`DAYOFMONTH`	One day of the month
`HOUR`	One hour
`MINUTE`	One minute
`SECOND`	One second
`MILLISECOND`	One millisecond

Creating and Using Random Objects

The `java.util` package also contains a useful class, `Random`, for creating pseudorandom numbers. Pseudorandom numbers are generated by a mathematical process that results in nearly, but not quite perfectly, random numbers. A `Random` object is, in effect, a little factory for churning out such pseudorandom numbers. There are two ways to create `Random` objects:

```
Random randomizerOne = new Random( );
Random randomizerTwo = new Random(123L);
```

The first creates a pseudorandom number generator using a mystery starting value, based on the system time. The second creates a pseudorandom number generator based on the specified seed value. Because the starting value of the first generator is unpredictable, this pseudorandom number generator will produce a different sequence of numbers each time the program is run. The second generator, on the other hand, will produce the same pseudorandom sequence each time it is run. The second form is useful for program testing: You'll use the first more often in actual operation.

The primary methods of the `Random` class are given in Table 4-6. The first four methods return uniformly distributed pseudorandom numbers. That means that each number in the sequence is equally likely to occur. The `nextGaussian( )` method, by contrast, returns numbers that approximate a normal or bell-shaped curve, where the central values are more likely to occur than the more remote values.

TABLE 4-6
USEFUL METHODS OF THE `java.util.Random` CLASS

METHOD	MEANING
`double nextDouble( )`	Return the next pseudorandom `double`, between 0.0 and 1.0.
`float nextFloat( )`	Return the next pseudorandom `float`, between 0.0 and 1.0.
`int nextInt( )`	Return the next pseudorandom `int`.
`long nextLong( )`	Return the next pseudorandom `long`.
`double nextGaussian( )`	Return a pseudorandom `double` from an approximately normally distributed sequence (that is, a bell-shaped curve) with mean 0.0 and standard deviation 1.0.

TIME TRAVEL MADE (ALMOST) PRACTICAL

What can you use `Random` objects for? Here's a useful application. The applet `TimeMachine` uses the date-related classes from `java.util`, the `Random` class from `java.util`, and several methods from the `java.lang.Math` class to simulate time travel. Press the button and you'll be automatically transported to a new date and time somewhere between 1996 and 2021.

This time machine does have one little flaw. Unfortunately for you, the would-be time traveler, there is no mechanism for choosing a date and time. The time machine simply chooses a random date and time for you. This significantly complicates returning to your original date and time. The only known solution is to keep trying until the machine eventually transports you back to the desired time. This may take a while, but because you now own a time machine, that shouldn't pose a serious problem.

Compile and run the `TimeMachine` applet in Listings 4-14 and 4-15, which you can see running in Figure 4-18. When you're finished, return to this date and time, and we'll take a look at how the `TimeMachine` works.

Listing 4-14 TimeMachine.java

```java
//   TimeMachine.java
import java.applet.*;
import java.awt.*;
import java.awt.event.*;
import java.util.Date;
import java.util.GregorianCalendar;
import java.util.Random;

public class TimeMachine extends Applet implements
ActionListener
{
    // Attributes
    Date    theDate         = new Date( );
    Label   theLabel        =⇐
      new Label ( "You started on " + theDate );
    Label   newLabel        =⇐
      new Label ( "You have arrived at " + theDate );
    Button pressMe          = new Button ( "Blast Off" );
    Random theRandomizer   = new Random( );

    // Methods
    public void init( )
    {
        theLabel.setFont( new Font("TimesRoman",⇐
          Font.BOLD, 18 ));
        add( theLabel );
        newLabel.setFont( new Font("Helvetica",⇐
          Font.ITALIC, 18 ));
        add( newLabel );
        add( pressMe );
        pressMe.addActionListener(this);
    }

    public void actionPerformed(ActionEvent theEvent)
    {
        theDate = timeTravel( );
        newLabel.setText("Your new date is " + theDate );
    }

    public Date timeTravel( )
    {
        int year, month, date;
        int hour, minute, second;

        year    = 1996 +⇐
          (int) (theRandomizer.nextFloat( ) * 25.0f);
        month   =    0 +⇐
          (int) (theRandomizer.nextFloat( ) * 12.0f);
        date    =    1 +⇐
          (int) (theRandomizer.nextFloat( ) * 28.0f);
        hour    =    0 +⇐
          (int) (theRandomizer.nextFloat( ) * 24.0f);
```

continued on next page

continued from previous page

```
            minute =      0 +⇐
               (int) (theRandomizer.nextFloat( ) * 60.0f);
            second =      0 +⇐
               (int) (theRandomizer.nextFloat( ) * 60.0f);
            GregorianCalendar cal
               = new GregorianCalendar(year, month, date, hour,⇐
                  minute, second);
            return cal.getTime( );
      }
}
```

Listing 4-15 TimeMachine.html

```
<HTML>
<HEAD>
<TITLE>Jumbo's Gets Random</TITLE>
</HEAD>
<BODY>
<IMG SRC="Jumbo.gif" ALIGN=LEFT>
<H1>Jumbo says, "It's time for pizza"</H1>
<HR>
"That slogan really didn't work very well, JG. We need
something with a little more oomph! Take a look at this
TimeMachine applet I built. It's so cool!" <P>
Brenda was waxing enthusiastic again. Jumbo, a little
miffed, said, "But I liked my slogan." But to himself he
thought, "I wish I could go back to when I bought all
this Rain-Forest pizza topping. What was I thinking?"
<APPLET CODE=TimeMachine.class HEIGHT=150 WIDTH=600>
</APPLET>
</BODY>
</HTML>
```

FIGURE 4-18

Running the
TimeMachine
applet

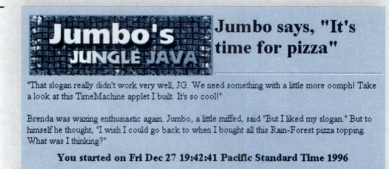

How does the `TimeMachine` work? The `TimeMachine` applet creates two labels: one to display your original date, because after traveling through time and space it's hard to remember where you started, and one to display the new date you've arrived at. The applet also creates a `Date` object, `theDate`, which is automatically given the current date and time by your system. The applet also creates a `Button` object, which is used to start your time travels, and a `Random` object, called `theRandomizer`. Because you don't pass any arguments when you create the `Random` object, it will start out with some mystery number, as was previously explained.

When you press the `Button`, the method `timeTravel( )` generates a new date using `theRandomizer`. How does it do that? It generates pseudorandom numbers for year, month, date, hour, minutes, and seconds, and then passes all of these on to the `GregorianCalendar` class, which hands back a new `Date` object when sent the `getTime( )` message. The `timeTravel( )` method then returns this new date and time to the `actionPerformed( )` method where it was invoked.

Notice how the pseudorandom numbers returned by the `Random` class are scaled. Because the `nextFloat( )` method of the `Random` class returns a value between 0.0 and 1.0 (exclusive of 1.0), you can multiply that number by 25F, and you end up with a number between 0.0 and 25.0 (exclusive of 25.0). Adding this number to 1996 makes sure your dates have a year between 1996 and 2031 (exclusive of 2031). As an interesting aside, the `Date` class can handle dates beyond the valid number of days in a given month. For example, specifying January 32 will produce a date of February 1. This facilitates performing date arithmetic.

Object-Oriented Design (OOD)

Now that you've learned to write methods and to explore some of the library objects supplied with Java, it's time to learn how to design your own classes. Of course, one of the best ways to learn about design is by studying the successful designs of others. For most software developers, this is a lifetime journey. One way to jump-start that journey is by learning a few concepts and rules of thumb that can save you time as you progress up the learning curve.

The object-oriented design process we'll follow consists of five steps:

1. Describe the problem and write a problem summary.
2. Find the objects and classes.
3. Find the attributes of the objects and classes.
4. Find the events the objects must respond to, and the actions the objects must perform.
5. Describe the desired object behavior.

DESCRIBING THE PROBLEM AND WRITING A PROBLEM SUMMARY

What's been happening at Jumbo's Jungle Java Joint? He'd originally thought that by hiring a few of those responsible for the "Elephants Rule" episode, he could "kill two birds with one stone." First, he'd help keep some basically good kids out of trouble. Second, he hoped to use some of this new technology to improve his business. True, his brief foray into adding pizza to the menu had come a cropper, but Jumbo was sure there was an angle here somewhere. Something that would let him settle down and lighten the load, so to speak. After all, at 152 years of age, he was no longer the young bull he'd once been.

Late one afternoon, sitting on the verandah with his favorite beverage, an Espresso-Surprise, he found himself talking this over with Brenda, the leader of the young cyberpachs.

"Automate," Brenda had said. "You don't want to be waiting tables 50 years from now when you start to get old. Why don't you think about building a machine that could do some of this work for you. Give me a description, and we'll see if we can't build something."

"Bless you," thought Jumbo to himself, fixing on the part about getting old, "50 years from now."

"I'll have to give that some thought," was what he said aloud. And that very night he did. Lying on his back next to his wife, Zenia, looking up at the stars, Jumbo began the slow gestation of the JavaMatic.

Describing the Problem

What should an automated coffee machine do? Surprisingly, the first step in constructing software is not writing programs. The first step is to figure out

☕ What's the problem?

☕ Where's the need?

☕ What should be done?

This process is called *analysis*. Analysis is the fact-finding part of developing software, and it concentrates on *what* should be done, not *how* it should be done. Discovering what should be done is often difficult, because the system may need to please several people, each with a different idea of what's needed. Sorting through inconsistent "facts" and contradictory perspectives is a large part of analysis, which is a communications-intensive process.

Writing a Problem Summary

An important aid to clear thinking in the analysis phase is writing a problem summary that describes what the system should do. Writing everything down often sharpens

FIGURE 4-19

The JavaMatic
version 1.0

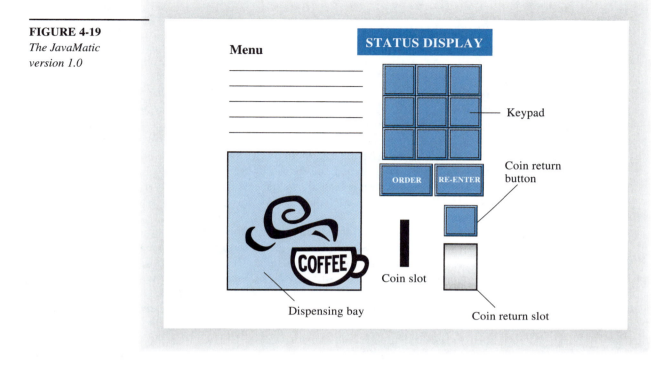

your thinking, and a written summary can be shared with others, who can point out errors and deficiencies. You may want to include some pictures to illustrate your points, but the most important thing is to be clear, complete, and correct. Here's a problem summary for the JavaMatic. Figure 4-19 illustrates the design graphically. Note that the important nouns in the description have been underlined, and the important verbs have been italicized, as discussed in subsequent steps of the OOD process.

PROBLEM SUMMARY FOR THE JAVAMATIC

The *JavaMatic* is an automatic vending machine that dispenses several different *hot beverages* in two *sizes*, large and small. The JavaMatic accepts *coins* and makes *change* when necessary.

In operation, the JavaMatic works as follows: A customer who wants to purchase a hot beverage can examine the attractive *menu*, which displays both the choices available and the *price* of each item. The *status display* instructs the customer to deposit

Continued...

PROBLEM SUMMARY FOR THE JAVAMATIC Continued...

money into the machine. To purchase a beverage, the customer deposits money into the *coin slot*. As money is deposited into the JavaMatic, the status display *changes* to let the customer know the total amount of money deposited. The customer can, at any time, decide to *cancel* the purchase by pressing the *Coin Return button*. At that point, the JavaMatic will *return* an amount of money equivalent to the amount entered by the customer in the *coin slot*. This need not be the same money deposited by the customer.

To select an appropriate beverage, the customer will use the *keypad* to enter the *product code* that appears beside each item on the menu. As each character of the product code is entered on the keypad, the status display *"echoes"* each button press. The keypad has a *Reenter button*, which allows the customer to start over on the selection, and an *Order button*, which tells the machine to dispense the beverage the customer entered.

To dispense a beverage, the machine first *chooses* the correct *cup size* and *drops* a *cup* of that size into position. The correct *beverage mix* is then *selected* and *dropped* into the cup, or the *filter* is *placed* in position. Hot water is then *dispensed* into the cup, the amount depending on the size of the cup. Finally, the *door* to the dispensing bay is *opened*, and the status display, which has been chronicling each step for the customer, *offers* up a cheery *"Thank you!"* If the customer deposited more money than was required to purchase the beverage, the JavaMatic *computes* the change required and then *dispenses* it into the *coin return slot*.

FINDING THE OBJECTS AND CLASSES

Who does *what*? That is the first order of business in designing an object-oriented program. When you learned about designing methods, remember that the focus was on *how* an object should respond to a particular message. When you order a pizza, the employees have a certain procedure or method—an ordered set of steps they go through—to get that large pepperoni-and-anchovies pizza delivered to your door. Designing methods is like that: You want to list the steps necessary to accomplish a certain task and you want to specify *how*.

Not so with designing programs. To design an object-oriented program, you begin by trying to find the objects, classes, and responsibilities in the problem space. And just what does that mean? All it means is that you are going to try to organize your program as a set of classes. Each of these classes has methods that will do certain things—have certain behaviors or responsibilities. As you've already seen, you will write methods to accomplish each of these responsibilities. These classes in your program will generally need to collaborate, or work together with each other. This collaboration will occur when specific objects—instances of each class—communicate with other objects by sending messages.

So, how do you discover the objects and classes in this problem? There are many techniques, but one of the easiest starts by analyzing the summary description you just produced. The first step in this technique is to underline all the nouns in the problem description, and then to create a list of potential objects. This list is then winnowed down to remove synonyms, duplicates, and things that are outside the program you are proposing to build. For instance, *customer* appears a multitude of times in the description, but you are not proposing to include a customer as part of your JavaMatic. If you were building a simulation that measured how different types of customers used a coffee machine, then a customer would remain as part of your list of potential objects and classes.

After you remove all the duplicates and the nouns that are outside the problem, the next step is grouping. For the JavaMatic you can see that there are many different potential objects derived from the problem summary. Are all those things objects? No, not by a long shot. Some of them will be synonyms; for instance, "JavaMatic" and "the machine" refer to the same thing. Some of them will be attributes of objects, rather than objects themselves. To start grouping things, a good first step is to put similar things together—especially if those related things operate on the same kind of information. In this example, things seem to fall pretty easily into four kinds of things, other than the JavaMatic itself.

TABLE 4-7
CANDIDATE CLASSES OF THE JAVAMATIC

CLASS	RELATED NOUNS
User interface	Keypad, Coin Return button, Reenter button, Order button, status display "Thank you!"
Machine parts	Beverage, hot water, beverage mix, filter, cup, door
Money	Coin, change
Menu	Product code, price

Again, note that the customer, though often mentioned in the problem summary, is not listed in Table 4-7. This is because the customer is outside the system you propose to automate: You're not trying to automate the customer, although this idea does present certain advantages! Instead, the customer will interact with the automated system through the user-interface components, which were identified as a candidate class.

FINDING THE ATTRIBUTES OF THE CLASSES AND OBJECTS

The next step is to identify the attributes of the classes and objects you've found. Remember that attributes are the things that make up a class—the parts, if you will. Finding these involves revisiting the problem summary, looking for explicit references to attributes as well as some good old-fashioned noodling about what's needed but *not* mentioned in the problem summary. Table 4-8 lists the attributes derived from the summary description.

After doing your best work, you'll probably feel that the list of attributes is complete. But usually *something* has been overlooked. You may detect this omission yourself, or a user may inform you of the omission. Hopefully, you'll find out about the problem *before* you've written too much code, because it's much, much easier to change a problem summary than to change a software program!

TABLE 4-8
ATTRIBUTES OF THE CANDIDATE CLASSES

CLASS	ATTRIBUTES
User interface	Product selected
Machine parts	Mix inventory, filter inventory, cup inventory
Money	Amount deposited, change available
Menu	Product code, price, ingredients

FINDING EVENTS AND ACTIONS

Finding the events the objects must respond to, and actions the objects must perform, is a lot like finding the attributes. Not every event or action will be mentioned explicitly in the problem summary. Again, there is a likelihood of overlooking some, hopefully unimportant, detail. Table 4-9 lists the events and actions identified by searching the problem summary. Notice that the events and actions are written by use of mixed uppercase and lowercase letters, conforming to the Java conventions for the naming of methods.

Can you think of some others that may be needed? What unusual circumstances might require actions not found in the table?

TABLE 4-9
EVENTS AND ACTIONS BY CLASS

CLASS	EVENT/ACTION	MEANING
User interface	selectProduct	Customer uses keypad to select a product.
	cancelSelection	Customer presses Reenter button.
	requestRefund	Customer presses Coin Return button.
	dispenseBeverage	Customer presses Order button.
	acceptCoin	Customer inserts a coin.
Machine parts	checkInventory	Get the inventory amount of the specified ingredient.
	makeBeverage	Make and dispense the specified beverage.

Table continued...

TABLE 4-9 EVENTS AND ACTIONS BY CLASS CONTINUED...

CLASS	EVENT/ACTION	MEANING
Money	creditCoin	Increase total amount of change tended.
	debitPurchase	Increase total amount purchased.
	refundChange	Refund remaining amount.
Menu	getPrice	Get the price of the specified product.
	getIngredients	Get the ingredients of the specified product.

DESCRIBING THE DESIRED OBJECT BEHAVIOR

The final step in the OOD process is the description of the desired object behaviors. Now you have to specify *how* each method is to be performed. The best way to initially describe a method is to do it in your native language—not the computer's. Your method description should be something that your Aunt Edna could understand. It should state the steps you would follow to respond to a particular message—how you would solve a particular problem. For instance, the description of a method to respond to the makeBeverage message might look like this:

```
makeBeverage(cup size, filter)
Put the proper size cup in place
Put the proper filter in position
Pour the proper amount of hot water through the filter and
into the cup
Open the door
Display "Thank you!"
```

Each of these steps, putting the proper filter into position, for example, could also be broken down into smaller steps. This process, called *procedural abstraction*, allows you to look at the top level and see if you are missing something, without getting distracted by extraneous details. Of course, this is nothing new to you. This is the same process you learned in freshman English, when Ms. McGillicuty made you hand in an outline of every paper.

In the next chapter you'll begin constructing the JavaMatic. You'll start with a highly simplified version that has only a few pieces, just those that can be implemented by use of the Java language features introduced up to that point. Over the course of the next several chapters, you'll progressively approximate the behavior described in the JavaMatic problem summary, plus a few additional details not yet included in the summary.

Summary

☕ Objects have methods that define their responses to messages.

☕ Every message must have a corresponding method, and vice versa.

☞ Methods must specify a return type; a message that returns no value has return type `void`.

☞ Identifiers must begin with a letter and may contain letters or digits.

☞ A method body contains statements executed when a message is received.

☞ A `return` statement can include an expression specifying the value returned by a method.

☞ Arguments are used to add variety to the behavior specified within a method.

☞ When a message is sent, its parameters correspond to the arguments specified in the related method header.

☞ The names used for the arguments of a method do not need to match those used when the message is sent.

☞ Arguments and parameters must have compatible types.

☞ Parameters are passed by value, so that changing them within a method does not affect the original value.

☞ Even though parameters are passed by value, the fact that objects are known by name allows a method to change the fields of an object passed as a parameter.

☞ Compound statements consist of a series of semicolon-terminated statements, surrounded by curly braces.

☞ When no message receiver is specified, the message is sent to the current object, known as `this`.

☞ `static` methods are associated with a class as a whole; the corresponding messages can be sent to the class, rather than to an object of the class.

☞ The `drawString( )` method can be used to draw text on an applet's window.

☞ The applet life-cycle methods—`init( )`, `start( )`, `stop( )`, and `destroy( )`—are used by a browser to communicate with an applet.

☞ Library objects can be accessed more easily with the help of an `import` statement.

☞ The `java.lang.Math` class provides useful methods for mathematics.

☞ The `java.util` package provides `Date` objects and `Random` objects, among others.

☞ The object-oriented design (OOD) process helps organize your thinking when constructing an object-oriented program.

☞ Writing a problem summary is an important part of constructing a good program.

Quiz

1. Objects contain methods that define their response to _____.

2. A method that returns no value has type _____.

3. In addition to letters and digits, identifiers can contain the _____ character and the dollar sign (`$`).

4. A method _____, which consists of a compound statement, contains statements executed when a message is received.

5. A return statement can include a(n) _____ that specifies a value returned by the enclosing method.

6. The formal arguments of a method are sometimes called _____, because they are arbitrarily named.

7. While formal arguments are specified in a method, corresponding _____ are specified in a method call or message.

8. The values provided by a message must have types _____ with those of the arguments of the corresponding method.

9. Parameters passed by _____ can be altered within a method without altering the original variable.

10. It's possible to use the fact that object variables reference values, rather than contain them, to allow a method to alter the value of _____ within the object.

11. Every method has a(n) _____ statement that includes one or more component statements.

12. The _____ object receives any messages that do not explicitly specify a receiver.

13. Static methods are associated with a(n) _____ rather than an object.

14. The `drawString( )` method can be used to draw text on a(n) _____ that runs inside a browser.

15. Methods such as `init( )`, `start( )`, `stop( )`, and `destroy( )` are used to facilitate communication between a(n) _____ and the _____.

16. The `import` statement makes it easier to refer to _____ objects.

17. Useful methods for mathematics are found in the `java.lang.Math` _____, while the `java.util` _____ contains useful classes such as `Date` and `Random`.

18. The object-oriented design (OOD) process begins with writing a problem _____.

19. The OOD process suggests that we find the _____ and _____, and then find their attributes and methods.

20. The OOD process directs attention to the _____ objects must respond to and the _____ they must perform.

Exercises

1. The area of a circle is pi times the square of its radius, which is one-half the diameter of the circle. Write an applet that gets the radius of a circle using a `TextField` and computes the area of a circle given its diameter. Use the value of pi given by the `java.lang.Math` class.

2. Use the `Random` class to create a set of computerized dice for playing board games. When the user presses a button, compute two random integers between 1 and 6 (inclusive) and display them.

3. Create an applet that accepts a time, entered as a local time, and displays the equivalent GMT.

4. Boyle's Law describes the behavior of gases at a constant temperature, by use of the relation

$$P_1V_1 = P_2V_2$$

where P_1 is the original pressure of the gas and V_1 is its original volume, and P_2 and V_2 are the new pressure and volume. Write an applet that accepts values for P_1, V_1, and P_2 and displays the computed value for V_2.

5. Ohm's Law states the relationship between the voltage, current, and resistance in an electric circuit as follows:

$$E = IR$$

where the voltage is given by `E` (measured in volts), the current is given by `I` (measured in amperes), and the resistance is given by `R` (measured in ohms). Write an applet that accepts values for the resistance and voltage of a circuit, displaying the computed value for the current which will flow.

6. In economics, the velocity of circulation of money is given by

$$V = PQ/M$$

where `V` is the velocity of money, `P` is the average price level, `Q` is the real Gross National Product (GNP), and `M` is the total money supply. Write an applet that accepts values for `P`, `Q`, and `M`, and displays the computed value of `V`.

7. The quadratic equation

$$ax^2 + bx + c = 0$$

has roots given by

$$(-b \pm (b^2 - 4ac))^{\frac{1}{2}} / 2a$$

Write an applet that solves for, and displays, the roots of the equation, given values for `a`, `b`, and `c`. Use the `Math.sqrt( )` method to compute the square root. Don't worry about the possibility of attempting to take the square root of a negative quantity; let Java handle that.

8. The trajectory of a projectile is expressed by the equation

y = vy * x / vx – 0.5 * g * x * x / vx / vx

where vx and vy give the initial velocity (in meters per second) of the projectile in the x and y directions, respectively; x and y give its position (in meters); and g is the gravitational constant, about 9.8 meters per second per second. At any point during the trajectory, the following relationship also holds:

t = x / vx

where t is the elapsed time (in seconds). Note that at time t = 0, the projectile is assumed to be at position x=0, y=0. Create an applet that will accept values for vx, vy, and t and which displays computed values for x and y.

5

Making Choices:

Teaching Your Objects About True and False

Computers are fast—really, really fast! Not only that, but computers are consistent. When a computer makes a decision, you can bet that if the same circumstances arise again, the computer will make that very same decision. How many of us can say that about ourselves? Consistency is one of the reasons computers are so useful. If you ask your brother-in-law, Fred, to take all the members of your lawn-bowling club and give you a printed list ordered by last name, you're never quite sure whether this week he'll put Ms. Quigley before Mr. Orlando, or vice versa. He'll also take a whole lot of time to do it. A computer, by contrast, can accomplish the task faster than you can blink your eyes; the output will always be the same; and the output will always be right. Or will it?

> *" Your computer's capability to make accurate decisions depends on the skill and knowledge of its programmer— you! "*

When it comes to making decisions, speed and consistency are not everything. Your computer's capability to make *accurate* decisions depends on the skill and knowledge of its programmer—you! A cynic once observed that a computer can make more mistakes in a minute than all the scientists and engineers in the world could make in a lifetime. In this chapter, you'll learn how your computer makes decisions and how to build objects that can choose between alternatives. But always remember, the important job of making accurate decisions is up to you!

In this chapter you will learn

How selection, or branching, works.

How to use the `boolean` family of variables and the relational operators that work with them.

How to use the logical operators—AND, OR, NOT—to create complex `boolean` expressions.

How Java's short-circuit evaluation affects the selection statements you write.

How to write single-condition branches using the `if` statement.

How to write multiway branches using `if`, `else`, and `switch`.

What *nested logic* is, and why and where you can use it.

How to deal with applets that have multiple buttons.

How to write Java console-mode applications for prototyping and testing.

What are Selection and Branching?

Imagine that you're driving down the highway, when you see a sign with a single line splitting into two arrows, one pointing left and one pointing right. Next to the left arrow is "New York." Printed by the right arrow is "Los Angeles." What information does this sign—shown in Figure 5-1—convey to you?

When you see this sign, there are several things you know immediately. First, you know that up ahead the road is going to split into two, much like the branches of a tree. Second, you realize that you are being asked a question, and the question could be phrased in one of two ways: "Do you want to go to New York?" or "Do you want to go to Los Angeles?" It's not necessary to ask both questions, because you can plainly see that if you turn left to go to New York, you won't end up in LA—the two choices are mutually exclusive.

One last question: What is the purpose of the sign? Is it simply to tell you that New York lies to the left, and Los Angeles to the right? Not really, as you'll quickly discover if you fail to act on the information the sign provides. The purpose of the sign is to control the flow of traffic—to make sure that every car, truck, and motorcycle turns either to the left or to the right, and doesn't keep traveling straight ahead.

FIGURE 5-1

What does this sign say?

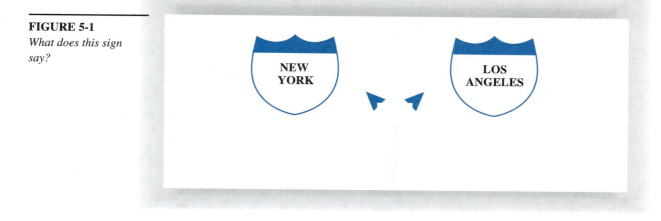

The Java language has statements that perform an analogous function within your programs. These statements are called *flow of control* statements because, like the highway split you just saw, they control the execution of your program. There are two types of flow of control statements. This chapter is about the first type, which allows you to make decisions. Such statements are called *selection* statements because you "select" between alternatives—you decide whether to go to Los Angeles or New York. The other type consists of *iteration* statements, which let you repeat a group of actions. These will be covered in Chapter 6, "Teaching Your Objects to Repeat Themselves."

DECISIONS, DECISIONS: if ONLY...

How do you make a decision? Suppose you were asked to record the grades for an entire class of students and were given the instructions that only students who obtained at least 70 points would pass the class. Most likely you'd outline the task like this:

1. Go through the class roster, getting every student's name and number of points.

2. If the number of points is at least 70, then write the student's grade as a PASS.

3. Otherwise, write the student's grade as a FAIL.

If you look closely at step 2, you'll notice the phrase "the number of points is at least 70." If you evaluate that statement in your head, you can see that either the number of points for a particular student is at least 70 points or it is not. In other words, the result of evaluating "the number of points is at least 70" is a *true* or *false* value. Such true/false values are called *Boolean values*, named after George Boole, the English mathematician of the 18th century who provided the theory for much of the logic that controls digital computers. In Java, `boolean` values can be stored in variables of the primitive type `boolean`. More often, however, `boolean` values arise from the use of expressions created by using the various comparison (relational) and logical operators that you'll meet in this chapter.

A QUICK VISIT WITH THE `boolean` FAMILY

When you first met the primitive types in Chapter 3, "The Atomic Theory of Objects: Working with Object Attributes," there was one family missing. This family, like the `char`, consists of one single primitive type—type `boolean`. A `char` can have any of 65,536 values, but a `boolean` can have only two possible values: `true` or `false`. To write a `boolean` literal, you simply write `true` or `false`. Recall, however, that Java is a case-sensitive language and so will not recognize `True` or `TRUE` in place of `true`.

Most of the time you will use literal `boolean` values in two places: first, to give a return value to a method that is declared as returning type `boolean`, and second, to store a `boolean` value in a `boolean` variable. You create a `boolean` variable just as you create a variable of any other type. Here is a declaration of two `boolean` variables:

```
boolean isAlive, isBuff = true;
```

The variable `isAlive` has not been given a value, while the variable `isBuff` is initialized with the literal value `true`. If `isAlive` and `isBuff` are field variables, then `isAlive` will be given a default initialization of `false` by the Java run-time system. If they are local variables, then `isAlive` will have to be given a value—by use of an assignment, for example—before it can be used.

JAVA BRANCHES

The Java programming language has three main ways of making decisions: the `if` statement, the `switch` statement, and the conditional operator. The `if` statement and the conditional operator both use a `boolean` expression. This expression is first evaluated, which yields a `true`/`false` result. Then action is taken, depending on whether the result was `true` or `false`. The old-fashioned term for this process is *branching*. It's called branching because a picture of the decision shows one branch leading into the decision but more than one branch leading out. Figure 5-2 shows a graphical representation of a program branch.

To understand how the `if` statement and the conditional operator work, it's helpful to first understand relational and logical operators. Together, the relational and logical operators allow you to construct the `boolean` expressions you'll use to control program flow. The `switch` statement, the other way of branching in Java, is somewhat more versatile than the `if` statement or the conditional operator, because it uses an integer expression, rather than a `boolean` expression. This allows a single `switch` statement to choose from among many possible actions, rather than only two. Let's take a look at some simple selections first, and then return to the `switch` statement near the end of this chapter.

FIGURE 5-2

A program branch

An Offer You Can't Refuse: Simple Single-Condition Branches

How did you learn to ride a bicycle? How would you teach someone else to ride a bicycle? It's almost a cliché, but the way we learn most behavior is by seeing it modeled. Despite your protests, your children are more likely to "do as you do" than to "do as you say." When learning to program, it is often easier to see how something should be done by looking at an example than through instruction. Often "show me" has greater impact than "tell me." But the greatest impact of all comes when you try to do it yourself.

Let's begin our study of decision making by looking at a program that contains no branching at all. You'll then see how the program can be improved by the addition of decisions. Listing 5-1 shows the program.

Listing 5-1 JavaMatic_1A.java

```java
// JavaMatic_1A:  no decisions
import java.io.*;

public class JavaMatic_1A
{
    public static void main(String args[])
    {
        System.out.println("Drop cup into position.");
        System.out.println("Pour hot water through filter.");
        System.out.println("Pour cream into cup.");
        System.out.println("Open door.");

    }
}
```

JAVA APPLICATIONS: WAIT JUST A DOGGONE MINUTE!

If you've been paying close attention, you'll probably find yourself thinking, "That doesn't look like any of the programs I've seen so far. Where's the `import java.awt.*;`? There's no `init( )` method. What's this `main( )` thing and what does `import java.io.*;` do? What's going on here?"

Those are all good observations. The JavaMatic_1A program really is different. It's not an applet, it's an application—specifically a *console-mode* application. Console-mode applications certainly don't have the flair and flash that graphical or GUI programs have, but there are areas where console applications have a distinct advantage. One of these is when you want to write a program that will run on your Internet server. A pretty interface on such a program is more than superfluous; it actually becomes a drain on efficiency.

A second area where console applications have an advantage over GUI applications is in the prototyping—or testing—of algorithms. An algorithm, you'll recall, is an unambiguous series of steps that can be followed to get some result. When you're creating algorithms, especially if they use branching or looping, you can use a console-mode application to follow the program step by step. In this chapter and the next, you will see how traditional I/O—specifically console-mode I/O—will give you a clearer picture of the fundamental concepts of selection and iteration. The "pretty face" of the graphical user interface has been stripped off, and you can see how things really work. Once you're sure that things are working well, you'll paste that pretty face back on. Let's start our look at console applications by seeing how input and output are done under the traditional model.

Traditional I/O

Traditional input and output don't use `TextField` and `Label` objects. Instead of being arranged around creating an object and sending it messages, a traditional program is arranged around following a set of sequential instructions that produces the desired output. If you want to do output in this type of system, you must find the particular command that the system uses and give the computer that command, along with the information you want the computer to display. The computer then displays the desired information on your terminal.

The terminal acts almost exactly as if you were printing on an old-fashioned computer printer, the sort that prints on fan-fold perforated paper. On such a printer, when a line of output is finished, the paper scrolls up to allow the printing mechanism to print on a fresh line. When you use this sort of input and output (dubbed *console I/O*) on a video monitor, each line of text automatically starts to display on the next line after printing. When a line of output is displayed on the last line of the terminal, the entire image scrolls up to provide a clean line to print the next output. In practice, this looks a little like the way the ancient printing terminals—the teletypes—worked. Thus, this scrolling sort of output has been dubbed the *glass teletype*.

The Glass Teletype Object: `System.out`

Because Java is an object-oriented language, it has no "commands" for doing input and output at all. Instead, as was mentioned before, a Java program is a community of objects, each of which has various abilities, and each of which can interact with the user and with each other. As luck and foresight would have it, Java comes complete with a built-in object that mimics the old-fashioned glass teletype.

The name of this object is `out`. That's right, `out`. But because it's a traditionalist sort of object, to get it to respond, you'll need to use its full name: `System.out`. Notice that `System.out` is an object, not a class such as `Label`. Of course, like all objects, `System.out` is an instance of some class—the class `PrintStream`, for those of you who just can't wait to know the details. Like other classes, the `PrintStream` class has several methods that allow its objects to do things. The two most important `PrintStream` methods are the `print( )` method and the `println( )` method.

Both the `print( )` and `println( )` methods take a single argument, which they display on the console. The argument can be of almost any conceivable type and is automatically converted to a `String` before being displayed. The only difference between `print( )` and `println( )` is that `println( )` adds the newline character (`'\n'`) to the end of the `String` it displays. That means the next `print( )` or `println( )` will take place on the next line of the console. If the text were already on the bottom line of the console, the whole console window would scroll up, and the new output would appear on the bottom line. A `println( )` with no argument just prints this newline.

A Running Console Application: The Java Program

"Yes," you agree, "`System.println( )` doesn't look that difficult, but how do I get the program to work? There's no HTML file, so to what do I point Appletviewer?" The answer is, you don't use Appletviewer for applications. Instead, you use a program called *Java*. As you know, the Javac program is the compiler that translates your Java source code into bytecodes. These bytecodes are stored in a CLASS file. Up until now, you have been using Appletviewer or your Web browser to load that CLASS file as part of a Web page, where the CLASS file has run as an applet.

To run an application, rather than an applet, you execute the Java program and give it the CLASS file as a command-line parameter, just as you provided the HTML file as a parameter when you launched Appletviewer. To run JavaMatic_1A as an application, all you have to say is

```
C:> java JavaMatic_1A
```

Like almost everything else in Java, the name of the CLASS file is case sensitive, so watch that [CAPS LOCK] key. Also, be sure you don't include the file name extension, `.class`, on the command line. Otherwise, Java will look for a file named `JavaMatic_1A.class.class` and will complain when it fails to find it. Figure 5-3 shows what you should see on your screen (if all goes well), in addition to the output of the process of compiling and running the JavaMatic_1A prototype.

FIGURE 5-3

Compiling and running the JavaMatic version 1A

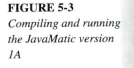

```
C:\OOP\Examples >javac JavaMatic_1A.java

C:\OOP\Examples >java JavaMatic_1A
Drop cup into position.
Pour hot water through filter.
Pour cream into cup.
Open door.

C:\OOP\Examples >
```

The `main( )` Event

There is one other thing about the JavaMatic_1A program that may be puzzling you. Just what does that line

```
public static void main(String args[])
```

mean? Each application, unlike an applet, contains a method called `main( )`. This is called the *entry point* of your application. That simply means it is the point where that particular application will begin running. By contrast, applets have an entire life-cycle they go through as they interact with your Web browser or Appletviewer, beginning with `init( )`.

An application has a life cycle too, but unlike an applet, that life cycle is fully visible and quite a bit more straightforward. When an application starts running, after all of the fields inside the class have been initialized, the Java interpreter executes the first line of code inside the `main( )` method. It then continues to execute the remainder of the lines inside `main( )`. After running the last line, the program ends.

The `main( )` method is a `public` method—meaning it can be invoked from outside the class. You always need to make `main( )` `public`. Furthermore, `main( )` is a `static` method. If you recall, that means it can be invoked before any objects are created. The `main( )` method returns no value, so you have to write its return type as `void`. Finally, the arguments to `main( )` are a collection—called an *array*—of `Strings`. These represent the command-line arguments passed into the program when it is started. For now you're just going to ignore these, but if you're anxious to read ahead, you can take a peek at Chapter 8, "Flocking Objects: Arrays and Exceptions," where `Strings` and arrays are covered in depth. Figure 5-4 shows the differences between applets and applications.

A SMARTER JAVAMATIC

The JavaMatic_1A models the operation of a simple coffee vending machine. Of course, the machine it mimics is a particularly stupid vending machine—everyone who buys a cup of coffee gets cream, whether they want it or not. Most vending machines have a button of some kind that the user presses to indicate that cream is desired. Let's add a similar capability to create the JavaMatic_1B, shown in Listing 5-2, using a one-way branch.

FIGURE 5-4

Applets versus applications

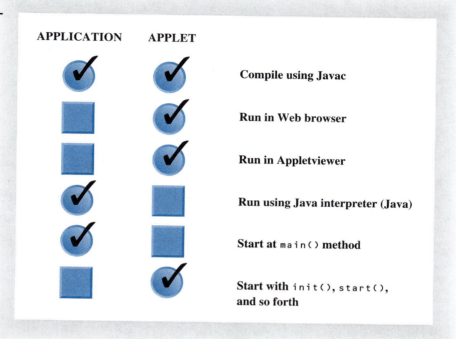

Listing 5-2 JavaMatic_1B

```java
// Illustrates a one-way branch
import java.io.*;

public class JavaMatic_1B
{
    public static void main(String args[]) throws Exception
    {
        // Create a char field to hold the selection
        char userChoice;

        // Tell the customer what the options are
        System.out.println("Enter 1 for cream:");
        System.out.println("Enter 2 for no cream:");
        // Get the user's selection
        userChoice = (char) System.in.read();

        System.out.println("Drop small cup into position.");
        System.out.println("Pour hot water through filter.");
        // Dispense a cream if the user enters '1',⇐
        // nothing otherwise
        if (userChoice == '1')
            System.out.println("Pour cream into cup.");
        System.out.println("Open door.");

    }
}
```

Your First Selection

JavaMatic_1B is the first step in giving your programs the capability to make decisions. The program works by first telling users to "Enter 1" if they want cream in their coffee. If the user inputs *1* and then presses ENTER, the program will print the line "Pour cream into cup." If the customer inputs anything else or just presses ENTER, that particular line will not print. This `if` statement

```
if (userChoice ==  1')
    System.out.println("Pour cream into cup.");
```

checks whether `userChoice`, the value input by the user, is equal to the `char` literal `'1'`. If so, the program prints the line that represents adding the cream; otherwise, the program simply omits the line. Figure 5-5 shows the output from the JavaMatic_1B. Notice that the first time the program was run, the number 1 was entered and the program dispensed cream. The second time the program was run, the number 2 was entered, indicating no cream was desired. Again, the output, which made no mention of cream, was appropriate to the number entered. The program correctly distinguishes between 1 and 2. So what do you suppose happens when you enter the number 3? Try it.

FIGURE 5-5

Running the JavaMatic_1B

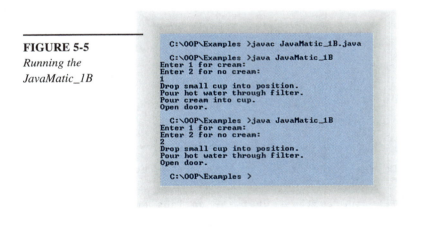

One if by Land: The Parts of an if

An if statement consists of three parts: the keyword if, a boolean condition, and a statement body. Remember that if, like all keywords, must be typed in lowercase. The boolean expression that represents the condition is enclosed in parentheses. It's a good idea to leave a space between the if and the opening parenthesis so that it doesn't look to a human reader as if you are invoking a method. Of course, the help provided by this convention is not needed by the Java compiler. The parentheses are necessary; you cannot just write the boolean condition without them as you can in many programming languages. The last part of the if statement is the statement body. This is the statement that will be executed if—and only if—the condition is true. If the condition is false, the statement will be skipped entirely. The syntax of the one-way if statement is shown in Figure 5-6.

The JavaMatic_1B provides cream to the customer who types 1 but not to the one who types 2, just as planned. Figure 5-7 is a flowchart of JavaMatic_1B. Flowcharts are often helpful in understanding program branches. You may find it useful to sketch a flowchart representing a piece of code you're designing or a piece of code you're trying to understand.

FIGURE 5-6

Syntax of the one-way if statement

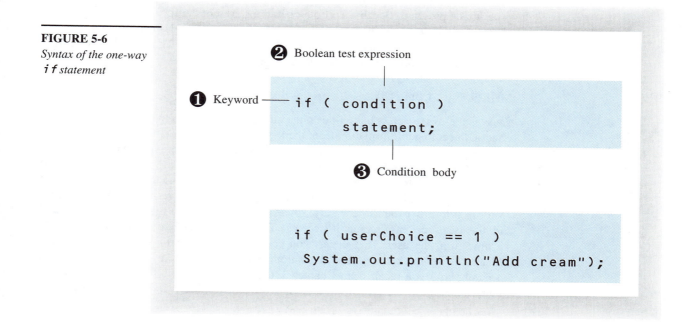

FIGURE 5-7
*Flowchart of the
JavaMatic_1B program*

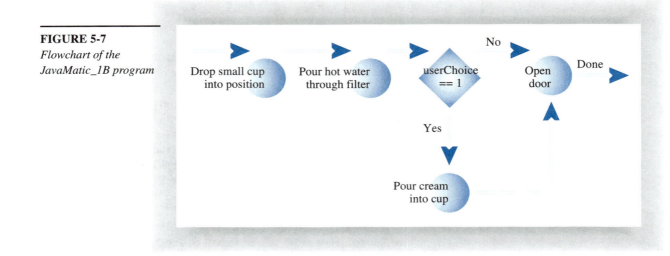

To give your vending machine the ability to choose between two alternatives, based on some information that the customer supplies, you made two other changes to the JavaMatic_1A program. These changes concerned getting input from the user in a console-mode program. Because console operations are not the focus of this chapter, and because console-mode input is not quite as simple as console-mode output, we will only touch briefly on that topic, returning to it in depth in Chapter 12, "The AWT: Containers, Components, and Layout Managers."

Meet `System.in`

Just as the `System` class has an `out` object to send information to the screen, it also has an `in` object to get information from the keyboard. The `System.in` object is a member of the class `java.io.InputStream`. Just as the `System.out` object has the methods `print( )` and `println( )` for displaying output, the `System.in` object has the useful method `read( )` for reading user input. Unlike the `print( )` methods, however, which allow you to display any type of object on your terminal screen (automatically converting it to a `String` as necessary), the `System.in.read( )` method is quite limited in the types of information it accepts. The `read( )` method gets only a byte at a time from the user. That means you cannot ask the user to enter an integer or a floating-point number and have Java automatically convert the byte from `read( )` into a number. As you recall from Chapter 3, though, a byte can be converted to a `char`; you'll rely on that fact as you experiment with your JavaMatic prototypes. This line

```
userChoice = (char) System.in.read();
```

" An if statement consists of three parts, the keyword if, a Boolean condition, and a statement body. "

pauses the program to allow the user to input some information at the keyboard. When the user presses ENTER, the information typed by the user is sent to the Java program. At that point, the first byte entered by the user is stored in the char variable, userChoice.

You might be wondering why you had to include the cast, (char), in front of System.in.read( ). After all, System.in.read( ) is reading a single byte of input, and a byte value can be stored in a char variable without the help of a cast.

The cast is necessary because System.in.read( ) returns an int value rather than a byte or a char. To store the int value in the char field userChoice, a cast is required, because the char field cannot accommodate all the bits of the int value.

Why does System.in.read( ) return an int? Sometimes your program may fail in trying to read from System.in, because no input is available. To notify the program that no input is available, System.in.read( ) returns the value -1. Why -1? Because the value -1 does not correspond to any possible byte value: bytes are never negative. This special value is often referred to as *end-of-file* or simply *eof*. When your program receives the end-of-file value from System.in.read( ), it knows that no input is available and can take appropriate action.

What if everything went well and System.in.read( ) actually read the requested byte? In that case, the value of the byte is returned. Although the value is returned as an int, it can be easily stored in a byte or char variable by using the appropriate cast.

The value returned by System.in.read( ), unless it is the end-of-file value, is the ASCII value of the character typed by the user. Digits have ASCII values, but these values are distinct from their numerical values. For example, the digit 0 has the ASCII value 48 and the digit 9 has the ASCII value 57. If you tried to initialize a char variable like this:

```
char theChar = 8;
```

your variable would not hold the ASCII value of the digit 8, it would hold the character that has 8 as its ASCII value, BACKSPACE. To properly initialize your char variable with the digit 8, you could use either of the following two declarations:

```
char theChar = '8';
char theChar = 56;
```

For those who have not memorized the ASCII table, the former method is a great deal clearer, although both methods have the same effect.

When Bad Things Happen: Input Exceptions

A problem with using System.in.read( ) is that things can go wrong. When something bad happens with input—the connection between your program and the input device is broken, for instance—Java "throws an exception." This is just a way of saying that *it* will tell *you* when something bad happens, so you don't always have to be checking. However, one of the consequences of this is that when Java does throw an exception, you need to be prepared to "catch" that exception. Because this is a fairly advanced concept, one you'll cover completely in Chapter 8, let's try an alternative strategy here.

Do you remember the childhood game "Hot Potato"? In Hot Potato, a ball or other small object is passed around a circle of children while a song is played. When the music ends, the person holding the hot potato is eliminated from the game. This continues until all but one—the winner—has been caught with the potato. The strategy for winning at Hot Potato is simple—don't hold onto the ball.

You can do the same thing with Java exceptions. Instead of preparing to catch an exception, you may instead pass it on—treat it as a hot potato, so to speak. You do this by telling the Java compiler that a particular method throws the specific exception you want to pass on. If you don't want to catch *any* exceptions, you can pass them all on by adding `throws Exception` to the end of the declaration for the `main( )` method like this:

```
public static void main(String args[]) throws Exception
{
    // Body of main( ) method goes here
}
```

After that you can use the `System.in.read( )` method inside the `main( )` method, and if something bad happens, your program will just pass notice back to the Java runtime system. In practice, that generally means your program will terminate when an exception is thrown inside `main( )`—not something you want in commercial software, but just the thing while you're working on a prototype. What if you forget to include the `throws Exception`? The Java compiler knows that `System.in( )` can throw an exception and insists that the exception be caught or thrown. If you neither catch it nor throw it, the Java compiler will refuse to compile your program.

IT'S ALL RELATIVE: THE RELATIONAL OPERATORS

Now that you're equipped with the ability to obtain input from the user, it's time to return to the topic of selections, where your new knowledge can be readily applied. Let's learn more about relational operators, which are the key to forming the condition part of selections. As you recall, the condition or "test" expression used in an `if` statement must evaluate to `true` or `false`: It must be a `boolean` expression. How do you create a `boolean` expression? The most common way is to use Java's six relational operators, which are listed in Table 5-1.

"What," you wonder, "is a relational operator? It sounds like some kind of Las Vegas lounge lizard." Never fear. The relational operators are called that because they allow you to test how two values are related to each other. If you are writing a program that calculates commissions based on sales, you might pay one commission rate if sales were over $1,000 and another if they were under that amount. To correctly program this, you would have to be able to ask the question, "Are sales greater than $1,000?" The relational operators allow you to find out whether this condition—or relationship—is true or false. The relational operators are used to form expressions such as (`sales > 1000`). These expressions are called *relational* expressions. Just as *integer* expressions such as (`3 + 4`) produce an *integer* result, `7`, relational expressions produce a `boolean`—true or false—result. This particular relational expression will have the value `true` if, and only if, the value of `sales` is greater than $1,000. It's easy to remember how this works, because the bigger side of the symbol faces toward the value that's bigger when the expression is `true`, in this case `sales`.

TABLE 5-1
JAVA'S RELATIONAL OPERATORS

RELATIONAL OPERATOR	MEANING
<	Less than
<=	Less than or equal (that is, not more than)
>	Greater than
>=	Greater than or equal (that is, not less than)
==	Equal
!=	Not equal

The relational operators can be used with literals, variables, and values returned by methods. Table 5-2 shows you some examples. See if you can figure out the results before you look at the answers. Note that the first two entries in the table are assignment statements that set values used in the following entries.

TABLE 5-2
EXAMPLES USING THE RELATIONAL OPERATORS

`int amount = 35;`	// Assignment statement
`int price = 50;`	// Assignment statement
`(amount < price)`	// True
`(price > amount)`	// True
`(amount != price)`	// True
`(price == amount)`	// False
`(amount <= price)`	// True
`(amount >= price)`	// False
`(amount < 40)`	// True
`(amount > 30)`	// True
`boolean b = false;`	// Assignment statement
`b = amount > price;`	// Assignment statement

The Equality Operators

The `==` and `!=` operators, listed in Table 5-1 as relational operators, are in some ways different from the other relational operators. That's why they're sometimes referred to as *equality* operators rather than relational operators. The other relational operators generally allow their *operands*—the variables or literals they operate on—to have only numerical data types, such as `int` or `float`. You can't compare two `Labels` or `Strings` by using the `<` operator, for instance. After all, what would you expect it to mean if you were told that one `Label` was "less than" another? However, you are allowed to compare `Strings` and other objects by using either equality operator, as Figure 5-8 illustrates.

Equality Versus Identity

You might say that two different Porsches were equal if they were both red 928s. You would be considering their *equality*. On the other hand, suppose you want to know if the insurance certificate and the loan papers both refer to the same car: You want to consider *identity*.

Similarly, when using the equality operators with `Strings` or objects, Java makes a distinction between the concepts of identity and equality. This is an important distinction and one that is best seen by use of an example. Suppose you create two integer variables, `x` and `y`, and store the same value, `10`, inside each.

```
int x = 10;
int y = 10;
```

FIGURE 5-8

Data types and relational operators

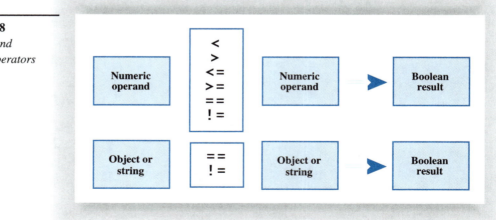

> *Instead of preparing to catch an exception, you may pass it on— treat it as a 'hot potato' so to speak*

If you now use the equality operator to compare these two variables, the expression (x == y) will be `true`. On the other hand, suppose you create two `Label` objects, `firstLabel` and `secondLabel`, and give each the text value `"Mom"`.

```
Label firstLabel  = new Label("Mom");
Label secondLabel = new Label("Mom");
```

In this case, the expression (`firstLabel == secondLabel`) will yield the value `false`. Why? The objects `firstLabel` and `secondLabel` are not the same *object*, although they have the same *value*. If you were to add the line

```
secondLabel = firstLabel;
```

to your code, the expression (`firstLabel == secondLabel`) would then evaluate to `true`, because both `secondLabel` and `firstLabel` would then refer to the same object—they would have the same identity. Though they are called equality operators, `==` and `!=` really test *identity* when they are applied to objects. They actually test *equality* only when applied to primitives.

Confusing these two types of equality is a common error, and one that the Java compiler doesn't warn you against. Figure 5-9 illustrates the distinction between identity and equality.

FIGURE 5-9

Identity and equality

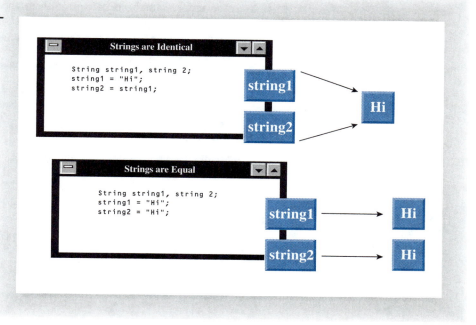

Testing Equality: The `equals( )` Method

Often, you may want to actually test the equality of two `Strings` or other objects, not their identity. The `equals( )` method is used to test whether two objects have the same contents or state. Consider the following code fragment, seen previously:

```
Label firstLabel  = new Label("Mom");
Label secondLabel = new Label("Mom");
```

The test `firstLabel.equals(secondLabel)` will return `true`, because the two `Strings` have the same value, even though they are not the same `String`. Most of Java's built-in objects have an `equals( )` method. However, when you learn how to create a class, you will need to provide your own implementation of the `equals( )` method if you want to compare objects of your class for equality.

Multiway Branches: Let a Hundred Branches Bloom

Single-condition branches have given Jumbo's JavaMatic a modicum of intelligence. Of course, real vending machines must implement more than one decision. Now that you've mastered relational expressions, how about programming the JavaMatic to offer different sizes of beverages? Jumbo is convinced that's the next logical step, and under Brenda's tutelage, he has programmed his prototype to offer a real Java jolt to those who need a little more caffeine. Listing 5-3 shows off their endeavors.

JUMBO THINKS MARKETING

Whenever Jumbo fretted, it always put Brenda on edge. Right now he was sitting silently in front of the prototype, slowly rocking back and forth. The tap, tap, tap, as his tusks brushed against the surface of the monitor was driving her crazy.

"Okay, J.G., What is it?" she blurted out.

Jumbo turned and looked up, focusing on his employee. "It's the payback period," he said at once. "Even at a dollar a cup, it'll take me a year to make my money back."

Brenda just grinned. "Wait till you see this. I've programmed the new JavaMatic to do multiway branches. Now we can offer a small Java for 75 cents, but it will cost us only half as much to make. Then we'll offer a large for a buck and a half."

Jumbo sat thinking for a few moments. Could he save money by using branches rather than Java beans? he wondered.

Listing 5-3 JavaMatic_1C.java

```java
// Using a two-way branch
import java.io.*;

public class JavaMatic_1C
{
    public static void main(String args[]) throws Exception
    {
        // Create a char field to hold the selection
        char userChoice;

        // Tell the customer what the options are
        System.out.println( );
        System.out.println("Enter S for small cup\n");
        System.out.println("Enter L for large cup\n");
        System.out.println("Enter your selection, please:");

        // Get the user's selection
        userChoice = (char) System.in.read();

        // Dispense a small cup if the user enters 'S',
        // a large cup otherwise
        if (userChoice == 'S')
            System.out.println(⇐
                "Drop small cup into position.");
        else
            System.out.println(⇐
                "Drop large cup into position.");
        System.out.println("Pour hot water through filter.");
        System.out.println("Open door.");
    }
}
```

A LARGE CUP, OR else

Jumbo's new JavaMatic works like a vending machine with a keypad. Entering product code *S* causes the if expression to evaluate to true, and the machine dispenses a small cup of coffee. Entering any other product code causes the if expression to evaluate to false. In this case, the statement under the else is executed, and the machine dispenses a large cup. The syntax of the if-else statement is shown in Figure 5-10, and Figure 5-11 shows what happens when you run the program and try each selection.

FIGURE 5-10
Syntax of the if-else statement

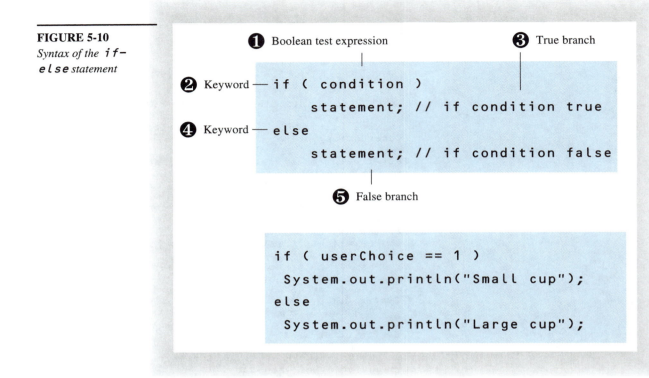

FIGURE 5-11
Running the JavaMatic version 1C

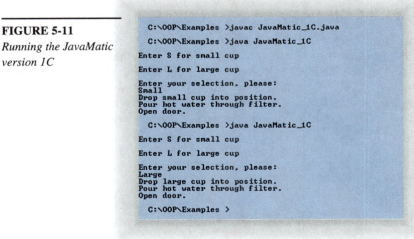

A SMALL FLAW

The JavaMatic_1C is still not perfect—not by a long shot. One failing is that, whether the cup is small or large, the program pours the same amount of water over the coffee filter and into the cup. This is wasteful, and it's inconvenient for the purchaser of a small beverage, who would doubtless prefer that the outside of the cup remain dry. To fix that, you need to use an amount of water appropriate to the cup size.

Remember from Chapter 4, "Simply Methods: One Step at a Time," that placing braces around a block of statements causes the statements to be treated as a unit. By splitting the statement that pours the water into two statements and placing one where it will be executed if the cup is small and the other where it will be executed if the cup is large, you can avoid drowning the defenseless cup. Listing 5-4 shows how to create the JavaMatic_1D, which incorporates this new feature.

AN INTERESTING WRINKLE

"That's amazing!" Jumbo exclaimed as he watched the latest JavaMatic go through its paces. Now when he pressed *S*, the new machine poured out a small cup. True, he was only charging 75 cents, rather than a dollar, but each cup only cost him about half as much.

"The only thing that worries me," began Jumbo.

"Everything worries you," thought Brenda to herself. But she continued to listen.

"Won't we sell a lot fewer large coffees now? It seems as if we'll have to offer folks a better deal on the large brews. Otherwise they'll just buy a small cup, and then order another if they find they want more later. I could actually make less money because I won't be covering my fixed costs!"

"Jumbo, Jumbo, Jumbo," repeated Brenda. She didn't usually use his nickname in that way, and he didn't like it. "You may be a first-class bean-crusher, but you don't know beans about marketing. We won't offer them twice the product for twice the price. We'll offer them half-again as much. And they'll think they're getting a bargain! We'll clean up!"

"You mean *I'll* clean up," thought Jumbo. To Brenda he said, "That's bean-counter."

Listing 5-4 JavaMatic_1D.java

```java
// Using a two-way branch with compound statements
import java.io.*;

public class JavaMatic_1D
{
    public static void main(String args[]) throws Exception
    {
```

continued on next page

continued from previous page

```
// Create a char field to hold the selection
char userChoice;

// Tell the customer what the options are
System.out.println();
System.out.println("Enter S for small cup\n");
System.out.println("Enter your selection, please:");

// Get the user's selection
userChoice = (char) System.in.read();

// Dispense a small cup if the user enters 'S',
// a large cup otherwise
if (userChoice == 'S')
{
    System.out.println(⇐
        "Drop small cup into position.");
    System.out.println("Dispense 8 oz. hot water.");
}
else
{
    System.out.println("Drop large cup into⇐
        position.");
    System.out.println("Dispense 12 oz. hot water.");
}
System.out.println("Open door.");
    }
}
```

Figure 5-12 shows the result of running the new JavaMatic with both cases, and Figure 5-13 shows the syntax of a multistatement `if-else`.

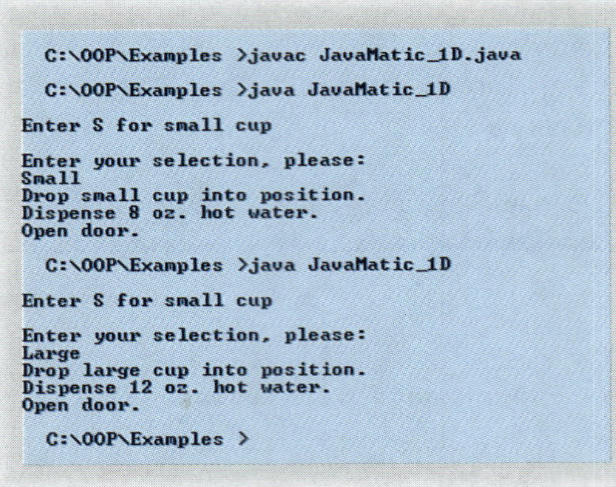

FIGURE 5-12

The JavaMatic version 1D

```
C:\OOP\Examples >javac JavaMatic_1D.java

C:\OOP\Examples >java JavaMatic_1D
Enter S for small cup

Enter your selection, please:
Small
Drop small cup into position.
Dispense 8 oz. hot water.
Open door.

C:\OOP\Examples >java JavaMatic_1D

Enter S for small cup

Enter your selection, please:
Large
Drop large cup into position.
Dispense 12 oz. hot water.
Open door.

C:\OOP\Examples >
```

FIGURE 5-13

Syntax of the multistatement `if-else`

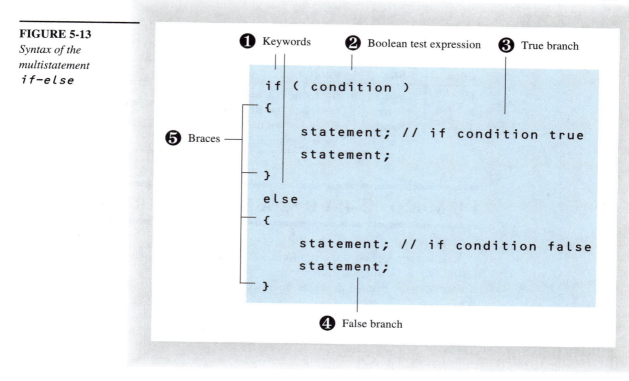

❶ Keywords ❷ Boolean test expression ❸ True branch

```
if ( condition )
{
        statement; // if condition true
        statement;
}
else
{
        statement; // if condition false
        statement;
}
```

❺ Braces

❹ False branch

THE JAVAMATIC GETS REAL

To make the JavaMatic into a viable contraption, it's still going to need a few features. One of them is the capability to dispense different types of beverages. After all, not everyone enjoys exactly the same thing—some may want regular (caffeine-laden) coffee, while others may prefer decaffeinated coffee. Or, perhaps in an upscale establishment such as Jumbo's, the clientele would prefer a more exotic selection.

The `if-else` combination can be put to good use creating more complex combinations of choices. Assume that the purchaser presses keys on a keypad to select the product desired. Table 5-3 shows Jumbo's product codes for his latest prototype, and their meanings.

Listing 5-5 shows how `if` and `else` statements can be used to expand Jumbo's product offerings. Note that the product codes, which are entered by the user, are digits. `System.in.read( )` returns the ASCII value of the digit typed by the user, which is tested against `char` literals holding product codes. The program displays appropriate messages, based on the results of the comparisons. This new version of the JavaMatic much more closely models the real world, giving its customers a choice of beverages.

TABLE 5-3
JAVAMATIC_1E PRODUCT CODES

CODE	SIZE	PRODUCT
1	Small	Bold, Brazilian Roast (Extra Strong)
2	Large	Bold, Brazilian Roast (Extra Strong)
3	Small	Super-Soother, Italian Espresso
4	Large	Super-Soother, Italian Espresso

JUMBO TRIES AN ALTERNATIVE

"Here, try this."

Brenda looked at the cup Jumbo held out with suspicion. "Why?" she said warily. "What's wrong with it?"

Jumbo was too excited to notice the reserve in her voice. "I call it Brazilian Roast," he said excitedly. "All your talk about branches got me thinking. What do we have too much of here in the forest? Branches! Why spend all that money on Java beans when I can just gather up a trunkful of branches on the way to work? Think of the money I'll save!"

"It's true, it doesn't say on the menu that it's really coffee," thought Brenda as she took a sip. A pile of floppies fell to the floor as she shuddered, trying to avoid spraying the monitor on the table. "If you think anyone will buy this, you've already had *more* than a trunkful on the way to work," she said.

```
Listing 5-5 JavaMatic_1E
// Using multi-way branches
import java.io.*;

public class JavaMatic_1E
{
    public static void main(String args[]) throws Exception
    {
        // Create a char field to hold the selection
        char userChoice;

        // Tell the customer what the options are
        System.out.println();
        System.out.println(⇐
          "Bold, Brazilian Roast (Extra Octane)");
```

```
System.out.println("   1   -   Small");
System.out.println("   2   -   Large");
System.out.println(⇐
   "\nSuper-Soother Italian Espresso");
System.out.println("   3   -   Small");
System.out.println("   4   -   Large");
System.out.print("\nEnter your selection, please:");
System.out.flush();

// Get the user's selection
userChoice = (char) System.in.read();

// Decide between Brazilian filter and Italian filter
if (userChoice == '1' || userChoice == '2')
    System.out.println(⇐
       "Put Brazilian Roast filter in place.");
else
       System.out.println("Put Italian Espresso filter
in place.");

// Decide between small cup and large cup
if (userChoice == '1' || userChoice == '3')
{
    System.out.println(⇐
       "Drop small cup into position.");
    System.out.println(⇐
       "Dispense 8 oz. hot water.");
}
else
{
    System.out.println(⇐
       "Drop large cup into position.");
    System.out.println("Dispense 12 oz. hot water.");
}
System.out.println("Open door.");
    }
}
```

By using two `if-else` statements, one following the other, the JavaMatic correctly dispenses either of two kinds of "coffee" in either of two sizes. Figure 5-14 shows what this looks like when you run it. The new version of the JavaMatic also allows the customer to enter the selection on the same line that prints the prompt. This is done by the `System.out.print( )` method, rather than `System.out.println( )`, which advances the cursor to the next line. Just adding `System.out.print( )` is not quite enough, however. To tell Java to actually send all output to the monitor before the user starts typing, you will also need to use the `System.out.flush( )` method. The reasons for this will be explained more fully in Chapter 14, "Streams and Files."

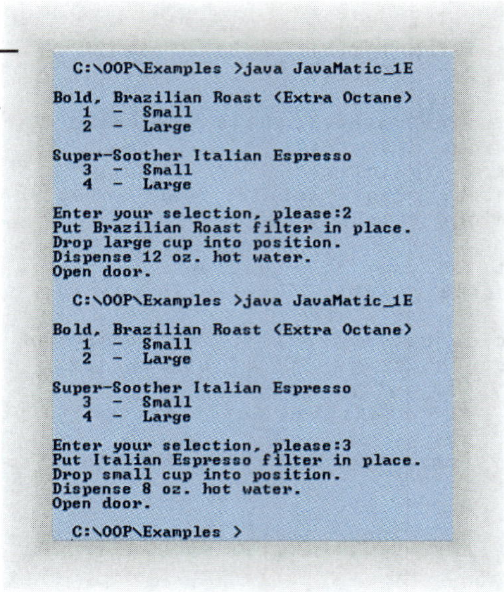

FIGURE 5-14

Running the JavaMatic version 1E

```
C:\OOP\Examples >java JavaMatic_1E

Bold, Brazilian Roast (Extra Octane)
    1  -  Small
    2  -  Large

Super-Soother Italian Espresso
    3  -  Small
    4  -  Large

Enter your selection, please:2
Put Brazilian Roast filter in place.
Drop large cup into position.
Dispense 12 oz. hot water.
Open door.

C:\OOP\Examples >java JavaMatic_1E

Bold, Brazilian Roast (Extra Octane)
    1  -  Small
    2  -  Large

Super-Soother Italian Espresso
    3  -  Small
    4  -  Large

Enter your selection, please:3
Put Italian Espresso filter in place.
Drop small cup into position.
Dispense 8 oz. hot water.
Open door.

C:\OOP\Examples >
```

Logical Operators

If you remember trying out the JavaMatic_1C, the one that had you enter an s to select a small cup, you might recall a small problem. What happened when you entered a lowercase s rather than the uppercase S? You ended up with a large coffee, right? It would be nice if Java offered some way for you to accept either S or s. It does.

The operators that allow you to build complex relational expressions are called the *logical* operators. Java provides logical operators that can be used to glue strings of relational expressions into a single boolean expression. Java's logical operators are shown in Table 5-4. Figure 5-15 shows how data types work with logical operators.

TABLE 5-4
JAVA'S LOGICAL OPERATORS

LOGICAL OPERATOR	MEANING
&&	AND
||	OR
!	NOT

FIGURE 5-15

Data types and logical operators

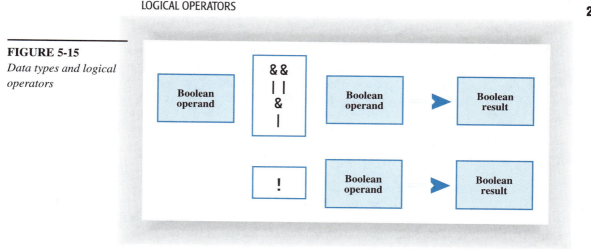

HOW LOGICAL OPERATORS WORK

The first logical operator is the AND operator, which uses the symbols **&&**. Two relational expressions joined with **&&** yield a `true` value only if *both* the relational expressions are `true`. For example, you might want the JavaMatic to dispense a beverage only if the user has entered sufficient change and if the requested product is available. You would want to use the **&&** operator this way:

```
if ( (amtEntered >= .75) && (javaAvailable > 0) )
    dispenseSomeJava();
else
    tellCustomerAboutProblem();
```

You certainly don't want your machine dispensing beverages the customer hasn't paid for, and your customer will get annoyed if your machine keeps the money when it is out of coffee. In this case, the extra parentheses around each logical subexpression are not necessary, but simply make the code more readable.

To Be, OR NOT to Be

The next logical operator, OR, is represented by use of a pair of vertical bars (**||**). These are typed on most keyboards by using the (SHIFT)-(\) key combination. Relational expressions joined with **||** yield a `true` value if either of the relational expressions is `true`. You might choose to wear a coat outdoors if the weather is cold or if the weather is wet like this:

```
if ( itsColdOutSide || itsRaining )
    wearYourCoat();
```

You wouldn't necessarily require that both conditions be `true` before donning your raincoat. The **||** operator is appropriate for this decision.

The final logical operator, NOT, is represented by the exclamation point symbol. The ! operator is called a unary operator, because it operates on only one operand, unlike most other operators, which take two operands. The ! operator converts a `true` value to `false` and vice versa. If the `boolean` variable `isTasty` has the value `true`, then the expression `!isTasty` has the value `false`. Note that using the ! operator does not change the value of `isTasty` itself; only the result of the expression is reversed.

Truth and the Table

The values returned by the logical operators are summarized in Table 5-5. This type of table is sometimes called a *truth table*. Table 5-6 gives some examples you might find helpful in understanding how logical operators are used. As before, the first few lines of Table 5-6 simply set some values to get things started.

TABLE 5-5
VALUES RETURNED BY JAVA'S LOGICAL OPERATORS

A	B	A && B	A || B	!A
false	false	false	false	true
false	true	false	true	true
true	false	false	true	false
true	true	true	true	false

TABLE 5-6
EXAMPLES USING THE LOGICAL OPERATORS

a = true;	// Assignment statement
b = true;	// Assignment statement
c = false;	// Assignment statement
d = false;	// Assignment statement
(a && b)	// True
(a && c)	// False
(c && b)	// False
(c && d)	// False
(a || b)	// True
(a || c)	// True
(c || b)	// True
(c || d)	// False
(!a)	// False
(!c)	// True

SHORT-CIRCUIT EVALUATION

The logical operators `&&` and `||` have one interesting property that contributes to the efficiency of Java programs but is not immediately obvious. Recall that a logical expression involving `&&` is `true` only if both parts of the expression are `true`. If the first part is `false`, the entire expression must be `false`. When the first part of an expression joined by `&&` is `false`, Java does not even bother to evaluate the second part of the expression, because it already knows that the result will be `false`. For example, in the expression `((a < b) && (b < c))`, if a is greater than b, the program will not take the time to see whether b is less than c. The result *must* be `false` in any case.

A similar situation exists with the `||` operator. In this case, because the result is `true` if either of the operands is `true`, when the first operand is `true`, Java can skip the evaluation of the second. As an example, in the expression `((a < b) || (b < c))`, finding that a is less than b allows the program to return the result `true`, without bothering to evaluate `(b < c)`.

Short-Circuit Caveats

Generally this short-circuit evaluation is a handy thing that makes programs run faster. It's also useful when you are working with arrays, as you'll see in Chapter 8. However, occasionally a problem occurs. For example, if an increment or assignment operator appears in the second expression, its evaluation may be skipped, depending upon the value of the first expression. This could occur in an expression like `((a < b) || (b++ < c))`. If `(a < b)` were found to be `true`, evaluation would short-circuit, and the expression `(b++ < c)` would not even be evaluated. This means that b would not be incremented, despite the presence of the increment operator. When writing such expressions, the programmer must make sure to take account of possible short-circuit evaluation.

Long-Circuits: Avoiding Short-Circuits

The operators `&` and `|` can be used to avoid this problem. Used in a logical expression, they yield the same result as `&&` and `||`, but evaluation is never short-circuited. The best advice is to avoid the use of increments and other side-effect operators within logical expressions. But, where this does not seem appropriate, the `&` and `|` operators can avoid unwanted short circuits.

Chapter 15, "Data Structures and Utility Classes," will introduce you to another use of these operators, the manipulation of bits within integers. Because of this capability, these operators are referred to as *bitwise* operators.

PRECEDENCE

In Chapter 4, Java's precedence rules were used to clarify the meaning of expressions such as `(3 + 4 * 5)`. The multiplication operator has a higher precedence than the addition operator, as can be seen from its higher position in the precedence table.

Multiplication's higher precedence causes the multiplication to be done before the addition, yielding a result of 23. Precedence is also used to clarify the meaning of expressions involving relational and logical operators, just as it's used for arithmetic expressions. Figure 5-16 gives a precedence table for the Java operators you've met. A complete table is given in Chapter 15. Table 5-7 gives some examples showing the use of precedence. Remember that operations higher in the precedence table are performed before those lower in the table unless parentheses are present in the expression.

FIGURE 5-16

Summary of operator precedence

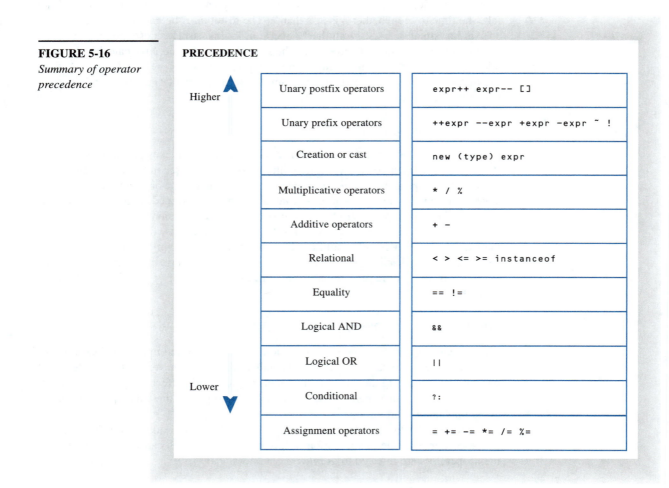

PRECEDENCE		
Higher	Unary postfix operators	`expr++ expr-- []`
	Unary prefix operators	`++expr --expr +expr -expr ~ !`
	Creation or cast	`new (type) expr`
	Multiplicative operators	`* / %`
	Additive operators	`+ -`
	Relational	`< > <= >= instanceof`
	Equality	`== !=`
	Logical AND	`&&`
	Logical OR	`||`
Lower	Conditional	`?:`
	Assignment operators	`= += -= *= /= %=`

TABLE 5-7
EXAMPLES USING PRECEDENCE OF RELATIONAL AND LOGICAL OPERATORS

EXPRESSION	MEANING
a && b || c	(a && b) || c
a || b && c	a || (b && c)
a < b == c < d	(a < b) == (c < d)

Nesting Logic

What does *nesting* mean? Simply that you can embed one statement or a set of statements inside another. The embedded statement is said to be nested. The if statement has this capability: An if statement can contain other if statements in its body. When one if is nested within another, the nested if is sometimes called the *inner* if, while the enclosing one is called the *outer* if. Listing 5-6, the JavaMatic version 1F, works just as the previous version, except that it is written by use of nested if statements.

Listing 5-6 JavaMatic_1F.java

```
// Using nested logic
import java.io.*;

public class JavaMatic_1F
{
    public static void main(String args[]) throws Exception
    {
        // Create a char field to hold the selection
        char userChoice;

        // Tell the customer what the options are
        System.out.println();
        System.out.println(⇐
            "Bold, Brazilian Roast (Extra Octane)");
        System.out.println("    1  -  Small");
        System.out.println("    2  -  Large");
        System.out.println(⇐
            "\nSuper-Soother Italian Espresso");
        System.out.println("    3  -  Small");
        System.out.println("    4  -  Large");
        System.out.print("\nEnter your selection, please:");
        System.out.flush();

        // Get the user's selection
        userChoice = (char) System.in.read();

        // Decide between Brazilian filter and Italian filter
        if (userChoice == '1' || userChoice == '2')
        {
```

continued on next page

continued from previous page

> **Think of of the**
> *switch* **statement**
> **as a large train-**
> **yard where**
> **incoming trains**
> **are routed to**
> **different**
> **sidings.**

```
                    System.out.println(⇐
                       "Put Brazilian Roast filter in place.");
                    if (userChoice == '1')
                    {
                        System.out.println(⇐
                           "Drop small cup into position.");
                        System.out.println(⇐
                           "Dispense 8 oz. hot water.");
                    }
                    else
                    {
                        System.out.println(⇐
                           "Drop large cup into position.");
                        System.out.println(⇐
                           "Dispense 12 oz. hot water.");
                    }
                }
                else
                {
                    System.out.println(⇐
                       "Put Italian Espresso filter in place.");
                    if (userChoice == '3')
                    {
                        System.out.println(⇐
                           "Drop small cup into position.");
                        System.out.println(⇐
                           "Dispense 8 oz. hot water.");
                    }
                    else
                    {
                        System.out.println(⇐
                           "Drop large cup into position.");
                        System.out.println(⇐
                           "Dispense 12 oz. hot water.");
                    }
                }
                System.out.println("Open door.");
        }
    }
```

The output from running JavaMatic_1F is the same as JavaMatic_1E, so it's not shown here. How does the nested version work? In JavaMatic_1F, the first (outer) if statement tests whether the customer wants to sample the Brazilian Roast (BR™). If so, the BR™ filter is placed in position and the second (inner) if statement is executed. This second if determines the proper cup size, small or large, which is then dispensed and filled.

If the first if statement tests false, this means the user has probably tried the Brazilian Roast on a previous visit and has had the good sense to order something else: the Italian Espresso. The Espresso filter is placed in position and a third (inner) if statement determines the proper cup size, just as before. Figure 5-17 shows the syntax of the nested if statement.

FIGURE 5-17
Syntax of the nested
i f statement

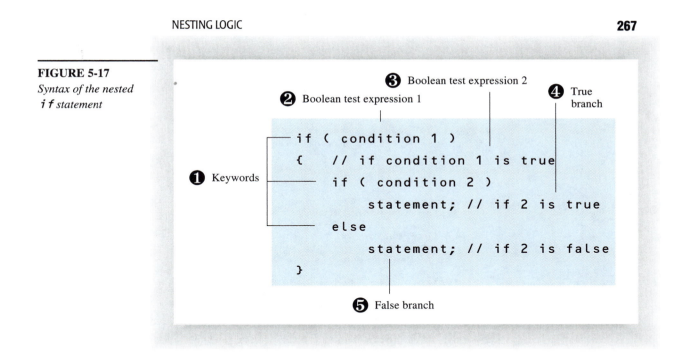

① Keywords
② Boolean test expression 1
③ Boolean test expression 2
④ True branch

```
if ( condition 1 )
{   // if condition 1 is true
    if ( condition 2 )
        statement; // if 2 is true
else
        statement; // if 2 is false
}
```

⑤ False branch

THE DANGLING else: DON'T LEAVE ME DANGLING AROUND

The nested if statement is easy to understand when both the outer and inner if state-ments have an associated else. When there are more ifs than elses, things can get a bit more confusing. The next prototype program attempts to use nested logic to allow the customer to order a beverage plain or to add cream and sugar. The different cup sizes have been removed from this example to make the logic easier to see. Take a look at Listing 5-7, which shows only the input and selection portions of the JavaMatic_1G.

JUMBO'S LEFT DANGLING

"Let me try," said Jumbo, rather rudely but not unkindly elbowing his way to the keyboard. "I want to use this nesting stuff to get the cream and sugar thing working. The Brazilian Roast needs a little something."

"Careful J.G.," Brenda started to say, but then thought better of it. After all, this was the first time he had really gotten excited about the programming part. What could go wrong?

Jumbo, muttering "Groovy" and "Far out" at the keyboard, was oblivious to all else.

Listing 5-7 The Dangling Else (JavaMatic_1G, partial)

```
// Caution: Dangling else
// This code doesn't do what it seems to do

// Get the user's selection
userChoice = (char) System.in.read();

// What happens when you press 2?
System.out.println("Drop small cup into position");

if (userChoice == '1' || userChoice == '2')
    System.out.println(⇐
      "Put Brazilian Roast filter in place.");
    if (userChoice == '1')
        System.out.println(⇐
          "Add cream & sugar");
else
    System.out.println(⇐
      "Put Italian Espresso filter in place.");
    if (userChoice == '3')
        System.out.println("Add cream & sugar");

System.out.println("Add 8 oz. of hot water.");
System.out.println("Open door.");
```

AN UNEXPECTED CONSEQUENCE

What would happen if you entered 2 as input to the program containing this fragment? The indentation of the statements might lead you to answer that the program would print the line that puts the Brazilian Roast filter in place and then skip the "Add cream & sugar" line. But recall that the Java compiler ignores whitespace during compilation. The correct answer is that the program would do those very things, but then it would also try to stuff the Italian Espresso filter on top of the Brazilian Roast filter, crumpling both in the process and, no doubt, spilling hot water everywhere. Take a look at Figure 5-18 to see what this would look like.

How could you tell this was going to happen? Fortunately, a simple rule applies in such a case. A dangling else is paired with the last if that had no matching else paired with it. A better approach than relying on this rule, one which you should use in your own programs, is to include braces that group the statements into blocks that help avoid such confusion in the first place. The braces make the inner if "invisible" to the following else. For example, if you really wanted the else to be matched with the first if, rewrite the code in the JavaMatic_1G to match that shown in Listing 5-8.

FIGURE 5-18

Running the JavaMatic version 1G

```
Bold, Brazilian Roast (Extra Octane)
    1  -  Cream & Sugar
    2  -  Plain

Super-Soother Italian Espresso
    3  -  Cream & Sugar
    4  -  Plain

Enter your selection, please:1
Drop small cup into position
Put Brazilian Roast filter in place.
Add cream & sugar
Add 8 oz. of hot water.
Open door.

  C:\OOP\Examples >java JavaMatic_1G

Bold, Brazilian Roast (Extra Octane)
    1  -  Cream & Sugar
    2  -  Plain

Super-Soother Italian Espresso
    3  -  Cream & Sugar
    4  -  Plain

Enter your selection, please:2
Drop small cup into position
Put Brazilian Roast filter in place.
Put Italian Espresso filter into place.
Add 8 oz. of hot water.
Open door.

  C:\OOP\Examples >
```

Listing 5-8 JavaMatic_1H.java

```java
// Avoiding the dangling else
import java.io.*;

public class JavaMatic_1H
{
    public static void main(String args[]) throws Exception
    {
        // Create a char field to hold the selection
        char userChoice;

        // Tell the customer what the options are
        System.out.println();
        System.out.println(⇐
            "Bold, Brazilian Roast (Extra Octane)");
        System.out.println("   1   -   Cream & Sugar");
        System.out.println("   2   -   Plain");
        System.out.println(⇐
            "\nSuper-Soother Italian Espresso");
        System.out.println("   3   -   Cream & Sugar");
        System.out.println("   4   -   Plain");
        System.out.print("\nEnter your selection, please:");
        System.out.flush();

        // Get the user's selection
        userChoice = (char) System.in.read();

        // What happens when you press 2?
        System.out.println("Drop small cup into position");
```

continued on next page

continued from previous page

```
        if (userChoice == '1' || userChoice == '2')
        {
            System.out.println(⇐
              "Put Brazilian Roast filter in place.");
            if (userChoice == '1')
                System.out.println("Add cream & sugar");
        }
        else
        {
            System.out.println(⇐
              "Put Italian Espresso filter into place.");
            if (userChoice == '3')
                System.out.println("Add cream & sugar");
        }
        System.out.println("Add 8 oz. of hot water.");
        System.out.println("Open door.");
    }
}
```

This explicitly pairs the `else` with the first (outermost) `if`. Use braces generously in your own programs, and you and your `else`s won't be left dangling.

CHUTES AND LADDERS: THE `else-if`

One problem with nested logic is its appearance. If you write a series of `if` statements that nest more than three or four levels, indenting each new `if` by four spaces, you may soon find that your statements are beginning perilously close to the right margin. Programmers refer to such code as code that "marches off the right side of the page." JavaMatic_1J, shown in Listing 5-9, illustrates this effect by adding additional products to the JavaMatic's repertoire. Figure 5-19 shows the results of running this application.

JUMBO TRIES AGAIN

"**S**top laughing at me," whined Jumbo, more than a little annoyed. "I'm just starting out with this programming thing. Everyone can make a little mistake. Everything's under control now. I've even expanded our menu. See?"

Brenda was still grinning. "I wasn't laughing at your programming skills," she said. "Everybody has to learn sometime, and the best way to learn is by making mistakes and then correcting them. I was really just laughing at... well..."

"What? What?!" Jumbo looked down to make sure his pen hadn't leaked and wrecked another shirt. Everything seemed to be in order. "What?" he asked again.

"Well, J.G., it's just that nobody says 'Groovy' anymore."

"They don't?" said Jumbo, mortified as the tips of his ears began to turn pink. "Bummer," he said.

> *Remember, the quickest and deadliest way to break a `switch` is to fail to take a needed break.*

Listing 5-9 JavaMatic_1J.java

```java
// The deeply nested if..else
import java.io.*;

public class JavaMatic_1J
{
    public static void main(String args[]) throws Exception
    {
        // Create a char field to hold the selection
        char userChoice;

        // Tell the customer what the options are
        System.out.println();
        System.out.println(⇐
            "1  - Bold, Brazilian Roast (Extra Octane)");
        System.out.println(⇐
            "2  - Super-Soother Italian Espresso");
        System.out.println(⇐
            "3  - Luscious Licorice-Lime (Served Hot)");
        System.out.println(⇐
            "4  - Zenia's Rain-Forest Chicken Soup)");
        System.out.print("\nEnter your selection, please:");
        System.out.flush();

        // Get the user's selection
        userChoice = (char) System.in.read();

        // Dispense the bounty of the forest
        System.out.println("Drop small cup into position");

        if (userChoice == '1')
            System.out.println(⇐
                "Put Brazilian Roast filter in place.");
        else
            if (userChoice == '2')
                System.out.println(⇐
                    "Put Italian Espresso filter in place");
            else
                if (userChoice == '3')
                    System.out.println(⇐
                        "Put Licorice-Lime mix in place");
                else
                    if (userChoice == '4')
                        System.out.println(⇐
                            "Put Soup mix in place");

        System.out.println("Add 8 oz. of hot water.");
        System.out.println("Open door.");
    }
}
```

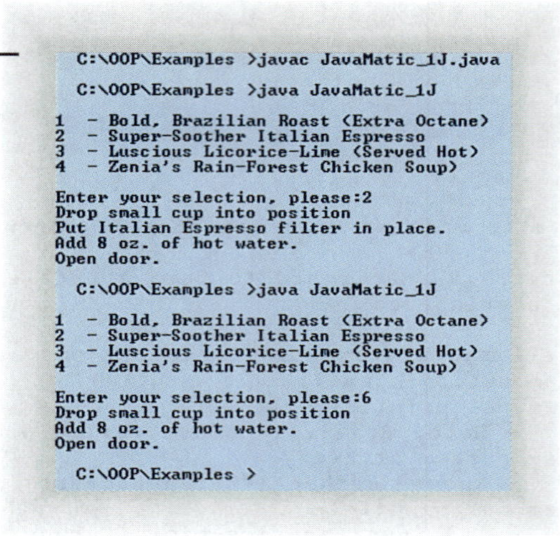

FIGURE 5-19

Running the JavaMatic version 1J

```
C:\OOP\Examples >javac JavaMatic_1J.java

C:\OOP\Examples >java JavaMatic_1J

1 - Bold, Brazilian Roast (Extra Octane)
2 - Super-Soother Italian Espresso
3 - Luscious Licorice-Lime (Served Hot)
4 - Zenia's Rain-Forest Chicken Soup)

Enter your selection, please:2
Drop small cup into position
Put Italian Espresso filter in place.
Add 8 oz. of hot water.
Open door.

C:\OOP\Examples >java JavaMatic_1J

1 - Bold, Brazilian Roast (Extra Octane)
2 - Super-Soother Italian Espresso
3 - Luscious Licorice-Lime (Served Hot)
4 - Zenia's Rain-Forest Chicken Soup)

Enter your selection, please:6
Drop small cup into position
Add 8 oz. of hot water.
Open door.

C:\OOP\Examples >
```

As you can see, it wouldn't take many more cases before you'd run out of room alto-gether. If Jumbo were to add in the code for cup sizes and cream and all the rest, you would be so far to the right that you'd fall off the page. One solution is to adopt a com-mon Java idiom, or standard programming style, known as *ladder-style* nesting. In ladder-style nesting, the nested `if` is placed on the same line as the `else`. Because whitespace is not considered in a Java program, the compiler doesn't care where you begin a statement, but this arrangement can be much easier to read for us humans. JavaMatic_1K, shown in Listing 5-10, shows the use of the `else-if` idiom.

JavaMatic_1K also corrects a small idiosyncrasy of earlier versions of the JavaMatic. A customer who entered an invalid product code into a previous version of the JavaMatic would be rewarded with a cup of delicious hot water. JavaMatic_1K gives the clumsy customer more value, by supplying a default beverage: Luscious Licorice-Lime, which just happens to be in over-supply at Jumbo's.

Listing 5-10 JavaMatic_1K.java

```java
// The "ladder style" if..else
import java.io.*;

public class JavaMatic_1K
{
    public static void main(String args[]) throws Exception
    {
        // Create a char field to hold the selection
        char userChoice;

        // Tell the customer what the options are
        System.out.println();
        System.out.println(⇐
            "1 - Bold, Brazilian Roast (Extra Octane)");
```

```
System.out.println(⇐
   "2  - Super-Soother Italian Espresso");
System.out.println(⇐
   "3  - Luscious Licorice-Lime (Served Hot)");
System.out.println(⇐
   "4  - Zenia's Rain-Forest Chicken Soup)");
System.out.print("\nEnter your selection, please:");
System.out.flush();

// Get the user's selection
userChoice = (char) System.in.read();

// Dispense the bounty of the forest
System.out.println("Drop small cup into position");

if (userChoice == '1')
    System.out.println(⇐
       "Put Brazilian Roast filter in place.");
else if (userChoice == '2')
    System.out.println(⇐
       "Put Italian Espresso filter in place.");
else if (userChoice == '3')
    System.out.println(⇐
       "Put Licorice-Lime filter into place.");
else if (userChoice == '4')
    System.out.println(⇐
       "Put Chicken-Soup filter into place");
else
{
    System.out.println(⇐
       "Invalid: serving Luscious Licorice Lime");
    System.out.println(⇐
       "Put Licorice-Lime filter into place.");
}
System.out.println("Add 8 oz. of hot water.");
System.out.println("Open door.");
    }
}
```

There's really nothing new in the source code for the JavaMatic_1K, except the way that whitespace is being used. But the `else-if` can be understood more easily than a set of deeply nested `if` statements. Simply read down the list of conditions. The first `true` condition will result in execution of the following statement. After that, any remaining statements in the `else-if` are skipped.

Multiple Choice with `switch`

The JavaMatic really seems to be coming along. By using `if` and `else`, you can not only choose between two alternatives, but by combining them using nested logic, you also can make multiple choices. Java has another conditional statement, one that allows you to choose between multiple alternatives in a single statement. It's called the `switch` statement. You might think that this is a strange name for a programming statement if you are thinking of a light switch that simply goes on and off. Instead, think of a large train-yard where incoming trains are routed to different railroad sidings by a series of switches.

The Java `switch` statement works in a similar manner. Rather than making a Boolean test, as the `if` statement, the `switch` uses an integer test expression. Think of the train yard again. The `switch` statement acts as the switch-operator looking at the incoming trains for their numbers. If the 403 comes in, it gets routed to a certain siding, while the 110 gets switched to another.

The `switch` statement is useful when it's necessary to choose different actions for each value from among a set of integer values, as the numbers on locomotives in the train yard. Listing 5-11, JavaMatic_1L, shows how the `switch` statement could replace the `if-else` of the previous version. The program operates identically to JavaMatic_1L. Note that the `switch` uses as its comparison values `char` literals, which behave as integers even though they represent characters.

Listing 5-11 JavaMatic_1L.java

```java
// The switch statement
import java.io.*;

public class JavaMatic_1L
{
    public static void main(String args[]) throws Exception
    {
        // Create a char field to hold the selection
        char userChoice;

        // Tell the customer what the options are
        System.out.println();
        System.out.println(⇐
            "1  - Bold, Brazilian Roast (Extra Octane)");
        System.out.println(⇐
            "2  - Super-Soother Italian Espresso");
        System.out.println(⇐
            "3  - Luscious Licorice-Lime (Served Hot)");
        System.out.println(⇐
            "4  - Zenia's Rain-Forest Chicken Soup)");
        System.out.print("\nEnter your selection, please:");
        System.out.flush();

        // Get the user's selection
        userChoice = (char) System.in.read();

        // Dispense the bounty of the forest
        System.out.println("Drop small cup into position");

        switch( userChoice )
        {
            case '1':
                System.out.println(⇐
                    "Put Brazilian Roast filter in place.");
                break;
            case '2':
                System.out.println(⇐
                    "Put Italian Espresso filter in place");
```

```
            break;
    case '3':
        System.out.println(⇐
          "Put Licorice-Lime filter into place.");
        break;
    case '4':
        System.out.println(⇐
          "Put Chicken-Soup filter into place");
        break;
    default:
        System.out.println(⇐
          "Invalid: serving Licorice-Lime");
        System.out.println(⇐
          "Put Licorice-Lime filter into place.");
    }

    System.out.println("Add 8 oz. of hot water.");
    System.out.println("Open door.");
  }
}
```

OPERATING A `switch`

The `switch` statement consists of three parts: the keyword `switch`, an integer test expression—enclosed in parentheses—and the body of the `switch`, which, as the body of the multistatement `if`, must be enclosed in braces. The body of the `switch` statement looks a little different than the body of an `if` statement. Inside the `switch` body is a series of labels. Each of these labels ends in a colon—not a semicolon—and consists of the keyword `case`, followed by a constant integer expression. Between each label are the statements that will be executed if that `case` is selected. In addition to the `case` labels, each `switch` body may also have one `default` label. Figure 5-20 shows the syntax of the `switch` statement.

In operation, the `switch` first evaluates its integer test expression. Then it scans down the list of enclosed `case` statements, looking for one that matches the value of the test expression. When it finds one, it executes the statements following the `case`. Note that the values included in the `case` statements must be constants, not variables. The Java compiler must be capable of mapping out the structure of the `switch` statement at the time it is compiled.

TAKE A break WHEN YOU NEED ONE

A tricky feature of the `switch` is that execution of statements following a `case` does not stop when a new `case` is encountered. Instead, execution proceeds right through the following `case` statement. This is known as *fall-through* execution, a common source of programming errors. To prevent this fall-through execution, the programmer should use a `break` statement. When the `switch` statement encounters a `break`, it immediately branches to the statement following the `switch`.

FIGURE 5-20

Syntax of the `switch`
statement

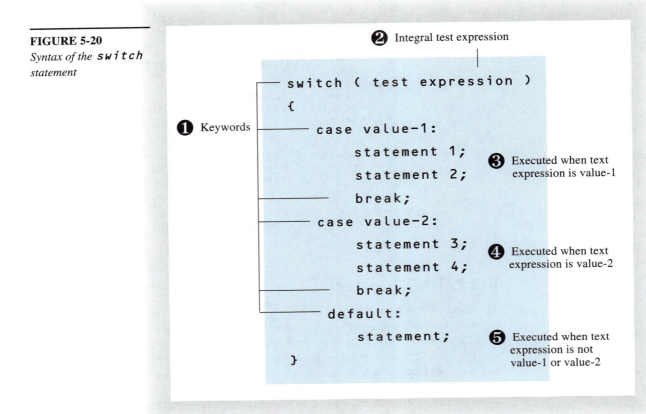

Sometimes, however, a programmer has arranged a `switch` in such a way that fall-through execution is desired, because the fall-through eliminates duplicate statements. In such a case, it is considered good programming practice to include a comment that makes it clear the fall-through is intended. If you include such a comment, the reader of your programs won't be distracted, wondering if you simply forgot to include a needed `break` statement.

As an example, consider the following code fragment:

```
switch (i)
{
    case 1:
        System.out.print("Fee "); // falls through: no break
    case 2:
        System.out.print("Fie ");
        break;
```

```
      case 3: // falls through: no break
      case 4:
          System.out.print("Foe ");
          System.out.print("Fum ");
          break;
   }
```

> " *To prevent*
> *fall-through*
> *execution, use*
> *a break*
> *statement.* "

The output printed by the fragment in response to various input values is shown in Table 5-8. Note how the input value 1 causes both `Fee` and `Fie` to be printed. This occurs because the first `case` statement is not terminated by a `break`; execution falls through to the next `case` statement, which prints the `Fie`. Similarly, the values 3 and 4 are treated identically because the third `case` statement and the fourth `case` statement are contiguous, with no `break` or other statements between them.

As is its companion the `break` statement, the `default` statement is also an important part of most uses of the `switch` statement. If the value of the test expression does not match any of the `case` statement values, a `switch` will normally transfer control to the next statement, without executing any of the `cases`. The `default` statement can be used to change this behavior. When a `default` appears and none of the `case` statement values matches the value of the test expression, the statements following the `default` are executed. It's generally a good idea to include an appropriate `default` in every `switch` statement.

SWITCHING VARIATIONS

While the JavaMatic_1L used a combination of a `switch` and an `if` to make its decisions, you could have done the same thing without using an `if`, by enclosing all of the necessary statements inside each `switch case`. Listing 5-12, which shows JavaMatic_1M, illustrates this usage.

TABLE 5-8
OPERATION OF THE `switch` AND `case`

INPUT VALUE	OUTPUT
1	Fee Fie
2	Fie
3	Foe Fum
4	Foe Fum
Other	N/A

JUMBO ELABORATES

"By Jove, I think I've got it," hummed Jumbo to himself. Both the tune and the allusion were lost on Brenda, who sauntered over to see what was going on.

"The rain in Spain stays mainly in the plain," began Jumbo. "Look at this. No ifs at all. Groov..., I mean Boss, huh?"

"Poor thing," thought Brenda as she headed back to the table where she'd set up her work. Jumbo, lost in admiration for his creation, didn't even notice her shaking her head.

Listing 5-12 JavaMatic_1M

```
// More elaborate switch statement
import java.io.*;
public class JavaMatic_1M
{
    public static void main(String args[]) throws Exception
    {
        // Create a char field to hold the selection
        char userChoice;

        // Tell the customer what the options are
        System.out.println();
        System.out.println(⇐
          "Bold, Brazilian Roast (Extra Octane)");
        System.out.println("  1 - Small      2 - Large");
        System.out.println("Super-Soother Italian Espresso");
        System.out.println("  3 - Small      4 - Large");
        System.out.print("\nEnter your selection, please:");
        System.out.flush();

        // Get the user's selection
        userChoice = (char) System.in.read();

        // Dispense the bounty of the forest
        switch( userChoice )
        {
            case '1':
                System.out.println(⇐
                  "Put Brazilian Roast filter in place.");
                System.out.println(⇐
                  "Drop small cup into position");
                System.out.println(⇐
                  "Add 8 oz. of hot water.");
                break;
            case '2':
                System.out.println(⇐
                  "Put Brazilian Roast filter in place.");
                System.out.println(⇐
                  "Drop large cup into position");
```

```
                       System.out.println(⇐
                          "Add 12 oz. of hot water.");
                       break;
                  case '3':
                       System.out.println(⇐
                          "Put Italian Espresso filter in place.");
                       System.out.println(⇐
                          "Drop small cup into position");
                       System.out.println(⇐
                          "Add 8 oz. of hot water.");
                       break;
                  case '4':
                       System.out.println(⇐
                          "Put Italian Espresso filter in place.");
                       System.out.println(⇐
                          "Drop large cup into position");
                       System.out.println(⇐
                          "Add 12 oz. of hot water.");
                       break;
                  default:
                       System.out.println(⇐
                          "Invalid: serving Luscious-Licorice⇐
                           Lime");
                       System.out.println(⇐
                          "Put Licorice-Lime filter into place.");
                       System.out.println(⇐
                          "Drop small cup into position");
                       System.out.println(⇐
                          "Add 8 oz. of hot water.");
              }
          System.out.println("Open door.");
      }
  }
```

The JavaMatic_1M certainly has a more regular pattern and is somewhat easier to read than the Javamatic_1K. Often, when more than two alternatives are present, a `switch` statement will be clearer than a series of `if` statements.

FALLING THROUGH ILLUSTRATED

What do you suppose would happen if you were to remove all of the `break` statements in JavaMatic_1M? Take a few minutes to put a single comment character, (`//`), in front of each `break` statement, so that it will not be executed. Then compile and run the program. Figure 5-21 shows what you'll see. It looks kind of like Jumbo's JavaMatic has broken down and gone haywire, doesn't it? Remember, the quickest and deadliest way to break a `switch` is to fail to take a needed `break`.

WHEN TO `switch`

Because the `if` statement and the `switch` statement both control program flow, it's reasonable to ask when it might be better to use one or the other. In some cases, the choice is made for you, as when you need to branch based on the value of a `float` or other noninteger expression. The `switch` statement does not readily lend itself to such uses, because its test expression must yield an integer value.

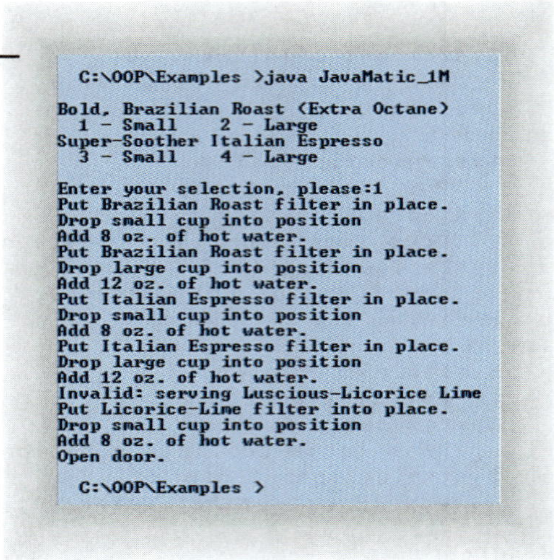

FIGURE 5-21

*Running the
JavaMatic_1M
without breaks*

```
C:\OOP\Examples >java JavaMatic_1M

Bold, Brazilian Roast (Extra Octane)
   1 - Small     2 - Large
Super-Soother Italian Espresso
   3 - Small     4 - Large

Enter your selection, please:1
Put Brazilian Roast filter in place.
Drop small cup into position
Add 8 oz. of hot water.
Put Brazilian Roast filter in place.
Drop large cup into position
Add 12 oz. of hot water.
Put Italian Espresso filter in place.
Drop small cup into position
Add 8 oz. of hot water.
Put Italian Espresso filter in place.
Drop large cup into position
Add 12 oz. of hot water.
Invalid: serving Luscious-Licorice Lime
Put Licorice-Lime filter into place.
Drop small cup into position
Add 8 oz. of hot water.
Open door.

   C:\OOP\Examples >
```

Similarly, when dealing with a wide range of integer values, the `switch` statement can become unwieldy, because it requires a `case` statement for each distinct value. Imagine the enormity of a `switch` statement intended to select one action for test expression values from 1 to 1,000 and another action for values from 1,001 to 10,000. Essentially, the `switch` is a special-purpose decision statement. When the problem fits the capabilities of the `switch`, a program using one is often easier to read and understand. But not every problem can be cast into the `switch`'s mold.

The Conditional Operator

The final Java language feature for decision making is the *conditional* operator. The conditional operator results in more compact code than the `if-else` statement, because it directly returns a value. This compactness can make a program easier to read or more confusing to read, depending upon where and how the conditional operator is used. Figure 5-22 shows the syntax of the conditional statement.

The conditional operator has three operands, rather than the usual two. That's why it's sometimes referred to as the *ternary* operator, in contrast to the more common *binary* operators. Each of the conditional operator's three operands is an expression. The first expression should be of type `boolean`, while the other two can be of any type, though they are normally of the *same* type as each other.

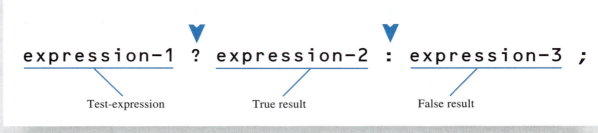

THE CONDITIONAL OPERATOR

expression-1 ? expression-2 : expression-3 ;

Test-expression   True result   False result

FIGURE 5-22

Syntax of expressions using the conditional operator

The conditional operator begins by evaluating the test expression. If the result of this evaluation is `true`, the second expression is evaluated, and the whole expression is given the result returned by evaluating that second expression. However, if the first expression evaluates to `false`, the third expression is evaluated, and the whole expression takes on the result given by that evaluation. Note that only one or the other of the second and third expressions will be evaluated. This is rather like the short-circuit evaluation of logical operators and poses some of the same complications.

Here's a program fragment demonstrating the use of the conditional operator:

```
int     theYear = 1998;
String  theCentury = (theYear < 1900) ? "19th" : "20th";
```

The conditional operator will cause the `String theCentury` to be assigned the value `"20th"` unless `theYear` is less than 1900, in which case `theCentury` will be assigned the value `"19th"`. The whitespace and parentheses are not needed because of the low precedence of the conditional operator; however, they make the expression much easier to read.

CONDITIONS FOR USE

What is the conditional operator used for? First, everything that can be done with the conditional operator can also be done by use of `if-else`. While the conditional operator may be more compact, frequently its use results in code that is less understandable than code using `if-else`s. But that is not always the case. Some natural uses of the conditional operator are computing functions as the maximum and minimum of two quantities and the absolute value of a quantity. The examples shown in Table 5-9 offer some possibilities.

TABLE 5-9
EXAMPLE USES OF THE CONDITIONAL OPERATOR

FUNCTION	EXPRESSION
maximum(a,b)	(a<b)?b:a
minimum(a,b)	(a<b)?a:b
absoluteValue(a)	(a<0)?(0-a):a

Summary

There's been quite a bit of material in this chapter, so you may find it worthwhile to read it more than once. We've covered the various ways of controlling program flow, including the `if` statement, the `switch` statement, and the conditional operator. We've learned how to form relational expressions and how to combine relational expressions into complex logical expressions.

- `boolean` values are always either `true` or `false`.

- Java has three selection mechanisms: the `if` statement, the `switch` statement, and the conditional operator.

- The `if` statement and the conditional operator make decisions using a `boolean` expression; the `switch` statement uses an integer expression.

- Console applications use text-based input and output, rather than GUI components.

- The `System.out.print( )` and `System.out.println( )` methods can be used in a console application to display information on the video monitor.

- A console application begins execution with the statements in its `main( )` method.

- The statement body of an `if` statement is executed if, and only if, the `boolean` condition is `true`.

- The `System.in.read( )` method can be used in a console application to read a byte of input.

- `System.in.read( )` returns an `int`, which has the value –1 when input is not available.

- `System.in.read( )` can throw an exception if an input error occurs.

- Adding `throws Exception` to the method header of the `main( )` method causes the Java interpreter to handle any run-time exceptions. It generally terminates program execution when an exception is thrown.

🖱 Java's relational operators allow comparison of numeric quantities and yield a `boolean` result.

🖱 Java's equality operators determine whether two variables refer to the same object, not whether the referenced objects have the same value.

🖱 The `else` statement can be used with an `if` to allow execution of a statement or block of statements when a `boolean` condition is `false`.

🖱 Logical operators can be used to build complex `boolean` expressions.

🖱 The `&&` (AND) operator and the `||` (OR) operator short-circuit evaluation of a second operand under certain circumstances.

🖱 Precedence is used to determine the order of evaluation of relational and logical expressions, just as it is used to determine the order of evaluation of arithmetic expressions.

🖱 Java's `if` statements can be nested. With a nested `if`, an `else` is paired with the immediately preceding `if` that has no matching `else`.

🖱 Braces can be used in nested `if` statements to minimize confusion.

🖱 Long sequences of `if` and `else` statements can be written as `else-if` statements.

🖱 The `switch` statement provides a multiway branch based on an integer expression.

🖱 A `switch` statement can include a `default` statement to handle test values not covered by any of the `case` statements.

🖱 A `break` statement can be used to prevent execution from falling through one `case` statement to another.

🖱 The conditional operator returns a value and can sometimes produce more compact and readable decisions.

Quiz

1. The two Java conditional statements are the _____ and the_____.

2. In addition to the two conditional statements, Java has the_____ operator.

3. Conditional expressions are built by use of the_____ operators and the _____ operators.

4. The `==` and `!=` operators are sometimes treated as a special type of operator. They are known as _____ operators.

5. Relational operators can be used to compare numeric values. The resulting value is a(n) _____ value.

6. For strings and other object data types, the equality operators actually test _____ rather than equality.

7. Logical operators take operands that have the _____ type.

8. Relational expressions joined with `&&` yield a `true` value if _____ expression(s) is/are `true`.

9. Relational expressions joined with `||` yield a `true` value if _____ expression(s) is/are `true`.

10. When the first operand of an expression joined with `&&` is `false`, the second operand will/will not be evaluated.

11. When the first operand of an expression joined with `||` is `false`, the second operand will/will not be evaluated.

12. In the expression `(a || b && c)`, the first operator evaluated will be _____.

13. In the expression `(a && b || c)`, the first operator evaluated will be _____.

14. When an `if-else` has an unmatched `else`, the `else` is paired with the last preceding `if` that has no matching _____.

15. An `if` statement can/cannot appear in the body of another `if` statement.

16. The `else-if` does/does not have a different syntax than the `if-else`.

17. While the `if` statement tests a `boolean` expression, the `switch` statement tests a(n) _____ expression.

18. `Break` statements are/are not generally needed within `switch` statements.

19. Fall-through execution occurs within a `switch` unless the _____ statement ends with a(n) _____ statement.

20. Most `switch` statements should generally include a(n)_____ statement, to handle the possibility that the value of the test expression matches none of the `case` values.

21. The conditional operator has _____ operands, each of which is a(n) _____.

22. The conditional operator tends to make program code more compact, but may also make it less _____.

Exercises

1. Improve the JavaMatic to offer a greater variety of hot and cold beverages, such as mocha, café au lait, and various sodas.

2. Modify the JavaMatic to display the amount the user must deposit to receive the selected beverage.

3. Modify the JavaMatic to allow a user to enter his/her initials, one character at a time. Cause the JavaMatic to display an appropriate greeting message, personalized with the user's initials.

4. Modify the JavaMatic to include three beverage sizes: small, medium, and jumbo.

5. The two-player game of stone, paper, and scissors is played as follows: Each player simultaneously chooses one of the three possible objects and then discloses his/her choice to the other player. If both players choose the same object, the game is a draw. Otherwise the following table determines the winner:

Player A	Player B	Winner
Paper	Stone	A
	Scissors	B
Stone	Paper	B
	Scissors	A
Scissors	Paper	A
	Stone	B

Write a console application that plays a single round of the game between the computer and a single human player. Use the `Math.random( )` method to determine the computer's choice of object.

6. The following table shows the predicted return of a stock investment, based on characteristics of the company issuing the stock. Write a console application that requests information about a company and then shows the predicted return on an investment in the company.

Industry	Chief Executive	Predicted Annual Return
Utilities	Young	3%
	Old	4%
Software	Marketer	15%
	Programmer	–5%
Entertainment	Financial	10%
	Artistic	5%

6

Teaching Your Objects to Repeat Themselves

Giving your JavaMatic Beverage Vendor the capability to make decisions goes a long way toward meeting one of the goals of object-oriented programming: to make classes that act like things in the real world. The prototype for your Virtual Vending Machine now acts a lot more like the one down the hall in the lunchroom. When you select Cafe au Lait, the machine now has the intelligence to give you what you asked for, instead of filling your cup with chicken soup. (On second thought, your virtual coffee machine may be *more* intelligent than the real one.)

What Is Iteration?

Iteration, the subject of this chapter, is just a computer science term for doing something over and over again. Other words that mean the same thing are *repetition* and *looping*. Iteration is the missing ingredient that will allow you to write more complex classes—grown-up classes, if you will. In real life, you know that your teenagers are

> *The three basic techniques of computer programming are sequence, selection, and iteration.*

reaching maturity when you can tell them to clean their rooms without giving explicit instructions about picking up every sock and shirt. They've learned the iterative algorithm:

```
while there are still clothes on the floor
    pick each item up
    put it in the laundry
```

In learning to program with Java, you will use iteration to process files, read lines of text, get input from the user, draw animations on the screen, add columns of numbers, and visit URLs around the world. Once you have mastered looping, you will have conquered the last of the three basic techniques that can be used to write any computer program: sequence, selection, and iteration.

WHAT YOU WILL LEARN

This chapter features several new concepts, keywords, and operators, as well as a few new objects you can use to move the JavaMatic out of the laboratory and into the wide world. When you have finished, you will have learned

☕ How to write counting loops using `for`

☕ How to write loops that test at the top using `while`

☕ How to write loops that test at the bottom using `do-while`

☕ How to write a loop-and-a-half using `break` and `continue`

☕ How to recognize common mistakes and pitfalls when writing loops

☕ How to decide which kind of loop to use

JavaMatic *Redux*?

In Chapter 5, "Making Choices: Teaching Your Objects About True and False," you built several prototypes of the JavaMatic beverage vendor. Starting with a machine that did nothing but mindlessly dispense the same tiny cup of virtual instant coffee to virtually everybody, you added `if`s, `else`s, and `switches` until you ended up with a program that faithfully models the best the world has to offer, at least in most respects. It does have one small problem, which you probably discovered while you were testing the program. Every time you want a cup of electronic Java, you have to restart the entire JavaMatic program! It's as if you had to plug the lunchroom vending machine into the wall for each cup of coffee.

Because real vending machines don't act like that, and because one of the goals of object-oriented programming is to make your classes model the real world, it seems obvious that the JavaMatic program needs a little bit of a tune-up. You'd like the program to keep running until you're done with it. You might also like to sort the

JavaMatic's actions into individual methods. Right now, the prototype does all its work in the `main()` method, which is getting rather complicated and unwieldy. Before adding loops to the JavaMatic, let's improve its organization a bit. Object-oriented programming is itself an iterative process; programmers often work and rework an object-oriented program before coming up with a final product.

THE METHODICAL MACHINE

What methods should the JavaMatic have? A good way to approach this question is to ask another: What does the JavaMatic do? So far, the JavaMatic is fairly simple—it doesn't collect money (yet!) or return change. It does three things:

☕ Shows the customer a menu

☕ Takes the customer's order

☕ Fills the customer's order

"That looks straightforward," you say, "We can start the JavaMatic off with three methods: `drawMenu()`, `getOrder()`, and `dispenseBeverage()`. This won't take any time at all." Well, there's one easy way to find out if you're right. You guessed it: Build a prototype. But building a prototype can sometimes be time-consuming—especially if you are not sure that your prototype is going to work. Rather than building a complete prototype, try a *stub*.

Despite what it sounds like, a stub is not some type of beverage in a very small bottle. A stub is a piece of code you use as a substitute for a method before you write the method. This allows you to work on and test the organization of your class even before you know all of the details about how the methods are going to work. Based on the three tasks we've identified for the JavaMatic, let's start writing the second-generation JavaMatic using stubs. Listing 6-1 contains the code for the JavaMatic 2A, and Figure 6-1 shows what happens when you compile it.

Listing 6-1 JavaMatic_2A.java

```
//   The JavaMatic Virtual Vending Machine - Version 2A
//   Caution: This version does not compile!
//   Uses methods
import java.io.*;

public class JavaMatic_2A
{
    // The application starts executing the main() method
    public static void main(String args[]) throws Exception
    {
        // Create a variable to hold the customer's selection
        char userChoice;

        // ----What does the JavaMatic_2A need to do?--------
        //     > Display its offerings
        //     > Accept the customer's selection
```

continued on next page

continued from previous page

```
            //      > Dispense the beverage chosen
            // ------------------------------------------------------
            // Call methods to accomplish objectives
            // ------------------------------------------------------
            drawMenu();
            userChoice = getOrder();
            dispenseBeverage( userChoice );
        }
        // "Stub" methods to implement object behavior
        // ******************************************************
        void drawMenu()
        {
            System.out.println("Now in method drawMenu()");
            System.out.println("Enter your selection:");
        }

        char getOrder()
        {
            return (char) System.in.read();
        }

        void dispenseBeverage( char choice )
        {
            System.out.println⇐
              ("Customer wants to receive " + choice );
        }
    }
```

JAVA OBJECTS

When you try to compile the JavaMatic 2A, you'll find that the Java compiler objects
to your program, quite strenuously, in at least four places. What's going on here? If
you look back at Chapter 4, "Simply Methods: One Step at a Time," you'll see that the
methods there are all defined exactly the same way you've defined your new methods
here. What then is the difference?

FIGURE 6-1

*Compiling the
JavaMatic_2A*

```
C:\OOP\Examples >javac JavaMatic_2A.java
JavaMatic_2A.java:21: Can't make static reference to method void drawMenu() i
lass JavaMatic_2A.
        drawMenu();
        ^
JavaMatic_2A.java:22: Can't make static reference to method char getOrder() i
lass JavaMatic_2A.
        userChoice = getOrder();
        ^
JavaMatic_2A.java:23: Can't make static reference to method void dispenseBeve
e(char) in class JavaMatic_2A.
        dispenseBeverage( userChoice );
        ^
JavaMatic_2A.java:35: Exception java.io.IOException must be caught, or it mus
e declared in the throws clause of this method.
        return (char) System.in.read();
        ^
4 errors

C:\OOP\Examples >
```

Take a close look at the first three of Java's four error messages (shown in Figure 6-1). It looks like this:

```
JavaMatic_2A.java:21: Can't make static reference to method
void drawMenu() in class JavaMatic_2A.
        drawMenu();
            ^
```

What is the compiler's message meant to tell you? First, it tells you that the problem Java is having is on line 21, or thereabouts. Sometimes the line number given in a compiler message can be misleading; every now and then, Javac has a little difficulty telling you exactly where the real error occurred—but it provides a place for you to start looking. Second, it tells you that the problem concerns the call to the `drawMenu()` method. Note that the problem is with the call, and not with the method definition. Apparently, the method itself is fine, as you can verify by checking it carefully.

As far as you can see, there is also no problem with the method call—it looks exactly like the method calls you used in Chapter 4. Of course, there is no object name in front of the method call, but as you recall, that simply means you are sending the message to the `this`, or current, object. As you're probably beginning to suspect, therein lies the rub. When you were creating applets in Chapter 4, your Web browser (or the Appletviewer) created an object for you when it loaded your applet—you didn't have to create an instance of your class in the same way you created `Button` and `Label` objects. With applications, however, things are different. There is no browser to automatically create a `JavaMatic` object for you, and Java simply won't take this responsibility. Instead, you need to create a new `JavaMatic` object when your program starts up. This `JavaMatic` object will be the one you will send your messages to, and the one that will perform the behavior you desire.

CREATING AN APPLICATION OBJECT: myMachine

Just how, then, are you supposed to create a `JavaMatic` object? Well, how did you create a `Label` or `Button` object? You used code that looked like this:

```
Label myLabel = new Label( "Hi Mom!");
```

You could do exactly the same thing to create, say, a new `JavaMatic_2B` object. In your `main()` method you'd say

```
JavaMatic_2B myMachine = new JavaMatic_2B();
```

This creates, or constructs, a `JavaMatic_2B` object and stores its reference in the variable `myMachine`. To send the `drawMenu()` message to your application object, you could write

```
myMachine.drawMenu();
```

Listing 6-2 shows a new version of the JavaMatic, `JavaMatic_2B`, that demonstrates how to create and use an application object. Figure 6-2 shows what your `JavaMatic_2B` looks like as it exercises your "stubby" methods.

Listing 6-2 JavaMatic_2B.java

```java
//  The JavaMatic Virtual Vending Machine - Version 2B
//  Uses methods and objects
import java.io.*;

public class JavaMatic_2B
{
    // The application starts executing the main() method
    public static void main(String args[]) throws Exception
    {
        // Create a variable to hold the customer's selection
        char userChoice;

        // Create a JavaMatic_2B object to carry out your
        //work
        JavaMatic_2B myMachine = new JavaMatic_2B();

        // Tell the object to do your bidding
        myMachine.drawMenu();
        userChoice = myMachine.getOrder();
        myMachine.dispenseBeverage( userChoice );
    }
    // Methods to implement object behavior
    // *****************************************************
    public void drawMenu()
    {
        System.out.println("Now in method drawMenu()");
        System.out.println("Enter your selection: ");
    }

    public char getOrder() throws Exception
    {
        return (char) System.in.read();
    }

    public void dispenseBeverage( char choice )
    {
        System.out.println(⇐
            "Customer wants to receive " + choice );
    }
}
```

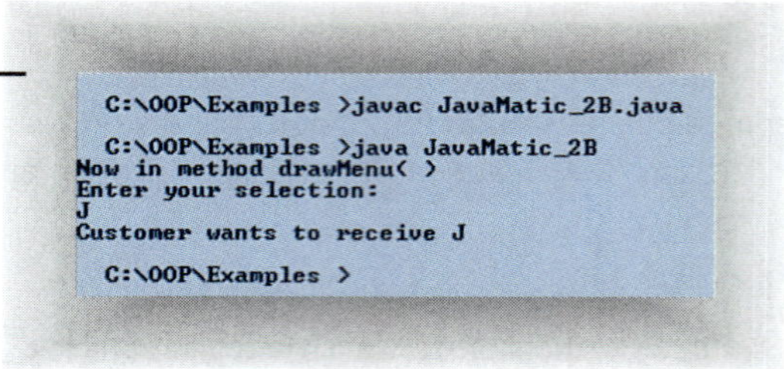

FIGURE 6-2

*Running the
JavaMatic_2B*

```
C:\OOP\Examples >javac JavaMatic_2B.java

C:\OOP\Examples >java JavaMatic_2B
Now in method drawMenu( )
Enter your selection:
J
Customer wants to receive J

C:\OOP\Examples >
```

CHANGES A' BREWIN'

You've now successfully created a JavaMatic prototype that creates the necessary application object and that uses methods. The new JavaMatic Virtual Vending Machine knows how to do three things. First, it displays its offerings to the customers lined up to purchase tasty beverages. It does this by invoking the method `drawMenu()`, which prints a list of choices and asks the user to enter a selection. The JavaMatic_2B then uses the `getOrder()` method to allow the user to type in a code representing the beverage he or she wishes to purchase. The `char` that the user types is stored in the local variable `userChoice`. This choice is then passed on to the method `dispenseBeverage()`, where the actual work of making sure the machine gives the user what he or she selected takes place.

In addition to creating the `myMachine` object, you had to make one other change to get the JavaMatic_2B to run. You had to add the line

```
throws Exception
```

to the definition of the `getOrder()` method, just as it was already included in the definition of the `main()` method. This was necessary because you moved the code that reads from the keyboard—`System.in.read()`—into the `getOrder()` method. You might be tempted at this point to remove the `throws Exception` from the `main()` method declaration, because `System.in.read()` no longer appears there. However, if you attempt that, you'll find that Java insists that you leave it in place. While `System.in.read()` no longer passes exception "hot potatoes" on to `main()`, there is still one method that does—your new `getOrder()`! As a general rule, if you use any method that throws an exception in any of your own methods, you will need to be prepared to handle that exception—as you'll learn to do in Chapter 8, "Flocking Objects: Arrays and Exceptions"—or you'll need to tell Java that your method can also throw that exception.

FILLING IN THE STUBS

Now that you have the JavaMatic "stubbed-out," you're ready to fill in the details. A good place to start is with the `drawMenu()` method. To finish `drawMenu()`, all you have to do is print each of the beverage options, along with the codes the customer must use, to the terminal. You'll probably also want to add a prompt telling the customer to enter a selection. As explained in Chapter 5, be sure to use `System.out.flush()` so that the prompt is visible before the user starts typing.

The second stub you'll need to fill out is the `getOrder()` stub. What do you need to do there? For now, you can leave it as it is, but in the future, this is where you'll check for errors such as entering an incorrect product code. Finally, you'll need to work on the `dispenseBeverage()` method, which receives the customer's selection as an argument. When you invoke `dispenseBeverage()`, you're telling a specific JavaMatic machine (`MyMachine` in this example) to dispense a beverage. But `MyMachine` needs to be told which beverage to dispense. To give the machine that additional information, you pass it an argument—a note, so to speak—telling it which beverage to serve. When the `dispenseBeverage()` method runs, it compares this value with the codes for the beverages the JavaMatic has in stock. If it finds a match, it performs the appropriate action: giving the customer a cup of Brazilian Roast or Zenia's chicken soup.

You'll want to pay particular attention to the `switch` statement inside the `dispenseBeverage()` method. Notice that if the customer enters a code that doesn't match one of the `cases`, the method simply returns (after printing a suitable message). No beverages are dispensed—not even the hot water dispensed by earlier versions of the JavaMatic. Listing 6-3 shows the JavaMatic_2C with its filled-in methods, and Figure 6-3 shows the JavaMatic_2C as it runs.

Listing 6-3 JavaMatic_2C.java

```java
//   The JavaMatic Virtual Vending Machine - Version 2C
//   Method stubs filled out
import java.io.*;

public class JavaMatic_2C
{
    // The application starts executing the main() method
    public static void main(String args[]) throws Exception
    {
        // Create a variable to hold the customer's selection
        char userChoice;

        // Create a JavaMatic_2C object to carry out your
        // work
        JavaMatic_2C myMachine = new JavaMatic_2C();

        // Tell the object to do your bidding
        myMachine.drawMenu();
        userChoice = myMachine.getOrder();
        myMachine.dispenseBeverage( userChoice );
    }
    // Methods to implement object behavior
    // ********************************************************
    //   method drawMenu(): display the JavaMatic offerings
    // ********************************************************
    public void drawMenu()
    {
        System.out.println();
        System.out.println(⇐
        "    The JavaMatic Virtual Vending Machine  ");
        System.out.println(⇐
        "    ----------------------------------------");
        System.out.println(⇐
        "  1 - Bold, Brazilian Roast (Extra Octane)");
        System.out.println(⇐
        "  2 - Super-Soother Italian Espresso      ");
        System.out.println(⇐
        "  3 - Luscious Licorice-Lime (Served Hot) ");
```

```java
        System.out.println(⇐
        "    4 - Zenia's Rain-Forest Chicken Soup)     ");
        System.out.println(⇐
        "   --------------------------------------");
        System.out.print⇐
        (  "                  What's Your Pleasure ? ");
        System.out.flush();
    }

    // ******************************************************
    //  method getOrder(): retrieve the user's selection
    // ******************************************************
    public char getOrder() throws Exception
    {
        return (char) System.in.read();
    }

    // ******************************************************
    //  method dispenseBeverage(): dispense chosen drink
    // ******************************************************
    public void dispenseBeverage( char choice )
    {
        System.out.println("");
        switch ( choice )
        {
            case '1':
                System.out.println(⇐
                "  Put Brazilian Roast" + "filter "in⇐
                place.");
                break;
            case '2':
                System.out.println(⇐
                "  Put Italian Espresso" + "filter in⇐
                place.");
                break;
            case '3':
                System.out.println(⇐
                "  Put Licorice-Lime mix into place.");
                break;
            case '4':
                System.out.println(⇐
                "  Put Chicken-Soup mix into place");
                break;
            default:
                System.out.println(⇐
                "  Invalid selection." + "Deposit more⇐
                money.");
                return;
        }
        System.out.println("  Drop cup into position.");
        System.out.println("  Add 8 oz. hot water.");
        System.out.println("  Open door.");
    }
}
```

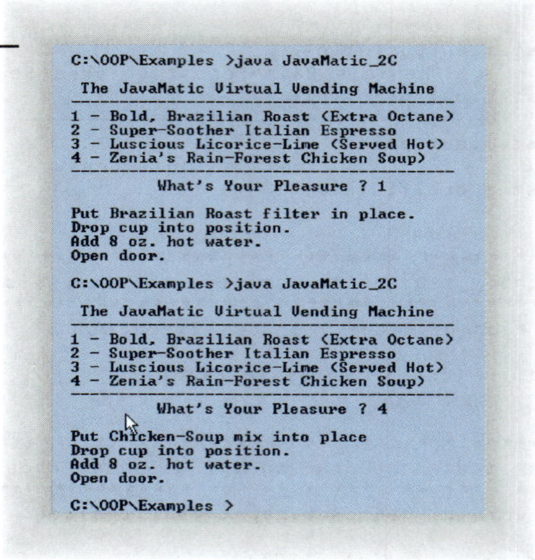

FIGURE 6-3

*Running the
JavaMatic_2C*

```
C:\OOP\Examples >java JavaMatic_2C

The JavaMatic Virtual Vending Machine
-------------------------------------
1 - Bold, Brazilian Roast (Extra Octane)
2 - Super-Soother Italian Espresso
3 - Luscious Licorice-Line (Served Hot)
4 - Zenia's Rain-Forest Chicken Soup)
-------------------------------------
          What's Your Pleasure ? 1

Put Brazilian Roast filter in place.
Drop cup into position.
Add 8 oz. hot water.
Open door.

C:\OOP\Examples >java JavaMatic_2C

The JavaMatic Virtual Vending Machine
-------------------------------------
1 - Bold, Brazilian Roast (Extra Octane)
2 - Super-Soother Italian Espresso
3 - Luscious Licorice-Line (Served Hot)
4 - Zenia's Rain-Forest Chicken Soup)
-------------------------------------
          What's Your Pleasure ? 4

Put Chicken-Soup mix into place
Drop cup into position.
Add 8 oz. hot water.
Open door.

C:\OOP\Examples >
```

"BREEEEEEENDA..."

Jumbo's bellow could be heard throughout the forest. "I thought you were going to fix this," he blustered, clearly annoyed. Brenda looked up from her desk with an air of resignation. She was tired from sitting all day, and, although she would have liked to, she couldn't exactly ignore him. After all, they didn't call him "Jumbo" for nothing.

"Calm down, J.G. What's the big deal? Restarting the program each time is not the end of the world, after all." Brenda spoke with quiet assurance, but Jumbo was not mollified.

"Taxes!" he said. "Did you ever think of taxes? The accountant wants these figures tomorrow, and I've got no idea how many cups of Brazilian Roast we've sold."

Brenda, for once, was at a loss for words.

Something Doesn't Add Up

Restarting your program each time the customer wants to make a selection is more than just a nuisance; it prevents you from providing one of the most basic features of a vending machine—keeping track of how much coffee it has sold. You *could* add this feature without having to learn a new concept such as iteration, of course. Let's

> *A stub is not a beverage in a very small bottle: A stub is a piece of code you use as a temporary substitute for a method.*

suppose you wanted to give your JavaMatic the ability to count the number of cups you've sold, along with the total amount you've collected when the day is done. How would you start?

THE JAVAMATIC_2D TAKES SHAPE

The easiest way to make the JavaMatic dispense multiple cups of coffee is to repeat each of the statements needed to dispense one cup of coffee. Here's how you could do this. First, create a variable to hold the total amount of money you collect. For this example, you can make things simple and just charge a quarter for each beverage, regardless of type. (Of course, you'll lose a little on each sale, but you can always make it up in volume!) Add the price of each sale to the total as each beverage is dispensed. At the end of the program, print the total sales. The JavaMatic_2D, shown in Listing 6-4, includes the appropriate changes. Let's look in detail at how to build the JavaMatic_2D.

Listing 6-4 JavaMatic_2D.java (partial)

```java
// The JavaMatic Virtual Vending Machine - Version 2D
// Works three times, and adds up total sales
import java.io.*;

public class JavaMatic_2D
{
    // This is the constant price for all beverages
    static final double PRICE = 0.25;

    // The application starts executing the main() method
    public static void main(String args[]) throws Exception
    {
        // Create a variable to hold the customer's selection
        char userChoice;

        // Create a variable to hold the total sales
        double totalSales = 0.0;

        // Create a JavaMatic_2D object to carry out your
        // work
        JavaMatic_2D myMachine = new JavaMatic_2D();

        // First sale --------------------------------
        myMachine.drawMenu();
        userChoice = myMachine.getOrder();
        myMachine.dispenseBeverage( userChoice );
        totalSales += PRICE;

        // Second sale --------------------------------
        myMachine.drawMenu();
        userChoice = myMachine.getOrder();
        myMachine.dispenseBeverage( userChoice );
        totalSales += PRICE;

        // Third sale --------------------------------
        myMachine.drawMenu();
```

continued on next page

continued from previous page

```
        userChoice = myMachine.getOrder();
        myMachine.dispenseBeverage( userChoice );
        totalSales += PRICE;

        System.out.println(⇐
           "\nYour JavaMatic sold " + totalSales);
   }

   // Methods to implement behavior go here (not shown)


}
```

BUILDING THE JAVAMATIC_2D

To build the JavaMatic_2D, simply save a copy of JavaMatic_2C.java—changing its name to JavaMatic_2D.java—and make changes to the new file. There are several such changes you'll need to make to allow it to keep track of how much money you have earned.

First, of course, you'll have to change the name of the class from JavaMatic_2C to JavaMatic_2D. Make sure that all the occurrences, such as the one in the line creating the `myMachine` object, are changed to correctly refer to your new class. Next, you'll need to add two new variables: one (`PRICE`) to store the price of each cup of coffee, and one (`totalSales`) to store the total amount of money collected. You'll want to make `totalSales` a `double`: first, so it can hold dollars and cents (represented as decimal numbers), and second, to make sure it is large enough to hold all the money you expect your JavaMatic to earn. (Remember from Chapter 4 that `doubles` can hold up to 15 significant digits. When your JavaMatic's sales start approaching this, be sure to remember where you started.)

The variable `PRICE` is declared outside the `main()` method. Remember that variables declared outside methods really belong to the whole class and are called fields. `PRICE` is declared as `static final` because it is a constant. Recall that constants are values that will not change during the life of your program. Using a `static final` field, rather than just using the literal `0.25` throughout your program, will make it easier for you to maintain your code if you decide to raise all the prices to $0.50! Rather than changing the price in several places, you'll have to make only one change.

To make the JavaMatic_2D handle more than a single customer, all you need do is duplicate the actions that the JavaMatic_2C performed when a customer selected a beverage. The new program behaves differently:

☕ Three customers can use the machine without restarting it.

☕ The JavaMatic_2D can keep track of how much money has been collected.

☕ When the third purchase has been made, the JavaMatic_2D gives you an accounting. It's just the thing to satisfy the IRS and help you avoid standing around the machine with a paper and pencil, making check marks as folks buy beverages.

A STRANGE OCCURRENCE

The JavaMatic_2D allows you to "purchase" up to three beverages. But there is a catch. If you purchase all three at the same time, all is well. For example, you could enter 212 followed by [ENTER] to receive an Italian Espresso (product code 2), followed by a Brazilian Roast (product code 1), followed by another Italian Espresso.

Unfortunately, things don't work out so well if you try to enter your selections one at a time. Figure 6-4 shows how the JavaMatic_2D program looks when you run it and enter 1 (the product code for Brazilian Roast) followed by [ENTER]. Notice that the JavaMatic correctly dispenses your 8 oz. Brazilian Roast and displays a menu to help you order a second beverage. However, it appears that someone must have entered a second selection, and an invalid one at that. Worse yet, the other customer appears to have received neither a beverage nor change. What's going on?

The problem is that the program doesn't wait for your second selection, due to some rather odd behavior on the part of the `System.in` object. Input from `System.in.read()` is *buffered*, meaning that characters typed on the keyboard are not sent to your Java program until you press [ENTER]. This delay is actually quite a handy thing, because it allows you to use [BACKSPACE] to make corrections before committing to your selection by pressing [ENTER]. When you press [ENTER], your selection is irrevocably transmitted to the JavaMatic.

But there's yet another complication in store. Pressing [ENTER] not only sends whatever you've typed along to your program, it also sends additional character codes for the [ENTER] key itself (the newline character, which has the ASCII value 10). So, when the second menu is displayed and the program uses `System.in.read()` to ask for

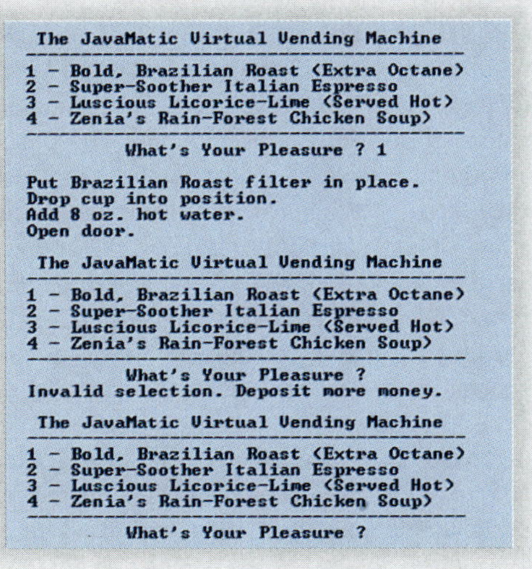

FIGURE 6-4

Running the JavaMatic_2D

❝ Remember that variables declared outside of methods really belong to the whole class and are called fields. ❞

another selection, it finds that it already has a character waiting in the buffer, the value for the ⌐ENTER⌐ key. Of course, this character is not a valid product code, so the program displays the error message, quite appropriately as it turns out; it seems there was no "second customer" at all.

What can you do to fix this behavior? An obvious attempt would be to send the flush() method to the System.in object, just as you used System.out.flush() to make sure the output buffer was sent to the screen. Unfortunately, the System.in object does not have a flush() method.

Until you learn a bit about loops, there's no good solution. This is something of an incentive to learn more about them, isn't it? For right now, you can simply add another System.in.read() to the getOrder() method. This will work if all your customers follow the rules, by entering product selections one at a time; the second System.in.read() will "eat" the unwanted ⌐ENTER⌐ key value waiting in the buffer. After you learn about loops, you'll find it simple to construct a much more robust solution. In the meantime, your modified getOrder() method should look like this:

```
// *********************************************************
//   method getOrder(): retrieve the user's selection
// *********************************************************
public char getOrder() throws Exception
{
    char ch = (char) System.in.read();
    System.in.read();
                    System.in.read();
    return ch;
}
```

Java and Iteration

While the JavaMatic_2D does solve the problem of totaling your sales without your having to plug in the machine each time you use it, it still lacks a little something from the flexibility standpoint. What you'd really like your machine to do is continue vending as long as there is still coffee in the machine. Suppose your machine holds 100 cups of coffee. Do you really want to write a main() method that consists of the same three lines of code repeated 100 times? What if you have some machines that can hold 100 cups of coffee and others that hold only 25? It seems wasteful (and it *is* wasteful) to simply repeat the same lines of code. Surely the computer could do that for us better than we could do it manually. The answer to this conundrum? Loops.

The Java programming language not only lets you create loops, but also provides three different loop statements from which you can choose: the for statement, the while statement, and the do-while statement. Like the decisions you studied in Chapter 5, loops are based on the idea of performing a Boolean test and then executing a block of code if the result of the test is true. The difference between writing a loop and writing a decision statement is that, in a loop, the block of code will be executed again and again—until the Boolean test comes up false.

DIFFERENT LOOPS

Why are there three kinds of loops? One difference between the various loops is *when* the test condition takes place. The `for` loop and the `while` loop are both entry-condition loops. In other words, they test the loop condition before they execute a block of code (which is called the *loop body*). This type of loop is also called a test-at-the-top loop. The other loop offered in Java, the `do-while`, performs its test at the bottom. As a result, a `do-while` loop will always execute the programming statements in the loop body at least one time. A `for` loop or a `while` loop might not execute the statements at all—provided the condition was initially `false`.

DIFFERENT USES

Each of these types of loops can be used in several ways. Some loops are used to do something a certain number of times. These are called *counting* loops. Other loops, called *indeterminate* or *testing* loops, don't have a fixed number of repetitions, but rely on a conditional test to decide whether to repeat a set of statements. One common example of a testing loop is reading all the lines of a file. When you start reading the file, you have no idea how many lines it contains, so you can't use a counting loop. You have to keep reading until you reach the end of the file. Indeterminate loops are very similar to the way most of us treat our checking accounts: We keep spending the money until it is gone. Finally, a special type of loop called an *event* loop is used for embedded systems such as missiles and automobiles, and in graphical user interfaces, such as the Abstract Window Toolkit, which you will learn about in Chapter 11, "Jumpin' Java: Menus, Graphics, Sound." This type of loop is sometimes called an *endless* loop, because it continues to repeat as long as the program is running.

THE SOLUTION IS: THE COUNTING LOOP

What you want for the JavaMatic is to take your repeating statements and wrap them up inside some type of controlling statements that tell the computer to execute the statements a certain number of times. Something like this would be nice:

```
while there are still some cups of coffee left in the machine,
do the following:
    myMachine.drawMenu();
    userChoice = myMachine.getOrder();
    myMachine.dispenseBeverage( userChoice );
end of looping section
```

This is exactly the type of control that loops give you. In computer science terms, these statements, along with the decision statements of Chapter 5, are called *flow of control* statements, because they control the order in which other statements are executed. Let's look at how you can use loops to control the JavaMatic.

Using the for Loop

The first type of loop provided by the Java language is called the `for` loop. The `for` is the Swiss Army knife among loops, because it contains a variety of useful features. Figure 6-5 shows the syntax of the `for` loop, along with a graphical illustration. The `for` loop has three parts:

- The keyword `for`, which, like other Java keywords, must be in lowercase
- A test condition
- A body, which consists of a simple statement or a block of statements enclosed by braces (that is, a compound statement)

The `for`'s test condition itself has three distinct components, each an expression. These expressions work together to control the loop. These three expressions are usually called

- The *initialization* expression
- The *test* expression
- The *update* expression

Each of these expressions is separated from its neighbor by a semicolon. You can leave out any expression you like—or even all of them—but you still need to put in the semicolons, which act as placeholders for the omitted expressions.

The `for` loop works almost exactly like the `if` statement. The big difference is what happens when all the statements in the loop body have run their course. Rather than continuing on with the next statement—as the `if` does—the `for` loop jumps back to the test condition and evaluates it again. If the expression is still `true`, the statements in the loop body start executing again. In fact, unless something happens to make the expression `false`, the loop will run the body over again forever. Figure 6-6 illustrates the difference between the `if` statement and the `for` loop.

In evaluating the expressions within its test condition, the `for` first evaluates the initialization expression. The initialization expression is usually an assignment expression used to set initial values of a loop variable (or variables). Next, the `for` evaluates the test expression. If the test expression is `false`, the `for` passes control to the following statement; otherwise, the `for` executes its body. Following execution of the body, the `for` evaluates its increment expression. Like the initialization expression, the increment expression is usually an assignment expression modifying the loop variable. After evaluating the increment expression, the `for` again evaluates the test expression and conditionally executes its body. Figure 6-7 illustrates the operation of the `for` loop.

Listing 6-5 shows how the `for` can be used to build a JavaMatic that dispenses 100 servings. The three actions that JavaMatic must perform—drawing a menu, getting the user's selection, and dispensing the proper beverage—have been grouped between braces as a compound statement that forms the body of a `for` loop. The loop itself uses

SINGLE STATEMENT BODY

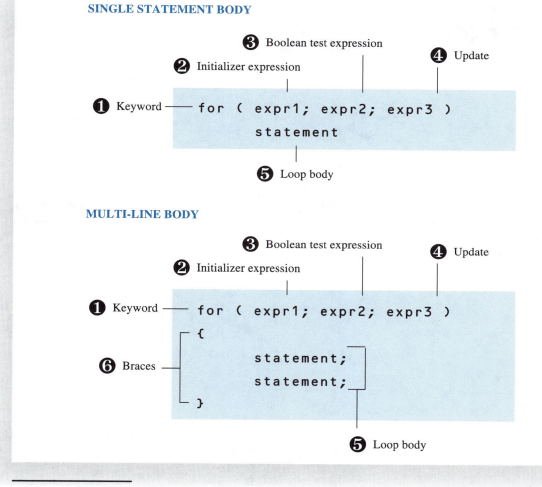

MULTI-LINE BODY

FIGURE 6-5

Syntax of the for loop

the `int` variable i to control its operation; such a variable is called a *loop variable* or *counter*. Loop variables are traditionally given names that consist of a single letter, the letters *i–n* being the ones most often pressed into such service.

The `for` initializes i to 0 and tests to make sure that the resulting value of i is less than 3. (Starting at 0 is a common programmer's way of counting that makes working with arrays easier, as you'll see in Chapter 8. Here, things would have worked just as well if i had been initialized to 1 and tested to make sure it was less than or equal to 3.) The value 3 is used because it takes less time to test a JavaMatic that can dispense

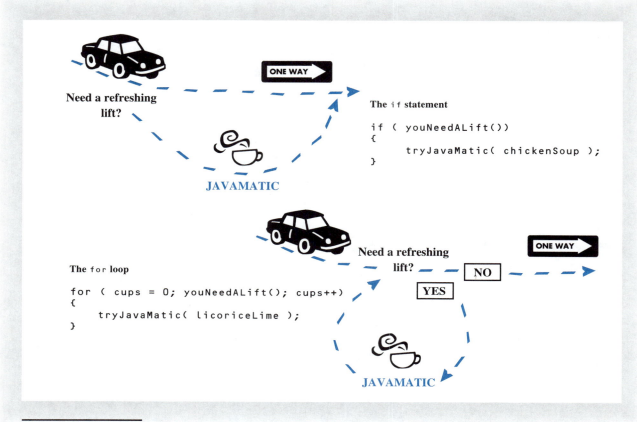

FIGURE 6-6

The **for** *loop versus the* **if** *statement*

three cups than one that can dispense 100 cups. After you're satisfied that it handles three cups properly, it's simple to change the program to provide full 100-cup service.

Listing 6-5 JavaMatic_2E.java (partial)

```java
// The JavaMatic Virtual Vending Machine - Version 2E
// Works 100 times, and adds up total sales
import java.io.*;

public class JavaMatic_2E
{
    // This is the constant price for all beverages
    static final double PRICE = 0.25;

    // The application starts executing the main() method
    public static void main(String args[]) throws Exception
    {
        // Create a variable to hold the customer's selection
        char userChoice;
```

FIGURE 6-7
Looking at the `for` loop

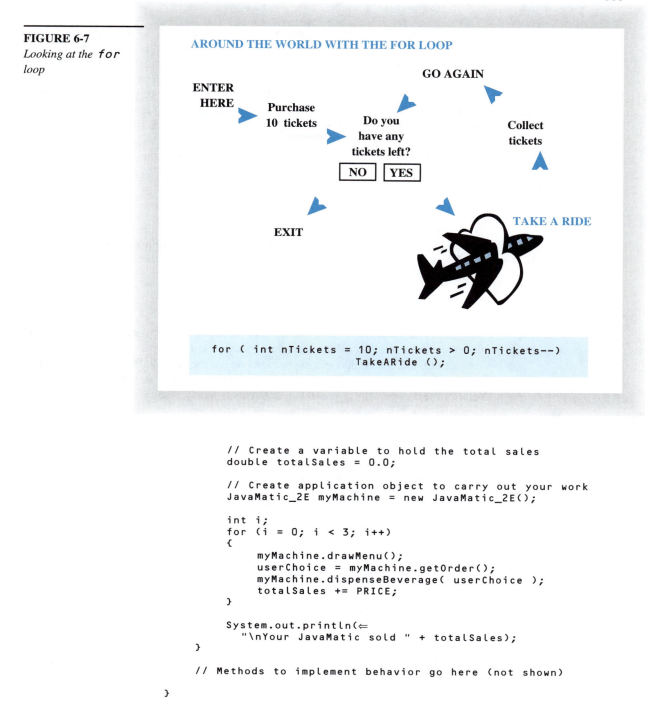

```
for ( int nTickets = 10; nTickets > 0; nTickets--)
              TakeARide ();
```

```
    // Create a variable to hold the total sales
    double totalSales = 0.0;

    // Create application object to carry out your work
    JavaMatic_2E myMachine = new JavaMatic_2E();

    int i;
    for (i = 0; i < 3; i++)
    {
        myMachine.drawMenu();
        userChoice = myMachine.getOrder();
        myMachine.dispenseBeverage( userChoice );
        totalSales += PRICE;
    }

    System.out.println(⇐
      "\nYour JavaMatic sold " + totalSales);
}

// Methods to implement behavior go here (not shown)

}
```

The first time the loop is executed, the value of i (which is 0) will certainly be less than 3, so the loop body will be executed. The program will draw the menu, get a product code, and dispense a beverage. After executing the loop body, the `for` will evaluate its increment expression (i++), which increments the value of i. So long as the resulting value of i continues to be less than 3, the body of the loop will again be executed. At some point, however, i will reach the value *3*. On this iteration, the test expression will evaluate to `false`, and the loop body will not be executed. Instead, `System.out.println()` will be used to display the total sales and the program will end. Figure 6-8 shows the middle and ending of a full run of the JavaMatic, serving all three cups in its inventory.

VARIATIONS ON THE for

Don't let the name of the third component of the `for`'s test condition (the increment expression) fool you: A `for` can count down as easily as it counts up. The loop

```
in i;
for (i = 3; i > 0; i--)
{
    // loop body statements
}
```

would execute three times, just like the loop in the JavaMatic—except, of course, that the value of i would decrease, rather than increase, as the loop executed.

As mentioned, the component expressions within the test condition of the `for` are all optional; however, the two semicolons must always appear as placeholders, whether each of the components is present or not. This is handy when you want to do some of

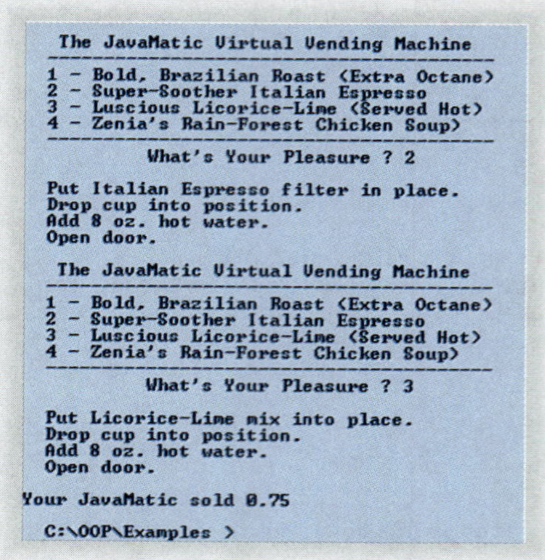

FIGURE 6-8

Running the JavaMatic_2E

```
The JavaMatic Virtual Vending Machine
----------------------------------------
1 - Bold, Brazilian Roast (Extra Octane)
2 - Super-Soother Italian Espresso
3 - Luscious Licorice-Lime (Served Hot)
4 - Zenia's Rain-Forest Chicken Soup)
----------------------------------------
        What's Your Pleasure ? 2

Put Italian Espresso filter in place.
Drop cup into position.
Add 8 oz. hot water.
Open door.

The JavaMatic Virtual Vending Machine
----------------------------------------
1 - Bold, Brazilian Roast (Extra Octane)
2 - Super-Soother Italian Espresso
3 - Luscious Licorice-Lime (Served Hot)
4 - Zenia's Rain-Forest Chicken Soup)
----------------------------------------
        What's Your Pleasure ? 3

Put Licorice-Lime mix into place.
Drop cup into position.
Add 8 oz. hot water.
Open door.
Your JavaMatic sold 0.75

C:\OOP\Examples >
```

the work of the `for` as part of other program statements. For example, the work of incrementing the loop variable could be done inside the body of the `for`:

```
int j;
for (j = 0; j < 3;)
{
    // loop body statements
    j++;
}
```

A `for` can also initialize or increment several variables. This is done by including several initialization or increment expressions, separated by commas:

```
for (i = 0, j = 0; (i+j) < 3; i++, j++)
```

This `for` initializes and increments both i and j, testing to make sure their sum is less than 3 on each iteration.

Another handy property of the `for` is that, as mentioned, it's a test-at-the-top loop. The following `for` will not execute its loop body at all, because the test expression is initially `false`:

```
int k;
for (k = 3; k < 3; k++)
```

Use of a `for` with a loop variable is so common that a special form of the `for` permits including the definition of the loop variable *within* the initialization expression:

```
for (int nServings = 1; nServings <= 3; n++)
{
    // body of loop goes here
}
```

When this special form is used, the definition of the loop variable is local to the loop— that is, the loop variable is known only inside the loop. When the loop variable is used elsewhere in the method, you must use the ordinary form.

Counting Loops with `while`

Once you've mastered the `for` loop, you'll find it easy to understand the `while` and `do-while` loops, because each of them does just a part of the larger job tackled by the `for`. The `while` and `do-while` "major" in testing, leaving the initialization and increment duties to other program statements.

WHISTLE `while` YOU WORK

Let's add a `while` loop to control a new version of the JavaMatic—the JavaMatic_2F. To get started, again copy your previous program—in this case JavaMatic_2E.java—to create the new file, using the same procedure you used to make JavaMatic_2E. Make the changes from Listing 6-6 to your main method. For this example, rather than assuming the JavaMatic can hold 100 cups of coffee, try using two or three, so that

" The for is the Swiss Army knife among loops: It contains a variety of useful features. "

you won't have to order 100 cups of Brazilian Roast to test whether your loop is working correctly. This value, stored in the `static final` member field `MAX_CUPS`, will be used as the value to test your counter.

Listing 6-6 JavaMatic_2F.java (partial)

```java
// The JavaMatic Virtual Vending Machine - Version 2F
// Now works until it's out of coffee
// Illustrates writing a counted loop using while
import java.io.*;

public class JavaMatic_2F
{
    static final double PRICE = 0.25;      // Constant price
for all
    static final int MAX_CUPS = 3;         // Set this to 3 to
test

    // The application starts executing the main() method
    public static void main(String args[]) throws Exception
    {
        // Create a JavaMatic_2F object to carry out your
        //work
        JavaMatic_2F myMachine = new JavaMatic_2F();

        // Local variables
        char userChoice;                   // User's selection
        double totalSales = 0.0;           // Is this big enough?

        int nServings = 0;                 // Nothing sold yet
        while ( nServings < MAX_CUPS )
        {
            myMachine.drawMenu();
            userChoice = myMachine.getOrder();
            myMachine.dispenseBeverage( userChoice );

            totalSales += PRICE;
            System.out.println(⇐
                "\nThis JavaMatic has earned " + totalSales);

            nServings++;
        }
    }

    // Methods to implement behavior go here (not shown)

}
```

When you compile and run the new, enhanced version of the JavaMatic, you'll see that you can now iteratively buy Zenia's Chicken Soup and Luscious Licorice-Lime until the expression

```java
( nServings < MAX_CUPS )
```

evaluates to `false`. Figure 6-9 shows the JavaMatic_2F in action, and as you can see, it nicely totals your sales.

FIGURE 6-9

The JavaMatic_2F totaling sales

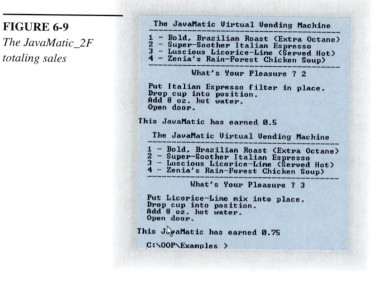

```
   The JavaMatic Virtual Vending Machine
-----------------------------------------------
1 - Bold, Brazilian Roast (Extra Octane)
2 - Super-Soother Italian Espresso
3 - Luscious Licorice-Line (Served Hot)
4 - Zenia's Rain-Forest Chicken Soup)
-----------------------------------------------
        What's Your Pleasure ? 2

Put Italian Espresso filter in place.
Drop cup into position.
Add 8 oz. hot water.
Open door.

This JavaMatic has earned 0.5
   The JavaMatic Virtual Vending Machine
-----------------------------------------------
1 - Bold, Brazilian Roast (Extra Octane)
2 - Super-Soother Italian Espresso
3 - Luscious Licorice-Line (Served Hot)
4 - Zenia's Rain-Forest Chicken Soup)
-----------------------------------------------
        What's Your Pleasure ? 3

Put Licorice-Line mix into place.
Drop cup into position.
Add 8 oz. hot water.
Open door.

This JavaMatic has earned 0.75

C:\OOP\Examples >
```

BROWSING A while

How does the while loop work? Figure 6-10 illustrates the syntax of a while loop. There are three parts you need to learn. The first part of a while loop is, surprise, the keyword while. Like all Java keywords, while needs to be spelled correctly and must be in lowercase.

The second part of the while loop is what is called the test expression. This is a boolean expression—one that has a true or false value when evaluated—and, like the test condition of an if or a for statement, the expression must be enclosed in parentheses.

The final part of the while loop is the loop body. The body of the loop is the statement (or statements) that will run if the condition part of the while statement is true.

WHEN DOES A LOOP EXIT?

As you can see, writing counted loops by use of a while is not too difficult. There are really only three main things you must always remember:

☕ Initialize your counter.

☕ Update your counter.

☕ Know when your loop will exit.

The for handles these tasks for you. Each of the component expressions of its test condition has responsibility for one of the tasks. When you use a while (or the do-while loop, which you'll soon meet) you have to make sure that you have provided for initialization, update (that is, increment), and exit of the loop.

FIGURE 6-10

The syntax of the
while loop

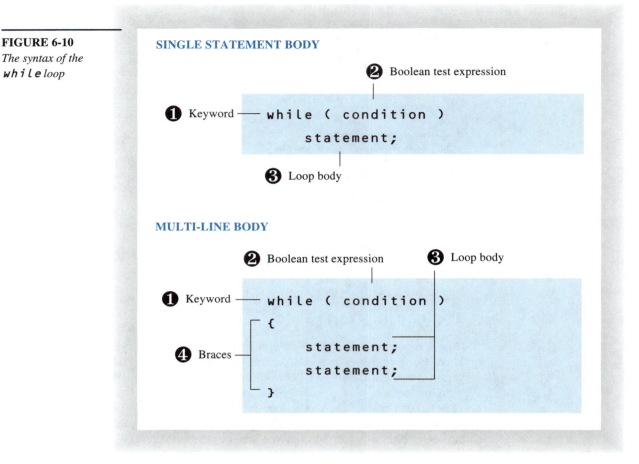

Initializing Your Counter

When you write a while loop that uses a counter, you need to make sure that you give the counter a value *before* you start the loop. This is less of a problem with Java than with some other programming languages. The Java compiler will warn you when you have a counter variable that has never been initialized. Still, a very common mistake is to reuse a counter variable that has already counted down. To avoid this problem, you should make it a habit to initialize your counter immediately before you enter the loop.

```
totalWidgets = 100;                  // initialize counters
for loops
while (totalWidgets > 0)
{

    doSomeStuffWithWidgets();        // do whatever Widgets do
```

```
        totalWidgets--;                           // update your counter
    }
```

Remember

> **Make sure you always initialize your loop counter. Put the initialization as close to the beginning of the loop as possible.**

Updating Your Counter

The Widget example illustrates the second thing you need to remember for your `while` loops to work correctly: You must do something inside the loop body that changes the value of the loop counter variable. If you fail to do this, the loop will just keep executing forever. Such an "endless" or "dead" loop is one of the most common programming errors. Furthermore, the Java compiler can't tell you when you've made this type of mistake. Forgetting to change the loop condition is not a *syntax* mistake, that is, a mistake in adhering to the grammar of the Java language. Instead, this type of error is a *logic* or semantic error. Your program will compile correctly; it simply won't do what it should. Specifically, it won't stop, so you will need to terminate it with the operating system (by pressing CTRL-C in an MS-DOS window, for example).

Another similar type of error is to make the wrong kind of change to the loop counter. The Widget loop, shown earlier, counts down instead of counting up like the JavaMatic_2F did. If you write your program to do this, just make sure your counter is counting in the right direction. If you changed the counter update in the Widget loop to `totalWidgets++`, the result would not be what you wanted.

Remember

> **Make sure that the counter variable in a counted loop is changed by the action of the loop. If the counter never changes, you have an endless loop.**

Knowing When Your Loop Will Exit

There is one last thing you need to understand if you want to avoid having big problems with your `while` loops. You have to know *when* a loop exits. Unfortunately, this is really easy to misunderstand. Consider the following code:

```
int cups = 0;
while (cups < 10)
{
    cups++;
    System.out.println(cups + " cups sold");
}
```

What do you expect to see printed? Because the test expression is `(cups < 10)`, many programmers say the numbers *1* through *9*. They expect that when `cups == 10`, as it does after the line `cups++` is executed, the test expression will be `false` and the loop will exit. Experienced programmers realize that they will see the numbers 1 through 10 instead.

Why the difference? Consider what happens when the value of cups is 9 and the loop is just beginning. Because the expression (cups < 10) is true, the body of the loop is entered. Next, the cups variable is incremented (cups++) and takes on the value 10. The condition is tested *before* the loop variable is incremented. If the loop test expression were *continuously evaluated*, the test expression, (cups < 10), would be false, and the last output statement would never appear. But that is not what happens. A loop does not exit when its condition *becomes* false, but when the condition is *tested* and found false.

Remember

> **The test expression of the while loop is not continually evaluated, but is examined only at the beginning of each repetition.**

What's New at the Dispensary?

WHATEVER POSSESSED ME...

"Whatever possessed me to start this JavaMatic thing?" groused Jumbo peevishly.

"That's the third customer today who's complained that my machine eats their money. I could give away the stuff free for all the trouble it's giving me."

Brenda, always sensitive to any indication that her program wasn't perfect, perked up her ears. "What's eating money?" she demanded.

"Guess," replied Jumbo, stubbornly. "Why don't you take your JavaMatic and try selecting item 5, and then see what happens?"

"But there are only 4 items on the menu," answered Brenda, frustrated. "Why would anyone put in a 5?"

If you haven't discovered it yet, it's high time you learned that the users of your program won't always do exactly what you expect. Part of the skill of writing programs is learning to anticipate things that can go wrong. Go ahead and try a little experiment with the JavaMatic_2F. Enter a 5 instead of one of the numbers 1 through 4. What happens? While the JavaMatic doesn't spill Luscious Licorice-Lime all over the floor, it does make one tiny little mistake. It takes your customer's money and doesn't deliver a beverage. This is probably not what you want to do—at least if you want to stay in business for any length of time. The JavaMatic_2G, shown in Listing 6-7, fixes this problem. It's worth a look to see how it works.

Listing 6-7 JavaMatic_2G.java

```
// The JavaMatic Virtual Vending Machine - Version 2G
// Money updated only when sold
//
```

```java
import java.io.*;

public class JavaMatic_2G
{
    static final double PRICE = 0.25;      // Constant price
    static final int MAX_CUPS = 3;         // Set this to 3
int nServings              = 0;        // No cups sold
double totalSales          = 0.0;

    // The application starts executing the main() method
    public static void main(String args[]) throws Exception
    {
        // Create a JavaMatic_2G object to carry out your
        // work
        JavaMatic_2G myMachine = new JavaMatic_2G();

        // Local variables
        char userChoice;                    // User's selection

        myMachine.nServings = MAX_CUPS;
        while ( myMachine.nServings > 0 )
        {
            myMachine.drawMenu();
            userChoice = myMachine.getOrder();
            myMachine.dispenseBeverage( userChoice );

            System.out.println(""); Servings Left
            System.out.println(⇐
              "    Total Servings = " + myMachine.nServings);
            System.out.println(⇐
              "    Total Sales    = " + myMachine.totalSales);
        }
    }

    // Methods to implement object behavior
    // ********************************************************
    //   method drawMenu(): display the JavaMatic offerings
    // ********************************************************
    public void drawMenu()
    {
        System.out.println();
        System.out.println(⇐
          "     The JavaMatic Virtual Vending Machine ");
        System.out.println(⇐
          "     -------------------------------------");
        System.out.println(⇐
          "    1 - Bold, Brazilian Roast (Extra Octane)");
        System.out.println(⇐
          "    2 - Super-Soother Italian Espresso      ");
        System.out.println(⇐
          "    3 - Luscious Licorice-Lime (Served Hot) ");
        System.out.println(⇐
          "    4 - Zenia's Rain-Forest Chicken Soup)   ");
```

continued on next page

continued from previous page

```
        System.out.println(⇐
            "  -------------------------------------");
        System.out.print(⇐
            "                What's Your Pleasure ? ");
        System.out.flush();
    }

    // ***********************************************************
    //   method getOrder(): retrieve the user's selection
    // ***********************************************************
    public char getOrder() throws Exception
    {
        char ch = (char) System.in.read();
        System.in.read();
        System.in.read();
        return ch;
    }

    // ***********************************************************
    //   method dispenseBeverage(): dispense chosen drink
    // ***********************************************************
    public void dispenseBeverage( char choice )
    {
        System.out.println("");
        switch ( choice )
        {
            case '1':
                System.out.println(⇐"
                    Put Brazilian Roast filter in place.");
                break;
            case '2':
                System.out.println(⇐
                    "  Put Italian Espresso filter in⇐
                    place.");
                break;
            case '3':
                System.out.println(⇐
                    "  Put Licorice-Lime mix into place.");
                break;
            case '4':
                System.out.println(⇐
                    "  Put Chicken-Soup mix into place");
                break;
            default:
                System.out.println(⇐
                    "  Invalid selection. Here's your⇐
                    money.");
                return;
        }
        System.out.println("  Drop cup into position.");
        System.out.println("  Add 8 oz. hot water.");
        System.out.println("  Open door.");

        // Sales now totalled here
        totalSales += PRICE;
        nServings--;
    }
}
```

FIELDING SOME DATA

As before, to build the JavaMatic_2G, the place to start is by making a copy of the file JavaMatic_2F.java, and renaming the copy to JavaMatic_2G.java. You'll then need to rename all occurrences of the word JavaMatic_2F to JavaMatic_2G throughout the new file.

Having done that, you need to make several more changes to rein in the errant JavaMatic. Start by noticing that the variables `totalSales` and `nServings` have been changed from local variables to fields. There are two reasons for this. One reason is purely practical. Previously, the number of servings and the total sales were updated inside the `main()` method, so they would be updated whether or not the beverage was successfully dispensed—thus creating the very problem you are trying to solve. To fix that problem, you are going to have to move the updating of these variables into the `dispenseBeverage()` method, where the coffee is actually served. By adding the lines

```
totalSales += PRICE;
nServings--;
```

to the very end of `dispenseBeverage()`, you ensure that only servings and sales that actually occur are counted.

Strictly Static

But you also are going to have to refer to the variables inside the `main()` method where `nServings` is used to control the loop, and `totalSales` is used to print the machine status. Only by making a variable a field can you ensure that it is visible in both the methods. There is one interesting side effect from doing this. Notice that you now have to refer to `nServings` as `myMachine.nServings` when you use it in the `main()` method. But inside `dispenseBeverage()` it is just called `nServings`. Why the difference? Remember the keyword `static` in the header of the `main()` method? Making `main()` static allows Java to execute `main()` even when no `JavaMatic_2G` objects yet exist, because a `static` method is associated with a class, rather than with an instance (object) of the class. However, *non*`static` methods and fields *are* related to objects. So, the fields `nServings` and `totalSales` exist only when an object exists; and when multiple objects exist, there are multiple values of `nServings` and `totalSales`, one set for each object. To refer to `nServings` in `main()`, you must explicitly specify which `nServings` you mean by prefixing it with the object's name. Specifying the object to which a field belongs is called *qualification*, and the "dot" used to separate the name of the object from the name of the field is called the *dot operator*. This same name, `dot` operator, is used to refer to the dot included when sending a message to a given object: the dot separates the name of the object from the name of the method.

Because the `dispenseBeverage()` method is not a static method like `main()`, it must be invoked by use of an object and the `dot` operator, as in the call

```
myMachine.dispenseBeverage( userChoice );
```

When `dispenseBeverage()` is invoked, it will always have a default object, referred to as `this`, which will be the object specified in the invocation of the method.

You might be wondering though, "When I'm designing my own classes, when should I use a `static` method, and when should I use a regular class method?" That's a good—and very profound—question. Fortunately, there's a short answer that provides a good rule of thumb:

Use a `static` method when the method does not read or change the state of the object—in other words, when it doesn't refer to an object's fields. In the JavaMatic example, you could make `drawMenu()` a `static` method, because it currently doesn't use any of an object's fields. Likewise, the `getOrder()` method could be written as a `static` method.

Otherwise, you should use a `nonstatic` method.

Storing State

The second reason that `totalSales` and `nServings` were made into field variables is really more conceptual. Fields should be used to store the state of an individual object. If you were to create 10 JavaMatic machines, at any one time, each of them would probably have sold a different number of beverages. Part of the state of each machine would be how many servings that particular machine had sold. Thus, `nServings` should be a field, and not a local variable. Contrast that with the local variable `userChoice`. Does `userChoice` store some information about what state your machine is in? No, not really. The `userChoice` variable is only used to store a temporary value while the user makes a purchase. Thus, `userChoice` should probably be a local variable. Recall that local variables have a limited lifetime: They exist only for the duration of a method. When the method is finished, the local variable goes away. Fields, by contrast, exist and hold their value for as long as the object exists.

The Fix Is In

Notice the change to the `dispenseBeverage()` method. The default case now contains a `return` statement that prevents an invalid product selection from causing a beverage to be dispensed. The `return` also prevents the updating of `totalSales` with the price of the invalid selection.

MAX_CUPS **AND THE LOOP**

Given the preceding, why isn't it necessary to refer to the variable `MAX_CUPS` by an object name? Like the method `main()`, `MAX_CUPS` is declared `static`. Any field or variable that is declared `static` can be used anywhere inside your class without any qualification.

Before you leave the JavaMatic_2G, take a look at this code fragment:

```
myMachine.nServings = MAX_CUPS;
while ( myMachine.nServings > 0 ) {
    // . . . loop body
}
```

Just as `fors` can count either up or down, so can `while` loops. Previously the counter `nServings` was initialized to 0 and then compared against `MAX_CUPS`. In this code fragment, it is initialized to `MAX_CUPS`, and then counted down until it reaches zero.

Using while to Build Testing Loops

MORE PROBLEMS WITH THE JAVAMATIC

"Good heavens! What's the problem now? Your customers are all happy. When they get a hankering for chicken soup, by golly, the JavaMatic gives them chicken soup!"

Brenda stood toe to toe with Jumbo, and she was really on a roll. That incident with the misplaced `break` was behind her, and her virtual vendor was humming away like the fine-tuned machine that it is.

"You're even keeping track of everything you sell for the IRS. What could go wrong?" she demanded.

"Well..." equivocated Jumbo, anxious to deflect some of her ire. "It's that accountant. You know he looks at things a little differently. He says that if we keep running the JavaMatic the way it's going, I'll be out of business in no time. I think it's all the fault of that counting loop."

"Loop, shmoop," muttered Brenda under her breath.

Adding loops to the JavaMatic was a big step forward, but it also brought some problems of its own. The machine you've designed, based on the use of a counting loop, continues to dispense refreshment to tired customers until `MAX_CUPS` has been dispensed. The problem is, you don't know exactly *what* your customers will purchase. All of them *might* decide to purchase Brazilian Roast, or Italian Espresso, or even Luscious Licorice-Lime. You don't know. Of course, if everyone purchases the Brazilian Roast, you'll run out long before you reach `MAX_CUPS` of Java. To avoid dealing with a mob of angry customers, you could stock your JavaMatic with four times as much inventory as you could possibly sell—not a formula for a profitable business. What you really need is the second kind of loop, a *testing* (that is, indeterminate) loop.

There's nothing to do but to roll up your sleeves and go back to the drawing board. Besides, because all programmers are optimists, you can clearly see the great opportunities that lie ahead for the next generation: the JavaMatic_2H. Maybe you can call it the Mark VI. But first you need to try out some of your ideas and build a few prototypes.

JAVAMATIC: THE NEXT GENERATION

To make the JavaMatic track inventories of individual items, you have three problems to solve:

☕ You need to keep track of how much of each beverage each machine holds.

☕ You have to monitor the inventory levels as part of your loop test, rather than just watch a counter variable.

☕ You need to make sure that the inventory is correctly managed. You don't want to dispense any empty cups, and you don't want machines that shut down when you run out of chicken soup, for instance.

Let's build a model program that will address each of these three problems.

The State of the Machine Revisited

How should you store the inventory levels of coffee, espresso, and soup? You could try to use local variables to store this kind of information, but you really need to store information about your machine. This type of information is part of an object's state, and an object's state should be stored as fields. So, you need to create fields to keep track of the amount of each individual beverage mix. (Thankfully, you can buy these as premeasured servings, rather than as raw ingredients.)

Look at the definition of the JavaMatic_2H in Listing 6-8. There are four fields defined to keep track of the number of each item served. These are called `nBrazilian`, `nItalian`, `nLicorice`, and `nChicken`. Putting an *n* in front of a variable name is a common programming shorthand for "number of something." In this case you are using it to stand for "number of Brazilian Roasts," "number of Italian Espressos," and so on.

In addition to the inventory amounts of each item, you'll also need fields to store the price you'll charge for each item. These fields are given the same name as the inventory fields, with the exception that they start with *p* (for price), rather than *n*. That helps you to avoid charging the wrong price when updating a particular inventory item. Also notice that every item is given an initial stock level. That way, when the machine is turned on, it starts out fully stocked.

Take some time to compile and run the JavaMatic_2H. The program starts with an inventory of 10 cups of each beverage. Notice, as you run the program, that once you have ordered 10 cups of Italian Espresso, for instance, it will not give you any more.

It's still more than willing to fill your cup with Luscious Licorice-Lime, however, just as it should. You might also want to try out the loop by ordering 10 of each item. When you order the next item, the loop will end. (You can always end the loop—and the program—at any time by pressing ⌷CTRL⌷-⌷C⌷.) Figure 6-11 shows how the JavaMatic_2H looks in action. When you're done with your virtual coffee break, come back here and get ready to look at the JavaMatic_2H in depth.

Listing 6-8 JavaMatic_2H.java

```java
//The JavaMatic Virtual Vending Machine - Version 2H
// An indeterminate loop to manage inventory and pricing
//
import java.io.*;

public class JavaMatic_2H
{
    // Attributes
    int nServings              = 0;        // No cups sold
    double totalSales       = 0.0;
    int    nBrazilian = 10, nItalian = 10, nLicorice = 10,⇐
           nChicken = 10;
    double pBrazilian =.25, pItalian =.55, pLicorice =.45,⇐
           pChicken =.75;

    // The application starts executing the main() method
    public static void main(String args[]) throws Exception
    {
        // Create a JavaMatic_2H object to carry out your
        // work
        JavaMatic_2H myMachine = new JavaMatic_2H();

        // Local variables
        char userChoice;                // User's selection

        while ( myMachine.nBrazilian > 0 ||⇐
                myMachine.nItalian > 0 ||
                myMachine.nLicorice  > 0 ||⇐
                myMachine.nChicken > 0 )
        {
            myMachine.drawMenu();
            userChoice = myMachine.getOrder();
            myMachine.dispenseBeverage( userChoice );

            System.out.println("");
            System.out.println("  Total Servings = " +⇐
            myMachine.nServings);
            System.out.println("  Total Sales     = " +⇐
            myMachine.totalSales);
        }
    }

    // Methods to implement object behavior
    // ****************************************************
    //   method drawMenu(): display the JavaMatic offerings
    // ****************************************************
    public void drawMenu()
    {
```

continued on next page

continued from previous page

> *Part of the skill of writing programs is learning to anticipate things that can go wrong.*

```
            System.out.println();
            System.out.println(⇐
              "    The JavaMatic Virtual Vending Machine   ");
            System.out.println(⇐
              "    ----------------------------------------");
            System.out.println(⇐
              "   1 - Bold, Brazilian Roast         " +⇐
                pBrazilian );
            System.out.println(⇐
              "   2 - Italian Espresso              " + pItalian⇐
                );
            System.out.println(⇐
              "   3 - Luscious Licorice-Lime        " + pLicorice⇐
                );
            System.out.println(⇐
              "   4 - Zenia's Chicken Soup          " + pChicken⇐
                );
            System.out.println(⇐
              "    ----------------------------------------");
            System.out.print(⇐
              "                 What's Your Pleasure ? ");
            System.out.flush();
    }

    // ******************************************************
    //   method getOrder(): retrieve the user's selection
    // ******************************************************
    public char getOrder() throws Exception
    {
        char ch = (char) System.in.read();
        System.in.read();
        System.in.read();
        return ch;
    }

    // ******************************************************
    //   method dispenseBeverage(): dispense chosen drink
    // ******************************************************
    public void dispenseBeverage( char choice )
    {
        System.out.println("");
        switch ( choice )
        {
            case '1':
                if ( nBrazilian > 0 )
                {
                    nBrazilian--;
                    totalSales += pBrazilian;
                    System.out.println(⇐
                      "    Insert Brazilian Roast filter.");
                    break;
                }
                else
                {
                System.out.println(⇐
                  "   Out of stock. ⇐
                    Make another selection.");
                return;
                }
            case '2':
```

```
                                    if ( nItalian > 0 )
                                    {
                                        nItalian--;
                                        totalSales += pItalian;
                                        System.out.println(⇐
                                            "   Insert Italian Espresso filter.");
                                        break;
                                    }
                                    else
                                    {
                                    System.out.println(⇐
                                        "   Out of stock. ⇐
                                        Make another selection.");
                                    return;
                                    }
                            case '3':
                                    if ( nLicorice > 0 )
                                    {
                                        nLicorice--;
                                        totalSales += pLicorice;
                                        System.out.println(⇐
                                            "   Put Licorice-Lime mix in place.");
                                        break;
                                    }
                                    else
                                    {
                                    System.out.println(⇐
                                        "   Out of stock. ⇐
                                        Make another selection.");
                                    return;
                                    }
                            case '4':
                                    if ( nChicken > 0 )
                                    {
                                        nChicken--;
                                        totalSales += pChicken;
                                        System.out.println(⇐
                                            "   Put Chicken-Soup mix in place");
                                        break;
                                    }
                                    else
                                    {
                                    System.out.println(⇐
                                        "   Out of stock. ⇐
                                        Make another selection.");
                                    return;
                                    }
                            default:
                                    System.out.println(⇐
                                        "   Invalid selection. Here's your money");
                                    return;
                        }
                        System.out.println("   Drop cup into position.");
                        System.out.println("   Add 8 oz. hot water.");
                        System.out.println("   Open door.");

                        // Sales now totalled here
                        nServings++;
            }
    }
```

FIGURE 6-11

*Running the
JavaMatic_2H*

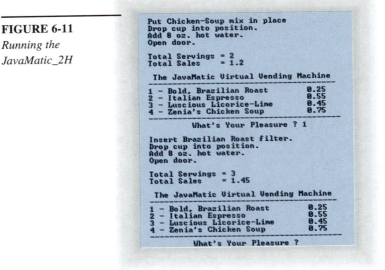

```
Put Chicken-Soup mix in place
Drop cup into position.
Add 8 oz. hot water.
Open door.

Total Servings = 2
Total Sales    = 1.2

The JavaMatic Virtual Vending Machine
-------------------------------------------
1 - Bold, Brazilian Roast          0.25
2 - Italian Espresso               0.55
3 - Luscious Licorice-Lime         0.45
4 - Zenia's Chicken Soup           0.75
-------------------------------------------
         What's Your Pleasure ? 1

Insert Brazilian Roast filter.
Drop cup into position.
Add 8 oz. hot water.
Open door.

Total Servings = 3
Total Sales    = 1.45

The JavaMatic Virtual Vending Machine
-------------------------------------------
1 - Bold, Brazilian Roast          0.25
2 - Italian Espresso               0.55
3 - Luscious Licorice-Lime         0.45
4 - Zenia's Chicken Soup           0.75
-------------------------------------------
         What's Your Pleasure ?
```

Improvements in the "Model H"

Probably the first thing you'll notice when running the new JavaMatic_2H, is that now your customers can see how much you are going to charge them for each item. Because chicken soup is everyone's favorite, you've decided to raise the price on it. In the previous version of the JavaMatic, you charged a fixed $0.25 per cup, which caused you to lose a few cents on every cup. Of course, you expected to make that up by increasing your volume, but somehow that didn't work out.

What did you need to do to add prices to your menu? First, you had to add the data members to store the price, which you did in the line

```
double pBrazilian =.25, pItalian =.55, pLicorice =.45,
pChicken =.75;
```

Now, when you change your prices, you have to change only this one line. The second thing you had to do was to add them to your menu. To do that, you had to concatenate each price to the end of the menu description inside the `drawMenu()` method by using the + operator like this:

```
System.out.println("  1 - Bold, Brazilian Roast        " +
pBrazilian );
```

What's Covered on the Test?

In addition to adding fields to track inventory and pricing, the JavaMatic_2H adds code to monitor those values, to make sure the loop will end. You want to make sure to "turn the machine off" when it's empty. The JavaMatic_2G stopped working when 100 beverages had been sold. You want the JavaMatic_2H to continue working until it is out of everything. In other words, you want to test a condition, rather than just executing the loop a fixed number of times.

Look carefully at the loop condition in Listing 6-8:

```
while ( myMachine.nBrazilian > 0 || myMachine.nItalian > 0 ||
        myMachine.nLicorice  > 0 || myMachine.nChicken > 0 )
{
    // . . . loop body goes here
}
```

This certainly looks a lot more complicated than the previous while loop, where you just made sure that you served 100 customers. What does that big expression inside the while condition mean? It means that the loop will continue while there is any Brazilian *or* Italian *or* licorice *or* chicken soup—that is, the JavaMatic_2H will continue to dispense its bounty to the world until it is out of every single beverage. When that happens—when the number of Brazilian Roasts remaining is 0 and the number of Italian Espressos remaining is 0 and the number of Chicken Soups remaining is 0, and so on—the loop will exit. The machine will be completely empty.

You might find a few things about this expression confusing at first. All of these expressions—nBrazilian > 0, and so on—are connected with ORs (||). "Shouldn't those be ANDs (&&)?" you wonder. "After all, when you talk about the condition in English, you use *AND*, not *OR*."

First, remember that while loops are entry-condition loops. When you write the code for a loop condition, you are specifying the conditions under which the loop will *continue*, not the conditions under which it will *exit*. The explanation in the previous paragraph specified the conditions under which the loop would *not* continue. As a programmer, though, you want to assure yourself that the loop will, indeed, end someday. You have enough experience at this point to know that a loop that never ends is a bad thing. So when analyzing the loop, it is natural to think about the condition that will cause it to finish: the "off" button, if you will. To recast the loop description in a positive manner, you could say that the loop will continue while there is Chicken Soup or Brazilian Roast or Italian Espresso, or even Luscious Licorice-Lime—that is, while any inventory at all exists.

Construction Assistance

Correctly writing the test condition is the most difficult part of constructing an indefinite loop, and requires the most thought from you, the programmer. The easiest way to understand a loop like this is to build up the test expression piece by piece, assuring yourself that the individual pieces work together. Start by just considering one case, the number of servings of Brazilian Roast remaining (nBrazilian). When your program starts, assume that you fill the machine with two servings of Brazilian Roast. When should your program stop? When nBrazilian is zero: that is, when the machine is empty. Put another way, you want to continue selling beverages while the machine is not empty. In code you would say

```
while ( nBrazilian > 0 )
{
    // Dispense some Brazilian Roast, decreasing nBrazilian
}
```

Once the operation of Brazilian Roast is clear in your mind, think about also selling Italian Espresso. Even though you may have sold all the Brazilian Roast, you don't want the machine to shut down. You want it to continue running until you are out of everything! You might start with this approach:

```
while ( nBrazilian > 0 && nItalian > 0)
{
    //Dispense some beverages, decreasing the appropriate field
}
```

If you walk through this example on paper—with a cup of java close at hand, of course—you'll see that it doesn't do exactly what you want. As long as both Brazilian Roast and Italian Espresso servings remain in the machine, it works fine. As soon as *either one* sells out, however, the machine shuts down. All of those Brazilian Roasts you could have sold are still sitting inside a machine that has stopped working. The correct "incantation" would be

```
while ( nBrazilian > 0 || nItalian > 0) {
    //Dispense some beverages, decreasing the appropriate field
}
```

If you have some difficulty with this, you may find Figure 6-12 helpful to work through the individual steps. It shows a hypothetical case with an inventory capacity of 2.

Dispensing the Brew

The final needed change to the JavaMatic is to make sure you correctly update the inventory of each item, and that you don't sell anything that is out of stock. You will again have to change your `dispenseBeverage()` method to handle this. You'll want to use a design that works something like this:

```
If the requested item is in stock
    Dispense the item
    Decrease the inventory items remaining
Else
    Politely suggest that the customer make another selection
End if
```

A good vending machine always invites the customer to purchase another item when something is out of stock. While some programmers might be tempted to insert an error message when the JavaMatic runs out of Licorice-Lime, that is not really the way to convince your customers to empty the machine, which is your goal, after all. For

FIGURE 6-12

Inventory levels and an indeterminate loop

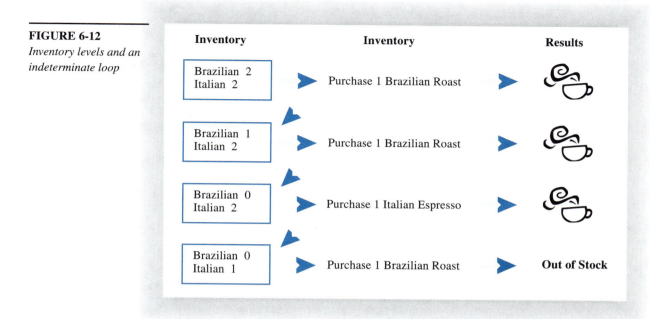

each of the different selection blocks in the `dispenseBeverage()` method, you will need to ask yourself how this affects the inventory. The code for the selection should end up looking like this:

```
switch ( choice )
{
    case '1':
        if ( nBrazilian > 0 )
        {
            nBrazilian--;
            totalSales += pBrazilian;
            System.out.println(⇐
              "  Insert Brazilian Roast filter.");
            break;
        }
        else
        {
            System.out.println(⇐
              "  Out of stock. Make another selection.");
            return;
        }
    case '2':

        // Rest of the cases will go here
}
```

More on Testing Loops

As you know, a testing loop is one that does not execute a predefined number of times. With a counting loop, you can tell by looking at the counter how many times the loop will execute. Telling when a testing loop will exit is not quite as easy. Because of this, testing loops are also called "indeterminate" or "indefinite" loops. Like a counting loop, the testing loop has both a body—the statements of code that will be repeated— and a test condition. In the counter loop, the test expression was a simple counter. There are two main types of testing loops: data loops and sentinel loops. These differ in the form of the test expression.

WHAT'S SO INDEFINITE?

Take a quick peek at this loop, and see if you can tell how many times it will execute:

```
someChar = getChar();
while ( someChar != 'Q' )
{
    System.out.println("You typed " + someCharacter);
    someChar = getChar();
}
```

This code uses the user-defined method `getChar()` to get input and then stores the result in a variable or field called `someChar`. The method `getChar()` could be reading from a file or the console. Notice that there are two assignments that use `getChar()` to store a value in `someChar`. Experienced Java programmers would be more likely to write the loop this way:

```
while ( ( someChar = getChar() ) != 'Q' )
{
    System.out.println("You typed " + someCharacter);
}
```

The second form behaves the same as the first. Each time the test expression is evaluated, the `getChar()` method is called. It returns a value that is stored in `someChar`. The value in `someChar` is then compared with the literal `'Q'`. Look closely at the parentheses surrounding the assignment in the second form. They make certain that the assignment to `someChar` will happen before any comparison to the character *Q*. As long as `someChar` does not have the value `'Q'`, the value of `someChar` is displayed. Although at first the second form is harder to read, it's more compact. You should use whichever form you're more comfortable with.

So, how may times will this loop execute? You really can't tell, can you? All you know is that it will stop executing when a particular value—the character *Q*—is found. This type of loop is called a *sentinel* loop, because it stops when it reaches a particular value: the sentinel. Another example of a sentinel loop would be searching a string for a particular character: a period or a space, perhaps.

Using a Sentinel Loop

A sentinel loop is just what you need to fix an annoying problem with the JavaMatic. As you might have noticed, the JavaMatic doesn't require a customer to put in exactly one selection at a time. The user can happily enter 123 before pressing ENTER. How does the JavaMatic respond? Not well. In response, it first dispenses a cup of Brazilian Roast—which is what you'd expect, because the input starts with 1. It then proceeds to "eat" the 2 the customer entered. Why? If you recall, the getOrder() method has a second call to System.in.read() that was designed to consume the extra character that got sent along because of pressing ENTER. But in the present case, because the customer has entered several characters instead of just one, the next character in the buffer is not the ENTER: it's the character 2, and getOrder() happily eats that instead. Finally, the next time through the main loop, System.in.read() still finds characters waiting for it—the 3 and the newline returned from pressing ENTER. The upshot is that your JavaMatic proceeds to dispense a cup of (hot!) Licorice-Lime all over your customer's hands while he or she is trying to retrieve the cup of Brazilian Roast.

What you'd really like to do—and what you can now do, using a sentinel loop—is to flush the input. Listing 6-9 shows a short test program that uses a method called getChar() and a method called flushInput() to make sure that getChar() always returns only a single character, no matter how many the user may enter. Figure 6-13 shows what happens when you exercise the GetChar program with various forms of input.

Listing 6-9 GetChar.java

```java
// GetChar.java
// Using a sentinel loop to flush the System.in buffer
//
import java.io.*;

public class GetChar
{
    // The application starts executing the main() method
    public static void main(String args[]) throws Exception
    {
        // Local variables
        char userEntry;                     // User's entry

        System.out.println("Enter characters. Enter a Q to
quit");
        while ( ( userEntry = getChar() ) != 'Q' )
        {
            System.out.println(⇐
                "User entered " + userEntry);
        }
    }

    // **********************************************************
    //   method getChar(): retrieve a single char
    // **********************************************************
```

continued on next page

continued from previous page

```
static public char getChar() throws Exception
{
    char ch = (char) System.in.read();
    flushInput();                    // This clears out
    return ch;
}

// *********************************************************
//  method flushInput: reads System.in until newline
// *********************************************************
static public void flushInput() throws Exception
{
    while ( (char) System.in.read() != '\n' )
        ; // do nothing
}

}
```

Some Sentinel Scrutiny

The GetChar program illustrates a few points that you have previously seen. The main loop is a sentinel loop that runs until the user enters the character *Q*. The method `getChar()` looks almost exactly like the `getOrder()` method in the JavaMatic, except that it uses the `flushInput()` method, rather than just issuing a single `System.in.read()`, as the JavaMatic's `getOrder()` method does. But how does `flushInput()` work?

The `flushInput()` method consists of a single sentinel loop. What is the sentinel in this case? It's the character value `'\n'`, the newline. This is the character that `System.in.read()` will return when the user presses ENTER. Because `System.in.read()` works only when the user sends data by pressing ENTER, all `flushInput()` need do is consume all of the characters up to, and including, this newline character.

Notice that the body of the sentinel loop consists of exactly nothing, and its end is marked by a semicolon. While the `null` statement is a valid Java statement, when you use one as the body of a loop (where all the actual action is in the loop condition), make sure that you clearly comment what you are doing so someone looking at your listing won't miss the semicolon or think it's a mistake. Also, while Java doesn't care,

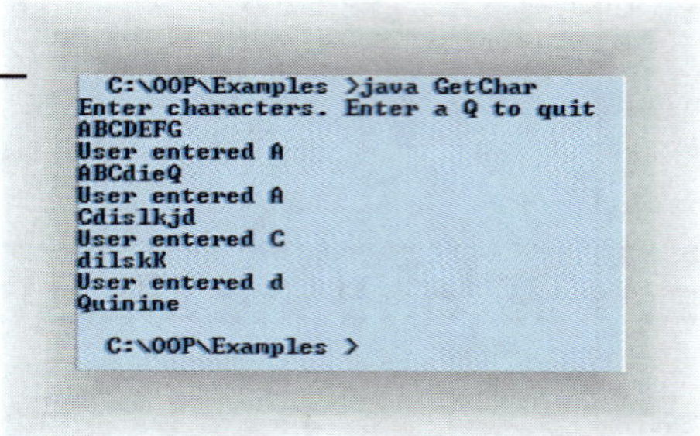

FIGURE 6-13

Running the GetChar application

```
C:\OOP\Examples >java GetChar
Enter characters. Enter a Q to quit
ABCDEFG
User entered A
ABCdieQ
User entered A
Cdislkjd
User entered C
dilskK
User entered d
Quinine

C:\OOP\Examples >
```

" Local variables have a lifetime limited to the duration of a method: Fields exist and hold their value for as long as the object exists. "

it's always a good idea to put a `null` statement on a line by itself, instead of putting the semicolon on the same line as the `while` statement, where it is easily missed.

Precedence in Loop Expressions

In the GetChar program, both the loop inside the `main()` method and the loop inside the `flushInput()` method are sentinel loops. But look closely and you'll see a difference in their format. The loop inside the `main()` method has an additional set of parentheses, while the `flushInput()` loop lacks these. Why? If you take those extra parentheses out of the `main()` loop, what happens? Your program stops compiling with an error saying that Java cannot "convert char to boolean." This happens because the expression

```
userEntry = getChar() != 'Q'
```

first compares the return value of `getChar()` to the literal `'Q'`. If they are not equal, it tries to assign the value `true` to the variable `userEntry`. But `userEntry` is a `char`, not a `boolean` variable, so you get a type mismatch. What causes all this confusion is precedence. You might know that you want Java to first assign the value from `getChar()` to `userEntry`, and then compare that value to `'Q'`, but to get Java to do so, you have to be explicit. You have to use parentheses to control the order of operations. To get the condition to compile, you have to write

```
( userEntry = getChar() ) != 'Q'
```

TESTING ON DATA

Sometimes a sentinel loop has to be combined with another type of loop. Look back at the GetChar program. What did you have to do to exit the `main()` loop? You had to test for a particular value, the sentinel `'Q'`. But what if you didn't want to give up the letter *Q* for this purpose? What if you needed to use all the possible input values? Or suppose that you wanted to find the letter *X* in some input typed by the user. You could use the sentinel `'X'`, but what about the case where you aren't always sure that the sentinel will occur? In those cases, you want to check two conditions. One, as you've seen, is the condition of finding your sentinel. The other, for lack of a better term, is the condition of being "out of input."

This is a case where you need to use a *data* loop. A data loop is one that gets some type of input, and then ends when the input is exhausted. You use this type of loop when you want to read all the records in a file, for instance. You are not looking for any special value. You want to stop when you have read the entire file. Recall that, in Java, this special "input is exhausted" condition is signaled by returning the `int` value −1 from `System.in.read()`. Because this value is not a legal `byte` value (because as an `int`, it requires more bits than can be represented in a `byte`), you can test for it without giving up any input character as a sentinel value. The program ReadChars, in Listing 6-10, shows how you would create a loop to exit when either a specific sentinel value is entered or when the "end of input condition" is reached. Figure 6-14 shows some possible interaction with the program. Note that, by outputting an integer value, you cause the program to output the numeric equivalent of each character entered. This program gives you a handy way to discover the ASCII value of any character.

Listing 6-10 ReadChars.java

```java
// ReadChars.java
// Using a sentinel loop and a data loop
//
import java.io.*;

public class ReadChars
{
    // The application starts executing the main() method
    public static void main(String args[]) throws Exception
    {
        // Local variables
        int userEntry;                   // User's entry

        System.out.println("Enter characters.");
        System.out.println("Quit by entering 'Q' or a ^Z");
        while ( (userEntry = System.in.read()) != -1 &&
                (char) userEntry != 'Q' )
        {
            System.out.println("User entered " + userEntry);
        }
    }
}
```

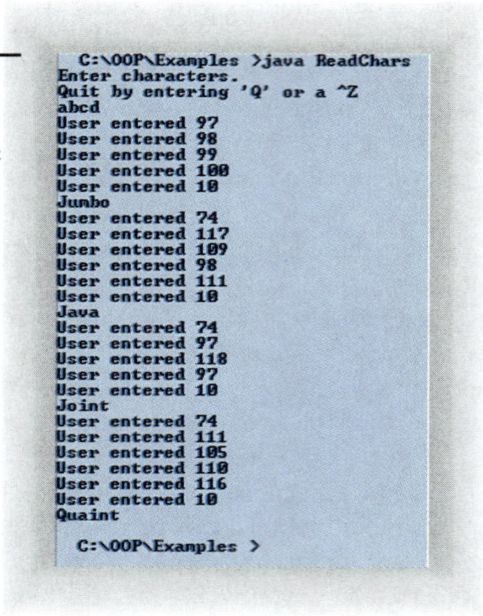

FIGURE 6-14

Running the ReadChars application

```
C:\OOP\Examples >java ReadChars
Enter characters.
Quit by entering 'Q' or a ^Z
abcd
User entered 97
User entered 98
User entered 99
User entered 100
User entered 10
Jumbo
User entered 74
User entered 117
User entered 109
User entered 98
User entered 111
User entered 10
Java
User entered 74
User entered 97
User entered 118
User entered 97
User entered 10
Joint
User entered 74
User entered 111
User entered 105
User entered 110
User entered 116
User entered 10
Quaint

C:\OOP\Examples >
```

Putting Loops to Work

BACK ON THE JAVAMATIC FRONT

"Okay, okay, okay!" Brenda heard Jumbo say into the phone. He was sitting at his desk, holding the phone to his ear with his trunk, while he typed fast and furiously at the keyboard. "Yes. I said okay, didn't I?" Jumbo continued. The conversation continued in that vein for several minutes, until, with a final flourish, the last "okay" poured forth and the telephone was untangled and back at rest. Jumbo's typing slowed, and Brenda knew that she would soon get a full replay of the conversation. She wasn't disappointed.

"You know," Jumbo began, "sometimes I don't know whether to kill Fred, or get him to marry you. Do you know he convinced the IRS that the little glitch with the miscounted money was all a misunderstanding? I don't know how he does it. But just when I think he's the greatest thing since sliced bread, he comes up with something new. Now you're going to have to fix the JavaMatic so it reports sales item-by-item. Not just totals. I told him it was all okay, and I figure you can just whip up one of those method thingies. Maybe you could call it `printSummary()`. What do you think? Brenda? ..."

"Hmmm," said Brenda, her mind obviously elsewhere. "I don't know about marriage, but I wouldn't object to dinner and a movie."

Now that you know about indefinite loops, you have the tools to add two new features to the JavaMatic. The first of these, `printSummary()`, simply reports the sales of each beverage when the machine is turned off—that is, when the loop ends. Writing the `printSummary()` method reveals the need for the second feature: How do you turn off the machine to print the summary? It turns off—exits the loop—only when it is out of beverages. That creates a problem. As it stands, to see the summary you must purchase all the remaining inventory inside the machine, which is counterproductive. You need to add the capability to input a password to stop the machine.

The JavaMatic_2I, shown in Listing 6-11, uses the new `printSummary()` method and allows a supervisor to exit the loop by typing in the magic word: "JUMBO" (of course). To accomplish this, it uses what is called a *priming read*. Figure 6-15 shows the JavaMatic_2I in action.

```
Listing 6-11 JavaMatic_2I.java
// The JavaMatic Virtual Vending Machine - Version 2I
//
// Simplifying an indeterminate loop, priming reads
//
```

continued on next page

continued from previous page

> **An n in front of a variable name is a common programming shorthand for "number of something."**

```java
import java.io.*;

public class JavaMatic_2I
{
    // Attributes
    int nServings = 0;          // No cups sold when starting
    double totalSales = 0.0;    // Is this big enough?

    // Inventory
    static final int startInventory = 25;
    int     nBrazilian = startInventory;
    int     nItalian   = startInventory;
    int     nLicorice  = startInventory;
    int     nChicken   = startInventory;
    double pBrazilian =.25, pItalian =.55, pLicorice =.45,⇐
    pChicken =.75;

    // The application starts executing the main() method
    public static void main(String args[]) throws Exception
    {
        // Create a JavaMatic_2I object to carry out your
        // work
        JavaMatic_2I myMachine = new JavaMatic_2I();

        // Priming read
        myMachine.drawMenu();
        String userChoice = getString(); // User's selection

        while ( (! myMachine.isEmpty()) &&⇐
          (! userChoice.equals("JUMBO")))
        {
            myMachine.dispenseBeverage(userChoice.charAt(0) );

            System.out.println("");
            System.out.println(⇐
              "  Total Servings = " + myMachine.nServings);
            System.out.println(⇐
              "  Total Sales    = " + myMachine.totalSales);

            myMachine.drawMenu();
            userChoice = getString();
        }
        myMachine.printSummary();
    }

    // Methods to implement object behavior
    // ******************************************************
    //  method isEmpty(): returns true if out of everything
    // ******************************************************
    public boolean isEmpty()
    {
        return (nBrazilian == 0 && nItalian == 0 &&
                nLicorice  == 0 && nChicken == 0);
    }
```

```java
// ***********************************************************
//   method printSummary(): how much have you sold today?
// ***********************************************************
void printSummary()
{
// Calculate sales for each beverage
    int salesBrazilian = startInventory - nBrazilian;
    int salesItalian   = startInventory - nItalian;
    int salesLicorice  = startInventory - nLicorice;
    int salesChicken   = startInventory - nChicken;

    System.out.println("\nNumber of Sales");
    System.out.println("-----------------");
    System.out.println(⇐
        "Brazilian Roast   :" + salesBrazilian);
    System.out.println(⇐
        "Italian Espresso :" + salesItalian);
    System.out.println(⇐
        "Licorice-Lime     :" + salesLicorice);
    System.out.println(⇐
        "Chicken Soup      :" + salesChicken);
    System.out.println("");
}

// ***********************************************************
//   method drawMenu(): display the JavaMatic offerings
// ***********************************************************
public void drawMenu()
{
    System.out.println();
    System.out.println(⇐
        "   The JavaMatic Virtual Vending Machine   ");
    System.out.println(⇐
        "   ---------------------------------------");
    System.out.println(⇐
        "  1 - Bold, Brazilian Roast      " + pBrazilian );
    System.out.println(⇐
        "  2 - Italian Espresso           " + pItalian );
    System.out.println(⇐
        "  3 - Luscious Licorice-Lime     " + pLicorice );
    System.out.println(⇐
        "  4 - Zenia's Chicken Soup       " + pChicken );
    System.out.println(⇐
        "   ---------------------------------------");
    System.out.print(⇐
        "            What's Your Pleasure ? ");
    System.out.flush();
}

// ***********************************************************
//   method getString(): retrieve a String
// ***********************************************************
public static String getString() throws Exception
{
    String retValue = "";
    int ch;
```

continued on next page

continued from previous page

```
        while ( ((ch = System.in.read()) != -1) &&
               ((char) ch != 1 1/2\n);
            if (ch!= '\n') retValue += (char) ch;

        return retValue;
    }

    // **********************************************************
    //  method dispenseBeverage(): dispense chosen drink
    // **********************************************************
    public void dispenseBeverage( char choice )
    {
        System.out.println("");

        if ( (choice == '1' && nBrazilian == 0) ||
             (choice == '2' && nItalian   == 0) ||
             (choice == '3' && nLicorice  == 0) ||
             (choice == '4' && nChicken   == 0) )
        {
            System.out.println(⇐
            "  *** Please make another selection ***");
            return;
        }

        switch ( choice )
        {
            case '1':
                nBrazilian--;
                totalSales += pBrazilian;
                System.out.println(⇐
                  "  Insert Brazilian Roast filter.");
                break;
            case '2':
                nItalian--;
                totalSales += pItalian;
                System.out.println(⇐
                  "  Insert Italian Espresso filter.");
                break;
            case '3':
                nLicorice--;
                totalSales += pLicorice;
                System.out.println(⇐
                  "  Put Licorice-Lime mix in place.");
                break;
            case '4':
                    nChicken--;
                    totalSales += pChicken;
                    System.out.println(⇐
                      "  Put Chicken-Soup mix in place");
                    break;
            default:
                System.out.println(⇐
                  "  Invalid selection. Here's your money");
                return;
        }
        System.out.println("  Drop cup into position.");
```

```
                 System.out.println("  Add 8 oz. hot water.");
                 System.out.println("  Open door.");

                 // Sales now totalled here
                 nServings++;
          }
    }
```

ALL NEW, ALL IMPROVED, ALL THE TIME

Take a moment to put the JavaMatic_2I through its paces and see what's changed. Try out a Licorice-Lime and a Chicken Soup. Then, when you're thoroughly sated, type the word "JUMBO", and see how many of each beverage your JavaMatic has sold for the day.

Besides the `printSummary()` method, many of the changes to the JavaMatic have improved efficiency, simplified the processing, or added capabilities that you can use in other applications. Let's start by taking a look at the simplification of the `dispenseBeverage()` method.

Simplify, Simplify, Simplify

In the `dispenseBeverage()` method used in the previous version of the JavaMatic, you might have noticed a lot of redundant code. For every possible selection, you had to add exactly the same instructions to tell the customer if you were out of a specific beverage. It is easier and more efficient to test for an out-of-stock condition at the

FIGURE 6-15

The JavaMatic_2I at work

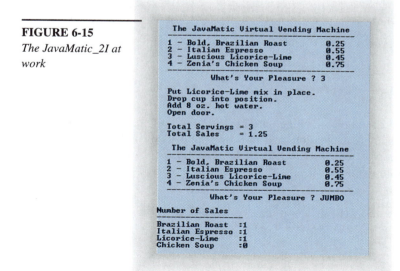

beginning. By testing whether the customer has requested Espresso and whether you are out of Espresso, you can use the same error-handling code for all cases like this:

```
if ( (choice == '1' && nBrazilian == 0) ||
     (choice == '2' && nItalian   == 0) ||
     (choice == '3' && nLicorice  == 0) ||
     (choice == '4' && nChicken   == 0) )
{
    System.out.println(⇐
    "  *** Please make another selection ***");
    return;
}
```

Pay special attention to the extra sets of parentheses around each subexpression, and the way that each subexpression is connected with ORs. You want to print an error message if you are out of Chicken Soup and the user *selected* Chicken Soup, but you don't want to print an error message if he or she selected Licorice-Lime and you are out of Espresso. Each of the subexpressions handles a situation in which the user selected a beverage that is out of stock.

Double Reads: Déjà Vu All Over Again

Another new feature with this version of JavaMatic is the priming read. Your `while` loop should stop when your supervisor types in "JUMBO" (the secret password). That means you need to get the `userChoice` before you enter the `while` loop—and you don't want to execute the loop body in that case. To make this work, you have to get input in *two* places—before you enter the loop and at the end of the loop—before you make another iteration. That is why this style of loop is called a priming read—the input primes the loop:

```
String userChoice = getString();        // User's selection
while ( (! myMachine.isEmpty())&&⇐
  (! userChoice.equals("JUMBO")))
{
    // Do stuff with the input

    userChoice = getString();           // Read again
}
```

The previous exit condition—running out of everything—still needs to be tested. That was already a complex expression, and moving it into its own method, `isEmpty()`, makes the loop expression easier to understand. The `isEmpty()` method itself returns `true` if every inventory item is 0.

```
public boolean isEmpty()
{
    return (nBrazilian == 0 && nItalian == 0 &&
            nLicorice  == 0 && nChicken == 0);
}
```

There is a downside to a loop that uses a priming read. Often you have to do several things in addition to reading input. You may read some input from the user and then process it in some way. With a priming read, you have to duplicate this information in two places, which potentially could be a liability if you change the processing in one place and forget to change it in the other. In such cases, many computer scientists recommend what is called a "loop-and-a-half," which is explained in the next section.

Stringing Along

To add the capability to exit the loop when a password is entered, the `userChoice` variable has been changed to a `String`. Previously the JavaMatic handled only `char` input. Because the `dispenseBeverage()` method expects to receive the product code as a `char`, when calling that method you need to use the `charAt()` method of the `String` class to pass the first character in the `String` `userChoice` to `dispenseBeverage()` like this:

```
myMachine.dispenseBeverage( userChoice.charAt(0) );
```

You'll recall from Chapter 3, "The Atomic Theory of Objects: Working with Object Attributes," that the characters in a `String` are numbered starting at zero, so `dispenseBeverage()` receives the first character.

There are two other questions raised by changing `userChoice` from a `char` to a `String`:

☕ How do you read `String` input?

☕ How do you compare `String`s for equality?

The `System.in` object you have been using for input does not have a method for reading a `String` from the keyboard. However, now that you know about testing loops, constructing one is relatively simple. In JavaMatic_2I.java, `getString ()` is a `static` method that reads `bytes` from the `System.in` object and constructs a `String` object by using concatenation. The logic for the `getString()` method is simply:

1. Create an empty, temporary `String` to hold the return value.

2. Continue reading `bytes` until the newline is encountered or end-of-input occurs.

3. On each iteration, add the character read to the temporary `String`.

4. Return the temporary `String`.

The code to implement this algorithm looks like this:

```
public static String getString() throws Exception
{
    String retValue = "";
    int ch;
```

continued on next page

continued from previous page

```
        while ( ((ch = System.in.read()) != -1) && ((char) ch !=
'\n'))
            retValue += (char) ch;

        return retValue;
    }
```

Using `equals()` with `Strings`

As you recall, the equality operators cannot be used with objects to compare equality of contents. With `Strings`, as with other objects, the equality operators actually compare identity. To compare two `Strings` to see if they have the same contents, you use one of the methods from the `String` class: `equals()`. The `equals()` method will return `true` if both `Strings` have exactly the same contents, and `false` otherwise. To compare two `String` objects, your code will look like this:

```
String s = "Hi Mom";

if ( s.equals("Hi Mom") )
    System.out.println(s + " is equal to " +"\"Hi Mom\"");
else
    System.out.println(s + " is NOT equal to " + ⇐
        "\"Hi Mom\"");

if (s.equals("HI MOM") )
    System.out.println(s + " is equal to " + "\"HI MOM\"");
else
    System.out.println(s + " is NOT equal to " +⇐
        "\"HI MOM\"");
```

The output for this looks like:

```
Hi Mom is equal to Hi Mom
Hi Mom is NOT equal to HI MOM
```

In the JavaMatic_2I, this method of the `String` class is used to test whether the supervisor has entered the "JUMBO" password. Because you want to exit the loop when `userChoice` equals "JUMBO", the condition, `userChoice.equals("JUMBO")` is negated with the NOT (`!`) operator.

```
while ( (! myMachine.isEmpty()) && ⇐
    (! userChoice.equals("JUMBO")))
{
    // Body of loop
}
```

Endless (Event) Loops

As you saw, the JavaMatic_2I uses a priming read to get and process the customer's input. But you could also write this program in another way. Instead of doing one read before the loop and one read at the bottom of the loop, you could put the exit condition in the middle of the loop and then exit the loop if the supervisor enters "JUMBO". A loop that exits in the middle of the body is sometimes called a *loop-and-a-half*. This method is also used to create *endless* or *event* loops.

Listing 6-12 shows the `main()` method of a new version of JavaMatic that uses a loop-and-a-half. Of course, this loop isn't endless, because it will terminate when the machine is empty, as can be seen by inspecting the test expression of the `while`:

```
while ( ! MyMachine.isEmpty() )
{
    userChoice = getString(); // only a single read!
    if ( userChoice.equals("JUMBO"))
            break;
    // . . . loop body here
}
```

This loop will also end if the user enters the password "JUMBO" when prompted for a product code. The program accomplishes this by using a `break` statement. The `break`, which you learned about in Chapter 5, can be used to leave a loop as well as to break out of a `switch`. Remember that, in a `switch`, the `break` causes "termination" of a `case` statement. It works similarly within a loop. When the computer finds a `break` statement, the code jumps out of the enclosing loop. This happens immediately, so any remaining statements inside the loop body are skipped. This ability to terminate a loop at will allows you to avoid the priming read required in the earlier version of this program.

Listing 6-12 JavaMatic_2J.java (main() method shown)

```
public static void main(String args[]) throws Exception
{
    // Create a JavaMatic_2J object to carry out your work
    JavaMatic_2J myMachine = new JavaMatic_2J();

     while ( ! myMachine.isEmpty() )
    {
        myMachine.drawMenu();
        String userChoice = getString();// Only a SINGLE read

        if ( userChoice.equals("JUMBO") )
            break;

        myMachine.dispenseBeverage( userChoice.charAt(0) );

        System.out.println("");
        System.out.println(⇐
         "  Total Servings = " + myMachine.nServings);
        System.out.println(⇐
         "  Total Sales    = " + myMachine.totalSales);
    }
    myMachine.printSummary();
}
```

Testing at the Bottom with do-while

AT LEAST ONCE

"Riiinnngggg." Without a pause, her eyes firmly fixed on the screen and her typing never missing a beat, Brenda snaked her trunk out over her shoulder, searching for the phone buried amongst the detritus piled high on her bookshelf.

"Riiinnnggggg. Craaasssshhh. Riiinnnnggggg."

Brenda stopped typing and turned. A pile of books lay in a haphazard heap on the floor. Atop them sat an ancient black telephone. "Riiinnnnggggg. Riiinnnnggggg," it continued.

"Sigh...." Brenda reacted as she reached over to pick up the receiver. The ringing stopped before she reached it.

"Some hi-tech establishment this is," Brenda mumbled to herself. "I don't know how Jumbo plans to manage a whole fleet of JavaMatics, when he can't even get someone to answer the phone!"

Sometimes you know in advance that you want to iterate at least once. Let's concoct an example. Once you get the JavaMatic perfected, you intend to stick a copy in every Java Joint from here to Timbuktu. How do you intend to collect your virtual fortune? Because your fortune is virtual, it should be easily transported over the Net. All you really need is some way to connect up with your fleet.

One way is to create an automatic telephone dialer that has the phone numbers for each of your JavaMatics. When you flip the dialer on, you want it to immediately request a telephone number to be dialed. Then, after the number has been dialed and you've downloaded your bouillon (pun intended), the dialer should prompt for another number. You could implement the dialer by using code like this:

```
String phoneNumber;
String yesOrNo;

phoneNumber = getInput("Phone number:   ");

dialNumber(phoneNumber);

yesOrNo = getInput("More? (yes/no):   ");

while ( yesOrNo.equals("yes") )
{
    phoneNumber = getInput("Phone number:   ");
    dialNumber(phoneNumber);
    yesOrNo = getInput("More? (yes/no):   ");
}
```

Of course, you'd have to actually write code for the `getInput()` method (which displays a prompt and then reads a `String`) and the `dialNumber()` method before the dialer would work. Notice that several of the program statements appear more than once; this looks much like the priming read problem that you saw in the last section. The repetition makes the program more difficult to understand and more difficult to change. One possible remedy is to initialize the variable yesOrNo with the value "yes":

```
String phoneNumber;
String yesOrNo = "yes";

while ( yesOrNo.equals("yes") )
{
    phoneNumber = getInput("Phone number:   ");
    dialNumber(phoneNumber);
    yesOrNo = getInput("More? (yes/no):   ");
}
```

Although this works all right, you must remember to initialize the String. However, Java provides a special type of loop that is ideally suited to such situations: the do-while loop. Your dialer program can be rewritten by use of the do-while like this:

```
String phoneNumber;
String yesOrNo;

do {
    phoneNumber = getInput("Phone number:   ");

    dialNumber(phoneNumber);

    yesOrNo = getInput("More? (yes/no):   ");
} while (yesOrNo.equals("yes"));
```

In Figure 6-16, you can see the syntax of the do-while loop. Unlike the while loop, the do-while evaluates its test expression only *after* executing the loop body. The shape of the loop should remind you of this, because the test expression appears after the body of the loop. The do-while is sometimes called a "hasty" loop, because it always runs its loop body at least once; it doesn't bother to evaluate the test expression until it's executed the loop body. In that sense it "leaps before it looks." Figure 6-17 shows how a do-while loop could be used to follow a recipe that asked you to "salt to taste."

THE continue STATEMENT

The break is useful in working with a switch or a loop, allowing you to easily and quickly exit the body of the switch or loop. Another statement that is useful when working with loops (though not switches) is the continue statement. While a break causes you to leave a loop entirely, a continue statement causes the remaining statements of the loop body to be skipped, without leaving the loop. That means that when your program encounters a continue statement within a while or a do-while, the control of the program will immediately go to the test condition. The continue acts a little differently when encountered inside a for loop. There it causes control to be transferred immediately to the increment expression, after which the test condition is evaluated.

FIGURE 6-16

The syntax of the
do-while loop

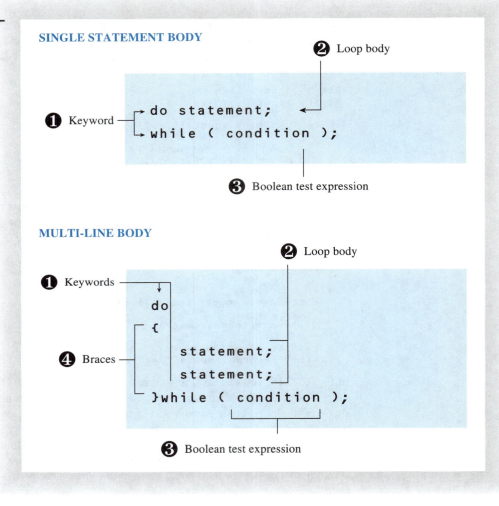

Because nothing helps like seeing some code in action, take a look at Listing 6-13, which shows a simple application that prints a list of even numbers, using the `continue` statement to avoid printing the odd values. Every time the condition (n % 2) evaluates to 0, you have a number evenly divisible by 2—an even number—and the number is printed to the console by use of the `System.out` object. However, when (n % 2) doesn't evaluate to 0, the program executes the `continue` statement, transferring control to the update expression in the `for` loop, and skipping the `System.out.println()` at the bottom of the loop. Obviously, you could achieve the same results by using an `if-else`. The `continue` simply gives you another way of writing your programs, which can sometimes be simpler and more readable if you use

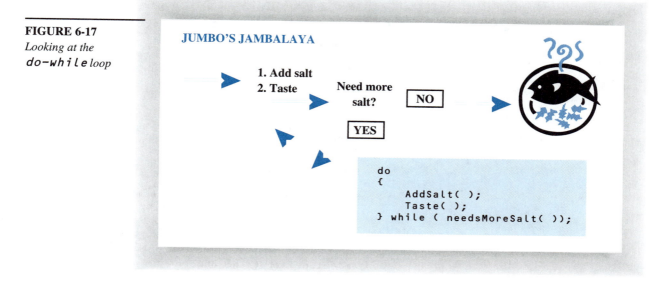

a `continue` rather than an `if-else`. By the way, what numbers should you see printed?

Listing 6-13 Evens.java

```java
public class Evens
{
    public static void main(String args[])
    {
        System.out.println("Even numbers from 1 to ????");
        for (int n = 1; n < 10; n++)
        {
            if ((n % 2) != 0)
                continue;
            System.out.print(n + " ");
        }
        System.out.println();
    }
}
```

LABELED breakS AND continueS

Just as it's possible to nest `if`s, it's also possible to nest loops. While `break` and `continue` work fine for single loops, nested loops require special forms of these two statements. These special forms can be used to exit—or skip execution of the loop body—of an outer loop, not just an inner loop. You can do this by giving the outer loop a name, called a *label*. The `PrimeSieve` application in Listing 6-14 shows how to use a labeled `continue` with nested loops.

> **A loop that exits in the middle of the body is sometimes called a loop-and-a-half.**

Listing 6-14 PrimeSieve.java

```java
public class PrimeSieve
{
    public static void main(String args[])
    {
        nextNumber:
        for (int n = 3; n <= 100; n += 2)
        {
            for (int divisor = 2; divisor <= n / 2;
                divisor++)
            {
                int remainder = n % divisor;
                if (remainder == 0)
                {
                    System.out.println("The number " + n +
                        " is evenly divisible by " +
                        divisor + ".");
                    continue nextNumber;
                }
            }
            System.out.println("The number " + n + "
                is prime.");
        }
    }
}
```

The program `PrimeSieve` prints a list of the odd prime numbers less than 100. A prime number is a number that is evenly divisible only by itself and 1.

The program contains two loops: an outer loop with loop variable n, and an inner loop with loop variable `divisor`. Right before the outer loop, look for the identifier `nextNumber`, which is followed by a colon. This type of identifier is a label—not to be confused with the `Label` class of the AWT. A label is used to give a name to a loop, in this case the `for` loop that immediately follows it. Now find the `continue` statement inside the inner loop. Notice how it refers to `nextNumber`? When this `continue` is executed, rather than just continuing with the update expression of the `for` loop that contains it, control is transferred to the increment expression of the outer loop, which has been named `nextNumber`.

What would have happened if you had used an ordinary `continue` instead? In that case, the program would continue to search for, and print, additional numbers that evenly divide n. Because you know that finding one number that divides into your potential prime disqualifies it as a candidate, there's no reason for you to keep on looking. This is very similar to the strategy of "short-circuit evaluation" employed by Java's logical operators.

You might also have used a `break` in place of the `continue`. This would, in fact, avoid continuing the search for additional factors by immediately exiting the inner loop. Notice, however, that the inner loop is followed by the `println()`, which actually identifies each of the prime numbers. If you had simply used a `break`, this statement would be executed, when, in fact, the number was not a prime number. To make the program work using a `break`, you'd need to use a variable to "remember" whether a factor had been found, as shown in Listing 6-15. By avoiding the need for such a variable, the labeled `continue` makes the program easier to read. However, overuse of labeled `breaks` and `continues` may result in a confusing program. Avoid them except where the alternative is even more difficult to read.

Listing 6-15 PrimeSieve2.java

```java
public class PrimeSieve2{

    public static void main(String args[])
    {

        for (int n = 3; n <= 100; n += 2)
        {
            boolean factored = false;
            for (int divisor = 2; divisor <= n / 2;⇐
                divisor++)
            {
                int remainder = n % divisor;
                if (remainder == 0)
                {
                    System.out.println("The number " + n
                        + " is evenly divisible by " +⇐
                        divisor + ".");
                    factored = true;
                    break;
                }
            }
            if (!factored)
                System.out.println("The number " + n +⇐
                    " is prime.");
        }
    }
}
```

Summary

☕ *Iteration* means doing something repeatedly, or "looping."

☕ Java has three iterative statements: the `while`, the `do-while`, and the `for`.

☕ The `while` and the `for` test before each iteration; the `do-while` tests after each iteration.

☕ Console applications and applications often create objects in the `main()` method; applets are themselves objects.

☕ The `read()` method returns bytes entered by the user, but does not make them available until the user presses ENTER. The newline character (`'\n'`) is sent along with the bytes entered by the user.

☞ A counting loop executes its body a fixed number of times.

☞ Loops continue to execute their body until the test expression is evaluated and found to be `false`.

☞ Once started, a loop that never changes the value of its test expression will never end.

☞ `static` methods are related to an entire class, rather than a specific object, and so do not have a `this` object.

☞ A sentinel loop stops when it finds a particular value.

☞ A data loop ends when its input is exhausted.

☞ Loops that read data can be primed by reading input before executing the loop statement.

☞ The `equals()` method can be used to test `Strings` for equality.

☞ Endless (event) loops can terminate on a specific condition by use of the `break` statement.

☞ The `do-while` always executes its loop body at least once.

☞ The `for` loop includes three expressions: an initialization expression, a test expression, and an update expression.

☞ The initialization expression of a `for` loop can define a variable to be used within the loop body.

Quiz

1. The three basic programming constructs are sequence, selection, and _____.

2. The three kinds of Java loop statements are the _____, the _____, and the _____.

3. The test expression of a loop has data type _____.

4. The two main parts of a loop are the _____ and the _____.

5. The body of a `do-while` loop will always execute at least _____.

6. Two kinds of program loops are counting loops and _____ loops.

7. Given a determinate loop, it is/is not possible to determine the number of iterations by examining the loop.

8. The _____ statement can be used to exit a loop.

9. The _____ method can be used to test strings for equality.

10. The value of a `static final` field can/cannot be changed during program execution.

11. One of the most common programming mistakes is the unintentional creation of a(n) _____ loop.

12. An object's _____ is stored in variables known as fields.

13. The test expression of a loop specifies the condition under which it will _____, not the condition under which it will _____.

14. Two types of testing loops are _____ loops and _____ loops.

15. The loop that is useful for inspecting the parts of a data collection, for example, the bytes of a file, is the _____ loop.

16. The loop that is useful in searching for a specific value is the _____ loop.

17. Reading a value before using it in the test expression of a loop is called _____.

18. A loop placed inside the body of another loop is called a(n) _____ loop.

19. The _____ statement causes statements in a loop body to be skipped.

20. It is possible to exit an outer loop by using a _____ `break` statement.

Exercises

1. Write a program that takes a number input by the user and computes the sum of each number from 1 to the given number. For example, entering **3** would produce the result **6** (1+2+3=6). Print the result, or print **0** if the input number is less than 1.

2. Write a program that prompts the user for two numbers, **a** and **b**. The program should output **ab** (**a** multiplied by itself **b** times) so long as **b** is an integer greater than or equal to zero. Otherwise, the program should display an error message. For example, entering **3** should produce the output **9** ($3^2=9$).

3. Write a program that prints the average of a series of assignment scores, where each score can range from 0.0 to 100.0. Decide how many scores to process by prompting the user to enter the number of scores. Create a second program version that simply processes scores until a score outside the valid range is found. Now, combine these into a single program that lets the user select the input method.

4. Write a program that reads a series of numbers and outputs the smallest number and the largest number. Use a negative number to indicate the end of the input series.

" A 'hasty' loop doesn't bother to evaluate the test expression until it's executed the loop body: In that sense it 'leaps before it looks.' "

5. Write a program that displays a table showing the lengths of the sides of all right triangles with shorter sides of length from 1 to 10, in steps of 1. Recall from geometry that the length of the longest side of a right triangle is the square root of the sum of the squares of the shorter sides:

$$l = (a^2 + b^2)^{1/2}$$

Use the `Math.sqrt()` method to compute the square root.

7

Testing and Debugging: When Things Go Wrong

" **J**ust what in the world is going on here?" you think, scratching your head. "That answer just can't be right." All of us have had such experiences. Your program doesn't work the way it should. Why? Did something go wrong? Has your program somehow emerged from the script of *The Exorcist*? Even though that might seem to be the case, the truth is even more unappetizing: You've made a mistake.

If you never make mistakes when you program, you can skip this chapter. However, most of you will need to read it carefully, because there don't appear to be any programmers who *never* make a mistake. John Von Neumann, credited by many with the invention of the computer as we know it, was one of the great geniuses of the 20th century, breaking new ground in such diverse areas as quantum mechanics, economics, and computation. Yet Von Neumann and his team were horrified to discover that, though they were expert mathematicians, they could not seem to write error-free programs. Bearing in mind that these first computer programs were quite simple by modern standards, we can perhaps be excused for the odd bug or two.

> *"If you never make mistakes when you program, you can skip this chapter. "*

In this chapter, you'll be introduced to the art of tracking down the wily bug. Like Sherlock Holmes on the track of a master criminal, you must focus all your energies on the "game." You must sift through enormous volumes of evidence, ignoring no clue, however small. You must apply the indispensable tool of all great detectives, logic. And, you must know when to seek out the advice of Dr. Watson, whose confused ramblings often contain the key that unlocks the baffling puzzle.

In this chapter you will learn

☕ The differences between compile-time and run-time errors

☕ Common compile-time and run-time errors and their causes

☕ How to create a debugging plan of action for repairing an unruly program

☕ How to use the JDK debugger, Jdb, to help you carry out your debugging chores

When Things Go Wrong

What kinds of things can go wrong with your programs? Well, you know that something's gone wrong when the Java compiler refuses to compile your program, announcing instead that it contains errors. Even when your program compiles successfully, you know that something's gone wrong if, when you run it, the results are not what you want.

These two cases identify the two major kinds of programming errors that you will encounter in your programs. In the first case, you find out about an error when you compile your program. Hence, this sort of error is called a *compile-time* error or sometimes a *syntax* error, since these errors occur when you have violated the grammar of the Java language.

You find out about the second kind of error when you run your program. This sort of error is called a *run-time* error, or sometimes a *semantic* error. "Semantic" refers to meaning, and if your program doesn't do what you intended it to do, you have communicated the wrong meaning, regardless of how correct your grammar seems to you. If you tell your computer program to turn left, when you meant for it to turn right, the program is not going to end up where you had planned, even though turning left and right are entirely valid commands.

These two sorts of errors—compile-time and run-time—arise from different sorts of mistakes on your part. Let's look at each of them in turn.

Compile-Time Errors

"CONTEXT BOB,"

S aid Brenda, talking into her headset while "tickling the ivories."
Jumbo, sitting at the next table, tried to make some sense of what she was saying.
He couldn't. Whenever Brenda got on the phone with one of her cyberpach group, the conversation became incomprehensible—it was as if she started talking another language. His brain idly tried to rearrange both words in different orders. No matter how he arranged them, they made no sense at all. Finally, he could stand it no longer.

"What," he asked with exasperation, turning to Brenda, who had finished her call, "does 'context Bob' mean?"

Brenda, a little taken aback to think that Jumbo would eavesdrop on her conversation, recovered quickly. "It means," she said archly, "that you should mind your own business."

When you speak with a friend, you can often violate the rules of English grammar and usage without causing a problem. Your friend knows what you mean even if you say something that isn't quite right. In fact, you and your friend may enjoy making up slang words that are not in the dictionary and which others might not understand.

As you've no doubt already learned, the Java compiler is not your friend in this way. A stern and pedantic taskmaster, it tolerates absolutely no departure from the official rules of the Java language. These official rules are called Java's syntax. If you'd rather write *Class* instead of *class* you're out of luck: The compiler will refuse to accommodate you. Perhaps even worse, it gives you no opportunity to explain or clarify something it didn't understand. Instead, it requires you to correct the program and recompile it completely. As an example, take a look at Listing 7-1, which shows a program that contains some compile-time errors. Figure 7-1 shows what happens when you ask the Java compiler to compile it.

Listing 7-1 Error_1.java

```
// Error_1.java shows a variety of compile-time errors
import java.Applet.*;
import java.awt.*;

public class error1 extends Applet
{
    int someNumber;
    someNumber = 32;

    public static void main(String args[])
    {
        int localVar;
        System.out.println("localVar = "+localVar);
```

continued on next page

continued from previous page

```
            System.out.println("I'm now " + someNumber);
            return true;
        )
    }
```

TRUTH AND CONSEQUENCES

"You don't love me!" Every parent has heard those words when they tell their off-spring that they can't catch that jellyfish with their bare hands, or drop out of school to become the first 10-year-old T-shirt salesperson. Most parents do love their children, however; parents prevent their children from doing everything that they want to do because the parents can see just a little farther down the road than the kids can. In this sense, the Java compiler is very much your friend. It is very concerned with accurate and precise communication. It wants to be very sure that it's understood *exactly* what you mean. That's why it's so picky. Some languages won't tell you about an error in your code until you actually try to run the code. That practice can have some devastating consequences. You don't want to press the "turn left" button while you are cruising at 30,000 feet using your JumboJavaJet Autopilot software, and have it tell you only then that it cannot understand what you are trying to say. Java's capability to detect syntax errors at compile-time allows you to catch some kinds of errors *before* you leave the ground.

Still, compile-time errors can be frustrating and are best avoided. When a compile-time error pops up, it's all too easy to quickly launch the editor and make a change that causes the error to disappear. Usually, you make the proper change. But sometimes, in the heat of the moment, you find yourself making a change that produces a syntactically correct program—one that contains no compile-time errors—that does something other than what you had intended. What you've done in that case is to convert a compile-time error into a run-time error. Now, instead of rearing its ugly head during compilation, the error can pop up when you least expect it, like during the rollout demonstration for those new investors.

FIGURE 7-1

Compiling `Error_1.java`

```
C:\OOP\Examples >javac Error_1.java
Error_1.java:2: Package java.Applet not found in import.
import java.Applet.*;
             ^
Error_1.java:5: Superclass Applet of class error1 not found.
public class error1 extends Applet
                            ^
Error_1.java:8: Identifier expected.
    someNumber = 32;
             ^
Error_1.java:10: '(' expected.
    public static void main(String args[])
                                         ^
Error_1.java:5: Public class error1 must be defined in a file called "error1
a".
public class error1 extends Applet
              ^
5 errors

C:\OOP\Examples >
```

Rather than "shooting from the hip," a better approach is to think before acting, to approach the correction of compile-time errors methodically. Study the error message produced by the compiler for clues that point to the nature of the error. These messages aren't always easy to understand. Because it's hard, almost impossibly hard, to write a compiler that produces clear and easy-to-use error messages, many compilers produce error messages that say little more than "invalid-bad-stuff somewhere around line so-and-so." But, combined with a strategy, even that little assistance will help narrow the focus of your search for the elusive error.

COMMON ERRORS

Most compile-time errors are obvious; often they're simply typographical errors. Note that being obvious and being easy to find are different things. Even when they're hard to find, compile-time errors are generally obvious *after* you've found them. You'll learn a process for locating the cause of a particularly difficult compile-time error in a moment. First, let's look at some of the more common mistakes that give rise to compile-time errors and how you can avoid them.

Missing Semicolon

Most Java statements, unless they end with a compound statement enclosed within braces (`{}`), end with a semicolon. Omitting the semicolon causes one statement to run into the next, confusing the compiler, which then is unable to sort out the results of the collision. You should include semicolons where required.

Omitting or Misspelling a Keyword or Identifier

Java uses keywords to mark off (delimit) the parts of statements. If you omit or misspell a keyword within a statement, Java will be unable to make sense of the statement. Similarly, if you omit or misspell an identifier (for example, the name of a field, method, or local variable), Java will be unable to compile the affected statement. You should include keywords and identifiers where required and take care to spell them correctly.

Using the Wrong Case

Recall that Java is a case-sensitive language. Using the wrong case (for example, writing *While* instead of *while*) is a common way of misspelling keywords and identifiers. Use the proper case in all keywords and identifiers.

Unmatched Single or Double Quotes

Single quotes are used to delimit character literals, and double quotes are used to delimit `Strings`. When, for example, you omit the closing double quotes of a `String`,

Java understands the following words of your program to be part of the `String`. When it scans the end of the line without finding the closing double quotes, it issues an error. To avoid this, you should be careful to match the single and double quotes used to form literals.

Unmatched Parentheses, Brackets, or Braces

Parentheses, brackets, and braces—like quotes—must occur in pairs. Unlike `Strings` that never extend beyond the end of a program line, constructs built using parentheses, brackets, and braces may extend across several program lines. When the paired elements are not properly matched, the compiler may scan several lines beyond the point where the missing element belongs before determining that an error exists. As a result, the line number reported by the compiler in its error message may be considerably removed from the point of the real error. You should take care to correctly match parentheses, brackets, and braces; a programming style that uses whitespace liberally will help.

Using Assignment in Place of Equality

A very common error is typing an assignment operator (`=`) in place of an equality operator (`==`) within a conditional expression. Remember that the main job of a condition is to form and test a `boolean` value, not to assign a value to a variable. Use the proper relational, equality, or logical operator in each condition you write.

Incompatible Types

Using incompatible types, especially within declarations and assignments, is an easy and common mistake. Recall, for example, that a floating-point literal is `double` by default and cannot be assigned to a `float` variable without a cast. Write literals of the appropriate type, and include casts where it is necessary to coerce the type of an operand.

Wrong Placement of Fields or Methods

Recall that fields and methods are declared within classes, though they can appear in any order within a class. You should be careful to declare each field and method within the enclosing braces (`{}`) of its class.

Missing or Incorrect `return`

The header of a method declares the type of value returned by the method. The actual `return` statement (or statements) within the method must agree with the declaration. For example, if the method is declared to return an `int` value, there must be at least one `return` statement within the method, and every such `return` statement must specify a value of type `int`.

You should be careful to match method headers with `return` statements and the types of values they return. If you don't want the method to return a value, you should declare the method to return type `void`, and make sure that no `return` within the method has an associated `return` value.

WHEN YOUR COMPILER FEEDS YOU A LINE: FINDING THE ERROR

Usually, when a compile-time error occurs, the error will be found in the line mentioned in the error message. Certainly that's where you should start your search: Look at the indicated line, and you'll probably find the error there. But when a statement that contains an error spans several lines, the compiler will often report the error with a line number a bit beyond that of the actual line that contains the error. If you don't see an error on the line reported, look back several lines. Usually you'll find the error there.

Sometimes, the line number reported is entirely incorrect—not even close. This happens most often with language elements that occur in pairs, like the braces used to enclose method bodies. If you are entering a method body and forget to type the ending brace, or you type something else by mistake, the compiler is not capable of telling where the method was supposed to end. If there is a subsequent brace that begins a compound statement, the compiler is only further confused. In such a case, the error can be very hard to locate. The best strategy to follow when that happens is to mark up a printed listing of the program, showing each pair of corresponding braces. Usually the missing or offending item will be obvious. Other language elements that should be examined for this problem include single quotes (`' '`), double quotes (`""`), brackets (`[]`), and parentheses. Often, your programmer's editor will help you by marking mismatched pairs of delimiters, or by specially coloring the contents of `String` constants.

DIVIDE AND CONQUER

Dealing with compile-time errors is easier if you have a firm knowledge of Java's syntax. Study the syntax diagrams for the statements involved, and look at sample code that uses the statements. But when all else fails, you can use what is called the "divide and conquer" tactic (or, as Julius Caesar first named it in Latin, *divide et impera*) to simplify your program to a point where the error will stand up and announce itself.

To use the divide-and-conquer approach, you start by placing comment symbols (either `//`, or `/*` and `*/`) around program lines that you believe are okay. Once you've added these comment symbols—this process is called *commenting out* lines of code— you recompile the program. The compiler will ignore the lines you commented out, even though they contain Java language elements. This code becomes temporarily inactive, without being removed from your source file. You have to be careful to avoid commenting out too many lines of code. For example, you need to make sure you don't comment out lines that give the class name or the line containing the ending brace (}). In addition, if you comment out only the body of a conditional or loop statement, make sure you don't include the beginning and ending braces in the text to be ignored. The conditional or loop must have a body of some sort, so comment out the contents of the body, but leave the opening and closing braces outside the comment.

When you compile the newly commented program, one of two things can happen. Either the error disappears, or it is still present. If the error disappears, that means the problem is in a line of code that you've commented out. You then should go back and uncomment a few lines and try again. Keep compiling and uncommenting additional lines until the compile-time error reappears. Eventually, you will locate the line that contains the error.

What happens if you comment out a section of code and the error is still present? In that case, you have an error on a line that hasn't yet been commented out. You'll want to comment out a few more lines of code and then try again.

Successive applications of this divide-and-conquer tactic should help you pinpoint the location of the error. At that point, a detailed study of the offending line itself will usually unmask the culprit. Figure 7-2 shows a program fragment undergoing divide-and-conquer debugging.

FIGURE 7-2

Divide-and-conquer
debugging

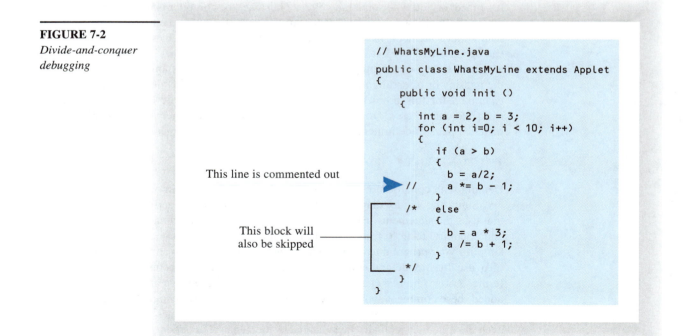

This line is commented out

This block will
also be skipped

```
// WhatsMyLine.java

public class WhatsMyLine extends Applet
{
    public void init ()
    {
        int a = 2, b = 3;
        for (int i=0; i < 10; i++)
        {
            if (a > b)
            {
                b = a/2;
//              a *= b - 1;
            }
/*          else
            {
                b = a * 3;
                a /= b + 1;
            }
*/
        }
    }
}
```

Run-Time Errors

Run-time errors, the second major sort of error your program can have, are different from compile-time errors, and a little more difficult to deal with. While compile-time errors always result in an error message (whether clear and helpful or otherwise), run-time errors often have no accompanying error message at all. In fact, there are three types of run-time errors:

☕ Errors that result in messages

☕ Errors that cause the program to produce a wrong result or wrong behavior

☕ Errors that cause the program to run endlessly or "hang"

TELL ME NO STORIES: ERRORS THAT ANNOUNCE THEMSELVES

The easiest sort of run-time error to deal with is the error that announces itself. When the Java run-time system encounters a problem in running the byte codes of your program, it will display an error message. Finding this error message, however, is sometimes easier said than done. The approach depends on what sort of Java program you're running and how you're running it. When you run an application, the error message will be displayed on the window that was used to start the interpreter—the place where you typed

```
java MyApp
```

This may be only one of several windows used by your program.

When you are running an applet using Appletviewer, the same thing happens. The error message is displayed in the window that you used to start the Appletviewer. However, when you are running an applet in a browser, you may have to search for the window containing the error message. In fact, the window may not be displayed at all unless you've set the proper option in the browser. For example, Netscape Navigator has an option that causes the "Java Console" to be displayed. Only if this option is enabled will you see the error messages displayed by the run-time system. Furthermore, your browser itself will catch many run-time errors, reporting no errors at all to you; this makes it advantageous for you to always test your program with the Appletviewer. Listings 7-2 and 7-3 show an applet that generates several different run-time errors. Figure 7-3 shows what the error messages look like when the applet is run in Appletviewer.

```
Listing 7-2 RuntimeError.java
// RuntimeError.java
// Illustrates several possible run-time errors
import java.applet.*;
import java.awt.*;
import java.awt.event.*;
```

continued on next page

continued from previous page

```java
public class RuntimeError extends Applet implements⇐
  ActionListener
{
    Button one    = new Button("How much is a Cat?");
    Button two    = new Button("Problems with Math");
    Button three = new Button("Nobody's Home");
    Button b;  // This has the value null

    public void init()
    {
        add( one );
        add( two );
        add( three );
        one.addActionListener(this);
        two.addActionListener(this);
        three.addActionListener(this);
    }

    public void actionPerformed( ActionEvent theEvent )
    {
        if (theEvent.getSource( ) == one) convertCat();
        if (theEvent.getSource( ) == two) divideZero();
        if (theEvent.getSource( ) == three) tryNull();
    }

    void convertCat()
    {
        // NumberFormatException
        String num = "Cat";
        int bad = Integer.parseInt( num );
    }

    void divideZero()
    {
        // ArithmeticException
        int numerator = 3;
        int denominator = 0;
        int problem = numerator / denominator;
    }

    void tryNull()
    {
        // NullPointerException
        b.setLabel("Uh Oh!");
    }
}
```

Listing 7-3 RuntimeError.html

```html
<HTML>
<HEAD>
<TITLE>RuntimeError.java</TITLE>
</HEAD>
<BODY>
<H1>RuntimeError.java</H1>
<H2>Run in appletviewer to see the output</H2>
<HR>
```

```
<H2>This code has three run-time errors</H2>
<UL>
<LI>A NumberFormatException trying to convert the
String "Cat" to an integer
<LI>A ArithmeticException trying to divide by zero
<LI>A NullPointerException trying to use a reference
to a Button that doesn't actually point to a button.
</UL>
<HR>
<APPLET CODE=RuntimeError.class HEIGHT=300 WIDTH=500>
</APPLET>
</BODY>
</HTML>
```

The applet produces predetermined errors when each appropriately labeled button is pushed:

Pressing the How much is a Cat? button causes the applet to try to convert the String "Cat" to an integer using the parseInt( ) method. This, of course, fails; the result is a NumberFormatException error, as you see in the figure.

Pressing the Problems with Math button causes the applet to perform a division by zero. This too fails; the result is an ArithmeticException error.

Pressing the Nobody's Home button tries to send a message to an object by use of a reference that is null. The result is a NullPointerException error.

These three run-time errors are exactly the three you're most likely to see in your programs. When your program displays an error message that includes one of these errors, you immediately know something about the kind of mistake that you made. Armed with that information, you should follow the strategy given in the section titled

FIGURE 7-3

Run-time error messages and Appletviewer

"A Debugging Plan of Action." Before that, however, let's look at the second kind of run-time error, the error associated with wrong output or behavior.

SOFTWARE MISBEHAVIOR: ERRORS IMPLICIT IN THE MIND OF THE BEHOLDER

Unless the run-time system has displayed an error message, in which case you *know* you have output you didn't want, the first problem with this sort of error is recognizing it when it occurs. Simply put, you cannot recognize wrong output or behavior unless you know clearly and precisely what good output or behavior should be.

Many programs are written without a clear idea of what the program should do or what the output should be. If you are writing programs for others, this often results in misunderstandings and disputes. Your client thinks the program should do one thing, and you think that it should do another. So, the first step in recognizing bad behavior is to precisely and unambiguously describe good behavior: what you expect of your program. This description is called a *program specification,* and if you're concerned that your program be error-free, you should prepare one before you begin to write your program.

Your specification should spell out, in detail, the proper output and behavior of your program under all relevant circumstances. The real value of such a specification is that it can be reviewed and approved by the final user of your program, thus avoiding or minimizing subsequent disputes about what the program should or should not do. There is no "official" form for a program specification, as there is for Java source code. You do need to be careful to cover all the important points. Figure 7-4 shows an example of such a program specification.

When a specification exists, it's possible to identify wrong output or wrong behavior as output or behavior contrary to the specification. The task then is to discover why the program doesn't do what it's supposed to do and what can be done about it. The section titled "A Debugging Plan of Action" will equip you with a suitable strategy. But first, let's deal with the final type of run-time error, programs that don't halt when they should.

THE ENDLESS PROGRAM: ERRORS FROM THE FOURTH DIMENSION

According to Einstein's General Theory of Relativity, time can be considered a fourth dimension, along with the three more familiar dimensions of height, width, and depth. Errors that cause your program to run endlessly or hang can therefore be considered errors from the fourth dimension.

The problem with such errors is deciding *when* to concede that an error exists. Perhaps if you waited just a few more seconds, the program would respond correctly. But, at some point, you become convinced that the program is malfunctioning. What

FIGURE 7-4

*A program
specification*

PROGRAM SPECIFICATIONS:
Prime Number Tester version 3.14159

INPUT:
An integer number, n

OUTPUT:
The string "The number n is prime" if n is prime
The string "The number n is evenly divisible by m"
otherwise, where m is a factor of n

NOTE:
A prime number is a number evenly divisible
only by 1 and itself.

PROCESSING:
Try each number m from 2 to n/2 to see if n is evenly
divisible by m. If any m evenly divides n, print the
message "The number n is evenly divisible by m,"
otherwise print the message "The number n is prime."

Identify the
program specification

Describe the
inputs and outputs

Define terms
or explain subtitles

Outlines steps
for processing

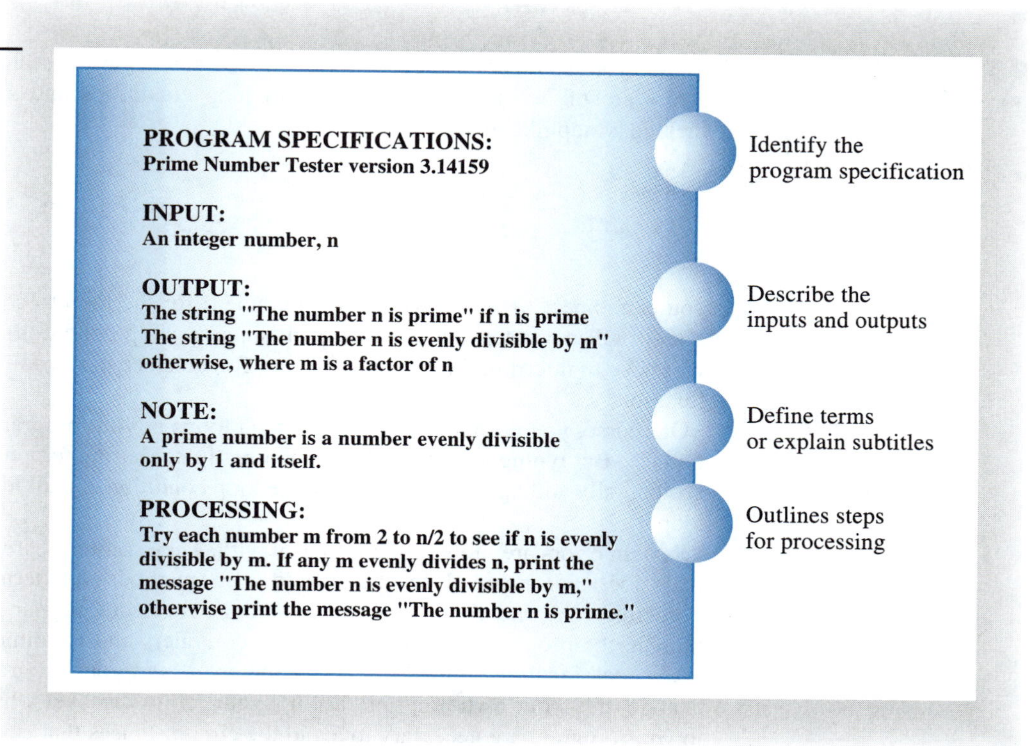

do you do to regain control of the system so that you can track down the bug? Here are
some suggestions, ranging from the mild to the drastic:

- Try the Stop, Exit, or Quit button included in your applet or GUI application.

- Try to load a different page into your browser.

- Click the Close icon in the upper-left corner of Appletviewer or your GUI
  application's window.

- Make the MS-DOS window you used to start Appletviewer or the MS-DOS
  window of your application the current window by clicking on its title bar.
  Then press CTRL-C, by holding down the CTRL key and simultaneously
  pressing C. This should cancel or terminate the program.

- Exit your browser.

- Use CTRL-ALT-DELETE to cancel the task.

- Shut down your computer.

- When all else fails, cycle power to your computer. This may result in serious
  loss of data, so it's definitely a last resort.

Once you regain control of your system, you can begin the search for the error. Such errors are of two basic types: errors in loop conditions and system errors. If you include a loop like this in your program:

```
int i;
while (i >= 0 || i < 0)
{
    i = i +1;
}
```

you can expect to wait a while (pun intended) for the loop to complete. In fact, such a loop will never terminate on its own, since its loop condition is always `true`; you will have to interrupt the program, or wait for a chance power failure or computer malfunction.

Of course, you normally won't write such loops in your programs, at least not intentionally. But typing a loop condition incorrectly, forgetting to update a loop counter, or accidentally adding a semicolon after the loop condition can all lead to such an endless loop.

System errors are more difficult to deal with. They commonly result in a hung system that does not respond to the less drastic methods for terminating a program. Sometimes the underlying cause of a system error is not in your program at all. Being human, the programmers who write Java compilers and run-time systems make mistakes occasionally. No matter whether the error is in your program or theirs, you can change only your own program. So, it's your job to discover what change or changes to *your* program are necessary to avoid the circumstances that expose the system error. The next section will show you how to do this.

A Debugging Plan of Action

"I JUST DON'T UNDERSTAND!"

Jumbo had sat, puzzled, staring at the same screen and the same listing for the last half hour. "This should work," he continued, secretly hoping Brenda, who was absorbed in her own efforts, hooking up the new computer to the espresso machine, would come over and help. No luck. "This must be some of Brenda's code," he muttered, just loudly enough to be sure Brenda would hear.

Distracted and annoyed, Brenda replied without taking her eyes off the screen. "Give me a break, J.G. I need to concentrate on this right now. You go ahead and break it, and when this is working I'll come over and fix it." Her voice trailed off at the end as she returned to her work.

Jumbo, tired and puzzled—and tired of being puzzled—thought for a moment, shrugged his massive shoulders, and with a swift and delicate motion, neatly broke off the locking-lever on the front of the ancient 5-1/4 inch floppy drive with his trunk. The "ping" as it snapped off brought Brenda's head up.

"OK," said Jumbo in an obedient and hopeful voice. "It's broken. What now?"

> *" System errors are more difficult to deal with than errors in loop conditions. "*

Debugging your code is a *process*—a series of steps that helps you find and fix the errors in your program. This process begins just as soon as you determine that your program is producing wrong output or behavior. The goal of the process is to fix the program, but this is best done in several disciplined steps. It is altogether too easy to fix one problem and, in the process, introduce another! To avoid that, you should perform each of the following steps of the debugging process:

1. Break it.
2. Pinpoint it.
3. Fix it.
4. Test it.

BREAK IT

Possibly it strikes you as odd that the first step in fixing your program is to break it. What could that possibly mean? If your program wasn't broken to begin with, you certainly wouldn't be debugging it now. Instead, you'd be packing for that jaunt to the Bahamas!

Breaking your program doesn't refer to introducing new errors, but rather to the process of forcing your program to fail reliably; that is, repeatedly and at will. Often some peculiar combination of circumstances is necessary for the error in your program to appear. A program involving dates may fail only for dates after February 28 and only for leap years. It may work perfectly under all other circumstances.

You want to avoid thinking you have fixed the program when, in fact, you haven't. That means that unless you're aware of the precise combination of circumstances under which the program fails, you won't know what values to use in testing the fixed program. This may lead you to believe that you've fixed the program when you really haven't.

Breaking the program involves reproducing the conditions under which it failed. To do this, you need to know as much as possible about the circumstances of failure. Ask the user (or yourself, if you were the user) what input was provided to the program, what controls were clicked, and in what order. Sit down and try to repeat the user's actions and find out what happens. You're done with this step when you can cause the program to fail in the same way it failed for the user and do so any time you please.

PINPOINT IT

The next step is usually the most difficult of the four, so be prepared to take your time. You need to find the exact place within the program that is responsible for the error. There are tools that can help you do this—for example, the Java debugger (Jdb) that we'll look at later in the chapter. For the moment, however, let's focus on somewhat more primitive techniques that are more widely applicable.

Remember from Chapter 2, "Programs: The Community of Objects," that there are two aspects of an object: the state of the object and methods that operate on the state.

To pinpoint the location of a bug, you normally will need to monitor the state of your objects (the values of their attributes) and to trace the instructions performed as the their methods are invoked and executed. How can you examine the state of an object or trace the instructions executed within an object method? One simple answer is the `println( )` method, usually invoked on the `System.out` object as `System.out.println( )`.

Using `println( )`

Examining the state of an object by using `println( )` is easy. You already know that the `println( )` method takes a single `String` argument and displays the value of this argument in the output window, the same window used by the runtime to print error messages. The handy thing about `println( )` is that it can also be called by use of many non-`String` argument types, such as `byte`, `int`, or `float`. Java provides these and similar types with an implicit `toString( )` "method," which can convert their value to a `String`. The `println( )` method automatically looks for such a method and will use it, if it exists, to convert the argument type to `String`. It's a good idea to include a `toString( )` method in classes you create, so that `println( )` can be called on your objects.

The argument to `println( )` can also be a straightforward `String` constant or expression. Writing a `println( )` with an argument like this:

```
System.out.println("Entered main loop");
```

or one like this:

```
System.out.println("Inside loop: i=" + i);
```

makes it easy to see what part of a program has been executed and what the program's state is at any point. One peculiarity of the `println( )` is that it gives the Java runtime permission to delay actually displaying the requested output, in order to improve program efficiency. This can be a problem when you're searching for a bug, because the bug may cause the program to terminate. When this happens, any pending output is simply discarded by the Java run-time system. To prevent this from happening, you should use the `flush( )` method, which instructs the Java run-time system to immediately display any pending output, just as you had to do when building the menu for the JavaMatic prototype. This will help avoid loss of the debugging output in the event the program terminates. You invoke `flush( )` like this:

```
System.out.flush( );
```

Putting `println( )` to Work

Take a look at the program in Listing 7-4. It was intended to display the sum of a range of integers. But be forewarned: There's a bug lurking inside. If you compile and run the program, the bug should come out and bite you on the nose.

Listing 7-4 TestSumRange.java

```
// A program with a bug
import java.io.*;
public class TestSumRange
{
    public static void main(String args[])
    {
        System.out.print(⇐
          "The sum of the range 1 to 3 (inclusive) is :");
        System.out.println( sumRange(1, 3) );
    }

    public static int sumRange(int i, int j)
    {
        int sum = 0;

        while (i < j)
        {
            sum += i;
            i++;
        }
        return sum;
    }
}
```

The sum of the integers from 1 to 3, inclusive, should be equal to $(1 + 2 + 3)$, or 6. When you invoke the method sumRange(1, 3), however, it returns 3, and the program prints that same value. It does this each time the program is run. What's the problem? Wrong output! Congratulations, you've completed the first step in the debugging process: discovering the error and getting the program to fail repeatedly. Now, how can you use println( ) to help with the second step of the debugging process, pinpointing the location of the bug?

Look at Listing 7-5. Notice how println( ) method calls have been distributed throughout the source code. Each invocation of println( ) allows you to monitor the state of the object—by examining the value of the variables i and j—or to monitor the operation of the method sumRange( )—by displaying messages about the current actions to the console. Figure 7-5 shows what the output generated by println( )s looks like as the program runs. Note how calls to flush are used to ensure that no output is lost in the event of a program termination. Can you spot the error by looking at Figure 7-5?

Listing 7-5 TestSumRange2.java

```
// Using System.out.println( ) to pinpoint the location of a bug
import java.io.*;
public class TestSumRange2
{
    public static void main(String args[])
    {
        System.out.print(⇐
          "The sum of the range 1 to 3 "+" (inclusive) :");
        System.out.println( sumRange(1, 3) );
    }
```

continued on next page

continued from previous page

```
public static int sumRange(int i, int j)
{
    int sum = 0;

    System.out.println("i=" + i);
    System.out.println("j=" +  j);
    System.out.flush( );

    while (i < j)
    {
        System.out.println("Before add, sum=" + sum);
        sum += i;
        System.out.println("After add,  sum=" + sum);

        System.out.println("Before increment, i=" + i);
        i++;
        System.out.println("After  increment, i=" + i);
        System.out.flush( );
    }
    System.out.println("The sum is : " + sum);
    System.out.flush( );

    return sum;
    }
}
```

> **“** *println( ) is more reliable than other debuggers currently offered in Java programming environments.* **”**

Nail That Puppy

"Hmmm," you think, examining the output. "If I'm summing up three numbers, then why does the output show only two numbers being added?" When you reach the point of asking that question, you know that you've located the error.

"What," you continue, "is causing the error? I know I need three numbers added and I'm getting only two. That must mean that the loop is going 'round too few times. There must be a mistake in the loop condition!" At that point, you've grasped both the location and the cause. The error is that the loop termination condition is wrong. It should be i <= j so that one additional iteration of the loop occurs when i finally reaches the same value as j.

FIGURE 7-5
Running SumRange2

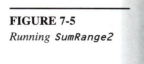

```
C:\OOP\Examples >javac TestSumRange2.java

C:\OOP\Examples >java TestSumRange2
The sum of the range 1 to 3 (inclusive) :i=1
j=3
Before add, sum=0
After add,  sum=1
Before increment, i=1
After  increment, i=2
Before add, sum=1
After add,  sum=3
Before increment, i=2
After  increment, i=3
The sum is : 3
3

C:\OOP\Examples >
```

Notice in the listing how the `println( )`s were strategically placed to show the progress of the computation. This is as much art as it is science; don't expect to put your `println( )`s in exactly the right places immediately. Debugging a program is an iterative process, meaning that you experiment a little, you learn a little from your experiments, and then you experiment some more.

The Joy of `println()`

If you've ever seen (or used) a modern, razzle-dazzle graphical debugger, the thought of inserting `println( )`s throughout your code might seem a crude anachronism. But the `println( )` technique has several advantages over even the highest-powered debugger. One nice thing about using `println( )` is that, no matter what Java environment you may be using, `println( )` always works the same. You don't have to learn the intricacies of a new debugger every time you switch systems.

Another nice thing is that `println( )` is more reliable than the debuggers currently offered in many Java programming environments. Writing a solid debugger is a formidable task, and current debuggers sometimes hang the system or otherwise refuse to work properly. You won't have these problems if you use `println( )` to do your debugging.

A Little Help from Your Friends

Sometimes, after thoroughly peppering your program with `println( )`s, you may still be unable to pinpoint the bug. When this occurs, it's time to call your "Dr. Watson." Get on the phone and invite a friend over for some java and pizza. Then, while you've got a captive audience, explain the program (and the bug), and invite your friend to ask questions.

Instead of slides from your vacation to Ohio, trot out your source code listings—especially if your guest can read C, C++, or Java. Usually, your efforts to clearly explain the situation will help *you* understand it better and will often lead rapidly to identification of the bug. Just having another pair of eyes look at a problem often brings obvious errors to light.

Occasionally, and it is to be hoped rarely, even your Dr. Watson will be unable to help. When this occurs, don't panic! Get away from the problem for a few hours. Work on an unrelated task, clean off your desk, get some exercise. Often your subconscious mind will continue to work on the problem. You may be struck with sudden inspiration while standing in the supermarket checkout line, or you may simply return to the problem the next day, only to find that what earlier seemed complicated seems oddly simple now. In any case, you'll benefit from the stress relief and will be a more effective detective when you return.

FIX IT

Once you've understood your program well enough to see why it malfunctions, you're ready to fix it. Think through the change you need to make. Some changes are easy and involve only a line of code. At other times you may realize that your whole concept was flawed and that you need to redesign an entire method or even an entire class.

If you've ever watched television, you've probably seen the situation-comedy episode where the well-meaning father decides to fix the roof or the shower or a light fixture, rather than calling in a tradesperson. This plot device has endured for many years because it is so true to human nature. All of us tend to rush in blindly, "fixing" things, but leaving the situation worse than when we began. The ancient proverb of the cure "…worse than the disease" aptly describes some of the possible fixes you might make.

To avoid the situation where you have to call in the "software plumber" after you've taken everything apart, it's a very good idea to save a copy of your unchanged program. In addition, you'll want to add comments that explain the change you're making and why it was necessary. Then, when you learn (perhaps much later) that your change has caused new problems—possibly even more serious than the one you've tried to fix—it's useful to be able to see exactly what it was that you did, and to be able to put things back the way they were.

TEST IT

At this point, 90 percent of the software developers pack up their tools and head for home. But a good craftsperson always performs one more step: He or she tests the repair to make sure that the new kitchen light actually can be turned on and off.

Testing and debugging are not the same thing. Debugging begins when you learn that your program contains an error. It is the process of isolating the bug and removing it from the program. Testing, on the other hand, is aimed at determining what bugs remain lurking in your program.

Testing turns into debugging when an error is found, and debugging should always transition back to testing, to make sure your fixes were good. In the testing-debugging process you will constantly bounce back and forth between these two until you're sufficiently confident that no serious bugs remain. At that point you can "release" your program. Figure 7-6 shows the testing and debugging process.

What to Test

Testing involves two major decisions. One decision is deciding what tests you should run. "I really want to make sure my program has no errors," you say, "so I'm going to test my program with all possible input values." While this is certainly a noble goal, unfortunately, it is one that usually cannot be achieved, you remind yourself.

"Balderdash!" you may be tempted to respond. "It can't be that much work." Well, let's think about that for a second. Let's assume that your program has only a single 10-byte input field. Since each byte has 8 bits, there are 2^8 (or 256) possible values for each byte. The entire field has 256^{10}, or 2^{80} possible values. To give you an idea of how many possible input cases that is, consider this: If you could run 10 million test cases each second, you would need 3,800,000,000 years to test this program. That is certainly more years than you have left until retirement! If that's not enough to convince

FIGURE 7-6

Testing and debugging

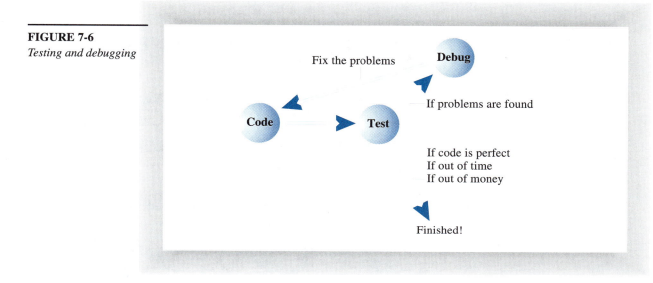

you this is an impossible task, imagine how long it would take you to go through the results, looking for one that is incorrect.

If you're still not convinced, think about this: Most programs have far more input values than can be accommodated by a single 10-byte field. Given that, testing all possible input values is simply not an option.

Your Friendly Representative

If you cannot test all possible values, then what values should you test? Or is there another way to test? Most testing relies on the idea that you can identify and run certain tests that are representative of a larger group of possible tests. If a representative test succeeds, you assume that any other member of this same group would have succeeded, so you don't bother even to try the other members of the group. Figure 7-7 shows how this works.

In applying this approach, most of the time you attempt to choose representative groups that have "geometric" relationships to other groups. Let's take a simple example. Assume that you've created a field inside one of the JavaMatic classes that will hold the product code of the last beverage the user has selected. In this version of the JavaMatic, the user's selection can range from 1 to 5 (Jumbo's decided to add a Decaf Mocha to the menu). The values 1 to 5 are *inside* your acceptable range of values, while other values are *outside* the range. Given such a range, you certainly would want to check at least these five values:

- The bottom of the valid range (here, 1)

- The middle of the valid range (here, 3)

- The top end of the valid range (here, 5)

FIGURE 7-7
Representative tests

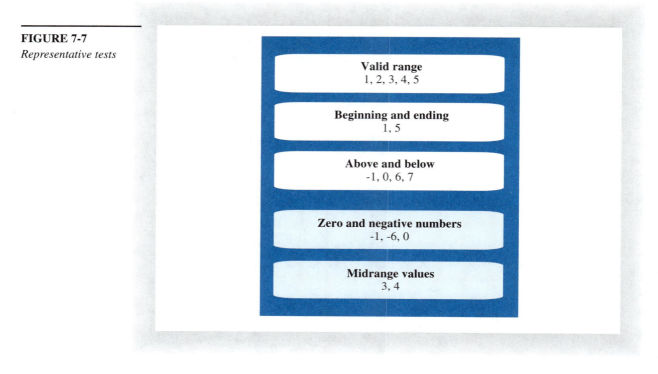

One step below the bottom of the valid range (here, 0)

One step above the top end of the valid range (here, 6)

Of course, there's no guarantee that testing the field with these values will uncover all possible errors. A famous computer scientist, Edgar Dijkstra, expressed the same sentiment with respect to testing generally: "Testing can prove only the presence of errors, never their absence." However, omitting one or more of these recommended test values means that your test has missed an opportunity to discover an entire group of possible errors. These are "high value" test cases.

COVERAGE AND CONDITIONS: KNOWING WHEN TO STOP

The first major testing decision is deciding what tests to run. The other major testing decision is deciding when to stop testing. Even using representative tests, a typical program will have many more tests than can be reasonably run. Since you cannot run them all, how do you decide when you're done testing? A good answer is that you're done testing when you've tested your program thoroughly. But how then can you measure how thoroughly a program has been tested? Fortunately, there are two useful measures: *statement coverage* and *condition coverage*. For languages of longer standing than Java, there are tools that can be used to measure statement and condition coverage. Although such tools are not yet widely available for Java programs, the underlying concepts are still useful. You can use these concepts to decide whether to continue testing a program.

Statement coverage measures the percentage of program statements that have been executed during testing. Obviously, you'd like to achieve 100 percent coverage of all statements, because a statement that has not yet been executed might contain a bug. Unless a statement is executed, you have no way of knowing whether it will produce correct output. When designing test cases—the sequence of input values that your program will be tested with—you should first examine the logic of your program, and then try to come up with cases that will cause each statement to be executed. When you cannot do this, you should at least inspect the untested code quite carefully, preferably with the aid of a friend or colleague.

A second, more rigorous, level of coverage is called condition coverage. A program that has achieved 100 percent condition coverage is one in which the condition part of every `if`, `switch`, and loop has been both `true` and `false`. That means there are no conditions in your program where only the `true` case or only the `false` case has been tested. An added bonus of condition coverage is that, if you fully exercise each condition, you will automatically achieve 100 percent statement coverage. Although it is difficult to achieve 100 percent condition coverage without the use of automated tools, you should design test cases with the idea of thoroughly exercising any conditions within your program. This will help you find test cases that have the highest possible value. When you've run all the test cases you designed with this criterion in mind, it's reasonable to stop testing.

Debugging Tools

Whatever Java development environment you choose to use, that environment is likely to have one or more tools intended to facilitate debugging. Sun's JDK provides Jdb, the Java debugger, for this purpose. The Jdb tool is far from being a perfect debugger and has been referred to as more of a "proof of concept" than an operationally satisfactory debugging tool. Despite its limitations, it is a useful part of every Java programmer's toolkit.

Debugging with Jdb is different from debugging with `println( )`s. When you used `println( )`s to debug the loop in Listing 7-5, you ran the whole program and then looked at the output. By noticing that there were only two add statements instead of three, your attention was directed to the condition statement that was controlling the loop. But think for a second. How quickly would you have spotted the error if the loop had repeated 100 times rather than three? At that point, inspection of "after the fact" output would lose much of its deductive power, due to the volume of output. You would want to turn to something that allowed you to look inside your program and to pick out only the parts you need at the moment. The Jdb debugger is the kind of tool that allows you to do that.

USING JDB

Let's use the Jdb debugger to examine the PrimeSieve program from the end of Chapter 6, "Teaching Your Objects to Repeat Themselves." Using Jdb involves several steps. You need to know

☕ How to prepare your programs for debugging

☕ How to start and give commands to the debugger

☕ How to quit the debugger when you are finished with your session

☕ How to set a breakpoint inside your code so that the program stops at a specific point and allows you to inspect it

☕ How to step through your code one line at a time

☕ How to inspect the data inside your objects and variables

Preparation

To start using Jdb, you must first compile your program using the special **-g** flag:

```
javac -g PrimeSieve.java
```

This flag causes the Java compiler to insert special information used by Jdb into the resulting CLASS file. Some versions of the JDK include a version of the Java compiler called Javac_G, which produces even better results working with Jdb. If you have a copy of that, you should type

```
javac_g -g PrimeSieve.java
```

Starting to Work

In either case, after you have prepared your CLASS file, you then can start the Jdb debugger by typing

```
jdb PrimeSieve
```

Once the Jdb program starts, you should see something like this on your screen:

```
Initializing jdb...
0x139fe30:class(PrimeSieve)
>
```

The > is a prompt character that lets you know that the system is now expecting a Jdb command. There are Jdb commands to list the statements of your program, to set *breakpoints* that let you control the execution of your program, to display the values of fields and local variables, and to perform other useful functions. Some of the most useful Jdb commands are summarized in Table 7-1.

TABLE 7-1
USEFUL JDB COMMANDS

COMMAND	FUNCTION
!!	Repeat the last command. May be followed by additional text, which is appended to the command before it is executed.
classes	List the classes that have been loaded.
clear	List the current breakpoints.
clear *class:line*	Clear the specified breakpoint.
cont	Resume execution (used after breakpoint has been reached).
dump *class*	Display all **static** methods and variables of the specified class and the identity of the superclass.
dump *object*	Display the value of all fields of the specified object.
exit	Quit Jdb.
help	Display a list of Jdb commands.
list	List the current line, in context.
list *line*	List the specified line, in context.
locals	Display the value of all local variables of the current method.
methods *class*	Display the names of each method of the specified class.
print *class* print *object* print *field* print *local—variable*	Print the value of the specified class, object, field, or local variable.
quit	Quit Jdb.
run run *class* run *class arguments*	Run the **main( )** method of the specified class, passing the method the specified arguments. If no class is specified, use the class specified on the command line when Jdb was started.
step	Execute the next line of code (not necessarily in the class being debugged).
stop at *class:line* stop in *class.method*	Set a breakpoint at the specified line or at the beginning of the specified method.

Looking at Code

The first thing you'll normally want to do after starting Jdb is to set a breakpoint by using the **stop** command. While Jdb executes your program, it checks each statement before it is executed to see if a breakpoint has been set. If so, Jdb temporarily suspends execution of your program and provides you with a > prompt so that you can enter new Jdb commands, such as those that display the values of fields and local variables. Using breakpoints this way lets you observe the progress of your program by watching the values of program fields and variables.

As you can see from looking at Table 7-1, there are two ways to set a breakpoint. You can specify a line number at which the breakpoint will be set, or you can specify a method, in which case the breakpoint is set at the beginning of the method. How do you know what line numbers or method names to use? The Jdb **run** command starts execution of your program by executing its `main( )` method, just as the Java interpreter does. So, to start out, you'll want to place a breakpoint at the beginning of the `main( )` method like this:

```
> stop in PrimeSieve.main
```

Once you do that, Jdb will display a response on the screen, just to let you know it got the message. You should see

```
Breakpoint set in PrimeSieve.main
>
```

which confirms that the breakpoint has been set. To further reassure yourself, you can type

```
clear
```

which will produce a display of all current breakpoints:

```
Current breakpoints set:
        PrimeSieve:6
>
```

Once you've set a breakpoint, you can start executing your program by typing the `run` command. If you type `run` but fail to set a breakpoint, the program will begin running, but you will not have a chance to stop it to examine its state. Since you have set a breakpoint—in this case on line 6—Jdb will execute your program until it reaches the code associated with line 6 of the source file, which is the beginning of the `main( )` method. When that happens, you'll see

```
> run
run PrimeSieve
running ...

Breakpoint hit: PrimeSieve.main (PrimeSieve:6)
main[1]
```

This lets you know that execution has been suspended at line 6. Notice that the prompt character has changed from > to `main[1]`. Now that a method of the `PrimeSieve` class is active, you can use the `list` command to view the source code:

```
main[1] list
2
3       public static void main(String args[])
4       {
5           nextNumber:
6=>         for (int n = 3; n <= 100; n += 2)
7           {
8               for (int divisor = 2; divisor <= n / 2; ⇐
                divisor++)
9               {
10                  int remainder = n % divisor; main[1]
```

Note how the => is used to mark the *next* statement that will be executed. Once your program is suspended, you can examine variables or set additional breakpoints to help you zero in on the code that you want to examine. Go ahead and try it by setting a breakpoint at line 10 and another at line 11:

```
main[1] stop at PrimeSieve:10
Breakpoint set at PrimeSieve:10
main[1] stop at PrimeSieve:11
Breakpoint set at PrimeSieve:11
main[1]
```

Now that you have several breakpoints in place, you can resume execution of the suspended program by using the `cont` command:

```
main[1] cont
Breakpoint hit: PrimeSieve.main (PrimeSieve:10)
```

Execution stops at the breakpoint on line 10. Resume the program by using the `cont` command:

```
main[1] cont
Breakpoint hit: PrimeSieve.main (PrimeSieve:11)
```

You can also execute a single line of code using the `step` command:

```
main[1] step
Source step: PrimeSieve.main (PrimeSieve:18)
The number 3 is prime.
main[1] step
Source step: PrimeSieve.main (PrimeSieve:10)
```

Looking at Data

The Jdb utility can also be used to inspect the value of program variables. Type the `locals` command to inspect local variables of the current method:

```
main[1] locals
Method arguments:
  args =
Local variables:
  n = 5
  divisor = 2
  remainder = 1
main[1]
```

USING JDB WITH APPLETVIEWER

You can also use the Jdb utility to debug applets. Listing 7-6 shows an applet that tests whether an input number is prime. Figure 7-8 shows the program at work.

Listing 7-6 PrimeApplet.java

```
import java.applet.*;
import java.awt.*;
import java.awt.event.*;
```

continued on next page

continued from previous page

```
public class PrimeApplet extends Applet implements ⇐
    ActionListener
{
    Label       theLabel   = new Label("Enter a number: ");
    TextField theNumber    = new TextField(4);
    Button      theButton  = new Button("Test"); " "
    Label       theResult  = new Label(
    );

    public void init( )
    {
        add(theLabel);
        add(theNumber);
        add(theButton);
        add(theResult);
        theNumber.addActionListener(this);
        theButton.addActionListener(this);
    }

    public void actionPerformed(ActionEvent theEvent)
    {
        int n = 0;
        n = Integer.parseInt(theNumber.getText( ));
        theResult.setText("The number " + n + " is prime.");

        for (int divisor = 2; divisor <= n / 2; divisor++)
        {
            int remainder = n % divisor;
            if (remainder == 0)
            {
                theResult.setText("The number " + n
                    + " is evenly divisible by " + divisor +
                    ".");
                break;
            }
        }

        invalidate( );
        validate( );
        repaint( );
    }
}
```

Setting Up an Applet

Starting Appletviewer with the −debug flag executes the specified applet under the control of Jdb. Since you don't have a main( ) method, you'll want to set a breakpoint when one of the special applet methods is invoked. In this applet, the test for whether a number is a prime number occurs in the `actionPerformed( )` method, so start by setting a breakpoint in that method. Just as with applications, you'll need to refer to the method using *class.method* notation.

FIGURE 7-8

Running
`PrimeApplet.java`

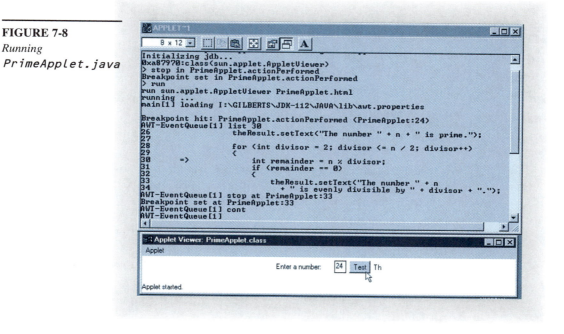

```
C:\OOP\Examples >appletviewer -debug PrimeApplet.html
Initializing jdb...
Oxa87970:class(sun.applet.AppletViewer)
> stop in PrimeApplet.actionPerformed
Breakpoint set in PrimeApplet.actionPerformed
> run
run sun.applet.AppletViewer PrimeApplet.html
running ...
main[1] loading I:\GILBERTS\JDK-112\JAVA\lib\awt.properties
```

Tripping the Breakpoint

Now to get back to the debugger, you'll need to do something that will cause the `actionPerformed( )` method to be called. This will trip or trigger the breakpoint. One way to do that is to type the number 23 in the `TextField` and press the Test button. You should see

```
Breakpoint hit: PrimeApplet.actionPerformed (PrimeApplet:24)
AWT-EventQueue[1]
```

Now that execution of your applet is suspended, set a new breakpoint at the line that handles a non-prime number and resume the program:

```
AWT-EventQueue[1] list 30
26 theResult.setText("The number " + n + " is prime.");
27
28 for (int divisor = 2; divisor <= n / 2; divisor++)
```

continued on next page

> *" Invest in an IDDE tool that includes an easier-to-use debugger than Jdb. "*

continued from previous page

```
29              {
30  =>      int remainder = n % divisor;
31        if (remainder == 0)
32        {
33              theResult.setText("The number  " + n
34                 + " is evenly divisible by " + divisor + ".");
AWT-EventQueue[1]
AWT-EventQueue[1] stop at PrimeApplet:33
Breakpoint set at PrimeApplet:33
AWT-EventQueue[1] cont
```

Now type the number 24, a non-prime number, into the `TextField` and press the Test button to see if your new breakpoint will get tripped. You should see that execution does, indeed, stop at each breakpoint, like this:

```
AWT-EventQueue[1]
Breakpoint hit: PrimeApplet.actionPerformed (PrimeApplet:24)
AWT-EventQueue[1] cont
AWT-EventQueue[1]
Breakpoint hit: PrimeApplet.actionPerformed (PrimeApplet:33)
AWT-EventQueue[1]
```

Applet Data

Just as with applications, you can use the `locals` command to obtain a list of the local variables in your applet. Normally, however, you aren't interested in seeing the values of all your variables. What if you want to see only a particular variable, or a field? In that case, you can use the `print` command to display its value. What actually gets displayed when you *print* an object depends on the object's `toString( )` method:

```
AWT-EventQueue[1] print theEvent
theEvent =
java.awt.event.ActionEvent[ACTION_PERFORMED,cmd=Test] on
button0
AWT-EventQueue[1]
```

The `locals` command allows you to see the values stored in all your local variables. Notice that `locals` also displays the values of method arguments and the special `this` argument:

```
AWT-EventQueue[1] locals
Method arguments:
  this =
PrimeApplet[panel1,0,0,628x40,layout=java.awt.FlowLayout]
  theEvent =
java.awt.event.ActionEvent[ACTION_PERFORMED,cmd=Test] on
button0
Local variables:
  n = 24
  divisor = 2
  remainder = 0
AWT-EventQueue[1]
```

CHOOSE YOUR WEAPONS

If you plan to do considerable Java programming, you'll want to invest in an IDDE (interactive development and debugging) tool that includes a debugger that is easier to use than Jdb. However, the debuggers within most IDDEs provide the same basic functions provided by Jdb. Understanding how Jdb works should make it easier for you to learn how to effectively use the debugger of any IDDE you encounter.

Summary

- The two major kinds of programming errors are compile-time errors and run-time errors.

- Compile-time errors can be diagnosed by use of the divide-and-conquer technique.

- There are three types of run-time errors: those that result in messages, those that result in wrong output, and those that result in a program that runs endlessly.

- A program specification describes the proper output and behavior of a program.

- The debugging process consists of four steps: break it, pinpoint it, fix it, and test it.

- Debugging involves searching for the cause of an error and fixing it; testing involves exercising a program in an attempt to discover what errors it contains.

- The `println( )` method can be used to trace program execution and inspect the value of program variables.

- Even very simple programs are too complex to be tested exhaustively.

- Input fields should be tested with values inside and outside their range of valid values.

- Thorough testing exercises every statement and both the `true` and `false` value of every conditional expression.

- The `continue` statement can be used to skip execution of the body of a loop.

- Labeled `continue` and `break` statements can affect the operation of outer loops.

- The Jdb utility included in the JDK can be used to debug an application or an applet.

- Breakpoints cause a program to be suspended before executing a specified statement.

Quiz

1. Syntax errors are also known as _____ errors because they are discovered when the program is compiled.

2. The second major kind of errors, _____ errors, are found when the program is run.

3. To use the divide-and-conquer technique, you _____ lines of code.

4. A program _____ describes the output and behavior of a program.

5. The goal of breaking a program during debugging is to find a way to make it fail _____.

6. The most useful method in attempting to pinpoint a program bug is the _____.

7. After locating and fixing a program bug, it's important to _____ the program, to find out if the original problem was really fixed and if additional problems were introduced.

8. A program should be tested by use of input values that are both _____ and _____ the valid range.

9. For even very simple programs, it is usually not possible to test _____ input value.

10. When every conditional expression within a program has been both `true` and `false`, 100 percent _____ coverage has been achieved.

11. The Jdb utility can be used to set _____, which suspends (s) execution when a specified statement is reached.

Exercises

1. Use `println( )`s to study the execution of an *application*. Show how the `println( )`s can be used to trace program execution and to inspect the value of fields and variables.

2. Use `println( )`s to study the execution of an *applet*. Show how the `println( )`s can be used to trace program execution and inspect the value of fields and variables.

3. Use the Jdb utility to study the execution of an *application*. Use commands to set breakpoints, print the value of local variables, and dump the fields of objects.

4. Use the Jdb utility to study the execution of an *applet*. Use commands to set breakpoints, print the value of local variables, and dump the fields of objects.

8

Flocking Objects:

Arrays and Exceptions

What is a community? Wake up some morning, before all of your neighbors get up, and look down your street. (Fortifying yourself with a large cup of java might help you to accomplish this.) What do you see? If you live in an average neighborhood, you'll see rows of houses, and each house will have a family living in it. From this perspective, your community is a collection of families, all arranged so that you can easily communicate with them. If you want to send a message to the Jones family, you can address a letter to 123 North Maple Street, or you can look them up in the phone book and give them a jingle. We arrange our human communities in ways designed to facilitate communication between us. The natural world, likewise, arranges its members not as random individuals, but as flocks and herds and prides.

Java has several facilities for grouping data and objects into collections. Just as an egg carton makes it easier for you to buy and store eggs, collections make it much more convenient for you to access and use the data in your programs. Imagine trying to arrive home from a trip to the market with a dozen eggs intact without the benefit of a carton! In this chapter, you'll learn about the Java *collections* known as `arrays`, `Strings`, and `Vectors`.

*" **One compact method call can replace three steps in converting text into a number.** "*

In addition to collections, you'll be introduced to the idea of *exceptions*. What's an exception? An exception is simply an unusual condition inside your program. When you expect your customers to type in numbers and they type in `Strings` instead, you have an exception. To handle exceptions, Java provides you with the ability to separate code that deals with usual situations from code that deals with unusual (exceptional) situations. This way you can often end up with two simple pieces of code, rather than one complex piece of code.

In this chapter you will learn

☕ How to use `TextAreas`, which provide applets and GUI applications with multiline input and output of text

☕ How to use `arrays` and `Vectors` to store data

☕ How to use the `Event` argument of the `action( )` method to identify the object that was the target of an action

☕ How to sort the data contained in `arrays` and `Vectors`

☕ How to use `GridLayout` to control the layout of user-interface controls

☕ How to use `Strings` to store and manipulate text

☕ How to use `try`, `catch`, and `throws` statements to detect and recover from exceptions

☕ How to use the `sleep( )` method to pause execution of a program

Arrays

One of the most important items of information you need to manage a vending machine is its daily sales. If you owned a fleet of JavaMatics, you'd need to keep track of daily sales from all of them. Then, if you had some machines with low daily sales, you could move them to a new location, where they might do better. Let's start with an applet that will let you calculate the average daily sales from your empire by entering the daily sales from each machine. Listings 8-1 and 8-2 are the source code for the applet. Figure 8-1 shows the `AverageSales` applet in action.

Listing 8-1 AverageSales.java

```
// AverageSales - computes average sales for a fleet of
JavaMatics
import java.applet.*;
import java.awt.*;
import java.awt.event.*;

public class AverageSales extends Applet⇐
   implements ActionListener
{
    TextField dailySalesTxt  = new TextField("", 15);
    TextArea  output         = new TextArea("", 8, 30);
```

```
    double totalSales = 0.0;
    double averageSales;
    int numMachines   = 0;

    public void init()
    {
        add( new Label("Enter daily sales, press Enter: "));
        add( dailySalesTxt );
        add( output );
        dailySalesTxt.addActionListener(this);
        output.setEditable(false          );
    }

    public void actionPerformed( ActionEvent theEvent )
    {
        calcDailySales();
    }

    public void calcDailySales()
    {
        // Convert TextField dailySales to a double
        String saleAmtStr = dailySalesTxt.getText();
        Double saleAmtDbl = Double.valueOf( saleAmtStr );
        double saleAmtdbl = saleAmtDbl.doubleValue();

        // Increment number of machines. Add sales to total.
        // Compute average.
        totalSales += saleAmtdbl;
        numMachines++;
        averageSales = totalSales/numMachines;

        // Display number, total, and average
        output.append(⇐
          "" + numMachines + ". " + saleAmtdbl + '\n' );
        output.append(⇐
          "   Total Sales   : " + totalSales +'\n' );
        output.append(⇐
          "   Average Sales : " + averageSales + '\n' );
    }
}
```

Listing 8-2 AverageSales.html

```
<HTML>
<HEAD>
<TITLE>Counting on Good Times</TITLE>
</HEAD>
<BODY>
<H1>Jumbo Counts His Loot</H1>
"If I were a rich man, duh-duh-dah-dah-dah-dah..." Jumbo
hummed to himself as he typed in the sales for his
burgeoning fleet of JavaMatics. His trunk, holding the
mouse, was swaying back and forth as he conducted his
imaginary orchestra.<P>
"Java's great. Java's good. JavaMatic in your 'hood!" he
said suddenly, stopping his humming and turning to Brenda,
who continued to ignore him. Undissuaded, he went on, "Wait.
How about this? In the jungle, in the veldt, JavaMatic for
your pelt!"<BR>
```

continued on next page

continued from previous page

```
Brenda, exasperated, sighed. "Boss, if you don't let me
get this work done, it's gonna be your pelt on the line."
<HR>
<IMG SRC="jumbo.GIF" ALIGN=RIGHT>
<APPLET CODE=AverageSales.class HEIGHT=200 WIDTH=300>
</APPLET>
</BODY>
</HTML>
```

EXAMINING AverageSales

With all your recent time in the console-mode jungle, it's been a while since you've seen an applet. Take a few minutes to read through the code, and then let's see what makes AverageSales.java tick.

The AverageSales class has one TextField object it uses to gather up the user's input and one TextArea object to display the output from its calculations. The class also has three primitive fields: totalSales, which is used to hold the accumulated sales every time a new amount is entered; numMachines, which keeps track of how many machines have been entered; and averageSales, which, as you might expect, holds the average sales from each of the vending machines entered so far. To use the AverageSales applet, you need to enter a number into the field dailySalesTxt. When you press [ENTER], the actionPerformed( ) method of the AverageSales class is invoked, and it, in turn, calls the calcDailySales( ) method, which processes the text you entered. The first step in that processing is to convert the text that you have entered into a number.

FIGURE 8-1

Running
AverageSales in
Netscape Navigator

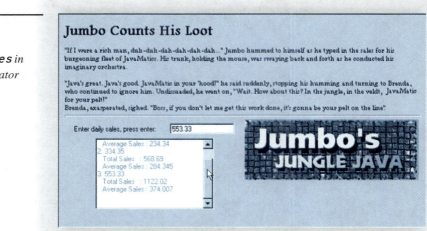

Revisiting Numeric Conversion

As you recall from Chapter 3, "The Atomic Theory of Objects: Working with Object Attributes," this is a three-step process. First, the text is retrieved from the `TextField` `dailySalesTxt` and stored in a local `String` named `saleAmtStr` by use of the call:

```
String saleAmtStr = dailySalesTxt.getText( );
```

Then, that `saleAmtStr` is converted into a `Double` object by use of the `static` method of the `Double` class, `valueOf( )`. The resulting `Double` object is stored in the local variable `saleAmtDbl`, like this:

```
Double saleAmtDbl = Double.valueOf( saleAmtStr );
```

Finally, remember that `Double` objects are "wrappers" around the primitive types you need to actually perform your calculations. To get the `double` value out of the `saleAmtDbl` variable, you use the `doubleValue( )` method of the `Double` variable `saleAmtDbl`, like this:

```
double saleAmtdbl = saleAmtDbl.doubleValue( );
```

Of course, because the only number you are actually interested in is the final `double` value, `saleAmtdbl`, you could have done the whole thing in one compact method call like this:

```
double saleAmtdbl =⇐
        Double.valueOf( dailySalesTxt.getText( ))⇐
        .doubleValue( );
```

The Rest of the `actionPerformed`

Once the `calcDailySales( )` method has retrieved the value you've entered for this new machine, it performs these steps:

1. Adds the sales from this machine to the total:

```
totalSales += saleAmtdbl;
```

2. Increments the number of machines:

```
numMachines++;
```

3. Calculates the new average daily sales and stores that value in the `averageSales` variable:

```
averageSales = totalSales/numMachines;
```

4. Displays the current sales, total, and average sales on the display:

```
output.append("" + numMachines + ". " + saleAmtdbl + '\n' );
output.append("    Total Sales   : " + totalSales +'\n' );
output.append("    Average Sales : " + averageSales + '\n' );
```

The display is updated by use of the `append( )` method for the `TextArea` object, `output`.

TextAreas for output

This applet introduces one new type of object, the `TextArea`. A `TextArea` is similar to a `TextField`, except that it can hold multiple lines of text, which can be scrolled. By putting a `TextArea` object on your applet, you have a roomy place for your program to write status messages and other output. Because it is so handy as an output device, the `TextArea` in the `AverageSales` applet has been named `output`.

To construct a `TextArea` object, you use the `new` operator, just as you do to create other objects. The constructor for `output` takes three arguments—the `String` you wish to initially display, the number of rows of text you wish to display, and the number of columns:

```
TextArea output = new TextArea("", 10, 40 );
```

This statement creates a `TextArea` object that displays 10 rows and 40 columns of characters. Just as with the `TextField` object, the number of columns is an approximation, based on the average character width of the current typeface. Your `TextArea` object can hold more lines of text than the number you specify in the constructor, but you will have to scroll the display to see them, by using the built-in scroll bars.

Normally, a `TextArea` object is both readable and writable; that is, you can type text into it, as well as programmatically add text to it. For the object, `output`, in the `AverageSales` applet, you really don't want to allow the user to type new values into it. You want it to act as the status display of your applet. You can make a `TextArea`— as well as a `TextField`—read-only by calling the `setEnabled( )` method of the field right after it has been added to the applet, like this:

```
add( output );
output.setEnabled(false);
```

After doing this, you cannot enter a new value into the field.

INTRODUCING AN ARRAY

Now that you have the ability to calculate the average daily sales for your entire fleet of JavaMatics, you need to know which ones have daily sales below this average in order to manage them intelligently. Those machines would be candidates for relocation. But how would you identify the low performers? At the time you enter the sales amount for a given machine, you don't yet know the average daily sales for the fleet. In fact, you don't know the average daily sales for the fleet until *all* the sales amounts have been entered. While you might write the applet so that the user was required to re-enter all of the sales amounts in order to get a listing of those that are below the daily average, that's not very user-friendly, to say the least.

Fortunately, Java has something called *arrays*, which allow you to conveniently store multiple data values for later use. By using arrays, you can enter your data once, but use it many times throughout your program. Essentially, an array consists of a collection of variables that share a single name. The individual variables are distinguished by use of a number—called the *index*, or preferably the *subscript*—to refer to a particular element of the array. You can see an example of an array in Figure 8-2.

Figure 8-2 shows an array called `dailySales`, which includes 100 distinct elements. All of the elements are known by this same name. Each element of the array has the same data type, which in this case is `double`.

Using Arrays

Because all of the elements in `dailySales` have the same name, how can you use subscripts to access the individual elements? To do this, you use a peculiar syntax. You refer to the first element of this array as `dailySales[0]` and the last element as `dailySales[99]`. The name of any element of the array can be formed by using the array name followed by an appropriate subscript within square brackets. Although it may seem odd at first to refer to the first element using `[0]` rather than `[1]`, you'll soon see that this often simplifies your programs.

Java arrays can hold primitive types, as you have seen with `dailySales`, or objects. Is an array also a primitive type? No. Java arrays are really themselves a kind of object. Any of the methods defined for the class `Object` can be invoked on a array, and any array can be assigned to a variable of class `Object`. In addition to methods, arrays also have fields. One field you may find useful is the `length` field of an array. For example, the length of the `dailySales` array can be accessed by use of the expression `dailySales.length`, which has the value 100.

FIGURE 8-2
An array

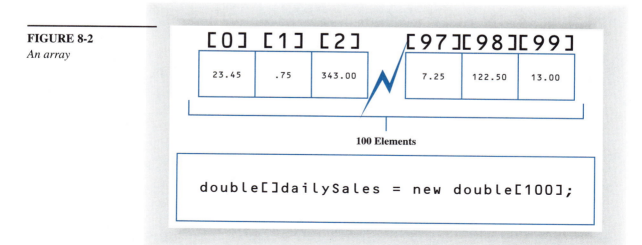

```
double[]dailySales = new double[100];
```

Adding Arrays

> *Java supports the idea of a multidimensional array.*

Now that you know a bit about Java arrays, let's modify your sales analysis program to use an array so that it can identify the machines with low sales. Compile and run the `LowSales` applet, shown in Listings 8-3 and 8-4. Then we'll take a look at how arrays add functionality to your applets. Figure 8-3 shows the `LowSales` applet in action.

Listing 8-3 LowSales.java

```java
// LowSales - computes average sales and then identifies the
slackers
import java.applet.*;
import java.awt.*;
import java.awt.event.*;

public class LowSales extends Applet implements ActionListener
{
    TextField dailySalesTxt = new TextField("", 15);
    TextArea  output        = new TextArea("", 8, 40);
    Button    findLowSales   =⇐
      new Button("Find Low Performers");

    // Array declared here
    double[] dailySales;

    double totalSales = 0.0;
    double averageSales;
    int numMachines    = 0;

    public void init()
    {
        // Array created here
        dailySales = new double[100];

        add( new Label("Enter daily sales, press Enter: "));
        add( dailySalesTxt );
        add( output );
        add( findLowSales );
        findLowSales.addActionListener(this);
        dailySalesTxt.addActionListener(this);
    }

    public void actionPerformed( ActionEvent theEvent )
    {
        // Check to see if button or enter key
        if ( theEvent.getSource( ) == findLowSales )
            printLowPerformers();
        else
            calcDailySales();
    }

    public void printLowPerformers()
    {
        output.append("\nLow performing machines\n");
        output.append("----------------------------\n");
```

```
        for ( int i = 0; i < numMachines; i++ )
        {
            if ( dailySales[i] < averageSales )
            {
                output.append("Machine # " + i + ". " );
                output.append("$" + dailySales[i] + '\n' );
            }
        }
    }

    public void calcDailySales()
    {
        // Convert TextField dailySales to a double
        // and store in dailySales
        double saleAmtdbl =
                Double.valueOf(⇐
                    dailySalesTxt.getText() ).doubleValue();
        dailySales[numMachines] = saleAmtdbl;

        // Increment number of machines. Add sales to total.
        // Compute average.
        totalSales += saleAmtdbl;
        numMachines++;
        averageSales = totalSales/numMachines;

        // Display number, total, and average
        output.append("" + numMachines + ". " +⇐
            saleAmtdbl + '\n' );
        output.append("   Total Sales   : " +⇐
            totalSales +'\n' );
        output.append("   Average Sales : " +⇐
            averageSales + '\n' );
    }
}
```

Listing 8-4 LowSales.html

```
<HTML>
<HEAD>
<TITLE>Separating the Sheep from the Goats</TITLE>
</HEAD>
<BODY>
<H1>Jumbo Finds the Slackers</H1>
"Where did I put that list?" Jumbo muttered. A large pile
of papers slid off the table and silently scattered themselves
across the floor. "Marvelous," he said to himself. <P>
"Why the mess, J.G.?" asked Brenda heedlessly, as she walked
through the door. <BR>
Jumbo pounced. "This is all your fault!" he exclaimed
unreasonably. How am I supposed to remember which machines
had low sales, after I've entered them all in?"<P>
Brenda, showing wisdom beyond her years, walked to the
keyboard and clicked the mouse. "Look at this," she said.
<HR>
<IMG SRC="jumbo.GIF" ALIGN=RIGHT>
<APPLET CODE=LowSales.class HEIGHT=300 WIDTH=300>
</APPLET>
</BODY>
</HTML>
```

FIGURE 8-3

Running the LowSales applet

EXAMINING LowSales

To use arrays inside your program, you need to do three things:

🖎 Declare an array variable (or reference).

🖎 Create an array and assign its reference to your variable.

🖎 Use the individual elements of the array.

Declaring and Defining Arrays

How do you create a variable that will hold an array? Look through the listing until you find the line where the variable dailySales is declared. Notice how the variable has a pair of brackets ([]) placed after the type. This marks dailySales as an array. You can change the order of this declaration somewhat if you want. It's perfectly okay to write the declaration as

```
double dailySales[];
```

Either way, the brackets say that dailySales is an array variable designed to hold an array of doubles.

After you have created an array variable, you then need to create the array that the variable refers to. As is the case with objects, the reference to an array and the array itself are two different things. In the LowSales applet, the array is created by use of the new operator, which creates an array of 100 doubles. The variable dailySales is then set to refer to the array by use of the line

```
dailySales = new double[100];
```

which takes place as the first line inside the `init( )` method. Of course, you could have created the array and declared the array variable all in one, by making the field declaration for `dailySales` look like this:

```
double[] dailySales = new double[100];
```

Arrays in Java always have a definite size and cannot hold more elements than permitted by their size. You've given this array space for 100 elements, which should be enough to accommodate your entire fleet of JavaMatics.

Looking at the `actionPerfomed( )`

When you press the `Find Low Performers` button, the `actionPerformed( )` method of the `LowSales` applet calls another method, `printLowPerformers( )`, to print to the status display those machines that have sales lower than the average sales of all of the machines. How does this work?

There are several steps that need to be taken. First, you store the sales amount of each machine as it is entered. In the `AverageSales` applet, this value was simply ignored, but now you need to modify the `calcDailySales( )` method to store this number in your array. That can be done with the lines

```
double saleAmtdbl =
    Double.valueOf( dailySalesTxt.getText( ) ).doubleValue( );
dailySales[numMachines] = saleAmtdbl;
```

These statements convert the text inside the field `dailySalesTxt` into a number using the compact notation discussed in the `AverageSales` applet. That number, `saleAmtdbl`, is then stored inside an array element. Note the use of brackets, which mark this as an assignment of a value to an array variable. The particular element into which the value is stored is determined by the current value of the field variable, `numMachines`. This field is initialized to zero in its declaration, and its value is increased by one every time you input data for another machine. The increment to the `numMachines` variable must take place after the first sales amount is stored in the array, because the first element of the array is `dailySales[0]`. If you incremented `numMachines` before storing the value, the first "slot" in the array would never be filled. Incrementing `numMachines` after storing the value causes successive sales amounts to be stored in distinct elements of the `dailySales` array.

There's another change to make to the `AverageSales` applet in order to build the `LowSales` applet. You need to call the `printLowPerformers( )` method when the user presses the button. But what happens when the user does press the button? The `actionPerformed( )` method is called, just as if the user had pressed ENTER after putting in the latest sales amount. You will need to have some way of distinguishing between the button press and the ENTER key in the `TextField`. To do that, you will need to be able to tell different kinds of `ActionEvent`s apart.

Who Did What?

To distinguish between different action events, you need to use the `ActionEvent` argument to the `actionPerformed( )` method, which you have heretofore ignored. An `ActionEvent` is an object, so it has fields and methods. One of the methods inside the `ActionEvent` object that you can use to learn about an `ActionEvent` is the `getSource( )` method. `getSource( )` will tell you which object is the source (sometimes called the *target*) of a particular action:

```
if ( theEvent.getSource( ) == findLowSales )
    printLowPerformers( );
else
    calcDailySales( );
```

If the source were the `findLowSales` button, you would know that the button had been pressed, and you could call the `printLowPerformers( )` method to handle that event.

The `printLowPerformers( )` method consists of a simple loop, which goes through each element of the `dailySales` array and prints the machine number and daily sales amount for any machines with below-average sales. Note that the array element is accessed, as always, by use of brackets. Here, the loop variable (`i`) determines which individual element is being accessed:

```
for ( int i = 0; i < numMachines; i++ )
{
    if ( dailySales[i] < averageSales )
    {
        output.append("Machine # " + i + ". " );
        output.append("$" + dailySales[i] + '\n' );
    }
}
```

What If?

It's reasonable to ask at this point what would happen if we had more than 100 JavaMatics. An attempt to access an element outside the actual range of elements of an array results in an `ArrayIndexOutOfBoundsException`. For example, this exception would be thrown by attempting to access `dailySales[101]`. Because the valid subscripts for an array of 100-element range from 0 to 99, attempting to access `dailySales[-1]` or `dailySales[100]` would raise the exception as well. You'll learn more about exceptions later in this chapter. For the moment, it's sufficient to know that, unless they're caught and handled, exceptions generally cause a program to terminate immediately. Though an error message is displayed when this occurs, often it's hard to find the error message if you're using a browser rather than the Appletviewer. When a program containing an array appears not to work, you should suspect that an `ArrayIndexOutOfBoundsException` has occurred, and search for the error message in the MS-DOS window or the Java console.

MULTIDIMENSIONAL ARRAYS

Arrays are not limited to a single dimension in Java. As do most other modern computer languages, Java supports the idea of a *multidimensional* array. If you think of an array as a single row or column of data, then a multidimensional array is similar to a matrix (think of a chessboard or spreadsheet), where there are both rows and columns of data. Figure 8-4 illustrates one way you can think about a two-dimensional array.

To create a two-dimensional array, you use two sets of brackets, rather than one, after the type or the name. To create an array that holds the grades for five tests for a class of 30 students, you would write

```
double[][] grades = new double[30][5];
```

You want a row every student—which is 30 in this case—and every row to have 5 columns.

Elements of a two-dimensional array are also accessed by use of the double pair of brackets. Conventionally, we think of the first subscript as designating a row and the second subscript as designating a column. So, `grades[3][2]` refers to an element representing the fourth student and the third test. Don't forget that the row and column numbers start with 0!

FIGURE 8-4

A two-dimensional array

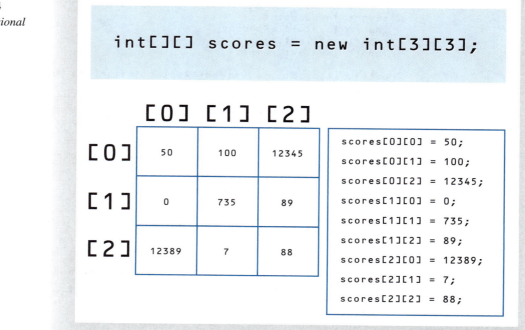

```
int[][] scores = new int[3][3];
```

	[0]	**[1]**	**[2]**
[0]	50	100	12345
[1]	0	735	89
[2]	12389	7	88

```
scores[0][0] = 50;
scores[0][1] = 100;
scores[0][2] = 12345;
scores[1][0] = 0;
scores[1][1] = 735;
scores[1][2] = 89;
scores[2][0] = 12389;
scores[2][1] = 7;
scores[2][2] = 88;
```

Java is not limited to two-dimensional arrays. You can also have arrays of three or more dimensions. You may find it easier to think of a multidimensional array as an array whose elements are themselves arrays, that is, an array of arrays. This is particularly helpful if an array has more than three dimensions, because few people can readily visualize such an array.

SORTING USING ARRAYS

One problem with your sales analysis program is that its output is displayed in the same sequence as its input. Because the program doesn't sort the data, the user must put the data in order before entering it. This is a time-consuming, error-prone, and boring process. Let's improve the program by making it capable of sorting the data.

Let's first create a class called `Bubble` to learn how to perform a sort; later you'll apply it to create an improved sales analysis program. Take a look at the `Bubble` applet in Listings 8-5 and 8-6. You can see the applet at work in Figure 8-5, but this is one you need to try for yourself. Press the Populate button to fill the `TextField`s with a random set of numbers. Then press the Sort button to watch the numbers rearrange themselves. Be sure to try pressing Sort a second time—after all the numbers are sorted, but before pressing Populate again—to see what happens. When you've finished playing—this applet may prove addictive—come back and we'll take a closer look.

Listing 8-5 Bubble.java

```java
// The Bubble applet shows how to sort an array
import java.applet.*;
import java.util.Random;
import java.awt.*;
import java.awt.event.*;

public class Bubble extends Applet implements ActionListener
{
    // -------- attributes ----------------------------------
    // declare and create the array
    TextField[] machine = new TextField[6];

    Random randGen      = new Random( );
    Button popBtn       = new Button("Populate");
    Button sortBtn      = new Button("Sort");

    // ------- init( ): set up the applet -------------------
    public void init( )
    {
        setLayout( new GridLayout(8,1) );

        for (int i = 0; i < machine.length; i++ )
        {
            // create the textfield object and store
            // in the array
            machine[i] = new TextField("", 10);
```

```
                add( machine[i] );
        }
        add( popBtn );
        add( sortBtn );
        popBtn.addActionListener(this);
        sortBtn.addActionListener(this);
    }


    // ------- action( ): choose between buttons ------------
    public void actionPerformed( ActionEvent theEvent )
    {
        if (theEvent.getSource( ) == popBtn)     populate( );
        if (theEvent.getSource( ) == sortBtn)    sort( );
    }


    // ------- populate( ): fill array with random values ---
    public void populate( )
    {
        for (int i = 0; i < machine.length; i++)
        {
            int n = (int) (randGen.nextFloat( ) * 500.0);
            machine[i].setText( "" + n);
        }
    }


    // ------- sort( ): arrange elements in order -----------
    public void sort( )
    {
        boolean swapped;

        do {
            swapped = false;
            for (int i = 0; i < (machine.length - 1); i++)
            {
                int a, b;
                a = Integer.parseInt(machine[i].getText( ));
                b = Integer.parseInt(machine[i+1].getText( ));
                setColor(i,   Color.blue);
                setColor(i+1, Color.red);
                pause(500);

                if (a > b)
                {
                  int temp = b;
                  machine[i+1].setText(machine[i].getText( ));
                    machine[i].setText("" + temp);
                    setColor(i,   Color.red);
                    setColor(i+1, Color.blue);
                    pause(500);
                    swapped = true;
                }
                setColor(i  , Color.white);
                setColor(i+1, Color.white);
            }
        } while (swapped);
    }
```

continued on next page

continued from previous page

```java
// ------- pause( ): sleep for milliseconds -------------
public void pause( int milliseconds )
{
    try
    {
        Thread.sleep( milliseconds );
    }
    catch( InterruptedException e )
    {
    }
}

// ------- setcolor( ): recolor a given member of the⇐
   array
public void setColor(int i, Color c)
{
    String text = machine[i].getText( );
    machine[i].setBackground(c);
}
}
```

Listing 8-6 Bubble.html

```html
<HTML>
<HEAD>
<TITLE>Jumbo Tries Some Bubbly</TITLE>
</HEAD>
<BODY>
<H1>Jumbo's Joy Bubbles Over</H1>
"Bubble, bubble, toil and trouble," read Jumbo aloud to
himself, as he thumbed his well-worn copy of Macbeth. "Ain't
it the truth," he said to no one in particular. <P>
Brenda, in a rare display of well-meaning but misguided
helpfulness, tried to distract him with the applet on the
screen. "There is no need for trouble. Just watch this applet
bubble." <BR>
Jumbo pressed the button and couldn't surpress his grin.
<HR>
<IMG SRC="jumbo.GIF" ALIGN=RIGHT>
<APPLET CODE=Bubble.class HEIGHT=200 WIDTH=150>
</APPLET>
</BODY>
</HTML>
```

FIGURE 8-5

Running the **Bubble** *applet*

BURSTING THE Bubble

This listing is somewhat longer than others you have studied, so extra care has been taken to organize the program for easier understanding. This is a good model for you to follow in writing your own programs. After the section of the program that contains the fields of the **Bubble** class, there are six methods:

- **init( )**, which initializes and sets up the applet to run

- **actionPerformed( )**, which calls either the **populate( )** or **sort( )** method, depending on which button was pressed

- **populate( )**, which fills each of the **TextField** objects in the applet with a random number

- **sort( )**, which uses a bubble-sort algorithm to successively swap adjacent elements until the entire array of **TextField** objects is in order

- **pause( )**, which causes the applet to wait for a few milliseconds between actions, so you can actually see what is happening

- **setColor( )**, which repaints a given **TextField** in a different color

The Attributes of Bubble

The **Bubble** applet has four fields. The first field, **machine**, is an array of **TextField** objects that will be used to hold the serial numbers of a number of JavaMatics. The **machine** variable is declared like this:

```
TextField[] machine = new TextField[6];
```

which can be read as saying "`machine` is an array of references to six `TextField` objects."

The second field is a `Random` object named `randGen`. Recall from Chapter 4, "Simply Methods: One Step at a Time," that `Random` objects can be used to create a series of pseudorandom numbers, especially handy for testing. To create objects from the `Random` class, you need to make sure that you have the line

```
import java.util.Random;
```

near the top of your file. The last two fields are `Button` objects, named `popBtn` and `sortBtn`, that will be used to tell the applet to populate the `machine` array and sort it.

The `init( )`ial Steps

`Bubble`'s `init( )` method will look familiar to you in some places and unfamiliar to you in other places. Let's start by looking at the first line:

```
setLayout( new GridLayout(8, 1) );
```

Just what does that mean? This line introduces a new feature that will be very handy as you build applets that present material in a tabular layout. Do you remember your very first applet, `Elephants_Rule`? In that applet, you created a `Label` object, and then displayed that `Label` on the screen by using the applet's `add( )` method. When you added the `Label` to the applet, it wasn't necessary for you to specify exactly where you wanted it to appear. In fact, much to your frustration, it was not *possible* for you to specify where you wanted the `Label` to appear—at least not without using the `move( )` method.

How does the `add( )` method know where to put your `Label`? The answer lies with something called the `LayoutManager`. The `LayoutManager`, like the maitre d' in a restaurant, is responsible for "seating" your components—`Label`s, `Button`s, and so forth—on the surface of the applet's display. There are several different types of `LayoutManager`s, and each has a different scheme for arranging your pieces.

The default `LayoutManager`, the one your applets use when you don't tell them to use another, is called `FlowLayout`. `FlowLayout` works by adding your components one after another, from left to right, starting in the upper-left corner of the screen. When a component will not fit in the current row, then a new row is started. On each row, all of the components are, by default, centered. While easy to use, `FlowLayout` does not really give you the control over the placement of your controls that you might like—especially for tabular material. An easy-to-use `LayoutManager` that does give you such control is called `GridLayout`.

Using `GridLayout`

The `GridLayout LayoutManager` arranges your components in a series of rows and columns. You can then add components to the resulting grid, starting in the upper-left corner, exactly as with `FlowLayout`.

To add a new `LayoutManager` to your applet, you use the `setLayout( )` method. You need to invoke it before you add any components to the applet. In the `Bubble` applet, the new `GridLayout` is created and set as the active `LayoutManager` of the applet by use of the single line

```
setLayout( new GridLayout( 8, 1 ) );
```

The `GridLayout` for this applet has eight rows and one column, and is made the default `LayoutManager` by invoking the `setLayout( )` method. Now when you use `add( )` to put your `TextFields` and `Buttons` on the screen, they will be nicely lined up in a spreadsheet-style grid.

`GridLayout` does have one other peculiarity you should be aware of. When a component is added to a cell of a `GridLayout`, the component expands to fill the space available for that cell. Thus, even if you specify a width of 10 for your `TextField` objects, they expand until they fill the width of the applet. How does the `GridLayout` decide what the proper width and height of each cell should be? It divides the total space devoted to the applet by the rows and columns required. You specify that amount of space by the numbers you put inside your `<APPLET>` tag to specify `HEIGHT` and `WIDTH` of the applet. You might want to experiment with some different numbers to see what it does to the sizes of your controls.

Java's `LayoutManagers` have a plethora of methods for controlling all aspects of an applet's display in a device-independent manner. `GridLayout` and the other `LayoutManagers` will be covered in considerable depth in Chapter 12, "The AWT: Containers, Components, and Layout Managers."

Creating TextFields and Adding Buttons

Once the `GridLayout LayoutManager` is in place, you need to add each of the `TextField` objects and `Buttons` to your applet. Because the variable `machine` is an array, it's convenient to use a loop to add each of the items in turn. But actually, your loop will need to do more than just add each element of `machine` to the applet. Recall that `machine` is an array of six `TextField` references. None of those references yet refers to an actual `TextField` object. So, inside your loop before you invoke the `add( )` method on each element of `machine`, you first need to initialize that element to a newly created `TextField` object by using the `new` operator. The loop that does both of those tasks looks like this:

```
for (int i = 0; i < machine.length; i++ )
{
    machine[i] = new TextField(10);
    add( machine[i] );
}
```

Looking at populate( )

The populate( ) method generates random values and places them into the array of TextFields called machine. Random values are handy here because it would be tiresome to enter sample values to be sorted. In your actual sales analysis program the user will enter the values.

The populate( ) method contains a loop, the body of which generates a random value and stores it into the machine array. A value is stored with each iteration of the loop, so you want the number of loop iterations to equal the number of elements in the machine array. You accomplish this by using the built-in length field of the array within the loop condition:

```
for (int i = 0; i < machine.length; i++)
{
    int n = (int) (randGen.nextFloat() * 500.0);
    machine[i].setText( "" + n);
}
```

The nextFloat( ) method of the Random class returns a randomly selected float value between 0.0 (inclusive) and 1.0 (exclusive). If you multiply this by 500.0 and convert it to an int, you will obtain a random integer value between 0 and 499. Note the parentheses in the expression. Without them it would read

```
int n = (int) randGen.nextFloat( ) * 500.0;
```

The (int) cast would then be performed first. Because nextFloat( ) always returns a number less than 1.0, and because the cast does not perform any rounding, the result would always be zero. This is clearly not what you want, so the parentheses are, indeed, necessary.

Zooming in on sort( )

The sort( ) method is the interesting part of this program. It's based on a very simple, though somewhat inefficient, method for sorting arrays. What you want is for the array to be sorted in ascending order, that is, elements at the beginning positions of the array ([0]) have low values, and elements at the end of the array ([6]) have high values. When placed on the screen, the first element of machine, machine[0], is at the very top of the applet. Thus, once the applet has run, you should see small numbers at the top, with increasingly larger numbers as you approach the bottom.

To use the bubble-sort algorithm, you start at the beginning of the array and look at each adjacent pair of array elements. If the pair is in the right order, all is well, but if not, you put them in the right order by swapping the values. Then you repeat the process for the next pair, and so on. When you've gone through the array once, you go back to the beginning and repeat the process. You keep doing this until a pass through the array results in no swaps, which means the array is in order.

The code for the sort( ) method contains few surprises. It uses a pair of nested loops. When the main loop is entered, the boolean variable swapped is set to false so you can later determine if the array has been completely sorted. When this occurs, the main loop is exited and the method returns. The variable `swapped` is set to `true` within the inner loop whenever a swap is necessary. The inner loop begins at the bottom (that is, first element) of the array and runs to the next-to-last element. This is because each element (`machine[i]`) is paired with the next higher element (`machine[i+1]`). Ending the inner loop with the next-to-last element allows it to be compared with the last element; these two together form the last pair of elements.

To swap the elements, the text of one `TextField` (`machine[i]`) is set to the value of that contained in another `TextField` (`machine[i+1]`). The first `TextField` also has its color set to blue, and the other has its color set to red. Swapping elements is performed by use of a temporary variable called `temp`. If `temp` were not used, storing the new text in one element would leave us with no way to access its previous value, which needs to be stored in the other element. The general pattern for swapping two values (`a` and `b`) by use of a temporary variable (`temp`) is

```
temp = b;
b = a;
a = temp;
```

In the `sort()` method, the place of `a` is occupied by `machine[i]` and that of `b` is occupied by `machine[i+1]`. Of course, the swapping done in `sort()` is also done by use of the `setText()` method rather than the assignment operator, so what you see in the listing is not quite as simple as the pattern itself.

Some Unnecessary Methods

The final two methods in the `Bubble` class are not strictly necessary—providing you comment out their invocation, of course. The method `setColor()` allows you to change the color of each `TextField` object as it becomes the active object. The `sort()` method uses the `setColor()` method to change the color of each pair of numbers being compared to red and blue. If the numbers need to be swapped, then the red and blue values are inverted again, to give you a visual indication that the swapping is taking place. Finally, the `setColor()` method is used to change the color of each `TextField` object back to white when its associated array element is no longer being processed.

You may wonder why a special method is necessary, when the `TextField` comes with the built-in `setBackground()` method. Without the `setColor()` method, which sends a `repaint()` message to the `TextField`, the `TextField` won't be redrawn. Setting the background color merely tells the `TextField` what color it should use to draw itself the next time it's drawn. Unless it is actually redrawn, you wouldn't see the color bubbling up and down the array—which is the whole point of the applet, after all.

Finally, there is the `pause()` method. Having a purpose similar to that of the `setColor()` method, `pause()` slows things down so you can see what is happening. The `pause()` method simply uses `sleep()` to tell the currently executing process to take a break for a few milliseconds. That allows the code that updates the display to catch up with the color changes. You will learn more about controlling the scheduling of your programs and applets when you study threads in Chapter 16, "Advanced Topics: Threads and Networking." The other parts of the `pause( )` method that may seem strange are the parts that start with `try` and `catch`. These are the Java instructions for dealing with exceptional situations, and you will learn how to use them toward the end of this chapter.

THE MOTHER OF ALL SALES ANALYSIS PROGRAMS

Let's return to the sales analysis report program and revise it to include sorting of the input data as well as the ability to use two-dimensional arrays. Look at the `SalesReport` applet in Listings 8-7 and 8-8. Figure 8-6 shows the program as it runs.

Listing 8-7 SalesReport.java

```java
// SalesReport - sorts and reports the weekly sales
// for up to 100 JavaMatics
import java.applet.*;
import java.awt.*;
import java.awt.event.*;

public class SalesReport extends Applet⇐
        implements ActionListener
{
    TextField[] dailySalesTxt = new TextField[8];
    TextArea    output         = new TextArea("", 8, 80);

    Button      addDailySales  =⇐
            new Button("Add Daily Sales to Total");
    Button      printReport     =⇐
            new Button("Print Sales Report");

    double[][] dailySales = new double[100][8];
    int numMachines    = 0;

    public void init()
    {
        for (int i = 0; i < dailySalesTxt.length; i++)
        {
            dailySalesTxt[i] = new TextField("", 6);
            add( dailySalesTxt[i] );
        }
        add( addDailySales );
        add( output );
        add( printReport );
        addDailySales.addActionListener(this);
        printReport.addActionListener(this);
    }

    public void actionPerformed( ActionEvent theEvent )
    {
        // Check to see which button was pressed
        if ( theEvent.getSource( ) == printReport )⇐
            printSalesReport();
        if ( theEvent.getSource( ) == addDailySales )⇐
            calcDailySales();
    }
```

```java
public void printSalesReport()
{
    sort();
    output.append("\nSales Report\n");
    output.append("------------------------------\n");
    for ( int i = 0; i < numMachines; i++ )
        printMachineSales( i );
}

public void printMachineSales(int row)
{
    output.append("Daily Sales for machine: " +
      dailySales[row][0]);
    for ( int j = 1; j < dailySales[row].length; j++ )
        output.append("  " + dailySales[row][j] );
    output.append("\n");
}

public double textToDouble( TextField tf )
{
    return Double.valueOf( tf.getText() ).doubleValue();
}

public void calcDailySales()
{
    // Convert TextFields dailySales to doubles
    // and store in dailySales
    for (int i = 0; i < 8; i++)
    {
        double saleAmt =
          textToDouble( dailySalesTxt[i]);
        dailySales[numMachines][i] = saleAmt;
    }
    printMachineSales( numMachines );
    numMachines++;
}

public void sort( )
{
    double temp;
    boolean swapped;
    do {
        swapped = false;
        for (int i = 0; i < (numMachines - 1); i++)
        {
            if ( dailySales[i][0] > dailySales[i+1][0] )
            {
                for (int j = 0; j < 8; j++)
                {
                    temp = dailySales[i+1][j];
                    dailySales[i+1][j] =
                      dailySales[i][j];
                    dailySales[i][j] = temp;
                }
                swapped = true;
            }
        }
    } while (swapped);
}
}
```

Listing 8-8 SalesReport.html

```
<HTML>
<HEAD>
<TITLE>Bringing in the Sheaves</TITLE>
</HEAD>
<BODY>
<IMG SRC="jumbo.GIF" ALIGN=RIGHT HEIGHT=50>
<H1>It Finally Adds Up</H1>
"Well, it certainly looks impressive," said Jumbo, failing to
remove the skeptical tone from his voice. <BR>
Brenda, ever sensitive, was a little miffed. "It is
impressive!"she said, controlling her temper. "All you need to
do is to put the machine number in the first field and then
enter the daily sales for the week in the remaining fields.
When you press the 'Print Sales Report' button, the applet
will sort by machine numbers, and you'll have a neatly
formatted list."<P>
"But where are the moving colors?" asked Jumbo.
<HR>
<APPLET CODE=SalesReport.class HEIGHT=300 WIDTH=500>
</APPLET>
</BODY>
</HTML>
```

A Closer Look

The new, revised `SalesReport` applet follows the template used in the `Bubble` class. Rather than using a `GridLayout`, as `Bubble` did, the `SalesReport` applet is laid out so that there are eight `TextField`s in a row across the top of the applet. Under the eight

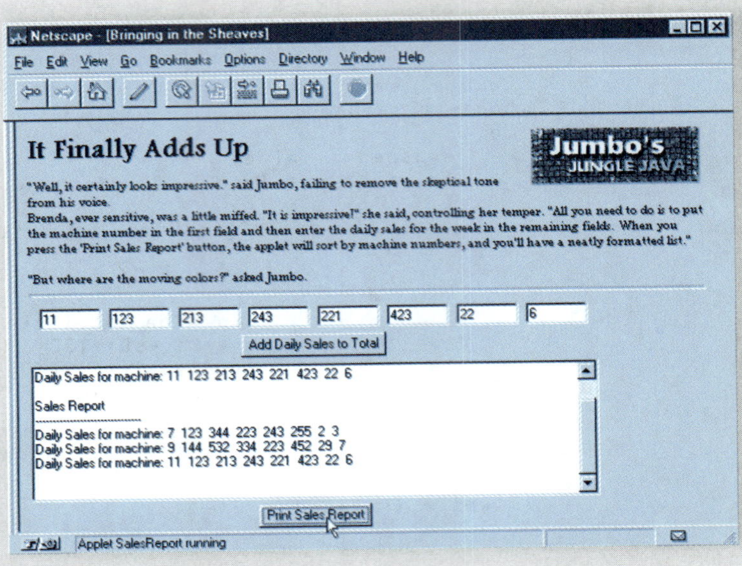

FIGURE 8-6

The `SalesReport`
applet in action

`TextField`s is a button labeled Add Daily Sales to Total. Below that is a `TextArea` that spans the entire width of the applet, and on the bottom is another button, this one labeled Print Sales Report.

To use the applet, the user enters a machine number in the first `TextField` and then enters the sales for each day of the week in the remaining seven fields. When the entire sales for a machine have been entered, the user presses the Add Daily Sales to Total button, and the `TextArea` displays the sales that were added. Echoing the sales back to the user at the time they are entered provides the user with useful feedback. Finally, after the user is finished entering the sales for all the machines—the `SalesReport` applet has room for up to 100 of them—the user presses the Print Sales Report button. The applet then sorts the sales by machine number and displays a listing of all the sales for each machine entered.

`SalesReport` Attributes

The `SalesReport` applet uses two array fields. The array `dailySalesTxt` contains eight `TextField` objects and is used to get the input values from the user. Notice how this array is declared and defined at the same time:

```
TextField[] dailySalesTxt = new TextField[8];
```

The second array, `dailySales`, is a two-dimensional array of `double`s. Each of the 100 rows in this array holds eight values. The first value, held in position `[0]`, holds the machine number. The other seven elements store the sales for each day of the week for that particular machine. The `dailySales` array is declared and defined in a manner similar to the `dailySalesTxt` array:

```
double[][] dailySales = new double[100][8];
```

In addition to these two arrays, the `SalesReport` applet has two `Button` objects—used to trigger the `calcDailySales()` method and the `printSalesReport()` method—and a `TextArea`, called `output`, consisting of 10 rows and 80 columns. The final attribute is a single integer, `numMachines`, that will hold the number of machines for which the user has entered values.

`SalesReport` Methods

The `SalesReport` applet has seven methods:

- `init()` performs two functions. First, it creates the eight `TextField` objects that the `dailySalesTxt` array actually refers to. Then it adds these, and all the other user-interface objects, to the applet.

- `actionPerformed()` simply invokes the `printSalesReport()` method or the `calcDailySales()` method, depending upon which button was pressed. As before, the `ActionEvent.getSource()` method is used to distinguish between these events.

🖉 `printSalesReport( )` first sorts the array, `dailySales`, by machine number, using the method `sort( )`. It then loops through all of the machines entered and prints the sales for each machine by calling the method `printMachineSales( )`.

🖉 `printMachineSales( )` prints the machine number and daily sales values for each machine. This method is called whenever a new row is added to the `dailySales` array by the `calcDailySales( )` method and is also used by the `printSalesReport( )` method to print the stats for each machine.

🖉 `textToDouble( )` is a utility method that takes a `TextField` reference as an argument and converts that argument to a `double`, which it then returns.

🖉 `calcDailySales( )` converts each of the eight `TextField`s in the `dailySalesTxt` array to a `double`—using the `textToDouble( )` method—and then stores those `double` values in a single row of the `dailySales` array. The method then calls the `printMachineSales( )` method to give the user some feedback and finally updates the `numMachines` attribute so that the next set of sales entered will go into the next row in the `dailySales` array.

🖉 `sort( )` uses the bubble-sort algorithm to order each row in the `dailySales` array by machine number. Within each row, the first column contains the identifying number of the vending machine, and the remaining seven columns contain sales data for each of the seven days of the week, Sunday through Saturday. Note that the `sort( )` method is careful to swap, where necessary, both the machine number and the seven sales amounts, using the innermost `for` loop.

INITIALIZING ARRAYS

Arrays, as other objects, are accessed by object references. Although an array seems to have a value, it actually has a reference to a value. Figure 8-7 illustrates this distinction.

When an array is first declared, it has the special value `null`. For instance, you cannot do this:

```
int[] someArray;    // someArray is null
someArray[3] = 7;   // Error: someArray[3] does not yet exist
```

After the `new` operator has been used to actually create an array object in memory, a reference to the array object may be stored in an array variable. Even after the array variable has received a reference to an actual array object, the elements of the array themselves have `null` values and should not be used until they are initialized.

```
someArray = new int[10];          // someArray is no longer null
int x = 3 + someArray[3];         // Error: someArray[3] is null
someArray[3] = 277;               // Now someArray[3] has a value
```

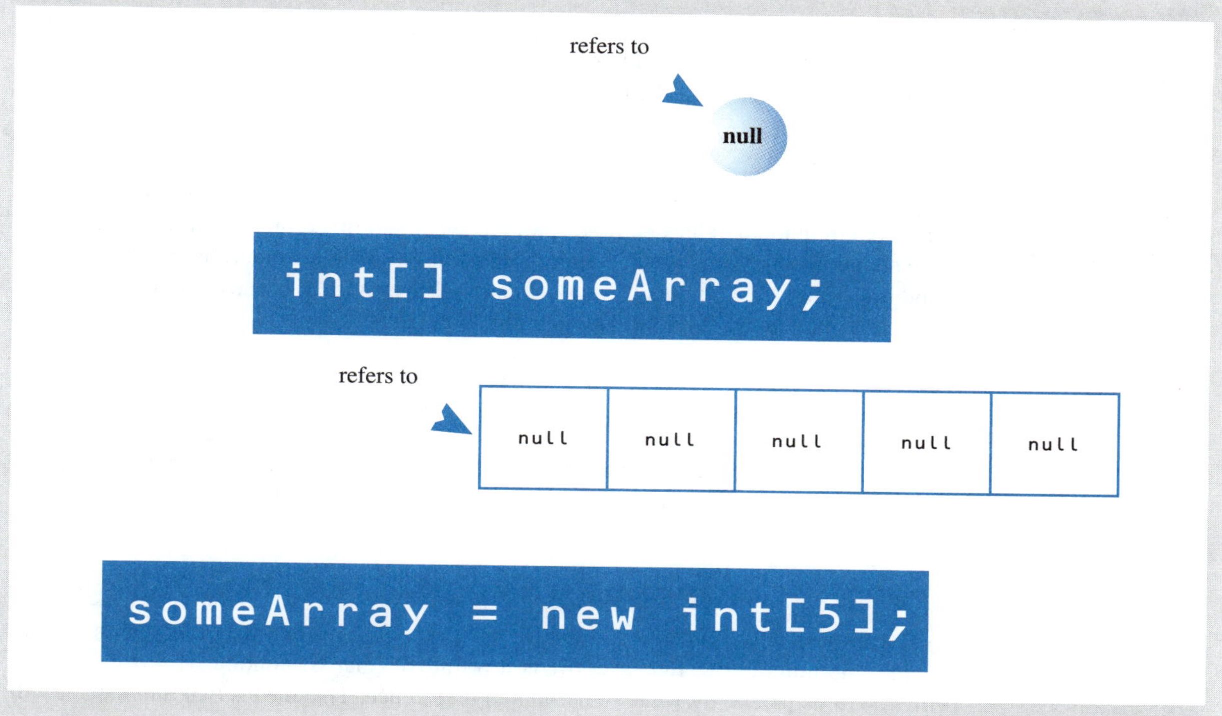

refers to

null

```
int[] someArray;
```

refers to

null	null	null	null	null

```
someArray = new int[5];
```

FIGURE 8-7

Array values and object references

In each example you have seen so far, values have been stored into arrays during program execution. Sometimes when writing a program, you already know the values you'd like to store. Java lets you specify array initializers to create an array with values already stored. For example, suppose you wanted to create an array of five `ints` initialized with the values 10, 20, 30, 40, and 50. The following array initialization would do exactly that:

```
int someArray[] = { 10, 20, 30, 40, 50 };
```

To initialize an array, you use a comma-separated list of values, enclosed in braces, and end the whole thing with a semicolon. Because blocks of code and class definitions—which are also enclosed in braces—are not followed by a semicolon, it is a common mistake to forget to put one at the end of a declaration that includes an initializer. Remember, a declaration is a statement, and all statements end with a semicolon. When you create an array using an initializer, you do not need to give the array a size by using the `new` operator. The size is automatically set to the number of initializing values.

Two-dimensional arrays and multidimensional arrays can be initialized similarly. For example, the following would create an array of three rows and three columns, initialized with the values from 1 to 9:

```
int twoDimArray[][] =⇐
    { { 1, 2, 3 }, { 4, 5, 6 }, { 7, 8, 9 } };
```

Again, notice that the values for the individual rows are each enclosed in braces, and both the individual values and the rows are separated by commas. There is only a single semicolon at the end of the entire initialization. Note also that the number of rows and the number of columns is not (and *cannot*) be specified, because the Java compiler will determine them from the values in the initialization list.

ARRAYS AS METHOD ARGUMENTS

Writing methods to operate on arrays can be both useful and tricky. For instance, when you pass the individual elements of an array to a method, the method treats those arguments as if they were ordinary nonarray variables. For example, given an array of `int`s declared as

```
int[] daysPerMonth =⇐
    { 31, 28, 31, 30, 31, 30, 31, 31, 30, 31, 30, 31 };
```

you can pass `daysPerMonth[3]` to a method, which will treat that element as an `int` value: the number 30. Because `int` is a primitive (that is, nonobject) type, the argument will be passed by value rather than by reference. This means that the method will be working with a copy of the `int` value rather than the original `int`. The method is free to change the value of its copy, but doing so will *not* affect the value of the original array element, as you can see from this code:

```
int[] daysPerMonth =⇐
    { 31, 28, 31, 30, 31, 30, 31, 31, 30, 31, 30, 31 };

System.out.println("daysPerMonth[3]=" + daysPerMonth[3]);
// prints 30
changeNumberOfDays( daysPerMonth[3] );
System.out.println("daysPerMonth[3]=" + daysPerMonth[3]);
// prints 30

public void changeDaysPerMonth(int month)
{
    System.out.println("Received: " + month);
    // prints 30
    --month;
    System.out.println("Changed to: " + month);
    // prints 29
}
```

Passing Arrays by Reference

Passing an entire array as an argument, however, is an entirely different matter from passing an individual primitive element. Although primitives are passed by value, objects are passed by reference. Because an array is an object, it is passed by reference rather than by value. Call by reference means that the method accesses the *original* array object, rather than a copy. Changes made by the method *do* affect the original copy, as you can see when the previous code is modified slightly:

```
int[] daysPerMonth =⇐
  { 31, 28, 31, 30, 31, 30, 31, 31, 30, 31, 30, 31 };

System.out.println("daysPerMonth[3]=" + daysPerMonth[3]);
// prints 30
changeNumberOfDays(daysPerMonth, 3);
System.out.println("daysPerMonth[3]=" + daysPerMonth[3]);
// prints 29

public void changeDaysPerMonth(int[] months, int month)
{
    System.out.println("Received: " + months[month]);
    // prints 30
    --months[month];
    System.out.println("Changed to: " + months[month]);
    // prints 29
}
```

Passing Rows or Columns

Sometimes, you don't want to pass an element of an array or the entire array. What you'd really like to do is pass just a column or row. While passing an individual row is straightforward, passing individual columns requires that you pass the entire array and then loop through each row, extracting the element of interest.

Listing 8-9, `PassArrays.java`, shows an application that deals with both situations. `PassArrays` creates a two-dimensional array of 3 columns and 3 rows, called `grades`. Each row in the `grades` array represents a particular student; each column represents a particular test. The method `printStudentScores( )` takes a single row from the `grades` array as an argument, and then prints the values in that row (in this case the second row). The method `printTestScores( )`, on the other hand, requires the user to pass in the entire `grades` array, as well as a second integer argument specifying which column to process. The method then loops through each row, extracting the values from the specified column.

Listing 8-9 PassArrays.java

```
// How to process individual rows and columns of a two-
dimensional array
import java.io.*;
public class PassArrays
{
    public static void main(String args[])
    {
        int grades[][] ={{ 100, 79, 83 },⇐
          { 44, 56, 67 }, { 95, 88, 99 }};
```

continued on next page

continued from previous page

```
        printStudentScores( grades[1] );
        printTestScores( grades, 1 );
    }

    public static void printStudentScores( int[] row )
    {
        System.out.print("Scores for student: ");
        for (int i = 0; i < row.length; i++)
            System.out.print(" "+ row[i]);
        System.out.println("");
    }
    public static void printTestScores( int [][] gradebook,⇐
      int testNo )
    {
        System.out.print("Scores for test " +⇐
          testNo + " : ");
        for (int row = 0; row < gradebook.length; row++ )
            System.out.print(" " + gradebook[row][testNo]);
        System.out.println("");
    }
}
```

Strings

Arrays, as you have seen, are useful collections. Another useful sort of collection is provided by the built-in String class. Strings facilitate the storage and manipulation of text in much the same way that arrays facilitate the storage and manipulation of other kinds of data. In fact, Strings are a great deal like arrays of type char. However, there are a lot of special features that make it much easier to use Strings for text manipulation than to use arrays of char.

For example, String constants can be easily created by enclosing text between a pair of double quote characters, as you know. When it's a String variable you need, you can create one using the String() constructor. This constructor can be used without any arguments, in which case an "empty" String is created. Use of the constructor with a String as an argument creates a new String with the same value as the String used as an argument. You don't have to specify the length of the text as you do the size of an array.

The convenient concatenation operator (+) can be used to join Strings, and the equally convenient equals() method (pun intended) can be used to compare String values. Recall that Strings are equal() when they contain the same contents. When you compare Strings using the equality operators (==, !=), you are actually testing identity. Strings can be equal (have the same contents) without being identical (being the same object). Listing 8-10 shows some examples of creating and manipulating strings.

Listing 8-10 Creating and manipulating Strings

```
String a;
String b = new String( );
String c = new String("Hi ");
String d = new String("Hi ");

a = b + c + "Mom!";
System.out.println(a);
if (c == d)
    System.out.println("Strings c and d are ==);
else
    System.out.println("Strings c and d are not ==);
if (c.equals(d))
    System.out.println("Strings c and d are equal( )");
else
    System.out.println("Strings c and d are not equal( )");
```

The output of the listing follows:
```
Hi Mom!
Strings c and d are not ==
Strings c and d are equal( )
```

ARRAYS OF StringS

Because it's possible to create arrays of any type, is it possible to create an array of Strings? Certainly! In fact, this is done quite often, because arrays of Strings are quite useful. Let's use an array of Strings to cause the JavaMatic to display a friendly message to each beverage purchaser. You can call this special version the PhraseMatic. Take a look at Listings 8-11 and 8-12. Figure 8-8 shows the PhraseMatic applet at work.

Listing 8-11 PhraseMatic.java
```
// A PhraseMatic class to draw customers
import java.applet.*;
import java.awt.*;
import java.awt.event.*;
import java.util.Random;

public class PhraseMatic extends Applet⇐
  implements ActionListener
{
    String phrase[];
    Random randGen = new Random( );

    TextField theInput  = new TextField("", 40);
    TextArea  theOutput = new TextArea("", 8, 40);
    Button    theButton =⇐
      new Button("Get Your Greeting Here!!!");

    public void init( )
    {
```

continued on next page

continued from previous page

```
            phrase = new String [5];
            phrase[0] = "Good morning, ";
            phrase[1] = "Enjoy your beverage, ";
            phrase[2] = "Come again soon, ";
            phrase[3] = "Hope it's how you like it, ";
            phrase[4] = "Your next purchase is free, ";

            add( theInput );
            add( theButton );
            add( theOutput );
            theInput.addActionListener(this);
            theButton.addActionListener(this);
            theOutput.setEditable(false);
        }

        public void actionPerformed(ActionEvent theEvent )
        {
            String name = theInput.getText();
            int n;
            n = (int) (randGen.nextFloat( ) * 4.0);
            theOutput.append( phrase[n] + name + ".\n" );
        }
    }
```

Listing 8-12 PhraseMatic.html

```
<HTML>
<HEAD>
<TITLE>Jumbo Tries Some Advertising</TITLE>
</HEAD>
<BODY>
<IMG SRC="Jumbo.GIF" ALIGN=RIGHT HEIGHT=50>
<H1>Jumbo Makes Friends</H1>
<HR>
"Oooh! Oooh! Oooh!" said Brenda, breathlessly. Jumbo,
dozing at the next table, was startled. "What?!" he
exclaimed. "Where?"<P>
"I've finally got it!" said Brenda, continuing on
heedless to Jumbo's confusion. "This'll bring the
customers in. I call it the PhraseMatic. The customer
types their name in here, see." Jumbo, now awake, was
getting interested. "When they press the button, we
give them a nice, personal greeting, like 'Good Morning,'
or 'Your next purchase is free'."<P>
Jumbo choked, while Brenda stood and grinned.
"Go ahead and try it," she urged.
<APPLET CODE=PhraseMatic.class HEIGHT=200 WIDTH=300>
</APPLET>
</BODY>
</HTML>
```

Inside the `PhraseMatic`

How does the `PhraseMatic` work? More importantly, from Jumbo's perspective, how many free beverages will he have to give away? The program consists of a single class,

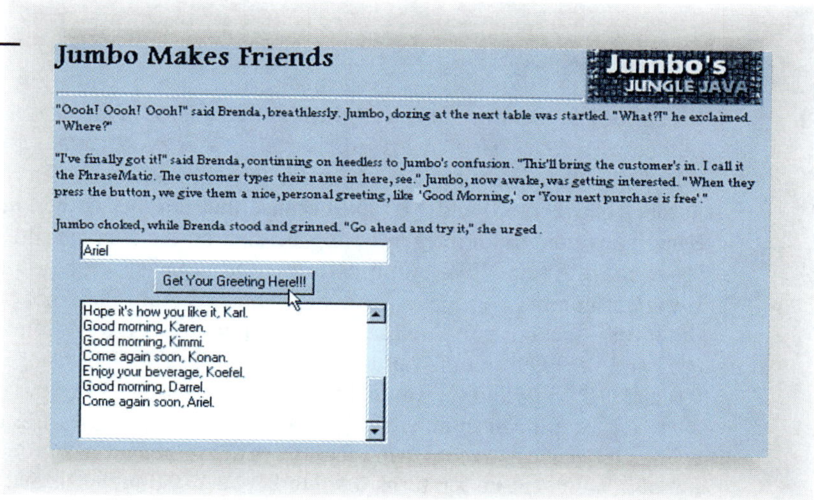

FIGURE 8-8

Running the
PhraseMatic
applet

PhraseMatic, which has five fields. One of the fields is an array of Strings, called, appropriately, phrase, which is used to hold a set of messages that will greet your customers when they use the PhraseMatic. A second field is a random-number generating object, named randGen, like the one used earlier in the Bubble class. Finally, the class contains a TextField, a TextArea, and a Button, which are used to gather the customer's name, display the personalized greeting, and start the whole thing rolling.

The init( ) method first creates an array of five Strings, using the new operator, and assigns the reference to that array to the array variable phrase:

```
phrase = new String [5];
```

Each of the individual Strings, [0] to [4], is then given a value through assignment like this:

```
phrase[0] = "Good morning, ";
phrase[1] = "Enjoy your beverage, ";
phrase[2] = "Come again soon, ";
phrase[3] = "Hope it's how you like it, ";
phrase[4] = "Your next purchase is free, ";
```

Finally, the init( ) method finishes up by adding the user-interface elements to the applet.

When a customer types his or her name into the TextField and then presses ENTER or presses the button labeled "Get Your Greeting Here!!!" the actionPerformed( ) method retrieves the name by using the getText( ) method. The actionPerformed( ) method then generates a random number from 0 to 4, which will be used as an index or subscript to select one of the Strings in the phrase array. This randomly selected phrase is then concatenated with the customer's name and displayed.

A Random Exploration

> **Java has several facilities for grouping data and objects into collections.**

If you look at the array `phrase`, you'll notice its last member is the `String` "Your next purchase is free." How many free beverages do you suppose you'll end up giving away? "Well," you may say, "because the `Random.nextFloat( )` method returns a number between 0.0 and 1.0, and because that number is then multiplied by 4 before being converted to an integer, I suppose that, on the average, I'd give away a free coffee every fifth time." The empirical way to test this is simply to run the `PhraseMatic` a sufficient number of times to convince yourself that this is not the case. Why? If you think for a second, you'll realize that, when multiplied by 4, random numbers between 0.75 and 0.99999 will all yield an integer value of 3. What range of numbers between 0.0 and 1.0 will yield the value 4? Only one, the value 1.0. So, your chances of giving away any significant numbers of Italian Espressos is minuscule. And actually, they're even smaller than that. As you recall from the explanation of the `Bubble` applet, while `Random.nextFloat( )` returns a value between 0.0 and 1.0, that range is *inclusive* of 0.0, but *exclusive* of 1.0. So you, as well as Jumbo, can breathe easier.

SPECIAL `String` FACILITIES

`String`s are convenient to use because of the large number of methods provided by the `String` class. One such method is `length( )`, which tells you the number of characters that a `String` contains. You'll want to note that, in the case of `String`s, this is a method, not a field as with arrays. Some of the most useful of the other `String` methods are summarized in Table 8-1.

TABLE 8-1
`String` METHODS

METHOD	RESULT	FUNCTION

`String a, b;`
`int i;`
`int n = 1;`
`boolean t;`
`char c;`
`b = "Ok";`
		Initialization.

`i = b.compareTo("Oh");`	`i = 1;`	i has zero if b is equal to "Oh", −1 if b is less than "Oh", and 1 if b is greater than "Oh".
`a = b.toUpperCase( );`	`a = "OK";`	a has uppercase letters in place of any lowercase letters from b.
`a = b.toLowerCase( );`	`a = "ok";`	a has lowercase letters in place of any uppercase letters from b.
`a = b.replace( k', h');`	`a = "Oh";`	a has all occurrences of k replaced by h.
`t = b.equalsIgnoreCase( "ok")`	`t = true;`	Test whether the strings are identical, except for case differences.
`t = b.endsWith("k");`	`t = true;`	Test whether the string ends with the specified string.

Table continued…

TABLE 8-1 String METHODS CONTINUED...

METHOD	RESULT	FUNCTION
t = b.startsWith("o");	t = false;	Test whether the string starts with the specified string.
c = b.charAt(1);	c = 'k';	Get the character at the indicated position in the string, relative to 0.
i = b.indexOf(j');	i = -1;	Get the index of the specified character within the string, or −1 if the specified character does not occur within the string.
i = b.length( );	i = 2;	Get the number of characters in the string.
a = toString(n);	a = "1";	Convert a primitive object to a string.

One way in which Strings are a little different from the other objects or variables you've seen, is that Strings cannot be modified—they are said to be *immutable*. When you assign a new value to a String variable, rather than changing the String object that the variable refers to, a new String object is actually created. The old String object is simply discarded, and a part of the Java run-time system, called the *garbage collector*, will reclaim its storage space for later reuse. (A related class, StringBuffer, does allow direct modification of characters and substrings within Strings.)

Another method that is very handy, although not exactly part of the String class, is the toString( ) method. This method is so handy, in fact, that you've been using it all along without calling it explicitly. The println( ) method uses toString( ) to convert its arguments to Strings when necessary. If you include a toString( ) method in objects you create, println( ) will use your toString( ) method for this purpose. This is a highly recommended practice.

A SPELLING CHECKER CLASS

Let's put some of these String methods to work and build a spelling checker. While our program will certainly be primitive compared with a commercial product, it does illustrate some useful principles. You could use the general spell-checking scheme to scan a user ID or password against a list, for example. Listings 8-13 and 8-14 show the code for the SimpleSpell applet, and Figure 8-9 shows it in action.

Listing 8-13 SimpleSpell.java

```
// A simple spelling checker applet
import java.applet.*;
import java.awt.*;
import java.awt.event.*;

public class SimpleSpell extends Applet⇐
    implements_ ActionListener
{
    String dictionary[] = new String [100];
    int nWords = 0;
```

continued on next page

continued from previous page

```
TextField theInput     = new TextField("", 40);
Button    checkButton = new Button("Check this word");
Button    addButton   = new Button("Add to dictionary");
Button    listButton  =⇐
  new Button("List the dictionary");
TextArea  theOutput    = new TextArea("", 8, 40);

public void init()
{
    addWord("aardvark");
    addWord("abacus");
    addWord("algebra");

    add( theInput );
    add( checkButton );
    add( addButton );
    add( listButton );
    add( theOutput );

    listButton.addActionListener(this);
    addButton.addActionListener(this);
    checkButton.addActionListener(this);

    theOutput.setEditable(false);
}

public String toString()
{
    String s;
    s = "Dictionary list:\n";
    for (int i = 0; i < nWords; i++)
    {
        s = s + dictionary[i] + "\n";
    }
    return ( s + "\n" );
}

public void actionPerformed( ActionEvent theEvent )
{
    String word = theInput.getText();

    if ( theEvent.getSource( ) == listButton )
        theOutput.append( "" + this );
    else if ( theEvent.getSource( ) == addButton )
    {
        addWord( word );
        theOutput.append( "The word: " + word +⇐
          " has been added.\n" );
    }
    else if ( theEvent.getSource( ) == checkButton )
    {
        theOutput.append( "Your word is " + word +⇐
          ": " );
        if ( isInDictionary( word ) )
            theOutput.append( "spelled correctly"⇐
              + "\n" );
        else
```

```
                                    theOutput.append( "Not in the dictionary" +⇐
                                       "\n" );
                }
        }

        public void addWord( String word )
        {
                if ( nWords > dictionary.length)
                    theOutput.append (⇐
                        "Sorry, the dictionary is full.\n");
                else
                {
                    dictionary[nWords] = word;
                    nWords++;
                }
        }

        public boolean isInDictionary( String word )
        {
                for ( int i = 0; i < nWords; i++ )
                    if ( word.equals( dictionary[i] ) ) return true;

                return false;
        }
}
```

Listing 8-14 SimpleSpell.html

```
<HTML>
<HEAD>
<TITLE>Jumbo Spells String</TITLE>
</HEAD>
<BODY>
<H1>Stringing in the Rain</H1>
"I before E, except in iced tea," chanted Jumbo as he
repeated the mantra he'd learned--unfortunately incorrectly--
in grammar school. "Somehow, it just doesn't look right,"
he said to himself, staring at the new menu item that now
read 'ECID TEA.'<P>
"New concoction, J.G.?" inquired Brenda, as she sauntered up,
looking quizzically at the menu. "It's iced tea,"
he retorted testily. "Can't you read?" he added unreasonably.
The hair rose on Brenda's back. "Yes," she said a little too
calmly. "Yes, I can. I can also spell. And if you're ever going
to learn, you'll need some help. Take a look at this applet."
<P>"Oh bother!" Jumbo muttered to himself, as he went looking
for iced tea.
<HR>
<IMG SRC="Jumbo.GIF" ALIGN=RIGHT>
<APPLET CODE=SimpleSpell.class HEIGHT=200 WIDTH=300>
</APPLET>
</BODY>
</HTML>
```

> **The reference to an array and the array itself are two different things.**

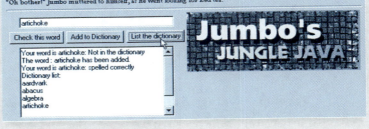

Checking Up on SimpleSpell

The SimpleSpell spelling checker has a capacity of 100 words, which are stored in the array dictionary. This field will contain all of the valid words. The init( ) method adds several useful, everyday words to the dictionary array by using the addWord( ) method, which takes as an argument a String containing the word to be added. Of course, in a real spelling checker, you would need to add thousands of words instead of only three.

The init( ) method then proceeds to add these user-interface pieces to the SimpleSpell applet:

- The TextField theInput, which will get words to check or add to the dictionary from the user.

- The TextArea theOutput, which provides a place for the SimpleSpell applet to talk back to the user.

- The Button checkButton, which the user presses to ask SimpleSpell to spell-check the word typed into theInput.

- The Button addButton, which the user presses to tell SimpleSpell to add the word in the TextField to the list of dictionary words.

- The Button listButton, which asks SimpleSpell to provide a list of all the words currently in the dictionary. The user can then scroll through the list of words to find the one of interest.

The `SimpleSpell` Methods

The `SimpleSpell` applet uses a few interesting `String` methods to do its work. When the user presses the List the dictionary button, the entire array of words stored in the `dictionary` array is listed on the display. But if you look at the code that actually does that, all you'll see is the line

```
theOutput.append( "" + this );
```

What in heaven's name does that mean? You know that the `TextArea.append( )` method displays a string at the end of a `TextArea` object, but what is the meaning of the argument (`""` + `this`)? The keyword `this`, you recall, refers to the current object. In this context, the current object is the copy of the `SimpleSpell` applet that is running. But an applet isn't a `String`. How can you concatenate a `String` and an applet? Simple. Just as the `System.out.println( )` method calls the `toString( )` method for any non-`String` argument, the `String` concatenation operator, `+`, attempts to convert any of its non-`String` operands to `Strings`. As you may have guessed, it does that by way of sending the `toString` message to the object, telling it to turn itself into a `String`. `SimpleSpell`'s `toString( )` method uses a loop to form a single `String`, by concatenating all the words in the dictionary. Words are separated by a newline character ("\n") so each word will be placed on a separate line when displayed.

Spelling is checked by the `isInDictionary( )` method, which returns `true` if the word is contained in the dictionary, and `false` otherwise. Note that `isInDictionary( )` uses case-sensitive comparison by using the `equals( )` method like this:

```
for ( int i = 0; i < nWords; i++ )
    if ( word.equals( dictionary[i] ) ) return true;
```

The `equalsIgnoreCase( )` method could have been used if case-insensitive comparisons were needed. The value returned by `isInDictionary( )` is used to decide which of two messages should be displayed.

Vector, Vectoria

Besides `arrays` and `Strings`, Java has a third built-in container class, `Vector`. The `Vector` class overcomes the main limitation of arrays: fixed size. You don't have to know the maximum number of elements before you create a `Vector`. A `Vector` is, in effect, a resizable array. When a `Vector` is created, a capacity is specified; but when this capacity is exhausted, the `Vector` obligingly grows to accommodate additional entries.

Creating and Using `Vectors`

To use `Vectors` in your program, you will first need to make sure you are importing the `java.util` package. Once you have done that, there are two ways you can create a

`Vector`. The first way uses the constructor `Vector(int)`, where the argument specifies the original number of elements allocated. For example

```
Vector littleVector = new Vector(10);
Vector bigVector = new Vector(1000);
```

Alternatively, a `Vector` can be created by use of the constructor `Vector(int, int)`, where the first argument is once again the original capacity, and the second argument specifies the amount of space that will be allocated each time the `Vector` runs out of space—how much it will grow by, in other words. For example

```
Vector mediumVector = new Vector(100, 10);
```

will create a `Vector` of 100 elements. Each time additional space is needed, space for 10 elements will be added to the current capacity.

You add elements to a `Vector` using the method `addElement(Object)`, which adds the specified object as a new element of the `Vector` like this:

```
mediumVector.addElement( someButton );
```

The type of the added element must be `Object`, but because every nonprimitive data type descends from `Object`, this is not a serious limitation. Even primitive types can be stored by casting them to a related nonprimitive type (for instance, from `int` to `Integer`). For example, here is how an `Integer` and an `int` could be added to a `Vector`:

```
// . . .
Integer i = new Integer(1);
int j = 2;
Vector v = new Vector(100);

v.addElement( i );
v.addElement( new Integer(j) );
// . . .
```

`Vector` Methods

Once you have created a `Vector`, what can you do with it? Java gives you many useful methods for working with `Vectors`. Table 8-2 presents some of the handiest methods. Many of these methods use an `int` value as an index to the `Vector`. An index functions as a subscript in the sense that its value ranges from zero to one less than the size of the `Vector`. Indexes make it possible to refer directly to an element of a `Vector`, just as you would do with an array, except that you don't use the brackets. Methods exist (for example, `removeElement( )`) that search an entire `Vector` for a given element, but these are less efficient than use of an index if the index is already known.

TABLE 8-2
`Vector` METHODS

METHOD	FUNCTION
`addElement(Object elem)`	Add the specified object, `elem`, to the vector.
`contains(Object elem)`	Return a `boolean` value indicating whether the vector contains `elem`.
`elementAt(int index)`	Return the element at the specified position of the vector (zero-relative).
`indexOf(Object elem)`	Return the index of `elem` in the vector if the vector contains `elem`, otherwise −1.
`size( )`	Return the number of elements of the vector.
`capacity( )`	Return the current capacity of the vector.
`isEmpty( )`	Return a `boolean` value indicating whether the vector is empty.
`setElementAt(Object value, int index)`	Set the value of the element at the specified index.
`removeElementAt(int index)`	Remove the element at the specified index.
`removeElement(Object elem)`	Remove the specified element.
`removeAllElements( )`	Remove all elements of the vector.

Exceptional Situations

Because Java was originally intended for the programming of high-reliability electronic devices, it comes with a built-in exception-handling facility that allows the programmer to detect, and recover from, unexpected occurrences and errors.

In Java terms, a method that detects an unusual condition can `throw` an exception. Such exceptions can be `caught`, or processed, by special blocks of code written for this purpose. Languages that lack exception-handling force you, the programmer, to deal with exceptions as they arise, sometimes resulting in code that is so cluttered with logic for exceptional conditions that the logic for the *usual* conditions is obscured. Java's exception-handling facility helps you write simpler code that is easier to understand.

Exception Objects

Exceptions are represented by objects, known appropriately as `Exceptions`, which have properties similar to all other Java objects. There are two basic classes of `Exceptions` in Java. Both are descendants of a parent class called java.lang.Throwable. The first of these subclasses, java.lang.Error, represents serious and usually unrecoverable exceptions, such as running out of memory or being unable to locate and load a needed class. The second subclass, java.lang.Exception, represents more or less unusual conditions that arise in the course of program execution, such as reaching the end of a file, or attempting to reference an array element outside the actual bounds of the array. Figure 8-10 shows some common exceptions and how they are related to their parent classes.

Suppose you were able to get hold of an Exception object. What kinds of things could you tell it to do? One of the most useful things would be to have it tell you about itself—to file a report, so to speak. Every Exception object inherits the ability to do this from the class java.lang.Throwable, which provides a message accessible via the method getMessage( ). This makes it easy to report the occurrence of an exception when that is desired.

FIGURE 8-10

Some common exceptions

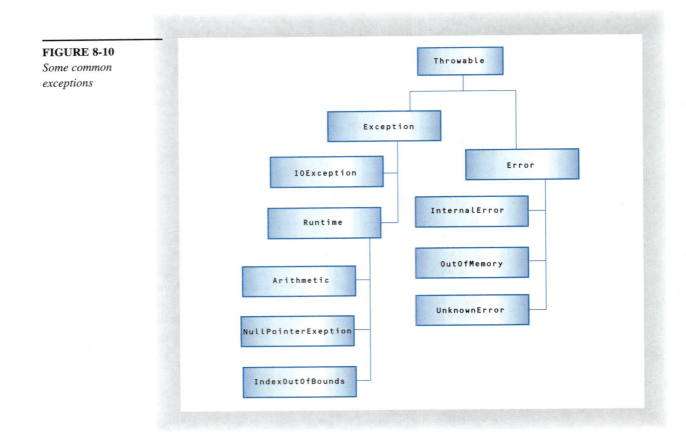

Using Exceptions

To actually use exceptions inside your program, you'll need to learn some new Java syntax. The language elements used for exception-handling are the keyword pair `try-catch` and the keyword trio `try-catch-finally`.

If you have a piece of code, a method, say, where something can go wrong, you can put that piece of code inside a `try` block. A `try` block starts with the `try` keyword and is delimited by braces like this:

```
try
{
    // Some potentially ill-behaved code
}
```

A `try` block is immediately followed by a series of `catch` blocks. Each `catch` block can catch one type or class of exception. An object of that exception type is declared in parentheses right after the `catch` keyword. This is followed by a set of braces, as with the `try` block. In essence, the `catch` block looks like a method named `catch` that takes an argument of a particular exception type. This is how the complete `try-catch` construct looks:

```
try
{
    // Some potentially ill-behaved code
}
catch( SomeExceptionType e1 )
{
    System.out.println( e.getMessage() );
}
catch( SomeOtherExceptionType e2 )
{
    // Do something if this exception occurs
}
```

Catching On?

When program execution reaches a `try` block, the block is entered and execution proceeds until the block is finished or an exception occurs. If execution of the block is completed without the raising of an exception, the immediately following series of `catch` blocks is skipped. However, if an exception does occur during execution of the `try` block, further execution of the `try` block is canceled. The `catch` blocks are then scanned sequentially for an exception type matching the exception that was thrown. If one is found, the code in the matching `catch` block is executed, and any remaining `catch` blocks are skipped. Figure 8-11 shows the syntax of a `try-catch`.

FIGURE 8-11
The try-catch block

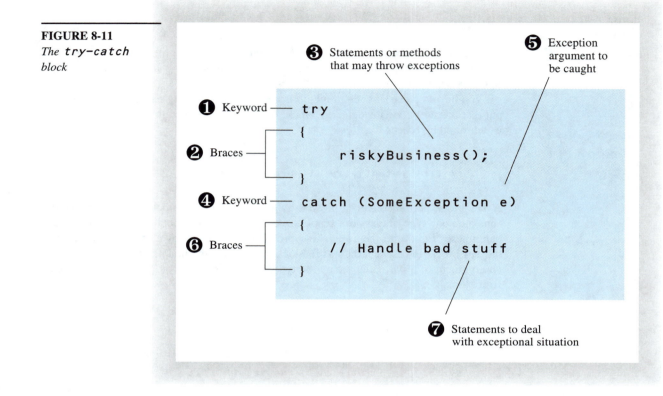

If no matching catch block is found, the exception is propagated to the next higher enclosing block of code. If a matching catch is found there, it is executed and any remaining catch blocks at that level are skipped. If ultimately the main( ) method is reached without finding a matching catch block, the Java run-time system will attempt to handle the exception, usually by displaying an error message and terminating the program. Figure 8-12 shows this propagation of an exception.

FIGURE 8-12
Exception propagation

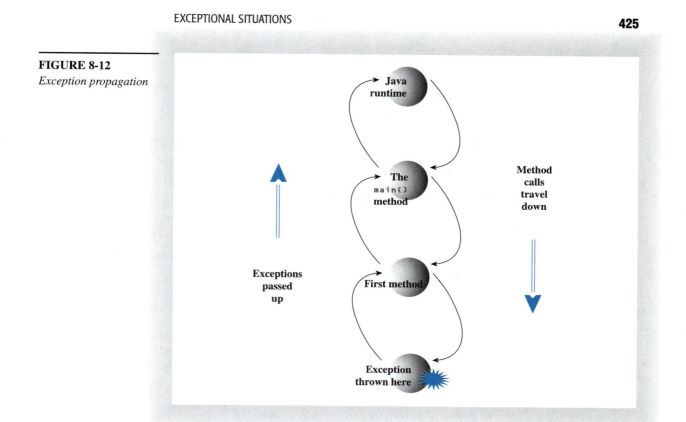

When the catch blocks are scanned looking for a match, Java takes into account the fact that Exceptions are arranged in an inheritance hierarchy. A catch specifying an Exception near the top of the hierarchy (a very general Exception) will match any Exception in the subtree below it. Thus, a catch specifying java.lang.Throwable, which is the root of the hierarchy, will catch *any* Exception. Figure 8-13 shows some examples of exception matching.

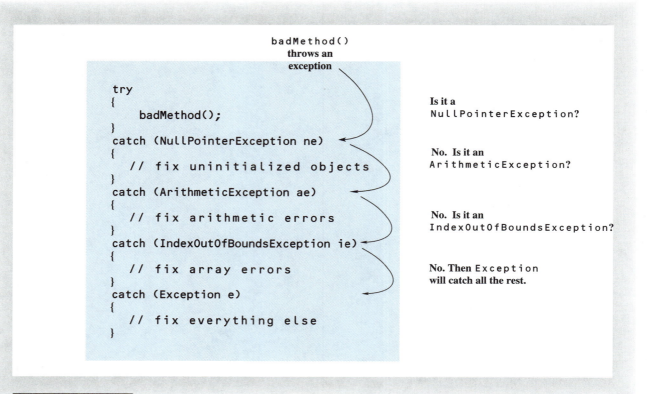

FIGURE 8-13
Exception matching

Ignoring the Problem

In principle, Java requires that every exception that could arise in a block of code be handled by use of a `try-catch`. However, there is a way to avoid this—as you have been doing from the start. If you don't want to catch an exception that may occur inside your method, Java requires that you "advertise" that fact by adding a `throws` clause to the end of your method declaration. This tells other methods that your method could raise an exception. Figure 8-14 shows a method with a `throws` clause.

Certain exceptions, such as `InternalError`, could arise in any block of code. It would really be a burden for you to catch every such potential error. Adding a `throws` clause to every program method would likewise be of dubious benefit. Accordingly, Java makes an exception for such exceptions and does not require them to be caught or thrown.

Actually, *most* exceptions fall into this category. You never need to catch exceptions that are descended from `java.lang.Error` or `java.lang.RuntimeException`, because they are ubiquitous. The only exceptions you're likely to be concerned with are `java.io.IOException`, which indicates an unusual input-output condition, and `java.lang.InterruptedException`, which is used in working with threads, discussed in Chapter 12.

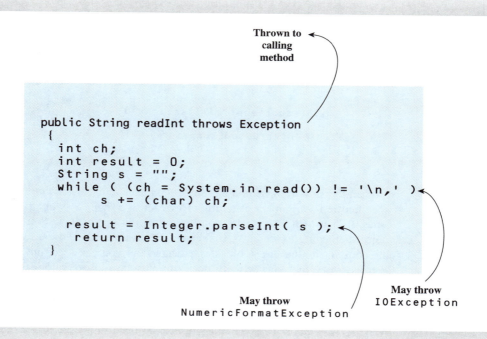

Thrown to calling method

```
public String readInt throws Exception
  {
    int ch;
    int result = 0;
    String s = "";
    while ( (ch = System.in.read()) != '\n,' )
        s += (char) ch;

    result = Integer.parseInt( s );
      return result;
  }
```

May throw NumericFormatException

May throw IOException

FIGURE 8-14

The throws clause

You may also want to handle `java.lang.NumberFormatException`, which occurs when an attempt to convert a supposed number discloses that the number is not valid. You are not required to do so because `java.lang.NumberFormatException` is descended from `java.lang.RuntimeException`. But it's difficult to test whether a `String` contains a valid number before passing the `String` to a conversion method. The easiest approach is usually to simply pass the `String` and handle the exception if one results.

How can you know if you're required to handle an exception? The easiest way is simply to compile your program. The compiler will inform you of any exceptions requiring a `catch` or `throw`, and you can easily add one or the other to eliminate the compiler error message.

A Few Short Examples

You've already seen an example of using `try-catch` blocks in the `Bubble` applet. The `pause( )` method—from the `Bubble` applet and reproduced in Listing 8-15—calls the `sleep( )` method of the `Thread` class. As you recall, the purpose of the `sleep( )` method is simply to suspend the running of the current code or `Thread`, and to allow other parts of your applet or application to have some of the CPU time for their own tasks. In the `Bubble` applet, the `sleep( )` method was used to allow the applet some time to update the screen as different elements were moved around in the array.

Listing 8-15 The pause( ) method from the Bubble class

```
// ------- pause(): sleep for milliseconds -------------------
public void pause( int milliseconds )
{
    try
    {
        Thread.sleep( milliseconds );
    }
    catch( InterruptedException e )
    {
    }
}
```

When the `sleep( )` method has suspended execution for the number of milliseconds specified in its argument, it returns. However, if `sleep( )` is interrupted before it finishes its "nap" (in Chapter 16, you'll see how this can occur), it throws an `Exception` object belonging to the class `InterruptedException`. When the exception is thrown, the code inside the `catch` block is executed. As you can see from this example, it is not necessary that you actually do anything with the exception. By not putting any code in the `catch` block, you are essentially saying, "ignore this exception." Note that if you remove the `try-catch` block, the compiler will not compile your program. The `InterruptedException` must be caught or thrown.

The second common exception you'll often need to handle is `IOException`. You've already had an encounter with it, although you may not have recognized it. `IOExceptions` occur, most often, from input operations. You may recall that when you built the first generation of JavaMatics, you needed to write the `main( )` method like this:

```
public static void main(String args[]) throws Exception
{
    // Code that could throw an exception here
}
```

The code inside your JavaMatic that forced you to add the `throws Exception` to the end of your `main( )` declaration was the use of the `System.in.read( )` method, which can throw an `IOException`. Because of that, you could have written the declaration of `main( )` to say `throws IOException` instead. But because `IOException` is a subclass of `Exception`, the `throws Exception` declaration means that `IOException` will be caught as well. To avoid adding the `throws` clause to the end of your `main( )` method, you could have simply put all of your calls to `System.in.read( )` inside `try-catch` blocks.

NOW, FINALLY, finally

An optional component of the `try-catch` structure that is sometimes helpful is the `finally` block. Code within a `finally` block is guaranteed to be executed if any part of the associated `try` block is executed, regardless of an exception being thrown or not. Code in a `finally` block is also guaranteed to be executed in the event that code in the associated `try` executes a `return`, `continue`, or `break`. Note that a `finally` can itself transfer control using one of these statements, in which case any pending transfer of control initiated within the `try` is abandoned. Figure 8-15 shows the syntax of the `try-catch-finally` block.

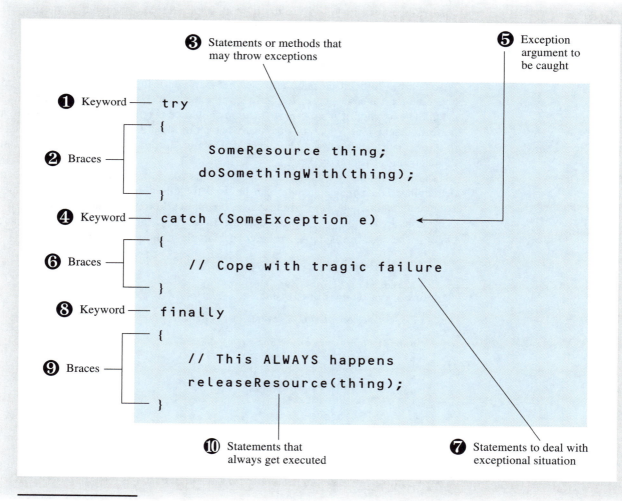

FIGURE 8-15
The `try-catch-finally` block

" *If you think of an array as a single row of data with separate columns, then a multi-dimensional array is like a matrix.* "

What are the rules for determining *when* the `finally` is executed? If an exception occurs in the related `try` and there is a matching `catch` in the local block, the `finally` is executed after the `catch`. If there is no matching `catch` in the local block, the `finally` is executed before propagating the exception to an enclosing block.

The `finally` is useful when there is "cleanup" that must be performed after the related `try`. Operations such as closing files and releasing resources are often performed in a `finally`. The properties of the `finally` guarantee that the cleanup is done. Sometimes it's even useful to write a `try-finally` without any associated `catches`.

EXCEPTION STRATEGIES

A sometimes difficult decision is the choice between using a `catch` block or merely appending a `throws exception` for a given exception. Usually the best advice is to catch the exception if it's clear what action should be taken and if the local block can perform that action. Where it's not clear what action should be taken, it's usually better to throw the exception to a higher level, where more information may be available and the decision is easier to make.

It's also occasionally useful to throw exceptions yourself, particularly for testing and debugging. The `throw` statement can be used for this purpose; it requires an object argument that is a subclass of `java.lang.Throwable`. You can create your own custom exceptions by writing a class that extends `java.lang.Throwable` or one of its subclasses. The code in Listing 8-16 shows an example of this.

Listing 8-16 TestException.java

```
// How to throw your own exceptions
import java.lang.Exception;

class CustomException extends Exception
{
    public CustomException( )
    {
        super( );
    }
    public CustomException(String s)
    {
        super(s);
    }
}

public class TestException
{
    public static void main(String args[])
    {
        try
        {
            throw new CustomException("Bad vibes!");
        }
        catch (CustomException e)
        {
```

```
        System.out.println(⇐
          "Bad vibes exception has occurred.");
      }
    }
  }
```

Summary

🔅 The `TextArea` is a user-interface component that provides multiline input and output of text.

🔅 Arrays can be used to store data items of a single type during program execution.

🔅 All the elements of an array have the same name—the name of the array—and are individually accessed by using subscript numbers placed within square brackets (`[]`).

🔅 Creating a variable that can hold an array reference does not create an actual array—an actual array should be created, and a reference to it should be stored in the array reference variable.

🔅 The `target` field of the `Event` object passed to the `action( )` method can be used to identify the object that was the target of the action generating the event.

🔅 An `ArrayIndexOutOfBoundsException` occurs when a program attempts to access an array element outside the range of valid elements.

🔅 Java supports multidimensional arrays by allowing the programmer to create arrays whose elements are themselves arrays.

🔅 The bubble-sort algorithm can be used to sort the data in an array or `Vector`.

🔅 The `GridLayout` object can be used to arrange user-interface controls in a series of rows and columns.

🔅 Entire arrays, or array rows or columns, can be passed as arguments to a method.

🔅 `Strings` are much like arrays of type `char`, but they are easily created by use of `String` literals.

🔅 There are many useful `String` methods that can be used to manipulate `Strings`.

🔅 `Strings` are immutable—changing a `String` involves creating an entirely new `String`.

Unlike arrays, `Vectors` have no predefined limit to their size.

`Vector` elements are accessed by use of special methods, rather than subscripts.

`Enumerations` make it easy to access all the elements of a `Vector`.

A method that detects an unusual condition may throw an exception.

Exceptions can be caught, or rethrown to a calling method.

The `try-catch-finally` block is used to catch exceptions.

When an exception occurs within a `try` block, its `catch` statements are searched for a matching exception type, and the statements of the matching `catch` block are executed.

A `finally` block is executed if any of the statements in the corresponding `try` block have been executed.

An uncaught exception is passed to the calling method when the enclosing method has a `throws` clause within its method header.

Certain exceptions must either be caught or thrown, otherwise the compiler will refuse to compile the program.

The `sleep( )` method can be used to pause execution of a program thread.

Quiz

1. The `TextArea` is similar to the `TextField`, except that the `TextArea` provides _____ for input or output.

2. The `setEditable( false )` method prevents a `TextField` or `TextArea` from _____.

3. The individual elements of an array are distinguished by use of a number called the _____.

4. Creating an array variable does not actually _____ the associated array unless an initializer is used.

5. Arrays in Java have a(n) _____ size.

6. The `target` field of the `Event` object passed to the `action( )` method identifies _____.

7. A multidimensional array can be created by creating a(n) _____ of arrays.

" Java has several LayoutManagers, each with a plethora of methods to control all aspects of an applet's display. "

8. A simple way to sort the elements of an array is to use an algorithm called the _____ sort.

9. Sorting an array by use of the simple method used in this chapter involves testing whether pairs of array elements are in the proper order and _____ the contents of those that are not.

10. A `GridLayout` object can be used to establish a layout that consists of _____ and _____ of user-interface components.

11. When an array is passed as an argument to a method, it is passed by reference, which means the method can/cannot alter the values of elements of the array.

12. When an array element is passed as an argument to a method, it is passed by value, which means the method can/cannot alter the value of the element.

13. `String` values can be created by use of the `String()` constructor or by specifying a `String` _____.

14. The `String` method _____ can be used to test `Strings` for equality.

15. The `String` method _____ can be used to access the `char` at a given position within a `String`.

16. The `String` method _____ can be used to determine the length of a `String`.

17. The `String` method _____ can be used to compare two `Strings` to determine which should be collated before the other.

18. The method _____ can be used with many types of objects to convert their contents to a form suitable for printing.

19. The largest value returned by the `Random.nextFloat()` method is just less than _____.

20. A `Vector` is like an array, except that the size of a `Vector` _____.

21. A method that detects an unusual condition can throw a(n) _____.

22. When an exception occurs inside a `try` block, the associated `catch` statements are searched for an exception with a(n) _____ matching that of the exception that occurred.

23. The statements of a(n) _____ are executed if any of the statements of the associated `try` are executed.

24. If a method contains statements that could cause an exception, but does not contain a `try-catch` to handle the exception, the method can include the _____ clause in its method header, which causes the exception to be rethrown to a calling method.

Exercises

1. Write an applet that accepts a series of numbers and then displays the three smallest numbers and the three largest numbers of the series. If the same value is entered several times, it may also appear several times in the list of smallest and largest numbers.

2. Write an applet that accepts a series of numbers, each between 0 and 100, representing scores on a quiz. The applet should determine the letter grade appropriate to each score, as follows:

Score	Letter Grade
90-100	A
80-89	B
70-79	C
60-69	D
Other	F

   The applet should then print the scores and letter grades, ordered from highest to lowest.

3. Write an applet that helps the user balance a checking account. The applet should allow the user to enter an opening balance and a series of deposits and checks. Checks can be entered as negative numbers and deposits entered as positive numbers. The applet should calculate the ending balance of the checking account. Because the user may enter an amount incorrectly, the program should allow the user to correct the opening balance or any check or deposit amount.

4. Improve the `SalesReport` applet by having it report sales by machine and product. For each machine, the user should enter the daily sales for each of three product types: Java, Extra Java, and Pseudo Java. The report should show the total sales for each machine and each product type.

5. Write an applet that can alphabetize a series of words, entered one-by-one into a `TextField`.

6. Write an applet that can alphabetize book titles, entered one-by-one into a `TextField`. Note that the word *the* is ignored when it occurs as the first word of a title.

7. Write an applet that accepts a line of text from a `TextField` and checks the spelling of each word in the line by use of a built-in array of valid words. You can identify words by scanning the input text character-by-character, looking for spaces and punctuation that mark the end of a word.

8. Write an applet that generates a newspaper headline, based on words supplied by the user. For example, the user can be requested to supply the name of a beverage, a movie star, and a European city, and the applet might display the result "Valentino sips tea in Prague." Use the `Random.nextFloat( )` to add variety to the result so that the same headline is unlikely to be produced consecutively.

9. Write an applet that generates an entire story of paragraph length, based on words supplied by the user, in a fashion similar to that described in the previous exercise.

9

Teams of Classes:

Using Classes Together

In football, no matter how stellar your quarterback, without the support of a solid group of players, your team will still end up in last place. Solitary objects, like individuals, increase their usefulness in the company of others. The programs you have written to this point have primarily been monolithic programs. You have used objects such as `Buttons` or `Labels`, but usually in service to a single applet or application. No longer! In this chapter you will create new classes and then arrange those classes to bring the JavaMatic application of Chapter 4, "Simply Methods: One Step at a Time," to life. The secret to your success will be teamwork: not only the capabilities of your workers, but also the way that they work together.

In this chapter you will learn

How to create "building-block" classes that can be assembled to solve a wide variety of problems

How to use the access modifiers `public` and `private` to build accessor and mutator methods that provide controlled access to the fields of your objects

> *By first designing the interface of each class—the methods accessed by its users—different teams can work on different parts without worrying about where they will meet.*

☕ How to use constructors to initialize objects when they are created

☕ How to cooperate with the garbage collector, which is responsible for recycling unused computer memory

☕ How to write and use finalizer methods that allow your objects to take action before they're recycled

Building the JavaMatic: A Beginning

Classes are nothing new to you, but until now all of your Java programs have consisted of a single class. All of the objects you have created—other than your applets and applications—have been instances of the classes provided with Java, such as `Label` and `Button`. Now, it's time for you to step out on your own, and start to build an *object team*, a group of classes that you can use to solve a wide variety of problems. What better way to accomplish this than to return to the JavaMatic? By starting with a single class and then adding methods and data, you'll learn about the process of building classes that are reusable and robust.

When you last looked at the overall design of the JavaMatic—at the end of Chapter 4—you saw that the JavaMatic naturally divides into four classes:

☕ A user interface class that contains the buttons necessary for the user to communicate with the JavaMatic, as well as a status display to let the customer know what's going on. This class not only needs to communicate with your customers, but also needs to direct the actions of the other classes, to have them carry out the customer's wishes. Let's call this the `Manager` class.

☕ In any organization, someone has to take care of the money. The JavaMatic needs a class to keep track of how much money has been deposited and the total amount of money on hand. This class must also make change when a beverage is purchased. Let's call this the `Banker` class.

☕ While a JavaMatic that accepts money and takes orders might be amusing, it won't attract many repeat customers unless it actually gives them a beverage for their money. Again, like most organizations, the JavaMatic needs someone who actually does the work and serves the coffee. The `Worker` class should handle this task just fine.

☕ Finally, someone needs to monitor the inventory. The `JavaMaticMenu` class keeps track of which items you have in stock and how much each one costs. It also makes sure that the `Banker` always charges the right price for each beverage and that the `Worker` has all the ingredients that are needed.

KEEPING THINGS ON TRACK USING OBJECT-ORIENTED DESIGN

Which class should you develop first? When using object-oriented design (OOD), there is no hard-and-fast rule about which class you should start with. That is one of the things that makes object-oriented development simpler than previous software development methodologies. Once you have decided on your classes and their responsibilities, you are free to start almost anywhere. Furthermore, if you have a team of programmers working together, it's possible to have different programmers working on different parts of the problem simultaneously.

How is that possible? You've probably seen pictures of tunnels dug from both ends, or railroad tracks laid from opposite directions. The problem with such endeavors is getting the two halves to meet in the middle. Imagine the problem of trying to simultaneously build five or ten rail lines that are to meet at a certain point, as in Figure 9-1. The measurement, checking, and double-checking required to make sure that everyone arrives in the same place, and not a mile, or a yard, or even an inch to the side of the target, is monumental. Much of the effort expended in creating large software projects is devoted to this task.

FIGURE 9-1

How do you get the tracks to meet?

But wait. Think for a second. Is there another way to solve this problem? Why not simply start at the meeting point and then build outwards? In a sense, that's what object-oriented design does. By first designing the interface of each class—the fields and methods accessed by its users—different teams can work on different parts without worrying about whether they will meet up with the others, much like building a freeway interchange before building the roads that lead into it, as Figure 9-2 shows.

DESIGNING A Keypad CLASS

Because you can start anywhere, let's start with a portion of the `Manager` class. Recall that the `Manager` is responsible for taking the customer's order and collecting the money. One of the attributes that the `Manager` class needs is a keypad. Let's start by designing an applet that creates a `Keypad` class. After a few rounds of improvements, you'll end up with a reusable keypad that can be used inside the JavaMatic, which you'll build in the last section of this chapter.

In using OOD to design a class, your first goal is to establish the interface of the class—the fields and methods that will be accessed by users of the class. Usually this process involves a considerable degree of iterative exploration and experimentation. In other words, it's largely trial and error. We'll simulate the process of OOD by showing you several versions of the keypad, each successive version being a little nearer to what's actually needed.

FIGURE 9-2

Starting at the interface and building out

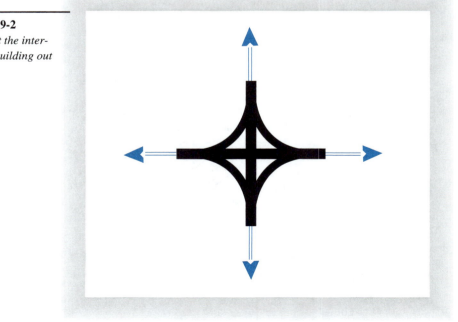

Listing 9-1 shows the `Keypad1` applet, while Listing 9-2 contains the HTML file you'll need to run the applet. Figure 9-3 shows the `Keypad1` applet in action.

Listing 9-1 Keypad1.java

```java
// A First Keypad Class
//
//
import java.applet.*;
import java.awt.*;
import java.awt.event.*;

public class Keypad1 extends Applet implements ActionListener
{
    String result = "";

    Button[] theKeys  = new Button[10];
    Button   clearBtn = new Button("Clear");
    Button   OKBtn    = new Button("Order");

    public void init()
    {
        setLayout( new GridLayout(4, 3) );

        for (int i = 0; i < 10; i++)
        {
            theKeys[i] = new Button(""+i);
            add( theKeys[i] );
            theKeys[i].addActionListener(this);
        }

        add( clearBtn );
        add( OKBtn );
        clearBtn.addActionListener(this);
        OKBtn.addActionListener(this);
    }

    public void actionPerformed(ActionEvent theEvent)
    {
        if (theEvent.getSource( ) == clearBtn) result = "";

        else
        {
            for (int i = 0; i < 10; i++)
                if (theEvent.getSource( ) == theKeys[i])
                    result += i;
        }
        ((ActionListener) getParent(⇐
          )).actionPerformed(theEvent);
          System.out.println( result );
    }
}
```

Listing 9-2 Keypad1.html

```html
<HTML>
<HEAD>
<TITLE>Jumbo's First Class</TITLE>
```

continued on next page

continued from previous page

```
</HEAD>
<BODY>
<H1>Brenda Pads Her Keys</H1>
"Drat!" exclaimed Jumbo. "This stupid machine."<BR>
Brenda rolled her eyes, as if to say "What now?" and
inquired in her most soothing, customer-service voice,
"Problem, J.G.?"<P>
Jumbo, perhaps a tad unreasonably, bit back. "I don't
have a problem. It's this moronic prototype. Why does
it let me type in letters if all it can use is
numbers? Who designed this anyhow?"<BR>
Brenda, stifling her impulse to reply, "You did," reached
over Jumbo's shoulder and pressed a key on his keyboard.
"I know just what you need," she said. "Look at this."
<HR>
<APPLET CODE=Keypad1.class HEIGHT=150 WIDTH=200>
</APPLET>
</BODY>
</HTML>
```

> **"** *Designing an interface usually involves a considerable degree of iterative exploration and experimentation: It's largely trial and error!* **"**

EXAMINING Keypad1

The `Keypad1` applet creates a rectangular grid filled with 12 buttons. Each of the buttons has a label consisting of a digit or the word *Clear* or *Order*. As you click each numbered button, the applet builds a `String` containing the digits you have pressed so far. This `String` is displayed in either the MS-DOS console window or your browser's

FIGURE 9-3

Running the **Keypad1** *applet*

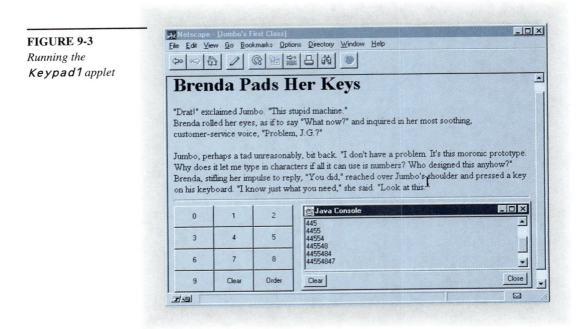

Java console after every button press, depending on whether you use Appletviewer or a browser. Clicking the Clear button sets the `String` to an empty `String`, clearing the entered digits. The Order button doesn't do anything at all, but the JavaMatic will need one, so it's been included for later use.

`Keypad1` uses almost all of the Java features you've learned about to this point. Let's take a brief look at the `Keypad1` applet before turning it into a reusable class. Figure 9-4 shows the fields and methods of the `Keypad1` applet.

`Keypad1` has four fields:

- `result` is a `String` object. It will be used to concatenate and store the individual digit keystrokes, building up a larger number. It is initially set to an empty `String` (`""`).

- `clearBtn` and `OKBtn` are `Button` objects that control the disposition of `result` by the `Keypad1` applet. When the `clearBtn` is pressed, the `String` `result` is reset to the empty `String`. When the `OKBtn` is pressed, the `Keypad1` applet signals the owner of the Keypad—the `Manager` in our case—that the user is finished with the entry.

FIGURE 9-4

Fields and methods of the Keypad1 applet

```
FIELDS

String result;      // Stores keystrokes
Button clearBtn;    // Set result to ""
Button OKBtn        // Ready to order
Button[] theKeys    // array of Buttons


METHODS
init ()
    // Create calculator buttons
    // Add buttons to array and surface
    // Add Clear and Order buttons
action ()
    // Clear result if Clear button
    // Add digit to result
    // Print result
```

theKeys is an array of Button objects. Each button is labeled with a digit. When one of them is pressed, the corresponding digit is concatenated onto the end of the result.

The two methods of Keypad1 are also straightforward:

init( ) performs four actions. First, it sets the LayoutManager for the Keypad1 applet to a GridLayout of three columns and four rows. Then it creates the individual Button objects for the theKeys array and adds each numbered Button object to both the array and the applet surface. Next, the init( ) method adds the clearBtn and OKBtn objects to the surface of the applet. Finally, it sets the applet itself as the ActionListener for messages originating with either of the buttons, by sending each of them an addActionListener message.

The other method, actionPerformed( ), handles Events generated by the buttons. First, if the source of the Event was the clearBtn, the result field is set to the empty String. If not, actionPerformed( ) loops through the array theKeys seeing if one of its buttons was pressed. If a match is found, actionPerformed( ) concatenates the value of the button that was pressed to the end of the String result. This works because the array index (i) and the button label are identical. So, you can concatenate i onto result without bothering to use getLabel( ) to retrieve the button's label. Next, the actionPerformed method informs the Manager (its parent container) that an AWT event has occurred, by forwarding the actionPerformed message to the Manager. Finally, the actionPerformed( ) method calls System.out.println( ) to display result after each action. Displaying result helps you make sure that your Keypad1 class is actually working.

PUTTING Keypad1 TO WORK

If you take a few minutes to work with the Keypad1 applet, you may find yourself both excited and frustrated. Excited, because with very little effort you've created an applet that looks good and works well. Frustrated, because it doesn't yet meet all the needs of the JavaMatic. If you recall from Chapter 4, your Manager class not only needs a keypad object to get user input, it also needs some type of "status display" object to "talk back" to the customer. The println( ) output is inadequate for customer use. A GUI display is needed.

While there are other ways to provide a status display, one of the easiest is to simply create another applet—let's call it PadUser1—that uses the Keypad1 class. Listing 9-3, PadUser1.java, does just that. Listing 9-4 contains the HTML file you'll need to see your applet run, and Figure 9-5 shows PadUser1 at work. When you compile PadUser1, make sure that the Keypad1 file, Keypad1.class, is in the same directory as PadUser1.java. Copy the file into the directory if necessary.

> *If a class has no constructor method, Java automatically provides an implicit constructor.*

Listing 9-3 PadUser1.java

```java
// Putting the Keypad1 class to work
//
//
import java.applet.*;
import java.awt.*;
import java.awt.event.*;

public class PadUser1 extends Applet implements ActionListener
{
    Keypad1 theKeypad = new Keypad1();
    TextField theOutput = new TextField("", 10);

    public void init()
    {
        theKeypad.init();
        add(theOutput);
        add(theKeypad);
        theOutput.setEditable(false);
    }

    public void actionPerformed( ActionEvent theEvent )
    {
        theOutput.setText( theKeypad.result );
    }
}
```

Listing 9-4 PadUser1.html

```html
<HTML>
<HEAD>
<TITLE>Classes Working Together</TITLE>
</HEAD>
<BODY>
<H1>Jumbo Reuses an Applet</H1>
"Why won't this thing fit?" said a pensive, puzzled,
Jumbo, as he tried to insert TAB-A into SLOT Q. The
pieces for his new ZoundsOMatic juicer and car-waxer
lay strewn across the table. "That's the last time
I buy something from late-night TV."<BR>
Brenda, in an uncharacteristic display of compassion,
replied. "I know what you mean," she began. "Be thankful
you didn't sign up for that computer dating service."<P>
A bit embarrassed by the revelation, she quickly changed
the subject. "At least you won't have any problem putting
these Java applets together. Look how these applets can
work together. That's what I call real teamwork."
<HR>
<APPLET CODE=PadUser1.class HEIGHT=300 WIDTH=300>
</APPLET>
</BODY>
</HTML>
```

FIGURE 9-5

Running the
PadUser1 applet

The PadUser1 Attributes

The PadUser1 applet contains two attributes. One of them, theOutput, is a TextField object, just like the TextFields you've added to your previous applets. The other, however, is a Keypad1 object. "What?" you say. "Keypad1 isn't an object, it's an applet!" Remember, in Java everything that's not a primitive type is an object. Looking back at Listing 9-1, you'll notice that the class Keypad1 is declared to extend the class Applet. The class Applet is used by Appletviewer (or a browser) to create an Applet object, based on the information you place in the <APPLET> tag of your HTML file. But it's also possible for you to create Applet objects inside your programs. Such Applet objects will act just like the familiar Button, Label, and TextField objects; that is, you can create a Keypad1 object, send messages to it, pass it as an argument to a method, or return it as the result of a method.

How do you create a Keypad1 object? The same way you create any other type of object: by using the operator new with a constructor method. The line

```
Keypad1 theKeypad = new Keypad1();
```

calls the constructor method Keypad1( ) to create a new Keypad1 object. A reference to the object returned by the Keypad1( ) constructor is then stored in the field theKeypad. "Wait just a minute," you say. "I read through the Keypad1 class very carefully. There wasn't any method named Keypad1( ). Where did this constructor thing come from?" You are entirely correct. If a class has no constructor method, Java automatically provides an implicit constructor. Because the name of a constructor is always the same as the name of the class, you can create an instance object of such a class by writing

```
SomeClass theClassObject = new SomeClass( );
```

The `PadUser1` Methods

Like many applets, `PadUser1` contains two methods, `init( )` and `actionPerformed( )`. When you compile and run `PadUser1`, you will find that both a `Keypad1` object and a `TextField` appear on the screen. When you press one of the numbered buttons on the `Keypad1` object, you can still see the output in the MS-DOS window or in the Java console. But, after each keystroke, output also appears inside the `TextField` object named `theOutput`. How does `PadUser1` get the `Keypad1` object to appear on the screen, and how do the keystrokes collected by the `Keypad1` object make their way to the `TextField theOutput`? Let's walk through the `PadUser1` class.

When you run the `Keypad1` applet, your Web browser automatically invokes the `Keypad1.init( )` method. But when you create a `Keypad1` object inside the `PadUser1` applet, the `init( )` method of `theKeypad` is *not* automatically called. You must call it yourself, as is done on the first line of the `PadUser1.init( )` method:

```
theKeypad.init();
```

If you fail to do this, the `Keypad1.init( )` method will not be called, and you will not see a keypad appear on your screen. What is true for the `init( )` method also holds true for the other applet life-cycle methods. If the `Applet` object you create has `start( )`, `stop( )`, `run( )`, or `destroy( )` methods, these will not be automatically called when your object is instantiated outside the usual cozy environment of a Web browser or Appletviewer. If you want these methods to be performed, you must provide code that invokes them.

The second method in the `PadUser1` applet is the `actionPerformed( )` method. All that the `actionPerformed( )` method does is tell the `TextField` object `theOutput` to set its text equal to the value of the `result` field inside the `Keypad1` object. But at what point does this `actionPerformed( )` method get invoked? You are really not doing anything to the `PadUser1` applet itself; all the action happens inside the `Keypad1` object, whose buttons are being clicked. Because the `Keypad1` object is already doing something about each button-press—sending the `String result` to the `System.out` console—how does the button-press action make it "outside" so that the `PadUser1` applet can see that something has happened? To answer that, you'll need to turn back to the `actionPerformed( )` method of the `Keypad1` class. Look at the line that reads

```
((ActionListener) getParent( )).actionPerformed(theEvent);
```

This line inside `Keypad1` invokes the `actionPerformed` method of `Manager` whenever an `ActionEvent` is handled by `Keypad1`. Thus, the `Manager` is always advised of interesting events happening within the `Keypad1`.

`PadUser1` contains a `Keypad1` object in two very different, but potentially confusing, ways. First, `PadUser1` contains a `Keypad1` object because the object reference `theKeypad` is a field inside the `PadUser1` class. This sort of a relationship—where one class contains objects of another class as fields—is called a `hasA` relationship. You can say that the `PadUser1` class `hasA` `Keypad1` object. Another word you may hear that means the same thing is "composition"—a `PadUser1` object is *composed* of a `Keypad1` object.

" A relationship in which one class contains objects of another class as fields is a `hasA` relationship. "

Second, the `Keypad1` is "contained" within the area of the screen owned by the `Applet`, as established by use of the `add( )` method to place the `Keypad1` on the surface of the `Applet`. This relationship is called a *containment relationship*. The `getParent( )` method makes it easy to pass information from `Keypad1` to its parent container, `Manager`. It's not even necessary to set the `Manager` to be an `ActionListener` in order to receive messages from the `Keypad1`, because we forward them explicitly, rather than depending upon the event system to do it for us.

In summary, there are four common ways that objects can be related:

☞ One object can send messages to another, as you've seen many times: the `usesA` relationship.

☞ One object can have another object embedded within it as a field: the `hasA` relationship.

☞ One GUI object can contain another GUI object within its screen area: the `containsA` relationship.

☞ One object can be related to another by means of inheritance: the `isA` relationship, which is the subject of Chapter 10, "Inheritance: Object Families."

Protecting Your Objects Against Unwanted Access

"BANG! WHAP! SCRCHHH!"

Startled, Brenda looked up from the Java manual she had been studying to see Jumbo standing over his monitor. On top of the display, balanced precariously, was a small, electronic clock-radio—its red LCD showing the time. Pressed against the top of the clock-radio was a screwdriver, which Jumbo was methodically hammering with one of his oversized Oxfords, while steadying the contraption with his knees.

"Whap!" went the Oxford once again.

"Stop it!" went Brenda, almost at once. "Whatever are you trying to do?" she asked with a touch of exasperation. Jumbo, grateful for the break, pulled a handkerchief out of his pocket with his trunk and wiped his forehead. "I need to get this thing open so I can reset the LCD for daylight saving time," he said.

"Don't be ridiculous," Brenda replied, retrieving the instrument before Jumbo could object. "You just use the Reset button on the back..." Brenda's voice trailed off. Jumbo, forgivably smug, replied, "What button?"

For all its simplicity and usefulness, the `Keypad1` class doesn't make a very useful, reusable class. As with Jumbo's clock-radio, the designers left a few things off. Writing classes that can be easily reused requires both forethought when designing the class, and discipline when implementing it. Java provides several features that will help you make the classes you write first-class members of your team.

INTERFACE AND IMPLEMENTATION REVISITED

In Chapter 4 you learned that an object's interface is its face to the world. The interface represents the services an object offers or the messages to which an object responds. The implementation of a service—the code necessary to carry out the task—is provided as the methods of the object. One of the primary techniques available to you for creating reusable and robust classes is to separate the *what* from the *how*—the interface from the implementation.

Suppose that you have created the `Keypad1` class for use by other programmers. What happens if, due to changing user requirements, you find yourself forced to modify the way some of its fields are defined? What happens if you have to change the `results` field from a `String` to a `double`, for instance? This is likely to make you very unpopular, because it will *break* code other programmers have written. To reflect the new class design, they will have to change every line of code that accesses the changed fields of your class.

Take another look at the way in which the `PadUser1` applet retrieves the `String` stored in the `result` field of `theKeypad`:

```
theOutput.setText( theKeypad.result );
```

Rather than asking the `Keypad1` object to give you the `String`, you are just going in and grabbing it. Not only is this rude, but it's also dangerous, because you are relying on the internal structure of another class. You are relying on the implementation, not the interface. Fortunately, there is an easy remedy. The problem lies not so much with `PadUser1` as with the `Keypad1` class. Much like Jumbo's clock-radio, it was never properly designed for reuse. It's time to change that.

ACCESSORS AND MUTATORS

If good OOP manners require you to avoid accessing the internal data of another class, how are you supposed to get the information you need? By asking the class for it, of course. And how do you ask the class for it? By calling a method rather than accessing the data directly.

The methods that provide you with information about the state of an object are called *accessor* methods. Frequently, programmers name these methods starting with *get*, creating such names as `getTemperature( )` or `getText( )`. Often, an accessor method will combine access to a field with some translation or conversion as well. If a class can hold a single value—as your `Keypad1` class can—your users might want to retrieve that value as either a number or a `String`. The `toString( )` method is a familiar accessor method provided by many classes. Users of such a class can retrieve the value of a class instance as a `String` by invoking the `toString( )` method. Similarly, by writing a `toDouble( )` method within your class, you could enable users of your class to retrieve the value stored in a `Keypad1` object as a `double`. Listing 9-5 shows these methods that could be added to provide access to the data stored inside the new, improved, `Keypad2` class.

Listing 9-5 The toString( ) and toDouble( ) methods of the Keypad2 class

```
// Accessor methods
public String toString()   { return result;    }
public double toDouble()   { return⇐
   Double.valueOf(result).doubleValue(); }
```

Similarly, methods used to change a field—to set Jumbo's clock-radio, for instance—are called *mutators*; not because they resemble fugitives from a 1950s horror movie, but because they change some of the attributes of an object. Again, courtesy and wisdom both demand that users refrain from changing fields directly, but instead use the class' interface to manipulate the state of an object.

Mutator methods insulate the users of your class from changes you might make to the implementation of the class. But they also do much more. Frequently, changing one field inside a class—for instance, a purchase amount—also requires changes to other fields, such as the total balance. Mutator methods ensure that the state of an object stays "in sync." Your `Keypad2` class has two places where the state of the object is changed: when the `result` field is cleared, and when characters are appended to its end. These are both candidates for mutator methods. Listing 9-6 shows `clear( )`, the first mutator method. The other method, `addDigit( )`, is discussed a little later.

Listing 9-6 The clear( ) method of the Keypad2 class

```
// Mutator methods
public void clear()                  { result = ""; }
```

By providing users of your classes with accessor and mutator methods, you are free at any time to change the way the related fields are defined. After changing the fields, you simply revise the accessor and mutator methods to work as they did before, despite the changes to the fields. The other programmers won't even know you've changed anything. You won't be a hero, but you'll also not be a goat.

This technique of structuring an object to present one face to the world, while hiding its true nature, is called *data hiding*. In building large systems that must continue in operation for long periods and undergo many changes, data hiding is essential. Figure 9-6 shows how data hiding protects your class, and the users of your class, from the undesirable effects of change.

FIGURE 9-6
Data hiding

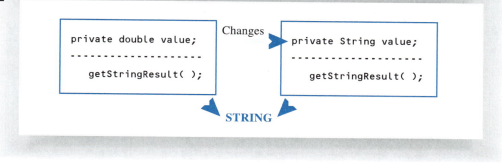

HIDING OUT: `public` AND `private`

Of course, all is well only so long as the users of your class conform to your wishes and use the accessor and mutator methods you've so thoughtfully provided. However, if even one rebellious rogue breaches the rules of software etiquette by directly accessing the fields, all your cleverness comes to ruin. Surely, you plead, there must be some way of *forcing* all those other programmers to do what is right and noble?

The good news is that *there is*. By including the keyword `private` before the declaration of a field, you prevent direct access to that field, except within methods of the same class. So, by changing the declaration of `result` to read

```
private String result = "";
```

you can prevent other programmers from accessing the field; they will be *forced* to use the accessor and mutator methods you wrote, whether they like it or not. This same device, by the way, can be used to limit access to the methods of a class, as well as the fields. By writing `private` at the beginning of a method header, you prevent access to that method outside its containing class.

What happens if someone attempts the impossible by trying to access a `private` field or method within a class? The Java compiler will refuse to compile the offending reference, issuing an error like this

```
PadUser2.java:29: Variable result in class Keypad2 not⇐
    accessible from class PadUser2.
          theOutput.setText( theKeypad.result );
                                          ^
1 error
```

Listing 9-7 shows how `Keypad2.java` has been changed to make all its fields `private`. The new accessor and mutator methods now allow the `PadUser2` applet to get the information from the `Keypad2` object without violating its privacy. Listing 9-8 shows the `PadUser2` applet, which uses the `Keypad2` object. The HTML file, `PadUser2.html`, is shown in Listing 9-9. Figure 9-7 shows the `PadUser2` applet in action.

" *Writing classes
that can be easily
reused requires
both forethought
in design and
discipline in
implementation.* "

Listing 9-7 Keypad2.java

```java
// A Second Keypad Class
//
import java.applet.*;
import java.awt.*;
import java.awt.event.*;

public class Keypad2 extends Applet implements ActionListener
{
    // Attributes
    private String result = "";

    private Button[] theKeys  = new Button[10];
    private Button   clearBtn = new Button("Clear");
    private Button   OKBtn     = new Button("OK");

    // Accessor methods
    public String toString() { return result;    }
    public double toDouble()
        { return Double.valueOf(result).doubleValue(); }

    // Mutator methods
    public  void clear()            { result = ""; }
    private void addDigit( int i ) { result += i; }

    public void init()
    {
        setLayout( new GridLayout(4, 3) );

        for (int i = 0; i < 10; i++)
        {
            theKeys[i] = new Button(""+i);
            add( theKeys[i] );
            theKeys[i].addActionListener(this);
        }

        add( clearBtn );
        add( OKBtn );
        clearBtn.addActionListener(this);
        OKBtn.addActionListener(this);
    }

    public void actionPerformed(ActionEvent theEvent)
    {
        if (theEvent.getSource( ) == clearBtn) clear();
        else
        {
            for (int i = 0; i < 10; i++)
                if (theEvent.getSource( ) == theKeys[i])
                    addDigit( i );
        }

        Object parent = getParent( );
        If (parent instanceof ActionListener)⇐
          ((ActionListener) parent).actionPerformed⇐
            (theEvent);
    }
}
```

Listing 9-8 PadUser2.java

```java
// Putting the Keypad2 class to work
//
//
import java.applet.*;
import java.awt.*;
import java.awt.event.*;

public class PadUser2 extends Applet⇐
   Implements ActionListener
   {
      private Keypad2 theKeypad = new Keypad2();
      private Label    theOutput = new Label();

      public void init()
      {
          theKeypad.init();
          setLayout( new BorderLayout() );
          theOutput.setAlignment(Label.RIGHT);
          add(theOutput, "North");
          add(theKeypad, "Center");
      }

      public void actionPerformed( ActionEvent theEvent )
      {
          theOutput.setText( theKeypad.toString() );
      }
}
```

Listing 9-9 PadUser2.html

```html
<HTML>
<HEAD>
<TITLE>Accessors and Mutators</TITLE>
</HEAD>
<BODY>
<IMG SRC="Jumbo.GIF" ALIGN=RIGHT HEIGHT=50>
<H1>Jumbo's Private Reserve</H1>
<HR>
<APPLET CODE=PadUser2.class HEIGHT=200 WIDTH=150 ALIGN=RIGHT>
</APPLET>
"Overdrawn? What do you mean I'm overdrawn?" said a
puzzled Jumbo, as he stared blankly at the phone
while Brenda vainly tried to get his attention from
across the room. "I can't be overdrawn. I just made
a deposit, and the only ones who can write checks on
this account...are..."<BR>
His voice slowed to a stop as he noticed Brenda's
frantic waving of a trunkful of receipts from across
the room, and the light began to dawn.<P>
"Brenda," he began, "did you..."<BR>
"You know J.G." Brenda broke in, "this reminds me of
why we need to make all of our fields private. That
way you'll never accidentally modify values that
another programmer doesn't know about. Look how I've
fixed the Keypad."<BR>
</BODY>
</HTML>
```

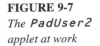

FIGURE 9-7
The `PadUser2`
applet at work

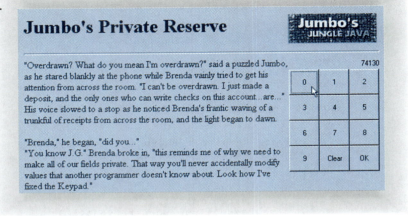

LOOKING AT Keypad2 AND PadUser2

The `Keypad2` class utilizes data hiding, and accessor and mutator methods. The two accessor methods, `toString( )` and `toDouble( )`, provide the only ways of looking at the data inside the `Keypad2` class. The two mutator methods, `clear( )` and `addDigit( )`, provide the only ways of modifying the `result` field. These are used inside the class as well as outside. Rather than just setting the value of `result` to the empty `String` when the Clear button is pressed, the `actionPerformed( )` method uses the `clear( )` method to change it. This means that if you decide tomorrow that `result` should be stored as a `double` rather than a `String`, you will need to change only the mutator and accessor methods.

Both the `Keypad2` class and the `PadUser2` class use the `private` keyword to keep "outside" methods from modifying any of their data. As recommended, all of the fields in each class are made `private`. When you learn about inheritance in Chapter 10, that recommendation will be modified slightly. For now, it's a good rule of thumb to make all fields `private`, and provide accessor and mutator methods as needed.

If all fields should generally be `private`, does it follow that all methods should be `public`? Certainly any methods designed for "outsiders" to call should be `public`, otherwise other programmers won't be able to use them. But every time you create a method, you need to ask yourself, "Will any outside objects need to use this method?" If the answer is no, you may have a candidate for a `private` "utility" method, like the `addDigit( )` method inside the `Keypad2` class:

```
private void addDigit( int i ) { result += i; }
```

The `addDigit( )` method can only be called from a method that is part of the `Keypad2` class. Because of this, no errant method can change the internal data of a `Keypad2` object, except through the `clear( )` method. The `PadUser2` applet uses the `private` keyword as well, and rather than attempting to read the `result` field directly, the `actionPerformed( )` method now uses the `toString( )` method to retrieve the value that is stored inside the `Keypad2` object.

NEW FEATURES: setAlignment AND BorderLayout

The `PadUser2` applet introduces two other new features that you have not seen before. These are not absolutely essential, but they greatly improve the appearance of the applet. The simpler of these new features is the use of the `setAlignment( )` method of the `Label` class. This method can take one of three arguments: the constants `Label.LEFT`, `Label.RIGHT`, and `Label.CENTER`. Sending the `setAlignment( )` message to a `Label` causes it to position its text starting at the left side, right side, or center of the `Label`. One small complication, however, is that `setAlignment( )` is ignored when the layout manager is set to the default `FlowLayout`.

To cure that problem, let's meet the second new feature of `PadUser2`, a new layout manager. You've already met `FlowLayout` and `GridLayout`. The new layout manager, called `BorderLayout`, is conceptually simple. There are only five possible locations at which objects can be placed in a `BorderLayout`. These are named for the four compass points ("North", "South", "East", and "West") and for the center of the applet ("Center"). Figure 9-8 shows the appearance of an applet with five buttons that uses `BorderLayout`. When a component is added to the center of an applet that uses `BorderLayout`, the component "swells" to fill all of the unused space. To add an object to a container controlled by `BorderLayout`, you use the `add( )` method with two

FIGURE 9-8
*The BorderLayout
layout manager*

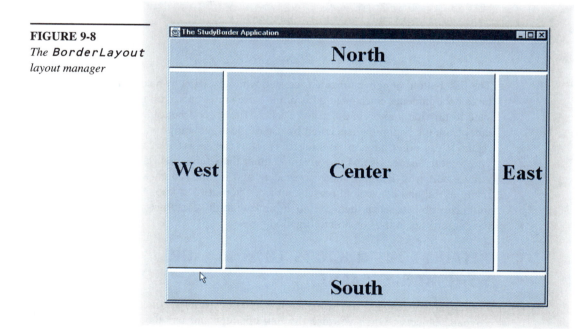

arguments, rather than one. The first specifies the component; the second specifies in which of the five possible positions the component should appear. Note that these names are case sensitive. If you erroneously try to

```
add(theOutput, "north"); //wrong
```

your `Label` will never be seen! Instead, you should write

```
add(theOutput, "North"); //right
```

Birth of an Object: Constructor Methods

When you create a class that is intended for use just once, in some particular program, you don't need to be very concerned with the initialization of new instances of the class. You can simply include appropriate initializers in the definition on each field, or set the fields to appropriate values in a method such as `init( )`. However, when you create a class intended for reuse, one whose objects must perform as part of a team of objects, initialization is a greater concern. Such a class must often be capable of providing customized initialization, so that created objects take on an individual personality from the start.

The designers of Java's Abstract Window Toolkit (AWT) provided most of the GUI classes with the capability to initialize objects when they are created by use of the `new` operator. For example, you can create a button like this:

```
Button genericButton = new Button( );
```

or like this:

```
Button customButton = new Button( "Custom" );
```

The first button, `genericButton`, is created without a label by a constructor method that takes no arguments. Such a button is of little use until you send it the `setLabel( )` message to provide appropriate text for a label. The second button, `customButton`, has a label from the beginning, specified by use of the argument provided to the constructor method. You don't have to send the `customButton` a `setLabel` message at all, unless you want to change its text to something other than `"Custom"`. The second way of creating a button is therefore more convenient and is much more widely used. To create really useful and convenient reusable objects, you need to know how the `new` operator initializes objects when there are no arguments to the constructor method, and how to pass arguments to the constructor method.

DEFAULT CONSTRUCTORS: CONSTRUCTORS WITHOUT ARGUMENTS

Earlier in this chapter, you saw that Java creates instances of your `Keypad2` class—`Keypad2` objects—when you use the `new` operator and use the `Keypad2` constructor. You also saw that even though you didn't write a constructor method, Java provided one for you.

When you provide no constructor for a class, as is the case with the `Keypad2` class, a default constructor is created by Java, telling the `new` operator how to create an instance of the class. The default constructor simply tells the `new` operator to create the object in memory and then to initialize each of its fields. For fields with initializers, the specified initial value is assigned to the field. For fields without initializers, a default value is used. The default value is

☕ `null` for `Strings` and object types

☕ Zero for numeric types and characters

☕ `false` for `boolean` types

For example, if your class has an `int` field called `theValue`, it is initialized to the value zero, just as if its declaration had been written

```
int theValue = 0;
```

instead of

```
int theValue;
```

Remembering that a constructor is a method with the same name as its enclosing class, you can see that it's as if Java had included the following constructor method in the `Keypad2` class:

```
public Keypad2( )
{
    result = "";

    theKeys  = new Button[10];
    clearBtn = new Button("Clear");
    OKBtn    = new Button("OK");
}
```

Because a constructor is never used to return a value, only to create an object, a constructor has no return type given in its method header. Otherwise a constructor is little different from a method that happens to be callable only by means of the `new` operator.

In fact, you can include a constructor just like this within the body of the `Keypad2` class. Such a constructor is referred to as a *no-argument* (or, for short, *no-arg*) constructor. If you do modify the `Keypad2` class to include a no-argument constructor, the class will work exactly as before, so there's little sense doing so. It just adds to the clutter within the class. On the other hand, the statements included inside the `init( )` method of the applet could instead be placed inside the no-argument constructor. By renaming the `init( )` method of `Keypad2` from:

```
public void init( ) { . . . }
```

to

```
public Keypad2( ) { . . . }
```

and thereby making the method into a no-argument constructor, you avoid the necessity of explicitly calling the `init( )` method of each `Keypad2` object when it's created, as you were required to do in the `PadUser2` applet. The `new` operator will use the statements in the no-argument constructor to initialize objects it creates, so the applet will have a proper layout manager and will have its component buttons added to its surface from the very time of its creation. Figure 9-9 shows the syntax of the no-argument constructor, using the constructor for the `Keypad2` class as an example.

CONSTRUCTORS WITH ARGUMENTS

Often it's desirable to include somewhat more elaborate constructors within a class. Such constructor methods may include one or more arguments. These allow you to create class instances (objects) that are customized; each one can be different.

Where might you use such capabilities? Perhaps you would like to have different numeric symbols on your `Keypad` objects. Listing 9-10 shows a new version of the `Keypad` class, christened `Keypad3`, that allows you to do just that. Listing 9-11, `PadUser3.java`, along with Listing 9-12, `PadUser3.html`, show how you can use this feature to create a keypad that uses regular Arabic numerals and another that labels its keys in Spanish. Figure 9-10 shows the applet at work.

FIGURE 9-9
The default constructor

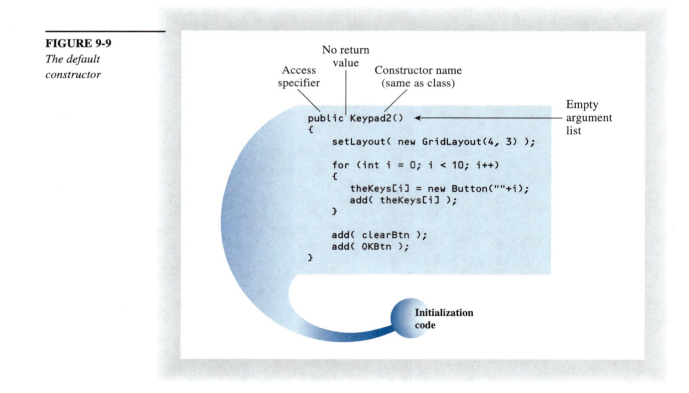

```
                    No return
                    value    Constructor name
         Access             (same as class)
         specifier
                                                              Empty
            public Keypad2()  ◄──────────────────────────── argument
            {                                                 list
                setLayout( new GridLayout(4, 3) );

                for (int i = 0; i < 10; i++)
                {
                    theKeys[i] = new Button(""+i);
                    add( theKeys[i] );
                }

                add( clearBtn );
                add( OKBtn );
            }
```

Initialization code

Listing 9-10 Keypad3.java

```
// A Third Keypad Class, with two constructors
//
import java.applet.*;
import java.awt.*;
import java.awt.event.*;

public class Keypad3 extends Applet implements ActionListener
{
    // Attributes
    private String result = "";

    private Button[] theKeys  = new Button[10];
    private Button   clearBtn = new Button("Clear");
    private Button   OKBtn    = new Button("Order");

    // Accessor methods
    public String toString() { return result;    }
    public double toDouble()
        { return Double.valueOf(result).doubleValue(); }

    // Mutator methods
    public  void clear()             { result = ""; }
    private void addDigit( int i ) { result += i; }

// Constructor method (no argument;⇐
    i.e., default constructor)
public Keypad3()
    {
        setLayout( new GridLayout(4, 3) );

        for (int i = 0; i < 10; i++)
        {
            theKeys[i] = new Button(""+i);
            add( theKeys[i] );
            theKeys[i].addActionListener(this);
        }
        add( clearBtn );
        add( OKBtn );
        clearBtn.addActionListener(this);
        OKBtn.addActionListener(this);
    }

// Constructor (three arguments)
    public Keypad3(String[] keyLabels, String clearLabel,⇐
      String OKLabel)
    {
        setLayout( new GridLayout(4, 3) );

        for (int i = 0; i < 10; i++)
        {
            theKeys[i] = new Button(keyLabels[i]);
            add( theKeys[i] );
            theKeys[i].addActionListener(this);
        }

        clearBtn = new Button( clearLabel );
        OKBtn    = new Button( OKLabel );
```

continued on next page

continued from previous page

```
            add( clearBtn );
            add( OKBtn );
            clearBtn.addActionListener(this);
            OKBtn.addActionListener(this);
        }

        public void actionPerformed(ActionEvent theEvent)
        {
            if (theEvent.getSource( ) == clearBtn) clear();

            for (int i = 0; i < 10; i++)
                if (theEvent.getSource( ) == theKeys[i])
                    addDigit( i );
            ((ActionListener) getParent( ))⇐
                .actionPerformed(theEvent);
        }
    }
```

Listing 9-11 PadUser3.java

```
// Putting the Keypad3 class to work
//
//
import java.applet.*;
import java.awt.*;
import java.awt.event.*;

public class PadUser3 extends Applet implements ActionListener
{
// Note:   arabicPad initialized using default constructor,
// spanishPad initialized in init( ) method, below.
    private Keypad3    arabicPad  = new Keypad3(), spanishPad;
    private TextField arabicOut  = new TextField("", 20);
    private TextField spanishOut = new TextField("", 20);

    public void init()
    {
        String[] spanish= { "Cero","Uno","Dos","Tres",⇐
                            "Quattro","Cinco","Seis",⇐
                            "Siete", "Ocho", "Nueve" };
// Note: spanishPad initialized using three-argument
constructor)
        spanishPad = new Keypad3( spanish, "  *  ", "  #  "⇐
            );

        add( arabicOut );
        add( spanishOut );
        add( arabicPad );
        add( spanishPad );
    }

    public void actionPerformed( ActionEvent theEvent )
    {
        spanishOut.setText( spanishPad.toString() );
        arabicOut.setText( arabicPad.toString() );
    }
}
```

Listing 9-12 PadUser3.html

```
<HTML>
<HEAD>
<TITLE>Overloaded Constructors</TITLE>
</HEAD>
<BODY>
<IMG SRC="Jumbo.GIF" ALIGN=RIGHT HEIGHT=50>
<H1>Jumbo Expands</H1>
<HR>
<APPLET CODE=PadUser3.class HEIGHT=300 WIDTH=200 ALIGN=RIGHT>
</APPLET>
"Que sera, sera," hummed Jumbo and Brenda, happily
working side by side on the latest version of the
JavaMatic.<BR>
"I have to admit," said Brenda, stopping and turning
to Jumbo, "I didn't really think this expansion thing
would take off like it did. And I really like what
you've done with these multi-lingual keypads."<P>
Jumbo, a little taken aback by the praise, deflected
the conversation with a witticism.
"If we overload our constructors, can they go out
on strike?" he asked.
</BODY>
</HTML>
```

The `Keypad3` class contains two constructors. Here are their headers:

```
public Keypad3( )
public Keypad3( String[] keyLabels, String clearLabel,⇐
    String OKLabel )
```

Note that each constructor is specified as `public`, so that it can be used by methods of other classes, and each is named the same as the enclosing class, `Keypad3`. The only

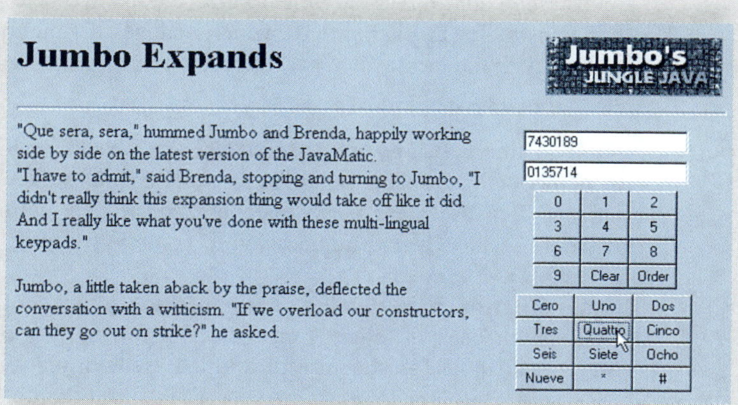

FIGURE 9-10

Running the
PadUser3 *applet*

difference is that the first constructor has no arguments and the second has three arguments:

- An array of `Strings` called `keyLabels` that will hold the text that appears on the face of each button

- The two `Strings`, `clearLabel` and `OKLabel`, which hold the text to appear on the face of the Clear button and the `OK` (or Order) button, respectively.

Most messages are sent to objects, but a constructor message is sent to a class. More precisely, a constructor message sent by the `new` operator is sent to a special object, hidden within the class named following the `new` operator, known as the *class object*. That such an object would exist is natural, because everything in Java other than primitives is represented as an object—even classes themselves. This special object is similar to a factory, shown in Figure 9-11, whose sole purpose is creating instances of the class. The nomenclature "class object" is unfortunate, because it is usually understood to refer to an instance of a class. Only context can disclose which of the two possible meanings is intended, but because both meanings concern object creation, this is admittedly not very helpful. Usually "*the* class object" refers to the special object, while "*a* class object" refers to an instance of the class. Knowing about the class object is important, because it supports several useful methods that you will meet in Chapter 10.

Two possible messages can be sent to the `Keypad3` class object:

```
new Keypad3( )
```

or

```
new Keypad3( theLabels, theClearText, theOrderText )
```

where the parameter `theLabels` is an array of `Strings`, and the parameters `theClearText` and `theOrderText` are both `Strings`. The first message would invoke the constructor that has no argument. The second message would be directed to the second constructor in Listing 9-10, which matches the number and type of arguments associated with the message. What if you tried to send the message

```
new Keypad3( theLabels )
```

with only a single `String` array argument? The Java compiler would look through the constructors defined inside the `Keypad3` class, trying to match the number and type of arguments. Because there is no matching constructor within the `Keypad3` class, an error would result when you attempted to compile the code containing the erroneous construction.

Besides differing in the number of arguments they take, how are the two constructors of the `Keypad3` class different from each other? What happens within their respective constructor methods? In the case of the first method, the one with no arguments, the object's field `clearBtn` is set to the text "Clear" and the field `OKBtn` has its text set to "Order." This occurs because each of these fields has an initializer

FIGURE 9-11

The class object

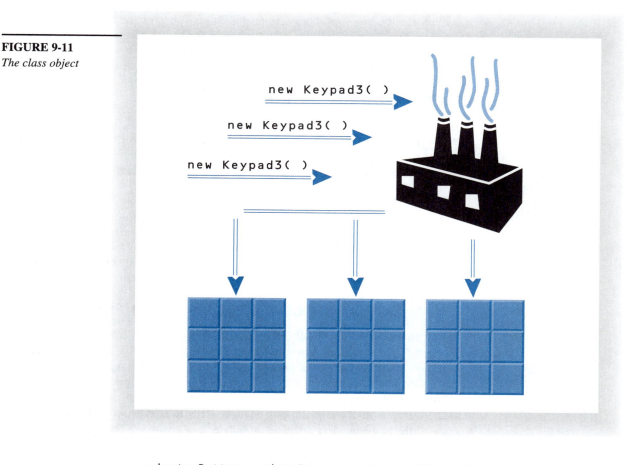

```
private Button    clearBtn = new Button("Clear");
private Button    OKBtn    = new Button("Order");
```

that is executed before the code inside the constructor method starts running. The loop inside the constructor is then used to put the number of each button on its face as the button's text.

In the case of the second constructor, which has three arguments, the arguments are used to specify the initial values of the fields. Although the `clearBtn` and `OKBtn` fields have already been initialized, the constructor uses the values passed into the constructor in the arguments `clearLabel` and `OKLabel` to create new buttons, and stores references to the buttons as new values for these fields, overwriting the previous values. The array argument `keyLabels` is then used to initialize the text to be displayed on each of the keypad buttons in place of its index number.

Why was it necessary to write a no-argument constructor? Because Java will provide a default constructor only if no constructors have been written at all. When you write any constructor, you must then take responsibility for writing a default constructor if you want one. Java will no longer supply this for you. If you fail to write a default constructor and nevertheless attempt to instantiate an object without providing the proper constructor arguments, the Java compiler will reject your program.

OVERLOADING CONSTRUCTORS

As you recall from Chapter 4, the word *overloaded*, when applied to a method, does not mean that the method has too much to do. Rather, overloading refers to the presence of two (or more) methods with the same name, differing in the number or type of their arguments. The two constructors inside the `Keypad3` class are thus called *overloaded constructors*.

Overloaded constructors are handled by Java in the same way that it handles overloaded methods. Java looks at the constructor message's *signature*—its name, and the number and types of its arguments—and determines which constructor method to use by looking for the best match. As with overloaded methods, Java will automatically perform compatible conversions in seeking this match. For example, an `int` argument in a message can be matched with a `long` parameter in a corresponding method.

THE `this( )` METHOD AND THE `this` OBJECT

You've already met the `this` object in Chapter 4. There it was used to name the default recipient of a message, the object that received the message that the current method is handling. A second use of the `this` object is to work around an unfortunate choice of name for a parameter or local variable. Sometimes a programmer will give a parameter or local variable the same name as an attribute. When that name is used inside a method, the value of the parameter or local variable is accessed. How, then, can the value of the corresponding attribute be obtained or changed? The best way is usually to change the name of the parameter or local variable and eliminate a possible source of confusion for readers of the class. When, for whatever reason, this is deemed inappropriate, Java allows the value of the attribute to be accessed by prepending `this.` to its name. For example, an attribute named `theValue` could be accessed by use of `this.theValue`. Let's emphasize that this is generally bad practice, which you should avoid. But when you read someone else's code, you may find that he or she has chosen the low road, rather than eliminating the name conflict.

This isn't the only way that `this` can be used. A special method, the `this( )` method, is often helpful in writing overloaded constructors. It allows one constructor to invoke another, usually more general, constructor. In the `Keypad3` class, most of the code inside each constructor is identical, which is wasteful in terms of space, and often leads to errors when changes are made to one constructor but not to the other. The `this( )` method provides a way to streamline such a class.

Let's return to the keypad one final time, exploiting the advantages of using the `this( )` method, demonstrating the use of the `this` object, and adding a few new features. The final version of the keypad consists of two classes, `Keypad` shown in Listing 9-13, and `KeypadWithDisplay` shown in Listing 9-14. The `KeypadWithDisplay` class contains a `Keypad` object within itself: It, in turn, can be used to create useful objects, as you'll see in the next section. The HTML file used to run the `Keypad` applet is shown in Listing 9-15, and the output is shown in Figure 9-12.

Listing 9-13 Keypad.java

```java
// A Keypad Class, with two constructors
//
import java.applet.*;
import java.awt.*;
import java.awt.event.*;

public class Keypad extends Applet implements ActionListener
{
    // Attributes
    private String result = "";
    private TextField theOutput;

    private Button[] theKeys  = new Button[10];
    private Button    clearBtn = new Button("Clear");
    private Button    OKBtn    = new Button("Order");

    // Accessor methods
    public String toString()  { return result;   }
    public double toDouble()
        { return Double.valueOf(result).doubleValue(); }

    // Mutator methods
    public  void clear() { result = ""; updateOutput(); }
    private void addDigit( int i ) { result += i; }

//  Constructor method (no argument; i.e., default
//  constructor)
    public Keypad()
    {
        this(null);
    }

//  Constructor method (single argument)
    public Keypad(TextField theOutput)
    {
        this.theOutput = theOutput;
        setLayout( new GridLayout(4, 3) );

        for (int i = 0; i < 10; i++)
        {
            theKeys[i] = new Button(""+i);
            add( theKeys[i] );
            theKeys[i].addActionListener(this);
        }
        add( clearBtn );
        add( OKBtn );
        clearBtn.addActionListener(this);
        OKBtn.addActionListener(this);
    }

    public void actionPerformed(ActionEvent theEvent)
```

continued on next page

continued from previous page

```
    {
        if (theEvent.getSource( ) == OKBtn)
            ((ActionListener) getParent(⇐
                )).actionPerformed(theEvent);
        if (theEvent.getSource( ) == clearBtn) clear();

        for (int i = 0; i < 10; i++)
            if (theEvent.getSource( ) == theKeys[i])
                addDigit( i );

        updateOutput();
    }

    void updateOutput()
    {
        if (theOutput != null)⇐
           theOutput.setText( toString() );
    }
}
```

> **" Accessor methods provide information about the state of an object. "**

Listing 9-14 KeypadWithDisplay.java

```
// Creating a Keypad With Display
//
//
import java.applet.*;
import java.awt.*;

public class KeypadWithDisplay extends Applet
{
    private TextField theOutput;
    private Keypad      theKeypad;

    public KeypadWithDisplay()
    {
        setLayout( new BorderLayout() );
        theOutput = new TextField( "", 20 );
        theKeypad = new Keypad( theOutput );
        add( theOutput, "North" );
        add( theKeypad, "Center" );
    }

    public String toString() { return theKeypad.toString(); }
    public void clear()      { theKeypad.clear(); }
    public double toDouble() { return theKeypad.toDouble(); }
}
```

Listing 9-15 Keypad.html

```
<HTML>
<HEAD>
<TITLE>Making Components</TITLE>
</HEAD>
<BODY>
<IMG SRC="Jumbo.GIF" ALIGN=RIGHT HEIGHT=50>
<H1>Jumbo Puts It Together</H1>
<HR>
```

```
<APPLET CODE=PadWithDisplayUser.class HEIGHT=180 WIDTH=200
ALIGN=RIGHT>
</APPLET>
"The secret of the JavaMatic," Jumbo droned on,
happily pontificating, buoyed up by a mug of
hot Brazilian Roast, "lies with its scalable
component-based architecture."<BR>
In the back of the room, Brenda, rolled her eyes
heavenward. "Come on boss," she thought, "don't lay
it on too thick."<P>
As if reading her thoughts, Jumbo went on. "But words
are cheap," he said. "Let me show you an example."<BR>
The crowd stirred and rustled 'round, expectantly, in
their seats.<P>
Glancing at his crib sheet buried in his palm, he went
on. "Our research on ergonomics here at J4.COM has shown
that 84% of the difficulty customers have experienced
with more primitive JavaMatics has to do with being
asked to press any key. This is our new modular keypad
with its display,"
began Jumbo. "You'll immediately notice that we've removed
the 'any' key."
</BODY>
</HTML>
```

Unraveling Keypad and Friends

The `KeypadWithDisplay` class contains a `Keypad` object and a `TextField` object that acts as the display for the `Keypad` object. If you already have a `TextField` named `myTextField`, for example, and you want to create a `Keypad` connected to it, you can do so like this:

```
KeypadWithDisplay theKeypad = new⇐
   KeypadWithDisplay(myTextField);
```

FIGURE 9-12

Output of the Keypad applet

Jumbo Puts It Together

Jumbo's JUNGLE JAVA

"The secret of the JavaMatic," Jumbo droned on, happily pontificating, buoyed up by a mug of hot Brazilian Roast, "lies with its scalable component-based architecture."
In the back of the room, Brenda, rolled her eyes heavenward. "Come on boss," she thought, "don't lay it on too thick."

As if reading her thoughts, Jumbo went on. "But words are cheap," he said. "Let me show you an example."
The crowd stirred and rustled 'round, expectantly, in their seats.

Glancing at his crib sheet buried in his palm, he went on. "Our research on ergonomics here at J4.COM has shown that 84% of the difficulty customers have experienced with more primitive JavaMatics has to do with being asked to press any key. This is our new modular keypad with its display," began Jumbo. "You'll immediately notice that we've removed the 'any' key."

74103		
74103		
0	1	2
3	4	5
6	7	8
9	Clear	Order

If, on the other hand, you want a `Keypad` that has no display, all you have to do is create a `KeypadWithDisplay` object like this:

```
KeypadWithDisplay theKeypad = new KeypadWithDisplay();
```

Either way, you no longer have to be concerned with creating both a `TextField` and a `Keypad` and then hooking them both together. Once you create a `KeypadWithDisplay` object and put it in your applet, you can treat it as you would any other object—you don't need to be concerned with the details. That is one of the real advantages of object-oriented programming.

Changes to `Keypad`

In previous versions of the `Keypad` class, each `Keypad` object notified the applet or container that contained it each time a key was pressed. It did this by forwarding the `actionPerformed` message. The new version of the `Keypad` class acts somewhat differently. Rather than informing its container whenever a key is pressed, each new `Keypad` object does so only when the Order button is pressed. All other events are handled entirely within the `Keypad` object itself. This is consistent with how you expect a `Keypad` object to behave. You want it to go about its business, doing `Keypad`-type stuff, until the user says, "I'm done entering numbers. Do something with them." Pressing the Order button sends that kind of notice to the `Keypad`'s container.

What does the new `Keypad` class do with the individual button-press events, if they are no longer passed out of the class? Each time one of the numeric buttons is pressed, the `actionPerformed( )` method now calls a new method named `updateOutput`, which prints the current value of the `Keypad` object to a `TextField` named `theOutput`, which was added to the `Keypad` class as a new field. The `updateOutput( )` method uses the `toString( )` accessor method rather than manipulating the `result` field directly. Also, before displaying the value, `updateOutput( )` first checks to make sure that `theOutput` is not equal to `null`.

The new `Keypad` class has two constructor methods. One, the default constructor

```
public Keypad( ) { . . . }
```

simply creates a `Keypad` object by using the `this( )` method to invoke the other, more powerful, constructor, sending it a `null` reference as a parameter. The second constructor

```
public Keypad( TextField theOutputRef ) { . . . }
```

sets the `TextField`, `theOutput`, equal to its parameter of the same name, using `this.theOutput` to refer to the instance variable. It then sets up a `GridLayout` layout manager, initializes the labels of the numeric buttons, and adds the various components to its own screen area.

If you create a `Keypad` object with no arguments, like this:

```
Keypad somePad = new Keypad( );
```

the created `Keypad` object will not echo digits to the display as the buttons are pressed. On the other hand, if you create a `Keypad` object like this:

```
TextField myTextField = new TextField("", 20 );
Keypad myPad = new Keypad( myTextField );
```

the `Keypad` object, `myPad`, and the `TextField` object, `myTextField`, will be linked, and `myPad` will print its output onto `myTextField`.

While you can use the `this( )` method to call the default constructor as you've seen here, you can also use it to call constructors with arguments. If you have a class with three constructors:

```
public Rabbit( ) { . . . }
public Rabbit( String breed ) { . . . }
public Rabbit( double milesPerGallon ) { . . . }
```

then you can use `this( )` in the following ways:

```
this( );            // Calls the default constructor
this( "Biloxi");    // Calls the Rabbit( String ) constructor
this( 55.3 );       // Calls the Rabbit( double ) constructor
```

Remember though, that you can only call `this( )` from within a constructor!

`KeypadWithDisplay`: Creating and Using

If the `Keypad` class now has the capability to manage its own display, then what is the purpose of the `KeypadWithDisplay` class? The `KeypadWithDisplay` class is really nothing more than an organizer class that integrates component classes. It contains both a `Keypad` reference, called `theKeypad`, and a `TextField` reference, called `theOutput`. The constructor, `KeypadWithDisplay( )`, first sets its `LayoutManager` to `BorderLayout`. It then creates a `TextField` object and a `Keypad` object (using the `Keypad( TextField )` constructor), and stores references to these inside the fields `theKeypad` and `theOutput`. Finally, both the `Keypad` and the `TextField` are added to the surface of the `KeypadWithDisplay` object, by use of the `add( )` method.

The `KeypadWithDisplay` class also has two accessor methods and one mutator method:

```
public String toString() { return theKeypad.toString(); }
public void clear()       { theKeypad.clear(); }
public double toDouble() { return theKeypad.doubleValue(); }
```

As you can see, these messages are simply passed on to the `Keypad` object stored inside the `KeypadWithDisplay`. "Why bother?" you might be asking. "Why not simply send the message directly to the `Keypad`?" There are two answers to that. First, because the field `theKeypad` is a `private` field, users of `KeypadWithDisplay` objects do not have access to `theKeypad`. This preserves the principle of data hiding you learned about earlier. Second, the `KeypadWithDisplay` class now has the opportunity to modify how the `Keypad` object works by intercepting the `toString( )`, `clear( )`, and `toDouble( )` messages. `KeypadWithDisplay` is free to change the color of the display if the user enters a negative number, for instance, or to prevent users of `KeypadWithDisplay` objects from calling the `clear( )` method. For example, by defining its own `clear( )` method as follows, `KeypadWithDisplay` could prohibit use of the `Keypad` Clear button:

```
public void clear()        { }
```

PUTTING KeypadWithDisplay TO WORK

The final class in our collection, `PadWithDisplayUser`, illustrates how you can put `KeypadWithDisplay` objects to work. The source code for the `PadWithDisplayUser` applet is shown in Listing 9-16, and an HTML file for the applet is provided in Listing 9-17. Figure 9-13 shows the applet being used to demonstrate the `KeypadWithDisplay` class.

The `PadWithDisplayUser` class has two fields, a `KeypadWithDisplay` object called `theKeypad`, and a `TextField` object called `theOutput`. This `TextField` object is different from the `TextField` object—also named `theOutput`—contained inside the `KeypadWithDisplay` object.

When you run the `PadWithDisplayUser` applet, notice that there are two `TextField`s displayed on the screen. One of them is attached to the `Keypad` object and displays the individual numbers as you press the `Keypad` buttons. The other one displays the finished number when you press the Order button. You'll recall that when you press the Order button, the original `Keypad` class forwards the `actionPerformed( )` message to its parent. As a result of this, the `PadWithDisplay` class will receive these events only when the Order key is pressed on the `Keypad`—it doesn't have to concern itself with handling the other individual button-presses. It then uses the `KeypadWithDisplay` object's `toString( )` method to display the final value of the `Keypad` in its own `TextField`.

FIGURE 9-13

Using the `KeypadWith-Display` *class*

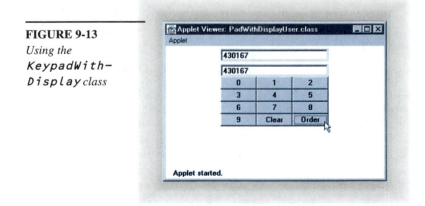

Listing 9–16 PadWithDisplayUser.java

```java
// Putting the KeypadWithDisplay class to work
//
//
import java.applet.*;
import java.awt.*;
import java.awt.event.*;

public class PadWithDisplayUser extends Applet⇐
   implements ActionListener
{
    private KeypadWithDisplay theKeypad =⇐
      new KeypadWithDisplay();
    private TextField theOutput = new TextField("", 20);

    public void init()
    {
        add( theOutput );
        add( theKeypad );
        theOutput.setEditable(false);
    }

    public void actionPerformed( ActionEvent theEvent )
    {
        theOutput.setText( theKeypad.toString() );
    }
}
```

Listing 9–17 Keypad2.html

```html
<HTML>
<HEAD>
<TITLE>Keypad.html</TITLE>
</HEAD>
<BODY>
<APPLET CODE=PadWithDisplayUser.class HEIGHT=300 WIDTH=300>
</APPLET>
</BODY>
</HTML>
```

Death of an Object: Garbage Collection and finalize( ) Methods

Knowing how objects are created, by use of constructors, is just half the story. It's also important to know what happens to objects that are no longer needed. Java obligingly recycles those objects so you can use the memory they previously occupied for other objects. In many programming languages, this process of recycling discarded objects is a task that falls upon the programmer. Java, however, takes care of it automatically, through a process called *garbage collection*. One of the joys of Java programming is that you don't have to take out the garbage. Java collects and discards the garbage for you.

Suppose, for example, that you have a `String` named `time` that holds the value "3:21 p.m." When 3:22 rolls around, your program replaces the old value of `time` with "3:22 p.m." What happens to the cells in memory that were holding the value "3:21 p.m."? The `String` variable called `time` no longer refers to them. If no other variable now refers to them, they're no longer needed: They've become "garbage," and the space they occupied will, at some point, be recycled.

Java's run-time system keeps track of every object and every cell of memory. It knows what objects reference what other objects and can determine what cells are being used at any time. Periodically it sweeps through memory, picking up the garbage and placing every unused memory cell in a pool of memory available for use.

This makes programming much easier than in languages such as C++, which force the programmer to keep track of which objects are in use and which memory cells are free. In those languages, program errors related to memory use are common, often resulting in "memory leaks" that cause system crashes, due to the failure to free memory that is no longer being used.

THE `finalize( )` METHOD

While Java programmers rarely need to give any thought to memory issues, memory is not the only system resource associated with objects. As you'll see in Chapter 14, "Streams and Files," Java programs can use files and other operating system resources.

Sometimes it's helpful to know that an object has been marked for garbage collection. If there are any special resources associated with the object, this gives you an opportunity to release them as a courtesy to the operating system, which might appreciate their early return because it's then able to allocate them to another process.

Each class can have a `finalize( )` method especially for this purpose, which will be invoked by the Java run-time before each related object is garbage collected. Note, however, that Java makes no guarantee about when, or even whether, garbage collection will occur. Java simply warrants that the `finalize( )` method will be called if and when the object is selected for garbage collection. In particular, it's possible for a Java program to exit without ever performing garbage collection. This could happen, for example, if a very small program runs on a computer having a very large memory. If the memory "garbage bin" never approaches full, Java may not ever have to empty the garbage.

GARBAGE COLLECTION ILLUSTRATED

The `CollectThis` applet, shown in Listing 9-18, circumvents this possibility by using the `System.gc( )` method, which forces the garbage collector to run immediately. This effectively coerces Java into running the `finalize( )` method associated with the `TrashClass` object, which displays a console message. Use Listing 9-19, `CollectThis.html`, to give the applet a try. Figure 9-14 shows the applet at work, with garbage collection in action.

Listing 9-18 CollectThis.java

```
// Demonstrates finalize( )
//
//
import java.applet.*;
import java.awt.*;
import java.awt.event.*;

public class CollectThis extends Applet implements⇐
    ActionListener
{
    TrashClass theTrash    = new TrashClass( );
    Button       emptyTrash = new Button("Empty Trash");
    Button       discardObj = new Button("New TrashClass⇐
        Object");
    TextField  theOutput   = new TextField("", 30);
    int numObjects = 0;

    public void init( )
    {
        add( emptyTrash );
        add( discardObj );
        add( theOutput  );
        theOutput.setEditable(false);
        emptyTrash.addActionListener(this);
        discardObj.addActionListener(this);
    }

    public void actionPerformed( ActionEvent theEvent )
    {
        if (theEvent.getSource( ) == emptyTrash )
        {
            System.gc( );
            numObjects = 0;
        }
        else
        {
        numObjects++;
        theOutput.setText( numObjects + " objects in the⇐
            trash" );
        theTrash = new TrashClass( );
        }
    }
}

class TrashClass
{
    int serialNo;
    static int nItems = 0;

    public TrashClass() { serialNo = nItems++; }

    public void finalize( )
    {
        System.out.println( "Help!, Object : " +
            serialNo + " I'm melting!!!" );
        System.out.flush( );
    }
}
```

Listing 9-19 CollectThis.html

```
<HTML>
<HEAD>
<TITLE>CollectThis.java</TITLE>
</HEAD>
<BODY>
<APPLET CODE=CollectThis HEIGHT=100 WIDTH = 300>
</APPLET>
</BODY>
</HTML>
```

EXAMINING CollectThis

The CollectThis applet contains two classes. The main class, CollectThis, is a child of the Applet class. It's not unlike classes you've seen before. The second class, however, is different. It's called TrashClass. Notice that TrashClass is not declared as a public class. The TrashClass is therefore accessible only to other classes and objects within the directory that contains the CollectThis.java file. As you'll see, the TrashClass does not perform a general-purpose function; it's unlikely that it would be used apart from the CollectThis class. It's reasonable in this case, then, to omit the keyword public because you don't expect to use the class except in this single source file anyway. Such single-use classes are often called *helper* classes.

In the applet, the line

```
TrashClass theTrash    = new TrashClass();
```

creates an instance of the TrashClass, storing its reference in the variable theTrash. It does this by running the default constructor, TrashClass(). The constructor assigns

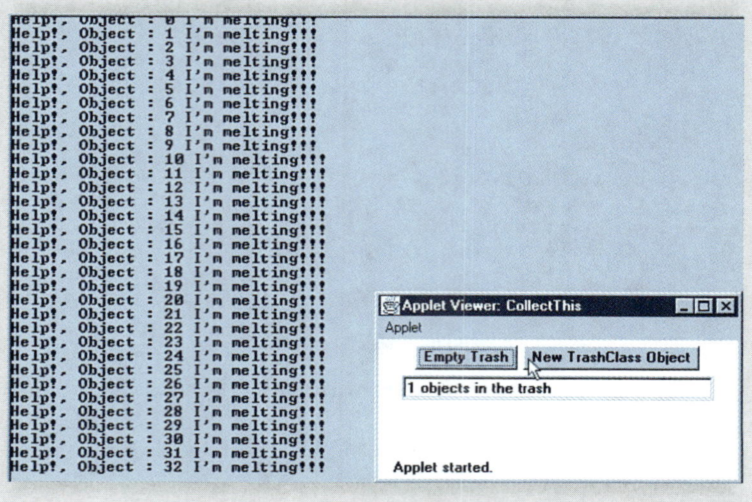

FIGURE 9-14

Running the CollectThis *applet with Appletviewer*

a serial number to each TrashClass object as it is created, by incrementing the static field nItems contained in the TrashClass class. Recall that, because nItems is a static field, there is only a single occurrence of nItems associated with the TrashClass class; all instances of the class share the same nItems field.

In addition to the field theTrash, CollectThis has

☕ Two buttons, discardObj and emptyTrash. When the user presses the discardObj button, the object reference theTrash is given a new TrashClass object to refer to. The old TrashClass object becomes garbage. When the user presses the emptyTrash button, the garbage collector is manually invoked by calling the System.gc( ) method.

☕ An integer field, numObjects, which keeps track of how many objects have been put into the trash.

☕ A TextField object, theOutput, that displays how many objects are currently awaiting garbage collection.

When you press the emptyTrash button, invoking the System.gc( ) method, all of the discarded TrashClass objects are garbage collected, and their finalizer( ) methods are run. By watching the console window, or the Java console, you can see their last gasp as they are discarded. It's possible, if you are very patient, to cause garbage collection to occur simply by pressing the discardObj button. But remember, Java collects the garbage only when it "feels like it," and it may take you a whole heap of button-presses before Java feels like the garbage is "full"—possibly several million or more.

Putting It All Together: The JavaMatic Applet

Now that you know the ins and outs of creating and destroying objects, and have some practice creating teams of classes, it's time to see how it all comes together in the JavaMatic applet. Based on the design of the JavaMatic presented at the end of Chapter 4, and using the Keypad and KeypadWithDisplay classes you've developed in this chapter, the JavaMatic applet illustrates many of the features you've learned about so far. You can see the JavaMatic applet in action in Figure 9-15. (The HTML file, JavaMatic.html, can be seen in Listing 9-25, at the end of the chapter.)

THE JavaMatic CLASS

Recall that the JavaMatic is made up of four classes, each of which does its assigned part of the work of dispensing Jumbo's best brew. The JavaMatic itself is created by a fifth class, JavaMatic, which contains instances—as fields—of each of the other four classes. Let's start your tour by looking at JavaMatic.java in Listing 9-20.

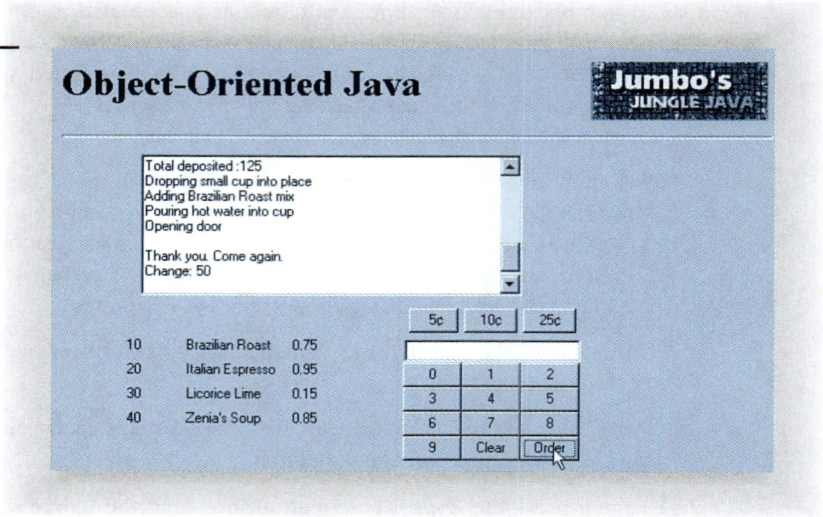

FIGURE 9-15
*The JavaMatic
applet*

```
Object-Oriented Java                    Jumbo's
                                        JUNGLE JAVA

Total deposited :125
Dropping small cup into place
Adding Brazilian Roast mix
Pouring hot water into cup
Opening door

Thank you. Come again.
Change: 50

                                   5c    10c    25c

  10    Brazilian Roast   0.75
  20    Italian Espresso  0.95      0     1      2
  30    Licorice Lime     0.15      3     4      5
  40    Zenia's Soup      0.85      6     7      8
                                    9    Clear  Order
```

Listing 9-20 JavaMatic.java

```java
// The JavaMatic Class
//
//
import java.awt.*;
import java.applet.*;

public class JavaMatic extends Applet
{

    private Banker          theBanker;
    private Worker          theWorker;
    private JavaMaticMenu   theMenu ;
    private TextArea        theDisplay = new TextArea("",⇐
                                8,50);
    private Manager         theManager;

    public JavaMatic()
    {
        theMenu    = new JavaMaticMenu();
        theBanker  = new Banker( 200, this );
        theWorker  = new Worker( theMenu, this );
        theManager = new Manager( theBanker, theWorker,⇐
                        theMenu, this);

        add( theDisplay );
        add( theMenu );
        add( theManager);
    }

    public void tell( String message )
    {
        theDisplay.append( message + "\n" );
    }
}
```

" Constructors with arguments allow you to create customized objects: Each one can be different. "

The JavaMatic class is simplicity itself, largely because much of the work is done inside the objects that make it up. Each JavaMatic object includes five fields:

- A Banker object, called theBanker, which controls the money inside the JavaMatic
- A JavaMaticMenu object, called theMenu, which displays the offerings of each machine and keeps track of the inventory
- A Worker object, named theWorker, which dispenses beverages to the customers
- A Manager object, which controls the activities of each of the other members of the team and does much of the communication with the customer
- A TextArea object, theDisplay, which provides a place for each JavaMatic machine to communicate with its customers

In addition to these five fields, the JavaMatic class has two methods. The first method is the constructor, JavaMatic( ), which simply creates new instances of the JavaMaticMenu, Banker, Worker, and Manager classes; assigns those objects to the appropriate fields; and then adds theDisplay, theMenu, and theManager to the surface of the applet. Because theWorker and theBanker work behind the scenes, it is unnecessary to add them to the applet surface. Notice, however, that both are passed as arguments to the Manager( ) constructor, because theManager needs to know to whom to give the money, and who should be doing the work. The second method, tell( ), simply provides a way for Manager, Worker, and Banker objects to communicate with the customer.

THE Banker CLASS

The Banker class creates objects that handle money. You can find the source code for this class in Listing 9-21. Each Banker object has three fields. Two of those, currentAmount and totalAmount, allow the Banker to keep track of the amount of money collected for a specific purchase and the total amount of money collected over a period of time. The other field, a JavaMatic object called theMachine, is required so that the Banker object can use the JavaMatic's tell( ) method to display its error messages.

The Banker class has five methods, including the constructor, Banker( ). Banker( ) requires a starting amount to initialize the field totalAmount and a JavaMatic object, which "owns" it. canCover( ) is an accessor method that allows the Manager to ask the Banker whether a customer has deposited enough money to cover the price of a particular beverage. The other three methods are mutator methods that change the state of the JavaMatic machine itself by depositing money, adding the price of a purchase to the totalAmount, or by making change.

Listing 9-21 Banker.java

```java
// The JavaMatic Banker Class
//
//
import java.awt.*;

public class Banker
{
    private JavaMatic theMachine;
    private double totalAmount;
    private double currentAmount = 0.0;

    public Banker(double startingAmount, JavaMatic j)
    {
        theMachine   = j;
        totalAmount = startingAmount;
    }

    // Accessor methods
    public boolean canCover( double amount )
    {
        return currentAmount >= amount;
    }

    // Mutator methods
    public void deposit( double amount )
    {
        currentAmount += amount;
        theMachine.tell("Total deposited :" + (int)⇐
            (currentAmount * 100));
    }

    public void creditJavaMatic( double amount )
    {
        totalAmount += amount;
        currentAmount -= amount;
    }

    public void makeChange()
    {
        if ( (int) (currentAmount * 100.0) > 1 )
            theMachine.tell("Change: " + (int)⇐
                (currentAmount * 100));
        currentAmount = 0.0;
    }
}
```

THE JavaMaticMenu CLASS

The most complex of the classes inside the JavaMatic, the JavaMaticMenu class, has a single field. However, that field is an array of JMenuItem objects. The JMenuItem class is a helper class you will find listed at the bottom of the JavaMaticMenu.java file (see Listing 9-22). Each JMenuItem object has four fields: the product code, the product description, the price for the item, and the inventory quantity of each item.

While these fields are declared as `public` inside the `JMenuItem` class, the array of `JMenuItems` inside the `JavaMaticMenu` class is declared as `private` and is initialized through an array initializer.

The constructor, `JavaMaticMenu( )`, sets a `GridLayout` layout manager and then adds `Labels` for the code, description, and price of each `JMenuItem` object. The `Label`'s `setAlignment( )` method is used to make the display of the menu attractive.

The `JavaMaticMenu` class has one `private` method, `getItem( )`, a utility method used by all the remaining methods to retrieve the appropriate `JMenuItem` when given a product code. One of the remaining methods, `getPrice( )`, is an accessor method that simply looks up the price for a given item, returning –1 if the item is not found. The second accessor method, `hasItem( )`, checks the inventory for an item when given a product code, and returns `true` if there is inventory left, and `false` in any other case. The last method, `getIngredients( )`, is a mutator that decreases the quantity on hand for a given product, and then returns the product description to the caller.

Listing 9-22 JavaMaticMenu.java

```java
// The JavaMatic Menu Class
//
//
import java.awt.*;
import java.applet.*;

public class JavaMaticMenu extends Applet
{
    private JMenuItem[] theItems =
    {
        new JMenuItem("Brazilian Roast",  "10",.75, 10),
        new JMenuItem("Italian Espresso", "20",.95, 20),
        new JMenuItem("Licorice Lime",    "30",.15, 30),
        new JMenuItem("Zenia's Soup",     "40",.85, 40)
    };

    public JavaMaticMenu()
    {
        setLayout( new GridLayout(theItems.length, 3));
        for (int i = 0; i < theItems.length; i++)
        {
            Label p = new Label( "" + theItems[i].code );
            p.setAlignment(Label.CENTER);
            add( p );
            add( new Label( theItems[i].description ) );
            add( new Label("" + theItems[i].price) );
        }
    }

    private JMenuItem getItem( String choice )
    {
        for (int i = 0; i < theItems.length; i++)
            if (theItems[i].code.equals( choice ))
                return theItems[i];
        return null;
    }
```

continued on next page

continued from previous page

```
    public double getPrice( String choice )
    {
        JMenuItem theItem = getItem( choice );
        return ( theItem == null ? -1 : theItem.price );
    }

    public boolean hasItem( String choice )
    {
        JMenuItem theItem = getItem( choice );
        return ( theItem == null ? false :⇐
            theItem.quantity > 0 );
    }

    public String getIngredients( String choice )
    {
        JMenuItem theItem = getItem( choice );
        theItem.quantity--;
        return theItem.description;
    }
}

class JMenuItem
{
    public String description;
    public String code;
    public double price;
    public int     quantity;

    public JMenuItem(String d, String c, double p, int q)
    {
        description = d;
        code        = c;
        price       = p;
        quantity    = q;
    }
}
```

> *Java obligingly recycles discarded objects so you can use the memory they previously occupied for other objects.*

THE Worker CLASS

In many ways, the `Worker` class is the simplest class inside the `JavaMatic`. Shown in Listing 9-23, each `Worker` has only two fields: `theMachine`, which it uses for its output, and `theMenu`, which provides it with ingredients for the beverages it is asked to dispense. Each of these is initialized in the `Worker( )` constructor. The single method, `dispenseBeverage( )`, first asks `theMenu` for the necessary ingredients, and then obediently reports to `theMachine` the results of its labors.

```
Listing 9-23 Worker.java
// The JavaMatic Worker Class
//
//
import java.awt.*;

public class Worker
```

```
{

    private JavaMatic      theMachine;
    private JavaMaticMenu  theMenu;

    public Worker(JavaMaticMenu m, JavaMatic j)
    {
        theMenu    = m;
        theMachine = j;
    }

    public void dispenseBeverage( String theBeverage )
    {
        String ingredients = theMenu.getIngredients(⇐
            theBeverage );

        theMachine.tell("Dropping small cup into place");
        theMachine.tell("Adding " + ingredients + " mix");
        theMachine.tell("Pouring hot water into cup");
        theMachine.tell("Opening door\n");
        theMachine.tell("Thank you. Come again.");
    }
}
```

THE Manager CLASS

The final class in the `JavaMatic`, the `Manager`, uses each of the remaining classes as well as the `Keypad` class you created earlier in this chapter. When you examine the source code in Listing 9-24, you can see that the constructor `Manager( )` first initializes each of these fields. Then it creates a `Panel` object—a `Panel` is a type of container that can hold other components—and adds a `KeypadWithDisplay` object and three coin-deposit buttons to the `Panel`. The entire `Panel` is then added to the applet by use of a `BorderLayout`. Using `Panel`s this way is something you'll learn more about in Chapter 10; Chapter 11, "Jumpin' Java: Menus, Graphics, Sound"; and Chapter 12, "The AWT: Containers, Components, and Layout Managers." The point of using a `Panel` here is that it allows the `Panel` itself to use a `FlowLayout` while the applet that contains the `Panel` uses a `BorderLayout`. The ability to mix and match layout managers is a very powerful means of designing attractive and useful applets and applications that are well-behaved even when the applet or application window is resized.

The only method inside the `Manager` class is the `actionPerformed( )` method. Because the `Keypad` object successfully handles its own interaction until the customer presses the Order button, the `Manager` class does not have to deal with other `Keypad` events. If one of the coin-deposit buttons is pressed, the `Manager` object just asks the `Banker` object to deposit the money.

When the customer finally orders a beverage by entering a choice and pressing the Order button on the `Keypad`, the `Manager` object follows a well-thought-out plan of action:

1. The `Keypad` object is asked to retrieve the user's selection by using its `toString( )` method. This is stored in the local `String` variable, `userChoice`.

2. The `Menu` object is asked to tell the `Manager` what the price is for that particular item, by use of the `getPrice( )` method. If `getPrice( )` returns a negative number, that means the `Menu` object was unable to locate that particular product code, and the `JavaMatic` object is asked to tell the customer to try another selection.

3. After the `Menu` object has given the `Manager` the price for the customer's selection, the `Manager` needs to clear the purchase with the `Banker` object by sending the `Banker` a `canCover( )` message. If the `Banker` says, "Yes, the customer has deposited enough money to afford that amount," then the `Worker` is told to dispense the beverage, and the `Banker` is told to credit the `JavaMatic`'s account and give the customer back the change, if any. If the customer doesn't have enough money to cover the selected beverage, the `JavaMatic` asks the customer to deposit more money.

Listing 9-24 Manager.java

```
// The JavaMatic Manager Class
//
//
import java.awt.*;
import java.awt.event.*;
import java.applet.*;

public class Manager extends Applet
implements ActionListener
{
    private KeypadWithDisplay theKeypad = new⇐
        KeypadWithDisplay();

    private Button nickelBtn     = new Button("⇐
        5"+(char)162+"   ");
    private Button dimeBtn       = new Button("⇐
        10"+(char)162+"   ");
    private Button quarterBtn    = new Button("⇐
        25"+(char)162+"   ");

    private Banker          theBanker;
    private Worker          theWorker;
    private JavaMaticMenu   theMenu ;
    private JavaMatic       theMachine;

    public Manager(Banker b, Worker w, JavaMaticMenu m,⇐
        JavaMatic j)
    {
        theBanker   = b;
        theWorker   = w;
        theMenu     = m;
        theMachine  = j;

        Panel p = new Panel();
        p.setLayout( new FlowLayout() );
        p.add( nickelBtn );
        nickelBtn.addActionListener(this);
```

> **" One of the joys of Java programming is that you don't have to take out the garbage; Java collects and discards the garbage for you. "**

```java
        p.add( dimeBtn    );
        dimeBtn.addActionListener(this);
        p.add( quarterBtn);
        quarterBtn.addActionListener(this);

        setLayout( new BorderLayout( ) );
        add( theKeypad, "Center" );
        add( p, "North" );
    }

    public void actionPerformed(ActionEvent event)
    {
        Object target = event.getSource( );

        if (target == nickelBtn )        theBanker.deposit⇐
            ( .05 );
        else if (target == dimeBtn    ) theBanker.deposit⇐
            ( .10 );
        else if (target == quarterBtn) theBanker.deposit⇐
            ( .25 );
        else
        {
            String userChoice = theKeypad.toString();

            double thePrice = theMenu.getPrice( userChoice );
            if (thePrice > 0)
                if ( theBanker.canCover( thePrice ))
                    if ( theMenu.hasItem( userChoice ))
                    {
                        theWorker.dispenseBeverage(⇐
                            userChoice );
                        theBanker.creditJavaMatic(⇐
                            thePrice );
                        theBanker.makeChange();
                        theKeypad.removeAll();
                    }
                    else
                        theMachine.tell("Out of stock.⇐
                            Choose another.");
                else
                    theMachine.tell("Please deposit more⇐
                        money");
            else
                theMachine.tell("Unrecognized selection.⇐
                    Choose again.");
        }

    }
}
```

Listing 9-25 JavaMatic.html

```html
<HTML>
<HEAD>
<TITLE>Jumbo's JavaMatic</TITLE>
</HEAD>
<BODY>
<IMG SRC="jumbo.GIF" ALIGN=RIGHT HEIGHT=50>
```

continued on next page

continued from previous page

```
<H1>Object-Oriented Java</H1>
<HR>
<APPLET CODE=JavaMatic HEIGHT=450 WIDTH=450>
</APPLET>
</BODY>
</HTML>
```

Summary

- Java programs can consist of a single class or multiple classes.
- `Applet` objects can be used inside other programs.
- Returning `false` from the `actionPerformed( )` method of an object causes the related `Event` to be sent to the object's container.
- Accessor methods provide access to the state of an object.
- Mutator methods allow change to the state of an object.
- Fields and methods specified `public` can be accessed outside their defining class.
- Fields and methods specified `private` cannot be accessed outside their defining class.
- Data hiding is implemented by use of `private` fields and `public` accessor and mutator methods that control access to the `private` fields.
- The `BorderLayout LayoutManager` places components at positions known as `"North"`, `"South"`, `"East"`, `"West"`, and `"Center"`.
- Java creates a default constructor for any class that is defined without an included constructor.
- A default constructor takes no arguments and is often referred to as a no-argument constructor.
- When two constructors are defined with the same name but different number or types of arguments, the constructors are said to be overloaded.
- When constructors are overloaded, Java determines which constructor to use based on the number and types of arguments in the call.
- The `this( )` method allows a constructor to invoke another constructor of the same class.
- Java automatically reclaims unused memory using its garbage collector.
- The `finalize( )` method is invoked on an object before it is garbage collected.

☕ Helper classes can be defined inside the same JAVA file as `public` classes; however, helper classes cannot be accessed publicly.

☕ When a local variable has the same name as a field, the local variable may shadow the field, making it more cumbersome to access.

☕ The `this` object can be used to access a field, the name of which has been shadowed by a local variable.

Quiz

1. A method that provides access to the state of an object is known as a(n) _____ method.

2. A method that allows change to the state of an object is known as a(n) _____ method.

3. Fields and methods with `public` access can/cannot be accessed outside the enclosing class.

4. Fields and methods with `private` access can/cannot be accessed outside the enclosing class.

5. To implement data hiding, you generally specify fields as having _____ access.

6. To implement data hiding, you generally specify methods as having _____ access.

7. The `LayoutManager` that allows placement of components at the four compass points or at the center of the container is _____.

8. The constructor provided by Java for a class that does not explicitly define a constructor is known as a(n) _____ constructor.

9. Two constructors defined with the same name but different number or types of arguments are known as _____ constructors.

10. The `this( )` method allows invoking a _____ method other than the one containing the call.

11. Unused memory is reclaimed by the _____.

12. The _____ method is called on an object that is about to be reclaimed.

Exercises

1. Write an applet that serves as an up/down counter. The applet should use a class `UpDownCounter` that encapsulates the capability to display an `int` value and methods `countUp( )` and `countDown( )` that increase and decrease,

respectively, the counter value. The applet should include a pair of buttons, one for "up" and one for "down," used to trip the counter.

2. Write an applet that serves as a calculator. The applet should include a keypad for entering numbers and should provide for the common arithmetic operations: addition, subtraction, multiplication, and division.

3. Write a program that uses two distinct classes to simulate aspects of a baseball game. One class should be called `Pitcher`, and the other should be called `Batter`. `Batter`s should be constructed based on statistics describing their past performance. For example, the statement

```
Batter theBatter = new Batter( 0.3F );
```

could be used to create a `Batter` with a 0.300 batting average, meaning that the batter has gotten a hit in 3 of his or her last 10 turns at bat. The `Pitcher` class should include a method that simulates pitching a ball to a specified `Batter`. The outcome of the pitch (hit or strike) should be determined by use of `Math.random( )` and reported by use of `System.out`.

4. Write a program that allows you to play the following oil-prospecting game. The game is played on a 25×25 grid. The player starts with a nest egg of $2.5 million and an oil rig. The rig starts at a random position and can be moved by use of any of four buttons labeled with compass points. The cost of moving the rig is

```
$5,000 + $15,000 x (number of cells moved - 1)
```

The object of the game is to discover one or more oil reservoirs, which have been randomly located on the grid. Successfully tapping a reservoir adds $1 million to the player's nest egg. Play continues until the player goes broke, finds all the oil, or quits. Your program should include an object representing the player and an object representing the grid and its hidden oil reserves.

5. Write a program that simulates a stock market. The market consists of 15 individuals who buy and sell. Individuals are created with a random amount of cash and random amounts of each of three stocks: GoGo Software (GGS), HighFlying Systems (HFS), and Consolidated Tomison (CT). Each individual has a (random) opinion concerning the value of the stock of each of the three companies. Use a loop to cycle through the simulation, and have each cycle represent one quarter of a year. During each cycle, each of the three companies posts an updated (random) estimate of the value of its stock. Those individuals who think the stock is worth more attempt to buy additional shares from other individuals. Those who think the stock is worth less attempt to sell their shares. The price at which a stock is bought or sold in a given transaction is the square root of the product of the seller's notion of its worth and the buyer's notion of its worth. As you should expect, buyers who lack sufficient funds cannot buy stock. You should devise a suitable interface for the simulation, making it possible for the user to track results over time.

10

Inheritance:

Object Families

W hat do you think of when you hear the word *inheritance*? You might think about the attributes you inherited from your parents: your mother's green eyes, your father's gift for numbers, or your grandfather's good looks. On the other hand, you may be reminded of the china that was passed down from your Great Aunt Bowline.

In Java, inheritance is the process of creating new classes from existing classes. The new classes receive all of the attributes and methods their parents had. In this sense, Java's inheritance is roughly analogous to genetic inheritance. But it's an imperfect metaphor. Human inheritance involves two objects—Mom and Dad—creating another object—you. In Java, inheritance creates new *classes*, not new objects, and each new class has only a single parent.

In Chapter 9, "Teams of Classes: Using Classes Together," you learned how to use objects as building blocks to create new and better classes. This chapter extends that knowledge in a new way as you learn to create families of objects with (figuratively speaking) brothers, sisters, nieces, nephews, and just good friends. You will then be able to put your newly won knowledge of "genetic engineering" to work automating some of the repetitive tasks that all Java programs have to accomplish.

" The isA relationship is called an inheritance relationship. "

You will learn

☕ More about inheritance, creating new classes by extending the capabilities of old classes

☕ How to use `protected` access to control access to a class, but nevertheless to allow programmers extending the class to access needed fields and methods

☕ How to use the `super( )` constructor to initialize child objects

☕ How to cope with name conflicts that "shadow" fields of a parent class

☕ How overridden methods work

☕ How to use `final` to prevent others from extending your class or overriding its methods

☕ How to use casts to convert an object to a different type

☕ How to use the methods of the `Object` class

☕ How to use packages to limit access to your classes

What Is Inheritance?

The easiest way to look at inheritance is in the form of a classification hierarchy, where you attempt to classify objects according to common characteristics and behaviors. All of us do this in our daily lives. You can think of your local mail-carrier and your senator as both belonging in the class `FederalGovernmentEmployee`. (Of course that's not true any longer since the Postal Service was privatized, but for the sake of the example, let's pretend it is.) They have certain things in common: They both have an employee ID number and a government salary, for instance. These similarities occur because they are members of the `FederalGovernmentEmployee` class. They also have several differences. The mail-carrier's salary will be computed on an hourly basis, while the senator receives an annual salary. Your senator won't be delivering your mail tomorrow—provided he or she is reelected—and you can't expect your mail-carrier to vote on the senate version of the latest tax bill, no matter how dearly he or she wants to. These differences arise because senators and mail-carriers really belong to different classes. So how can they belong to the same class—`FederalGovernmentEmployee`—and different classes—`PostalWorker` and `ElectedOfficial`—at the same time? The answer lies with classification and the processes of inheritance.

INTRODUCING JavaDrinkingAnimals

Because classifying public servants according to their attributes and behaviors is trying even for experienced journalists, let's take a look at a simpler classification hierarchy: the class `JavaDrinkingAnimal`, which you can see in Figure 10-1.

FIGURE 10-1
The class of
`JavaDrinking-`
`Animal`

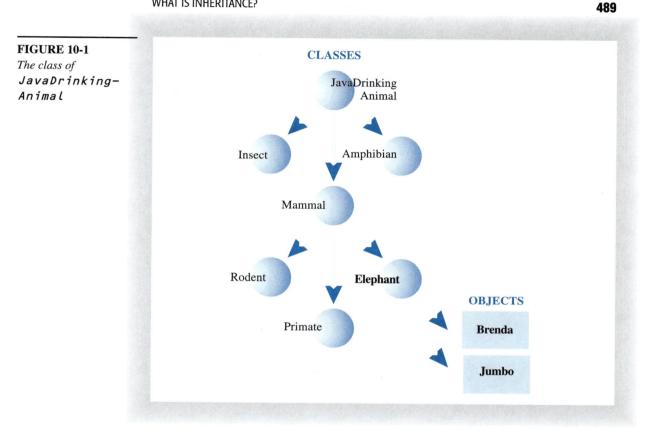

It's well known that not every animal drinks java, even in cyberbia. Whether they should is open to debate. Assume that, through lengthy observation and empirical study, you have decided—for purposes of your program—that the universe of animals can be divided into those animals who drink java and those who don't. Because you are not concerned with those who don't, you might create a class that looks something like Listing 10-1.

```
Listing 10-1 JavaDrinkingAnimal.java
// The class of all animals that drink Java
//
import java.io.*;

public class JavaDrinkingAnimal
{
    // Attributes
    double changeInPocket = 0.0;
    double weightInGrams;

    public void earnMoney( double wages )
```

continued on next page

continued from previous page

```
    {
        changeInPocket += wages;
        System.out.println(⇐
          "Yahoo, it's payday. I'm now worth $" +
                            (changeInPocket / weightInGrams)+⇐
                            " per gram" );
    }

    public boolean canAfford( double cost  )
    {
        if ( cost > changeInPocket )
            System.out.println(⇐
              "What? $"+ cost + " for that? No way!" );

        return changeInPocket  >= cost;
    }

    public void buyJava( double price )
    {
        if ( canAfford( price ) )
        {
            System.out.println(⇐
              "I'll have one please!");
            changeInPocket -= price;
        }
        else
            System.out.println(⇐
              "Come on! Lend me " + (price - changeInPocket));
    }
}
```

Looking at `JavaDrinkingAnimal`

Your `JavaDrinkingAnimal` class has two attributes. The `changeInPocket` lets you know how much a particular animal can afford to spend—because you have very wisely decided that it is generally a bad idea to extend credit to java-drinking animals. The other attribute, `weightInGrams`, represents each animal's weight in grams. Once your class is in place, you can then create several instances of the class (objects) and manipulate them like this:

```
JavaDrinkingAnimal Fred, Sally;
Fred.earnMoney( 10.50 );
Fred.earnMoney( 12.75 );

// See if Fred wants to spring for the Chateau Le Foot '93
if ( Fred.canAfford( 15.00 ) ) Fred.buyJava( 15.00 );

// Sally, disillusioned with Fred's bad taste, buys her own
// drink
if ( Sally.canAfford( 2.50 ) ) Sally.buyJava( 2.50 );
// A nice Latte
```

Using `JavaDrinkingAnimals`

From your point of view as a user of the `JavaDrinkingAnimal` class, java-drinking animals have only three behaviors that are of interest. First, they can earn money, which increases their ability to purchase more java. In this class the method `earnMoney( )` produces that behavior.

Second, they can purchase some java from you. This behavior, their whole reason for existence, is implemented in the `buyJava( )` method. Unfortunately, it is possible that a particular java-drinking animal will not have enough `changeInPocket` to purchase a beverage. In that case, such objects have the annoying habit of trying to borrow money from the proprietor or the other customers. To allow you to suppress this behavior—as well as to respect the principle of data hiding presented in Chapter 9—you can exploit the third useful behavior of the `JavaDrinkingAnimal` class, implemented in a method called `canAfford( )`, which you can use to query each patron's credit before preparing the ordered beverage.

The second attribute of the `JavaDrinkingAnimal` class, `weightInGrams`, might come in handy (if you added more methods) in determining the feasibility of removing patrons who solicit funds too aggressively once their `changeInPocket` runs out. You might handle a very large patron in a different manner from one that was more your size.

One possible use of the `JavaDrinkingAnimal` class would be to simulate the behavior of java-drinking animals under different conditions. Listing 10-2 shows an applet that simulates the behavior of a herd of java-drinking animals under conditions of wage inequity. As you can see from the results of running this applet in Figure 10-2, conditions of wage inequity lead to an increasing number of mendicant patrons, which lowers the overall Java Joint experience for everyone.

Listing 10-2 `WageEquitySimulation.java`

```java
// An applet to simulate the behavior of JavaDrinkingAnimals
// under conditions of severe wage inequity.
//
import java.applet.*;
import java.awt.*;
import java.awt.event.*;

public class WageEquitySimulation extends Applet ⇐
   implements ActionListener
{
    JavaDrinkingAnimal[] theHerd = new JavaDrinkingAnimal[5];
    Button paydayButton = new Button("Payday");
    Button orderButton  = new Button("Buy Now");

    public void init( )
    {
        for (int i = 0; i < theHerd.length; i++)
        {
                theHerd[i] = new JavaDrinkingAnimal( );
```

continued on next page

continued from previous page

```
                theHerd[i].weightInGrams = (i + 10) / 1000.0;
        }
        add( paydayButton );
        add( orderButton  );
        paydayButton.addActionListener(this);
        orderButton.addActionListener(this);
    }

    public void actionPerformed( ActionEvent theEvent )
    {
        // Assume each Java costs 5.00
        for (int i = 0; i < theHerd.length; i++)
            if (theEvent.getSource( ) == paydayButton)
                theHerd[i].earnMoney( (i+1) * 10 );
            else
                theHerd[i].buyJava( 5.00 );
    }
}
```

SUBCLASSES AND SUPERCLASSES

It's been said that the world is divided into two classes of people: those who divide everyone into two classes of people and those who don't. While your computer simulation may prove valuable in such a limited universe, the classification scheme it proposes—JavaDrinkingAnimal and non-JavaDrinkingAnimal—is really too simplistic

FIGURE 10-2

Running the
WageEquity–
Simulation

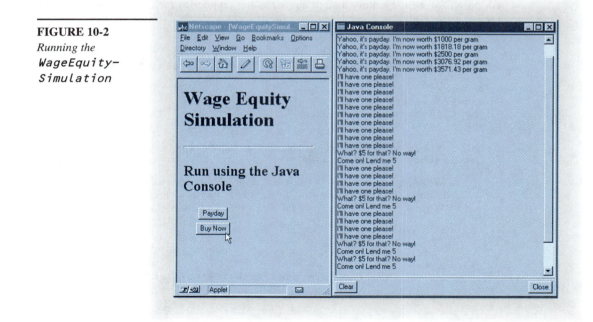

"An object of a subclass generally has more attributes or capabilities than an object of its more generic superclass."

to model the real world. The characteristics of some patrons—not individually but as a group—require that they be treated differently from others. Take a look back at Figure 10-1. Notice that there are three distinct groups of `JavaDrinkingAnimals`: `Insects` (chiefly Army Ants on leave), `Mammals`, and `Amphibians`.

Each of these groups has certain characteristics that separate it from the others: The `Insects` have exoskeletons, for instance, that limit their ability to perform certain aerobic exercises. Furthermore, each of these groups can, itself, be subdivided: `Mammals` can be separated into `Rodents`, `Primates`, and `Elephants`. At the very bottom of the pyramid, you have individuals (objects). Each of the individuals—Jumbo and Brenda in this case—is a member of all the classes above it in the hierarchy. You can say that an `Elephant` isA `Mammal`; but an `Elephant` isA `JavaDrinkingAnimal` as well.

This `isA` relationship is called an inheritance relationship. You might recall from Chapter 2, "Programs: The Community of Objects," that in an inheritance relationship, the more general class is called the *superclass*. In this case, `JavaDrinkingAnimal` is the superclass of the `Mammal`, `Insect`, and `Amphibian` classes. These three classes are the *subclasses* of `JavaDrinkingAnimal`. Subclasses are below, or subordinate to, their superclass in a hierarchy diagram as shown in Figure 10-1. Many people find the words *superclass* and *subclass* confusing, because they erroneously think that superclass implies a class that has more capabilities than one termed a subclass. Actually, an object of a subclass generally has *more* attributes or capabilities than an object of its more bland and generic superclass. While `JavaDrinkingAnimals` are, in general, trunkless and lack mobility methods, `Elephant` objects possess both a trunk and the ability to `stampede( )`.

IMPLEMENTING A SUBCLASS

To avoid the confusion arising from the terms "superclass" and "subclass," Java uses the `extends` keyword to specify an inheritance relationship between classes. By saying that one class `extends` another, Java reminds you that the new class you are creating may contain both additional data (in the form of new fields) and more specialized behavior (in the form of new methods). Let's see how this works with the `Mammal` class.

Mammals differ from other animals in several ways. Mammals have lungs and breathe air. Mammals, with a few exceptions, give birth to live young, which they nurse with milk. At some stage in their development, mammals have hair. Mammals have a four-chambered heart. Finally, mammals are endotherms, meaning that they maintain a fairly stable, high body temperature (35–42° C, 95–105° F). Maintaining this high temperature requires a high metabolic rate, which, in the real world is measured by the rate of oxygen consumption. In cyberspace, of course, Java consumption is the index of choice for measurement of metabolic rate. The average cyberbian `Mammal`, for example, requires 20 to 30 times more java per day than that required by non-`Mammals`.

The actual metabolic rate can be measured in the amount of java consumed per day per gram of body weight. Because smaller mammals have a larger surface area with respect to their overall weight, they have to drink much more java for each gram of body weight than larger mammals. Thus, the average cyberbian mouse has to daily drink 2,500 milliliters per gram of body weight; the average human, 200; and the average elephant, just 148. For the human, this works out to slightly over 6,000 cups per day, which is about average for programmers here in the real world. (Remember folks, these are `JavaDrinkingAnimals` that only exist in cyberspace. Please don't try feeding java to your real pets—particularly not in these quantities!)

Listing 10-3 shows how the `Mammal` class extends the `JavaDrinkingAnimal` class to provide essential information on java consumption. Listing 10-4 puts the `Mammal` class to work helping Jumbo predict how much coffee he'll need to have on hand for various situations.

Listing 10-3 Mammal.java

```
// A class that models Mammals (that drink Java)
//
import java.io.*;

public class Mammal extends JavaDrinkingAnimal
{
    static final double mlPerCup = 236.59;

    double mlPerGramPerDay; // milliliters per gram per day

    public double cupsOfJavaNeeded( )
    {
        return (( mlPerGramPerDay / weightInGrams ) / ⇐
        mlPerCup );
    }
}
```

Listing 10-4 HowMuchJava.java

```
// A console application to simulate
// the Java consumption of several Mammals
//
import java.io.*;

public class HowMuchJava
{
    public static void main(String args[] )
    {
        Mammal tom               = new Mammal( );
        JavaDrinkingAnimal harry = ⇐
          new JavaDrinkingAnimal( );

        // Mammals have both weightInGrams and ⇐
        // mlPerGramPerDay
        tom.weightInGrams   = ( 90000 );
        tom.mlPerGramPerDay = 200;
```

```
// JavaDrinkingAnimals have only weightInGrams
harry.weightInGrams   = ( 28.56 );
// harry.mlPerGramPerDay = 2500;   // ILLEGAL

// Both Mammals and JavaDrinkingAnimals can earn
// money
tom.earnMoney( 500.0 );
harry.earnMoney( 500.0 );

// Both Mammals and JavaDrinkingAnimals can buyJava()
tom.buyJava( 1.75 );
harry.buyJava( 2.50 );

// Calculate the Daily Java Requirement (DJR) -
// Mammals ONLY
double dJR = tom.cupsOfJavaNeeded( );

System.out.println(⇐
   "Tom's DJR is " + dJR + " cups per day");

   }
}
```

RUNNING THE HOWMUCHJAVA APPLICATION

```
Yahoo, it's payday. I'm now worth $0.00555556 per gram
Yahoo, it's payday. I'm now worth $17.507 per gram
I'll have one please!
I'll have one please!
Tom's DJR is 6340.24 cups per day
```

EXAMINING HOWMUCHJAVA AND THE Mammal CLASS

The first thing you should notice about the Mammal class is the header:

```
public class Mammal extends JavaDrinkingAnimal { . . . }
```

This specifies that the Mammal class is going to add something to, or extend, the JavaDrinkingAnimal class. The Mammal class itself has only a single field, mlPerGramPerDay, which measures the daily amount of java required, in milliliters, for each gram of body weight. In addition to this one field, Mammal also has a single method, cupsOfJavaNeeded( ), which calculates the DJR (daily java requirement) for each Mammal object.

The HowMuchJava application is a console-mode application that consists of a single `main( )` method and no attributes. Inside the `main( )` method, two local variables are created. The first, `tom`, is a `Mammal`. The second, `harry`, is a `JavaDrinkingAnimal`.

```
Mammal tom                   = new Mammal( );
JavaDrinkingAnimal harry     = new JavaDrinkingAnimal( );
```

Next, the `weightInGrams` fields of both `tom` and `harry` are given values, and `tom`'s `mlPerGramPerDay` field is also assigned a value:

```
tom.weightInGrams    = ( 90000 );
// Average 198 lb. weakling
tom.mlPerGramPerDay  = 200;
harry.weightInGrams  = ( 28.56 );
```

At this point, if you're following along closely, you may be tempted to throw up your hands in frustration, because no matter how hard you look, the `Mammal` class doesn't seem to have a `weightInGrams` field. How did `tom` get his `weightInGrams` field? Remember that the `Mammal` class `extends` the `JavaDrinkingAnimal` class. Because of this, each instance of the subclass (`Mammal`) automatically inherits the fields and methods of the superclass (`JavaDrinkingAnimal`). The `JavaDrinkingAnimal` class also contains fields—`weightInGrams` and `changeInPocket`—and methods `earnMoney( )` and `buyJava( )`—which do not appear in the `Mammal` class.

So, each `Mammal` object actually contains a `weightInGrams` field and can respond to `earnMoney` and `buyJava` messages. This is demonstrated by the following four statements inside the `main( )` method:

```
tom.earnMoney( 500.0 );
harry.earnMoney( 500.0 );
tom.buyJava( 1.75 );
harry.buyJava( 2.50 );
```

The first invokes the inherited `earnMoney( )` method using the `Mammal` object as the message receiver. As you can see from the output, `tom` obediently displays the message "Yahoo, it's payday. I'm now worth $0.00555556 per gram." Likewise, both `tom` and `harry` can `buyJava( )`.

There is one last thing you need to make sure you understand about this example. Although `Mammal` objects contain the fields and methods of their ancestor, `JavaDrinkingAnimal`, the reverse is not true. Because `harry` is simply a `JavaDrinkingAnimal`, and *not* a `Mammal`, he has no `mlPerGramPerDay` field and cannot respond to invocations of `cupsOfJavaNeeded( )`. These fields and methods are only available to members of the `Mammal` class, and their descendents. Figure 10-3 illustrates how objects inherit the data and methods of their superclass.

In this example, the parent and child classes are given in separate source files. An even more common situation is to derive a new subclass from a superclass written by someone else, for which you have no source code at all, only a CLASS file. This works no differently than when you have the source file. So long as the Java compiler (Javac) can find the CLASS file for the class you want to `extend`, it will let you `extend` it. The Java compiler does not need, or even look at, the source code for the extended class.

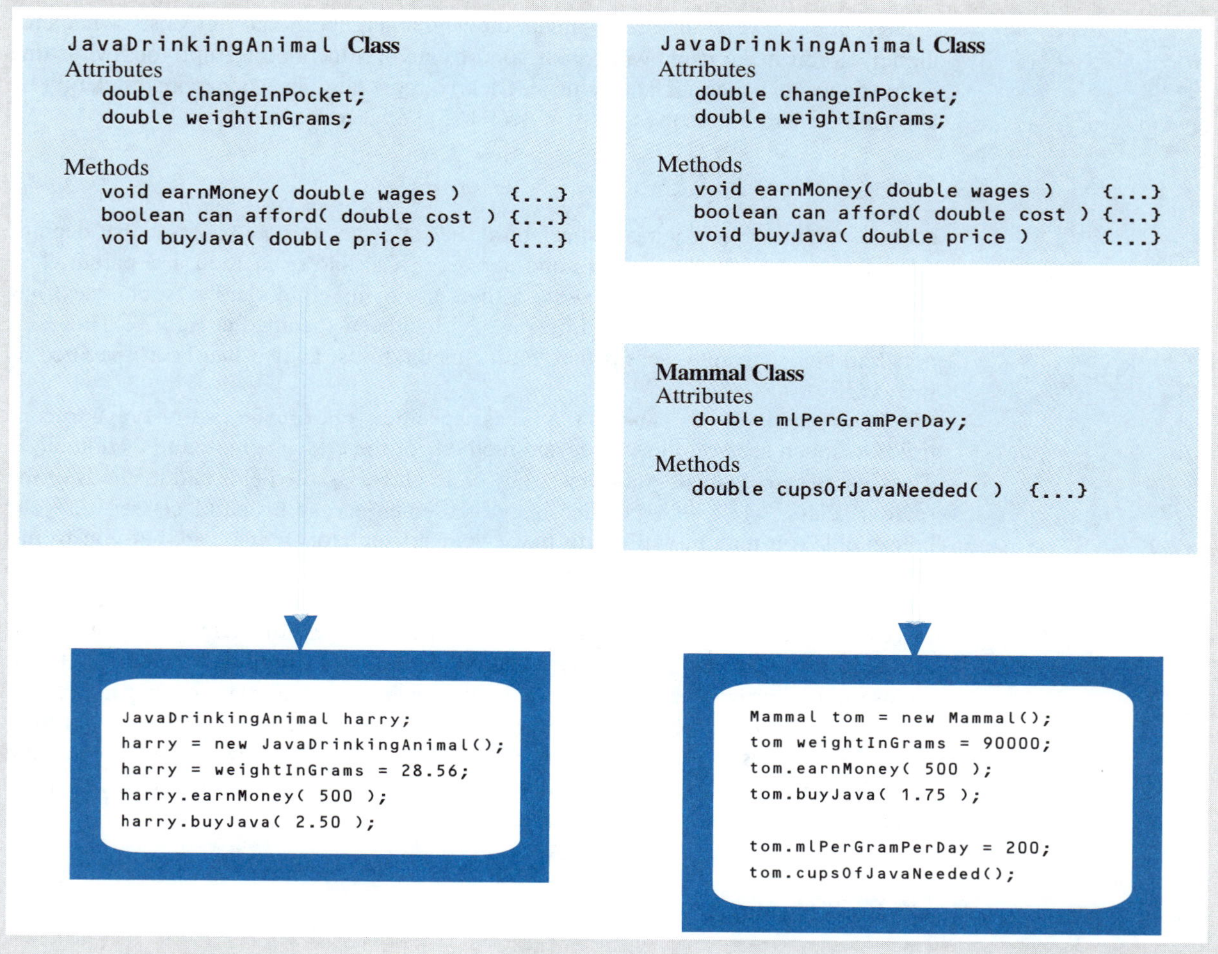

```
JavaDrinkingAnimal Class
Attributes
    double changeInPocket;
    double weightInGrams;

Methods
    void earnMoney( double wages )    {...}
    boolean can afford( double cost ) {...}
    void buyJava( double price )      {...}
```

```
JavaDrinkingAnimal Class
Attributes
    double changeInPocket;
    double weightInGrams;

Methods
    void earnMoney( double wages )    {...}
    boolean can afford( double cost ) {...}
    void buyJava( double price )      {...}
```

Mammal Class
```
Attributes
    double mlPerGramPerDay;

Methods
    double cupsOfJavaNeeded( )  {...}
```

```
JavaDrinkingAnimal harry;
harry = new JavaDrinkingAnimal();
harry = weightInGrams = 28.56;
harry.earnMoney( 500 );
harry.buyJava( 2.50 );
```

```
Mammal tom = new Mammal();
tom weightInGrams = 90000;
tom.earnMoney( 500 );
tom.buyJava( 1.75 );


tom.mlPerGramPerDay = 200;
tom.cupsOfJavaNeeded();
```

FIGURE 10-3

Subclass and super-class: fields and methods

KEEPING IT IN THE FAMILY: ACCESS CONTROL

Do you remember the access specifiers `public` and `private`? If a field or method is declared to be `private`, no class outside of the current class has access to it. If a field or method is declared `public`, any class has access to the field or method through an object of the respective class. The use of access control can enforce the idea of data hiding by allowing you to protect critical fields and methods from unauthorized manipulation.

When inheritance enters the picture, though, things begin to get a little more complicated—just as in real life. If you were to write a Java program to model your own family, for instance, would you make your refrigerator a `public` or `private` field? If you make it `public`, you—in effect—invite the whole neighborhood over to see what's for dinner. If you make it `private`, your son or daughter has to interrupt you every time he or she wants a glass of orange juice. Clearly, most families work more efficiently by allowing the children in the family a special kind of access.

Protected ACCESS

As you might hope, Java has a special, third access specifier, `protected`, that denotes a level of access between `public` and `private`. If a field or method in a parent class (superclass) is specified as `protected`, then any of its child classes (subclasses) has full access to the field or method, just as if it had been specified as `public`. However, nonchild classes cannot access the field or method, just as if it had been specified as `private`.

In writing a class, you can use the access specifiers `protected` and `private` to control how much access to the fields and methods of the class is granted to a child class. The specifier `protected` grants access by child classes to the fields and methods of the (parent) class, while the specifier `private` denies access by child classes. In your household, you may be willing to make your refrigerator `protected`, but you would probably want to make your checkbook `private`. Then, at least, your child's need for those special $200 sneakers has to get your approval first. When you declare a field as `private`, the author of the child class cannot directly access the field, and must instead use accessor or mutator methods you provide for this purpose. Of course, if you choose not to provide such methods, the author of the child class cannot access the field at all! On the other hand, specifying fields as `protected` prevents the world at large from accessing the sensitive fields of your class, but allows inheritance of the fields by child classes that extend your class. And remember, methods as well as fields can be specified as `public`, `protected`, or `private`.

Constructors

Just as inheritance adds some complications to access modifiers, it also adds a few new wrinkles to the subject of constructors. Constructors, as you know, are the special methods Java uses to create objects. These methods are never called directly, but are invoked by the Java run-time when the `new` operator is encountered in an expression. Constructors are useful things, because they establish the initial state of an object, ensuring that all the object's fields have correct and consistent values.

A SUBTLE IMPLICATION

Java decides at compile-time which of a set of overloaded constructors to use in creating an object. It's possible to later revise and recompile the class that defines the

Continued...

A SUBTLE IMPLICATION Continued…
object in a way that makes a different constructor the "best" constructor. However, once the determination to use a particular constructor has been made, it will not be reconsidered until the class containing the constructor invocation is recompiled. This is one of those occasional situations when it's a good idea to recompile even the classes that *haven't* changed.

INHERITANCE AND THE DEFAULT CONSTRUCTOR

It's possible to define a class that has no explicit constructor at all, as you did for `JavaDrinkingAnimal` and `Mammal`. In such a case (as you learned in Chapter 9), Java creates a default constructor that requires no arguments. This is necessary because classes *always* extend other classes; if no `extends` specifier is present in a class header, the class is taken to extend the built-in class `Object`.

A child object *must* inherit the allowable fields and methods of its parent, and a parent object *must* be created to support this. One duty of the default constructor is simply to create the necessary parent object. Here's an example of a class for which Java will build a default constructor:

```
public class NoteOnFinger extends Object
{
    private Color stringColor;
}
```

The default constructor generated by Java will look like this:

```
public NoteOnFinger( )
{
    super( );
}
```

Calling the `super( )`

The method `super( )` in the `NoteOnFinger( )` constructor is not the invocation of a superhero, or a call to a supervisor object. Rather, the method named `super( )` is related to the `this` object. The `super( )` method invokes the constructor of the parent class of the `this` object; in the `NoteOnFinger` class, that's `Object`. The only place you can call `super( )` is in a constructor, and then it must be the first statement inside the constructor. If you don't make this necessary call, Java will make it for you. Java is quite serious about its responsibility for ensuring that a necessary parent object is created. If you had written the `NoteOnFinger` class like this:

```
public class NoteOnFinger extends Object
{
    private Color stringColor;

    public NoteOnFinger( )
```

continued on next page

> " *Each instance of the subclass (* Mammal *) automatically inherits all the fields and methods of its superclass (* JavaDrinking- Animal.*)* "

continued from previous page

```
        {
                stringColor = Color.red;
        }
}
```

Java would call the `super( )` constructor before executing the assignment, just as though you'd written

```
public NoteOnFinger( )
        {
                super( );
                stringColor = Color.red;
        }
```

Note that, as specified here, `super( )` takes no arguments. There must be a corresponding no-argument constructor for the parent class, or a compile-time error will result. Fortunately, the class `Object` has just such a default constructor.

Construction Tasks

Every constructor, default or not, has three tasks which it performs in a set order:

1. Construct the parent object and initialize its fields.
2. Initialize any fields having initializers.
3. Perform the statements in the body of the constructor.

If the first statement of a constructor does not invoke a constructor for the parent using `super( )`, Java inserts the call for you. You can write the `super( )` yourself, so long as you write it as the first statement within the constructor body. The `super( )` method cannot be used in any other way.

It is possible, however, to pass arguments in the call to `super( )` so that the parent object will be properly initialized. Java, of course, cannot do this when it creates a default constructor, because it has no way of knowing what the appropriate arguments might be.

Listing 10-5 shows the FunCar application, which demonstrates the use of the `super( )` method with arguments and the implicit call to `super( )` made by constructors. The application consists of a main class, `FunCar`, which extends the helper class `Car`, which is defined in the same source file.

Figure 10-4 shows the output of the application. Notice that `momsCar`, created by use of the default constructors for `FunCar` and `Car`, is a blue wagon, as determined by the initializers of the fields of the `Car` class. Mom's car may not be fun to drive, but at least it has a CD player, as the output of the `playCD( )` method shows. Only a `FunCar` has a CD player, because the instances of the parent class, `Car`, are not so equipped. Dad's car, on the other hand, is created by use of the two-argument constructor, so Dad is able to drive a red convertible. It, too, is equipped with a CD player.

Listing 10-5 FunCar.java

```
// Demonstrates initialization of parent with super( )
//
public class FunCar extends Car
```

```
    {
        public static void main(String args[])
        {
            FunCar momsCar = new FunCar( );
            System.out.println(⇐
              "Mom's car is a " + momsCar.toString( ));
            System.out.println( momsCar.playCD( ) );

            System.out.println( );
            FunCar dadsCar = new FunCar("red", "convertible");
            System.out.println(⇐
              "Dad's car is a " + dadsCar.toString( ));
            System.out.println( dadsCar.playCD( ) );
        }

        // default constructor
        public FunCar( )
        {
            // implicit call to super( ), which is Car( )
        }

        public FunCar(String color, String body)
        {
            super(color, body);
        }

        public String playCD( )
        {
            return ⇐
            "(Beautiful music fills the passenger compartment.)";
        }
    }

    class Car
    {
        String theColor = "blue";
        String theBody  = "wagon";

        // default constructor creates a blue wagon
        public Car( )
        {
            System.out.println(⇐
              "Called the default constructor Car( ).");
        }

        // constructor creates car of specified color
        public Car(String color, String body)
        {
            System.out.println(⇐
              "Called the two-argument constructor Car( ).");
            theColor = color;
            theBody  = body;
        }

        // accessor method to report car color and model
        public String toString( )
        {
            return theColor + " " + theBody + ".";
        }
    }
```

FIGURE 10-4

The FunCar application

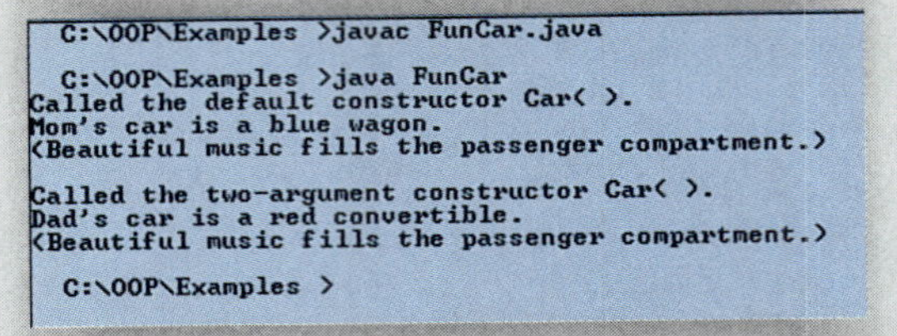

```
C:\OOP\Examples >javac FunCar.java

C:\OOP\Examples >java FunCar
Called the default constructor Car( ).
Mom's car is a blue wagon.
(Beautiful music fills the passenger compartment.)

Called the two-argument constructor Car( ).
Dad's car is a red convertible.
(Beautiful music fills the passenger compartment.)

C:\OOP\Examples >
```

INHERITANCE FOR APPEARANCE'S SAKE

Reusable classes make your life easier by moving repetitive tasks "further up" the class hierarchy so that they don't have to be repeated in every subclass you write. This same principle can bring big benefits when applied to all of Java's built-in components.

Suppose you were hired to create a large Java application—a loan application package, for example. The one thing you know about such an application is that there will be a *lot* of TextField objects. A common request you might anticipate is that your client will change the requirements for these TextField objects several times over the life of the project. If you have 1,000 of these fields scattered throughout your application, you are not going to take kindly to the suggestion "You know, it would really look better if all of these fields were in 14-point text with a yellow background." On the other hand, if you have followed a strategy of subclassing all components before use, you'll only have to make a single change that will then ripple throughout your application. Listing 10-6 shows the source code for the JumboTextField class, and Listing 10-7 puts the JumboTextField class to work, as you can seen in Figure 10-5.

Listing 10-6 JumboTextField.java

```java
// A subclass that can be used in place of the TextField
//
import java.awt.*;

public class JumboTextField extends TextField
{
    private static Font theFont = new Font(⇐
      "Helvetica", Font.BOLD, 14);
    private static Color theColor = new Color(255,255, 0);

    private void setFontAndColor()
    {
        this.setBackground( theColor );
        this.setFont( theFont );
    }

    public JumboTextField()
    {
        super("", 20 );
```

```
            this.setFontAndColor();
    }

    public JumboTextField(String s)
    {
        super( s );
        this.setFontAndColor();
    }

    public JumboTextField(String s, int n)
    {
        super( s, n );
        this.setFontAndColor();
    }

    public JumboTextField( int n )
    {
        super("", n );
        this.setFontAndColor();
    }
}
```

Listing 10-7 LoanApplication.java

```
// Using the JumboTextField class
//
import java.awt.*;
import java.awt.event.*;

public class LoanApplication extends Frame
                             implements ActionListener,
                                        WindowListener
{
    JumboTextField theName = new JumboTextField();
    JumboTextField theAddr = ⇐
      new JumboTextField("Put your address here ");
    JumboTextField theCity = new JumboTextField("City", 20);
    JumboTextField theZip  = new JumboTextField("", 10);
    Button          theQuit = ⇐
      new Button("Go away and leave me alone");

    public LoanApplication()
    {
        setTitle("LoanApplication");
        setLayout(new FlowLayout( ));
        add( theName );
        add( theAddr );
        add( theCity );
        add( theZip );
        add( theQuit );

        theName.addActionListener(this);
        theAddr.addActionListener(this);
        theCity.addActionListener(this);
        theZip.addActionListener (this);
        theQuit.addActionListener(this);
        addWindowListener(this);
```

continued on next page

continued from previous page

```
    }

    public void actionPerformed(ActionEvent theEvent)
    {
        if (theEvent.getSource( ) == theQuit) ⇐
         quitApplication( );
    }

    public void windowClosed      (WindowEvent e) { }
    public void windowClosing     (WindowEvent e)
                                    { quitApplication( ); }
    public void windowDeiconified(WindowEvent e) { }
    public void windowIconified  (WindowEvent e) { }
    public void windowOpened      (WindowEvent e) { }
    public void windowActivated  (WindowEvent e) { }
    public void windowDeactivated(WindowEvent e) { }

    public void quitApplication( )
    {
        setVisible( false );
        dispose( );
        System.exit(0);
    }

    public static void main( String args[] )
    {
        LoanApplication oLA = new LoanApplication();
        oLA.setSize(400, 150);
        oLA.setVisible( true );
    }
}
```

Looking at `JumboTextField`

The `JumboTextField` class has two `static` fields, called `theFont` and `theColor`, respectively. The field `theFont` is set to 14-point Helvetica Bold. The field `theColor`

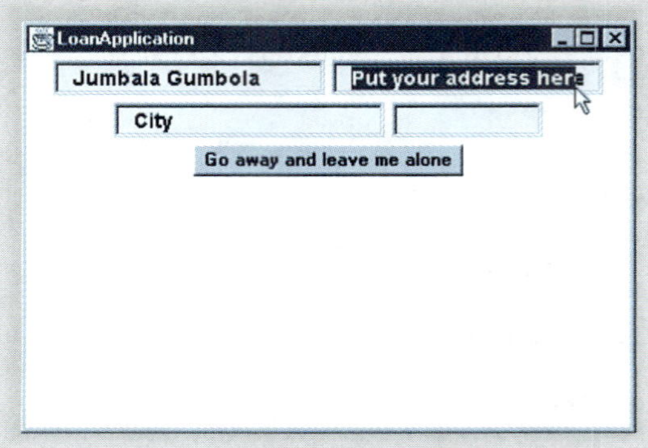

FIGURE 10-5

Running the LoanApplication application

is a `Color` object that is set to yellow. The `Color( )` constructor used takes three 8-bit values that represent red, green, and blue values. A zero means there is no color, and 255 means that there is maximum color. Because this `Color` object is constructed with both red and green set to maximum and blue turned off, the resulting color is a bright yellow. The `Color` class itself has a set of constants that represent common colors, so that the line initializing `theColor` could have been written as:

```
private static Color theColor = new Color( Color.yellow );
```

However, you won't find the constant `Color.mauve` defined with the `Color` class; using the three-argument constructor for `Colors` gives you more flexibility. You'll want to note that despite the convention of writing constants in all capitals, the color constants inside the `Color` class are written by use of lowercase letters.

The body of the `JumboTextField` class consists of four public constructors and a private method named `setFontAndColor( )`. Each constructor calls the `TextField` constructor by using `super( )`. The default constructor makes this call by saying

```
super("", 20 );
```

This means that all `JumboTextField`s have a default width of 20 if none is provided.

The rest of the constructors take various combinations of field width (`int`s) and `String`s. After the parent `TextField` object is created, each constructor calls the `setFontAndColor( )` method, which first sets the font by using the `setFont( )` method, and then sets the background color by using the `setBackground( )` method.

Looking at LoanApplication

Now that you have your new component, using it is just as easy as using any of the built-in objects provided with Java. To create a new `JumboTextField` object, you proceed exactly as you would for a `TextField` object. The LoanApplication application creates four such objects, using each of the various constructors contained in the `JumboTextField` class. It then adds them to its surface in its constructor, `LoanApplication( )`, along with a button to close the application.

The real importance of the LoanApplication program is that you can change every field to use a new `Font` or `Color` by simply making changes to the two variables at the beginning of the `JumboTextField` class. You don't even have to recompile the LoanApplication program for the changes to take effect. Go ahead, try it. By changing the color inside `theColor` field to `Color.pink` and then recompiling just `JumboTextField.java`, you've just saved yourself hours of tedious labor. As a general rule, for large systems you will want to subclass any of the built-in controls whose appearance or behavior you've customized.

Parents and Children: The Name Game

Although a subclass (child) inherits the fields of its superclass (parent), the child can also define a field having the same name as a field of its parent. This new field *shadows* the identically named field of the parent. Sometimes though, you may still need to access the identically named field inside the parent class. Java provides ways for you to do so. Listing 10-8 shows the application `ShadowField`, which demonstrates one such technique.

Listing 10-8 ShadowField.java

```java
// Demonstrates field adding and shadowing
//
import java.awt.*;
import java.awt.event.*;

public class ShadowField extends ShadowBase ⇐
                         implements ActionListener
{
    private String perpetrator = "<unknown>";
    private Button theButton    = new Button("Solve!");
    private boolean solved       = false;

    public static void main(String args[])
    {
        ShadowField theFrame = new ShadowField( );
        theFrame.setSize( 500,300 );

        theFrame.add( theFrame.theButton );
        theFrame.theButton.addActionListener(theFrame);
        theFrame.setVisible( true );
    }

    public void actionPerformed(ActionEvent theEvent)
    {
        if (theEvent.getSource( ) == theButton)
        {
            solved=true;
            repaint( );
        }
    }

    public void paint(Graphics g)
    {
        if (solved)
        {
            g.drawString("Child  perpetrator is " + ⇐
                perpetrator, 20, 80);
            g.drawString("Parent perpetrator is " + ⇐
                super.perpetrator, 20, 100);
        }
    }
}

class ShadowBase extends Frame implements WindowListener
{
    String perpetrator = "Ghengis Khan (G.K.) Chesterton";

    public ShadowBase( )
    {
        super("Only the Shadow knows");
        setLayout(new FlowLayout( ));
```

```
            addWindowListener(this);
    }

    public void windowClosed       (WindowEvent e) { }
    public void windowClosing      (WindowEvent e) {⇐
      quitApplication( ); }
    public void windowDeiconified(WindowEvent e) { }
    public void windowIconified    (WindowEvent e) { }
    public void windowOpened       (WindowEvent e) { }
    public void windowActivated    (WindowEvent e) { }
    public void windowDeactivated(WindowEvent e) { }

    public void quitApplication( )
    {
        setVisible(false);
        dispose( );
        System.exit(0);
    }

}
```

MEET THE SHADOW

This application consists of two classes: `ShadowField` and `ShadowBase`. The `ShadowField` class extends `ShadowBase` and defines a field named `perpetrator`. The problem is that an identically named field already exists in the `ShadowBase` class. What is the Java compiler supposed to do? If you take a look at the `paint( )` method, you'll see how you can use Java to gain access to both fields. The field in the child class can be accessed simply as

```
perpetrator
```

Because the child field has initialized the perpetrator field to hold the `String` `"<unknown>"`, that is what will be printed when the line

```
g.drawString("Child perpetrator is " + perpetrator, 20, 80);
```

is executed. In the parent class, `ShadowBase`, the field perpetrator holds the `String` `"Ghengis Khan (G.K.) Chesterton"`, a conglomeration of the name of the nomadic general of the Mongols with the name of the famous English detective novelist who created the Father Brown character. To access this value, Java requires you to "unshadow" it by referring to

```
super.perpetrator
```

Another way to accomplish the same result is to cast the type of a child object to that of its parent. The `this` object is handy for this purpose. In `ShadowField`, you could have written

```
((ShadowBase) this).perpetrator
```

instead of

```
super.perpetrator
```

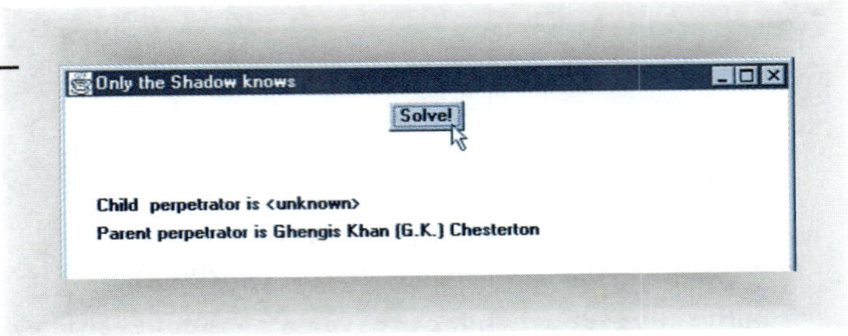

FIGURE 10-6

Running the ShadowField application

Figure 10-6 shows the ShadowField application at work.

Table 10-1 summarizes ways in which shadowed fields and the fields that shadow them can be accessed from a child object. Note that the shadowed field need not be a field of the child class's immediate parent; it may actually be a field of a superclass of the parent. The technique works in either case.

TABLE 10-1
ACCESSING SHADOWED FIELDS

FORM	MEANING
`this.theField`	Access the field named `theField`, defined in the child class.
`super.theField`	Access the field named `theField`, defined in a parent class.
`(ParentClass) this.theField`	Access the field named `theField`, defined in a parent class.
`super.super.theField`	Not valid.

ACCESS RESTRICTIONS

While the ShadowField application works as advertised, you might notice that the `perpetrator` field was not specified as `private` or `protected`. What would happen if it were? If perpetrator were declared as `private` in the `ShadowBase` class, you would not be able to access it at all in the `ShadowField` class. If `perpetrator` were `protected`, you would be able to access the field using the `super.perpetrator` notation. Note, however, that although `protected` fields are inherited as part of the child object, the child object is not allowed to access `protected` fields *in* the parent object.

Listing 10-9 shows the RentVideo application, which demonstrates this restriction. The class `Child` extends the class `Parent`, which contains the protected field `rentalID`. Every `Child` object inherits the `Parent`'s `rentalID` field. Thus, they can go to the video store and check out movies, but only movies that the parents have approved. To get around this restriction, the `Child` may be tempted to "pretend" to be a `Parent`. In Java, this is accomplished by casting `this` to the `Parent` type:

```
((Parent) this).methodCall( );
```

❝ *Every*
constructor,
default or not,
has three tasks
which it performs
in a set order. **❞**

However, because the `rentalID` field is protected inside the `Parent`, the `Child` is prohibited from pretending to be a `Parent` object, and is thus spared the trauma, not to mention the boredom, of watching *Mutant Monsters from Outer Space Discuss the National Economy.*

Listing 10-9 RentVideo.java

```
// Demonstrates inheritance, but not access, to parent
//

public class RentVideo
{
    public static void main(String args[])
    {
        Child theChild   = new Child( );
        theChild.rentVideo( );
    }
}

class Child extends Parent
{
    void rentVideo( )
    {
        System.out.println("I'm just a child!");
        System.out.println(⇐
         "My parent's rental ID is " + rentalID );

        // This does NOT COMPILE, preventing a child from
        // masquerading as a Parent object
        // System.out.println(⇐
        //    "Of course I'm old enough to rent that!");
        // System.out.println(⇐
        //    "My rentalID is " + ((Parent)this).rentalID );
    }
}

class Parent
{
    protected int rentalID = 1246;
}
```

USING final CLASSES

Another way to restrict use of your class is to declare it as `final`:

```
public final class Childless
```

A `final` class can be used, but cannot be extended. Given the `Childless` class declared earlier, it's not possible to create a new class by writing

```
public class Child extends Childless
```

Declaring a class as final often also allows the Java compiler to take some shortcuts that can improve the efficiency of your program. Several of Java's built-in classes are declared as final, including the `System` class.

"You Act Just Like Your Father!"

Just as a field defined in a child class can shadow an identically named field in its parent class, a method can be defined in a child class even though a method of the same name already exists in its parent. When referring to methods, this is not called "shadowing"; instead, it's called *overriding*, and it works somewhat differently than shadowing.

"Didn't I already read about this?" you might think. "I thought when two methods had the same name, that was called overloading. Why are you changing the name now?" Good point. Overriding should not be confused with overloading, which was presented in Chapter 9. An *overloaded* method has the same name as another method, but has a *different number* of arguments or has arguments that *differ in type* from those of the other method. An overridden method has the *same number and types* of arguments as the overriding method, only the overridden method is in a superclass of the class that contains the overriding method. Figure 10-7 distinguishes overloading from overriding.

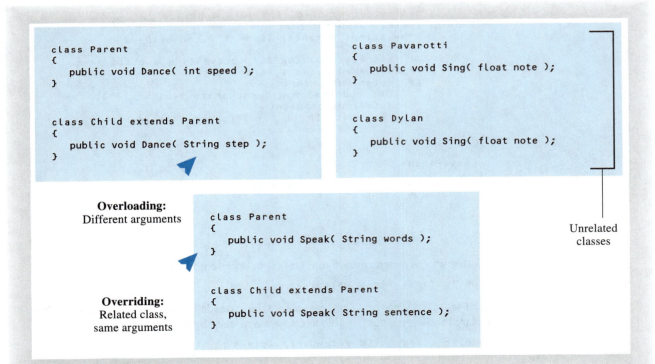

FIGURE 10-7

Overloading and overriding methods

When you write a new method in a subclass that has the same name and argument signature as a method in a superclass, the messages that are sent to child objects will invoke this new method, rather than the original method that still exists in the parent class. The child class, therefore, overrides or overrules the behavior defined by the parent class for the message. This is what makes it possible for child classes to exhibit new varieties of behavior not supported by their parents, an important feature of object-oriented programming.

Listing 10-10, the TalkToMe application, shows how methods can be overridden in a subclass.

Listing 10-10 TalkToMe.java

```
// How overridding methods works
//
import java.io.*;

public class TalkToMe
{

    public static void main( String args[] )
    {
        Cat         theCat      = new Cat( );
        Dog         theDog      = new Dog( );
        Frog        theFrog     = new Frog( );
        Flamingo    theFlamingo = new Flamingo( );

        System.out.println("The CAT says: ⇐
          " + theCat.speak());
        System.out.println("The DOG says: ⇐
          " + theDog.speak());
        System.out.println("The FROG says: ⇐
          " + theFrog.speak());
        System.out.println("The FLAMINGO says: ⇐
          " + theFlamingo.speak());
    }
}

class Pet
{
    String speak() ⇐
      { return "Hi, I'm a happy and contented pet"; }
}

class Dog extends Pet
{
    String speak() ⇐
      { return super.speak() + ". Arf, Arf"; }
}

class Cat extends Pet
{
    String speak() ⇐
      { return super.speak() + ". Meow, meow"; }
}
```

continued on next page

continued from previous page

```
class Frog extends Pet
{
}

class Flamingo extends Pet
{
    String speak() ⇐
        { return "They're holding me captive. You must help!"; }
}
```

RUNNING THE TALKTOME APPLICATION

```
The CAT says: Hi, I'm a happy and contented pet. Meow, meow
The DOG says: Hi, I'm a happy and contented pet. Arf, Arf
The FROG says: Hi, I'm a happy and contented pet.
The FLAMINGO says: They're holding me captive. You must help!
```

INHERITED AND OVERRIDDEN METHODS

The TalkToMe application shows several different relationships between methods in a subclass and methods in a superclass. TalkToMe creates a class called Pet, which has a single method, speak( ). This method returns the String "I'm a happy and contented pet." TalkToMe then creates four subclasses of the Pet class: Dog, Cat, Frog, and Flamingo.

The Dog and Cat class act similarly. They both first call super.speak( ) to allow their "higher nature" (the Pet class) to speak( ) before each of them contributes its own unique vocabulary. Then each of them responds as appropriate. The Frog class does not have a speak( ) method, so Java will search for a method in its super-classes, where it will find and execute the speak( ) method in the Pet class. Finally, the Flamingo class—not a happy and contented pet in the best of circumstances—doesn't call its superclass speak( ) method at all, but attempts to tell the world that it is being held prisoner.

SHADOWING AND OVERRIDING

Both overriding and shadowing can be used inside an application. The SuperMethod application, shown in Listing 10-11, demonstrates how methods can be overridden. It also shows how it is possible to access the overridden method of a parent class.

> **Reusable classes make your life easier by moving repetitive tasks further up the class hierarchy.**

Listing 10-11 SuperMethod.java

```java
// Demonstrates method overriding
//
import java.awt.*;
import java.awt.event.*;

public class SuperMethod extends SuperMethodBase ⇐
                         implements ActionListener
{
    String perpetrator = "Dr. No";

    Button theParentButton = new Button("Solve via parent!");
    Label  theParentLabel  = ⇐
        new Label("--------------------");
    Button theChildButton  = new Button("Solve via child!");
    Label  theChildLabel    = ⇐
        new Label("--------------------");

    public static void main(String args[])
    {
        SuperMethod theFrame = new SuperMethod( );
        theFrame.seteSize(300,100);
        theFrame.add(theFrame.theParentButton);
        theFrame.add(theFrame.theParentLabel);
        theFrame.add(theFrame.theChildButton);
        theFrame.add(theFrame.theChildLabel);
        theFrame.theParentButton.addActionListener(theFrame);
        theFrame.theChildButton.addActionListener(theFrame);
        theFrame.setVisible( true );
    }

    public String solve( )
    {
        System.out.println("Child method invoked");
        return perpetrator;
    }

    public void actionPerformed(ActionEvent theEvent)
    {
        if (theEvent.getSource( ) == theChildButton)
            theChildLabel.setText(solve( ));
        else
            theParentLabel.setText(super.solve( ));
    }
}

class SuperMethodBase extends Frame implements WindowListener
{
    String perpetrator = "<unknown>";

    public SuperMethodBase( )
    {
        setTitle("Only the Shadow knows");
        setLayout(new FlowLayout( ));
        addWindowListener(this);
    }
```

continued on next page

continued from previous page

```
public String solve( )
{
    System.out.println("Parent method invoked");
    return perpetrator;
}

public void windowClosed      (WindowEvent e) { }
public void windowClosing     (WindowEvent e) { ⇐
    quitApplication( ); }
public void windowDeiconified (WindowEvent e) { }
public void windowIconified   (WindowEvent e) { }
public void windowOpened      (WindowEvent e) { }
public void windowActivated   (WindowEvent e) { }
public void windowDeactivated (WindowEvent e) { }

public void quitApplication( )
{
    setVisible( false );
    dispose( );
    System.exit(0);
}
```

}

This application includes two classes: the class `SuperMethodBase` and the class `SuperMethod`, which extends `SuperMethodBase`. Each class defines the method `solve( )`, which returns the value of the `String` field `perpetrator`. Pressing the buttons labeled "Solve" causes the invocation of the `solve( )` and `super.solve( )` methods. Run the application and see what happens.

When you press the button to tell the child object to execute its `solve()` method, the result is `"<unknown>"`. However, pressing the button that directs the child to use its parent's `solve( )` method via `super.solve( )` produces the result `"Dr. No"`.

Here's how it works. The `solve( )` method defined in the `SuperMethod` class works as you would expect, returning the value of the field defined in the child. The output of the `println( )` confirms that the child method has been invoked. The `super.solve( )` method, however, has a different result. Although the `return` statement in the `SuperMethodBase` class's `solve( )` method has an expression identical to that in the corresponding method in the `SuperMethod` class, it returns a different value. It returns the value of the `perpetrator` field in the `parent` class. The `super.solve( )` method invokes the parent method, but it invokes it within the context "shadowed" by the identically named `perpetrator` field in the child.

OVERRIDING CONCERNS

In addition to the examples you've seen so far, here are some other rules you'll need to learn and remember to make good use of overridden methods.

Perhaps surprisingly, you can't use a cast to access an overridden method in a parent class. Using

```
((SuperMethodBase)this).solve( ) ;
```

would invoke the method of the child class, despite the cast. Casting never changes the actual nature of an object. The `this` object was, and remains, a `SuperMethod`, and its `solve( )` method will be accessed.

IMPORTANT TO REMEMBER

Access to fields is governed by the form of the reference. Casting an object to a different type will permit access to fields shadowed by the type of the original object.

Access to methods, however, is governed by the nature of the object. Casting an object to a different type will have no effect on which method is invoked in response to a given message. Once overridden, methods remain overridden.

☞ Only the nonstatic methods of a class can be overridden. If you need to modify the behavior associated with a static method, you must change the source code for the defining class.

☞ It's possible for an overriding method to have an access specifier that differs from that given in the overridden method. In such cases Java requires that the overriding method not have more restrictive access than that of the overridden method. For example, a method specified as `public` in the parent class cannot be overridden by a method specified as `private` in the child class. But it's perfectly okay to override a `private` method with a new `public` method.

THE final WORD ON METHODS

Just as a class can be specified as `final`, preventing another class from extending it, it is also possible to specify that individual methods of a class are `final`. In that case, you can still extend the class, but you're not allowed to override the method specified as `final`. As with `final` classes, this gives you greater control over how others, who might want to extend your classes, can use them.

Specifying a method as `final` (or `private`) also permits the Java compiler to emit faster code for a method invocation. Because such methods cannot be overridden, the compiler doesn't need to generate code that searches through the related classes at run-time, looking for an overriding method definition. However, this optimization is only performed if the `-O` flag is specified when the compiler is invoked:

```
javac -O SourceFile.java
```

Use of this flag may also allow the compiler to include small methods inline, duplicating the code for each invocation. This is useful when the overhead involved in invoking the method is large compared with the processing performed by the method. For very small methods, the program may actually be smaller and faster if they are duplicated.

Constructors, by the way, cannot be specified as `final`. The proper way to limit extension of a class is by specifying the class itself as `final`.

FINALIZERS REVISITED

Do you remember finalizers, the methods called before an object is collected as garbage? You might expect that the finalizer of a child class would automatically invoke the finalizer of a parent class, in much the same way that the constructor of a parent is automatically called by the constructor of a child.

Unfortunately, this does not occur. If your program defines finalizers, you should end each `finalize( )` method with the line

```
super.finalize( )
```

to guarantee that any overridden `finalize()` methods of superclasses are actually invoked.

Casting Your Cares Away

A cast is a way to tell the Java compiler to treat an object or variable as if it were of a different type. Thus, the expression

```
System.out.println("The value is :" + (int) 3.999);
```

prints the number *3* and not *3.999*. You have told Java to treat the expression **3.999** as if it were an `int`. Casts can be used with objects just as with primitive types, as you've seen. One place where this is handy is when you are using collections, such as vectors or arrays. Collections usually require their elements to have type `Object`. When you store something in a collection and later retrieve it, you usually have to cast it back from `Object` to its original type.

However, some care is needed when performing casts with objects. Just as with primitive types, there are "good" casts and there are "bad" casts. Suppose you have a set of classes related as in Figure 10-8. The base class, `Mammal`, is extended to create two subclasses, `HerbivorousMammal` and `CarnivorousMammal`. Because of their relationship through inheritance, an `HerbivorousMammal` is a `Mammal`, as is a `CarnivorousMammal`. However, not every `Mammal` is an `HerbivorousMammal`; nor is every `Mammal` a `CarnivorousMammal`.

If you have an `HerbivorousMammal` object, you can safely cast it to a `Mammal` object:

```
HerbivorousMammal hm = // some value
Mammal m = (Mammal) hm;
```

Similarly, you can safely cast a `CarnivorousMammal` object to a `Mammal` object:

```
CarnivorousMammal cm = // some value
Mammal m = (Mammal) cm;
```

FIGURE 10-8

*An example community
of classes*

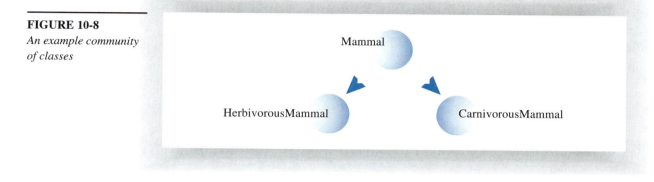

However, you *cannot* cast an `HerbivorousMammal` to a `CarnivorousMammal` or vice versa. Nor can you, ordinarily, cast a `Mammal` object to either an `HerbivorousMammal` or a `CarnivorousMammal`.

```
Mammal m = . . .              // some value
HerbivorousMammal hm = . . .  // some value
CarnivorousMammal cm = . . .  // some value

HerbivorousMammal hm1 = (HerbivorousMammal) m;
CarnivorousMammal cm1 = (CarnivorousMammal) m;
HerbivorousMammal hm1 = (CarnivorousMammal) hm;
CarnivorousMammal cm1 = (HerbivorousMammal) cm;
```

If you attempt to perform these casts, the Java interpreter will throw a `ClassCastException`. But there is one exception to this general rule. Some times you know perfectly well that the object whose reference is contained in a `Mammal` field is, in fact, an `HerbivorousMammal`. In such a case, when you attempt such a cast, all will be well, and the cast will succeed. What if you're not sure what kind of object you have, but you'd like to do the cast if it's possible? In that case, you can turn to the `instanceof` operator. Recall that the `instanceof` operator allows you to test the type of an object. By writing the test

```
if (m instanceof HerbivorousMammal)
```

you can determine, in advance, whether the cast will succeed. Then, if the test succeeds, you can actually perform the cast.

The general rule is that using an object in a context that is permissible for its superclass or casting an object to its superclass is *always* safe. In other cases, the `instanceof` operator should be used to verify the type of the object before proceeding. Some people express this concept by saying it's okay to cast "up" the inheritance hierarchy but not "down" the inheritance hierarchy. Listing 10-12, `Casting.java`, illustrates these principles.

Listing 10-12 Casting.java

```java
// How casting works
//

public class Casting
{
    public static void main( String args[] )
    {
        Parrot          theParrot     = new Parrot( );
        ColorfulPet thePet            = new Goldfish( );

        Parrot          tempParrot;
        ColorfulPet tempPet;

        if (thePet instanceof ColorfulPet)
            System.out.println("thePet is a ColorfulPet:    "
                + thePet.move( ));
        if (theParrot instanceof ColorfulPet)
            System.out.println("theParrot is a ColorfulPet: "
                + theParrot.move( ));
        if (theParrot instanceof Parrot)
            System.out.println("theParrot is a parrot:      "
                + theParrot.move( ));

        /*
        ClassCastException due to unsafe (downwards) cast:

        tempParrot = (Parrot) thePet;

        */

        // safe cast (upwards)
        tempPet = (ColorfulPet) theParrot;
        if (tempPet instanceof ColorfulPet)
            System.out.println("tempPet is a ColorfulPet:   "
                + tempPet.move( ));
        if (tempPet instanceof Parrot)
        {
            // safe cast (verified by instanceof)
            tempParrot = (Parrot) tempPet;
            System.out.println("tempPet is a parrot:        "
                + tempParrot.move( ));
        }
    }
}

class ColorfulPet
{
    String move() ⇐
        { return "Hi, I'm a happy and colorful pet"; }
}
```

```
class Parrot extends ColorfulPet
{
    String move()  { return super.move() + ". Walk, Fly"; }
}

class Goldfish extends ColorfulPet
{
    String move()  { return super.move() + ". Swim, swim"; }
}
```

Using the `Object` Class

Although the `JavaDrinkingAnimal` class in the `WageEquitySimulation` applet shown near the beginning of the chapter does not appear to extend another class, it actually does. Java's built-in `Object` class is the implicit superclass of classes that do not explicitly extend another class. The class header is interpreted just as if it had been written

```
public class JavaDrinkingAnimal extends Object
```

The benefit of this arrangement is that, except for primitive types, everything is an `Object`. This means, for example, that an `Object` variable can hold a reference to any other nonprimitive type. This is an extremely useful feature of the Java language for building *container objects*—objects that can contain other objects—as you'll see in Chapter 15, "Data Structures and Utility Classes."

The `Object` class has some unique and useful properties:

- It is the only class that has no superclass.

- Every other class is ultimately a subclass of `Object`.

- An object of any type can be assigned to a variable of type `Object`.

- It defines several useful methods, including `equals( )`, `toString( )`, and others you'll meet in Chapter 16, "Advanced Topics: Threads and Networking."

Figure 10-9 shows a portion of the hierarchy that descends from the `Object` class.

OVERRIDING `Object` METHODS

The methods defined by the `Object` class are particularly important. Often the default behavior implemented within the `Object` class is not the kind of base (groan) behavior you want your objects exhibiting. In such a case, you can override the inherited behavior by writing a method that is specific to your class.

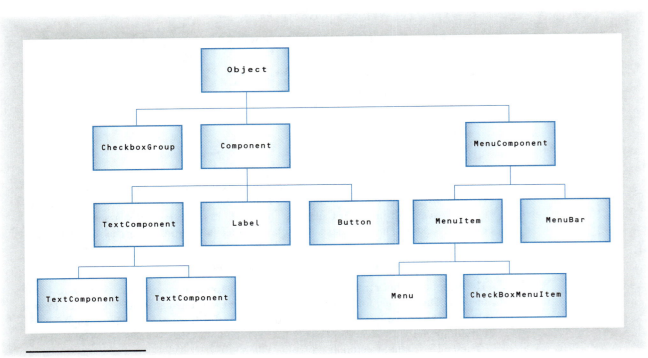

FIGURE 10-9

A portion of Java's object hierarchy

IMPLEMENTING toString( )

The first method you should consider implementing is toString( ). This method is called to convert an object to a String whenever the object appears within a String expression or inside a println( ) call. By giving each of your classes a toString( ) method, you make debugging considerably easier. Having written toString( ), you can display the state of an entire object with a single, simple call to println( ). For example, if you implemented a class representing a circle, you might include a toString( ) method like this:

```
public class Circle
{
    float x;
    float y;
    float radius;

    // Other stuff, including constructor(s)

    public String toString( )
    {
        return "Circle at (" + x + "," + y + "), of radius ⇐
        " + radius;
    }
}
```

ALL OTHER THINGS BEING equals( )

Another important method is `equals( )`. Whenever your class includes objects as fields, you need to consider what the notion of "equality" means for that class. That is, what relationships should hold between the fields of two objects in order that they be regarded as equal? That's not always as easy a question as it might seem.

For example, you might choose to consider two `Circles` of the same radius equal, even though they were located at different positions. In such a case you'd write a method like this:

```java
public boolean equals(Circle c)
{
    if (radius == c.radius)
        return true;
    else
        return false;
}
```

The `equals( )` method takes a single argument, of the same type as the class containing the `equals( )` method, and compares this argument with the `this` object.

The Package Tour

You've now seen two basic ways that classes can be related to each other. In Chapter 9, you saw that classes could contain objects of other classes as fields. This is called containment, or a `hasA` relationship. You can say that a `Car` object `hasA Door`. In this chapter you saw that classes can also be specializations of other classes. This is the inheritance relationship, known as an `isA` relationship; a `Mammal isA Animal`.

The access specifiers—`public`, `private`, and `protected`—are designed to facilitate these relationships. Fields that should be shared among all classes can be declared `public`, while fields and methods that only make sense inside a particular class can be declared `private`. Fields and methods that should be extended in a subclass can be declared `protected`. You're not quite finished with class relationships, however. The world is bigger than parents, children, and strangers. The Java facility, packages, allows you to add some additional possibilities.

FILES, CLASSES, AND PACKAGES

Let's start by looking back at files and classes. Java's source files, which are named with the extension `.java`, contain definitions of classes. Each source file can contain the definitions of more than one class, but only one `public` class can be defined in each source file. A `public` class must be defined in a source file that has the same name as the class (with the exception, of course, that the source file has the extension `.java`). Even if your operating system's file system is not case sensitive, the Java compiler is. The name of the source file and the name of its `public` class must match even with respect to capitalization.

> *A cast is a way to tell the Java compiler to treat an object or variable as if it were of a different type.*

Java also allows you to group your classes into units called *packages*. Packages are important when you are creating Java programs of substantial size, because they help you organize your program better. The classes within a package can share fields and members that cannot be seen outside the package, as you'll see when you return to access modifiers at the end of this section.

Java has several rules for creating a package. First, all the classes of a package must be stored in a single directory. Second, if a class belongs to a named package, the source file must identify the package to which it belongs. This is done by use of the `package` statement as the first statement within the source file of each class:

```
package MyPackage;
```

A source file that lacks a `package` statement is considered part of a special "unnamed" package. The classes it defines and other classes stored in the same directory are all part of this unnamed package.

PACKAGE NAMING

The Java compiler will implicitly add the name of the package to the front of each class inside the package. If the package `MyPackage` contains a class named `MyClass`, the full name of the class becomes `MyPackage.MyClass`. Inside a package, class names must be unique. `MyPackage` can have only one class named `MyClass`. For this reason, when you refer to `MyPackage.MyClass` within any of the other classes contained in `MyPackage`, you only need use the name `MyClass`; the shorter name is sufficient. However, classes outside `MyPackage` must use the longer form, `MyPackage.MyClass`.

As you might have guessed by now, this is what the `import` statements you've been using do behind the scenes. You could *always* refer to your hypothetical class as `MyPackage.MyClass`. But to avoid getting keyboard cramp, you would normally include an `import` within your program:

```
import MyPackage.*;
```

The import would allow you to refer to the class as simply `MyClass`.

What if two packages, `PackageA` and `PackageB`, each define a class named `MyClass`? Again, you can *always* refer to one class as `PackageA.MyClass` and the other as `PackageB.MyClass`. If one class—say `PackageA.MyClass`—is used more than the other, then you could import the classes of that package:

```
import PackageA.*;
```

or, more specifically, import only the needed class:

```
import PackageA.MyClass;
```

Now when you refer to `MyClass`, you will be understood as meaning `PackageA.MyClass`. When you need to use `PackageB.MyClass`, you would use the longer form.

PACKAGES AND ACCESS

A fourth type of access, apart from `public`, `protected`, and `private`, is package access. If no access specifier is given, access defaults to `package` access, which allows access only from within classes of the same package. Remember that source files that do not begin with a `package` statement are part of an unnamed package that includes similar files stored in the same directory. Don't try to actually add `package` as an access modifier. Remember that the absence of `public`, `protected`, and `private` signifies `package` access.

Listing 10-13 shows how access control works, as applied to fields. The class `Parent` defines four fields: one for each of the three access specifiers and one with no access specifier. The `Child` class, which `extends` the `Parent` class, is capable of accessing all fields of the `Parent` other than the `private` field. The `WideWorld` class, which is not part of the family, can access only the `public` and default (`package` access) fields; both the `private` and `protected` fields are invisible to it.

Listing 10-13 Access control

```
public class Parent
{
    public    int publicField;
    protected int protectedField;
    private   int privateField;
              int defaultField;   // package access
}

public class Child extends Parent
{
    // . . .
    publicField =      10;
    protectedField =   20;
    defaultField =     30;
    // . . .
}

public class SamePackageClass
{
    // . . .
    publicField =      10;
    defaultField =     30;
    // . . .
}


public class DifferentPackageClass
{
    // . . .
    publicField =      40;
    // . . .

}
```

Figure 10-10 shows how access modifiers affect visibility of fields and methods.

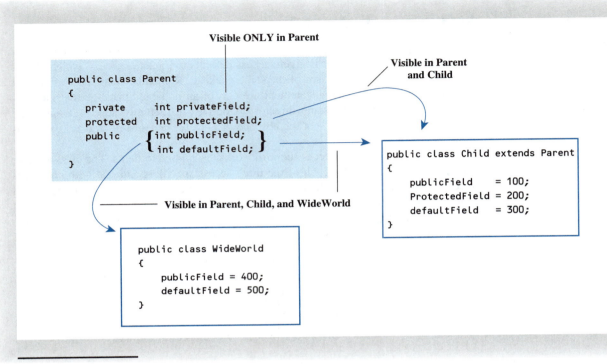

FIGURE 10-10

Access modifiers and visibility

Tables 10-2, 10-3, and 10-4 summarize the rules for access to classes, fields, and methods.

TABLE 10-2
ACCESS TO CLASSES

ACCESS	ACCESS WITHIN SAME PACKAGE	ACCESS FROM DIFFERENT PACKAGE
public	Yes	Yes
package	Yes	No

TABLE 10-3
ACCESS TO FIELDS

	SAME CLASS	DIFFERENT CLASS, SAME PACKAGE		DIFFERENT PACKAGE	
		CHILD CLASS	NONCHILD CLASS	CHILD CLASS	NONCHILD CLASS
`public`	A	A,I	A	A	A
`package`	A	A,I	A	NA	NA
`protected`	A	A,I	NA	I	NA
`private`	A	NA	NA	NA	NA

A = Accessible; I = Inherited; NA = No access

TABLE 10-4
ACCESS TO METHODS

	SAME CLASS	DIFFERENT CLASS, SAME PACKAGE		DIFFERENT PACKAGE	
		CHILD CLASS	NONCHILD CLASS	CHILD CLASS	NONCHILD CLASS
`public`	Yes	Yes	Yes	Yes	Yes
`package`	Yes	Yes	Yes	No	No
`protected`	Yes	Yes	No	Yes	No
`private`	Yes	No	No	No	No

SOME USEFUL RULES OF THUMB FOR CHOOSING ACCESS SPECIFIERS

Deciding which access specifier to use in defining a class, field, or method can be difficult. Here are some rules of thumb that work well in most cases:

- Helper classes should have package visibility and should not have an access specifier; all other classes should be specified as `public`.

- Fields and methods you wish everyone to be able to access should be specified as `public`.

- The decision to specify a field as `public` should not be made lightly. Fields that, when manipulated directly, can lead to an inconsistent object state should not be made `public`. Create `public` accessor and mutator methods instead.

- Fields and methods used only inside a class should be specified as `private`.

If you're designing a library of classes that other programmers will use and extend, you'll find these simple rules of thumb inadequate. In such a case, you'll need to anticipate the needs of future programmers and specify certain fields and methods that are presently used only inside your classes as `protected`, so that programmers extending your classes can access them. Which fields should be specified as `protected`? Only accurate foreknowledge of the intended use of your classes can lead to an accurate answer. The bottom line: If you open your class too much, others may break the class by manipulating it into an inconsistent state. If you fail to open it enough, desired extensions may not be possible—truly a decision for Solomon!

NAME THAT CONFLICT

What if two programmers create packages with the same name? How is it possible to sort out the classes? The designers of Java thought that this was a problem better avoided than solved. To this end, they published a convention for naming packages, designed to prevent programmers from creating identically named packages.

Remember from Chapter 1, "What's All This Java Stuff?" that every company with a network attached to the Internet has a unique domain name. By use of the domain name as part of the package name, it becomes much simpler to avoid duplicate package names, as long as the programmers within a single company communicate effectively enough to give their packages unique names.

For example, assume that Jumbo's Jungle Java Joint's domain name is `j4.com`. If a package named `MyPackage` were created by a programmer there, the package should be named this way:

```
package COM.j4.MyPackage;
```

According to the convention, the order of the domain name is reversed (`COM.j4`, rather than `j4.com`), and the first component is capitalized.

Of course, it would still be possible for a programmer within Jumbo's Information Systems and Technology department to create a package with the same name as one created by a programmer within the JavaMatic Embedded Systems department. To avoid this, Jumbo could assign a subdomain to each department:

```
package COM.j4.jes.MyPackage;
```

Only programmers within the JavaMatic Embedded Systems department would use the `jes` subdomain; therefore, conflicts would be unlikely.

STORING AND LOCATING PACKAGES

Packages must be stored in a directory whose name matches the name of the package. It's your responsibility to create the proper directory and place your CLASS files in it. The Java compiler does not do this for you.

On a Windows 95 system, the dots within a package name are translated to back-slashes (\) to form the directory name. The package `COM.j4.jes.MyPackage`, for example, must be stored in a directory named `COM\j4\jes`. This is a relative directory reference, not a reference from the root directory, such as `\COM\j4\jes`. When searching for a class, Java uses the `CLASSPATH` environment variable to identify a series of directories that may contain packages. These will automatically be searched by Java to find a needed class.

For example, suppose the `CLASSPATH` variable has been set as follows:

```
CLASSPATH=c:\java\lib;c:\oop;.
```

Let's also suppose your source file contains these two `imports`:

```
import java.util.*;
import oop.*;
```

If your code uses the class name `TheClass`, Java will look for it in the following locations:

```
c:\java\lib\java\util\TheClass.class
c:\java\lib\oop\TheClass.class
c:\oop\java\util\TheClass.class
c:\oop\oop\TheClass.class
.\java\util\TheClass.class
.\oop\TheClass.class
```

The dot at the end of the `CLASSPATH` stands for the current directory. It's important to include it within the `CLASSPATH`, or Java may be unable to find classes you've written stored "right under its nose" in the current directory!

N O N – J D K   D E V E L O P M E N T   E N V I R O N M E N T S

Java development environments other than the JDK may use methods other than `CLASSPATH` to identify directories that will be searched. Consult your documentation.

If you check out the contents of the `java\lib` subdirectory of the JDK, you won't find CLASS files there. Instead you'll find a file named `classes.zip`. This file contains many separate CLASS files, stored as a single file to improve efficiency. You may be able to view the names of these CLASS files using a ZIP file viewer. However, don't attempt to unzip the file. You could inadvertently corrupt important JDK classes, rendering Java inoperative.

Summary

- In an inheritance relationship, the superclass (parent class) is the more general class, and the subclass (child class) is the more specific class.

- The `extends` keyword is used to specify a subclass.

- A `protected` field or method can be accessed from a subclass of its enclosing class, but not from other classes.

- The `super` object can be used to refer to a field of a parent class, which is shadowed by a similarly named field in the related child class.

- To access a shadowed parent field, an object can be cast to its parent type.

- Specifying a class as `final` prevents it from being extended.

- Specifying a method as `final` prevents it from being overridden in a child class.

- A method cannot be overridden by a method that has more restrictive access.

- `Finalizer` methods should generally end with `super.finalize( )`.

- Inheritance can often be used to simplify selection logic within a program.

- Casting an object to its superclass (parent class) is safe.

- Casting an object to a subclass (child class) may result in an exception.

- The `instanceof` operator can be used to test the type of an object in order to determine whether a cast to a subclass is safe.

- Classes not defined as extending another class actually extend the `Object` class.

- Important methods of the `Object` class include `toString( )` and `equals( )`.

- Packages are used to group related classes.

- The `import` statement allows the abbreviation of class names by prespecifying possible package names.

- Package-level access is specified by the absence of the keywords `public`, `private`, and `protected`.

- A special naming convention can be used to avoid conflicting package names.

- A package must be stored in a location that relates to its name in order for the Java run-time to be able to locate its CLASS files.

- The `CLASSPATH` environment variable specifies how directories are to be searched for CLASS files.

Quiz

1. In an inheritance relationship, the more general class is known as the _____.

2. In an inheritance relationship, the more specific class is known as the _____.

3. The Java keyword that denotes inheritance is _____.

4. In addition to `public` and `private`, Java includes the access specifier _____, which is useful within the context of inheritance relationships.

5. The _____ object can be used to refer to a field of a parent class, which is shadowed by a field in the current class.

6. To prevent a class from being used as a Parent class, the class can be specified as _____.

7. Specifying a method as _____ prevents it from being overridden in a child class.

8. Casting an object to the type of its superclass/subclass is always safe.

9. An unsafe cast may result in a(n) _____ event.

10. To avoid an unsafe cast, the _____ operator can be used to test the type of an object.

11. Every class is a subclass of the class _____.

12. When a `String` expression includes a non-`String` operand, the _____ method is used to generate a `String` value for the non-`String` operand.

13. A package is a group of related _____.

14. An `import` statement allows the abbreviation of _____ names.

15. Package-level access is specified by _____ the keywords `public`, `private`, and `protected`.

Exercises

1. Implement a family of classes describing at least five types of vehicles. Each type should, at a minimum, be characterized by its weight (in pounds), maximum speed (in miles per hour), and maximum number of passengers. Include a method `travel()` that simulates movement of a vehicle by printing the type of the vehicle and the mode of locomotion.

2. Create a class `Employee` that encapsulates data about employees. Then derive new subclasses `Manager` and `Programmer` from the `Employee` class; each new class should include additional fields relevant to the specific type of employee represented by the class.

3. Modify the classes created in exercise 2 by adding annualSalary as a field in the Employee class. Also include a method, updateSalary( ), that calculates an employee's revised salary based on the result of the employee's annual review. The result of the employee's review is passed as an argument to the updateSalary( ) method, coded as a float value between 0.0F and 1.0F (inclusive), where 1.0F denotes a perfect review. Decide how the method should operate for Managers and Programmers and implement that behavior; any behavior you choose is acceptable, so long as the behavior of the two subclasses is distinct.

4. Create an applet that maintains a database of employees, based on exercise 3. The employees should be stored in a vector to permit an indefinitely large staff. The applet should allow the user to add, delete, or inspect the data related to any employee. The format of the screen should be adjusted to reflect the type of employee; for example, the fields related to a manager should not appear when you are inspecting the record of a programmer.

5. From the base class Button, derive the new class StopGoButton. A StopGoButton initially contains the text "Stop," but when the button is pressed, the text is changed to "Go." The class StopGoButton should contain the method getState( ), which returns the int value 0 if the button is in the "Stop" state and the value 1 if the button is in the "Go" state. Create an applet that contains a StopGoButton and uses the button to control an action of your choice by querying the getState( ) method.

11

Jumpin' Java:

Menus, Graphics, Sound

"The journey of a thousand miles begins with a single step." Congratulations! A thousand miles, 10 chapters—it's all the same thing. When you began Chapter 1, "What's All This Java Stuff?", you were not a programmer. Now you are. But learning to program is only the beginning of the story. It's like learning to drive. Once you've learned, it's time to go someplace!

While the first half of this book taught you about object-oriented programming using Java, the rest is devoted to a tour of Java's features and capabilities. Your tour will not be exhaustive by any means. But as on the seven-day grand tour of Europe, you'll visit all the capitals, climb the Eiffel Tower, see the Colosseum in Rome, quaff a brew in Munich, and take a quick trip around Piccadilly Circus. By the time you're done, you'll have met and used the major classes in Java. You'll try your hand at graphics and GUI creation. You'll learn about networking, sound, and animation. You'll find out what a thread is and, although Java doesn't have any rivers, you'll get to spend a considerable time floating down its wide variety of `streams`. In short, we hope to leave you both satisfied and happily planning your next trip, just as a good tour company should.

THE CODER'S CODA

Jumbo unfolded the wrinkled notice and read the familiar lines one last time.

The Powers That Be, Inc.

Dear Sir or Madame (as the case may be),

This is to inform you that your domain name, `j4.com`, is in conflict with the registered name of Justin, Jason, James, and Jorowitz, Attorneys at Law, and is hereby suspended. They're lawyers. They might sue us. You're not. You're history.

Have a nice day.

Sincerely,

Tammi

At first, he had been at a total loss. How would he tell Zenia? How would he tell Brenda? What about all the work the "pachs" had done on the JavaMatic? What about his retirement?

"J.G.," said Brenda, herself looking unusually glum, "I've got some news."

"Marvelous!" thought Jumbo sarcastically to himself. "She knows. It doesn't get any worse than this."

"I don't know how to tell you. I've thought long and hard," Brenda forged ahead in a breathless rush. "I'm leaving. I've got an offer—me and the whole gang—an offer we can't refuse." Somehow, Brenda thought, saying "we" made the whole thing less personal.

"Huh?" said Jumbo stupidly, still thinking about the notice, open in his hand. Brenda's words refused to arrange themselves in any meaningful way. "What?" he almost repeated himself, a dazed look on his face. It was his look, more than anything, that caused Brenda to stop her headlong recitation. Looking down she noticed the letter Jumbo was holding. Reaching out and taking it from his unresisting hand, she quickly scanned the page, and, much to Jumbo's amazement, let out an uncharacteristically girlish "Yowza!"

"This is soooo cool. Things couldn't get any better!" Brenda ran on in a completely different direction now. "I just didn't know how to tell you, and I knew you'd never leave the 'Joint,' but this is a really, really big opportunity. I talked it over with the whole gang. We can't pass it up. And all of us agree, we'd like you to come with us and head up the effort."

"Huh?" said Jumbo, still stupidly.

"Oh," Brenda went on, "I almost forgot. We all pitched in and got you this." From behind her back she produced a package, wrapped with a bow. "It was going to be a 'going-away' present, but now that you're coming with us"—somehow that had become an inevitable occurrence in Brenda's mind—"it seems almost prescient."

"What's 'prescient' mean?" asked Jumbo, a little warily, as he tore away the wrapping paper to reveal a truly Jumbo-sized black leather jacket. Turning it over he saw the legend, emblazoned with rhinestones:

The Leader of the Pachs

Continued...

THE CODER'S CODA Continued...

...time passes...

Jumbo stood, his laptop in its vinyl leopard-print case slung carelessly across his shoulder, and held his arm out for Zenia. The late afternoon sun shone through the thatched shutters and glinted off the empty table tops, strangely clean and arranged as if awaiting the evening crowd. He felt, or at least he thought he should feel, a little sad. But, as he turned to Zenia, he was not surprised to feel an entirely different set of emotions: elation and euphoria. Zenia grinned back at him—a stunning, wild smile—and together she and Jumbo raised their trunks to face the setting sun.

Miles away, stowing the last package of freeze-dried, instant Licorice-Lime mix into the minivan, Brenda heard the trumpeting note as it carried on the breeze, and smiled to herself. "I'm sure glad we have Jumbo on our side," she said to herself as she settled into the driver's seat and headed over to the Java Joint for the last time. "Those other guys don't have a prayer."

Pulling the map down from its hiding place behind the visor, she unfolded it and handed it to Jumbo as he got into the passenger seat. "You can navigate," she said. Jumbo strapped himself in, turned to make sure Zenia was comfortable, and only then focused his attention on the map. He snorted. "What kind of strange name is 'Redmond'?" he asked no one in particular.

Even those who know only a little about Java have heard about Java's ability to make Web pages sing and dance. So far, the vocal and jitterbugging skills of your Java programs have resembled those of Frankenstein more than those of Fred Astaire. However, in this chapter you'll learn how to teach your programs the "Monster Mash." Frankie is really quite light on his feet once he discovers he's not the wallflower he thought himself to be. And can he ever sing the blues!

In this chapter you'll learn

- How to use color to enliven your applets and applications
- How to create a subclass of `Canvas` that gives you a place to draw figures and text
- How to use the `paint( )`, `repaint( )`, and `update( )` methods to maintain the integrity of your artwork
- How to draw text and figures
- How to include images on your applet or application window
- How to add a soundtrack or sound effects to your applet or application
- How to add a menu to your application

Colors

Scientists tell us that most elephants do not perceive color—their view of the world is that of a 1940s *film noir*, entirely black and white. Fortunately, Java was designed for human use and provides a simple model for specifying colors that lets your programs display everything from rainbows to rhinestones.

If you've studied art or disassembled a color TV, you know that it's possible to generate any color by combining just three fundamental colors in proper proportions. Starting with only red, green, and blue you can make brown, violet, fuchsia, or mauve—you can even make heliotrope if you have the urge.

COLOR MECHANICS

To accomplish this feat in your Java programs, you use the AWT class `Color`. The `Color` class, which you met briefly in your previous Java forays, has two constructors. One allows you to specify levels of the fundamental colors using `int` values ranging from 0 to 255. Another lets you specify them using `float` values from 0.0F to 1.0F, which represent the relative amount of each color. Table 11-1 summarizes the `Color` constructors.

TABLE 11-1
PUBLIC CONSTRUCTORS OF THE `Color` CLASS

```
Color (int red, int green, int blue)
Color (float red, float green, float blue)
```

A number of popular colors are included as `static final` constants of the `Color` class. These constants are collected in Table 11-2. Using the `Color` constructors and constants is easy. For example, any of the following could be used to create a `Color` variable and initialize it with the color red:

```
Color a = new Color(255, 0, 0);
Color b = new Color(1.0F, 0.0F, 0.0F);
Color c = Color.red;
```

TABLE 11-2
COLOR CONSTANTS

black
blue
cyan
darkGray
gray
green

Table continued...

TABLE 11-2 COLOR CONSTANTS CONTINUED…

lightGray
magenta
orange
pink
red
white
yellow

The `Color` class also lets you analyze a `Color` object to obtain the values of each of the three fundamental colors. The methods used are summarized in Table 11-3. Each returns an `int` from 0 to 255.

TABLE 11-3
KEY `public` METHODS OF THE `Color` CLASS

METHOD	FUNCTION
`int getBlue( )`	Return the blue component of the `Color`.
`int getGreen( )`	Return the green component of the `Color`.
`int getRed( )`	Return the red component of the `Color`.

COLOR AT WORK

Listing 11-1 shows the `Colors` applet, which lets you experiment by combining the fundamental colors in various proportions to generate interesting colors. `Colors` was built as an "appletcation" allowing you to run the `Colors` program as an applet, using either Appletviewer or your Web browser, or as an application, using the Java interpreter. You'll see how this was done shortly. Figure 11-1 shows the program running in all three environments.

The `Colors` applet gives you a pair of "up" (+) and "down" (−) buttons for each of the three fundamental colors. Every time you press one of the buttons, the background color of the applet is changed by use of the `setBackground( )` method. The value of each of the three fundamental colors is displayed in a separate `TextField` so you can jot down the numbers and re-create colors you find pleasing. Note that each time the button is pressed, the color value changes by 16. If the value were changed by only 1, the resulting color change would generally be imperceptible, and it would take a long time to travel from the minimum value (0) to the maximum value (255). The step value of 16 was chosen as a compromise between the speed with which colors are changed and the variety of colors possible. If you'd prefer a different compromise, just change the value of the `STEP` variable to something other than 16. You can also type a specific value into each of the `TextField`s shown on the screen, and see the resulting swatch displayed below when you press ENTER.

COLOR CONFUSION

You may be dismayed to find out that your brand new super-gonzo monitor with 16 gazillion colors does not, in fact, display all of the colors you might expect. As a matter of fact, you may see a great difference between running the applet through your browser and running the same applet as an application. Moreover, display adapters and monitors do not all render colors consistently. The color red on one system may be a little darker than on another. It might even contain a little green or blue. If your program requires precise rendering of colors, you shouldn't count on it working portably on various systems. The fault, of course, is not with Java—it arises from the variety of hardware and software that might be found on the "other end" of your program. Many systems restrict the range of available colors in the interest of efficiency.

Listing 11-1 Colors.java

```java
// Illustrates the use of the Color class
import java.applet.*;
import java.awt.*;
import java.awt.event.*;

public class Colors extends Applet implements ActionListener
{
    ColorControl[] control = new ColorControl[3];

    public Colors()
    {
        setLayout( new GridLayout(6,1) );

        control[0] = new ColorControl( "Red" );
        control[1] = new ColorControl( "Green" );
        control[2] = new ColorControl( "Blue" );

        for (int i = 0; i < 3; i++)
        {
            add( control[i] );
        }
    }

    public void actionPerformed( ActionEvent theEvent )
    {
        Color c = new Color( control[0].getValue(),
                             control[1].getValue(),
                             control[2].getValue() );

        setBackground( c );
        repaint();
    }

    public static void main(String arg[])
    {
        Colors theApp = new Colors( );

        AppletFrame af = ⇐
           new AppletFrame(theApp, "The Colors Applet");
```

```
            af.add( theApp, "Center" );
            af.setSize( 200, 300 );
            af.setVisible( true );
            theApp.init( );
            theApp.start( );
        }
    }

class ColorControl extends Applet implements ActionListener
{
    final static int STEP = 16;

    private Label name;
    private int    value   = 255;
    private TextField input = new TextField( "255" );
    private Button upButton = new Button( " + " );
    private Button dnButton = new Button( " - " );

    public int getValue() { return value; }

    public ColorControl( String s )
    {
        setLayout( new GridLayout(1,4) );
        name = new Label( s );

        add( name );
        add( input );
        add( upButton );
        add( dnButton );
        input.addActionListener(this);
        upButton.addActionListener(this);
        dnButton.addActionListener(this);
    }

    public void actionPerformed(ActionEvent theEvent)
    {
        value = Integer.parseInt(input.getText());

        if (theEvent.getSource( ) == upButton)
            value+=(value + STEP > 255 ? 0 : STEP);
        if (theEvent.getSource( ) == dnButton)
            value-=(value - STEP < 0 ? 0 : STEP);

        input.setText( "" + value );
        ((ActionListener) getParent( )) ⇐
          .actionPerformed(theEvent);
    }
}

class AppletFrame extends Frame implements WindowListener
{
    Applet theApplet;

    public AppletFrame(Applet anyApplet, String title)
    {
        super(title);
        theApplet = anyApplet;
        addWindowListener(this);
```

continued on next page

continued from previous page

```
        }
        public void windowClosed       (WindowEvent e) { }
        public void windowClosing      (WindowEvent e) { ⇐
          quitApplication( ); }
        public void windowDeiconified (WindowEvent e) { }
        public void windowIconified    (WindowEvent e) { }
        public void windowOpened       (WindowEvent e) { }
        public void windowActivated    (WindowEvent e) { }
        public void windowDeactivated (WindowEvent e) { }

        public void quitApplication( )
        {
            setVisible( false );
            theApplet.setVisible( false );
            theApplet.stop( );
            theApplet.destroy( );
            dispose( );
            System.exit(0);
        }

    }
```

HOW Colors WORKS

As mentioned, Colors is an unfamiliar type of Java program: an appletcation. An appletcation is simply an applet, along with some "scaffolding" code that allows the applet to be run as an application. You can run Colors using Appletviewer (see Figure 11-1), a browser, or the Java interpreter. You'll see the details of how this is accomplished in a moment. For now, let's focus on the "bread and butter" of the program.

Colors uses three classes: the Colors class, and the helper classes ColorControl and AppletFrame. Each color—red, green, and blue—is controlled by a different

FIGURE 11-1

Running the Colors "appletcation"

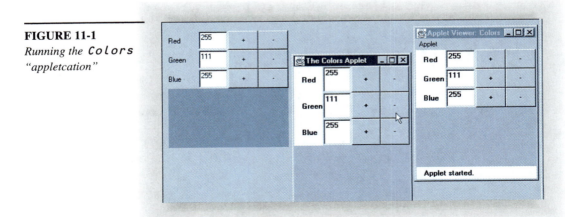

ColorControl object. The Colors program puts three of these ColorControl objects on the screen and retrieves the appropriate color value from each of them when the user makes a change by pressing the increase/decrease button, or by typing in a new value and pressing ENTER. Once the program retrieves the values from each control, the applet combines the three pieces to form a new Color object and then uses that object to repaint the applet in that color.

The ColorControl Class

Each ColorControl object has five fields:

- The Label name will hold a String—red, green, or blue—to let the user know which control to manipulate.

- The int field value holds the numeric value for each ColorControl—from 0 to 255—and is initially set to 255.

- The TextField named input displays the current value as a String. It can act as either an input area—as it is named—or as an output area when the value of the ColorControl is changed by pressing the appropriate button. Like the value field, it is set to reflect a value of 255.

- The two Button objects, upButton and dnButton, allow the user to change the value of each ColorControl by clicking, rather than by typing in a new value.

In addition to these fields, the ColorControl class has three methods: a constructor, an actionPerformed( ) method, and an accessor method that allows the users of the ColorControl class to retrieve the appropriate value. To preserve encapsulation, all of ColorControl's fields are private, and only the getValue( ) method allows access to its data. Since the constructor and actionPerformed( ) methods are more complex than the getValue( ) method, we'll need to look at them a little more closely.

- The constructor, ColorControl( ), takes a single argument, which is used to identify the name of the control. The constructor then establishes a GridLayout of four columns, and the name, input, upButton, and dnButton components are added in that order.

- The actionPerformed( ) method has four steps. In the first step, the value field is updated by retrieving the text from the field input, by way of the getText( ) method. Next, both upButton and dnButton are checked to see if either was the source of the event. If so, then the value field is increased or decreased by the amount defined in the static final field STEP. Note the use of the conditional operator to restrict the range of value to 0–255. Next, value is once again translated back into text—this time by the simple expedient of using String arithmetic—and then placed back in the input field. Last, the actionPerformed( ) method forwards the ActionEvent to its parent, notifying the parent that an event has occurred.

The Colors Class

The Colors applet has a single data field, the array named control, which will contain three ColorControl objects. In addition, the applet contains three methods: a constructor, an actionPerformed( ) method, and—because Colors is an appletcation—a main( ) method. Let's look at the main( ) method first, before returning to the other two.

☞ When you look at the main( ) method of Colors, you may think, "Boy, that appletcation thing looks a whole lot more complicated than a plain old applet. What's going on in there?" You're right. An appletcation has to contain code to do the things that your Web browser normally does. That includes sending init( ) and start( ) messages to your applet, as well as providing a place for your applet to live. The main( ) method in Colors creates a Colors object and an AppletFrame object, and then proceeds to add the applet to the AppletFrame. The frame is then displayed, and the applet messages, init( ) and start( ), are sent to the applet. In an appletcation, the main( ) method needs to do all of the work that your browser would normally do for the applet, including calling the applet life-cycle methods.

☞ The constructor method, Colors( ), begins by setting its layout to a GridLayout one column wide and six rows high. It then proceeds to create and add three new ColorControl objects, one each for red, green, and blue. The references to these ColorControl objects are stored in the array named control. Although only three controls are being added to the applet, the layout was made six rows high. Why? The remaining three rows of space—roughly half the height of the applet—will be used to display the color as the user changes the color values.

☞ The last method, actionPerformed( ), performs three tasks. First, a new Color object is created by retrieving the value of each control, by use of getValue( ). Next, the background color of the applet—the three rows not covered with ColorControls—is set to the new color, by use of the setBackground( ) method. Finally, by invoking the repaint( ) method, the applet is asked to redisplay itself.

The AppletFrame Class

The third and final class inside the Colors applet is called AppletFrame, which provides a suitable host environment for an applet run outside Appletviewer or a browser. The AppletFrame class was written as a separate class to make it easier for you to use it to convert your own applets into appletcations. Let's take this class apart so you can see what it does.

The `AppletFrame` class is structured like this:

```
class AppletFrame extends Frame
{
    // Fields (attributes)
    // Constructor method
    // Event handler method
}
```

The `AppletFrame` class is an extension of the `Frame` class provided in the Java AWT class library, which you'll meet in more detail in Chapter 12, "The AWT: Containers, Components, and Layout Managers." There are three parts inside the `AppletFrame` class. First, there is a field, of type `Applet`, called `theFrame`. The whole point of having the `AppletFrame` is to hold an `Applet`. The second part of the `AppletFrame` class is the constructor method. The `AppletFrame( )` constructor will be invoked when you want to build an `AppletFrame` object. Finally, the last part of the `AppletFrame` class is a method to handle events, or interactions with the user. Again, because the `AppletFrame` class is replacing the browser when your appletcation is run through the interpreter, it must handle the events that would normally be handled by your browser, and it must pass them on to your applet.

The constructor for the `AppletFrame` class, which has the same name as its class—like all constructors—looks like this:

```
public AppletFrame(Applet anyApplet, String title)
{
    super(title);
    theApplet = anyApplet;
}
```

To construct an `AppletFrame` object, you must provide it with an `Applet` object, which it stores as a field. It will use this object reference to communicate with the applet contained inside the frame. In addition to the applet, the `AppletFrame` constructor also needs to receive a `String` argument. `AppletFrame` takes this `String` argument and passes it to its parent, `Frame`, where it is typically used to decorate the title bar. This "pass-up" is done by calling the `super( )` method, which really isn't a method at all. Calling `super( )`, which is only valid inside a constructor, is simply a way of saying "Call my parent's constructor." In addition to the `Applet` field and the constructor, the `AppletFrame` class also implements the `WindowListener` interface, making it possible to close the applet and its frame by clicking on the Close icon in the window title bar.

To convert any of your existing applets to an appletcation, you can follow the same pattern. Create a `main( )` method for your applet, and then use the `AppletFrame` helper class. You will then be able to execute your applet under control of the Java interpreter.

What Are Canvases and Graphics?

Learning to specify colors is sort of like getting a set of oil paints as a gift. Without a canvas and brush, there's only so much you can do with them—and most of those things will get you sent to your room without any dinner. The good news is that Java provides canvases free for the asking; the `Canvas` is an AWT component specifically designed for drawing. Not only that, Java even provides you with some of the skill you might lack. Whether you can draw a straight line or not, Java's resident artist—Jacques the `Graphics` guy—is there to do your bidding, with a plethora of methods for drawing lines and shapes.

Java's `Canvas` object is an appropriate place for you to create your masterpieces, so let's dive right in. Listing 11-2 shows the `CanvasExample` applet, which creates three canvases, each in a different color. Like the real article, Java's `Canvas`es need shape and form if they're to be of any use. To give them shape and form, the `CanvasExample` applet creates a subclass called `PlainCanvas` that implements the methods `getMinimumSize( )` and `getPreferredSize( )`. These are special methods that let the applet know how much space to set aside for a `PlainCanvas` when one is added to the applet by use of the `add( )` method. If you were to try to use a `Canvas` directly, without subclassing it, it would be zero pixels high and zero pixels wide. Though you could add it to the applet, you'd be unable to see it.

Like other AWT components, the `Canvas` has a rectangular shape, so specifying the size of a `PlainCanvas` simply involves setting its height and width. These are given by a `Dimension` object. A `Dimension` object contains two `public` variables of type `int`, called `height` and `width`. That means if you had a `Dimension` object named `dim`, you could use it like this:

```
dim.height = 50;
dim.width = 100;
```

There are three constructors for the `Dimension` class—these are summarized in Table 11-4. The second of these three forms is the one used in the `CanvasExample` applet, setting both the width and height of the `PlainCanvas` to 50 pixels.

The familiar `setBackground( )` method is used to change the background color of each `PlainCanvas`. Figure 11-2 shows the applet itself running.

TABLE 11-4
PUBLIC CONSTRUCTORS OF THE `Dimension` CLASS

```
Dimension( )
Dimension(int width, int height)
Dimension(Dimension d)
```

Listing 11-2 CanvasExample.java

```java
// Demonstrates using and extending the Canvas class
import java.applet.*;
import java.awt.*;

public class CanvasExample extends Applet
{
    PlainCanvas redCanvas   = new PlainCanvas();
    PlainCanvas greenCanvas = new PlainCanvas();
    PlainCanvas blueCanvas  = new PlainCanvas();

    public CanvasExample()
    {
        add( redCanvas );
        add( greenCanvas );
        add( blueCanvas );
        redCanvas.setBackground  ( Color.red );
        greenCanvas.setBackground( Color.green );
        blueCanvas.setBackground ( Color.blue );
    }
}

class PlainCanvas extends Canvas
{
    public Dimension getMinimumSize()
    {
        return new Dimension(50, 50);
    }

    public Dimension getPreferredSize()
    {
        return getMinimumSize();
    }
}
```

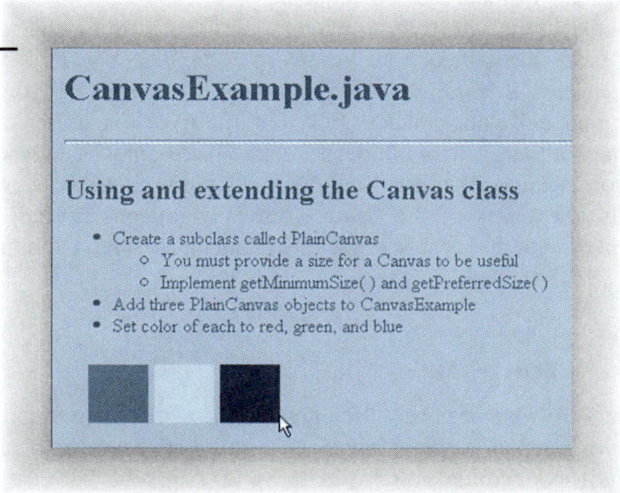

FIGURE 11-2

Running the
CanvasExample
applet

THE paint( ), repaint( ), AND update( ) METHODS

Now that you can set up a Canvas and choose its background color, you're ready to learn to draw. Drawing on a canvas requires the cooperation of three distinct methods: paint( ), repaint( ), and update( ). When you subclass a Canvas, your subclass will inherit the default implementation of each of these methods. The default implementations of repaint( ) and update( ) may work just fine the way they are, but it's always necessary for you to override the default implementation of the paint( ) method if you want to draw on your Canvas.

Whenever the AWT wants to redraw your Canvas, it will invoke the paint( ) method. Why would the AWT want to redraw *your* Canvas, you ask? Well, say you minimize the applet that contains your Canvas and then restore it. Obviously, it must be redrawn on the screen. The same thing happens if you move a window in front of your applet and then move it away. The applet is no longer obscured by the other window; the applet and the Canvas it contains must be redrawn. Such things happen often on a typical desktop.

ASSIGNING RESPONSIBILITY

Whose job is it to redraw the Canvas? A compromise was worked out by the designers of Java. On the one hand, the AWT doesn't know what you want to draw on your Canvas, so *it* can't redraw it. On the other hand, you *don't* want to be forced to include code in your program to handle such routine events as minimizing and restoring windows. You could end up writing more code to handle these routine events than you write to handle "real" functions.

The compromise works as shown in Figure 11-3: You promise to put all your drawing statements inside a method called paint( ). In return, the AWT frees you from the burden of dealing with routine window events, by promising to call your paint( ) method whenever it needs to redraw your Canvas. You also promise never to call paint( ) yourself. Instead, you agree to call repaint( ) if you ever need to change the appearance of your Canvas. This gives the AWT exclusive control of the paint( ) method and allows it to avoid debacles like half-painted Canvases. Observe the terms of this contract and all will be well. Violate its terms, and problems inevitably follow.

Happily, the terms of the compromise are gracious indeed. It's easy to call the repaint( ) method, because it has no arguments. Inside your applet you could use

```
repaint()
```

to repaint your applet or

```
MyCanvas.repaint()
```

to repaint only your subclassed Canvas called MyCanvas. Of course, you only need to repaint your applet if you want to change its appearance in some way, perhaps by changing its background color as in the Colors applet.

FIGURE 11-3
The AWT painting contract

DEALING WITH paint( )

The `paint( )` method is not quite as simple as the `repaint( )` method, but it's still pretty straightforward. To draw text or figures, you first have to have an object that knows how to draw and that has the requisite tools. Fortunately, Java provides you such an object in the form of the `Graphics` class, which encapsulates things like the current font and line color and has methods for drawing text and figures. Even better, when the AWT calls the `paint( )` method, it knows you're going to need a painter, so it provides the appropriate `Graphics` object as an argument. All you need to do is define the `paint( )` method and include in its body the drawing statements that create the picture you want:

```
public void paint(Graphics g)
{
    // your drawing statements go here
}
```

UPDATING YOUR DISPLAY

What about the `update( )` method, the third member of the `paint( )`, `repaint( )`, `update( )` trio? This method is called by the AWT every time you call the `repaint( )`

method. The default implementation of `update( )` provided by Java simply erases the background with the proper color and then calls `paint( )` like this:

```
public void update(Graphics g)
{
    g.setColor( getBackground() );
    g.fillRect( 0, 0, width, height );
    g.setColor( getForeground() );
    paint( g );
}
```

Notice how `update( )` sends the `setColor( )` and `fillRect( )` messages to the `Graphics` object. The `setColor( )` method sets the current color used for drawing, and the `fillRect( )` method draws a solid rectangle the size of the entire component being painted, whether that's an applet, a `Canvas`, or something else. It then sets the proper foreground color, again using `setColor( )`.

What's unusual about `update( )` is that, although it's called by the AWT in response to your `repaint( )` message, it's not necessarily called immediately. Sometimes a program will call `repaint( )` repeatedly during a short interval. Because each call to `update( )` paints the background color over the result of the previous call to `update( )`, only the most recent call leaves a visible image. In such a case the AWT will discard pending calls to `update( )` and perform only the last one in the sequence. This saves processing time without changing the final result. As you'll see later, there are some occasions when this behavior has some undesirable side effects, so it's important that you know what's going on behind the scenes. But usually you can work with just `paint( )` and `repaint( )` without concern for `update( )`, which quietly and efficiently goes about its business. If you *don't* want to clear the entire window every time you get a `paint( )` message, then you must override `update( )`.

Painting Text on Your Window

Let's try painting some text. Listing 11-3 shows the `StackedText` applet, and Figure 11-4 shows how the applet looks as it runs. The applet uses the `drawString( )` method to paint the text. As required by the AWT, the `drawString( )` method is called inside the `paint( )` method, and the `repaint( )` method is called whenever the appearance of the applet is changed. The `drawString( )` method, as you might recall from Chapter 4, "Simply Methods: One Step at a Time," takes three arguments: a `String` containing the text to be drawn, the `x` (horizontal) position at which the text is to be drawn, and the `y` (vertical) position at which the text is to be drawn. Figure 11-5 shows how the drawing coordinate system works.

Listing 11-3 StackedText.java

```
// Demonstrates use of FontMetrics
import java.applet.*;
import java.awt.*;
import java.awt.event.*;
```

```java
public class StackedText extends Applet ⇐
  implements ActionListener
{
    // Strings to display
    private String line1 = "Once upon a midnight dreary,";
    private String line2 = ⇐
      "While I pondered, weak and weary . . . .";

    // Buttons and labels
    private Button fontButton    = new Button("Font");
    private Button sizeButton    = new Button("Size");
    private Button metricsButton = new Button("Metrics");
    private Label  metricsLabel  = new Label("Off");

    // Font families and sizes
    Font[]  fonts = { new Font("TimesRoman", Font.PLAIN, 10),
                      new Font("Helvetica", Font.PLAIN, 10),
                      new Font("Courier", Font.PLAIN, 10)
                    };

    int[]   fontSizes = { 10, 12, 14, 18 };

    int font     = 0;
    int fontSize = 0;
    boolean metrics = false;

    public void init()
    {
        setBackground( Color.yellow );
        add( fontButton );
        add( sizeButton );
        add( metricsButton );
        add( metricsLabel );
        fontButton.addActionListener(this);
        sizeButton.addActionListener(this);
        metricsButton.addActionListener(this);
    }

    public void actionPerformed(ActionEvent theEvent)
    {
        if (theEvent.getSource( ) == fontButton)
        {
            if ( font == fonts.length - 1 ) font = 0;
            else ++font;
        }

        if (theEvent.getSource( ) == sizeButton)
        {
            if ( fontSize == fontSizes.length -1 ) ⇐
                fontSize = 0;
            else ++fontSize;

            fonts[font] = new Font( fonts[font].getName(),
                                    Font.PLAIN,
                                    fontSizes[fontSize]);
        }

        if(theEvent.getSource( ) == metricsButton)
```

continued on next page

continued from previous page

```
            {
                metrics = ! metrics;
                metricsLabel.setText( metrics ? "On" : "Off" );
            }
            repaint();
        }

        public void paint(Graphics g)
        {
            Point origin1 = new Point(10, 100);
            Point origin2 = new Point(origin1.x, origin1.y + 10);

            g.setColor(Color.black);
            g.setFont(fonts[font]);

            if (metrics)
            {
                FontMetrics fm = g.getFontMetrics();
                origin1.x = (getSize().width - ⇐
                  fm.stringWidth(line1)) / 2;
                origin2.x = (getSize().width -⇐
                  fm.stringWidth(line2)) / 2;
                origin2.y = origin1.y + fm.getHeight();
            }

            g.drawString(line1, origin1.x, origin1.y);
            g.drawString(line2, origin2.x, origin2.y);
        }
    }
```

FIGURE 11-4

Running the
StackedText
applet

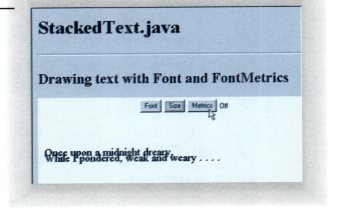

FIGURE 11-5

The drawing coordinate system

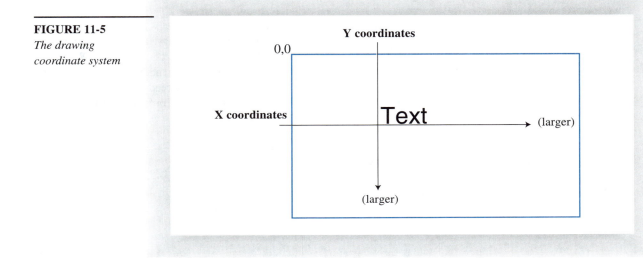

INSIDE StackedText

When you run the StackedText applet, you will notice three buttons and a label across the top of the screen. In the center of the screen, two lines from Edgar Allan Poe's "The Raven" are drawn, slightly offset from each other. The user can choose to see this excerpt displayed in any of three typefaces, which are stored in the array named fonts:

```
Font[]  fonts = { new Font("TimesRoman", Font.PLAIN, 10),
                  new Font("Helvetica", Font.PLAIN, 10),
                  new Font("Courier", Font.PLAIN, 10)
               };
```

When the user presses the Font button, the index variable, font, is incremented unless it is pointing to the last element in the array, in which case the index is simply set back to zero. This is accomplished by using the following lines in the actionPerformed( ) method:

```
if (theEvent.target == fontButton)
{
    if ( font == fonts.length - 1 ) font = 0;
    else ++font;
}
```

Each typeface can also be displayed in any of three sizes. These sizes are stored in the array fontSizes, which is indexed by use of the integer variable fontSize.

```
int[]   fontSizes = { 10, 12, 14, 18 };
```

> *" To draw text or figures, you first must have an object that knows how to draw and that has the requisite tools. "*

Naming the array and its index variable with similar names helps ensure that you don't forgetfully use the wrong index variable with the wrong array. If you had chosen to call your index variables i and j, it would be much easier to confuse them. When the user presses the Size button, the `actionPerformed( )` method increments the `fontSize` subscript, setting the number back to zero if it is already on the last element. Then a new `Font` object is created and stored in the current fonts array, by use of the newly specified size:

```
if (theEvent.target == sizeButton)
{
    if ( fontSize == fontSizes.length -1 ) fontSize = 0;
    else ++fontSize;

    fonts[font] = new Font( fonts[font].getName(),
                            Font.PLAIN,
                            fontSizes[fontSize]);
}
```

Notice that when the new `Font` is created, it calls the `Font.getName( )` method to retrieve the name of the current `Font` object.

INTRODUCING THE FontMetrics CLASS

The `StackedText` applet lets the user select various fonts and sizes with which to draw text, but it also includes a third button which controls *how* the text string is placed on the applet window. It does this by defining two *modes*. In the first mode, the two lines of text are drawn at fixed positions, one 10 pixels below the other:

```
Point origin1 = new Point(10, 100);
Point origin2 = new Point(origin1.x, origin1.y + 10);
```

These locations are represented by using `Points`. A `Point` object is an object that contains two `public` fields that can store x,y coordinates. Appropriately, the fields are called x and y. Here, two `Point` objects are created: The first contains the coordinates (10, 100), and the second has the vertical (y) coordinate increased by 10. When the applet first draws the text in a small 10-point font, everything looks just fine. But try increasing the font size, as shown in Figure 11-4. As you can see, using such fixed positions doesn't work really well when a large font is used to draw the text: The lines can overlap one another if the letters are too large. To fix that, the applet also has a second mode, in which special font information is used to better position the lines.

In this second mode, font information is obtained by use of the `getFontMetrics( )` method. This method supplies you with a `FontMetrics` object that you can use to find useful information about the characteristics of the current font. Figure 11-6 illustrates these key characteristics that can be discovered by using the methods of the `FontMetrics` class.

FIGURE 11-6
FontMetrics

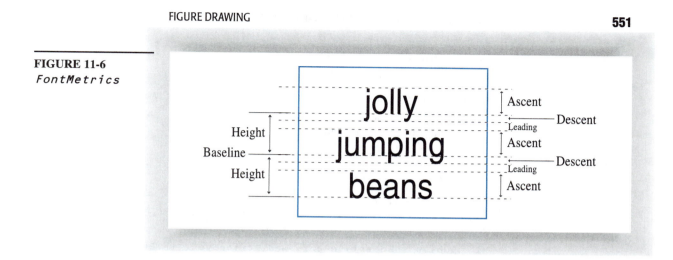

One useful method provided by the `FontMetrics` class is `stringWidth( )`, which returns the number of pixels needed to draw a given text string in the font described by the `FontMetrics` object. The `StackedText` applet uses the `FontMetrics` information to center the text within the applet window.

```
FontMetrics fm = g.getFontMetrics();
origin1.x = (getSize().width - fm.stringWidth(line1)) / 2;
origin2.x = (getSize().width - fm.stringWidth(line2)) / 2;
origin2.y = origin1.y + fm.getHeight();
```

The `getSize()` method returns a `Dimension` object (such as you saw in the `CanvasExample` applet), which has a `height` and `width` field. The call to `getSize( )` used here returns the dimensions of the applet. The `FontMetrics` method, `getHeight( )`, is used to vertically position the lines so they are properly spaced, regardless of the size of the font.

Figure Drawing

Drawing lines and figures is even easier than drawing text. Listing 11-4 shows the `Figures` applet, which decorates its screen with rectangles, ovals, and arcs. The applet includes a button named "Draw," which is used to select from four different pictures. Each picture also includes the previous picture: Picture number 4 is an all-inclusive picture that includes pictures 1 through 3, plus some arcs. Figure 11-7 shows how this masterpiece looks when it runs, but you really won't get the full effect unless you run it yourself.

```
Listing 11-4 Figures.java
// Illustrates drawing figures and text
import java.applet.*;
import java.awt.*;
```

continued on next page

continued from previous page

```java
import java.awt.event.*;

public class Figures extends Applet implements ActionListener
{
    int drawingNumber = 0;
    final static int MAX_NUM = 4;

    Button theButton = new Button("Draw");

    public void init()
    {
        add(theButton);
        theButton.addActionListener(this);
    }

    public void actionPerformed(ActionEvent theEvent)
    {
        drawingNumber =(drawingNumber == MAX_NUM ? 0 : ⇐
          drawingNumber + 1);
        repaint();
    }

    public void paint(Graphics g)
    {
        if ( drawingNumber > 0 )
        {
            g.setColor(Color.red);
            g.drawRect(100, 25, 100, 100);
            g.fillRect(150, 50, 100, 100);
        }

        if ( drawingNumber > 1 )
        {
            g.setColor(Color.green);
            g.drawRoundRect(200,  75, 100, 100, 50, 50);
            g.fillRoundRect(250, 100, 100, 100, 50, 50);
        }

        if ( drawingNumber > 2 )
        {
            g.setColor(Color.blue);
            g.drawOval(300, 125, 100, 200);
            g.fillOval(350, 150, 200, 100);
        }

        if ( drawingNumber > 3 )
        {
            g.setColor(Color.yellow);
            g.drawArc(400, 200, 100, 100,   0, 180);
            g.fillArc(450, 250, 100, 100, 180, 270);
        }
    }
}
```

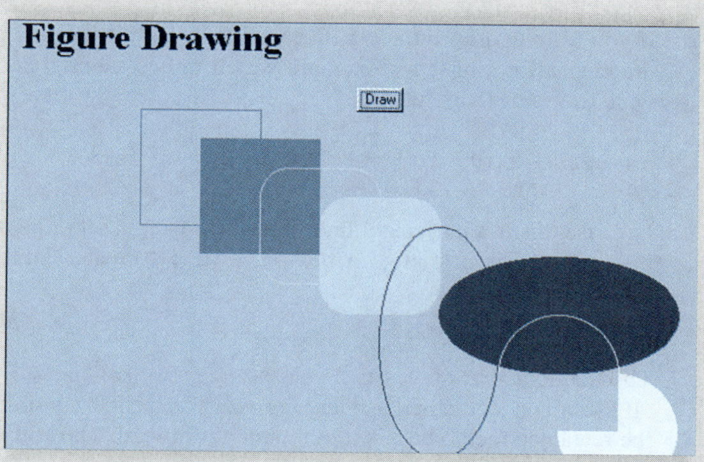

FIGURE 11-7
*The Figures applet
at play*

THE BOUNDARIES OF ART

The `Figures` applet illustrates the use of several of the drawing methods provided by the `Graphics` class. You can divide these drawing methods into three general categories:

☕ Methods that draw lines or unclosed figures.

☕ Methods that draw simple closed figures such as rectangles and ovals. These figures can be drawn as outlines—with `drawRect( )` and `drawOval( )`—or they can be drawn as solid, filled figures—with `fillRect( )` and `fillOval( )`. To draw a filled rectangle that also has an outline, you will need to first call `fillRect( )` to draw the filled portion, and then `drawRect( )` to draw the border. Normally you will also have to change the drawing color between these calls to make sure the border is visible. Other figures can be similarly drawn by use of the methods shown in Table 11-5.

☕ Methods that draw complex shapes or polygons.

SIMPLE LINES

The `drawLine( )` method is the simplest of all the drawing methods. It simply draws a line (1 pixel wide) between two points, using the current foreground color. To draw a line between the position `0,0` and `200,200`, you use

```
drawLine( 0, 0, 200, 200 );
```

If you want to draw a thicker line, you have to do it yourself by repeatedly moving and drawing a line, like this example which draws a horizontal line that is three pixels wide from 10,10 to 100,10:

```
drawLine( 10,   9, 100,   9 );
drawLine( 10,  10, 100,  10 );
drawLine( 10,  11, 100,  11 );
```

Because this is a horizontal line, simply drawing a set of parallel lines on either side of the single-pixel line between 10,10 and 100,10 creates a three-pixel-wide line.

CLOSED FIGURES

The methods that draw simple closed figures, drawRect( ), drawOval( ), and so on, all use a concept called a *bounding box* to describe the dimensions of the figure. For the rectangle methods, this is very straightforward: The arguments represent the upper-left corner (x,y) and the height and width of the rectangle. Drawing an oval or circle is a little different, however. When you are drawing an oval, an invisible rectangle is first drawn by use of the x,y, height, and width arguments. The oval itself is then drawn so that it touches this invisible rectangle at the midpoints on each side. To draw a circle, you would specify a bounding rectangle with equal height and width—in other words, a square.

The methods used in the Figures applet, plus several additional methods, are summarized in Table 11-5. Figure 11-8 shows how the parameters of each method are used to determine the position and shape of each figure.

TABLE 11-5
public METHODS OF THE Graphics CLASS USED TO DRAW LINES AND FIGURES

METHOD	FUNCTION
drawLine(int x1, int y1, int x2, int y2)	Draw a line from (x1,y1) to (x2,y2).
drawRect(int x, int y, int width, int height)	Draw a rectangle of specified size at (x,y).
fillRect(int x, int y, int width, int height)	Draw a solid rectangle of specified size at (x,y).

drawRoundRect(int x, int y,
              int height,
              int width,
              int arcwidth,
              int archeight)
	Draw a rectangle with rounded corners of specified size at (x,y). The rounded corners are drawn within a bounding rectangle with width given by arcwidth and height given by archeight.

fillRoundRect(int x, int y,
              int w, int h,
              int arcwidth,
              int archeight)
	Draw a solid rectangle with rounded corners of specified size at (x,y). The rounded corners are drawn within a bounding rectangle with width given by arcwidth and height given by archeight.

Table continued...

TABLE 11-5 `public` METHODS OF THE `Graphics` CLASS USED TO DRAW LINES AND FIGURES CONTINUED...

METHOD	FUNCTION
`drawOval(int x, int y,` `        int width, int height)`	Draw an oval within the given bounding rectangle.
`fillOval(int x, int y,` `        int w, int h)`	Draw a solid oval within the given bounding rectangle.

`drawArc(int x, int y,int width,`
`        int height,int start,`
`        int angle)`
	Draw an arc whose circle is within the given bounding rectangle. The start position and angle of the arc are given in degrees, with clockwise rotation indicated by positive values and counterclockwise rotation indicated by negative values. The 0-degree line is at the 3 o'clock position.

`fillArc(int x, int y,int width,`
`        int height,int start,`
`        int angle)`
	Draw a solid arc whose circle is within the given bounding rectangle. The start position and angle of the arc are given in degrees, with clockwise rotation indicated by positive values and counterclockwise rotation indicated by negative values. The 0-degree line is at the 3 o'clock position.

`drawPolygon(int x[],int y[],int n)`	Draw a polygon, consisting of n points. Each point is indicated by its x and y positions.
`fillPolygon(int x[],int y[],int n)`	Draw a solid polygon, consisting of n points. Each point is indicated by its x and y positions.

The Polygon

A *polygon* is a many-sided figure. Java does not require polygons to be closed figures, your geometry class notwithstanding. Thus, a polygon can be used to render any sort of shape as a series of line segments, similar to the connect-the-dots pictures you created in grade school. To use the `drawPolygon( )` or `fillPolygon( )` methods, you supply two *parallel* arrays. One array should have the horizontal coordinates of all the points, and the other should have the vertical coordinates of all the points. The last argument is the number of elements in each array, which should be identical for both. When called, the `drawPolygon( )` method matches up the points from these two arrays, effectively making a call to

```
drawLine( x[0], y[0], x[1], y[1]);
```

and then following that up with

```
drawLine( x[1], y[1], x[2], y[2]);
```

until all the elements of the arrays have been processed.

FIGURE 11-8

Drawing figures

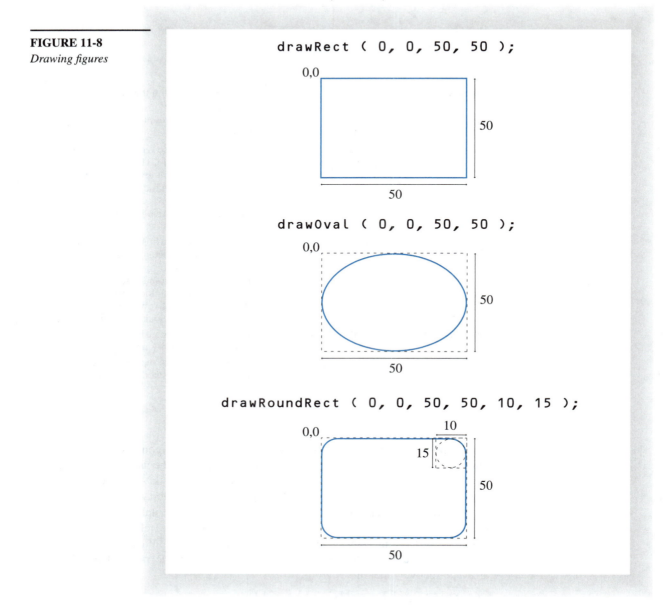

The `drawPolygon()` method and the `fillPolygon()` method can also be used with an argument which is an instance of the `Polygon` class, which encapsulates the number of points of the polygon and the coordinates of its points as public instance variables named `npoints`, `xpoints`, and `ypoints`. The constructors for the `Polygon` class are shown in Table 11-6. The `Polygon` class provides several useful methods, which are summarized in Table 11-7.

TABLE 11-6
public CONSTRUCTORS OF THE Polygon CLASS

```
Polygon( )
Polygon(int [] xpoints, int [] ypoints, int npoints)
```

TABLE 11-7
KEY public METHODS OF THE Polygon CLASS

METHOD	FUNCTION
void addPoint(int x, int y)	Add an additional point to the polygon.
Rectangle getBoundingBox( )	Obtain the bounding rectangle of the polygon.
boolean inside(int x, int y)	Return a value that indicates whether the specified point is inside the polygon.

The PolyGone applet, shown in Listing 11-5 and Figure 11-9, shows how each of these methods can be used. Although polygons are not closed figures in Java, the fillPolygon( ) method will attempt to close the polygon it draws, by connecting the first and last members of the set of points. The PolyGone applet creates several integer arrays that represent screen locations. The arrays headX and headY give the coordinates of a set of points that draw the head of a parrot on the screen. Likewise, the arrays beakX and beakY are the points to draw the parrot's beak. A Polygon object is then created by use of the beakX and beakY arrays. Inside paint( ), both versions of the fillPoly( ) method are used, one for the head and one for the beak of the parrot.

```
Listing 11-5 PolyGone.java
// Illustrates drawing polygons using arrays and Polygon ⇐
    objects
import java.applet.*;
import java.awt.*;
import java.awt.event.*;

public class PolyGone extends Applet implements ActionListener
{
    boolean drawing = false;

    int[] headX ={ 105, 80, 100, 110, 140, 165, 160, 190, ⇐
                   145, 185, 110 };
    int[] headY ={  90, 75,  80,  40,  65,  45,  75,  70, ⇐
                   140, 175, 175 };

    int[] beakX ={ 110, 100,  90,  80,  70,  60,  50,  40, ⇐
                    30,  20,  10,   8,  10,  15,  40,  55, ⇐
                    67,  80,  90, 100,  90,  80,  70,  60, ⇐
                    50,  40,  45,  57,  70,  85, 100, 110, ⇐
                   120,  130, 132 };
```

continued on next page

> *A Java program can support a number of threads, each of which executes independently.*

continued from previous page

```java
        int[] beakY = { 110, 107, 104, 101, 100, 101, 105,  ⇐
                        110,  120, 130, 140,  150, 160, 170, ⇐
                        160, 170, 155, 165, 145, 160, 180, 175, ⇐
                        190, 180, 192, 187, 200, 210, 213,  ⇐
                        213, 210, 205, 200, 175, 170 };
    Polygon theBeak = new Polygon( beakX, beakY,  ⇐
        beakX.length );

    Button   theButton = new Button("Feed Me");

    public void init()
    {
        add(theButton);
        theButton.addActionListener(this);
    }

    public void actionPerformed(ActionEvent theEvent)
    {
        drawing = ! drawing;
        repaint();
    }

    public void paint(Graphics g)
    {
        if ( drawing )
        {
            // Draw head using arrays
            g.setColor(Color.green);
            g.fillPolygon( headX, headY, headX.length );

            // Draw beak using Polygon object
            g.setColor(Color.orange);
            g.fillPolygon( theBeak );

            // Fill in the eyes
            g.setColor(Color.white);
            g.fillOval( 108,  95, 10, 15 );
            g.fillOval( 118,  90, 10, 15 );
            g.setColor(Color.blue);
            g.fillOval( 110, 100, 5, 10 );
            g.fillOval( 120,  95, 5, 10 );
        }
    }
}
```

FIGURE 11-9
Running the
PolyGone applet

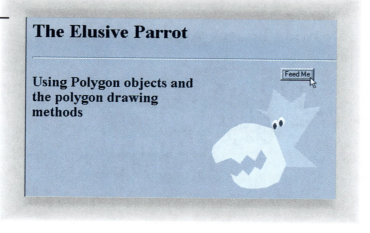

Putting Images on the Screen

In addition to giving you tools for drawing pictures by hand, Java also gives you the ability to display images that have been stored in files using coding schemes supported by Appletviewer or your browser. Among the most popular of these coding schemes are GIF and JPEG. The ShowImage applet, presented in Listing 11-6 and shown running in Figure 11-10, shows you how easy it is to retrieve and display an image stored in a GIF file. (Changing the file name to that of a file containing a JPEG image is all that is necessary to make the applet display a JPEG image instead.)

Listing 11-6 ShowImage.java

```java
// Retrieving and displaying an image
import java.applet.*;
import java.awt.*;

public class ShowImage extends Applet
{
    Image theImage;

    public void init()
    {
        theImage = getImage(getDocumentBase(), "Jumbo.gif");
    }

    public void paint(Graphics g)
    {
        g.drawImage(theImage, 0, 0, this);
        g.drawImage(theImage, 100, 50, this);
        g.drawImage(theImage, 200, 100, this);
    }
}
```

FIGURE 11-10
The ShowImage
applet

The first step in displaying an image is to call the `getImage( )` method, which returns an `Image` object. The form of the `getImage( )` method used here makes it easy to obtain an image stored on the local hard drive, in the same directory as the CLASS file. The `getDocumentBase( )` method returns a URL that refers to this directory. When an image is stored on a server, you can use another form of the `getImage( )` method:

```
Image getImage(URL url)
```

However, to use this form you'll need to know how to create a URL object, a topic you'll study in Chapter 16, "Advanced Topics: Threads and Networking."

Displaying the image is done by use of the `drawImage( )` method, called from within the `paint( )` method. The first parameter to `drawImage( )` specifies the `Image` to be drawn. The second and third parameters give the `x,y` position at which its upper-left corner is to be placed. The fourth parameter specifies the applet itself. This is necessary because of some "handshaking" that occurs while the image is loaded. If the image is large and stored on a server, loading it can take considerable time. In this event, the `drawImage( )` method keeps the applet informed of the progress of loading, using the reference to the applet included as the final parameter. When you try this example yourself, be sure the file `Jumbo.gif` is in the same directory as the file `ShowImage.class`, or the example won't work. Copy the file to the directory if necessary.

Animating Images

It's finally time to make your applet dance, by use of a process called *animation*. Animation is performed by rapidly displaying a sequence of images. When you watch this sequence, your eyes are unable to individually resolve the rapidly changing images, and you perceive the result as motion. Listing 11-7 shows the

`AnimateExample` applet, and Figure 11-11 shows a single animation frame produced by the applet. This is one example that must be run to be understood and appreciated, so be sure you fire up your PC and give this applet a try before reading on.

Listing 11-7 AnimateExample.java

```java
// Simple animation with Java
import java.applet.*;
import java.awt.*;

public class AnimateExample extends Applet implements Runnable
{
    Thread theThread;
    String theString = "Boing!!!";
    int x = 20;
    int y = 20;
    int dx = 1;
    int dy = 1;
    final static int STEP = 5;
    final static int MIN  = 0;
    int maxX  = 0;
    int maxY  = 0;
    int stringTop, stringBottom, stringWidth;

    public void start()
    {
        theThread = new Thread(this);
        theThread.start();
    }

    public void stop()
    {
        if (theThread != null)
            theThread.stop();
        theThread = null;
    }

    public void run()
    {
        while (true)
        {
            x += dx * STEP;
            if (x < MIN || x + stringWidth > maxX) dx *= -1;
            if (x < MIN ) x = MIN;
            if (x + stringWidth > maxX) x = maxX - ⇐
             stringWidth;

            y += dy * STEP;
            if (y - stringTop < MIN || y + stringBottom > ⇐
             maxY) dy *= -1;
            if (y - stringTop < MIN ) y = MIN + stringTop;
            if (y + stringBottom > maxY) y = maxY - ⇐
             stringBottom;

            repaint();
```

continued on next page

continued from previous page

```
                    try { Thread.sleep(30); }
                    catch (InterruptedException interrupted) ⇐
                      { /* null action */ }
            }
    }

    public void paint(Graphics g)
    {
        maxX = getSize().width;
        maxY = getSize().height;
        g.drawString(theString, x, y);
    }
    public void init()
    {
        setFont( new Font("TimesRoman", ⇐
          Font.BOLD+Font.ITALIC, 24));
        setBackground(Color.yellow);
        setForeground(Color.red);

        Graphics g        = getGraphics();
        FontMetrics fm    = getFontMetrics(g.getFont());
        stringWidth       = fm.stringWidth(theString);
        stringTop         = fm.getAscent();
        stringBottom      = fm.getDescent();
    }
  }
```

INSIDE AnimateExample

The AnimateExample applet, like all the applets you have seen to date, starts with the init( ) method. The init( ) method in this program needs to perform two basic tasks. The first task is to set up the visual environment for the applet. This includes selecting the font that will be used for all text painted while the applet is running, and also setting the background and foreground colors for the applet—a nice red text on a yellow background.

FIGURE 11-11

A single animation frame from the AnimateExample *applet*

The second `init()` task is to get some information about the font that has just been created. This requires a `FontMetrics` object, as you saw earlier in this chapter. The problem is, to get a `FontMetrics` object, you need to have a `Graphics` object. Inside the `paint()` method, Java obligingly furnishes you with a `Graphics` object, but inside the `init()` method, you need to get your own by calling the `getGraphics()` method.

Once you get a `Graphics` object, you can use it to get a `FontMetrics` object, here named `fm`. This is used to initialize the `stringWidth`, `stringTop`, and `stringBottom` fields. Remember that when you paint text in Java, the number of pixels any `String` uses depends on the font, size, and characters that the `String` contains. The `stringWidth()` method calculates the width of the `String` (in pixels) for you, taking into account these variables. Likewise, the height of any `String` depends on the font used. Recall that when you use the `drawString()` method to display text, the y coordinate you supply represents the baseline position of the selected font. The height of the characters above and below the baseline can be retrieved by use of the `getAscent()` and `getDescent()` methods.

While this applet probably looks familiar up to this point, the rest of the program introduces several new features. As you noticed when you ran the `AnimateExample` applet, the text string "Boing!!!" is not just painted on the screen, but bounces around as its name suggests. To do this, the applet needs to rapidly redisplay the text in several different locations. To display the images rapidly, the `AnimateExample` applet uses Java's thread capability.

INTRODUCING THREADS

"What," you ask, "is a thread?" One way to think of a program is to compare it to a scavenger hunt. When you start a scavenger hunt, you're given a list of things you need to collect before you can cross the finish line. There are many different paths you could follow to collect all of the items, but you still have to collect them sequentially: first you get one, and then you get another. Now, imagine that, instead of working individually, you were allowed to assemble a team to help you gather the necessary loot. You could put Paul to work finding the Elvis painting on black velvet, while Mary could head uptown to get that salami-on-rye. Each of you would work individually to do one of the tasks necessary to complete the entire task.

Java's threads work something like that. A Java program can support a number of threads, each of which executes independently. On a computer equipped with multiple CPUs, threads can even execute *simultaneously*, but on the pedestrian single-CPU computers most of us presently own, threads simply take turns using the CPU. One useful property of threads is that they make it possible to ensure that very important tasks take priority over less important tasks. This is done by running the important tasks in a separate thread and by giving that thread a high priority. The less important tasks can then run in a thread by themselves and will only use the CPU when more important tasks are idle.

There are several ways to create a thread in Java; you'll see these when you look at threads in more detail in Chapter 16. For now, let's concentrate on the broader issues.

IMPLEMENTING THREADS

If you look at the header for the `AnimateExample` applet, you'll see that it has a new clause in its class header:

```
implements Runnable
```

This is one way you can tell Java that `AnimateExample` can be run as a thread. In addition to this, the applet also contains a field, called `theThread`, which is used to hold a reference to the special thread the applet creates.

Unlike most other applets you've seen, `AnimateExample` includes definitions for the `start( )` and `stop( )` applet life-cycle methods. The `start( )` method uses the `new` operator to create a new thread that uses the data and methods of the applet:

```
public void start()
{
    theThread = new Thread(this);
    theThread.start();
}
```

The newly created thread is then sent a `start` message of its own, which causes it to start executing. What, exactly, does the thread do when you tell it to `start`? Well, what would you do if you were a thread? You'd start running, right? That's exactly what Java's threads do. When you tell a thread to `start`, it immediately looks to its creator—in this case, the applet—and attempts to find a `run( )` method. When it finds it, it starts executing the statements contained inside.

LOOKING AT run( )

The `run( )` method inside `AnimateExample` loops indefinitely, performing its three steps over and over again. The first thing that `run( )` does is update the x and y positions where `theString` will be displayed. It does this by adding the value `STEP` to the x and y fields. It then checks to see if the new values for x or y have wandered past the edge of the screen. If they have, then the direction of change, `dx` or `dy`, is reversed—from 1 to −1 and back. Once the x and y positions have been updated, a `repaint( )` call is issued to redraw the screen. Finally, `run( )` uses the `sleep( )` method, which is a static method of the `Thread` class, to pause for 30 milliseconds after each picture is drawn. This allows about 30 pictures to be drawn each second, which yields smooth animation without drawing more often than is necessary.

Because the `run( )` method loops indefinitely, how does the applet stop? Recall that the applet implements the `stop( )` method, which is called by the browser when the user moves to a new page or when Appletviewer is shut down. In the `stop( )` method, the applet sends the `Thread` a `stop` message, which causes it to cease execution:

```
public void stop()
{
    if (theThread != null)
        theThread.stop();
    theThread = null;
}
```

The applet also sets the field `theThread` to `null`, to avoid any possibility of sending the `stop` message to a `Thread` that's already stopped, because this is treated by Java as an error condition.

Sounding Swell

Now that your applets can "dance," it's time to teach them to "sing" as well. This is done in a manner similar to displaying an image: First a sound object is loaded from a file or a URL, and then the sound object is played. Listing 11-8 shows the `SoundExample` applet, which demonstrates the technique. Of course, if your computer lacks a sound card, this example won't work. Java does not support the PC speaker as an output device.

Listing 11-8 SoundExample.java

```
// Playing sounds in your applet
import java.applet.*;
import java.awt.*;

public class SoundExample extends Applet
{

    AudioClip theClip;

    public void init()
    {
        try
        {
            theClip = getAudioClip(getDocumentBase(), ⇐
                "spacemusic.au");
        }
        catch (Exception e)
        {
            showStatus("Unable to load audio clip.");
        }
    }

    public void start()
    {
        theClip.loop();
    }

    public void stop()
    {
        theClip.stop();
    }
}
```

The `getAudioClip( )` method is used in a fashion similar to the `getImage( )` method of the `ShowImage` applet. Of course, `getAudioClip( )` returns an `AudioClip` object, rather than an `Image`. When you try to load an audio clip, there is always the chance that you will fail—the file might not exist, or some other error may occur. In this example, the `getAudioClip( )` method call is placed inside a `try-catch` block to deal with the possibility that the desired audio file, `spacemusic.au`, cannot be found in the same directory as the CLASS file.

To play an audio file, you use the `loop( )` method; when you tire of the sound, you can use the `stop( )` method to obtain relief. A picture fails to do this applet justice, so you'll have to try it yourself. Be sure the `spacemusic.au` file is in the same directory as the `SoundExample.class` before you begin. This file can be found in the `java\demo\Animator\audio` directory created when you installed the JDK. Of course, you may substitute any other AU file that you prefer.

Adding a Menu to Your Application

Used even more often than animation or sound, menus are a standard feature of GUI applications. Menus are convenient to use because they allow new users to see the operations and choices available in your program, reducing the time it takes them to learn their way around a new application.

The fundamental class used to construct menus in Java is the `MenuBar` class. A `MenuBar` can be attached to a `Frame` by sending the `Frame` a `setMenuBar` message with a parameter that specifies the `MenuBar`, like this:

```
Frame f = new Frame(. . .);
Menubar m = new Menubar();
f.setMenuBar( m );
```

Individual pull-down menus, represented by the class `Menu`, can be added to a `MenuBar`. Each `Menu` consists of a number of items, represented by instances of the `MenuItem` class. There is also a `CheckboxMenuItem`, which can be toggled. Figure 11-12 shows the inheritance hierarchy of the menu-related classes.

MAKING A MENU

Creating a menu is fairly straightforward. A simple example shows how easy adding menus can be. Listing 11-9 shows the SimpleMenuExample application, which adds a simple menu to an application's `Frame`. Figure 11-13 shows this application in action.

FIGURE 11-12

The hierarchy of menu-related classes

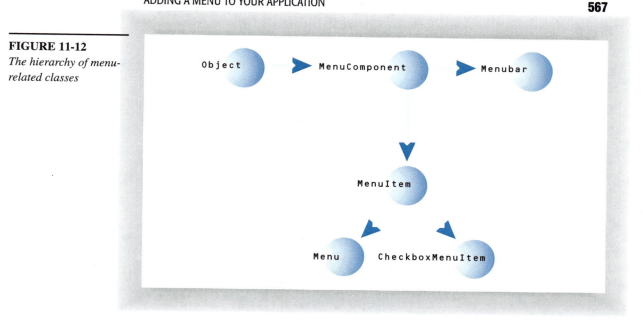

Listing 11-9 SimpleMenuExample.java

```
// Constructing a simple menu
import java.awt.*;
import java.awt.event.*;

public class SimpleMenuExample extends Frame
                               implements ActionListener, ⇐
                                                WindowListener
{
     MenuBar    theBar       = new MenuBar();
     Menu       theMainMenu  = new Menu("Main");
     Menu       theQuitMenu  = new Menu("Quit");
     MenuItem   theRedItem   = new MenuItem("Red");
     MenuItem   theBlueItem  = new MenuItem("Blue");
     MenuItem   theExitItem  = new MenuItem("Exit");

     public static void main(String args[])
     {
          SimpleMenuExample theApp = new SimpleMenuExample();
     }

     public SimpleMenuExample()
     {
```

continued on next page

continued from previous page

```
            super( "A Simple Menu Example" );

            setMenuBar(theBar);
            // 1. Attach menubar to frame

            theBar.add(theMainMenu);
            // 2. Add menus to menubar
            theBar.add(theQuitMenu);

            theMainMenu.add(theRedItem);
            // 3. Add items to MainMenu
            theMainMenu.addSeparator();
            theMainMenu.add(theBlueItem);

            theQuitMenu.add(theExitItem);
            // 4. Add item to QuitMenu

            theRedItem .addActionListener(this);
            // 5. Add Listeners for items
            theBlueItem.addActionListener(this);
            theExitItem.addActionListener(this);
            addWindowListener(this);

            setSize( 320, 240 );
            setVisible( true );
        }

    public void actionPerformed(ActionEvent theEvent)
    {
        // Handle the various menu actions
        if ( theEvent.getSource( ) == theExitItem) ⇐
          quitApplication();
        if ( theEvent.getSource( ) == theRedItem ) ⇐
          setBackground(Color.red);
        if ( theEvent.getSource( ) == theBlueItem) ⇐
          setBackground(Color.blue);

        repaint();
    }

    public void windowClosed      (WindowEvent e) { }
    public void windowClosing     (WindowEvent e) { ⇐
      quitApplication( ); }
    public void windowDeiconified (WindowEvent e) { }
    public void windowIconified   (WindowEvent e) { }
    public void windowOpened      (WindowEvent e) { }
    public void windowActivated   (WindowEvent e) { }
    public void windowDeactivated (WindowEvent e) { }

// Quit the application ---------------------------------
    public void quitApplication()
    {
        setVisible( false );
        dispose( );
        System.exit(0);
    }
}
```

FIGURE 11-13

The SimpleMenu Example in action

SimpleMenuExample at Work

SimpleMenuExample has one `MenuBar`, two `Menus`, and three `MenuItems`—all defined as fields. The constructor, `SimpleMenuExample( )`, has several responsibilities. First, the constructor calls the `Frame` parent constructor, which it does by using `super( )`. Second, the `MenuBar` object must be added to the application's frame, by use of `setMenuBar( )`. Third, both of the `Menus`—`MainMenu` and `QuitMenu`—must be added to the `MenuBar`. Fourth, the appropriate `MenuItems` must be added to each of the respective `Menus`. Finally, the applet is made an `ActionListener` of each `MenuItem`, so that it will receive an `ActionEvent` when a `MenuItem` is selected.

When a menu item is selected, the Java run-time system will call an `actionPerformed( )` method if you've provided one. Inside `actionPerformed( )` you can use the `getSource( )` method to see which menu selection was made:

```
// Handle the various menu actions
if ( theEvent.getSource( ) == theExitItem) quitApplication();
if ( theEvent.getSource( ) == theRedItem) ⇐
  setBackground(Color.red);
if ( theEvent.getSource( ) == theBlueItem) ⇐
  setBackground(Color.blue);
```

Menus at the `MenuBar`

The `MenuBar` class includes a default constructor and several useful methods. These methods are summarized in Table 11-8. The `MenuBar` class, along with other menu-related classes, also inherits several useful members from its base class (`MenuComponent`). These are summarized in Table 11-9.

TABLE 11-8
KEY `public` METHODS OF THE `MenuBar` CLASS

METHOD	FUNCTION
`add (Menu m)`	Adds the specified menu to the menu bar.
`int countMenus( )`	Returns the number of menus in the menu bar.
`Menu getHelpMenu( )`	Returns a reference to the designated help menu.
`Menu getMenu(int i)`	Returns the specified menu on the menu bar.
`remove(int index)`	Removes the specified menu from the menu bar.
`remove(MenuComponent m)`	Removes the specified menu from the menu bar. `MenuComponent` is a parent class of `MenuItem`, `Menu`, and `MenuBar`.
`setHelpMenu(Menu m)`	Adds the specified menu as the designated help menu.

TABLE 11-9
KEY `public` METHODS OF THE **MenuComponent** CLASS

METHOD	FUNCTION
`Font getFont( )`	Gets the current font used to draw menu text.
`MenuContainer getParent( )`	Gets a reference to the container that holds this menu component.
`setFont(Font f)`	Sets the font used to draw menu text.

Individual `Menu`s can be constructed by use of a simple constructor that requires a `String` containing the name of the `Menu`:

```
Menu theFileMenu = new Menu("File");
```

There are also several useful methods in the `Menu` class; these are summarized in Table 11-10.

TABLE 11-10
KEY `public` METHODS OF THE **Menu** CLASS

METHOD	FUNCTION
`add(MenuItem item)`	Adds the specified item to the menu.
`add(String label)`	Creates a menu item with the specified label and add it to the menu.
`addSeparator( )`	Adds a separator item to the menu.
`int countItems( )`	Returns the number of items in the menu.
`MenuItem getItem(int index)`	Returns the specified menu item.
`remove(int index)`	Removes the specified menu item.
`remove(MenuComponent item)`	Removes the specified menu item. `MenuComponent` is a parent class of `MenuItem`, `Menu`, and `MenuBar`.

The `MenuItem`s contained in a menu are created with a simple constructor that requires a `String` containing the name of the `MenuItem`:

```
MenuItem theFileOpenItem = new MenuItem("Open");
```

Useful methods of the `MenuItem` class are summarized in Table 11-11.

TABLE 11-11
KEY `public` METHODS OF THE `MenuItem` CLASS

METHOD	FUNCTION
`setEnabled(boolean state)`	Sets the menu item to respond to selection (argument is **true**) or to ignore selection (argument is **false**).
`String getLabel( )`	Gets the label associated with the menu item.
`boolean isEnabled( )`	Returns a value indicating whether the menu item is enabled.
`setLabel(String label)`	Sets the label associated with the menu item to the specified text.

EMPOWERED MENUS

Once your application has a menu, there are times when some menu items may be inappropriate. If you create a word processing applet, choosing the `SpellCheck` menu item is inappropriate when there is no document loaded. One alternative is to check for each of these conditions when you process your `actionPerformed( )` method. Another, better, alternative is to enable and disable the individual menu items themselves. That way Java can keep track of the necessary conditions for you. Thus, if you only enable the `SpellCheck` menu item once a document has been loaded, you can safely spell-check when you receive that menu selection in your `actionPerformed( )` method.

To see how this is done, look at Listing 11-10. It shows the MenuExample application, which demonstrates how to enable and disable menu items. Figure 11-14 shows the application in action.

Listing 11-10 MenuExample.java
```
// Enabling and disabling menu items
import java.awt.*;
import java.awt.event.*;

public class MenuExample extends Frame ⇐
                    implements ActionListener, ⇐
                          WindowListener
{
    MenuBar     theBar       = new MenuBar();
    Menu        theMainMenu  = new Menu("&Main");
    Menu        theQuitMenu  = new Menu("&Quit");
    MenuItem    theBWItem    = new MenuItem("B&&W");
    MenuItem    theColorItem = new MenuItem("Color");
    MenuItem    theRedItem   = new MenuItem("&Red");
    MenuItem    theBlueItem  = new MenuItem("&Blue");
    MenuItem    theExitItem  = new MenuItem("E&xit");

    public static void main(String args[])
    {
        MenuExample theApp = new MenuExample();
    }
```

continued on next page

continued from previous page

```java
public MenuExample()
{
    super( "A Java Menu Example" );

    setMenuBar(theBar);

    theBar.add(theMainMenu);
    theBar.add(theQuitMenu);

    theMainMenu.add(theBWItem);
    theMainMenu.add(theColorItem);
    theMainMenu.addSeparator();
    theMainMenu.add(theRedItem);
    theMainMenu.add(theBlueItem);

    theQuitMenu.add(theExitItem);

    theColorItem.setEnabled(false);

    theBWItem.addActionListener(this);
    theColorItem.addActionListener(this);
    theRedItem.addActionListener(this);
    theBlueItem.addActionListener(this);
    theExitItem.addActionListener(this);
    addWindowListener(this);

    setSize( 320, 240 );
    setVisible( true );
}

public void actionPerformed(ActionEvent theEvent)
{
    if ( theEvent.getSource( ) == theExitItem ) ⇐
     quitApplication();

    if ( theEvent.getSource( ) == theBWItem)
    {
        setBackground(Color.white);
        theBWItem.setEnabled(false);
        theColorItem.setEnabled(true);
        theRedItem.setEnabled(false);
        theBlueItem.setEnabled(false);
    }

    if ( theEvent.getSource( ) == theColorItem)
    {
        setBackground(Color.white);
        theBWItem.setEnabled(true);
        theColorItem.setEnabled(false);
        theRedItem.setEnabled(true);
        theBlueItem.setEnabled(true);
    }

    if ( theEvent.getSource( ) == theRedItem  )
        setBackground(Color.red);
    if ( theEvent.getSource( ) == theBlueItem )
        setBackground(Color.blue);

    repaint();
```

```
        }


        public void windowClosed      (WindowEvent e) { }
        public void windowClosing      (WindowEvent e) { ⇐
           quitApplication( ); }
        public void windowDeiconified(WindowEvent e) { }
        public void windowIconified   (WindowEvent e) { }
        public void windowOpened       (WindowEvent e) { }
        public void windowActivated    (WindowEvent e) { }
        public void windowDeactivated(WindowEvent e) { }

        // Quit the application --------------------------------
    public void quitApplication()
        {
            setVisible( false );
            dispose( );
            System.exit(0);
        }
    }
```

Examining MenuExample

The MenuExample application adds an additional menu item, named **B&&W**, to **theMainMenu**. If you look closely at Figure 11-14 though, you'll notice that on the screen the text looks like **B&W**. Some of the other menu items also seem to have gratuitous ampersands added to their text. What's going on here?

Adding an ampersand in front of a character in a menu item makes that character an *accelerator key* or *hotkey*. Do you see the & in front of *Main*? When the word *Main* appears on the screen, the *M* is underlined. Under Windows 95, you can pull down the main menu by holding the ALT key while pressing *M*. (This may or may not work when the application is used under other Java run-time systems.)

Making MenuExample Behave

Besides having a different appearance, MenuExample also acts differently from SimpleMenuExample. When you start MenuExample, pull down the main menu and notice that the **Color** menu choice appears gray. Try to select that item. You'll find you

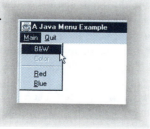

FIGURE 11-14
The MenuExample in action

cannot, because `theColorItem` has been disabled in your `init( )` method with the line:

```
theColorItem.setEnabled(false);
```

Now, click on the `B&W` menu item, and then pull down the `Main` menu again. Now `Color` appears normal, and all the other choices are gray. Logically, that makes sense. You don't want to allow your users to select Red when you are in black-and-white mode. They need to switch back to color mode first. By disabling the inappropriate code, you prevent senseless errors. This switching back and forth between enabled and disabled modes is done in the `actionPerformed( )` method whenever the `Color` or `B&W` menu items are selected, like this:

```
if ( theEvent.getSource( ) == theBWItem)
{
    setBackground(Color.white);
    theBWItem.setEnabled(false);
    theColorItem.setEnabled(true);
    theRedItem.setEnabled(false);
    theBlueItem.setEnabled(false);
}

if ( theEvent.getSource( ) == theColorItem)
{
    setBackground(Color.white);
    theBWItem.setEnabled(true);
    theColorItem.setEnabled(false);
    theRedItem.setEnabled(true);
    theBlueItem.setEnabled(true);

}
```

When `B&W` is selected, `theColorItem` is enabled and all others are disabled. When color mode is selected, all others are enabled and `theColorItem` is disabled. Note that when you compare `theObject` against the menu text, you must compare the text exactly as you entered it when you created the menu item, superfluous ampersands and all.

ADDING MENU FEATURES

In addition to their regular fare, menus also offer two additional "blue plate specials." The first of these is the ever tasty *nested* menu. This has nothing to do with old birds' nests or other exotic delicacies. Rather, a nested menu is a menu that contains another menu as an item. If you add a menu to an existing menu using the `add( )` method, Java will add the text to the original menu. But when the item is selected, rather than generating an `actionPerformed( )` event, the new menu will open up. Under Windows 95, these submenu items can be recognized by the triangle that the operating system places after the text.

The second sort of menu item is the `CheckboxMenuItem`. A `CheckboxMenuItem` can be created by use of a simple constructor specifying its text label:

```
CheckboxMenuItem thePowerStatus = new ⇐
  CheckboxMenuItem("Power");
```

The state of a `CheckboxMenuItem` can be set by use of the `setState( )` method and can be queried by use of the `getState( )` method:

```
thePowerStatus.setState(false);
                      // set power status off
boolean powerStatus = thePowerStatus.getState( ); ⇐
   // get the state of the //    power status
```

These can be added to a menu anywhere you would normally add a `MenuItem`. A `CheckboxMenuItem` acts just like a regular `MenuItem`, except that it also contains a boolean "checked" or "unchecked" value. You can retrieve the value of a `CheckboxMenuItem` by using the `getState( )` method:

```
if ( theItem.getState( ) ) . . .
```

You can also programmatically toggle the checked state of a `CheckboxMenuItem` by using the `setState( )` method:

```
theItem.setState( true );
```

When a `CheckboxMenuItem` is selected, it generates an `actionPerformed( )` event, exactly like a plain `MenuItem` object. The operating system will also automatically toggle the checked state of the item—from checked to unchecked, and back. Listing 11-11 shows the MoreMenus application, which shows how to create menus that contain submenus, as well as how to use `CheckboxMenuItems` to create a menu that stores only one of many possible values. Figure 11-15 shows the application in action.

Listing 11-11 MoreMenus.java

```
// How to create nested and checkbox menus
import java.awt.*;
import java.awt.event.*;

public class MoreMenus extends Frame ⇐
                   implements ActionListener, ⇐
                              WindowListener⇐
                              ItemListener{

    MenuBar              theBar        = new MenuBar();
    Menu                 theMainMenu   = new Menu("&Main");
    Menu                 theColorMenu  = new Menu("&Color");
    CheckboxMenuItem     theBWItem     = ⇐
      new CheckboxMenuItem("B&&W");
    CheckboxMenuItem     theLightRed   = ⇐
      new CheckboxMenuItem("Light Red");
    CheckboxMenuItem     theDarkRed    = ⇐
      new CheckboxMenuItem("Dark  Red");
    CheckboxMenuItem     theLightBlue  = ⇐
      new CheckboxMenuItem("Light Blue");
```

continued on next page

continued from previous page

```java
CheckboxMenuItem   theDarkBlue  = ⇐
    new CheckboxMenuItem("Dark  Blue");
MenuItem              theExitItem  = ⇐
    new MenuItem("E&xit");

final static Color LIGHT_RED  = ⇐
    new Color(1.0f, 0.0f, 0.0f);
final static Color DARK_RED   = ⇐
    new Color(0.5f, 0.0f, 0.0f);
final static Color LIGHT_BLUE = ⇐
    new Color(0.0f, 0.0f, 1.0f);
final static Color DARK_BLUE  = ⇐
    new Color(0.0f, 0.0f, 0.5f);

public static void main(String args[])
{
    MoreMenus theApp = new MoreMenus();
}

public MoreMenus()
{
    super( "Nested and Checkbox Menus" );

    setMenuBar(theBar);

    theBar.add(theMainMenu);
    theMainMenu.add(theColorMenu);
    theMainMenu.addSeparator();
    theColorMenu.add(theBWItem);
    theColorMenu.add(theLightRed);
    theColorMenu.add(theDarkRed);
    theColorMenu.add(theLightBlue);
    theColorMenu.add(theDarkBlue);
    theMainMenu.add(theExitItem);

    theBWItem.addItemListener(this);
    theLightRed.addItemListener(this);
    theDarkRed.addItemListener(this);
    theLightBlue.addItemListener(this);
    theDarkBlue.addItemListener(this);
    theExitItem.addActionListener(this);


    setSize( 320, 240 );
    setVisible( true );
}

public void actionPerformed(ActionEvent theEvent)
{
    if ( theEvent.getSource( ) == theExitItem ) ⇐
        quitApplication();
public void item stateChanged(ItemEvent theEvent)
    if ( theEvent.getSource( ) == theBWItem )
        setBackground(Color.white);
```

```
                       if ( theEvent.getSource( ) == theLightRed )
                          setBackground(LIGHT_RED);
                       if ( theEvent.getSource( ) == theDarkRed )
                          setBackground(DARK_RED);
                       if ( theEvent.getSource( ) == theLightBlue )
                          setBackground(LIGHT_BLUE);
                       if ( theEvent.getSource( ) == theDarkBlue )
                          setBackground(DARK_BLUE);

                    theBWItem.setState   ( ⇐
                       theEvent.getSource( ) == theBWItem    );
                    theLightRed.setState ( ⇐
                       theEvent.getSource( ) == theLightRed  );
                    theDarkRed.setState  ( ⇐
                       theEvent.getSource( ) == theDarkRed   );
                    theLightBlue.setState( ⇐
                       theEvent.getSource( ) == theLightBlue );
                    theDarkBlue.setState ( ⇐
                       theEvent.getSource( ) == theDarkBlue  );

                    repaint();
                 }

            public void windowClosed       (WindowEvent e) { }
            public void windowClosing      (WindowEvent e) { ⇐
               quitApplication( ); }
            public void windowDeiconified (WindowEvent e) { }
            public void windowIconified    (WindowEvent e) { }
            public void windowOpened       (WindowEvent e) { }
            public void windowActivated    (WindowEvent e) { }
            public void windowDeactivated (WindowEvent e) { }

            // Quit the application ---------------------------------
      public void quitApplication()
         {
              setVisible(false);
              dispose( );
              System.exit(0);
         }
      }
```

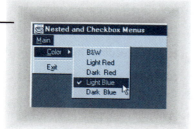

FIGURE 11-15
The MoreMenus
application in action

Summary

All Java's colors are created by combining specified amounts of the primary colors: red, green, and blue.

A number of useful colors are prespecified as static members of the Color class.

A Canvas is an AWT component on which it is possible to draw text and figures.

To use a Canvas, it's necessary to create a child class that overrides the getMinimumSize( ) and getPreferredSize( ) methods.

Whenever the AWT wants to redraw a component, it invokes the component's paint( ) method.

All your drawing statements must be placed in the paint( ) method.

Your program should call repaint( ) (not paint( )) if you need to redraw a component.

The default update( ) method clears the background of a component by painting a rectangle of the proper size and color.

Text is drawn by use of the drawString( ) method.

The FontMetrics class can be used to determine information about a Font, such as the width of a given String when drawn in the Font.

Lines are drawn by use of the drawLine( ) method.

Java's AWT includes methods to draw outlines and solid figures, including rectangles, rounded rectangles, ovals, arcs, and polygons.

Images are acquired by use of the getImage( ) method and drawn by use of the drawImage( ) method.

Animation is based on the use of threads, which allow a program to be started and stopped at defined time intervals.

When a Thread is started, it begins executing its run( ) method.

Sound clips are acquired by use of the getAudioClip( ) method and played by use of the loop( ) method.

Menus, which can be nested, consist primarily of a MenuBar and one or more Menus having MenuItems.

Quiz

1. Colors in Java are created by use of specified amounts of three colors: _____, _____, and _____.

2. Though it's possible to draw on a(n) _____ component, the component has no fixed size and must be subclassed in order to be used.

3. When the AWT needs to draw a component, it invokes the component's _____ method.

4. When a component needs to be redrawn, a program should invoke the component's _____ method.

5. The _____ method, by default, clears the surface of a component by painting it with the proper background color.

6. Text contained in a `String` is drawn by use of the _____ method.

7. Information about a `Font`, such as the width of a `String` drawn in the `Font`, can be obtained by use of a(n) _____ object.

8. A line can be drawn by use of the _____ method.

9. The outline of a rectangle can be drawn by use of the _____ method.

10. A filled rectangle can be drawn by use of the _____ method.

11. An `Image` can be drawn by use of the _____ method.

12. An audio clip can be played by use of the _____ method.

13. Java threads are needed to support _____, which is performed by rapidly displaying a sequence of static images.

14. A Java thread, when started, executes its _____ method.

15. A menu can be used with an application but not with a(n) _____.

Exercises

1. A variant form of the `drawImage( )` method can be used to scale an image to a size larger or smaller than the size specified in the file that stores the image. The method header is

   ```
   drawImage(Image theImage, int x, int y, int width, int height, ⇐
   ImageObserver theObserver);
   ```

   where `width` and `height` specify the desired image size. The `this` object may be used as the final parameter, just as in the form of `drawImage( )` described in the text. Use this second form of the method to create an applet that displays an image and allows the user to adjust the size of the image using buttons.

2. Write an applet that displays a small image, or drawn figure, on the screen. When the mouse is moved, determine whether the mouse is "close" to the position occupied by the image. If so, redraw the image at a new position further away from the mouse than its original position. If the image "strikes" a "wall" of the screen, cause it to either "bounce" off the wall, reenter the screen from the opposite wall, or vanish and reappear at a random position, according to your preference.

3. Write a "light show" applet that displays random shapes of random sizes and colors and moves them about the screen in a random fashion. Allow the user to select the number of shapes that will appear.

4. Write an application that includes a menu that allows the user to choose from the colors defined as `static` members of the `Color` class. The selected color is used to determine the color of a line, drawn between the positions at which the mouse button is clicked. Allow the user to draw an indefinite number of lines. Include a menu item used to erase the screen and another used to exit the application.

5. Write an applet that functions as an alarm clock. You may want to use method `java.lang.System.currentTimeMillis( )`, which returns a `long` containing the elapsed time (in milliseconds) since January 1, 1970. You may also want to use the constructor `java.util.Date(long date)`, which returns a `Date` object given the time (in milliseconds). Your applet should run as a `Thread` so that it doesn't squander CPU time.

6. Using an audio clip, add a "wake to music" feature to the applet you created in the previous exercise.

12

The AWT:

Containers, Components, and Layout Managers

T he package `java.awt`, known as the Abstract Window Toolkit (AWT), makes it quick and easy for you to implement Java programs that have graphical user interfaces. This may not seem like much of an accomplishment, because most computer languages have libraries to help build such interfaces. But remember that Java programs are designed to be portable. A Java program that provides a graphical user interface must work on Sun workstations, IBM-compatible PCs, Macintoshes, and many other platforms. That *is* a big challenge, and it's the job of the AWT to make this happen.

Chapter 11, "Jumpin' Java: Menus, Graphics, Sound"; this chapter; and Chapter 13, "Advanced AWT," each give you different information about the AWT. Chapter 11 taught you how to use the `Graphics` primitives provided by the AWT to draw lines and shapes, how to render images, and even how to play sounds. Chapter 12 gives you

" A Java application will look like a Windows 95 application on a PC and like a Macintosh application on a Mac! "

more information about the user-interface components that are provided by the AWT. These include the container classes—`Frame`, `Panel`, and `Dialog`—as well as the control classes—`Button`, `Label`, `List`, and so on. Finally, in Chapter 13, you will learn about the way `Events` are handled in the AWT, along with printing and some advanced inheritance topics.

More specifically, in this chapter, you will learn

- How to use the container classes—`Frame`, `Panel`, and `Dialog`—to organize the various components used in your application

- How you can design the appearance of your application by using `Panels`

- How to use the basic layout managers—`FlowLayout`, `BorderLayout`, and `GridLayout`—as well as two advanced layout managers—`CardLayout` and `GridBagLayout`

- About the basic methods that apply to all the subclasses of `Component`

- More about the attributes and methods of the `Label`, `Button`, `TextField`, and `TextArea` classes

- How to use the `Checkbox` and `CheckboxGroup` classes to simplify providing user options

- How to use the `List` and `Choice` classes to present alternatives for your users to pick from

- How to use the attributes and methods of the `Scrollbar` class

How Does the AWT Work?

How is a program using the AWT capable of working on so many different computers? The AWT does its magic by sitting on top of your computer's native windowing system, whether that's Windows, OS/2, X-11 Motif, or the Macintosh. This allows Java programs running on a given platform to approximate the familiar look and feel of other programs running on that platform. Because of this, a Java application will look like a Windows 95 application on a PC, while looking like a Macintosh application on a Mac!

There is a small downside to this approach, however. Because the AWT, at least in its present form, is something of a "lowest common denominator" toolkit, you may find areas where it provides less functionality than a particular native windowing system. The bright side of these limitations is that the AWT is somewhat less involved, and therefore simpler to learn and use, than many other windowing systems. While it might be difficult to accomplish certain advanced operations by use of the current incarnation of the AWT, doing simple things is pretty simple. And, at the rate Sun is improving and updating the Java libraries, you won't have long to wait for new releases that improve and extend the functionality of the AWT.

INSIDE THE AWT

The AWT provides several major subsystems that support the development of graphical user interface (GUI) programs. These subsystems are

- Graphics primitives that allow the drawing and rendering of lines and images. These were covered in Chapter 11.

- Components such as Labels, Buttons, and TextFields.

- Containers including Frames, Panels, and Dialogs.

- Layout managers that control the appearance of your display in a portable manner.

- The event system, which allows you to respond to interactions between the components and containers in your application. The event system will be covered in more detail in Chapter 13.

Components

Components, known to some as *widgets* or *controls*, are the labels, buttons, and other objects that the user views and with which he or she interacts. Many components are clickable, meaning that the user can click them with the mouse, triggering an appropriate response. Components make graphical user interfaces fun, because they're active: They do things. The AWT provides a small set of built-in components, but it also allows you to construct your own custom components. And not only can you "roll your own" components, but as a Java programmer you also can look forward to a rich variety of new components, created by other programmers, that can be used in your programs.

Containers

By using containers, you can group your components and treat the group as a unit. Typically, a container takes on the appearance of a window that holds components, and that can be moved, resized, minimized, and restored by your users. Containers allow users to see and use the video monitor as a desktop: They shuffle aside windows relating to low-priority tasks and bring to the front and enlarge windows relating to urgent tasks.

Layout Managers

Layout managers, another basic subsystem of the AWT, are not provided by most windowing systems. Yet they are an important part of the AWT, because they allow AWT programs to be portable. Most windowing systems require you to lay out the components of a container using fixed positions. These fixed positions might suit a given platform well, but are unlikely to be appropriate for other platforms, which may have very different video resolutions and other properties.

The AWT provides a family of layout managers that you can use to arrange the components of a container in a more flexible way, relative to one another and to the borders of the container. Once you have installed a layout manager, the AWT then determines the exact sizes and positions of your components each time the window is drawn. This unusual division of responsibility is akin to that used to display hypertext documents on the Web. Layout managers (such as browsers) interpret specifications and constraints given by the author of a program (or HTML document) and determine a suitable appearance that satisfies those requirements.

Events

The final main contribution of the AWT to the health and well-being of Java programmers is the event system. The event system is an orderly way of informing programs that something interesting has happened: The user has clicked a button, or the user has pressed the PAGEUP key, or whatever. When an event occurs, the event system creates an Event object and sends it as part of an event message to potentially interested components. By use of a standard protocol, components can handle the message or pass the buck, causing the message to be forwarded to another component. You might want to look ahead to Chapter 13 if you are very interested in the details of how this is done.

OBJECTS: WHAT KIND OF TOOL AM I?

Because you know that everything in Java—other than the primitive types—is an object, you might conclude that the various classes provided by the AWT are related. You'd be right! Because Java's classes form a hierarchy rooted in the Object class, all the AWT classes are part of the Object family. Figure 12-1 shows relationships among the classes of the AWT.

This figure has been somewhat simplified. Certain classes have been omitted. Also, some classes are actually related by use of the implements mechanism (which you'll meet in Chapter 13) rather than extends. These are nevertheless shown in the figure as though the classes were related by simple inheritance, because this correctly reflects their actual behavior. Also note that most of the AWT classes are descendents of the class Component: Even Containers and Applets are actually Components!

A SECOND HIERARCHY: "CONTAINS"

You'll recall from Chapter 9, "Teams of Classes: Using Classes Together," that in addition to the hierarchy based on inheritance, the components of an AWT program are also related as part of a second hierarchy. We mentioned earlier that Containers contain Components, and you can see from Figure 12-1 that Containers *are* Components. Why is this important? Because Containers can contain other Containers. In other words, Containers can be nested.

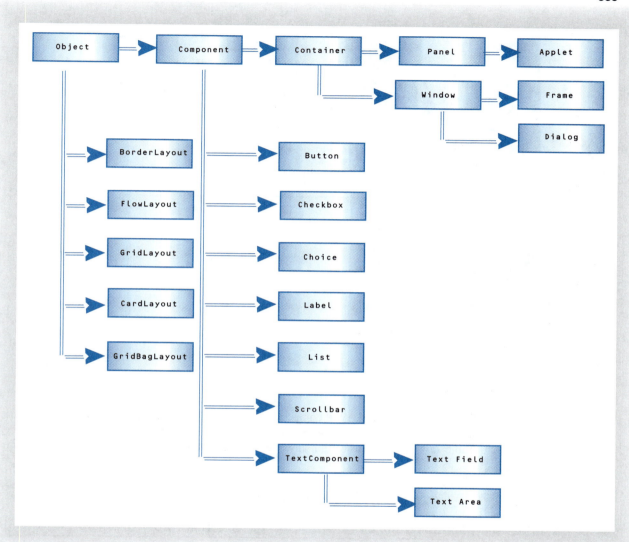

FIGURE 12-1

A simplified inheritance hierarchy of the AWT classes

When this occurs, `contains` hierarchies such as that in Figure 12-2 coexist with the familiar `extends` hierarchies. This can cause headaches when someone talks about a `Component`'s "parent," which can be either the superclass of the `Component` or the `Container` in which the `Component` has been placed. Only context can make clear which is meant.

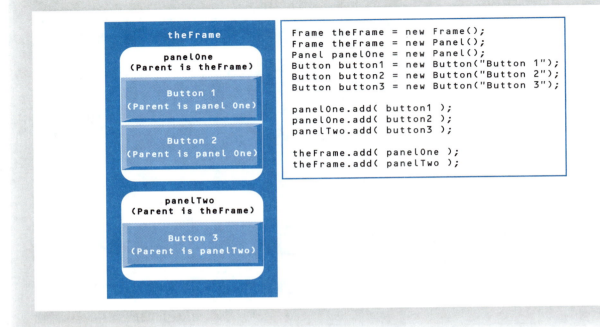

FIGURE 12-2
A contains
hierarchy

What Are Components?

Because many of the AWT components are descended from the Component class, an understanding of the Component class is fundamental to effective use of the AWT. Table 12-1 summarizes certain key public methods of the Component class.

TABLE 12-1
KEY public METHODS OF THE Component CLASS

METHOD HEADER	FUNCTION
Rectangle getBounds( )	Get the rectangle that encloses the component.
Font getFont( )	Get the font used to draw the component.
Container getParent( )	Get the container (if any) which holds the component.
Dimension getSize( )	Return the size of the component.
boolean isEnabled( )	Return value indicating whether component is set to respond to user (see setEnabled( )).
boolean isShowing( )	Return value indicating whether component is visible and not obscured by other components.
boolean isVisible( )	Return value indicating whether component is visible (see setVisible( )).

Table continued...

TABLE 12-1 KEY **public** METHODS OF THE **Component** CLASS
CONTINUED...

METHOD HEADER	FUNCTION
repaint( )	Request that the component be scheduled for painting.
void setBounds(int x, int y, int width, int height)	Move the component to position x,y within the containing component and adjust its size (values in pixels).
void setEnabled(boolean cond)	Set the component so that it will (**true**) or will not (**false**) respond to the user.
void setFont(Font f)	Set the font used to draw the component.
void setLocation(int x, int y)	Move the component to position x,y within the containing component (**x, y** in pixels).
void setSize(int width, int height)	Adjust the size of the component (values in pixels).
void setSize(Dimension d)	Adjust the size of the component (values of components of **d** in pixels).
void setVisible(boolean cond)	Make the component visible (**true**) or invisible (**false**).
String toString( )	Return a **String** describing the component and its state.

Components, though they are not always rectangular in shape, always occupy a rectangular area on the screen. The getBounds( ) method can be used to obtain the value of this rectangle. When a Component is first created, it cannot be seen on the display. At a given time, a Component may be *visible* or *hidden*. A hidden Component, even though it has position and size, cannot be seen on the display. Similarly, Components can be *enabled* or *disabled*. A disabled Component does not perform its characteristic and usual action; for example, a disabled button does not respond when clicked. Disabled Components are visible on the display, but their appearance is altered to indicate that they are disabled. Under Windows 95, for example, this is done by "graying out" the Component.

USING ComponentS

The Component class itself is an *abstract* class. That doesn't mean that it's hard to understand or is obscure. It simply means that, while the Component class provides methods and attributes that all Components will share, you cannot create a Component object: your search for a Component( ) constructor will be in vain. Instead, you construct objects using the specific subclasses of Component: Frames, Labels, and so on. This allows the Component class to implement certain behavior—setting the Font used in the Component, for instance—only once, and frees the subclasses from the necessity of implementing redundant functionality. Chapter 13 will give you more information on implementing and using abstract classes.

`Components`, like most AWT objects, are not painted—drawn on the display surface—on demand. Instead, the `repaint( )` method can be used to request that a `Component` be redrawn at a time convenient to the AWT.

A number of other methods are important to those planning to extend components or implement custom components. These are not included in Table 12-1. If you're curious about them, you might consult *Java Networking and AWT API SuperBible*, by Nagaratnam, Maso, and Srinivasan (Waite Group Press, ISBN 1-57169-031-X).

THE `Rectangle` CLASS

Chapter 11 focused on graphics and graphics-related classes, but three graphics classes are important even to nondrawing uses of `Components`. These are `Point`, `Dimension`, and `Rectangle`. The first two were discussed in Chapter 11, so it's now time to meet the `Rectangle`. A `Rectangle` includes both a position, given by its `x` and `y` `public` instance fields, and a size, given by its `width` and `height` `public` instance fields. Useful constructors, methods, and fields of the `Rectangle` class are given in Tables 12-2, 12-3, and 12-4.

TABLE 12-2
KEY `public` CONSTRUCTORS OF THE `Rectangle` CLASS

```
Rectangle( )
Rectangle(int x, int y, int width, int height)
```

TABLE 12-3
KEY `public` METHODS OF THE `Rectangle` CLASS

METHOD HEADER	FUNCTION
`boolean equals(Object obj)`	Test whether another `Rectangle` is equal to this one.
`boolean inside(int x, int y)`	Test whether the specified point is inside the `Rectangle`.
`Rectangle intersection(Rectangle r)`	Find the intersection of another `Rectangle` with this one.
`boolean intersects(Rectangle r)`	Test whether the specified `Rectangle` intersects this one.
`void move(int x, int y)`	Move the `Rectangle` to the specified location.

> *"Components make graphical user interfaces fun because they're active: They do things."*

TABLE 12-4
KEY `public` INSTANCE FIELDS OF THE `Rectangle` CLASS

FIELD	TYPE	MEANING/USE
width	int	Width (pixels)
height	int	Height (pixels)
x	int	Coordinate (pixels)
y	int	Coordinate (pixels)

Containing Your Enthusiasm

Because the `Component` class is an abstract class, you cannot write an application that allows you to exercise a "pure" `Component`. Likewise, the `Container` subclass of `Component` is also an abstract class, so to see a `Container` in action you will need to look at one of *its* children. Looking back at Figure 12-1, you'll notice that the `Container` class has two major subclasses: `Window` and `Panel`. Because these classes extend the `Container` class, they are both `Containers` and `Components`.

The `Window` class itself, although not an abstract class, is rarely used, because its two children, `Frame` and `Dialog`, provide so much more built-in functionality. Let's start your exploration of the `Container` classes by looking at the `Frame` class and its parent, `Window`.

FRAMING YOUR APPLICATION

`Frames` are the top-level windows in which applications live, but your applications and applets can also create additional `Frames`. `Frames` have a title bar that contains a caption identifying the `Frame`. In addition, `Frames` have a set of icons that can be used to control their appearance—to minimize, maximize, or restore them, for instance. From their parent class (`Window`), `Frames` inherit the methods shown in Table 12-5.

When first created, a `Frame` is not automatically visible. To make a `Frame` appear on your display once it has been created, you can use its `setVisible( )` method, which will also recursively show any components that the `Frame` contains. The `pack( )` method is useful when you want to automatically resize a `Frame` to accommodate its `Components`. The `dispose( )` method should be called whenever there is no further need for a `Frame`. It releases the display resources held by the `Frame`, which are often a scarce commodity within a windowing system.

TABLE 12-5
KEY `public` METHODS OF THE `Window` CLASS

METHOD HEADER	FUNCTION
`void dispose( )`	Release the `Window`'s peer object in the native environment, freeing the `Window`'s resources.
`void pack( )`	Set the `Window` size according to the preferred sizes of its `Components`.
`void setVisible( boolean cond )`	Make the `Window` visible (`true`) or invisible (`false`).
`void toBack( )`	Send the `Windows` to the back of the desktop, behind other `Windows`.
`void toFront( )`	Bring the `Window` to the front of the desktop.

Table 12-6 shows the two constructors provided by the `Frame` class. The first results in a `Frame` unhappily titled "Untitled." If you use this constructor, you should follow it up with a call to `setTitle( )` to provide an appropriate title for your `Frame`. The `setTitle( )` method, and others, are summarized in Table 12-7. An interesting property of the `Frame` class is its support for the various types of cursors that can be used to indicate the current position of the mouse. `Public` fields giving values corresponding to these cursor types are shown in Table 12-8.

TABLE 12-6
KEY `public` CONSTRUCTORS OF THE `Frame` CLASS

`Frame( )`
`Frame(String title)`

TABLE 12-7
KEY `public` METHODS OF THE `Frame` CLASS

METHOD HEADER	FUNCTION
`int getCursor( )`	Get the current cursor.
`String getTitle( )`	Get the `Frame` title.
`boolean is Resizable( )`	Determine if the `Frame` is resizable.
`void setCursor(int cursor)`	Set the `Frame`'s cursor to the specified shape.
`void setResizable(boolean resizable)`	Set the `Frame` to be resizable (`true`) or nonresizable (`false`).
`void setTitle(String title)`	Set the `Frame` title.

TABLE 12-8
CURSOR SHAPES IN THE Frame CLASS (USED WITH setCursor( ))

FIELD	TYPE
DEFAULT_CURSOR	int
CROSSHAIR_CURSOR	int
HAND_CURSOR	int
MOVE_CURSOR	int
NE_RESIZE_CURSOR	int
NW_RESIZE_CURSOR	int
N_RESIZE_CURSOR	int
SE_RESIZE_CURSOR	int
SW_RESIZE_CURSOR	int
S_RESIZE_CURSOR	int
E_RESIZE_CURSOR	int
W_RESIZE_CURSOR	int
TEXT_CURSOR	int
WAIT_CURSOR	int

To demonstrate the various types of cursor that can be used, Listing 12-1 shows the StudyCursor application. This application provides a button that can be used to cycle through the entire set of defined cursor types, permitting each to be viewed. Figure 12-3 shows the application window itself.

FIGURE 12-3

Output of the StudyCursor application

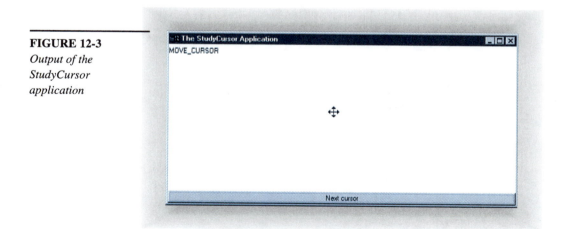

Listing 12-1 StudyCursor.java

```java
// Cursors and Frames
import java.awt.*;
import java.awt.event.*;

public class StudyCursor extends Frame
                        implements ActionListener, ⇐
                                   WindowListener
{
    Button theButton = new Button("Next cursor");
    Label  theLabel  = new Label();

    int cursorNo = 0;

    int cursor[] =  {
        Cursor.DEFAULT_CURSOR,     Cursor.CROSSHAIR_CURSOR,
        Cursor.TEXT_CURSOR,        Cursor.WAIT_CURSOR,
        Cursor.SW_RESIZE_CURSOR,   Cursor.SE_RESIZE_CURSOR,
        Cursor.NW_RESIZE_CURSOR,   Cursor.NE_RESIZE_CURSOR,
        Cursor.N_RESIZE_CURSOR,    Cursor.S_RESIZE_CURSOR,
        Cursor.W_RESIZE_CURSOR,    Cursor.E_RESIZE_CURSOR,
        Cursor.HAND_CURSOR,        Cursor.MOVE_CURSOR
        };


    String desc[] = {
        "DEFAULT_CURSOR", "CROSSHAIR_CURSOR", "TEXT_CURSOR",
        "WAIT_CURSOR", "SW_RESIZE_CURSOR", SE_RESIZE_CURSOR",
        "NW_RESIZE_CURSOR", "NE_RESIZE_CURSOR",
        "N_RESIZE_CURSOR",
        "S_RESIZE_CURSOR", "W_RESIZE_CURSOR",
        "E_RESIZE_CURSOR", "HAND_CURSOR", "MOVE_CURSOR"
        };

    public static void main(String args[])
    {
        StudyCursor theApp = new StudyCursor( );
    }

    public StudyCursor()
    {
        super( "The StudyCursor Application" );
        setSize(600, 300);

        add( theButton, "South" );
        add( theLabel,  "North" );

        theButton.addActionListener(this);
        addWindowListener(this);

        updateCursor();
        setVisible(true);
    }

    public void updateCursor()
    {
        setCursor(new Cursor(cursor[cursorNo]));
        theLabel.setText( desc[cursorNo] );
        theLabel.repaint();
```

```
    }

    public void actionPerformed(ActionEvent theEvent)
    {
        cursorNo++;
        if (cursorNo >= cursor.length) cursorNo = 0;
        updateCursor();
    }

    public void windowClosed      (WindowEvent e) { }
    public void windowClosing     (WindowEvent e) { ⇐
       quitApplication( ); }
    public void windowDeiconified (WindowEvent e) { }
    public void windowIconified   (WindowEvent e) { }
    public void windowOpened      (WindowEvent e) { }
    public void windowActivated   (WindowEvent e) { }
    public void windowDeactivated (WindowEvent e) { }

    public void quitApplication( )
    {
        setVisible(false);
        dispose();
        System.exit(0);
    }
}
```

Container BASICS

You've already met one `Container`, the `Frame`. Because applications live inside some type of `Container`, you may have guessed that applets must also live inside a `Container`. Take a look back at the AWT tree in Figure 12-1, and see what you can discover. You should see that there are two main types of `Containers`: `Windows` and `Panels`. `Frames` and `Dialogs` are both `Windows`, and `Applets` are `Panels`. So, actually, an `Applet` doesn't merely live inside a `Container`: An `Applet` *is* a `Container`.

The basic difference between `Windows` and `Panels` is that `Panels` are not top-level windows. They lack the window bar containing a title and icons. `Panels` usually live inside `Windows`, just as your `Applet` (a `Panel`) lives inside the `Frame` provided by the Appletviewer application or your Web browser. But in many ways the similarities between `Windows` and `Panels` are more important than the differences. These similarities stem from the common methods provided by the `Container` class, shown in Table 12-9. Remember that every `Container` is also a `Component`, so the `Component` methods of Table 12-1 are also available for `Containers`.

TABLE 12-9
KEY `public` METHODS OF THE `Container` CLASS

METHOD HEADER	FUNCTION
`Component add(Component comp)`	Use with `null` layout, `FlowLayout`, `GridLayout`, `GridBagLayout`.
`Component add(Component comp, String name)`	Use with `BorderLayout`, `CardLayout`.
`int getComponentCount( )`	Get the number of components in the `Container`.
`Component getComponent(int n)`	Get the specified `Component`.
`Component[] getComponents( )`	Get an array of the `Components` within the `Container`.
`LayoutManager getLayout( )`	Get the `Container`'s `LayoutManager`.
`void remove(Component comp)`	Remove the specified `Component`.
`void removeAll( )`	Remove all `Components`.
`void setLayout(LayoutManger mgr)`	Set the `Container`'s `LayoutManager`.
`void validate( )`	Validate the `Container` and its `Components`.

LAYOUT BASICS

The two most important things done with a `Container` are establishing the `Container`'s layout manager and adding components to the `Container`. You set the `Container`'s layout manager by using the `setLayout( )` method, which takes a `LayoutManager` as its argument. Once a layout manager has been set, you can add components to the `Container` using the `add( )` method. Note that the `add( )` method has two forms. The one-argument form can be used without a layout manager as well as with `FlowLayout`, `GridLayout`, and `GridBagLayout`. The two-argument form, which specifies a position along with the component, is used with `BorderLayout` and `CardLayout`. Let's begin our study of layout managers by looking at what happens when no layout manager is used.

Using a `null` Layout

It's possible to forego use of a layout manager altogether, placing components into containers according to absolute positions in the same way that nonportable windowing systems usually work. The downside of doing your own layout is that your application may not look good if a user has a display with dimensions unlike those assumed in your program. One way to avoid this problem is by using a limited portion of the display area, so that even low-resolution monitors (640×480 pixels) can render your application acceptably.

There are five steps you'll need to follow to use a `null` layout:

1. Send the `setLayout( null )` message to the `Container`. This overrides any existing or default layout manager that may be in place.

2. Send the `setSize(int width, int height)` message to the `Container` to set its size. (This method is inherited from the `Component` class.)

3. For each component you wish to add to the `Container`, send an `add( Component comp )` message to the `Container`.

4. Send each component a `setBounds( int x, int y, int width, int height )` message to establish its location and size.

5. Finally, send the `Container` a `setVisible( true )` message to make the `Container` and its components visible.

This might look like a lot of work. It is! You should also be aware that the task of picking positions and sizes for your components can be tricky. If you choose inappropriate positions or sizes, you will end up with a jumbled mess, rather than a usable `Container`. For this reason it's generally better to use one of the layout managers discussed next.

Using `BorderLayout`

The layout manager called `BorderLayout` is so named because it arranges components around the four borders of a rectangular container. Every `Frame` has `BorderLayout` installed as its default layout manager, so if you have a `Frame` and are satisfied with the capabilities provided by `BorderLayout`, you don't even need to call `setLayout( )`. If you have a container other than a `Frame` and you want to install a `BorderLayout`, you can do so by sending this message to your container:

```
setLayout(new BorderLayout( ));
```

There are two constructors provided for the `BorderLayout` class. These are shown in Table 12-10. The second form allows you to explicitly specify the size of the gaps that you want to appear between adjacent components within the container. There are no commonly used methods within the `BorderLayout` class. The `Container` class defines the `add( Component comp, String position )` method used to add components to the container managed by `BorderLayout`. There are only five possible locations at which components can be placed. These are named for the four compass points (`North`, `South`, `East`, and `West`) and for the center of the container (`Center`). Remember that these names are case-sensitive. If you erroneously try to

```
add("north", new Button("Phone home"));
```

your `Button` will never be seen!

TABLE 12-10
KEY public CONSTRUCTORS OF THE BorderLayout CLASS

```
BorderLayout( )
BorderLayout(int hgap, int vgap)
```

Because you've already used the first form of BorderLayout in several of your applications, Listing 12-2 shows you how to use the second form of BorderLayout. This application simply creates five Buttons and places them inside a Frame, leaving 5 pixels for the horizontal gap, and 5 pixels for the vertical gap between components. The result is shown in Figure 12-4. Note how components placed in a container managed by BorderLayout "swell" to fill the available space. The components at the top and bottom take all the horizontal space available, while those to the left and right take the remaining vertical space. The lone component in the center expands to take all the space that's left. Depending upon the nature of the components in your container, this can be rather disconcerting. You'll see later in this chapter how to use Panels to overcome this potential problem.

Listing 12-2 StudyBorder.java

```java
// Shows how to use BorderLayout with spacing between
components.
import java.awt.*;
import java.awt.event.*;

public class StudyBorder extends Frame implements
WindowListener
{
    Button northButton  = new Button ("North");
    Button southButton  = new Button ("South");
    Button eastButton   = new Button ("East");
    Button westButton   = new Button ("West");
    Button centerButton = new Button ("Center");

    public static void main(String args[])
    {
        StudyBorder theApp = new StudyBorder( );
    }

    public StudyBorder( )
    {
        setTitle( "The StudyBorder Application" );
        setFont( new Font( "TimesRoman", Font.BOLD, 36 ));

        setLayout( new BorderLayout( 5, 5 ) );

        add( northButton,  "North" );
        add( southButton,  "South" );
        add( eastButton,   "East" );
        add( westButton,   "West" );
        add( centerButton, "Center" );

        addWindowListener(this);
```

```
            pack( );
            setVisible(true);
      }

public void windowClosed     (WindowEvent e) { }
public void windowClosing    (WindowEvent e) { ⇐
  quitApplication( ); }
public void windowDeiconified(WindowEvent e) { }
public void windowIconified  (WindowEvent e) { }
public void windowOpened     (WindowEvent e) { }
public void windowActivated  (WindowEvent e) { }
public void windowDeactivated(WindowEvent e) { }

public void quitApplication( )
{
    setVisible(false);
    dispose();
    System.exit(0);
}
   }
```

Using `FlowLayout`

Another layout manager you are already somewhat familiar with is `FlowLayout`, which is the default layout manager for `Applets` and `Panels`. `FlowLayout` simply places components row-by-row into the container. When one row is full, a new one is

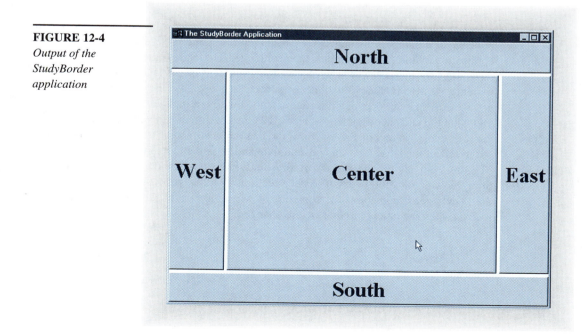

FIGURE 12-4
Output of the StudyBorder application

started below it. Each row is aligned to the left or right, or centered within the container, according to an alignment parameter. Unlike components managed by `BorderLayout`, those placed in a `FlowLayout`-managed container do not swell to fill the available space—they retain their normal proportions and sizes.

The constructors of the `FlowLayout` class are shown in Table 12-11. The alignment values used with the second and third forms are given in Table 12-12.

TABLE 12-11
KEY `public` CONSTRUCTORS OF THE `FlowLayout` CLASS

```
FlowLayout( )
FlowLayout(int alignment)
FlowLayout(int alignment, int hgap, int vgap)
```

TABLE 12-12
KEY `public` FIELDS OF THE `FlowLayout` CLASS

FIELD	TYPE	MEANING/USE
CENTER	int	Specify alignment within rows.
LEFT	int	Specify alignment within rows.
RIGHT	int	Specify alignment within rows.

The simple `add( Component comp )` form of the `add( )` method is used to add components to containers managed by `FlowLayout`. Listing 12-3 shows the StudyFlow application, which demonstrates the technique. The StudyFlow application creates three `Buttons` that allow you to change the alignment of the layout, from left to right to center. It also includes `Buttons` to increase and decrease the amount of horizontal and vertical spacing between the components. Finally, it includes three `Labels` that tell you what the current alignment is, as well as the horizontal and vertical spacing. When the user clicks on any of the `Buttons`, the `actionPerformed( )` method resets the layout to reflect the necessary change, and the window is then repainted.

Figure 12-5 shows the output of the StudyFlow application. You should run the StudyFlow application yourself to get a feel for how this works. You'll also notice how the `FlowLayout` repositions the components when the window is reshaped by users, as well as when the layout parameters are changed.

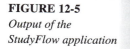

FIGURE 12-5

*Output of the
StudyFlow application*

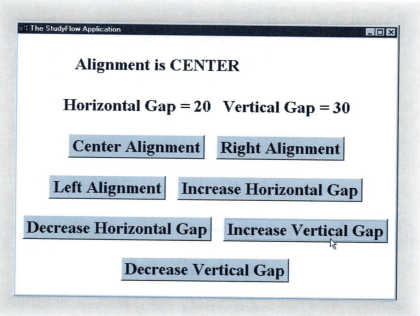

Listing 12-3 StudyFlow.java

```
// Shows how FlowLayout works

import java.awt.*;
import java.awt.event.*;

public class StudyFlow extends Frame
                       implements ActionListener, ⇐
                                  WindowListener
{
    Button centerAlign = new Button( "Center Alignment" );
    Button rightAlign  = new Button( "Right Alignment" );
    Button leftAlign   = new Button( "Left Alignment" );
    Button incHGap     = ⇐
      new Button( "Increase Horizontal Gap" );
    Button decHGap     = ⇐
      new Button( "Decrease Horizontal Gap" );
    Button incVGap     = ⇐
      new Button( "Increase Vertical Gap"   );
    Button decVGap     = ⇐
      new Button( "Decrease Vertical Gap" );

    int hGap = 0, vGap = 0;
    int alignment = FlowLayout.CENTER;

    Label  alignLabel  = ⇐
      new Label( "Alignment is FlowLayout.CENTER" );
```

continued on next page

continued from previous page

```
Label   hGapLabel   = ⇐
  new Label( "Horizontal Gap = " + hGap );
Label   vGapLabel   = ⇐
  new Label( "Vertical Gap = " + vGap );

public static void main(String args[])
{
    StudyFlow theApp = new StudyFlow( );
}

public StudyFlow( )
{
    setTitle( "The StudyFlow Application" );
    setFont( new Font( "TimesRoman", Font.BOLD, 28 ) );
    setLayout(new FlowLayout( FlowLayout.CENTER, hGap, ⇐
      vGap ) );

    add( alignLabel  );
    add( hGapLabel   );
    add( vGapLabel   );

    add( centerAlign );
    add( rightAlign  );
    add( leftAlign   );
    add( incHGap     );
    add( decHGap     );
    add( incVGap     );
    add( decVGap     );

    centerAlign.addActionListener(this);
    rightAlign.addActionListener(this);
    leftAlign.addActionListener(this);
    incHGap.addActionListener(this);
    decHGap.addActionListener(this);
    incVGap.addActionListener(this);
    decVGap.addActionListener(this);

    addWindowListener(this);

    setSize( 320, 240 );
    setVisible(true);
}

public String getAlignment()
{
    if ( alignment == FlowLayout.CENTER ) ⇐
      return "CENTER";
    if ( alignment == FlowLayout.RIGHT  ) return "RIGHT";
    if ( alignment == FlowLayout.LEFT   ) return "LEFT";
    return "OOPS";
}

public void setNewLayout()
{
    setLayout( new FlowLayout( alignment, hGap, vGap ) );
}

public void actionPerformed( ActionEvent ev )
{
```

```
        if ( ev.getSource() == centerAlign) ⇐
          alignment = FlowLayout.CENTER;
        if ( ev.getSource() == rightAlign ) ⇐
          alignment = FlowLayout.RIGHT;
        if ( ev.getSource() == leftAlign  ) ⇐
          alignment = FlowLayout.LEFT;
        if ( ev.getSource() == incHGap    ) hGap += 5;
        if ( ev.getSource() == decHGap    ) ⇐
          hGap -= ( hGap > 0 ? 5 : 0 );
        if ( ev.getSource() == incVGap    ) vGap += 5;
        if ( ev.getSource() == decVGap    ) ⇐
          vGap -= ( vGap > 0 ? 5 : 0 );

        alignLabel.setText( "Alignment is " + ⇐
          getAlignment() );
        hGapLabel.setText( "Horizontal Gap = " + hGap );
        vGapLabel.setText( "Vertical Gap = " + vGap );

        setNewLayout();
        invalidate();
        validate();
        repaint();
    }

    public void windowClosed      (WindowEvent e) { }
    public void windowClosing     (WindowEvent e) { ⇐
      quitApplication( ); }
    public void windowDeiconified (WindowEvent e) { }
    public void windowIconified   (WindowEvent e) { }
    public void windowOpened      (WindowEvent e) { }
    public void windowActivated   (WindowEvent e) { }
    public void windowDeactivated (WindowEvent e) { }


    public void quitApplication( )
    {
        setVisible(false);
        dispose();
        System.exit(0);
    }
}
}
```

Using `GridLayout`

The last of the layout managers you've already seen is `GridLayout`, which establishes a system of rows and columns, allowing components to be placed within the resulting grid. The components are placed in the same sequence as that used by `FlowLayout`: left to right, top to bottom. You don't have to specify a destination for every component; each simply goes to its place in turn. As with `BorderLayout`, components used with `GridLayout` swell to fill their cells. Table 12-13 shows the constructors you can use to create a `GridLayout`.

TABLE 12-13
KEY public CONSTRUCTORS OF THE GridLayout CLASS

GridLayout(int rows, int cols)

GridLayout(int rows, int cols, int hgap, int vgap)

Listing 12-4 shows the StudyGrid application, which demonstrates use of the GridLayout layout manager with a 3×4 grid. StudyGrid first creates a nine button array. The Buttons are then placed in the container by use of the add( ) method. Then, three additional Buttons are added to the last row of the application. By pressing the "+" Button, the GridLayout is changed to increase the horizontal and vertical gaps between buttons by 2 pixels. When the "-" is pressed, the horizontal and vertical gaps are decreased. Output of the application is shown in Figure 12-6.

Listing 12-4 StudyGrid.java

```java
// How to create a GridLayout
import java.awt.*;
import java.awt.event.*;

public class StudyGrid extends Frame
                        implements ActionListener, ⇐
                                    WindowListener
{
    Button aButton[] = new Button[9];
    Button plusBtn    = new Button( " + " );
    Button minusBtn   = new Button( " - " );
    Button quitBtn    = new Button( "Quit" );
    int hGap = 0, vGap = 0;

    public static void main( String args[] )
    {
        StudyGrid theApp = new StudyGrid();
    }

    public StudyGrid()
    {
        setTitle( "The StudyGrid Application" );
        setFont( new Font( "Helvetica", Font.BOLD, 28 ) );
        setLayout( new GridLayout( 4, 3 ) );

        for (int i = 0; i < aButton.length; i++)
        {
            aButton[i] = new Button("Button " + i);
            add(aButton[i]);
        }

        add( plusBtn  );
        add( minusBtn );
        add( quitBtn  );

        plusBtn.addActionListener(this);
        minusBtn.addActionListener(this);
        quitBtn.addActionListener(this);
        addWindowListener(this);
```

```
            pack( );
            setVisible(true);
    }

    public void actionPerformed( ActionEvent theEvent )
    {
        if ( theEvent.getSource( ) == plusBtn )
        {
            hGap += 2;
            vGap += 2;
            reShow();
            return;
        }

        if ( theEvent.getSource( ) == minusBtn )
        {
            hGap -= ( hGap > 0 ? 2 : 0 );
            vGap -= ( vGap > 0 ? 2 : 0 );
            reShow();
            return;
        }

        if ( theEvent.getSource( ) == quitBtn )
quitApplication();
    }

    public void windowClosed      (WindowEvent e) { }
    public void windowClosing      (WindowEvent e) { ⇐
        quitApplication( ); }
    public void windowDeiconified(WindowEvent e) { }
    public void windowIconified   (WindowEvent e) { }
    public void windowOpened       (WindowEvent e) { }
    public void windowActivated   (WindowEvent e) { }
    public void windowDeactivated(WindowEvent e) { }

    public void quitApplication()
    {
        setVisible(false);
        dispose();
        System.exit(0);
    }

    public void reShow()
    {
        setLayout( new GridLayout( 4, 3, hGap, vGap ) );
        pack();
    }
}
```

BOXES IN BOXES IN BOXES: USING Panels

If you're as tired of large Buttons as we think, you'll be relieved to learn to make them smaller. The simple remedy is to use your friend, the Panel. A Panel can be made by use of a default constructor, Panel( ), and can be placed in a container like any other component. However, because a Panel is itself a Container, you can place other components in the Panel. Even though the Panel may swell under the influence of

FIGURE 12-6
Output of the StudyGrid application

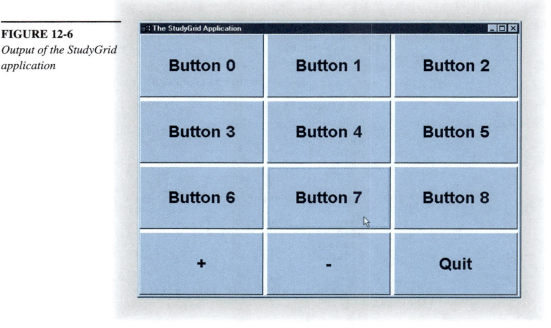

BorderLayout or GridLayout, its contents will not—assuming, of course, you set something other than BorderLayout or GridLayout as the layout manager of the Panel.

Listing 12-5, the StudyPanel application, shows how this is done. The application uses GridLayout to divide the surface of a Frame into a single row of three cells. Each of the three cells becomes the home of a Panel, each using a different layout manager: GridLayout, FlowLayout, and BorderLayout. Buttons are then placed in each of the three Panels to show the effects of the layout managers. Figure 12-7 shows the result. Resizing the Frame causes each layout manager to reconsider its chosen layout in a distinctive way. The StudyPanel application is worth running so you can see firsthand the different behaviors of the three layout managers used.

Listing 12-5 StudyPanel.java

```
// How to use Panels with LayoutManagers
import java.awt.*;
import java.awt.event.*;

public class StudyPanel extends Frame implements
WindowListener
{
    Panel   aPanel [] = new Panel [3];
    Button aButton[] = new Button[23];
    String compass[] = { "North", "South", "East", ⇐
                         "West", "Center" };
```

```
public static void main(String args[])
{
    StudyPanel theApp = new StudyPanel();
}

public StudyPanel()
{
    setTitle( "The StudyPanel Application" );
    setLayout( new GridLayout( 1, 3 ) );

    // Give the first Panel a GridLayout and add it to
    // the Frame
    aPanel[0] = new Panel();
    aPanel[0].setLayout( new GridLayout( 3, 3 ) );
    add( aPanel[0] );

    // Give the second Panel a FlowLayout and add it
    aPanel[1] = new Panel();
    aPanel[1].setLayout( new FlowLayout() );
    add( aPanel[1] );

    // Give the third Panel a BorderLayout and add it
    aPanel[2] = new Panel();
    aPanel[2].setLayout( new BorderLayout() );
    add( aPanel[2] );

    // Add nine Buttons to the first (GridLayout) Panel
    for (int i = 0; i < 9; i++)
    {
        aButton[i] = new Button("Button " + i);
        aPanel[0].add(aButton[i]);
    }

    // Add the next nine to the second (FlowLayout) Panel
    for (int i = 9; i < 18; i++)
    {
        aButton[i] = new Button("Button " + i);
        aPanel[1].add(aButton[i]);
    }

    // Add next five to the BorderLayout panel
    int j = 0;
    for (int i = 18; i < 23; i++)
    {
        aButton[i] = new Button(compass[j]);
        aPanel[2].add(aButton[i], compass[j]);
        j++;
    }

    addWindowListener(this);

    setSize( 600, 400 );
    setVisible(true);
}

public void windowClosed     (WindowEvent e) { }
public void windowClosing    (WindowEvent e) { ⇐
 quitApplication( ); }
```

continued on next page

continued from previous page

```
public void windowDeiconified(WindowEvent e) { }
public void windowIconified (WindowEvent e) { }
public void windowOpened     (WindowEvent e) { }
public void windowActivated  (WindowEvent e) { }
public void windowDeactivated(WindowEvent e) { }

public void quitApplication( )
{
    setVisible(false);
    dispose();
    System.exit(0);
}
}
```

Looking at Controls

Another way of looking at the matter of `Components` and `Containers` is to focus on those `Components` that are *not* `Containers`. Looking back at Figure 12-1, you can see a set of sibling classes that fits this bill. It includes the following classes:

 `Button`

`Checkbox`

`Choice`

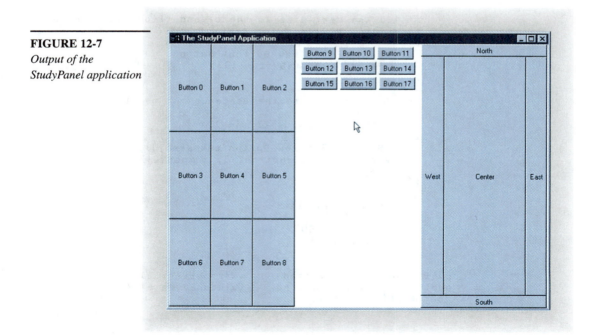

FIGURE 12-7

Output of the StudyPanel application

☕ `Label`

☕ `List`

☕ `Scrollbar`

☕ `TextComponent`, and its children, `TextArea` and `TextField`

These, along with an uncle class, `CheckboxGroup`, are the AWT classes you'll meet in this section. These classes are sometimes called *controls*, because they provide a way for the user to control the way that your program behaves.

EXAMINING CONTROLS

To thoroughly examine the controls you are going to use in your Java program, it would be helpful to have a "microscope" to let you look at their attributes and methods. Using your newfound knowledge of `Containers`, you can easily construct such an instrument that will allow you to exercise the methods of each new component, as well as to watch the messages and events that occur while you interact with each component you create.

The ComponentLab application, shown in Listing 12-6, provides a class that you can use to study and exercise new components as they are created, all without rewriting a lot of redundant code. The ComponentLab will allow you to change the visibility and accessibility of any component, experiment with different dimensions and placement, and modify the font characteristics used for each component. In addition to that, you can use the ComponentLab to examine the way that a component responds to events as you interact with it.

Listing 12-6 ComponentLab.java

```
// A tool for examining components
import java.awt.*;
import java.awt.event.*;

public class ComponentLab extends Frame
                          implements ActionListener, ⇐
                                     WindowListener
{
    // The ComponentLab and its attributes
    protected Component   theComponent;
    protected CPanel      theSurface    = new CPanel();
    protected Panel       theWorkbench  = new Panel();
    protected TextArea    theDisplay    = new TextArea();
    protected TextField   theInput      = new TextField();
    private   Label       theOutput     = new Label();
    private   Label       fontDesc      = new Label();

    // Position and size attributes
    protected int theX = 50, theY = 50, theWidth = 200, ⇐
             theHeight = 25;

    // Font attributes
```

continued on next page

> **" Remember: Every Container is also a Component, so all of the Component methods are also available for Containers. "**

continued from previous page

```
    private int font=0, style=0, size=0;

    private String fontName[]  = { "TimesRoman", ⇐
                                   "Helvetica", "Courier", ⇐
                                   "Dialog","DialogInput", ⇐
                                   "ZapfDingbats"
                                 };
    private int     fontStyle[] = { Font.PLAIN, Font.BOLD, ⇐
                                   Font.ITALIC, (Font.BOLD+ ⇐
                                   Font.ITALIC)
                                 };
    private int     fontSize[]  = { 12, 15, 18, 21, 24, 27, ⇐
                                   30, 33, 36, 39, 42, 45, ⇐
                                   48,  8, 10
                                 };

// Main method
public static void main(String args[])
{
    ComponentLab theApp = new ComponentLab();
}

// Constructor
public ComponentLab()
{
    super( "Component Lab" );
    setLayout( new BorderLayout() );
    setSize(600,400);

    // Main window divided into two panes
    Panel p1 = new Panel();
    p1.setLayout( new GridLayout( 2, 1 ));

    // Construct the top pane
    Panel p2 = new Panel();
    p2.setLayout( new BorderLayout());
    p2.add( theOutput, "North" );
    p2.add( fontDesc,  "South" );

    // Divide center into control panel and surface
    Panel p3 = new Panel();
    p3.setLayout( new GridLayout( 1, 2 ));

    // Surface for controls
    theSurface.setLayout( null );
    theSurface.setBackground( Color.gray );
    theSurface.setForeground( Color.yellow );
    p3.add( theSurface );

    // Control panel (with input area at top)
    Panel p4 = new Panel();
    Panel p5 = new Panel();
    p4.setLayout( new GridLayout( 5, 3 ) );
    String[] s = { "Left",       "Up",         "Right",
                   "Hide",       "Down",       "Enable",
                   "Show",       "Taller",     "Disable",
                   "Wider",      "Shorter",    "Thinner",
                   "Type Face", "Type Style", "Type Size"
```

```
                            };
        for ( int item = 0; item < s.length; item++ )
        {
            Button b = new Button( s[item] );
            p4.add( b );
            b.addActionListener(this);
        }
        p5.setLayout( new BorderLayout() );
        p5.add( theInput, "North" );
        p5.add( p4, "Center" );
        p3.add( p5 );
        p2.add( p3, "Center" );

        // Bottom panel of the screen
        theWorkbench.setLayout( new BorderLayout() );
        theWorkbench.add( theDisplay, "Center" );

        // Add top and bottom panels to the main panel
        p1.add( p2 );
        p1.add( theWorkbench );

        addWindowListener(this);

        // Add main panel to the screen
        add( p1, "Center" );
        reShow();
        setVisible( true );
    }

// Respond to action events
public void actionPerformed( ActionEvent theEvent )
{
    String theText = "";
    if (theEvent.getSource( ) instanceof Button)
        theText = ((Button) ⇐
            theEvent.getSource( )).getLabel( );

    if ( theText.equals( "Show" ) ) ⇐
      theComponent.setVisible(true);
    if ( theText.equals( "Hide" ) ) ⇐
      theComponent.setVisible(false);
    if ( theText.equals( "Disable" ) ) ⇐
      theComponent.setEnabled(false);
    if ( theText.equals( "Enable" ) ) ⇐
      theComponent.setEnabled(true);

    if ( theText.equals( "Wider" ) )        ⇐
      theWidth  += 10;
    if ( theText.equals( "Thinner" ) )      ⇐
      theWidth  -= 10;
    if ( theText.equals( "Taller" ) )       ⇐
      theHeight += 10;
    if ( theText.equals( "Shorter" ) )      ⇐
      theHeight -= 10;

    if ( theText.equals( "Left" ) )         theX -= 10;
    if ( theText.equals( "Right" ) )        theX += 10;
    if ( theText.equals( "Up" ) )           theY -= 10;
    if ( theText.equals( "Down" ) )         theY += 10;
```

continued on next page

continued from previous page

```java
                    if ( theText.equals( "Type Face" ) )
                    {
                        if ( font < fontName.length - 1 ) font++;
                        else font = 0;
                    }
                    if ( theText.equals( "Type Style" ) )
                    {
                        if ( style < fontStyle.length - 1 ) style++;
                        else style = 0;
                    }
                    if ( theText.equals( "Type Size" ) )
                    {
                        if ( size < fontSize.length - 1 ) size++;
                        else size = 0;
                    }
                    if ( theEvent.getSource( ) == theComponent )
                        log( "" + theEvent );

                reShow();
            }

            protected void log( String s )
            {
                theDisplay.append( s + "\n" );
            }

            // Redisplay and position the component
            public void reShow()
            {
                if ( theComponent != null )
                {
                    theComponent.setFont( new Font( fontName[font],
                                                    fontStyle[style],
                                                    fontSize[size] ) );
                    theComponent.setBounds(theX, theY, theWidth,
                                           theHeight);
                    theOutput.setText( "Component:" + theComponent );
                    fontDesc.setText("Font : " +
                                        theComponent.getFont());
                }
            }

            public void windowClosed       (WindowEvent e) { }
            public void windowClosing      (WindowEvent e) {
              quitApplication( ); }
            public void windowDeiconified(WindowEvent e) { }
            public void windowIconified    (WindowEvent e) { }
            public void windowOpened       (WindowEvent e) { }
            public void windowActivated    (WindowEvent e) { }
            public void windowDeactivated(WindowEvent e) { }

            public void quitApplication( )
            {
                setVisible(false);
                dispose();
                System.exit(0);
            }
        }
```

```
// A helper class to display the panel
class CPanel extends Panel
{
    // Paint the panel that holds the component
    public void paint( Graphics g )
    {
        int rows    = getSize().height;
        int cols    = getSize().width;

        for ( int r = 0; r < rows; r += 10 )
            for ( int c = 0; c < cols; c += 10 )
                g.drawLine( c, r, 1, 1 );
    }
}
```

EXAMINING THE COMPONENTLAB

The ComponentLab consists of several `Panels` that allow you to insert a component and then monitor the event activity and change the attributes of the component you are studying. While understanding the ComponentLab class is not difficult, you don't have to understand exactly how it works to find it useful. Figure 12-8 shows the ComponentLab and each of its major parts.

FIGURE 12-8

The ComponentLab

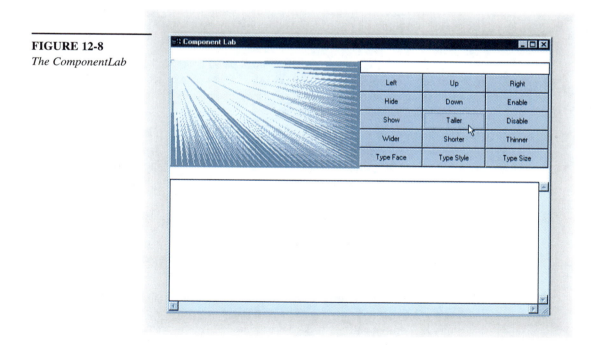

The main parts of the ComponentLab are

☕ The *surface*, where you will place the components you are studying. This is a CPanel object named theSurface. The CPanel class is a helper class designed to hold components. The only method defined inside the CPanel class is paint( ), which draws an attractive pattern on its face, making it easy to see the components placed there. This field is protected so you can add components to it in the subclasses you create.

☕ A *control pad* of Buttons that allow you to control various aspects of each component as it is added to the ComponentLab. Using these Buttons, you can change the position of the component, by moving it left, right, up, and down. You can change the dimensions of your component, by making it taller, shorter, wider, or thinner. You can change the accessibility of the component, making it hidden or visible, enabled or disabled. You can even change the Font attributes used with the component, cycling through a set of typefaces, styles, and sizes.

☕ A Label that displays the attributes of the component. This field, named theOutput, is positioned at the top of the ComponentLab Frame, directly under the title bar. Another Label, fontDesc, shows the characteristics of the currently selected Font used by the component. Like theOutput, this stretches the full width of the window, but appears below theSurface and the control panel.

☕ Directly above the Buttons in the control panel is a TextField called theInput. This field is also protected so that you can access it in subclasses of ComponentLab. Its purpose is to provide you a place to change the text associated with a particular component.

☕ The bottom half of the ComponentLab is taken up with a BorderLayout Panel, whose central component is a TextArea called theDisplay. Also protected, the purpose of theDisplay is to provide a place to monitor the various events that occur as you interact with the components you place in the ComponentLab.

The ComponentLab class has the following methods:

☕ The constructor, ComponentLab( ), which lays out all the parts of the display. Figure 12-9 shows how the constructor assembles and nests the various Panels to create a pleasing display.

☕ The actionPerformed( ) method, which only responds to actionPerformed events. These are events caused by a Button-press, or by choosing a menu item. In ComponentLab, these are used to control the appearance of the component.

- The `windowClosing()` method, which closes the application when it receives a `WINDOW_CLOSING` message. Four other window methods handle other window-related events, but take no actual action in response to such events.

- The `reShow()` method, which applies any changes to the current component, displays it in its new position, and repaints the ComponentLab.

- The `log()` method, which is used in `ComponentLab` and its subclasses to display events on the `TextArea`, `theDisplay`.

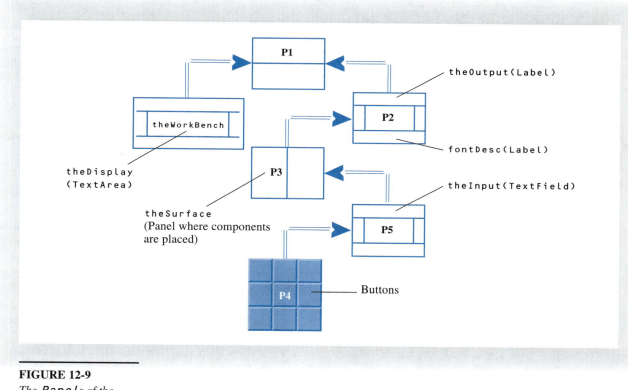

FIGURE 12-9
*The **Panel**s of the* `ComponentLab` *class*

Meeting the Controls

To put the ComponentLab to work, you create a subclass of `ComponentLab` and add your own control. The `ComponentLab` class will then allow you to modify, manipulate, and examine the control to your heart's content. The sample programs for each control will use the same basic form:

1. Create a subclass that `extends` the `ComponentLab`.

2. Add a field whose type is that of the particular component—`Label`, `Button`, and so on—that you want to study.

3. Assign the `Label` or `Button` to `theComponent` reference in the parent class, `ComponentLab`.

4. Add your component to the `Panel`, named `theSurface`.

You can also add additional `Button`s (or other components) to the `Panel` that holds the `TextArea` used to display events. This `Panel` is a `protected` field called `theWorkBench`, and it uses a `BorderLayout`. To add a `Button`, as the `StudyLabel` application below does, you simply say

```
theWorkBench.add( theButton, "North" );
```

You might want to add such additional components to study special methods that are only contained in the specific class you are studying, such as the alignment methods of the `Label` class.

THE `Label` CLASS

Probably the simplest and most humble, but also most useful, of the children of the `Component` class is the `Label`, which you've been using in your applets and applications from the very beginning of this book. A `Label` is simply a piece of text that can be used to identify another control, or to communicate information to the user. Most of the capabilities of `Label`s are based on the fact that they are `Component`s: They have position and size, they can be drawn with various `Font`s, and they can be hidden or shown. A `Label` can be disabled, but because a `Label` doesn't do anything to begin with (other than sit there), there's little point in doing so.

To the capabilities afforded it by heredity, the `Label` class adds two new capabilities. A `Label` can display a text `String`, and it can justify its text to the left, the right, or the center of its bounding rectangle. Both the value of the text `String` and the choice of alignment can be specified when the `Label` is constructed, or changed on-the-fly by use of methods. The key constructors, methods, and fields of `Label`s are given in Tables 12-14, 12-15, and 12-16, respectively.

TABLE 12-14
KEY public CONSTRUCTORS OF THE Label CLASS

```
Label( )
Label(String label)
Label(String label, int alignment)
```

TABLE 12-15
KEY public METHODS OF THE Label CLASS

METHOD HEADER	FUNCTION
int getAlignment( )	Get alignment of text within Label.
String getText( )	Get text contained within Label.
void setAlignment(int alignment)	Set alignment of text within Label.
void setText(String label)	Set text contained in Label.

TABLE 12-16 KEY
public FIELDS OF THE Label CLASS

FIELD	TYPE	MEANING/USE
CENTER	int	Specify Label alignment.
LEFT	int	Specify Label alignment.
RIGHT	int	Specify Label alignment.

The StudyLabel application, shown in Listing 12-7, demonstrates the use of Labels. As you run the application, you can use the ComponentLab application to configure a Label with a specified font, locate the Label at a specified position within a window, as well as change the dimensions and visibility of the Label. The StudyLabel application is a great way to experiment with and to observe the effects of creating various kinds of Labels. Figure 12-10 shows sample output of the StudyLabel application. Don't be too concerned with the details of the source code; focus on the calls to the methods of the Label object known as theLabel.

Listing 12-7 StudyLabel.java

```
// Examining the Label Component
// Built upon ComponentLab.java
import java.awt.*;
import java.awt.event.*;

public class StudyLabel extends ComponentLab
                        implements ActionListener
{
```

continued on next page

continued from previous page

```
private Label   theLabel    = ⇐
   new Label("This is a Label object");
private Button leftAlign    = new Button("Left Align");
private Button rightAlign   = new Button("Right Align");
private Button centerAlign = new Button("Center Align");

public static void main(String args[])
{
    StudyLabel theApp = new StudyLabel();
}

public StudyLabel()
{
    super();
    setTitle( "Studying the Label object" );

    Panel p = new Panel();
    p.setLayout( new GridLayout( 1, 3, 5, 0 ) );
    p.add( leftAlign );
    p.add( rightAlign );
    p.add( centerAlign );
    theWorkbench.add( p, "North" );

    theComponent = theLabel;
    theLabel.setBackground( Color.lightGray );
    theLabel.setForeground( Color.red );
    theSurface.add( theLabel );

    theInput.addActionListener(this);
    leftAlign.addActionListener(this);
    rightAlign.addActionListener(this);
    centerAlign.addActionListener(this);

    reShow();
}

public void actionPerformed( ActionEvent theEvent )
{
    if ( theEvent.getSource( ) == theInput )
    {
        theLabel.setText( theInput.getText() );
        reShow();
        return;
    }

    if ( theEvent.getSource( ) == leftAlign)
        theLabel.setAlignment( Label.LEFT );
    else if ( theEvent.getSource( ) == rightAlign )
        theLabel.setAlignment( Label.RIGHT );
    else if ( theEvent.getSource( ) == centerAlign )
        theLabel.setAlignment( Label.CENTER );

    super.actionPerformed( theEvent );
}
}
```

FIGURE 12-10

Output of the StudyLabel application

THE Button CLASS

One step up from the Label in terms of capability is the Button. A Button is much like a Label, except that a Button is clickable and lacks the ability of the Label to align the text it contains. Oddly, to change the text associated with a Label, you use the setText( ) method, but to perform the corresponding task with a Button, you have to use setLabel( ). The key constructors and methods of the Button class are shown in Table 12-17 and Table 12-18, respectively.

TABLE 12-17
KEY public CONSTRUCTORS OF THE Button CLASS

Button( )
Button(String label)

TABLE 12-18
KEY public METHODS OF THE Button CLASS

METHOD HEADER	FUNCTION
String getLabel( )	Get the text contained within the Button.
void setLabel(String label)	Set the text contained within the Button.

The StudyButton application, shown in Listing 12-8, was written to show how to work with Buttons. It is very similar to the StudyLabel application, except that there are no additional Button methods, as there were for the Label class. However, unlike Labels, Buttons do generate Events, as you can see by clicking the Button with the mouse or by pressing a key when the Button has *focus*. When a control has focus, it means that Java will send keystroke events to that control. You can usually tell when a Button has focus, because the operating system will change its appearance. Windows 95, for instance, draws a dashed line around the interior of Buttons that have focus.

You can give your `Button` focus by first clicking on it with the mouse. Figure 12-11 shows the StudyButton application in operation.

Listing 12-8 StudyButton.java

```
// Examining the Button Component
// Built upon ComponentLab.java
import java.awt.*;
import java.awt.event.*;

public class StudyButton extends ComponentLab
                              implements ActionListener
{
    private Button theButton   = new Button( "Button" );

    public static void main(String args[])
    {
        StudyButton theApp = new StudyButton();
    }

    public StudyButton()
    {
        setTitle( "Studying the Button object" );

        theComponent = theButton;
        theButton.setForeground( Color.black );
        theSurface.add( theButton );

        theButton.addActionListener(this);
        theInput.addActionListener(this);

        reShow();
    }

    public void actionPerformed( ActionEvent theEvent )
    {
        if ( theEvent.getSource( ) == theInput )
        {
            theButton.setLabel( theInput.getText() );
            reShow();
            return;
        }
        super.actionPerformed( theEvent );
    }
}
```

THE Checkbox CLASS

A `Checkbox` is something like a combination of a `Label` and a `Button`, only the `Button` part of a `Checkbox` acts more like a switch than a push-button. A `Checkbox` consists of a square `Button` that can be clicked to cause it to change from the "off" state to the "on" state. The "on" state is denoted by a check mark or an *x* drawn over the `Checkbox`. The "off" state is denoted by the absence of such a mark. The `Checkbox` has a bit of text near it—that's the `Label` part—used to explain the `Checkbox`.

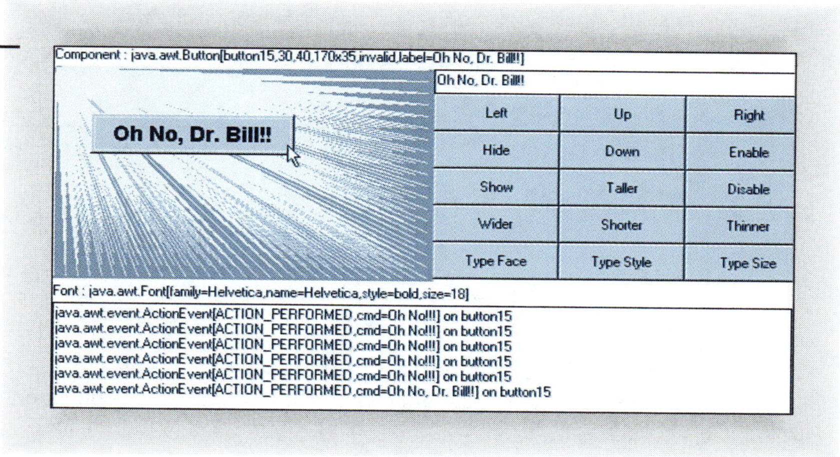

FIGURE 12-11
The StudyButton application

The key constructors and methods of the `Checkbox` class are given in Table 12-19 and Table 12-20, respectively. Note that one constructor and one method refer to an argument of type `CheckboxGroup`. These are used to make the `Checkbox` function as part of a group of `Checkboxes` that act like old-fashioned radio buttons: Only one member of the group can be "on" at any time. Creating and using such "radio buttons" is discussed under the topic of the `CheckboxGroup` class shortly.

As is the case with `Buttons`, it's possible to create the `Checkbox` either without an initial `Label` or with one. In either case, it's possible to later change the `Label` by use of the `setLabel( )` method. To support its two-state property, the `Checkbox` adds the `getState( )` and `setState( )` methods that allow you to obtain the current state of the `Checkbox` and to alter its state programmatically. The state of the `Checkbox` is represented as a `boolean` value: `true` indicates "on" and `false` indicates "off."

TABLE 12-19
KEY `public` CONSTRUCTORS OF THE `Checkbox` CLASS

```
Checkbox( )
Checkbox(String label)
Checkbox(String label, boolean cond, CheckboxGroup g)
```

TABLE 12-20
KEY `public` METHODS OF THE `Checkbox` CLASS

METHOD HEADER	FUNCTION
`String getLabel( )`	Get the text that labels the `Checkbox`.
`boolean getState( )`	Get the state of the `Checkbox`.
`void setLabel(String label)`	Set the text that labels the `Checkbox`.

Table continued...

TABLE 12-20 KEY `public` METHODS OF THE `Checkbox` CLASS CONTINUED...

METHOD HEADER	FUNCTION
void setCheckboxGroup(CheckboxGroup g)	Make the `Checkbox` part of a "radio button" group (see `CheckboxGroup` component).
void setState(boolean cond)	Set the state of the `Checkbox`.

The StudyCheckbox application, in Listing 12-9, was created for experimenting with `Checkboxes`. Figure 12-12 shows the StudyCheckbox application as it runs.

Listing 12-9 StudyCheckbox.java

```
// Examining the Checkbox Component
// Built upon ComponentLab.java
import java.awt.*;
import java.awt.event.*;

public class StudyCheckbox extends ComponentLab
                                implements ActionListener, ⇐
                                           ItemListener
{
    private Checkbox   theCheckbox = ⇐
       new Checkbox( "This is a Checkbox object" );
    private Button     trueButton  = new Button( "True" );
    private Button     falseButton = new Button( "False" );

    public static void main(String args[])
    {
        StudyCheckbox theApp = new StudyCheckbox();
    }

    public StudyCheckbox()
    {
        setTitle( "Studying the Checkbox object" );

        Panel p = new Panel();
        p.setLayout( new GridLayout(1, 2) );
        p.add( trueButton );
        p.add( falseButton );
        falseButton.setEnabled(false);
        theWorkbench.add( p, "North" );

        theComponent = theCheckbox;
        theCheckbox.setForeground( Color.black );
        theSurface.add( theCheckbox );

        theCheckbox.addItemListener(this);
```

```
        trueButton.addActionListener(this);
        falseButton.addActionListener(this);
        theInput.addActionListener(this);

        invalidate();
        validate();
        reShow();
}

public void actionPerformed( ActionEvent theEvent )
{
    if ( theEvent.getSource( ) == theInput )
    {
        theCheckbox.setLabel( theInput.getText() );
        reShow();
        return;
    }

    if (theEvent.getSource( ) == trueButton)
        theCheckbox.setState( true );

    if (theEvent.getSource( ) == falseButton)
        theCheckbox.setState( false );

    updateState( );

    reShow();
    super.actionPerformed( theEvent );
}

public void itemStateChanged( ItemEvent theEvent )
{
    updateState( );
    reShow();
    log( theEvent.toString() );
}

public void updateState( )
{
    if ( theCheckbox.getState() )
    {
        trueButton.setEnabled(false);
        falseButton.setEnabled(true);
    }
    else
    {
        trueButton.setEnabled(true);
        falseButton.setEnabled(false);
    }
}
}
```

FIGURE 12-12
*The StudyCheckbox
application*

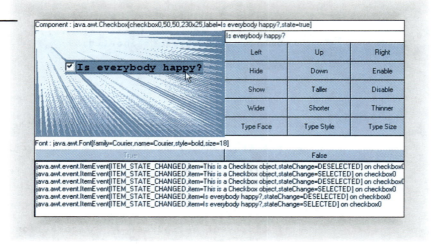

THE CheckboxGroup CLASS

The CheckboxGroup class is used to create an object that can constrain a set of Checkboxes so that only one of them can be "on" at any time. Such a set is commonly referred to as *radio buttons*.

The CheckboxGroup can be created either before or after its member Checkboxes. One Checkbox constructor allows you to specify an existing CheckboxGroup when a Checkbox is first created. Alternatively, you can use the setCheckboxGroup() method of the Checkbox class to add an existing Checkbox to a CheckboxGroup. Here's a short example showing how the first method can be used:

```
CheckboxGroup cbg = new CheckboxGroup( );
Checkbox chocolateSyrup = new Checkbox("Chocolate Syrup", ⇐
    true, cbg);
Checkbox caramelSyrup  = new Checkbox("Caramel Syrup", ⇐
    false, cbg);
```

The setSelectedCheckbox( ) method can be used to programmatically set one of the radio buttons to the "on" state like this:

```
cbg.setSelectedCheckbox(chocolateSyrup);
```

Similarly, the getSelectedCheckbox( ) method can be used to determine which of the member Checkboxes is currently "on":

```
Checkbox onBox = cbg.getSelectedCheckbox( );
```

The lone constructor of the CheckboxGroup class is given in Table 12-21. The methods are summarized in Table 12-22.

TABLE 12-21
KEY **public** CONSTRUCTOR OF THE **CheckboxGroup** COMPONENT

```
CheckboxGroup( )
```

TABLE 12-22
KEY **public** METHODS OF THE **CheckboxGroup** COMPONENT

METHOD HEADER	FUNCTION
`Checkbox getSelectedCheckbox( )`	Get the currently selected **Checkbox**.
`void setSelectedCheckbox(Checkbox box)`	Select the specified **Checkbox**.

As with the previous examples in this chapter, the StudyCheckBoxGroup application will help you experiment with, and learn about, `CheckboxGroups`. The source code for this application is shown in Listing 12-10, and you can see it running in Figure 12-13.

Listing 12–10 StudyCheckboxGroup.java

```java
// Examining the CheckboxGroup component
// Built upon ComponentLab.java
import java.awt.*;
import java.awt.event.*;

public class StudyCheckboxGroup extends ComponentLab
                              implements ActionListener, ⇐
                                         ItemListener
{
    private CheckboxGroup theGroup    = ⇐
      new CheckboxGroup( );
    private Checkbox       countryBox = ⇐
      new Checkbox("Country", true,  theGroup);
    private Checkbox       rockBox    = ⇐
      new Checkbox("Rock",    false, theGroup);

    private Button         countryButton = ⇐
      new Button( "Country" );
    private Button         rockButton    = ⇐
      new Button( "Rock" );
    private Label          currentItem   = new Label();

    public static void main(String args[])
    {
        StudyCheckboxGroup theApp = ⇐
          new StudyCheckboxGroup( );
    }

    public StudyCheckboxGroup( )
    {
```

continued on next page

continued from previous page

```
            super();
            setTitle( "Studying the CheckboxGroup object" );

            Panel theButtons = new Panel();
            theButtons.setLayout( new GridLayout(1, 2) );
            theButtons.add( countryButton );
            theButtons.add( rockButton    );
            rockButton.setEnabled(false);
            rockButton.addActionListener(this);
            countryButton.addActionListener(this);
            theWorkbench.add( theButtons,  "North" );
            theWorkbench.add( currentItem, "South" );

            Panel theGroupPanel = new Panel();
            theComponent = theGroupPanel;
            theGroupPanel.setForeground( Color.black );
            theGroupPanel.setLayout( new GridLayout(2, 1) );
            theGroupPanel.add( countryBox );
            theGroupPanel.add( rockBox    );
            countryBox.addItemListener(this);
            rockBox.addItemListener(this);
            theSurface.add( theGroupPanel );

            theInput.setEnabled(false);
            updateState( );
    }

    public void actionPerformed( ActionEvent theEvent )
    {
        if (theEvent.getSource( ) == countryButton)
            countryBox.setState( true );

        if (theEvent.getSource( ) == rockButton)
            rockBox.setState( true );

        updateState( );

        super.actionPerformed( theEvent );
    }

    public void itemStateChanged (ItemEvent theEvent )
    {
        updateState( );
        log( theEvent.toString() );
    }

    public void updateState( )
    {
        if ( rockBox.getState() )
        {
            rockButton.setEnabled(false);
            countryButton.setEnabled(true);
        }
        else
        {
            rockButton.setEnabled(true);
            countryButton.setEnabled(false);
        }
```

```
currentItem.setText("Current button = ⇐
  "+theGroup.getSelectedCheckbox());
theComponent.invalidate();
theComponent.validate();
reShow();
    }
  }
```

THE Choice CLASS

The Choice class is a somewhat different component from those you've met so far. The Choice class contains a list of items from which the user can select a single item. (In fact, the Choice is called a ListBox by MS Windows programmers.) The currently selected item is visible in the component; clicking the Choice drops down a menu that shows the alternatives.

A Choice is built by use of a no-argument constructor. To place the items within the Choice, you use the add( ) method, which is shown in Table 12-23 along with other useful methods of the Choice class. For example, the statements

```
Choice theChoice = new Choice( );
theChoice.add("C");
theChoice.add("C++");
theChoice.add("Java");
theChoice.select("Java");
```

would create a Choice allowing the user to pick a language and would make Java the initially selected item. Obtaining the selected item is easily done by use of the getSelectedItem( ) method:

```
String currentItem = theChoice.getSelectedItem( );
```

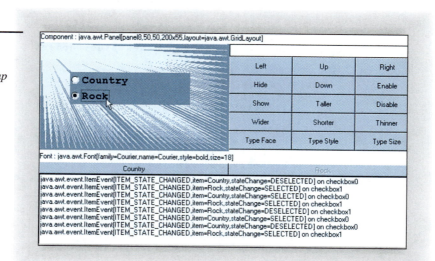

FIGURE 12-13

The StudyCheckboxGroup application

TABLE 12-23
KEY public METHODS OF THE Choice CLASS

METHOD HEADER	FUNCTION
void add(String item)	Add the item to the Choice.
String getItem(int index)	Get the item at the specified position within the Choice.
int getItemCount( )	Get the number of items in the Choice.
int getSelectedIndex( )	Get the index of the currently selected item.
String getSelectedItem( )	Get the currently selected item.
void select(int pos)	Select the specified item.
void select(String item)	Select the specified item.

The ComponentLab for the Choice component, the StudyChoice application, is shown in Listing 12-11. Figure 12-14 shows the application as it runs.

Listing 12-11 StudyChoice.java

```
// Examining the Choice Object
// Built upon ComponentLab.java
//
import java.awt.*;
import java.awt.event.*;

public class StudyChoice extends ComponentLab
                         implements ActionListener, ⇐
                                    ItemListener
{
    Choice theChoice     = new Choice( );
    Label  theSelection = new Label( );

    public static void main(String args[])
    {
        StudyChoice theApp = new StudyChoice( );
    }

    public StudyChoice( )
    {
        setTitle( "Studying the Choice object" );

        theChoice.add("Atlantic");
        theChoice.add("Pacific");
        theChoice.add("Arctic");
        theChoice.add("Indian");
        theChoice.add("Antarctic");

        theComponent = theChoice;
        theChoice.setForeground( Color.black );
        theChoice.setBackground( Color.white );
        theSurface.add( theChoice );
```

```
        theWorkbench.add( theSelection, "South" );

        theInput.addActionListener(this);
        theChoice.addItemListener(this);

        reShow();
    }

    public void actionPerformed( ActionEvent theEvent )
    {
        if ( theEvent.getSource( ) == theInput )
        {
            theChoice.add( theInput.getText() );
            reShow();
            return;
        }
        super.actionPerformed(theEvent);
        theChoice.invalidate();
        theChoice.validate();
    }

    public void itemStateChanged( ItemEvent theEvent )
    {

        String theIndex = "Index = " + ⇐
           theChoice.getSelectedIndex();
        String theItem  = "Item  = " + ⇐
           theChoice.getSelectedItem();
        theSelection.setText( theIndex + " : " + theItem );
        reShow();
        log( theEvent.toString() );
    }
}
```

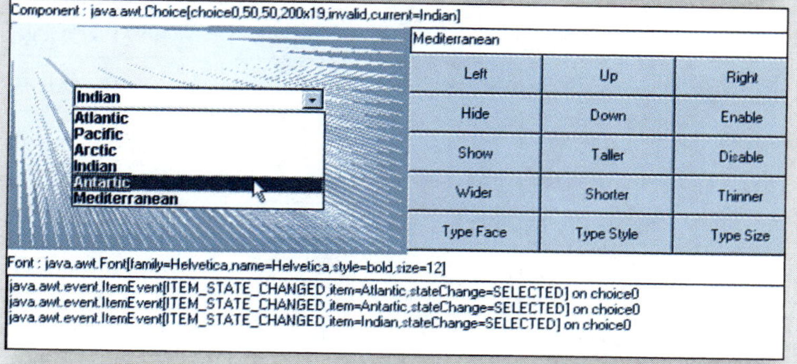

FIGURE 12-14

The StudyChoice application

THE List CLASS

The List is something like a Choice, except that in a Choice, only the selected item is visible. In a List, it's normal to have a number of visible items along with scroll bars that allow the user to view and choose from among many possible items. Also, the List, unlike the Choice, can be configured to accept multiple selections. With a List, users can truly have their cake and eat it too!

The constructors for the List class are shown in Table 12-24 and its methods are shown in Table 12-25. The following example creates a List allowing multiple selections. This could also be done by use of the second form of the constructor.

```
List happiness = new List( );
happiness.add("Have cake");
happiness.add("Eat cake");
happiness.add("Take vacation");
happiness.add("Complete assignment");
happiness.setMultipleSelections(true);
// . . .
// user selects items, generating action event(s)
// . . .
String[] goals = happiness.getSelectedItems( );
```

TABLE 12-24
KEY public CONSTRUCTORS OF THE List CLASS

List( )
List(int rows, boolean multipleSelections)

TABLE 12-25
KEY public METHODS OF THE List CLASS

METHOD HEADER	FUNCTION
void add(String item)	Add an item to the List.
void add(String item, int index)	Add an item at the specified position within the List.
void deselect(int index)	Deselect the specified item.
String getItem(int index)	Get the text of the specified item.
int getItemCount( )	Get the number of items in the List.
int getRows( )	Get the number of rows used to construct the List.
int getSelectedIndex( )	Get the index of the selected item.
int[] getSelectedIndexes( )	Get an array of indexes of the selected items.
String getSelectedItem( )	Get the text of the selected item.
String[] getSelectedItems( )	Get an array of text strings of the selected items.

Table continued…

TABLE 12-25 KEY `public` METHODS OF THE `List` CLASS CONTINUED...

METHOD HEADER	FUNCTION
`boolean isMultipleMode( )`	Determine if the `List` allows multiple selections.
`boolean isSelected(int index)`	Determine if the specified item is selected.
`void makeVisible(int index)`	Make the specified item visible.
`void remove(int position)`	Delete the specified item from the `List`.
`void removeAll( )`	Clear all items from the `List`.
`void replaceItem(String newText, int index)`	Replace the specified item.
`void select(int index)`	Select the specified item.
`void setMultipleMode(boolean cond)`	Set the `List` to allow (`true`) or disallow (`false`) multiple selections.

The application for studying `List`s is named—you guessed it—StudyList, and it can be found in Listing 12-12. Figure 12-15 shows StudyList as it runs, along with some of the events generated by the `List`.

Listing 12-12 StudyList.java

```java
// Examining the List Object
// Built upon ComponentLab.java
import java.awt.*;
import java.awt.event.*;

public class StudyList extends ComponentLab
                       implements ActionListener, ItemListener
{
    private List      theList      = new List( );
    private Label     theSelection = new Label( );
    private Button    multButton   =
       new Button("Multiple Selection");
    private Button    clrButton    = new Button("Clear List");
    private Button    delButton    = new Button("Delete Item");

    private boolean multiSelect    = false;

    public static void main(String args[])
    {
        StudyList theApp = new StudyList( );
    }

    public StudyList( )
    {
        setTitle( "Studying the List object" );

        Panel theButtons = new Panel();
```

continued on next page

continued from previous page

```
            theButtons.setLayout( new GridLayout( 1, 3 ) );
            theButtons.add( multButton );
            theButtons.add( clrButton );
            theButtons.add( delButton );
            multButton.addActionListener(this);
            clrButton.addActionListener(this);
            delButton.addActionListener(this);
            theWorkbench.add( theButtons, "North" );

            theList.add("Atlantic");
            theList.add("Pacific");
            theList.add("Arctic");
            theList.add("Indian");
            theList.add("Antartic");

            theComponent = theList;
            theHeight *= 3;
            theList.setForeground( Color.black );
            theList.setBackground( Color.white );
            theSurface.add( theList );
            theWorkbench.add( theSelection, "South" );

            theInput.addActionListener(this);
            theList.addItemListener(this);
            theList.addActionListener(this);

            theList.setVisible( true );
            reShow();

    }

    public void actionPerformed( ActionEvent theEvent )
    {
        if ( theEvent.getSource( ) == theInput )
        {
            theList.add( theInput.getText() , 0);
            theList.select( 0 );
            reShow();
            return;
        }

        if ( theEvent.getSource( ) == delButton )
            theList.remove( theList.getSelectedIndex() );

        if ( theEvent.getSource( ) == clrButton )
            theList.removeAll();

        if ( theEvent.getSource( ) == multButton )
        {
            if (multButton.getLabel( ).equals(⇐
              "Multiple Selection"))
            {
                multButton.setLabel( "Single Selection" );
                theList.setMultipleMode( true );
            }
            else
            {
                multButton.setLabel( "Multiple Selection"
);
```

```
                    theList.setMultipleMode( false );
            }
            reShow();
            return;
        }


        super.actionPerformed( theEvent );
    }

    public void itemStateChanged( ItemEvent theEvent )
    {
        String theIndex = "Index = " + ⇐
          theList.getSelectedIndex();
        String theItem  = "Item  = " + ⇐
          theList.getSelectedItem();
        theSelection.setText( theIndex + " : " + theItem );
        reShow();
        log( theEvent.toString() );
    }
}
```

THE Scrollbar CLASS

Scroll bars, also known as *sliders*, are an interesting sort of graphical input device. Figure 12-16 shows a typical scroll bar and explains its operation. The current position of the thumb is translated to a numerical value somewhere between the minimum and maximum values assigned to the extreme possible positions of the scroll bar. Scroll bars can be either horizontal or vertical. It is common to have a pair of scroll bars that

FIGURE 12-15

The StudyList application

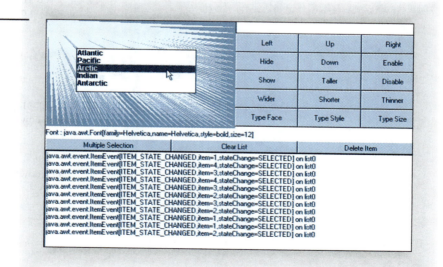

allows a user to page left and right, up and down, through a large document. In the ComponentLab applications you have been building, the event display `TextArea` has a set of scroll bars that allow you to see the text for very long events.

The constructors of the `Scrollbar` class are given in Table 12-26, and the methods of the class are given in Table 12-27. The default range of values for a `Scrollbar` is 0 to 100. If you want the `Scrollbar` to track a different set of values, you can use the `setValues( )` method to specify them. If you're using the `Scrollbar` to scroll a window, the "visible area" refers to the size of the window. If you're using the `Scrollbar` as a slider, you can select this value to zero.

TABLE 12-26
KEY `public` CONSTRUCTORS OF THE `Scrollbar` CLASS

```
Scrollbar( )
Scrollbar(int orient)
Scrollbar(int orient, int value, int visible, int min, int max)
```

FIGURE 12-16
*Components and opera-
tion of a* `Scrollbar`

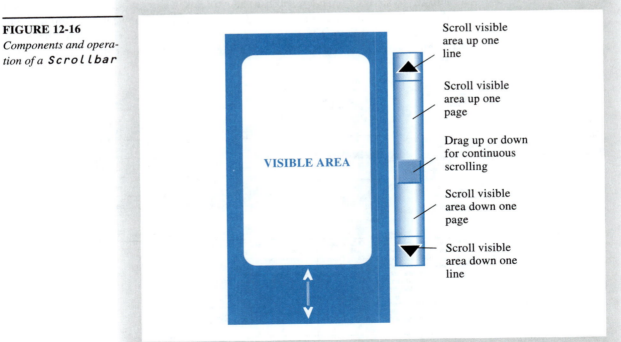

TABLE 12-27
KEY `public` METHODS OF THE `Scrollbar` CLASS

METHOD HEADER	FUNCTION
`int getMaximum( )`	Get the maximum possible value of the thumb, as set by `setValue( )`.
`int getMinimum( )`	Get the minimum possible value of the thumb, as set by `setValue( )`.
`int getBlockIncrement( )`	Get the increment value associated with a page up/down operation.
`int getUnitIncrement( )`	Get the increment value associated with a line up/down operation.
`int getValue( )`	Get the current value of the thumb.
`int getVisible( )`	Get the size of the object being scrolled.
`void setBlockIncrement(int step)`	Set the increment value associated with a page up/down operation.
`void setUnitIncrement(int step)`	Set the increment value associated with a line up/down operation.
`void setValue(int value)`	Set the current position of the thumb.
`void setValues(int value, int visible, int min, int max)`	Set the current position of the thumb, the size of the object being scrolled, and the minimum and maximum values of the thumb.

An application for learning about `Scrollbars`, StudyScrollbar, is shown in Listing 12-13. Figure 12-17 shows the StudyScrollbar application and the various events generated by use of the `Scrollbar`.

Listing 12–13 StudyScrollbar.java

```
// Using a Scrollbar as a slider
// Built upon ComponentLab.java (Listing 12-6)
import java.awt.*;
import java.awt.event.*;

public class StudyScrollbar extends ComponentLab implements
AdjustmentListener
{
    Scrollbar theSB  = new Scrollbar(Scrollbar.HORIZONTAL, ⇐
                                    50, 40, 0, 255);

    public static void main(String args[])
    {
        StudyScrollbar theApp = new StudyScrollbar( );
    }

    public StudyScrollbar( )
    {
        setTitle( "Studying the Scrollbar object" );

        theComponent = theSB;
```

continued on next page

continued from previous page

```
        theSurface.add( theSB );
        theSB.addAdjustmentListener(this);

        reShow();
    }

    public void adjustmentValueChanged( ⇐
      AdjustmentEvent theEvent )
    {
        int newColor = theSB.getValue();
        theSurface.setForeground( ⇐
          new Color( 255, newColor, newColor ));
        theSurface.repaint();
        reShow();
        log( theEvent.toString() );
    }
}
```

THE TextComponent CLASS

The `TextComponent` is the parent of two talented children: the `TextField` and the more ambitious `TextArea`. The methods of the `TextComponent` class, shown in Table 12-28, are available to each of these extended classes.

Both the `TextField` and the `TextArea` define boxes in which the user can enter text. The text can be obtained from the component by use of the `getText( )` method. The value it returns does not include any ending carriage return (`'\n'`). The text can also be changed by use of the `setText( )` method. User input can be prohibited without disabling the component (which would alter its appearance) by passing the argument `false` in the `setEditable( )` method.

FIGURE 12-17

The StudyScrollbar application

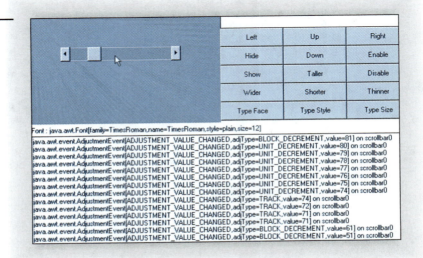

The user can also drag the mouse across text within a TextComponent to select some, or all, of the text. Several methods allow determination of the position or contents of the selected text. Position is expressed relative to the start of the text, which is position 0.

TABLE 12-28
KEY public METHODS OF THE TextComponent CLASS

METHOD HEADER	**FUNCTION**
String getSeletectedText( )	Get the currently selected text.
int getSelectionEnd( )	Get the ending position of the selection, if any.
int getSelectionStart( )	Get the starting position of the selection, if any.
String getText( )	Get the text.
boolean isEditable( )	Get a value indicating whether the text component is editable by the user.
void select(int selStart, int selEnd)	Select the specified portion of the text.
void selectAll( )	Select the entire text.
void setEditable(boolean cond)	Set the component to allow editing (true) or disallow editing (false).
void setText(String text)	Set the text.

THE TextField CLASS

The TextField class inherits the capabilities of its TextComponent superclass and adds a few of its own. A TextField can hold a single row of text. Its width will be set to accommodate a String used in the constructor or can be specified by use of an int parameter giving a number of columns. The latter method may prove unreliable if the TextField is drawn with a proportional Font. It is best used with a Font, such as Courier, in which every letter has the same size.

It's possible to use setFont( ) to change the Font in which text will be drawn, but, of course, this can only be done *after* the TextField has been created. How, then, can you set the Font for a TextField *before* it's created? Simply by setting the Font of the container that will hold the TextField, by use of the familiar setFont( ) method: remember Containers are Components and share all the methods of the Component class. In this case, the Font of the Container becomes the default Font for Components placed inside it.

The constructors of the TextField class are given in Table 12-29, and the methods are given in Table 12-30. The methods allow use of a TextField to enter passwords and other sensitive information. By use of setEchoChar( ), every key typed by the user can be echoed as some specified character. For example, the following

```
TextField passwordField = new TextField( );
passwordField.setEchoChar('*');
```

would cause every character typed in the `TextField` to be displayed as an asterisk, regardless of the actual character typed. The text actually typed could then be retrieved by use of `getText( )`.

TABLE 12-29
KEY public CONSTRUCTORS OF THE TextField CLASS

```
TextField( )
TextField(String text, int cols)
TextField(String text, int cols)
```

TABLE 12-30
KEY public METHODS OF THE TextField CLASS

METHOD HEADER	FUNCTION
boolean echoCharIsSet( )	Determine if an echo character has been set.
char getEchoChar( )	Get the echo character ('\0' if none).
void setEchoChar(char c)	Set the echo character ('\0' to remove).

You can do some `TextField` aerobics using the StudyTextField application shown in Listing 12-14. Figure 12-18 shows the application as it runs.

Listing 12-14 StudyTextField.java

```java
// Using a TextField
// Built upon ComponentLab.java
import java.awt.*;
import java.awt.event.*;

public class StudyTextField extends         ComponentLab
                            implements ActionListener, ⇐
                                       KeyListener
{
    TextField theText      = ⇐
       new TextField( "This is a TextField" );
    Button     editButton = new Button( "No Edit" );
    Button     echoButton = new Button( "No Echo" );

    public static void main(String args[])
    {
        StudyTextField theApp = new StudyTextField( );
    }

    public StudyTextField( )
    {
        setTitle( "Studying the TextField object" );

        Panel theButtons = new Panel();
        theButtons.setLayout( new GridLayout( 1, 2 ) );
        theButtons.add( editButton );
```

```
            theButtons.add( echoButton );
            editButton.addActionListener(this);
            echoButton.addActionListener(this);
            theWorkbench.add( theButtons, "North" );

            theComponent = theText;
            theText.setBackground( Color.white );
            theText.setForeground( Color.black );
            theSurface.add( theText );
            theText.addActionListener(this);
            theText.addKeyListener(this);

            reShow();
    }

    public void actionPerformed( ActionEvent theEvent )
    {
        if ( theEvent.getSource( ) == theInput )
        {
            theText.setText( theInput.getText() );
        }

        else if (theEvent.getSource( ) == editButton)
        {
            if ((editButton.getLabel( )).equals("No Edit"))
            {
                theText.setEditable(false);
                editButton.setLabel("Edit");
            }
            else
            {
                theText.setEditable(true);
                editButton.setLabel("No Edit");
            }
        }

        else if (theEvent.getSource( ) == echoButton)
        {
            if ((echoButton.getLabel( )).equals("No Echo"))
            {
                theText.setEchoChar('*');
                echoButton.setLabel("Echo");
            }
            else
            {
                theText.setEchoChar('\0');
                echoButton.setLabel("No Echo");
            }
        }
        reShow();
        super.actionPerformed( theEvent );
    }

    public void keyPressed( KeyEvent theEvent )    ⇐
        { log( "" + theEvent ); }
    public void keyReleased( KeyEvent theEvent )   ⇐
        { log( "" + theEvent ); }
    public void keyTyped( KeyEvent theEvent )      ⇐
        { log( "" + theEvent ); }
}
```

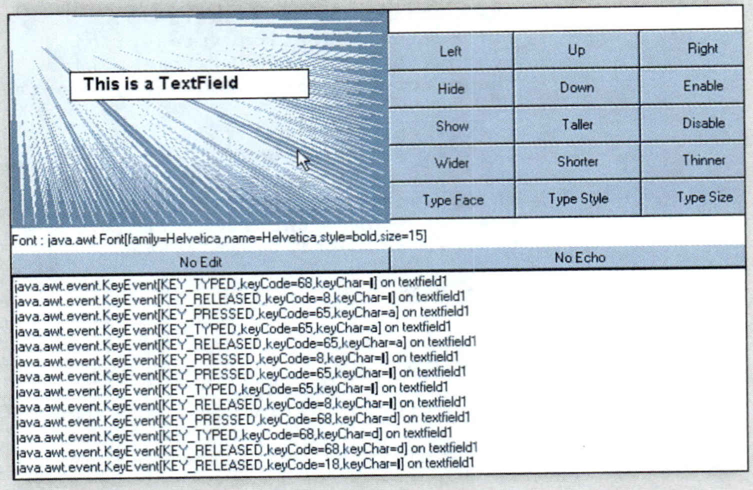

FIGURE 12-18

The StudyTextField application

THE TextArea CLASS

The TextArea class, like its sibling TextField, allows the user to enter text. The TextArea, however, is a multiline input area that includes scroll bars, so that large amounts of text can be entered and displayed. The class also includes methods used to insert, append, and replace text within the TextArea. The constructors for TextArea are given in Table 12-31. The methods are shown in Table 12-32.

The TextArea is easy to use. For example, the following code fragment would delete text within the TextArea that has been selected by the user:

```
TextArea block = new TextArea( );
// . . .
// user types in value and causes an "action event"
// . . .
int startSel = block.getSelectionStart( );
int endSel = block.getSelectionEnd( );
block.replaceText("", startSel, endSel);
```

TABLE 12-31
KEY public CONSTRUCTORS OF THE TextArea CLASS

TextArea( )

TextArea(int rows, int cols)

TextArea(String text)

TextArea(String text, int rows, int cols)

TABLE 12-32
KEY public METHODS OF THE TextArea CLASS

METHOD HEADER	FUNCTION
void append(String text)	Append text to the TextArea.
int getColumns( )	Get the number of columns used in constructing the TextArea.
int getRows( )	Getthe number of rows used in constructing the TextArea.
void insert(String text, int pos)	Insert text at the indicated position within the TextArea.
void replaceRange(String text, int start, int end)	Replace text at the indicated position within the TextArea.

An application for study of the TextArea class, StudyTextArea, is presented in Listing 12-15. Figure 12-19 shows the StudyTextArea application at work.

Listing 12-15 StudyTextArea.java

```java
// Using a TextArea
// Built upon ComponentLab.java
import java.awt.*;
import java.awt.event.*;

public class StudyTextArea extends ComponentLab
                                 implements ActionListener, ⇐
                                            KeyListener
{
    TextArea theText         = ⇐
      new TextArea( "This is \na TextArea" );
    Button    editButton   = new Button( "No Edit" );
    Button    replButton   = new Button( "Replace" );
    Button    insertButton = new Button( "Insert" );
    Button    appendButton = new Button( "Append" );

    public static void main(String args[])
    {
        StudyTextArea theApp = new StudyTextArea( );
    }

    public StudyTextArea( )
    {
        setTitle( "Studying the TextArea object" );

        Panel theButtons = new Panel();
        theButtons.setLayout( new GridLayout( 1, 4 ) );
        theButtons.add( editButton );
        theButtons.add( replButton );
        theButtons.add( insertButton );
        theButtons.add( appendButton );
        editButton.addActionListener(this);
        replButton.addActionListener(this);
        insertButton.addActionListener(this);
```

continued on next page

continued from previous page

```
                appendButton.addActionListener(this);
                theWorkbench.add( theButtons, "North" );

                theComponent = theText;
                theText.setBackground( Color.white );
                theText.setForeground( Color.black );
                theSurface.add( theText );
                theText.addKeyListener(this);

                reShow();
        }

        public void actionPerformed( ActionEvent theEvent )
        {
                if ( theEvent.getSource( ) == theInput )
                   theText.setText( theInput.getText() );

                else if (theEvent.getSource( ) == appendButton)
                   theText.append( theInput.getText() );

                else if (theEvent.getSource( ) == insertButton)
                   theText.insert( theInput.getText(),
                                    theText.getSelectionStart() );

                else if (theEvent.getSource( ) == replButton)
                   theText.replaceRange( theInput.getText(),
                        theText.getSelectionStart(),
                        theText.getSelectionEnd() );

                else if (theEvent.getSource( ) == editButton)
                {
                     if ((editButton.getLabel( )).equals("No Edit"))
                     {
                         theText.setEditable(false);
                         editButton.setLabel("Edit");
                     }
                     else
                     {
                         theText.setEditable(true);
                         editButton.setLabel("No Edit");
                     }
                }

                reShow();
                super.actionPerformed( theEvent );
        }

        public void keyPressed( KeyEvent theEvent )   ⇐
           { log( "" + theEvent ); }
        public void keyReleased( KeyEvent theEvent )  ⇐
           { log( "" + theEvent ); }
        public void keyTyped( KeyEvent theEvent )      ⇐
           { log( "" + theEvent ); }
}
```

FIGURE 12-19

The StudyTextArea application

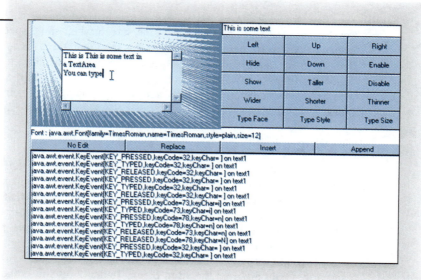

More Containers

You might be forgiven if your eyes are beginning to glaze over at the thought of YAC—Yet Another Component! Never fear, the end is in sight. In addition to the `Containers` you have already met, Java provides a type of temporary window, called a `Dialog`. There are also two new layout managers, `CardLayout` and `GridBagLayout`, which you'll want to meet before you close up your Java AWT toolbox.

CREATING A CONSTRUCTIVE `Dialog`

When you place user-interface components on the surface of an application's `Frame` or on the surface of an `Applet`, those components are visible for the entire lifetime of the application or applet. Sometimes, however, this is not appropriate. For example, you might want the user to enter a password so that your program can authenticate the user's identity before allowing access to sensitive information. If your design for the input screen includes a `TextField` for entering the password, the `TextField` will be there long after it's needed, pointlessly cluttering the screen and consuming potentially scarce and valuable pixels.

What Are `Dialog`s?

You can hide the `TextField` (using `setVisible(false)`) or even `remove()` it if you choose. You can even use a series of screens rather than a single screen. But a more common solution is to use a `Dialog`. A `Dialog` is a type of `Window` that is a great deal like a `Frame`. It has a title bar and a Close icon; but it lacks the Minimize and Restore icons possessed by a `Frame`.

A `Dialog` is usually popped up on the screen when some special input is required, such as a password. After the user provides the input, the `Dialog` is then normally hidden. In most cases, a `Dialog` causes the program that created it to *block*—that is, wait—until input is available. Such a `Dialog` is called a *modal* `Dialog`. However, it is also possible to create *modeless* `Dialogs` that do not cause their "owner" program to block.

Creating `Dialogs`

A `Dialog` can be owned by a parent `Frame`, which you can specify when the `Dialog` is created. A `Dialog` created by specifying `null` as the `parent` parameter has no parent `Frame`. Events sent to, but not handled by, a `Dialog` with a parent `Frame` are forwarded to the parent. This makes it possible to handle `Dialog` events in the parent `Frame`: it's sometimes convenient to handle all AWT events in a single place. Because AWT `actionPerformed()` processing is performed in a special thread, the events forwarded by a `Dialog` to its parent `Frame` can be processed even if the `Dialog` is modal, and has caused the main program thread to block. Table 12-33 shows the constructors used to instantiate `Dialogs`, and Table 12-34 shows important methods implemented by `Dialogs`.

TABLE 12-33
KEY **public** CONSTRUCTORS OF THE **Dialog** CLASS

`Dialog( Frame parent, boolean modal)`
`Dialog( Frame parent, String title, boolean modal)`

TABLE 12-34
KEY **public** CLASS METHODS OF THE **Dialog** CLASS

METHOD HEADER	FUNCTION
`String getTitle( )`	Get the title of the `Dialog`.
`boolean isModal( )`	Determine if the `Dialog` is modal (`true`) or modeless (`false`).
`boolean isResizable( )`	Determine if the `Dialog` is resizable.
`void setResizable (boolean resizable)`	Set the resizability of the `Dialog`, according to the parameter.
`void setTitle(String title)`	Set the title of the `Dialog`.

A `Dialog` Example

Listing 12-16 shows the StudyDialog application, which demonstrates how to create and use a `Dialog`. Figure 12-20 shows the application and its `Dialog` as they run. The application includes a `TextField`, used simply to display messages, and two `Buttons`.

One Button is used to pop up a Dialog that allows the user to enter a secret password (which is Java). The other allows the user to request riches beyond imagination, which are forthcoming only if the correct password has been entered.

The Dialog itself is actually an instance of the helper class PasswordDialog, which extends the built-in java.awt.Dialog class. An instance of the PasswordDialog class is created in the constructor StudyDialog(). Like most AWT objects, a Dialog is initially hidden; no PasswordDialog appears on the screen until showDialog() is called. The method, showDialog(), is only called in the application's actionPerformed() method, when the user clicks the mouse on the Enter Password Button. Showing the PasswordDialog causes the application to block until the PasswordDialog is hidden.

The PasswordDialog itself includes three components: a Label, a TextField, and a Button. The Label is simply used to direct the user's attention to the TextField, where the user must enter the password. Although not done in StudyDialog, you could use the setEchoChar() method to prevent the typed contents of the TextField from being displayed, to increase the security of the password. After entering the password, the user must press the OK Button or click the Close icon. The actionPerformed() method of the PasswordDialog simply hides the PasswordDialog in response to either event.

When the user presses the Acquire Riches Button on the application window, the application verifies the password entered by the user. This is done by use of the PasswordDialog.checkPassword() method, which returns true if the user entered Java and returns false otherwise. The application generates and displays a message appropriate to whichever situation actually occurs.

Listing 12-16 StudyDialog.java

```
// How to use a Dialog class
import java.awt.*;
import java.awt.event.*;

public class StudyDialog extends Frame
                    implements ActionListener, ⇐
                                    WindowListener
{
    Button      passwordButton = new Button("Enter password");
    Button      richesButton   = new Button("Acquire riches");
    boolean     passwordOK     = false;
    TextField theText          = new TextField("", 48);
    PasswordDialog theDialog;

    public static void main(String args[])
    {
        StudyDialog theApp = new StudyDialog();
    }

    public StudyDialog()
    {
        setTitle("Studying the Dialog class");
        setLayout(new BorderLayout());
        Panel centerPanel = new Panel();
```

continued on next page

continued from previous page

```
                centerPanel.setLayout(new FlowLayout());

                centerPanel.add(passwordButton);
                centerPanel.add(richesButton);
                passwordButton.addActionListener(this);
                richesButton.addActionListener(this);
                add(centerPanel, "Center");
                add(theText, "South");

                addWindowListener(this);

                pack();
                setVisible(true);
                theDialog = new PasswordDialog(this);
        }

        public void actionPerformed(ActionEvent theEvent)
        {
                if (theEvent.getSource( ) == passwordButton)
                {
                    theText.setText("");
                    theDialog.showDialog();
                }
                if (theEvent.getSource( ) == richesButton)
                {
                    passwordOK = theDialog.checkPassword( );
                    if(passwordOK)
                        theText.setText(⇐
                        "Ed McMahon is here to see you.");
                    else
                        theText.setText(⇐
                        "There's a man from the IRS here to see ⇐
                        you.");
                }
        }

        public void windowClosed      (WindowEvent e) { }
        public void windowClosing     (WindowEvent e) { ⇐
          quitApplication( ); }
        public void windowDeiconified (WindowEvent e) { }
        public void windowIconified   (WindowEvent e) { }
        public void windowOpened      (WindowEvent e) { }
        public void windowActivated   (WindowEvent e) { }
        public void windowDeactivated (WindowEvent e) { }

        public void quitApplication( )
        {
                setVisible(false);
                dispose();
                System.exit(0);
        }
}

class PasswordDialog extends Dialog
```

```
                                implements ActionListener, ⇐
                                           WindowListener
{
    Label      theLabel    = new Label("Password: ");
    TextField  thePassword = new TextField("", 16);
    Button     okButton    = new Button("OK");

    public PasswordDialog(Frame f)
    {
        super(f, "Enter the secret password", true);
        setLayout(new GridLayout(2, 1));
        Panel p1 = new Panel();
        Panel p2 = new Panel();
        add(p1);
        add(p2);
        p1.setLayout(new FlowLayout());
        p1.add(theLabel);
        p1.add(thePassword);
        p2.setLayout(new FlowLayout());
        p2.add(okButton);
        okButton.addActionListener(this);
        addWindowListener(this);
        setSize(400, 100);
    }

    public boolean checkPassword()
    {
        if (thePassword.getText().equals("Java")) ⇐
            return true;
        return false;
    }

    public void actionPerformed(ActionEvent theEvent)
    {
        setVisible(false);
    }

    public void showDialog()
    {
        thePassword.setText("");
        setVisible(true);
    }

    public void windowClosed      (WindowEvent e) { }
    public void windowClosing     (WindowEvent e) { ⇐
        quitApplication( ); }
    public void windowDeiconified (WindowEvent e) { }
    public void windowIconified   (WindowEvent e) { }
    public void windowOpened      (WindowEvent e) { }
    public void windowActivated   (WindowEvent e) { }
    public void windowDeactivated (WindowEvent e) { }
}
```

FIGURE 12-20
*The StudyDialog
application and its*
Dialog

DEALING WITH THE CardLayout

The penultimate layout manager provided by the AWT is the CardLayout. CardLayout is different from the other layout managers in that it allows only one of its Components to be visible at a time, and it provides methods for cycling from one Component to the next. It's useful for implementing an interface that resembles a card file, in which only a single card can be viewed, but it's possible to flip forward or backward to view another. The relevant constructors are shown in Table 12-35, and the methods are shown in Table 12-36. Note that the methods, though sent to the CardLayout object, require the parent Container object as a parameter.

TABLE 12-35
KEY public CONSTRUCTORS OF THE CardLayout CLASS

CardLayout( )
CardLayout(int hgap, int vgap)

TABLE 12-36
KEY public METHODS OF THE CardLayout CLASS

METHOD HEADER	FUNCTION
void first(Container parent)	Show the first **Component** in the **Container**.
void last(Container parent)	Show the last **Component** in the **Container**.
void next(Container parent)	Show the next **Component** in the **Container**.
void previous(Container parent)	Show the previous **Component** in the **Container**.
void show(Container parent, String name)	Show the specified **Component** in the **Container**.

The StudyCard application, shown in Listing 12-17, demonstrates the use of CardLayout. It places five Buttons at the top of the screen. The Buttons are used to select the appropriate Panel from among five different Panels, each containing a descriptive message. Figure 12-21 shows the output of the application. You might find it interesting to modify StudyCard to use the next( ) and previous( ) methods instead of, or along with, the existing method of selection.

Listing 12-17 StudyCard.java

```
// Shows how to use the CardLayout layout manager
import java.awt.*;
import java.awt.event.*;

public class StudyCard extends Frame
                       implements ActionListener, ⇐
                                  WindowListener
{
    Button[]    aButton      = new Button[5];
    Panel       northPanel   = new Panel( );
    Panel       centerPanel  = new Panel( );
    Panel[]     aPanel       = new Panel[5];
    CardLayout  theLayout    = new CardLayout( );
    Label[]     aLabel       = new Label[5];
    Font        theFont      =
     new Font("Courier", Font.BOLD, 36);
    Color[]     aColor       = { Color.pink, Color.yellow, ⇐
     Color.blue, Color.red, Color.green};
    String[]    aColorDesc   = { "Pink", "Yellow", "Blue", ⇐
     "Red", "Green"};

    public static void main(String args[])
    {
        StudyCard theApp = new StudyCard( );
    }

    public StudyCard( )
    {
        setTitle( "The StudyCard Application" );

        northPanel.setLayout( new FlowLayout( ) );
        centerPanel.setLayout( theLayout );
        add( northPanel, "North" );
        add( centerPanel, "Center" );

        for ( int i = 0; i < aButton.length; i++ )
        {
            aButton[i] = new Button( "" + aColorDesc[i] );
            northPanel.add( aButton[i] );
            aButton[i].addActionListener(this);

            aLabel[i] = new Label( "This is a " + ⇐
              aColorDesc[i] + " page", Label.CENTER );
            aLabel[i].setFont( theFont );
```

continued on next page

continued from previous page

```
                aPanel[i] = new Panel( );
                aPanel[i].setBackground( aColor[i] );
                aPanel[i].setLayout( new BorderLayout() );
                aPanel[i].add( aLabel[i], "Center" );

                aLabel[i] = new Label( "" + ⇐
                    aColor[i], Label.CENTER );
                aLabel[i].setFont( new Font( "Helvetica", ⇐
                    Font.BOLD, 14));
                aPanel[i].add( aLabel[i], "North" );

                centerPanel.add( aPanel[i], aColorDesc[i] );
            }
        addWindowListener(this);
        pack( );
        setVisible(true);
    }

    public void actionPerformed(ActionEvent theEvent)
    {
        theLayout.show(centerPanel, ⇐
            ((Button)theEvent.getSource()).getLabel() );
    }

    public void windowClosed      (WindowEvent e) { }
    public void windowClosing     (WindowEvent e) { ⇐
     quitApplication( ); }
    public void windowDeiconified(WindowEvent e) { }
    public void windowIconified   (WindowEvent e) { }
    public void windowOpened      (WindowEvent e) { }
    public void windowActivated   (WindowEvent e) { }
    public void windowDeactivated(WindowEvent e) { }

    public void quitApplication( )
    {
        setVisible(false);
        dispose();
        System.exit(0);
    }
}
```

USING GridBagLayout

The "king" of the layout managers is GridBagLayout, not to be confused with its less-than-noble cousin, GridLayout. GridBagLayout is highly configurable to provide flexibility, but that flexibility comes at the price of complexity. With GridBagLayout, you can create complex displays such as the keypad pictured in Figure 12-22.

FIGURE 12-21

Output of the StudyCard application

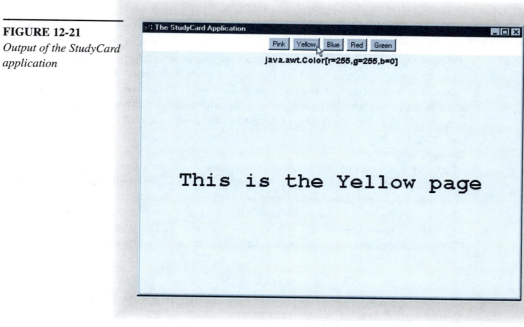

FIGURE 12-22

A more complex keypad layout

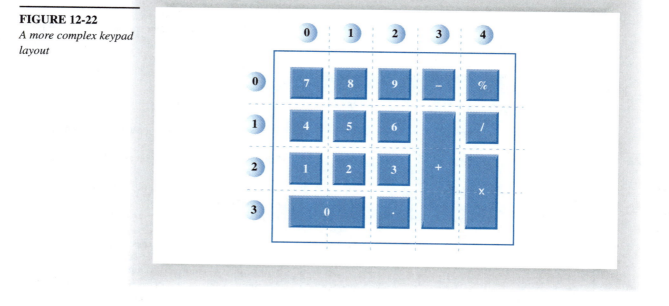

The first thing you'll notice about this display is that the Buttons are not all the same size. The "+" Button is three times as tall as any of the others, for example, and the "0" Button is twice as wide. This is the sort of layout where GridBagLayout excels.

The GridBagLayout is based on the idea of rows and columns. When you place a Component into a Container that is controlled by GridBagLayout, you don't need to place them in any specific order, as you do with the other layout managers. Instead, you specify the row and column where the Component should be placed. In addition, you can say how many rows tall and how many columns wide you want the Component to be.

The way that you tell the GridBagLayout that you want a Component to appear at a particular location is by associating an object called a GridBagConstraint with the Component before it is added to your Container. This GridBagConstraint object has a whole family of public fields that control almost every aspect of the manner in which the GridBagLayout will display your Component. These fields are given in Table 12-37 and associated constants used in setting their values are given in Table 12-38.

TABLE 12-37
KEY public INSTANCE FIELDS OF THE GridBagConstraints CLASS

FIELD	TYPE	MEANING/USE
anchor	int	Set the anchor position of a Component. Use when the Component's row (column) is larger than the Component's horizontal (vertical) size, based on the Component's fill constraint.
fill	int	Determine whether the Component is resized to fill its row or column.
gridheight	int	The number of grid rows occupied by the Component.
gridwidthint		The number of grid columns occupied by the Component.
gridx	int	The grid position (column) of the Component's northeast corner.
gridy	int	The grid position (row) of the Component's northeast corner.
insets	Insets	Specify margins appearing on all sides of the Component.
ipadx	int	Increase size of the Component beyond its default horizontal size.
ipady	int	Increase size of the Component beyond its default vertical size.
weightx	double	Maximum value over all Components in a column determines the proportion of any excess space that will be distributed to the column.
weighty	double	Maximum value over all Components in a row determines the proportion of any excess space that will be distributed to the row.

TABLE 12-38
KEY `public` FIELDS OF THE `GridBagConstraints` CLASS

FIELD	TYPE	MEANING/USE
CENTER	int	Use to set **anchor** instance variable.
EAST	int	Use to set **anchor** instance variable.
NORTH	int	Use to set **anchor** instance variable.
NORTHEAST	int	Use to set **anchor** instance variable.
NORTHWEST	int	Use to set **anchor** instance variable.
SOUTH	int	Use to set **anchor** instance variable.
SOUTHEAST	int	Use to set **anchor** instance variable.
SOUTHWEST	int	Use to set **anchor** instance variable.
WEST	int	Use to set **anchor** instance variable.
HORIZONTAL	int	Use to set **fill** instance variable.
VERTICAL	int	Use to set **fill** instance variable.
BOTH	int	Use to set **fill** instance variable.
NONE	int	Use to set **fill** instance variable.

`GridBagLayout`, Step By Step

`GridBagLayout` is so complex that it's quite easy to get overwhelmed. The easiest way to avoid that is to walk through a minimal example. The keypad pictured in Figure 12-22 is just the ticket.

☕ As you would with the other layout managers, you start by creating an instance of `GridBagLayout`, using the `GridBagLayout()` constructor:

```
GridBagLayout theBag = new GridBagLayout();
```

☕ Save the `GridBagLayout` object, because you will need it later. To actually apply the `theBag` to a `Frame` or `Panel`, you call `setLayout()` just as you did with the other layout managers:

```
setLayout( theBag );
```

☕ You will also need to have a `GridBagConstraints` object, which you can get by using the default constructor. You don't need a separate `GridBagConstraints` object for each `Component` you add to your `Container`—a single instance will do:

```
GridBagConstraints theGBC = new GridBagConstraints();
```

☕ Next, you have to tell your `GridBagConstraints` object how you want it to treat `Components` that are smaller than their assigned cells. You do this by setting the `fill` `public` field. To have `Components` expand in both directions, you can use the defined constant, `GridBagConstraints.BOTH`. A list of the constants used to specify component fill can be found in Table 12-39.

If you specify a value for `fill` that prevents a `Component` from expanding either horizontally or vertically, you should specify a value for `anchor`. The `anchor` value controls how the `Component` is aligned within any extra available space. Legal values for `anchor` are shown in Table 12-40.

You may also want some space or padding around each `Component` as it is added—similar to the `hgap` and `vgap` arguments you used when using the `GridLayout` constructor. To do this, you set the `insets` field, by assigning a new `Insets` object, constructed with integers representing the space to leave around each side of the `Component`.

```
theGBC.fill     = GridBagConstraints.BOTH;  // Fill both
directions
theGBC.insets   = new Insets( 5, 5, 5, 5 ); // 5 pixels
around each
```

For each `Component` you want to add, you need to

1. Set the row and column position where the `Component` will appear. This is the position where the upper-left corner will be placed. You do this by assigning values to the `gridx` and `gridy` variables in the `GridBagConstraints` object.

   ```
   theGBC.gridx = 0;
   theGBC.gridy = 0;
   ```

2. Set the number of rows and columns that each `Component` spans. Like the position parameters, these are set by assigning values to the `gridwidth` and `gridheight` fields in your `GridBagConstraints` object.

   ```
   theGBC.gridwidth  = 1;
   theGBC.gridheight = 1;
   ```

3. Associate the `GridBagLayout`, the `Component`, and the `GridBagConstraints` object by using the `setConstraints( )` method of the `GridBagLayout`, passing your `Component` and the `Constraints` you set as the arguments to the method.

   ```
   theBag.setConstraints( b, theGBC );
   ```

4. Finally, add your new `Component` to the `Container` using the plain old `add( )` method.

   ```
   add( b );
   ```

TABLE 12-39
CONSTANTS USED TO SPECIFY COMPONENT FILL

NAME	TYPE
HORIZONTAL	int
VERTICAL	int
BOTH	int
NONE	int

TABLE 12-40
CONSTANTS USED TO SPECIFY COMPONENT ALIGNMENT

NAME	TYPE
CENTER	int
EAST	int
NORTH	int
NORTHEAST	int
NORTHWEST	int
SOUTH	int
SOUTHEAST	int
SOUTHWEST	int
WEST	int

Because this process needs to be done repeatedly for layouts that are complex enough to warrant using GridBagLayout, the wisest strategy is to place all of these details in a method such as the addComponent() method used in the StudyGridBagLayout application. Browse through Listing 12-18 until you feel comfortable with the basic ideas behind GridBagLayout. Then you'll want to modify some of the fields in your GridBagConstraints object to see their effect. You can see what the application display looks like in Figure 12-23.

Listing 12-18 StudyGridBagLayout.java

```
// Shows how to use the GridBagLayout layout manager
import java.awt.*;
import java.awt.event.*;

public class StudyGridBagLayout extends Frame
                                implements ActionListener, ⇐
                                           WindowListener
{
    GridBagLayout       theBag = new GridBagLayout();
    GridBagConstraints theGBC = new GridBagConstraints();

    public static void main(String args[])
    {
```

continued on next page

continued from previous page

```
              StudyGridBagLayout theApp = new StudyGridBagLayout(
                );
    }

    public StudyGridBagLayout( )
    {
        setTitle( "A Simple GridBagLayout" );
        setFont( new Font( "Courier", Font.BOLD, 36 ) );

        setLayout( theBag );

        theGBC.fill    = ⇐
          GridBagConstraints.BOTH;    // Fill both directions
        theGBC.insets  = ⇐
          new Insets( 5, 5, 5, 5 ); // 5 pixels around each
        theGBC.weightx = ⇐
          1.0;                        // Allow X expansion
        theGBC.weighty = ⇐
          1.0;                        // Allow Y expansion

        addComponent( 0, 0, 1, 1, new Button( "7" ) );
        addComponent( 0, 1, 1, 1, new Button( "8" ) );
        addComponent( 0, 2, 1, 1, new Button( "9" ) );
        addComponent( 0, 3, 1, 1, new Button( "-" ) );
        addComponent( 0, 4, 1, 1, new Button( "%" ) );

        addComponent( 1, 0, 1, 1, new Button( "4" ) );
        addComponent( 1, 1, 1, 1, new Button( "5" ) );
        addComponent( 1, 2, 1, 1, new Button( "6" ) );
        addComponent( 1, 3, 3, 1, new Button( "+" ) );
        addComponent( 1, 4, 1, 1, new Button( "/" ) );

        addComponent( 2, 0, 1, 1, new Button( "1" ) );
        addComponent( 2, 1, 1, 1, new Button( "2" ) );
        addComponent( 2, 2, 1, 1, new Button( "3" ) );
        addComponent( 2, 4, 2, 1, new Button( "X" ) );

        addComponent( 3, 0, 1, 2, new Button( "0" ) );
        addComponent( 3, 2, 1, 1, new Button( "." ) );

        addWindowListener(this);

        setSize( 400, 300 );
        setVisible(true);
    }

    public void addComponent( int row, int col, int high, ⇐
      int wide, Component theComponent )
    {
        theGBC.gridx      = col;
        theGBC.gridy      = row;
        theGBC.gridwidth  = wide;
        theGBC.gridheight = high;
        theBag.setConstraints( theComponent, theGBC );
        add( theComponent );
        if (theComponent instanceof Button)
            ((Button) theComponent).addActionListener(this);
    }
```

```
public void actionPerformed(ActionEvent theEvent)
{
    if (theEvent.getSource( ) instanceof Button)
    {
        String s = ((Button) ⇐
            theEvent.getSource( )).getLabel( );
        System.out.println( s );
    }
}

public void windowClosed      (WindowEvent e) { }
public void windowClosing     (WindowEvent e) { ⇐
    quitApplication( ); }
public void windowDeiconified(WindowEvent e) { }
public void windowIconified  (WindowEvent e) { }
public void windowOpened      (WindowEvent e) { }
public void windowActivated   (WindowEvent e) { }
public void windowDeactivated(WindowEvent e) { }

public void quitApplication( )
{
    setVisible(false);
    dispose();
    System.exit(0);
}
}
```

FIGURE 12-23

*Running the
StudyGridBagLayout
application*

Looking Into StudyGridBagLayout

When you run StudyGridBagLayout, the actual size of each row and column is determined by the `GridBagLayout` each time the container is resized. Each row and column has a designated minimum size, based on the largest component each contains. If the container has excess space, it is proportionally distributed to rows and columns. If you wish, you can control which columns or rows expand—that is, the percentage of excess space that column or row will receive—by setting the `GridBagConstraints` fields `weightx` and `weighty`. While you can use any positive number, it's usually good to initially use *only* the values 0.0 or 1.0 for `weightx` and `weighty`. If a row or column has a 0.0 weight, it will not receive any of the excess space. Excess space will then be divided equally among the remaining rows or columns with weight 1.0. By use of positive values less than 1.0 (or greater than 1.0), it's possible to cause a row or column to receive a smaller or greater share of the excess space.

Remember that the `fill` and `anchor` values are used to specify whether a component swells to fill its cell. Permissible values for `fill` are NONE, HORIZONTAL, VERTICAL, and BOTH. The associated component will swell in only the indicated direction. Components that are not specified as swelling in both dimensions use the anchor parameters to specify their position with their cell. The compass-point values and CENTER are used for this purpose.

The values of the `GridBagConstraints` object are not altered by the call to `setConstraints( )`, so it is possible to set the values once and call `setConstraints( )` repeatedly, changing between calls only those values that are different from one call to the next. For example

```
GridBagConstraints gbc = new GridBagConstraints( );
gbc.fill = gbc.NONE;
gbc.anchor = gbc.CENTER;
gbc.gridwidth = 1;
gbc.gridheight = 1;
gbc.gridx = 0;
gbc.gridy = 0;
setConstraints(componentOne, gbc);
gbc.gridx = 1;
gbc.gridy = 0;
setConstraints(componentTwo, gbc);
gbc.gridx = 2;
gbc.gridy = 0;
setConstraints(componentThree, gbc);
```

positions three components along the top row of a container.

GridLook, a second application demonstrating the use of `GridBagLayout`, is included on the CD-ROM. Figure 12-24 shows this application at work. GridLook allows you to vary the constraints applied to a container and to observe the effects. Time spent experimenting with the GridLook application will greatly improve your understanding of the powerful, but tricky, `GridBagLayout` class.

FIGURE 12-24

Output of the GridLook application

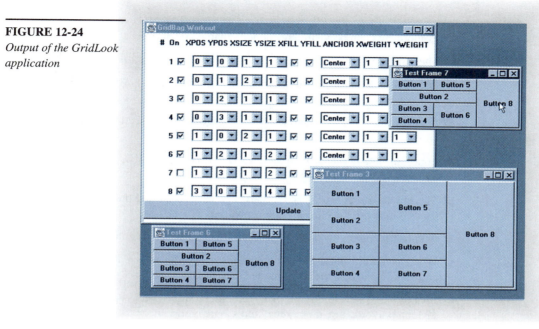

Summary

☕ The Abstract Window Toolkit (AWT) permits Java programs with graphical user interfaces (GUI) to work on a wide variety of computers and operating systems.

☕ The major subsystems of the AWT are graphics, components, containers, layout managers, and the event system.

☕ Components are the widgets or controls with which the user interacts with a GUI program.

☕ Containers allow components to be grouped together and treated as a unit.

☕ Layout managers allow components to be placed in containers, without fixing them at definite positions.

☕ Because a container is a component, it is possible to place a container within another container.

☕ Components of a GUI program form a hierarchy of containment relationships.

☕ Components always occupy a rectangular area on the screen.

☕ Components can be visible or hidden, enabled or disabled.

☕ The `repaint()` method can be used to request that a component be redrawn.

☕ The classes `Dimension` and `Rectangle` are important for working with components.

☕ A `Frame` is a top-level window, with a title bar, often used to host an application.

☕ Important `Frame` methods include `setVisible()`, `pack()`, and `dispose()`.

☕ The `Frame.setCursor()` method can be used to choose the type of cursor used to indicate the current mouse position.

☕ A `Panel` is a window with no title bar that can act as a container.

☕ When you are using a `null` layout manager, components can be positioned and sized by use of the `setBounds()` method.

☕ Java provides several layout managers, including `FlowLayout`, `GridLayout`, `GridBagLayout`, `BorderLayout`, and `CardLayout`.

☕ The `add()` method is used to add components to containers.

☕ `BorderLayout` allows components to be placed at the four compass points, or at the center of a container.

☕ `FlowLayout` allows components to be placed row-by-row and left-, right-, or center-aligned within the resulting rows.

☕ `GridLayout` allows components to be placed on a grid with a specified number of rows and columns; each component is resized to fill its cell in the grid.

☕ `Panels` using various layout managers can be nested to create desired screen layouts.

☕ A `Label` is used to place a `String` of text on the screen.

☕ A `Button`, when clicked, generates an `Event` that can be detected and handled by a program.

☕ A `Checkbox` is always in either the "on" (`true`) or "off" (`false`) state. Clicking a `Checkbox` toggles its state and generates an `Event`.

☕ A `CheckboxGroup` can be used to combine `Checkboxes` into a set in which only one member can be `true`. When used this way, the `Checkboxes` are referred to as radio buttons.

A `Choice` contains a list of items, only one of which is normally visible, from which the user can select one item. Selecting a `Choice` item generates an `Event`.

A `List` is similar to a choice, except that multiple items are normally visible, and scroll bars can be used to select from many possible items.

A `Scrollbar` features a sliding thumb that can be positioned to indicate a value between two limits.

The `TextComponent` class is the parent class of `TextField` and `TextArea`.

A `TextField` allows the user to enter a single line of text input.

A `TextArea` allows the user to enter multiple lines of text input.

A `Dialog` is a special temporary window used for tasks such as entering passwords.

Quiz

1. The widgets or controls used to create a graphical user interface (GUI) are known as _____.

2. `Frames`, `Panels`, and objects that can contain other GUI objects are known as _____.

3. The screen area occupied by a component is always _____ in shape.

4. A component that is _____ cannot be seen on the screen.

5. A component that is _____ does not respond to user actions.

6. A _____ is used to indicate the current position of the mouse.

7. `Frames` have a title _____ and `Panels` do not.

8. `BorderLayout` allows components to be placed at the four positions of the _____.

9. Components added to a container by use of _____ are added row-by-row, from left to right.

10. When you are using `GridLayout`, each component in the container is _____ according to the size of the grid cell it occupies.

11. A(n) _____ is used to place text on the screen, but cannot receive input.

12. A(n) _____ can be clicked to generate an `Event`, but does nothing else.

13. A(n) _____ can be clicked to toggle its state.

14. A(n) _____ can be used to combine `Checkboxes` into a set of radio buttons.

15. A(n) _____ can be used to select a single item from a list, but never allows selection of multiple items.

16. A(n) _____ can be used to select multiple items from a list.

17. A Scrollbar has a value that can be changed by moving its _____.

18. Both the TextField and TextArea extend the class _____.

19. A(n) _____ can be used to obtain a single line of input.

20. A(n) _____ can be used to obtain multiple lines of input.

21. A(n) _____ is a temporary window often used to obtain small amounts of input.

Exercises

1. Write an applet that mimics the operation of an automated teller machine. The applet should allow the user to make both withdrawals and deposits. Use a keypad object (see Chapter 9) to simplify building the applet.

2. Write an applet that functions as a travel advisor. Your applet should provide components that let users define their interests, based upon which it should recommend a set of appropriate destinations.

3. Write an applet that functions as a calculator, similar to the MS Windows 95 Calculator program. You do not need to include memory functions or a menu.

4. Convert the applet of your choice so that it can be run as an applet *or* as an application. Such a program is called a standalone applet or an "appletcation." To allow the applet to be run as an application, your application's main( ) method should create a Frame, create an instance of the applet, and then add the applet to the Frame. The main( ) method will also need to invoke any of the applet life-cycle methods defined by the applet, for example, init( ). For additional "credit" you can add a menu similar to that provided by Appletviewer.

5. Write an applet that presents a checkerboard and allows players to take turns using the applet to move checkers. A checker is picked up by clicking on it and is deposited by clicking on the desired new location, or by clicking beside the board to return the checker to its original location. Your applet does not need to check that moves are valid or allow pieces to be jumped. Include a scoreboard that keeps track of the number of games won by each player. The score for a player is incremented by simply pushing a button.

6. Improve the checkerboard applet by checking for valid moves. You do not need to handle jumps. When an invalid move is attempted, the applet should display a message and play an audio file.

7. Continue to improve the checkerboard by implementing the capability for pieces to jump other pieces. You do not need to handle multiple jumps.

8. Continue to improve the checkerboard by implementing multiple jumps.

9. Continue to improve the checkerboard by adding the capability to automatically detect a "win" by one player when none of the other player's pieces remain. Also include a button that allows the players to declare the game a "draw" and that updates a visual display of the number of games drawn.

10. Continue to improve the checkerboard by implementing "kinging" of pieces that reach the final row. Remember that kings can move in any direction.

Advanced AWT

A primary purpose of object-oriented programming is to help you manage complexity. Just as a map of the world helps you to see the relationships between the continents and countries spread out over the globe without getting bogged down in unnecessary details, so object-oriented programming, through the process of abstraction, allows you to separate the essential elements of your program from all the nitty-gritty coding minutiae. Abstract classes and interfaces are features of the Java language that allow you to step back from your code and design your programs and classes at a level closer to the problem they solve.

Abstract classes and interfaces may sound as if they're, well, sort of "abstract"or theoretical and of no use in the real world. Nothing could be further from the truth. These features allow you to write programs that are not only more robust, but are also easier to understand. And, as you look at the way Java's AWT delivers events to your programs, you'll see that interfaces are an integral part of programming `Components` to respond to different messages.

This chapter addresses three main topics: abstract classes and interfaces; the way events are delivered in the AWT; and several advanced uses of the AWT, including printing, dynamic creation of objects at run-time, and the art of component subclassing. You will learn

☞ How to use abstract classes and interfaces to build reusable components

☞ Additional details about how events are delivered

☞ How to print text and figures

" A primary purpose of object-oriented programming is to help you manage complexity. "

☕ How to create arbitrary objects, those whose type you can't predict at the time you write your program

☕ How to create your own `Component`s that have capabilities beyond those provided by the standard AWT `Component`s

Abstract Classes and Methods

In Chapter 10, "Inheritance: Object Families," you looked at the process of creating families of objects through inheritance. You saw that subclasses (child classes) could override methods in their superclasses (parent classes). In the `TalkToMe` class, reprinted in Listing 13-1, you created a virtual menagerie—`Dog`s, `Cat`s, `Frog`s, and `Flamingo`s—all derived from the `Pet` class. When asked to speak, each of your pets responded according to type: the Dog said "Arf," the Cat "Meow," and so forth.

Listing 13-1 TalkToMe.java

```java
// How overridding methods works
//
import java.io.*;

public class TalkToMe
{

    public static void main( String args[] )
    {
        Cat        theCat      = new Cat();
        Dog        theDog      = new Dog();
        Frog       theFrog     = new Frog();
        Flamingo   theFlamingo = new Flamingo();

        System.out.println("The CAT says :" + ⇐
          theCat.speak());
        System.out.println("The DOG says :" + ⇐
          theDog.speak());
        System.out.println("The FROG says:" + ⇐
          theFrog.speak());
        System.out.println("The FLAMINGO says :" + ⇐
          theFlamingo.speak());
    }
}

class Pet
{
    String speak()   ⇐
      { return "Hi, I'm a happy and contented pet"; }
}

class Dog extends Pet
{
    String speak()   { return super.speak() + ". Arf, Arf"; }
}
```

```
class Cat extends Pet
{
    String speak()  { return super.speak() + ". Meow, meow";
}
}

class Frog extends Pet
{
}

class Flamingo extends Pet
{
    String speak() ⇐
        { return "They're holding me captive. You must help!"; }
}
```

This program, however, has a subtle conceptual flaw. The `speak()` method in the superclass `Pet` is defined like this:

```
class Pet
{
    String speak() ⇐
        { return "Hi. I'm a happy and contented pet."; }
}
```

Now think for a second, and then answer this question: What kind of creature is a `Pet`? Most likely you'll answer, "It can be any kind of pet." And you'd be entirely correct. The idea of a `Pet` class is an abstraction. It describes the *general* characteristics of a group of animals for which you provide food and shelter, not expecting any utilitarian benefits in return. Your pets agree not to work, and you, in return, agree not to eat them.

When you have a parent class that includes only general or abstract characteristics, sometimes you don't know exactly how the objects in the real class (usually called the *concrete* class) will act, even though you know that they will all respond to some particular message. One solution to that dilemma is to include in the parent class a dummy method that either does nothing or does something innocuous, like the `speak()` method in the `Pet` class. But a better solution is to add an `abstract` method, and to thus create an `abstract` class.

CREATING abstract METHODS AND CLASSES

There are two steps to creating an `abstract` method. The first is to add the keyword `abstract` before the method definition. The second is to put a semicolon where the body of the method would normally go. To make the `Pet.speak()` method into an `abstract` method, you would write

```
class Pet
{
    abstract String speak();
}
```

Making the `speak()` method `abstract` in the superclass `Pet` accomplishes several things. First, any class with an `abstract` method automatically becomes an `abstract` class, and, as a result, cannot be instantiated. Thus, before you made `speak()` an `abstract` method, it would have been perfectly acceptable to write

```
Pet unknownPet = new Pet( );
```

although this doesn't make much sense. This is the conceptual flaw referred to earlier. But now, because `Pet` is an `abstract` class, you cannot create an "unknown" pet object. `Abstract` classes cannot instantiate objects. However, even though you cannot create an instance of the `Pet` class, you can create a `Pet` variable like this:

```
Pet anyPet;
```

and then assign an instance of any concrete `Pet` class to that variable like this:

```
anyPet = new Cat( );
anyPet = new Dog( );
```

A second and more useful consequence of making `Pet` an `abstract` class is that all subclasses derived from `Pet` are required to implement the `speak()` method. If a subclass fails to do so, it also becomes an `abstract` class. Thus, trying to create a `Frog` object as in Listing 13-1 (provided the `Pet` class were rewritten as an `abstract` class) would result in a compile-time error, because `Frog` does not have a `speak()` method. You'll find this an especially powerful feature when you begin writing classes that other programmers will extend, because you can force those programmers to make sure they don't forget to put in a needed method. This technique is used extensively throughout the Java class libraries themselves, including the `java.awt` and `java.io` packages.

MIXING abstract AND NORMAL METHODS

Just because a class is an `abstract` class does not mean it cannot have normal methods. Exactly the opposite is true: you *want* your `abstract` classes to contain as much information and functionality as possible. You should declare as `abstract` only those methods that cannot reasonably be implemented in the superclass, owing to its generality.

By making the `Pet.speak()` method `abstract`, you lost the ability to provide default speaking behavior. In considering how to provide this useful default behavior, you might reason that "contentedness" is really a property of the `Pet` class in general. You might add a `satisfied()` method to the `Pet` class, which would then look like this:

```
class Pet
{
    String satisfied()  ⇐
      { return "I'm a happy and contented pet"; }
    abstract String speak( );
}
```

The `Cat` and `Dog` classes can call this method from their own `speak()` methods and do not have to duplicate that code:

```
class Cat extends Pet
{
        String speak( ) ⇐
        { return "Meow, meow!" + super.satisfied( ); }
}
```

Now your `Pet` class offers the benefits of both `abstract` methods and default behavior.

RUN-TIME POLYMORPHISM AND DISPLAY LISTS

"I thought you said this was going to make things simpler. The `TalkToMe` program was easier to understand *before* you added all this `abstract` stuff!" As usual, you're correct. In a very simple program, you normally don't need `abstract` classes, but when things start to get complex, `abstract` classes can be a big help.

The `Figure` Class

For example, suppose you wanted to create a class library to be used for drawing geometric figures: triangles, parallelograms, rhombuses, and so on. Because each of the figures shares certain properties—size and location, for instance—you might write a base class `Figure` and extend the `Figure` class to create a class `Triangle`, class `Parallelogram`, and so forth. Your `Figure` class would define `abstract` methods such as `paint()` and `move()`. Each subclass of `Figure` would implement the `paint()` method with a behavior appropriate to its species of `Figure`: the `paint()` method in the subclass `Triangle` would draw a triangle, and the `paint()` method in `Parallelogram` would draw a parallelogram. Similarly, each subclass would also implement the `move()` method so that it could relocate a triangle or parallelogram, as appropriate.

But what statements would you put in the body of the `paint()` method within the superclass `Figure`? Because every figure is drawn differently, there's no obvious answer. If you were to define an empty method body and then later subclass `Figure` to create a `Dodecagon` class, you would have to remember to override the `paint()` method. Otherwise, when you tried to tell the `Dodecagon` to draw itself, nothing would happen. The `move()` method presents the same problem: It's not at all clear what the body of `Figure.move()` should contain. And forgetting to override it within a subclass results in a broken subclass that doesn't do everything it should.

This, then, is a situation that demands an `abstract` class. You could define your `Figure` class like this:

```
public abstract class Figure
{
    public abstract void paint( );
    public abstract void move( );
}
```

Note that `Figure`, implicitly `abstract` by virtue of having `abstract` methods, is made explicitly `abstract` by including the keyword `abstract` in the class header. Because

`Figure` is an `abstract` class, you won't be able to create a `Figure`. That's OK, because you really don't want to create a `Figure` anyway: You want to create a `Triangle`, or a `Parallelogram`, or some other specific kind of `Figure`.

To create your `Triangle` class, you'll need to implement every method that is declared as `abstract` in `Figure`. Remember, a class that contains an `abstract` method or that fails to define an inherited `abstract` method is considered to be `abstract`, whether it's declared as such or not. If you were to create a `Triangle` class that defined only `paint( )`, and not `move( )`, the `Triangle` class would be an `abstract` class and could not instantiate instances of itself. However, providing definitions of each `abstract` method is all that's required to empower an implicitly `abstract` class to create new objects. So long as your `Triangle`, `Parallelogram`, and `Dodecagon` classes provide definitions of the inherited `abstract` methods, `paint( )` and `move( )`, you'll have no trouble populating your geometric world.

Building the List

As you recall from the `Pet` example, when you declare a class as `abstract`, you're allowed to directly assign subclass objects to variables with superclass type. For example, you can do this:

```
Figure theFigure = ⇐
   new Triangle( /* arguments to constructor here */ );
```

Note that no cast is necessary in the assignment, which would otherwise have to be written as:

```
Figure theFigure = (Figure) new Triangle( /* arguments */ );
```

What good is assigning a `Triangle` object to a `Figure` variable? When you invoke an `abstract` method on a superclass object, the method in the `subclass` is actually run. That means, for example, that you can create an array containing `Figure` variables, and then `paint( )` all of them on the screen without knowing what kinds of `Figures` are actually contained in the references. That means, instead of writing code like this:

```
for ( i = 0; i < figureList.length( ); i++ )
{
    if ( figureList[i] instanceOf Triangle )
        (Triangle) figureList[i].paint( );
    else if
    . . .
    // Different test for each possible type of figure
    . . .
}
```

you can write code like this:

```
for ( i = 0; i < figureList.length( ); i++ )
{
    figureList[i].paint( );
}
```

Now that really is simpler! Furthermore, when you add additional `Figure` types, you won't have to rewrite this portion of your code; it will work with *any* type derived from `Figure`.

This principle has wide applicability:

Consider writing a program to play the game of chess. All chess pieces know how to move, but a pawn, a bishop, and a rook move differently. By using `abstract` classes, you can encapsulate the special information about how to move into each of the subclasses of the `abstract` superclass `ChessPiece`.

Think about writing a space exploration game. You might have hundreds of types of spaceships: battlestars, fighters, cruisers, drones. Each of these ships would move at different speeds and be drawn differently on the screen, but by putting that information inside distinct subclasses of `SpaceShip`, you reduce the work of updating your display to a simple loop.

Listings 13-2 to 13-5 show how `abstract` methods and classes can be used. Listing 13-5 shows the `FigureTest` applet, which uses the members of the `Figure` family, and Figure 13-1 shows the applet's output.

Listing 13-2 Figure.java

```java
// Figure.java
import java.awt.*;

public abstract class Figure
{
    public abstract void paint(Graphics g);
}
```

Listing 13-3 Triangle.java

```java
// Triangle.java
import java.awt.*;

public class Triangle extends Figure
{
    int[] pointX;
    int[] pointY;

    public Triangle(int[] x, int[] y)
    {
        pointX = x;
        pointY = y;
    }

    public void paint(Graphics g)
    {
        g.drawLine(pointX[0], pointY[0], pointX[1], ⇐
                            pointY[1]);
        g.drawLine(pointX[1], pointY[1], pointX[2], ⇐
                            pointY[2]);
```

continued on next page

> **The idea of a Pet is an abstraction. It describes the general characteristics of a group of animals for which you provide food and shelter.**

continued from previous page

```
                g.drawLine(pointX[2], pointY[2], pointX[0], ⇐
                           pointY[0]);
        }
}
```

Listing 13-4 Parallelogram.java

```java
// Parallelogram.java
import java.awt.*;

public class Parallelogram extends Figure
{
    int[] pointX, pointY;
    int   width,  height;

    public Parallelogram(int[] x, int[] y)
    {
        pointX = x;
        pointY = y;
        height = x[2];
        width  = y[2];
    }

    public void paint(Graphics g)
    {
        g.drawLine(pointX[0], pointY[0], pointX[0] + width, ⇐
                   pointY[0]);
        g.drawLine(pointX[1], pointY[1], pointX[1] + width, ⇐
                   pointY[1]);
        g.drawLine(pointX[0], pointY[0], pointX[1], ⇐
                   pointY[1]);
        g.drawLine(pointX[0] + width, pointY[0], ⇐
                   pointX[1] + width, pointY[1]);
    }
}
```

Listing 13-5 FigureTest.java

```java
// FigureTest.java
import java.applet.*;
import java.awt.*;
import java.awt.event.*;
import java.util.*;

public class FigureTest extends Applet implements
ActionListener
{
    Figure[] figureList = new Figure[100];

    Button newTriangle  = new Button( "Triangle" );
    Button newParallel   = new Button( "Parallelogram" );
    Random randomizer    = new Random();

    int cur = 0;

    public void init()
    {
```

```
            setLayout( new BorderLayout() );
            Panel p = new Panel();
            p.setLayout( new GridLayout(1, 2) );
            p.add( newTriangle );
            p.add( newParallel );
            add( p, "South" );
            newTriangle.addActionListener(this);
            newParallel.addActionListener(this);
    }

    public void paint(Graphics g)
    {
    for ( int i = 0; i < figureList.length ; i++ )
            if ( figureList[i] != null )
                figureList[i].paint( g );
    }

    public void actionPerformed( ActionEvent theEvent )
    {
        if ( cur >= figureList.length ) return;

        if      ( theEvent.getSource() == newTriangle )
            figureList[cur++] =
                new Triangle( randArray(3), randArray(3) );
        else if ( theEvent.getSource() == newParallel )
            figureList[cur++] =
                new Parallelogram( randArray(3), ⇐
                    randArray(3) );

        repaint();
    }

    public int[] randArray( int arraySize )
    {
        int[] ar = new int[arraySize];

        for ( int i = 0; i < ar.length; i++ )
            ar[i] = (int) (randomizer.nextFloat() *
                            (getSize().width * .75));

        return ar;
    }
}
```

Inside the `FigureTest` Applet

The `Figure` class is an `abstract` class that declares a single method, `paint()`. The `Triangle` class and the `Parallelogram` class both `extend` `Figure`, and `implement` the `paint()` method; so each is a concrete class. The `Triangle` class stores two `int` arrays that hold the x and y coordinates of the three corners of the `Triangle`. Its `paint()` method simply connects the points by using the AWT's `drawLine()` method. Likewise, the `Parallelogram` class contains two arrays holding the coordinates of the corners of the `Parallelogram`, while the fourth corner is calculated based on those values.

FIGURE 13-1

The Figures family at play

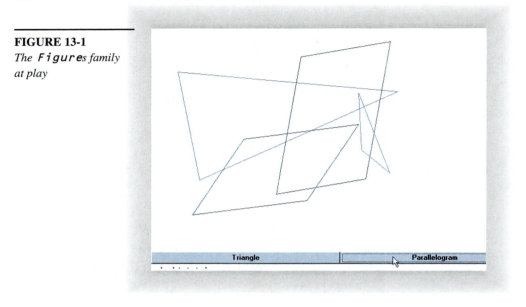

The FigureTest applet has five fields:

- figureList is an array of 100 Figures. When filled, this will hold the Triangles and Parallelograms that the user creates.

- The Buttons—newTriangle and newParallel—cause the applet to create a new Triangle or Parallelogram and store its reference in the figureList array.

- The Random object randomizer is used to create random dimensions for the Figures that are created.

- The int cur is used as the subscript for the figureList array so you can tell when the array is full. If you use a Vector, rather than an array, you will not need to keep track of how many elements are in the array.

The FigureTest applet has four methods:

- The init() method adds the Buttons to the bottom of the screen.

- The paint() method iterates through the elements of figureList. If the element is not null, it calls the Figure's paint() method.

- The actionPerformed() method first checks to make sure there is room in the array figureList, returning if there is not. If room is found, then the identity of the Button is checked, and a new Triangle or Parallelogram is created and added to figureList.

- randArray() is a utility method that creates arrays of random numbers and is used in the actionPerformed() method to create each Figure.

USING abstract POWER

If you think about it, you'll realize that `abstract` classes and methods don't enable you to write even one program that you couldn't write without them. But that doesn't mean that they are unimportant. They're simply much more important to the software designer than to the programmer. Similar to the access specifiers `private` and `protected`, abstraction lets you design classes for use by others and yet retain a degree of control over how your classes will be used.

Many of the classes of the AWT are `abstract` classes, including such classes as `Component`, `Container`, `Graphics`, `Image`, and `MenuComponent`. Much of the simplicity and flexibility of the AWT is rooted in the power of abstraction. For example, the AWT provides many types of `Containers`, yet each type of `Container` shares important similarities with its kin, because each must implement the methods of the `abstract class Container`. Learning to use one type of `Container` makes it easy to learn to use the other types, because each implements these methods specified by the `abstract` superclass.

Moreover, `Containers` hold members of another `abstract` class: `Component`. All that's necessary to achieve this impressive feat is an array of type `Component` defined as a field of the `Container` class.

Many AWT classes descend from `Component` (including the `Container` class itself), so the ability to hold `Components` allows a `Container` to hold such varied concrete objects as `Buttons`, `Canvases`, `Checkboxes`, `Choices`, `Labels`, `Lists`, `Scrollbars`, and `TextComponents`. Because a `Component` must implement such methods as `repaint()`, `setLocation()`, and `setVisible()`, the `Container` can depend upon the capability of its contained objects to respond to these messages.

The use of `abstract` classes and methods gives the AWT great simplicity and flexibility. In designing your own reusable classes, you'll do well to study and follow the example of the AWT and make liberal use of abstraction.

Inherited Tools: Implements and Interfaces

The next time you visit your doctor, take a look at the diplomas and certificates displayed on the office wall. What purpose do they serve? The diplomas are there to assure you that your doctor has been certified to perform a specific kind of work. Doctors receive one type of certification for brain surgery, and quite another for heart surgery. Their diplomas act as a kind of "broadcast" that they are willing and able to carry out these types of operations.

Java classes make a similar sort of claim when they use the `implements` keyword. A class that says it `implements Runnable` is claiming that it is prepared to receive and handle the `run()` message. The "requirements" that a class `implements` are contained in a Java construct called an `interface`. An `interface` looks almost identical to a class definition, except that all its methods are `abstract`, and all its fields (if any) are declared as `static final`. Interfaces are useful when you are building reusable objects that respond to events (among many other things).

SPECIFYING AN INTERFACE

> *" Just because a class is abstract does not mean it cannot have normal methods. "*

One common situation is the need to have your objects take some action when an interesting event occurs. This is quite simple when the action you want to take is always the same: You simply add a method that does what you want. But what happens when you want your object to do something different the next time that same event occurs? A good example is some type of alarm-clock object. You'd like to start it up and then perform action "X" when its time arrives. Then you could put one alarm-clock object inside your virtual microwave to tell you when your virtual coffee is reheated, and another inside your virtual appointment book to tell you when you need to leave for the dentist.

As things stand now, your object must be rewritten afresh for every new circumstance. This is not consistent with the mother of all programming virtues, laziness. What you'd really like is a reusable object that can do *anything* when the interesting event occurs, one that allows you to specify the desired action whenever you create a new instance of the object, not once and for all time when you first write the class.

The secret to accomplishing this trick, which is termed a *callback*, is to write a Java `interface`. An `interface` is a lot like a class, except that it specifies only the messages an object responds to, not the behavior that the object performs in response to these messages. An object that is declared as implementing a given interface gives notice that it will accept any and all of the messages identified in the interface.

Listing 13-6 shows a simple interface, named `Action`. The `Action` interface identifies a single method, `action( )`. The `action( )` method has no arguments and returns no value; if it had arguments or returned a value, these would have been specified in the method header in the usual way.

Listing 13-6 Action.java

```
// Action.java
public interface Action
{
    public void action( );
}
```

USING AN INTERFACE

To use the `Action` interface with a client class, you need to do only two things to the client class:

1. Add the `implements Action` clause to the end of its class declaration.

2. Write a method named `action( )` that has exactly the same signature—taking no arguments and returning no value—as the `Action` interface.

The `TimerTest` class, shown in Listing 13-7, implements the `Action` interface. Note the class header, which specifies that the `TimerTest` implements the `Action` interface. Consistent with this specification, the class includes a definition for the `action()` method; if it did not, Javac would not compile it.

Listing 13-7 TimerTest.java

```java
// TimerTest.java
public class TimerTest implements Action
{
    public static void main(String args[])
    {
        TimerTest theApp = new TimerTest();
        Timer theTimer = new Timer(15, theApp);
    }

    public void action()
    {
        System.out.println("R i i i n g!");
        System.exit(0);
    }
}
```

The TimerTest application uses a `Timer` object to wait for a specified interval. When the interval (given in seconds) has expired, the `Timer` invokes the `action( )` method of the `TimerTest` object. Listing 13-8 shows the `Timer` class itself. There are several things you'll want to notice about the `Timer` class:

☕ It contains an `Action` variable, named `theAction`, and takes an `Action` argument as the second parameter of its constructor. An `Action` variable can reference an object of *any* class that implements the `Action` `interface`. Thus, TimerTest, shown earlier, passes a `TimerTest` object as the argument to the `Timer` constructor, which is then assigned to the field `theAction`.

☕ After initializing itself, a `Timer` object runs as a private thread, sleeping for one second (1000 milliseconds) and then waking up to check the current time. If the timer interval has expired, the `Timer` sends the `action( )` message to the object passed to the `Timer` constructor, stored by the constructor in the variable `theAction`. This causes the `action( )` method of the `TimerTest` object to be invoked.

Listing 13-8 Timer.java

```java
// Timer.java
import java.util.Date;

public class Timer extends Thread
{
    long targetTime;
    Action theAction;

    public Timer(int numSeconds, Action myAction)
    {
        long now = System.currentTimeMillis( );
        targetTime = now + 1000 * numSeconds;
        System.out.println("Time now:      " + ⇐
         new Date(now));
        System.out.println("Alarm set for: " + ⇐
         new Date(targetTime));
```

continued on next page

continued from previous page

```
        theAction = myAction;
        start();
    }

    public void run()
    {
        while (true)
        {
            try { Thread.sleep(1000); }
            catch (InterruptedException e) { /* ⇐
             null statement */ }

            long now = System.currentTimeMillis();
            if (now >= targetTime)
            {
                theAction.action();
                break;
            }
        }
    }
}
```

OUTPUT OF THE TIMERTEST APPLICATION

```
C:\Ch13\Examples>java TimerTest
        Time now:      Wed Dec 18 17:44:00 PST 1996
        Alarm set for: Wed Dec 18 17:44:15 PST 1996
        R i i n g!
```

Abstract CLASSES AND INTERFACES

It's easy to confuse `abstract` classes and interfaces. They are indeed similar, but there are also differences between them. Interfaces and `abstract` classes are similar because

☞ Both contain `abstract` methods.

☞ Neither an interface nor an `abstract` class can be used to instantiate objects, although you can create variables from either of them.

Abstract classes and interfaces are different because

☞ A class can implement many interfaces. However, it can be derived only from a single `abstract` class; that is, it can have only a single immediate parent.

Many classes can implement the same interface, and those classes do not have to be related to each other. By contrast, only subclasses explicitly derived from an `abstract` class can implement the `abstract` methods of that class.

An `abstract` class may include methods which are concrete (not `abstract`). All the methods contained in an interface are `abstract` methods.

An interface can extend interfaces other than `Object`, which is the implicit base type of an interface that extends no other interface.

While an interface, like an `abstract` class, can include fields, the fields of an interface must all be declared `static final`.

USING interfaceS TO SIMULATE MULTIPLE INHERITANCE

Unlike Java, many object-oriented languages (for example, C++ and Smalltalk) allow a child class to inherit fields and methods from more than one parent class. This capability is called *multiple inheritance*. Java avoids multiple inheritance because it can lead to very complicated and error-prone relationships among classes. However, the fact remains that it is often necessary to combine in a single class the properties of several other classes. Java's `interface` facility can be used to accomplish this.

For example, suppose you had two parent classes defining two sorts of animals, each derived from the base class `Animal`:

```
public class Animal
{
    // Shared animal characteristics and behavior
    // defined here
}

public abstract class FlyingAnimal extends Animal
{
    public abstract void fly( );
}

public abstract class SwimmingAnimal extends Animal
{
    public abstract void swim( );
}
```

You could extend these classes to create a host of child classes representing sparrows, eagles, sharks, porpoises, and so on. But what about the duck, which both flies and swims? How should it be represented by your classes? Obviously, there's a problem. A better design would be one that draws on the power of interfaces:

```
public class Animal
{
```

continued on next page

continued from previous page

```
    // Shared animal characteristics and behavior
    // defined here
}

public interface Flier
{
    public void fly( );
}

public interface Swimmer
{
    public void swim( );
}
```

This improved design allows you to populate your zoo with animals (including ducks) that fly, swim, or both fly and swim (the bodies of the class definitions are omitted):

```
public class Sparrow extends Animal implements Flier ⇐
  { . . . }
public class Shark    extends Animal implements Swimmer ⇐
  { . . . }
public class Duck     extends Animal implements Flier, ⇐
  Swimmer { . . . }
```

WHEN TO USE AN interface

Choosing when to use an abstract class and when to use an interface is usually straightforward. You should use abstract classes whenever you want to provide substantial functionality or data in the superclass, and yet want to force the users of your class to override a particular method or set of methods. You should use interfaces when you know what methods a task requires, but you have no default implementation, or when you want a class to implement behavior from multiple parents.

Coping with Current Events

One of the most important uses of interfaces within Java is in handling events. Java's AWT Components are attractive enough, but they're not very useful unless you know how to trap and process the Events they generate. Java actually supports two distinct models for handling events: an original model and a new model implemented as part of the 1.1 release of the JDK. These models cannot be mixed within a single program, but each is supported by JDK 1.1. Examples in this book have used the JDK 1.1 model, which will now be explained more fully.

JDK 1.1 offers a new event-related object, java.util.EventObject. EventObjects are sent by a *source* directly to a *listener* or *listeners*. Objects that want to receive event notifications from a source have to *register* with that source as a listener, similar to signing up for a mailing list. Whenever a relevant event occurs, the source object notifies all registered listeners, using a callback. Listeners must implement the interface EventListener (or one of its subclasses) and are typically application objects; sources are typically AWT Components.

Most `EventObjects` are already subclassed, providing unique object types for common AWT events. Table 13-1 shows how the events of the original model and the new model are related.

TABLE 13-1
ORIGINAL MODEL AND NEW MODEL EVENT CROSS-REFERENCE

ORIGINAL MODEL	NEW MODEL		
SOURCE OBJECT	**EVENT/METHOD**	**INTERFACE**	**METHODS**
Button, List, MenuItem, TextField	ACTION_EVENT /action	ActionListener	actionPerformed (ActionEvent)
Checkbox, Choice	ACTION_EVENT /action	ItemListener	itemStateChanged (ItemEvent)
Dialog, Frame	WINDOW_DESTROY	WindowListener	windowClosing (WindowEvent)
	WINDOW_EXPOSE	WindowListener	windowOpened (WindowEvent)
	WINDOW_ICONIFY	WindowListener	windowIconified (WindowEvent)
	WINDOW_DEICONIFY	WindowListener	windowDeiconified (WindowEvent)
	WINDOW_CLOSED	WindowListener	windowClosed (WindowEvent)
	WINDOW_MOVED	ComponentListener	componentMoved (ComponentEvent)
	WINDOW_MOVED	ComponentListener	componentHidden (ComponentEvent)
	WINDOW_MOVED	ComponentListener	componentResized (ComponentEvent)
	WINDOW_MOVED	ComponentListener	componentShown (ComponentEvent)
Scrollbar	SCROLL_LINE_UP	AdjustmentListener	adjustmentValueChanged (AdjustmentEvent)
	SCROLL_LINE_DOWN	AdjustmentListener	adjustmentValueChanged (AdjustmentEvent)
	SCROLL_PAGE_UP	AdjustmentListener	adjustmentValueChanged (AdjustmentEvent)
	SCROLL_PAGE_DOWN	AdjustmentListener	adjustmentValueChanged (AdjustmentEvent)
	SCROLL_ABSOLUTE	AdjustmentListener	adjustmentValueChanged (AdjustmentEvent)
	SCROLL—BEGIN	AdjustmentListener	adjustmentValueChanged (AdjustmentEvent)
	SCROLL_END	AdjustmentListener	adjustmentValueChanged (AdjustmentEvent)

Table continued...

TABLE 13-1 ORIGINAL MODEL AND NEW MODEL EVENT CROSS-REFERENCE CONTINUED...

ORIGINAL MODEL	NEW MODEL		
SOURCE OBJECT	**EVENT/METHOD**	**INTERFACE**	**METHODS**
Checkbox, CheckboxMenuItem, Choice, List	LIST_SELECT	ItemListener	itemStateChanged (ItemEvent)
	LIST_DESELECT	ItemListener	itemStateChanged) (ItemEvent)
Canvas, Dialog, Frame, Panel, Window	MOUSE_DRAG /mouseDrag	MouseMotionListener	mouseDragged(MouseEvent)
	MOUSE_MOVE /mouseMove	MouseMotionListener	mouseMoved(MouseEvent)
	MOUSE_DOWN /mouseDown	MouseListener	mousePressed(MouseEvent)/ mouseClicked(MouseEvent)
	MOUSE_UP /mouseUp	MouseListener	mouseReleased(MouseEvent)/ mouseClicked(MouseEvent)
	MOUSE_ENTER /mouseEnter	MouseListener	mouseEntered(MouseEvent)
	MOUSE_EXIT /mouseExit	MouseListener	mouseExited(MouseEvent)
Component	KEY_PRESS /keyDown	KeyListener	keyPressed(KeyEvent)
	KEY_RELEASE /keyUp	KeyListener	keyReleased(KeyEvent)/ keyTyped(KeyEvent)
	KEY_ACTION_RELEASE /keyUp	KeyListener	keyReleased(KeyEvent)/ keyTyped(KeyEvent)
	GOT_FOCUS /gotFocus	FocusListener	focusGained(FocusEvent)
	LOST_FOCUS /lostFocus	FocusListener	focusLost(FocusEvent)

LOOKING AT ALL THE EVENTS

Listing 13-9, the CurrentEvents application, gives you a taste of each event-handling method and prints the contents of each Event when it occurs. While this might seem like overkill, such an application can be a valuable tool when you want to discover exactly which events are triggered by some interaction with your program. You can see the results of running CurrentEvents in Figure 13-2.

Listing 13-9 CurrentEvents.java

```
// CurrentEvents.java

import java.awt.*;
import java.awt.event.*;

public class CurrentEvents extends Frame
   implements ActionListener,
             ItemListener,
             WindowListener,
             ComponentListener,
             AdjustmentListener,
             MouseMotionListener,
             MouseListener,
```

> *An abstract class is one that contains an abstract method or that fails to define an inherited abstract method.*

```
                     KeyListener,
                     FocusListener
   {
   // Attributes
   Button          theButton  = new Button("Button");
   Scrollbar       theScroll  = ⇐
     new Scrollbar(Scrollbar.HORIZONTAL,
                                        0, 10, 0, 100);
   Choice          theChoice  = new Choice();
   TextField       theText    = ⇐
     new TextField("Jumbo WAS here.");
   SimpleCanvas theCanvas     = ⇐
     new SimpleCanvas("Mouse! Come here!!");

   TextArea        theOutput  = new TextArea("", 10, 80);

   // The main method - creates a single instance
   public static void main(String args[])
   {
       new CurrentEvents( );
   }

   // Constructor
   public CurrentEvents( )
   {
       setTitle("CurrentEvents: Exercising the JDK 1.1 ⇐
                Event Model");

       // Top panel
       Panel p1 = new Panel( );
       p1.setLayout(new GridLayout(1, 2, 10, 10));

       // Canvas panel (top, left)
       Panel p2 = new Panel( );
       p2.setLayout(new BorderLayout());
       p2.setFont( new Font("Dialog", Font.BOLD, 10) );
       p2.add(new Label("Canvas"), "North");
       p2.add(theCanvas, "Center");
       p1.add( p2 );

       // Labels for controls
       Panel p3 = new Panel( );
       p3.setFont( new Font("Dialog", Font.BOLD, 10) );
       p3.setLayout(new GridLayout(4, 1, 5, 5));
       p3.add(new Label("Button :", Label.RIGHT));
       p3.add(new Label("Scrollbar :", Label.RIGHT));
       p3.add(new Label("Choice :", Label.RIGHT));
       p3.add(new Label("TextField :", Label.RIGHT));

       // Other controls panel (top, right)
       Panel p4 = new Panel( );
       p4.setLayout(new GridLayout(4, 1, 5, 5));
       p4.add(theButton);
       p4.add(theScroll);
       p4.add(theChoice);
       p4.add(theText);
```

continued on next page

continued from previous page

```
            // Panel to hold controls and labels
            Panel p5 = new Panel( );
            p5.setLayout(new BorderLayout());
            p5.add(p3, "West");
            p5.add(p4, "Center");
            p5.add(new Label("Controls"), "North");
            p5.add(new Label(""), "South"); // Added for spacing
            p5.add(new Label(""), "East");
            p1.add( p5 );

            // Add top panel and output to main screen
            add(p1, "North");
            add(theOutput, "Center");

            // Initialize controls
            theChoice.add("Java");
            theChoice.add("More Java");
            theChoice.add("Most Java");

            theOutput.setEditable(false);

            // Add listeners for each event
            theButton.addActionListener(this);
            theChoice.addItemListener(this);
            addWindowListener(this);
            addComponentListener(this);
            theScroll.addAdjustmentListener(this);
            addMouseMotionListener(this);
            addMouseListener(this);
            theText.addKeyListener(this);
            theText.addFocusListener(this);
            theCanvas.addMouseMotionListener(this);
            theCanvas.addMouseListener(this);

            setSize(640, 480);
            setVisible(true);
        }

        // =========================================================
        // Event handling (listener) routines
        // =========================================================
        public void windowClosing(WindowEvent event)
        {
            theOutput.append(event.toString( ) + "\n");
            setVisible(false);
            dispose( );
            System.exit(0);
        }

        public void actionPerformed         ⇐
          (ActionEvent e)        { report(e); }

        public void itemStateChanged         ⇐
          (ItemEvent e)          { report(e); }

        public void windowOpened         ⇐
          (WindowEvent e)        { report(e); }
```

```
    public void windowIconified             ⇐
       (WindowEvent e)     { report(e); }
    public void windowDeiconified           ⇐
       (WindowEvent e)     { report(e); }
    public void windowActivated             ⇐
       (WindowEvent e)     { report(e); }
    public void windowDeactivated           ⇐
       (WindowEvent e)     { report(e); }

    public void componentMoved              ⇐
       (ComponentEvent e)  { report(e); }
    public void componentHidden             ⇐
       (ComponentEvent  e) { report(e); }
    public void componentResized            ⇐
       (ComponentEvent  e) { report(e); }
    public void componentShown              ⇐
       (ComponentEvent  e) { report(e); }

    public void adjustmentValueChanged  ⇐
       (AdjustmentEvent e) { report(e); }

    public void mouseDragged                ⇐
       (MouseEvent e)      { report(e); }
    public void mouseMoved                  ⇐
       (MouseEvent e)      { report(e); }
    public void mousePressed                ⇐
       (MouseEvent e)      { report(e); }
    public void mouseReleased               ⇐
       (MouseEvent e)      { report(e); }
    public void mouseEntered                ⇐
       (MouseEvent e)      { report(e); }
    public void mouseExited                 ⇐
       (MouseEvent e)      { report(e); }
    public void mouseClicked                ⇐
       (MouseEvent e)      { report(e); }

    public void keyPressed                  ⇐
       (KeyEvent e)        { report(e); }
    public void keyReleased                 ⇐
       (KeyEvent e)        { report(e); }
    public void keyTyped                    ⇐
       (KeyEvent e)        { report(e); }

    public void focusGained                 ⇐
       (FocusEvent e)      { report(e); }
    public void focusLost                   ⇐
       (FocusEvent e)      { report(e); }

    public void windowClosed                ⇐
       (WindowEvent e)     { }

// =========================================================
// Helper method report: display event to TextArea
// Note type of parm: AWTEvent, not Event!
// =========================================================
public void report(AWTEvent event)
{
    theOutput.append(event.toString() + "\n");
```

continued on next page

continued from previous page

```
        }
}

class SimpleCanvas extends Canvas
{
    String theString;

    public SimpleCanvas(String string)
    {
        theString = string;
        setBackground(Color.lightGray);
    }

    public Dimension getPreferredSize()
    {
        return new Dimension(100, 100);
    }

    public void paint(Graphics g)
    {
        g.drawString(theString, 5, 15);
    }
}
```

FIGURE 13-2

Running the CurrentEvents application

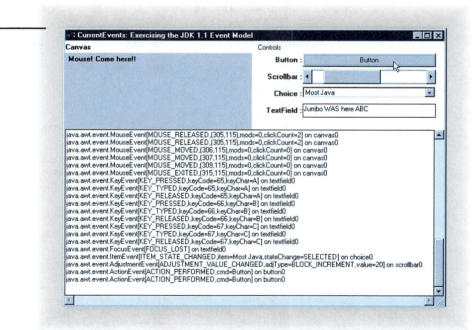

Java's Original Event Model

This section explains Java's original event model, which you should not use in your own programs because it will not be supported indefinitely. However, you will find it useful to know something about the original model, because you may need to read code written for the original event model, or you may wish to convert such code to use the newer event model.

EVENT HANDLING IN THE ORIGINAL MODEL

As in the JDK 1.1 model, events are generated when something of interest happens to a `Component`. In response, the system creates an `Event` object and sends a `handleEvent` message to the affected `Component`. Programs can override the default `handleEvent()` method of the `Component` class, to provide customized handling of events. If you write a method to handle messages sent to a `Component`, your method should first check to see if the message is of interest. If it is, your `handleEvent()` method should process the message and then return the value `true`. This indicates to the event system that the event was processed. If you don't process the event, you should return the value `false`, in effect telling the AWT, "No, I didn't handle this event." The default `handleEvent()` method included in the `Component` class always returns `false`, signifying it has not handled any `Event` sent to it.

When a `handleEvent()` method returns `false`, the AWT arranges for the message to be re-sent to the `Container` in which the `Component` resides. This process, shown in Figure 13-3, continues until the `Event` is processed or until the topmost `Container` returns `false` from its `handleEvent()` method. Returning `true` from a `handleEvent()` method causes the `Event` to be consumed rather than propagated up the container hierarchy.

To avoid subclassing the many `Components` used in a typical program, programmers usually implement the `handleEvent()` method at the `Frame` or `Applet` level, where all messages generated by the contained `Components` will eventually end up. The method normally consists of one or more selection statements that check for "interesting" `Events`. When one is found, the method processes it or, if processing is extensive, sets a flag to request subsequent processing. It is important that processing performed in the `handleEvent()` method be minimal. Performing lengthy operations in the `handleEvent()` method will cause AWT `Components` to respond sluggishly, something users profoundly dislike.

THE Event OBJECT

Each `Event` object received by `handleEvent()` encapsulates a wealth of information that you can mine to learn the details of the occurrence that caused it to be created. The key public instance fields of an `Event` are shown in Table 13-2. Chief among these is the `id` field, which indicates the type of occurrence that the `Event` represents. Possible values of the `id` field are shown in Table 13-3.

FIGURE 13-3
The Event life cycle

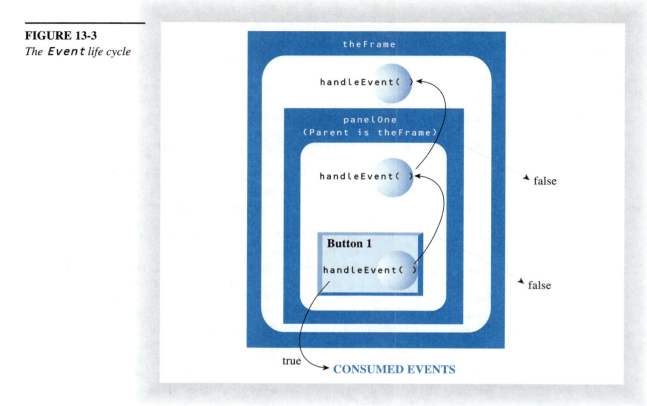

TABLE 13-2
KEY public INSTANCE FIELDS OF THE Event CLASS

FIELD	TYPE	MEANING/USE
arg	Object	An arbitrary argument describing the event. The meaning depends on the type of event.
ClickCount	int	The number of consecutive clicks for the MOUSE_DOWN event.
id	int	The type of event.
key	int	The key associated with a keyboard event.
modifiers	int	The state of the modifier keys—associated with a keyboard or mouse event—decoded by use of mask fields.
target	Object	The Object over which the event occurred, or with which the event is associated.
when	long	Time stamp of the event.
x	int	Coordinate of the event (x).
y	int	Coordinate of the event (y).

TABLE 13-3
`public` FIELDS OF THE Event CLASS USED TO IDENTIFY Event TYPES

EVENT CATEGORY	EVENT	DESCRIPTION
Mouse	MOUSE_DOWN	Mouse button was pressed.
	MOUSE_UP	Mouse button was released.
	MOUSE_DRAG	Mouse was moved with a button pressed.
	MOUSE_MOVE	Mouse was moved with no button pressed.
	MOUSE_ENTER	Mouse entered a `Component`.
	MOUSE_EXIT	Mouse exited a `Component`.
Keyboard	KEY_PRESS	A normal key was pressed.
	KEY_RELEASE	A normal key was released.
	KEY_ACTION	An "action" key was pressed.
	KEY_ACTION_RELEASE	An "action" key was released.
Action Key	F1, F2, ..., F12	A function key was pressed.
	LEFT, RIGHT, UP, DOWN, HOME, END, PG UP, PGDN	A cursor movement key was pressed.
Window	WINDOW_EXPOSE	A window has become exposed.
	WINDOW_ICONIFY	A window is to be iconified.
	WINDOW_DEICONIFY	A window is to be deiconified.
	WINDOW_DESTROY	A window is to be destroyed.
	WINDOW_MOVED	A window has moved.
Action Component	ACTION_EVENT	An "action" has been requested.
	LIST_SELECT	A `List` item has been selected.
	LIST_DESELECT	A `List` item has been deselected.
	LOAD_FILE	A file-loading event.
	SAVE_FILE	A file-saving event.
	SCROLL_ABSOLUTE	A `Scrollbar` thumb has been moved.
	SCROLL_LINE_UP	A `Scrollbar` "line up" area has been pushed.
	SCROLL_LINE_DOWN	A `Scrollbar` "line down" area has been pushed.
	SCROLL_PAGE_UP	A `Scrollbar` "page up" area has been pushed.
	SCROLL_PAGE_DOWN	A `Scrollbar` "page down" area has been pushed.
Focus	GOT_FOCUS	A `Component` has received the focus.
	LOST_FOCUS	A `Component` has lost the focus.

TYPES OF `Events`

There are six basic types of `Events`, distinguished by the `id` field:

- Mouse events
- Keyboard events
- Action-key events
- Window events
- Action-component events
- Focus events

Each type has a series of specific `Events` associated with it, as shown in the table. To force your application window to stay in the upper-left corner of the screen, for instance, you could write

```
public boolean handleEvent( Event theEvent )
{
    if ( theEvent.id == Event.WINDOW_MOVED )
    {
        ((Frame)theEvent.target).move( 0, 0 );
    }
}
```

The `target` field contains a reference to the actual object that initiated the message. To call a method inside that object, you can cast the `target` field as is done here, or you can assign it to a variable of the correct type.

`Events` also encode the status of certain keys and of the mouse buttons. Table 13-4 shows mask values that can be ANDed (by use of the `&` operator) with the `modifiers` field to determine the status of modifier keys and the use of alternate mouse buttons. For example,

```
    if ( (theEvent.modifiers & theEvent.ALT_MASK) != 0)
```

can be used to determine if the middle button of a three-button mouse was used to generate the `Event`. You can also use the methods in Table 13-5 to determine the status of modifier keys at the time an `Event` occurred.

TABLE 13-4
`public` FIELDS OF THE `Event` CLASS USED IN DECODING THE MODIFIERS FIELD

FIELD	DESCRIPTION
ALT_MASK	AND with modifiers to determine if mouse middle button was used.
CTRL_MASK	AND with modifiers to determine if CTRL key was down when event occurred.

Table continued...

TABLE 13-4 `public` FIELDS OF THE `Event` CLASS USED IN DECODING THE MODIFIERS FIELD CONTINUED…

FIELD	DESCRIPTION
META_MASK	AND with modifiers to determine if meta [ALT] key was down when event occurred (keyboard event) or if right mouse button was used (mouse event).
SHIFT_MASK	AND with modifiers to determine if [SHIFT] key was down when event occurred.

TABLE 13-5
KEY `public` METHODS OF THE `Event` CLASS

METHOD HEADER	FUNCTION
boolean controlDown( )	Determine if [CTRL] key was down when event occurred.
boolean metaDown( )	Determine if meta [ALT] key was down when event occurred.
boolean shiftDown( )	Determine if [SHIFT] key was down when event occurred.

CONVENIENCE METHODS

The key event-related methods of the `Component` class are shown in Table 13-6. Chief among these is the `handleEvent( )` method, which was introduced earlier. For certain common `Event`s, if no `handleEvent( )` method accepts the `Event`, the AWT generates a call to one of the "convenience" methods listed in the table. It is sometimes more convenient to override one of these methods than to include the additional statements in a `handleEvent( )` method. `handleEvent( )` methods have a tendency to become cluttered and complex, so this feature is a quite welcome way of simplifying programs.

TABLE 13-6
KEY EVENT-RELATED `public` METHODS OF THE `Component` CLASS

METHOD HEADER	MEANING
boolean action(Event event, Object argument)	An action event occurred inside the `Component`.
boolean gotFocus(Event event, Object argument)	The `Component` received the focus.
boolean handleEvent(Event event)	An event occurred inside the `Component`.
boolean keyDown(Event event, int key)	A key was pressed while the `Component` had the focus.
boolean keyUp(Event event, int key)	A key was released while the `Component` had the focus.

Table continued…

TABLE 13-6 KEY EVENT-RELATED **public** METHODS OF THE **Component**
CLASS CONTINUED…

METHOD HEADER	MEANING
`boolean lostFocus(Event event, Object what)`	The **Component** lost the focus.
`boolean mouseDown(Event event, int x, int y)`	A mouse button was pressed inside the **Component**.
`boolean mouseDrag(Event event, int x, int y)`	The mouse was moved inside the **Component** while the mouse button was pressed.
`boolean mouseEnter(Event event, int x, int y)`	The mouse entered the **Component**.
`boolean mouseExit(Event event, int x, int y)`	The mouse exited the **Component**.
`boolean mouseMove(Event event, int x, int y)`	The mouse was moved inside the **Component** while the mouse button was not pressed.
`boolean mouseUp(Event event, int x, int y)`	A mouse button was released inside the **Component**.

THE `super.handleEvent()` IDIOM

A `handleEvent()` method must return `true` or `false`, but you won't necessarily want
to specify these as literals. A common Java idiom is to write

```
return super.handleEvent(theEvent);
```

where `theEvent` is the name by which the `Event` argument is known within the
`handleEvent()` method. This clever device forwards the `Event` up the `inheritance`
hierarchy to determine if a superclass of the current class has a `handleEvent()`
method interested in processing the current `Event`. This is particularly useful if the
`handleEvent()` method is part of an object that subclasses `Frame` or `Applet`, because
it permits the default action of the superclass to occur. This will normally cause the
`Event` to be forwarded up the `container` hierarchy. Returning `false` from such a
method will prevent messages not handled in the current method from being forwarded up the container hierarchy. In general, you should not return `false` from your
`handleEvent()` method; you should return `true` if you've handled the `Event` or
`super.handleEvent(theEvent)` otherwise.

Printing

In addition to the new event model, Java 1.1 also introduced platform-independent
printing. Now obtaining printed output from a Java application is as straightforward as
painting on the screen. You need to be aware, however, that applets are forbidden to
print, because the capability to print opens the door to potential mischief.

STARTING A PRINT JOB

To start printing, you'll need a `PrintJob` object, which you can obtain by calling the `Toolkit.getPrintJob()` method like this:

```
PrintJob thePJ = Toolkit.getPrintJob( this, "Output", ⇐
    (Properties) null);
```

This method requires three parameters: the application's frame, a `String` giving a suitable title for the printed output (used by the operating system to identify the print job), and a `java.util.Properties` object specifying any special properties of the print job. For most purposes, it's sufficient to specify the `Properties` as `null`, with an appropriate cast to type `Properties`. You'll learn more about `Properties` in Chapter 15, "Data Structures and Utility Classes."

When you request a `PrintJob` object, the `Toolkit` class will display the platform-specific dialog box that allows you to select a printer on your system. Figure 13-4 shows how this appears after calling `Toolkit.getPrintJob()` on Windows 95. According to the documentation, if the user cancels the printer selection dialog box, `getPrintJob()` should return `null`. (At the time of this writing, using JDK 1.1B2, that does not yet occur, and you have to wrap your printing setup code in a `try-catch` block to handle the possibility that the user cancels printing.)

FIGURE 13-4

Calling
`Toolkit.get`
`PrintJob()` on
Windows 95

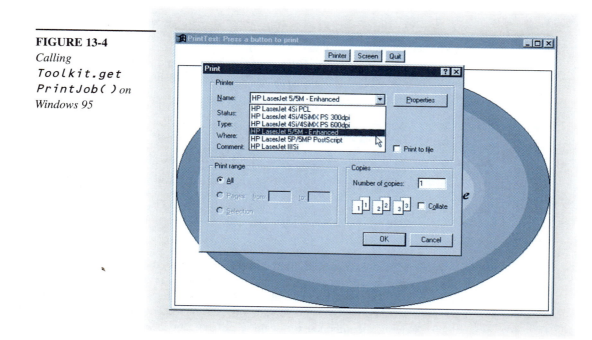

OBTAINING A `Graphics` OBJECT

Once you've obtained a `PrintJob` object, you can send it the `getGraphics` message, which causes it to return a special `Graphics` object adapted for printing:

```
Graphics output = thePJ.getGraphics( );
```

This `Graphics` object implements an interface known as `PrintGraphics`, which equips it with a number of useful methods that facilitate your printing. Printing under Java is a page-at-a-time operation. When you call `getGraphics( )`, you get a blank page that you can draw (that is, print) on. When you are finished, you send your page to the printer by using the `dispose( )` method. To print multiple pages, you simply repeat the process. Note that Java does no pagination; pagination is your responsibility.

RENDERING OUTPUT

The `Graphics` object returned by `PrintJob.getGraphics( )` is scaled so that it closely resembles your display. This makes it easy for you to write code that works identically on both your display and on your printer. The `PrintJob` object also implements two new informational methods, shown in Table 13-7, that help you to position your printed output by letting you know the logical dimensions and logical resolution of your printer. Note that this will not necessarily be the same as the physical resolution of your printer. Thus, when you write

```
output.drawString( "Hi Mom", 100, 100 );
```

it will print in the same position on a 600 dpi printer as on a 300 dpi printer. Otherwise, you would have to find the printer resolution and scale all your output accordingly. By providing logical dimensions, Java does the hard part for you.

TABLE 13-7
USEFUL METHODS FOR PRINTING

METHOD	DESCRIPTION
`Dimension PrintJob.getPageDimension( )`	Get the height and width of the printable area of the page in logical units.
`int PrintJob.getPageResolution( )`	Get the printer resolution in logical units.

All the normal graphics methods of the AWT work with this printing `Graphics` object, just as they do on the screen. Thus, you can `drawString( )`, `drawRect( )`, `fillOval( )`, and so forth. You can also change `Fonts` by using `setFont( )`, and space and align your textual output by using `FontMetrics( )`. In addition, you can print a representation of your Java components by calling `paint( )` or `print( )` and passing the special `Graphics` object as a parameter—the result is identical no matter which method is used, because the default implementation of `print( )` simply calls `paint( )`.

A handy alternative is the printAll( ) method. When invoked on a Container, it calls print( ) on each Component within the Container; nested Containers are handled without a hitch, making things easy for the programmer. Listing 13-10 shows an example of a printing application, and Figure 13-5 shows its output.

Listing 13-10 PrintTest.java

```java
// PrintTest.java
import java.awt.*;
import java.awt.event.*;
import java.util.*;

public class PrintTest extends Frame
                          implements ActionListener, ⇐
                                     WindowListener
{
    Button      thePrintButton   = new Button("Printer");
    Button      theScreenButton  = new Button("Screen");
    Button      theQuitButton    = new Button("Quit");
    Panel       theScreen        = new Panel();
    public static void main(String args[])
    {
        new PrintTest( );
    }
    public PrintTest( )
    {
        setTitle("PrintTest: Press a button to print");
        Panel p = new Panel( );
        p.setLayout(new FlowLayout( ));
        p.add(thePrintButton);
        p.add(theScreenButton);
        p.add(theQuitButton);

        add(p,          "North" );
          // New BorderLayout syntax
        add(theScreen, "Center");
        thePrintButton.addActionListener(this);
        theScreenButton.addActionListener(this);
        theQuitButton.addActionListener (this);
        addWindowListener(this);

        setSize(640, 480);
        setVisible(true);


        // The Toolkit class has a new beep!
        getToolkit( ).beep( );
    }
    public void actionPerformed(ActionEvent event)
    {
        Object target = event.getSource( );

        if (target == thePrintButton)
        {
            // 1. Get a PrintJob object
            //by calling getPrintJob( )
```

continued on next page

continued from previous page

```
PrintJob    pjob   = null;
Properties props = null;
pjob = getToolkit( ).⇐
       getPrintJob(
          this, "Printing Test", props);

// pjob SHOULD BE null if user canceled,
//(not currently implemented)
if (pjob != null)
{

    // 2. Get a Graphics object
    //from the PrintJob object
    Graphics pg = null;
    // Catch error resulting
    //from cancellation of dialog
    try
    {
        pg = pjob.getGraphics();
    }
    catch (InternalError e)
    {
        return;
    }

    // 3. Print the page
    if (pg != null)
    {
        printTestPage(pg, pjob);

        // flush page
        pg.dispose( );
    }

    // 4. End the print job
    pjob.end( );
    }
}

else if (target == theQuitButton)
{
    setVisible(false);
    dispose( );
    System.exit(0);
}

else if (target == theScreenButton)
{
    Graphics pg = theScreen.getGraphics( );
    printTestPage(pg, (PrintJob)null);
}
}

public void printTestPage(Graphics pg, PrintJob pj)
{
    // This code calculates how many pixels per inch
    // by first selecting a 72 point font into the
    // graphics context, and then calculating the
```

A class that says it implements Runnable *is claiming that it is prepared to receive and handle the* run() *message.* ''

```
    // pixels per inch from that context
    // Set a font (act as a placeholder)
    pg.setFont(new Font("Helvetica", Font.BOLD, 72));

    // Use the FontMetrics to get spacing
    FontMetrics metrics = pg.getFontMetrics( );
    int pixPerInch = metrics.getHeight( ) +
                     metrics.getLeading( );

    int width, height, margins;

    if (pg instanceof PrintGraphics)
    {
        // Find out some info about the printer
        // The following functions return inconsistent
        // results from different printers and drivers
        // under Windows 95
        //   pixPerInch = pj.getPageResolution( );
        //   Dimension pageSize = pj.getPageDimension( );
        // Calculate 1/4" margins
        margins    = pixPerInch / 4;

        // Assume 8.5 x 11 pages
        width      = 825 * pixPerInch / 100;
        height     = 105 * pixPerInch / 10;

    }
    else
    {
        Dimension screenSize = theScreen.getSize();
        margins = 5;
        width    = screenSize.width  - (margins * 2);
        height   = screenSize.height - (margins * 2);
        pixPerInch = 72;
    }

    // Set a new font
    pg.setFont(new Font("Helvetica", ⇐
                    Font.BOLD, pixPerInch / 2));

    // Use the FontMetrics to get spacing
    metrics = pg.getFontMetrics( );
    int lineHeight = metrics.getHeight( ) + ⇐
                    metrics.getLeading( );

    // Draw a circle filling the drawing area
    int ringWidth = pixPerInch / 4;
    int step = 0;
    for (int i = 0; i < 191; i += 16)
    {
        pg.setColor( new Color( 255, 64 + i, 0 ));
        pg.fillOval( margins + step, margins + step,
                    width - step * 2, ⇐
                    height - step * 2);
        step += ringWidth;
    }
    pg.setColor( Color.black );
    pg.drawOval( margins, margins, width, height );
    pg.drawRect( margins, margins, width, height );
```

continued on next page

continued from previous page

```
            // Find the width of the greeting
            String s = "Greetings from" ;
            int    sWidth = metrics.stringWidth( s );

            // Draw it centered above the circle in red
            pg.setColor( Color.red );
            pg.drawString( s, width/2 - (sWidth/2), ⇐
                              height/2 - (lineHeight/2) );

            // Change the font again and get new size
            pg.setFont(new Font("TimesRoman", ⇐
                        Font.BOLD+Font.ITALIC, pixPerInch/3));
            metrics = pg.getFontMetrics( );

            // Add signature
            if ( pg instanceof PrintGraphics )
                s = "your Printer";
            else
                s = "your Monitor";
            pg.setColor( Color.black );
            pg.drawString( s, width/2, ⇐
                              height/2 + (lineHeight/2) );


    }

    public void windowIconified      (WindowEvent event) { }
    public void windowDeiconified    (WindowEvent event) { }
    public void windowOpened         (WindowEvent event) { }
    public void windowClosed         (WindowEvent event) { }
    public void windowActivated      (WindowEvent event) { }
    public void windowDeactivated    (WindowEvent event) { }

    public void windowClosing        (WindowEvent event)
    {
            setVisible(false);
            dispose( );
            System.exit(0);
    }
}
```

FIGURE 13-5

Output of the printing application

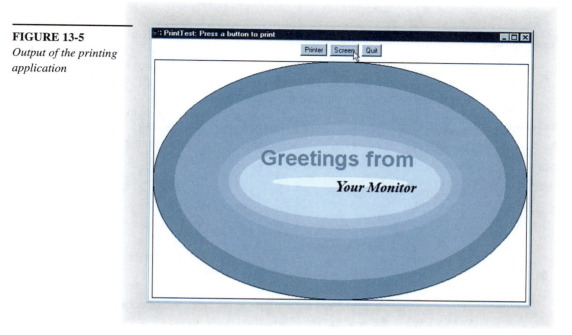

Dynamic Object Creation

Up to this point you've used the `new` operator to create objects, by following `new` with the name of the class of the object you want to create. What if, depending upon the value of some condition, you want to create any one of several possible types of objects? To do this, you could use a `switch` or a series of `if`s:

```
Object theObject;
switch (objectType)
{
    case 1:
        theObject = new Object1( );
        break;

    case 2:
        theObject = new Object2( );
        break;

    // etc.
}
```

> *Abstract classes and interfaces are similar and easy to confuse, but there are differences between them.*

However, you need to know in advance exactly what different types of objects you may need to create, because you must code a `case` statement for each one. What if, at the time you write a program, you don't know what types of objects you need? Is there a way to create an object without hard coding the class names? Java's `forName()` and `newInstance()` methods answer this need.

The `forName()` method is a `static` method of `java.lang.Class`, which returns a `Class` object for the class specified by its `String` argument, throwing `ClassNotFoundException` if the argument doesn't hold the name of a known class. To create a `Class` object, you would write

```
Class c = null;
String s = "java.lang.String"); // Or any other class name
try
{
    c = Class.forName( s );
}
catch (ClassNotFoundException e)
{
    System.err.println("Couldn't create class:" + e);
}
```

Once you have a `Class` object, it's simple to create an instance of the related class. You simply use the `newInstance()` method of the `Class` object, which returns a reference to the specified object, or throws `InstantiationException` or `IllegalAccessException` if an error occurs:

```
String theString = (String) c.newInstance( );
```

Notice that when the object is returned, it has the type `Object`. To use it to call a method, you will need to cast it to the appropriate type.

Listing 13-11 shows a class named `Factory`, which shows how you can create objects you specify at run-time. The actual creation of the object is performed by the `makeObject()` method. The `main()` method tests the operation of `makeObject()` by using it to create an instance of a `StringBuffer`. (A `StringBuffer` is a variety of `String` that supports methods for changing the value of the contained text.) The result is tested to prove that it is indeed a `StringBuffer`. The `makeObject()` method contains several `catch` blocks which trap possible error events and display helpful messages intended to assist you in tracking down any problems.

Listing 13-11 Factory.java

```
// Factory.java
public class Factory
{
    public static void main(String args[])
    {
        Object theObject = ⇐
          makeObject("java.lang.StringBuffer");
        if (theObject instanceof StringBuffer)
        {
            System.out.println("The String is good.");
            ((StringBuffer) theObject).append("Hi!");
            System.out.println((StringBuffer) theObject);
```

```
        }
        else
        {
            System.out.println("The String is bogus!");
        }
    }

    public static Object makeObject(String classname)
    {
        Class theClass;
        Object theObject = null;
        try
        {
            theClass = Class.forName(classname);
            theObject = theClass.newInstance();
        }
        catch (ClassNotFoundException e1)
        {
            System.out.println("Class not found");
            System.out.println(⇐
                "You should specify the full class name");
        }
        catch (IllegalAccessException e2)
        {
            System.out.println("Illegal access");
        }
        catch (InstantiationException e3)
        {
            System.out.println("Instantiation exception");
        }
        catch (NoSuchMethodError e4)
        {
            System.out.println("No such method exception");
            System.out.println(⇐
                "Class should have a default constructor");
        }
        catch (Exception e)
        {
            System.out.println("Unknown exception: " + e);
            e.printStackTrace();
        }

        return theObject;
    }
}
```

OUTPUT OF THE FACTORY APPLICATION

```
C:\Ch13\Examples>java Factory
    The String is good.
    Hi!
```

DYNAMIC OBJECT CREATION AND interfaceS

Dynamic object creation is often, and powerfully, used in combination with an interface implemented by a family of related classes. By dynamically creating an appropriate object and storing a reference to it in a variable with the same type as the interface, you can polymorphically access a range of extensible behaviors. The following code fragment shows how this might be done:

```
String classname = // some value;
Class theClass;
Object theObject = null;
try
{
    theClass = Class.forName(classname);
    theObject = theClass.newInstance();
    if (theObject instanceof Speaker)
        theObject.speak();
    else throw new NoSuchMethodError();
}
catch (Exception e)
{
    e.printStackTrace( );
}
```

The code fragment assumes the existence of an interface named Speaker, which might look like this:

```
public interface Speaker
{
    public void speak( );
}
```

As before, the forName( ) and newInstance( ) methods are used to dynamically create an object from a String holding the name of its type. Here, the created object is checked to make sure it implements the Speaker interface. If so, it must have a speak( ) method, which is invoked. If the object doesn't implement the Speaker interface, some sort of error has allowed an invalid object type to be specified. To deal with this situation, the code simply creates and throws an appropriate exception object.

Dynamic object creation allows you to create programs that can be extended by simply creating new classes. The power to instantiate an object whose type is not known until run-time makes it easy to access the new behaviors contributed by these classes.

Component Subclassing

The AWT contains many useful Components, but even within its extensive repertoire, you may not find exactly the Component you need. Never fear: It's possible to create your own Component, which looks and behaves almost any way you prefer. Once created, such a Component can be reused in your programs, making them faster and easier to develop than if you had to create the Component from scratch each time.

For example, suppose many of your programs have to work with dates. You could create a special "spinner" control, similar to a Choice, that lets the user quickly pick one of the 12 calendar months by name. Or suppose your users often mistype telephone numbers. You could create a special sort of `TextField` `Component` that makes sure that only digits are entered, and that properly groups the digits into area code, telephone exchange, and number.

Creating a new `Component` is simple if you go about it properly. The class `Component` is itself an `abstract` class, so subclassing `Component` is recommended only if you're up to implementing several dozen methods. It's easier instead to subclass one of `Component`'s subclasses; `Canvas` is the class most often chosen for this purpose. Of course, if you're interested in creating a new type of `Container`, you might choose to subclass `Panel` instead.

As an example, Listing 13-12 shows the class `ImageButton`, which extends `Canvas` to create a `Component` that behaves similar to a `Button`, but uses a GIF file to determine its appearance. `ImageButton` illustrates the following steps you should follow to construct a custom component:

☕ Subclass `Canvas`, implementing any necessary event-related interfaces.

☕ Implement `preferredSize( )` and `minimumSize( )`, returning an appropriate `Dimension` from each.

☕ Implement `paint( )` to give your `Component` its distinctive appearance.

☕ Handle any events that should be communicated to objects that use your `Component`. Usually, this will require constructing new events from those your `Component` receives, and forwarding them to a registered listener.

Listing 13-12 ImageButton.java

```
// ImageButton.java
import java.awt.*;
import java.awt.event.*;
import java.awt.image.*;

public class ImageButton extends Canvas ⇐
                         implements MouseListener
{
    private boolean pushState = false;
    private Image theImage;
    private ActionListener theListener;

    public ImageButton(String image)
    {
        theImage = ⇐
          Toolkit.getDefaultToolkit().getImage(image);
        setSize(getminimumSize());
        setBackground(Color.black);
        addMouseListener(this);
    }

    public Dimension getpreferredSize() ⇐
      { return getminimumSize(); }
```

continued on next page

continued from previous page

```
public Dimension getminimumSize() ⇐
  { return new Dimension(80, 40); }

public void paint(Graphics g)
{
    int width  = getSize().width;
    int height = getSize().height;
    int thickness = 3;

    if (pushState)
    {
        g.drawImage(theImage, 0, 0, width, height, this);
        g.setColor(getBackground());
        for (int i = 0; i < thickness; i++)
        {
            g.drawLine(0, i, width, i);
            g.drawLine(i, 0, i, height);
        }
    }
    else
    {
        g.drawImage(theImage, 0, 0, width, height, this);
        g.setColor(getBackground());
        for (int i = 0; i < thickness; i++)
        {
            g.drawLine(0, height - i - 1, width, ⇐
                height - i - 1);
            g.drawLine(width - i - 1, 0, width - i - 1, ⇐
                height);
        }

    }
}

public void addActionListener(ActionListener listener)
{
    theListener = listener;
}

public void mousePressed (MouseEvent e)
{
    if (!pushState) repaint();
    pushState = true;
}

public void mouseReleased(MouseEvent e)
{
    if (pushState) repaint();
    pushState = false;
}

public void mouseEntered(MouseEvent e) { }
public void mouseExited (MouseEvent e) { }

public void mouseClicked (MouseEvent e)
{
```

```
        ActionEvent event = new ActionEvent(this,
            ActionEvent.ACTION_PERFORMED, "Button", ⇐
                e.getModifiers( ));
        if (theListener != null) ⇐
                theListener.actionPerformed(event);
    }

}
```

INSIDE ImageButton

The `ImageButton` class begins by importing `java.awt.*` and `java.awt.image.*`. The classes of the latter package are necessary when loading an `Image` from an application. Loading an `Image` from within an applet is a simple thing, but it's a bit more complex from within an application or from within a class, such as `ImageButton`, that is intended for use within both applets and applications.

The `ImageButton` class has three fields:

☕ `pushState` is a `boolean` variable that is used to keep track of whether the `ImageButton` is pushed. When your `Component` receives a `MOUSE_DOWN` event, it will set `pushState` to `false`, and reset it back to `true` when it receives a `MOUSE_UP`.

☕ `theImage` is a reference to the `Image` that will be used to draw the `ImageButton`.

☕ `theListener` is an `ActionListener` object that's notified when the `ImageButton` is clicked.

The class also has a constructor and several methods:

☕ The constructor, `ImageButton( String )`, takes the name of an image file as an argument. `ImageButton( )` then uses the `static getDefaultToolkit( )` method to get a reference to a default AWT, which includes a method `getImage( )` capable of retrieving an `Image` stored in a file. The constructor then resizes the button, using the method `minimumSize( )`, and sets the background color to black.

☕ The methods `minimumSize( )` and `preferredSize( )` are used by layout managers to decide how big your buttons should be. `ImageButton` creates buttons that have a default size of 80×40 pixels.

☕ `ImageButton` paints its image in its `paint( )` method as required by the AWT, drawing some additional black lines used to give the illusion of movement when an `ImageButton` is pressed by clicking the mouse button.

☕ The `mouseClicked( )` method contains the code that makes your `ImageButton` behave like one of the built-in `Buttons`. It does this by constructing the `ActionEvent` expected by an `ActionListener` from the information included with the `MouseEvent` received as a parameter of `mouseClicked( )`. The identity of the `ActionListener`, if there is one, is established by the `addActionListener( )` method, which stores a reference to the `ActionListener` in the field `theListener`.

Listing 13-13 shows the applet `ImageButtonTest`, which demonstrates the use of the `ImageButton`. Figure 13-6 shows the output of `ImageButtonTest`.

Listing 13-13 ImageButtonTest.java

```java
// ImageButtonTest.java
import java.applet.*;
import java.awt.*;
import java.awt.event.*;

public class ImageButtonTest extends Applet ⇐
                             implements ActionListener
{
    ImageButton[] theImageButton = new ImageButton[10];
    Button clearButton = new Button("Clear This");

    public void init()
    {
        theImageButton[0] = new ImageButton("Jumbo.Gif");
        add(theImageButton[0]);
        theImageButton[0].addActionListener(this);

        for (int i = 1; i < 10; i++)
        {
            theImageButton[i] = ⇐
              new ImageButton("T"+i+".gif");
            add(theImageButton[i]);
            theImageButton[i].addActionListener(this);
        }

        add( clearButton );
        clearButton.addActionListener(this);
    }

    public void actionPerformed(ActionEvent theEvent)
    {
        if (theEvent.getSource( ) instanceof ImageButton)
        {
            setBackground( Color.red );
            System.out.println("Hit image button");
            repaint();
            return;
        }
        System.out.println("Hit regular button");
        setBackground( Color.green );
        repaint();
    }
}
```

FIGURE 13-6
The ImageButton
in action

Summary

☕ Abstract classes are classes that are declared as `abstract` or that contain a method declared as `abstract`.

☕ An `abstract` class cannot be instantiated.

☕ Interfaces are a mechanism for ensuring that classes can handle specified messages.

☕ A class that satisfies the requirements of an interface advertises the fact by declaring that it implements the interface.

☕ Callbacks, which allow flexible specification of behavior, are created by use of the interface-implements mechanism.

☕ Java's original model for event handling propagated `Event`s through the container hierarchy by means of the `handleEvent()` method and special convenience methods.

☕ The Java 1.1 event model relies on special interfaces to propagate various kinds of events.

☕ Java programs print in much the same way they draw, by using a special kind of `Graphics` object adapted for printing.

☕ A Java program can dynamically instantiate an object given a `String` containing the name of the class of the desired object.

☕ By extending the `Canvas` class, it's possible to create new AWT `Components` with special appearance and behavior.

Quiz

1. An `abstract` class cannot be used to _____ objects.
2. Any class with an `abstract` method is implicitly _____.
3. A class that is not `abstract` is called a(n) _____ class.
4. To specify that a class satisfies the requirements of a given interface, the class is declared to _____ the interface.
5. A mechanism that allows a programmer to associate an arbitrary action with an object is the _____.
6. All the fields of an interface must be declared as _____.
7. The primary method used to handle events in Java's original event model is the _____ method.
8. The _____ field of an `Event` object specifies the type of event that the `Event` describes.
9. The JDK 1.1 event model sends events directly from a(n) _____ object to a(n) _____.
10. Printing is performed in Java by the use of a special form of `Graphics` object that implements the _____ interface.
11. When your program is finished drawing a page of printed output, your program should call the _____ method.
12. When invoked on a `Container`, the _____ method calls `print()` on each `Component` within the `Container`, including nested `Containers`.
13. The `forName()` method returns a(n) _____ for the class specified as its sole argument.
14. The `newInstance()` method can be used to create a(n) _____.
15. The easiest way to create a new AWT `Component` is usually to subclass the class _____.

Exercises

1. Write a program that prints a set of geometric figures on the printer, arranging the figures to form the image of a familiar object, such as a snowman.
2. Write a simple drawing program that allows the user to draw lines and shapes on the screen. Pressing a button should send the drawing to the printer.
3. Create an alarm-clock applet that you can use to remind yourself of important appointments.

4. Create an appointment-book applet, with an easy-to-use interface that allows you to book appointments a month or more in advance. At some specified interval (say 15 minutes) before the appointment is to begin, the appointment book should warn you of the impending appointment and remind you of any necessary last-minute preparation.

5. By subclassing `Canvas`, create a novel AWT `Component` such as a progress bar that shows a value from 0 percent to 100 percent by displaying the number along with a bar that grows as the value approaches 100 percent, or a resettable counter that increases its numeric value each time it's clicked.

14

Streams and Files

Objects store their data in fields, which is a reasonable thing unless the power to your computer is interrupted. When power is removed, all the data stored in the fields of objects is lost along with everything else in memory. This is perfectly okay for some sorts of data, but not at all acceptable for others. Imagine the world if every power failure caused your local ATM to simply forget the last dozen cash withdrawals: People would steer their cars into light poles hoping to cause a power failure so they could pick up a little extra cash.

To avoid this scenario, Java gives your objects the ability to save their data in files. Files are stored on a permanent storage medium such as a floppy disk, the hard drive of your computer, or the drive on your network server. Then whenever one of your objects needs to recall what it was doing last Thursday, it can just go find the data where it last left it. To do this, the object uses a facility called a *stream*. Java provides an especially rich variety of streams in the package `java.io`.

In this chapter you will learn

☕ How to use the built-in standard input, standard output, and standard error streams

☕ How to use the `read( )` and `write( )` methods to send and receive data with a stream

☕ How to read and process command-line arguments

☕ How to create hybrid streams by combining existing stream classes

☕ How to process text files, character-by-character and line-by-line

How to read and write platform-independent binary data files

How to create and use random-access data files

How to use the `File` class to access the file system of your computer

How to use `FileDialog` objects to let your users select a file

How to use pipes to transfer data within your program and between processes

> *" A stream is simply a moving flow: It has a source and it has a destination, called a sink. "*

What are Streams and Files?

What do reading and writing have to do with streams? The image that might occur to you is reading a book by your favorite author while camped out beside a mountain brook, or perusing a sonnet while punting on a lazy afternoon. Java streams, while not as pleasant, are much more useful because they are streams of data.

In this sense, a stream is simply a moving flow. It has a source and it has a destination, called a *sink*. The data moving in and out of a program can be thought of as a stream. Data from input sources first streams into your program, where it is processed, and then goes streaming out of your program to a video monitor, printer, or file. Of course, such data streams are not composed of water. They're composed of bytes, the smallest commonly used unit of data. Figure 14-1 illustrates the relationship among sources, streams, and sinks.

The `java.io` package contains quite a few classes that you can use to provide your Java programs with support for streams and files. Figure 14-2 shows an abbreviated hierarchy of the `java.io` classes.

A HIGH-LEVEL LOOK AT `java.io`

The three major classes of the `java.io` package are `InputStream`, `OutputStream`, and `RandomAccessFile`. As you might (correctly) guess from the names, an `InputStream` models a data source, and an `OutputStream` models a data sink. `RandomAccessFiles` are a rather more sophisticated sibling that you'll meet toward the end of this chapter.

FIGURE 14-1

Sources, streams, and sinks

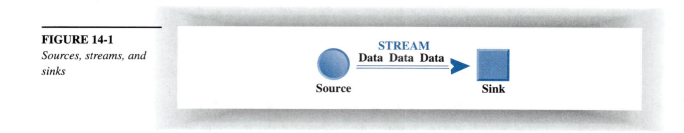

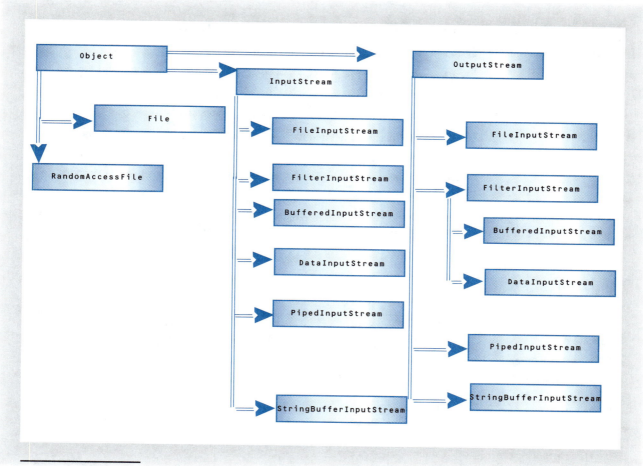

FIGURE 14-2

The classes of
java.io
(abbreviated)

Both `InputStream` and `OutputStream` are abstract classes. As you recall from Chapter 13, "Advanced AWT," an abstract class is similar to a placeholder in a class hierarchy. It's not possible to create an instance of an abstract class, but it's quite possible to use an abstract class to create a new subclass. Abstract classes can and do have children, but not instances. Most of the classes you will study in this chapter are subclasses of `InputStream` and `OutputStream`. These abstract classes provide basic behavior—reading, writing, and so on—and the child classes implement that behavior in specialized ways—using different sources, sinks, and buffering strategies.

"Why are there so many different subclasses of `InputStreams` and `OutputStreams`, and how do I decide which one to use?" is a question you'll probably ask upon meeting the `java.io` package for the first time. Java's designers have certainly provided you with an array of choices. But in a given situation, the choice is usually fairly easy to make.

When trying to decide which class to use, you need to ask

☕ Do I need an input stream or an output stream?

☕ What sort of object is the source of the input data stream or the sink of the output data stream?

☕ Is buffering needed to speed input-output processing?

☕ Are special methods needed to support platform-independent input and output?

☕ Does the class provide `print( )` and `println( )` methods used to support print formatting?

Table 14-1 describes the various classes in terms of these characteristics. The rest of this chapter will be devoted to an explanation of these classes and what their characteristics mean.

TABLE 14-1
CHARACTERISTICS OF KEY `java.io` CLASSES

CLASS	INPUT/ OUTPUT	SINK/ SOURCE TYPE	BUFFERED	PLATFORM- INDEPENDENT	PRINT FORMATTING
BufferedInputStream	Input	stream	Yes	No	No
ByteArrayInputStream	Input	byte array	No	No	No
DataInputStream	Input	stream	No	Yes	No
FileInputStream	Input	file	No	No	No
PipedInputStream	Input	pipe	No	No	No
StringBufferInputStream	Input	string	No	No	No
BufferedOutputStream	Output	stream	Yes	No	No
ByteArrayOutputStream	Output	byte array	No	No	No
DataOutputStream	Output	stream	No	Yes	No
FileOutputStream	Output	file	No	No	No
PipedOutputStream	Output	pipe	No	No	No
PrintStream	Output	stream	No	No	Yes
StringBufferOutputStream	Output	string	No	No	No
RandomAccessFile	Both	file	No	No	No

HYBRID STREAMS

While the variety of streams provided by Java is indeed impressive, as they say on late-night TV, "That's not all!" Suppose you need a class to perform buffered, platform-independent file output. If you look at Table 14-1, you'll notice that there is no line in the table that corresponds to such a class. Does this mean you can't have your wish? Not at all. Java's support for inheritance lets you create hybrid objects whose properties and capabilities combine those of several distinct classes. You'll learn later in the chapter how this can be accomplished; let's start with something a little simpler.

Built-In Streams

> **❝ Data from input sources streams into your program, where it is processed, then goes streaming out to your screen or printer. ❞**

The good news is that you've been using streams throughout the book, even if you weren't aware of it. Almost every modern operating system, including Windows 95 and UNIX, creates three standard streams and attaches them to every program. These are called the standard *input* stream (`System.in`), the standard *output* stream (`System.out`), and the standard *error* stream (`System.err`). As an illustration, look at Table 14-2, which describes these standard streams. Notice that the standard output stream is connected to the Java object `System.out`. When you use the `System.out.println( )` method, what you are doing is invoking the `println( )` method of the `System.out` object, which is a `PrintStream` connected, by default, to the video monitor. Figure 14-3 shows how the standard streams work.

TABLE 14-2
STANDARD PROGRAM STREAMS

JAVA OBJECT	JAVA CLASS	INPUT/OUTPUT	PURPOSE
System.in	InputStream	Input	Standard input stream (keyboard)
System.out	PrintStream	Output	Standard output stream (monitor)
System.err	PrintStream	Output	Error output stream (monitor)

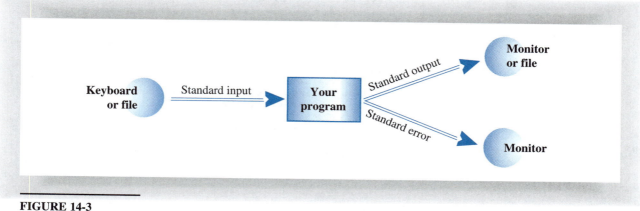

FIGURE 14-3

Standard input, standard output, and standard error

USING SIMPLE STREAMS

To use the standard input, output, and error streams, all you need to do is write to an output stream and read from an input stream. The fastest way to start working with streams is to try an example. Listing 14-1 shows the SimpleStream application, which performs some simple input and output on the standard streams. It uses the `read( )` method to obtain a `byte` of data from `System.in`, and the `println( )` method to write formatted data to both `System.out` and `System.err`. The `read( )` method acquires characters typed on the keyboard by the user, but it does not transmit them to the program until the user presses ENTER. Another way of saying this is that the program *blocks* until the input-output operation is completed.

Read through the source code and see if you can guess what happens if you type in the text *Java #1*, pressing ENTER after each character. Then compile and run the SimpleStream application, and see if you were right. Were there any results you didn't expect? You'll note that SimpleStream has no "polite" way of stopping. Just press CTRL-C, which terminates the running program, when you want to exit. Figure 14-4 shows output of the SimpleStream application.

Listing 14-1 SimpleStream.java

```java
// Illustrates using System.in, System.out, and System.err
import java.io.*;

public class SimpleStream
{
    public static void main(String args[]) throws IOException
    {
        int n;
        char c;

        while (true)
        {
            System.out.println(⇐
              "\nEnter a lowercase letter, please.");
            n = System.in.read();
            System.in.skip(2);   ⇐
              // skip the carriage return/line feed pair
            c = (char) n;
            if (Character.isLowerCase(c))
                System.out.println(⇐
              "You entered the lowercase letter " + c);
            else if (Character.isUpperCase(c))
                System.err.println(⇐
              "You entered an uppercase letter!");
            else
                System.err.println("What ARE you doing???");
        }
    }
}
```

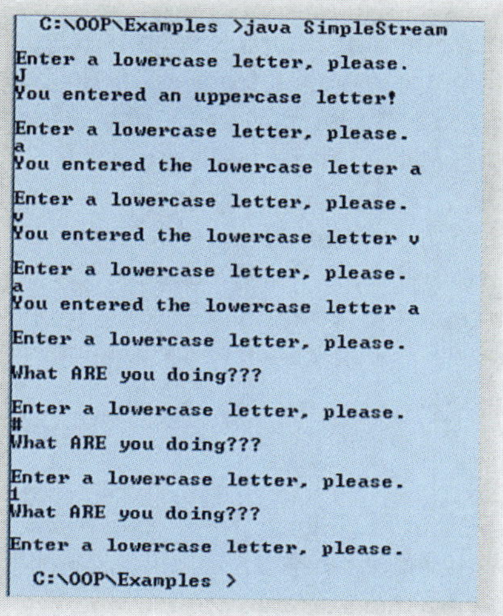

FIGURE 14-4

Output of the SimpleStream application

```
C:\OOP\Examples >java SimpleStream
Enter a lowercase letter, please.
J
You entered an uppercase letter!
Enter a lowercase letter, please.
a
You entered the lowercase letter a
Enter a lowercase letter, please.
v
You entered the lowercase letter v
Enter a lowercase letter, please.
a
You entered the lowercase letter a
Enter a lowercase letter, please.
What ARE you doing???
Enter a lowercase letter, please.
#
What ARE you doing???
Enter a lowercase letter, please.
1
What ARE you doing???
Enter a lowercase letter, please.
C:\OOP\Examples >
```

INSIDE SIMPLESTREAM

SimpleStream begins by using `System.out.println( )` to prompt you to enter a lowercase letter. The program then uses `System.in.read( )` to retrieve the first `byte` from the input stream—the keyboard in this case—and to store that `byte` in the integer `n`. A small complication with the `read( )` method on `System.in` is that both a carriage return character (`'\r'`) and a line feed character (`'\n'`) are sent to the program as input, along with all the other characters you type. In the SimpleStream application, you're not interested in doing anything with these extra characters, so you can use the `skip( )` method to simply read past them without returning them to the program. The argument provided to `skip( )` tells it how many `bytes` of input you want to skip, in this case 2 `bytes`.

Once `System.in.read( )` has retrieved the character you've typed at the keyboard, SimpleStream then performs some tests to make sure you've followed orders. The first order of business is to store the value read as a `char`. This is accomplished with the help of a simple cast. Next, SimpleStream checks to see if you actually *did* enter a lowercase character. It does this by using the `Character.isLowerCase( )` static method from the `Character` wrapper class. If you didn't type a lowercase character, SimpleStream then looks to see if you inadvertently entered an uppercase character using the `Character.isUpperCase( )` method. If the application finds you have entered something other than a lowercase letter, the program prints an error message. To accomplish this, it uses the `System.err.println( )` method. While `System.out` does not necessarily display its output on your monitor, `System.err` is guaranteed to always send its messages to your console, so you won't miss any important warnings.

Notice that the `main( )` method of SimpleStream is flagged as possibly throwing an `IOException`. As you might remember from your first encounter with `System.in` (Chapter 5, "Making Choices: Teaching Your Objects About True and False"), this is necessary because most input-output methods can trigger an `IOException`, and such exceptions must be caught, or the enclosing method must be flagged as a potential thrower. Much of the time there's no reasonable recovery action that can be taken when an input-output operation fails. However, some `IOExceptions` (such as reaching the end of a file) are common and require fairly straightforward processing. You'll see later in the chapter how to use a `try-catch` block to handle such situations.

Redirection

If you think about the output in Figure 14-4, it may occur to you that the output directed to `System.err` is intermingled with the output directed to `System.out`. What's the purpose of having two "separate" streams if both end up in the same place? Modern operating systems support the idea of input-output redirection that allows you to redirect an output stream to write to a new sink or redirect an input stream to read from a new source.

Try running the SimpleStream application using the following command:

```
java SimpleStream > Java1.txt
```

If you enter the same sequence of characters as before—*Java #1*—pressing ENTER after every character, just as you did before, your output should now look similar to that shown in Figure 14-5. Some of the output that was previously displayed on your console is now nowhere to be seen. It hasn't been lost, however. It's been saved for you in a file named `Java1.txt`. If you use the Edit program to open that file and inspect its contents, you'll see that all is well.

The reason for having separate output and error streams is that it's often useful to connect the output of one program to the input of another, in bucket-brigade fashion. The UNIX operating system makes this a way of life by providing numerous *filter* programs designed to be used in exactly this way. A filter program is a program that reads some input—from a file or from `System.in`—does some processing on the input, and then writes the processed data to the `System.out`. Redirection allows the output to be captured in a file or sent on to some other program quickly and easily, as Figure 14-6 illustrates.

Sometimes, however, things go wrong in a filter program, which then displays an error message. Of course, if the filter program attempts to display the error message by using the standard output stream, then the message won't be seen. It will simply be passed to the receiving filter program and processed along with any other data. Having a separate error stream, `System.err`, allows programs to display error messages even when their standard output stream has been redirected. Redirecting the error stream itself is not supported under MS-DOS, but can be accomplished under UNIX like this:

```
java SimpleStream 2>input.txt
```

FIGURE 14-5

Output of the SimpleStream application after redirecting standard output

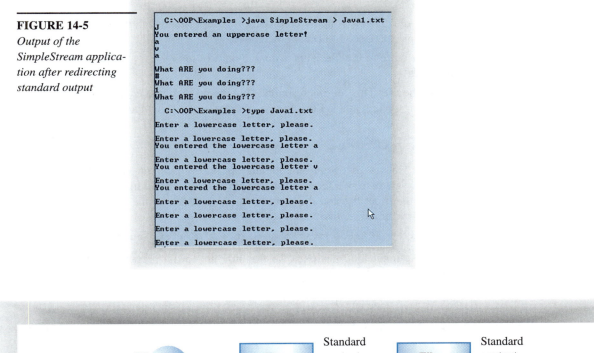

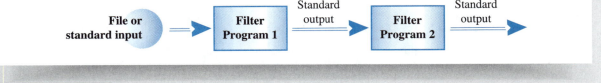

FIGURE 14-6

Redirection and filter programs

It's also possible to redirect a program's input stream so that it comes from a file:

```
java SimpleStream <input.txt
```

This will cause SimpleStream to obtain its input from the file input.txt, rather than from the keyboard. You can still use CTRL–C to interrupt the program, even though its input has been redirected to the file.

File Streams: Using Disk Files

While redirection is a useful facility, it really isn't flexible enough to meet all of the requirements you'll have for storing and retrieving your data. What you need is the ability to read and write files. Java has two classes for processing byte streams that are connected to files: FileInputStream and FileOutputStream. As you might have guessed, these are subclasses of InputStream and OutputStream, respectively. To work with either of these classes, there are three steps you'll need to perform:

1. Open a file: This is done by construction of an instance of either `FileInputStream` or `FileOutputStream`.

2. Read or write to the file: This is done by use of the `read( )` and `write( )` methods.

3. Close the file: This returns resources that are no longer needed back to the operating system and is done by use of the `close( )` method.

A SIMPLE EXAMPLE

Listing 14-2 shows the StudyFileStream application, which uses classes of the `java.io` package to copy a file. To use StudyFileStream, you will need to specify both the name of the input file and the name of the output file on the command line when the Java interpreter is run, like this:

```
java StudyFileStream c:\temp\input.txt c:\temp\output.txt
```

Of course, the input file must exist for the program to run properly. If it doesn't, the `FileNotFound` exception will cause the program to terminate.

Listing 14-2 StudyFileStream.java

```java
// Reading and writing disk files
import java.io.*;
import java.util.*;

public class StudyFileStream
{
    public static void main(String args[]) throws IOException
    {
        // How to use command-line arguments
        StudyFileStream theApp = ⇐
        new StudyFileStream(args[0], args[1]);
    }

    // How to use FileInputStream and FileOutputStream
    //objects
    public StudyFileStream(⇐
      String fromFile, String toFile) throws IOException
    {
        long start = new Date().getTime();
        System.out.println( "Starting : " + start );
        System.out.println( "Copying from file: " + ⇐
          fromFile );
        System.out.println( "Copying to   file: " + toFile );

        // How to open a FileInputStream and FileOutputStream
        // -----------------------------------------------
        FileInputStream  theInput  = null;
        FileOutputStream theOutput = null;

        try
        {
            theInput  = new FileInputStream( fromFile );
            theOutput = new FileOutputStream( toFile );
```

> *Java's stream classes let you create hybrid objects whose properties and capabilities combine those of several distinct classes.*

```
    }
    catch ( FileNotFoundException filenotfound )
    {
        System.out.println( "Could not open files." );
        System.exit( 0 );
    }

    // How to read and write using byte arrays
    // --------------------------------------------------
    int valueRead;

    while ( (valueRead = theInput.read()) != -1 )
        theOutput.write( valueRead );

    // How to close file stream objects
    // -------------------------------
    theInput.close();
    theOutput.close();

    long end = new Date().getTime();
    System.out.println( "Finished : " + end );
    System.out.println( "Elapsed  : " + (end - start) );
    }
}
```

COMMAND-LINE ARGUMENTS

How does the StudyFileStream application get the names of the files it opens? From the *command line*. Every Java program has the ability to accept arguments that are typed by the user when the program is run. These arguments are typed on the same line as the one that launches the Java interpreter and the application itself, appearing after the name of the application (CLASS) file. Because they appear on the same line as the command to start the program, they are called *command-line arguments*.

Java passes these arguments to your program as the `String` array argument you've included in the header of every `main()` method you've written. If you've wondered what `args` was for, now you'll find out. Each word typed after your application name appears as a separate element of the array `args`, with the first element being element [0]. If you want your program to accept several words as a single argument, the words that you want to bundle together should be enclosed in quotes.

An example should clarify this. Given a program called `EchoArgs` that has a `main()` method like this:

```
public static void main( String[] args ) { . . . }
```

and the command line

```
java EchoArgs One "Two Three" Four
```

the array `args` will contain

args[0]   "One"

args[1]   "Two Three"

args[2]   "Four"

CREATING A FILE STREAM AND OPENING A FILE

The first of the three steps in working with a file is to open it. This is done by creating a file stream object in any of several ways. The most straightforward way is to use a constructor that takes the name of the file you want to open. In the StudyFileStream application, that is done in the lines

```
FileInputStream   theInput  = null;
FileOutputStream  theOutput = null;

try
{
    theInput  = new FileInputStream( fromFile );
    theOutput = new FileOutputStream( toFile );
}
catch ( FileNotFoundException filenotfound )
{
    System.out.println( "Could not open files." );
    System.exit( 0 );
}
```

You can use a similar pattern whenever you want to open a file for reading and writing:

Create a reference to a `FileInputStream` or `FileOutputStream`, and set the reference to `null`. The reference can be stored in either a local variable or in a field. Fields, of course, are automatically initialized to `null` by Java.

Associate the reference with a disk file by using the appropriate constructor. The constructor used in StudyFileStream accepts the name of the file to open (as a `String`). The constructor will locate the specified file and open it for reading and writing.

What happens if you type the name of the file incorrectly on the command line? You normally will want to anticipate this common error by putting the constructor inside a `try-catch` block. If you catch the `FileNotFoundExeception`, as in the example, you can print a message and then exit the program. Alternatively, you could put the code in a loop and ask the user to enter another file name. Notice that no attempt is made to deal with other possible errors, such as failure to open the output file due to a full hard drive, or failure to open the file due to lack of permissions. Because the `main( )` method is flagged as potentially throwing an `IOException`, those errors will percolate up to the Java run-time system, which will terminate the program.

READING AND WRITING BYTE-BY-BYTE

Once you have the file open, actually reading and writing the data is simple. File streams read and write data one byte at a time, so the first thing you need is a variable to store the byte you read. Unfortunately, you can't just declare a `byte` variable and be done with it. When you have read all of the bytes in your `FileInputStream`, rather than throwing an `EndOfFileException`, Java will give you back an `end-of-file` value, the `int` −1. To be on the lookout for this `end-of-file` value, you have to make sure the variable you use will be large enough to store it. Thus, when you read from a stream, you have to declare your input variable as an `int`. Except for checking for the `end-of-file` value, you will treat your input variable as a `byte`.

The central part of StudyFileStream is a loop that reads all the data in the `FileInputStream theInput`, writing each byte of data after it is read:

```
int valueRead;
while ( (valueRead = theInput.read()) != -1 )
    theOutput.write( valueRead );
```

Although an `int` is passed to the `write( )` method, the method (internally) casts that `int` to a `byte` and writes only a `byte`. The condition inside the `while` loop is written by use of a common Java idiom. The value returned by the `read( )` method is assigned to the variable `valueRead`. Remember that an assignment expression, such as this, returns a value, namely the value assigned. This value, originally returned by the `read( )` method, is then compared with −1, which signifies `end-of-file`. The loop will terminate immediately if `end-of-file` is returned by `read( )`, without executing the body of the loop. This, of course, is exactly the desired behavior. As you recall from Chapter 6, "Teaching Your Objects to Repeat Themselves," you could rewrite the loop this way if you find it clearer:

```
int valueRead;
valueRead = theInput.read();
while ( valueRead != -1 )
{
    theOutput.write( valueRead );
    valueRead = theInput.read();
}
```

CLOSING FILES

After reading all of the input bytes and writing them back to the output file, the polite and proper thing to do is to close the files:

```
theInput.close();
theOutput.close();
```

While the Java run-time system *may* close your files when your Java application ends, you really shouldn't rely on this behavior. It's always safer and clearer if you do it yourself. Closing a stream frees operating system resources that are often scarce. Prompt closing of files is one mark of a considerate and wise programmer.

Figure 14-7, which features the work of the American poet Edgar Allan Poe, shows that the input and output files of the StudyFileStream application are indeed the same after the application has been run. Thus, you can see that the file has been correctly copied.

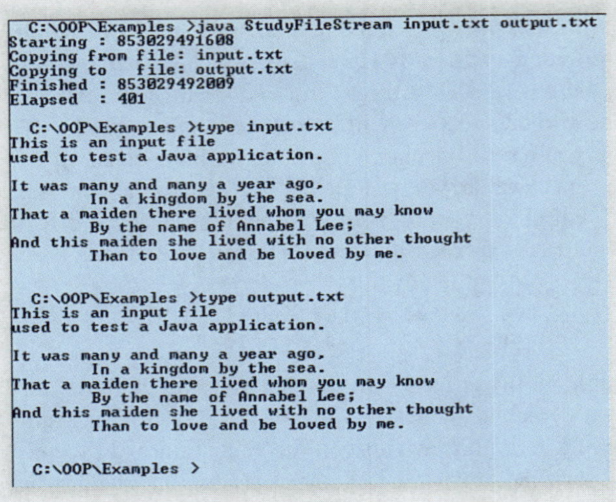

FIGURE 14-7

Output of the StudyFileStream application

```
C:\OOP\Examples >java StudyFileStream input.txt output.txt
Starting : 853029491608
Copying from file: input.txt
Copying to   file: output.txt
Finished : 853029492009
Elapsed  : 401

C:\OOP\Examples >type input.txt
This is an input file
used to test a Java application.

It was many and many a year ago,
       In a kingdom by the sea.
That a maiden there lived whom you may know
       By the name of Annabel Lee;
And this maiden she lived with no other thought
       Than to love and be loved by me.

C:\OOP\Examples >type output.txt
This is an input file
used to test a Java application.

It was many and many a year ago,
       In a kingdom by the sea.
That a maiden there lived whom you may know
       By the name of Annabel Lee;
And this maiden she lived with no other thought
       Than to love and be loved by me.

C:\OOP\Examples >
```

READING AND WRITING BYTE ARRAYS

Probably the first thing you noticed about StudyFileStream was that it is *sloooooow*. Reading and writing a byte at a time is not really the most efficient way to copy a file. It would be much faster if you could read and write all of the `bytes` in a file at once. Both `FileInputStream` and `FileOutputStream` overload the `read( )` and `write( )` methods to make this possible. You can modify the StudyFileStream application to process its data using a `byte` array by replacing the central loop with these three statements:

```
byte[] bytesBuffer = new byte[ theInput.available() ];
theInput.read( bytesBuffer );
theOutput.write( bytesBuffer );
```

The `available( )` method asks the `FileInputStream` object, `theInput`, how many bytes are ready to be read. This number is used to create a `byte` array, `bytesBuffer`, of that size. The `read( )` method then reads all the bytes into the buffer `byteBuffer`, and the `write( )` method writes them back out. Try the modified version of StudyFileStream (stored on the CD-ROM as `StudyFileStreamArray.java`), and see how much faster a little array can make things. Of course, this technique is most useful with small files, because the buffer must be large enough to accommodate the entire file. You would instantly exhaust the system's memory if you tried this technique on a several-hundred-megabyte file.

PROCESSING DATA BYTE-BY-BYTE

After running the StudyFileStreamArray application, you might be wondering why anyone would ever process data a byte at a time when using a `byte` array is so much faster. The answer is simple. When you read the data a byte at a time, you have an opportunity to process the bytes as they go by. While using `byte` arrays is certainly a better idea for copying a whole file, looking at each byte lets you do many wondrous and interesting things, and lets you handle large files.

Suppose you want to translate an entire file so that all lowercase characters are translated to uppercase. Replace the central loop of StudyFileStream with this:

```
while ( (valueRead = theInput.read()) != -1 )
    theOutput.write( Character.toUpperCase( valueRead ) );
```

How about making it all lowercase? Replace the central loop with this:

```
while ( (valueRead = theInput.read()) != -1 )
    theOutput.write( Character.toLowerCase( valueRead ) );
```

How about encrypting the file? Replace the central loop with this:

```
while ( (valueRead = theInput.read()) != -1 )
    theOutput.write( valueRead + 128 );
```

This program, (stored on the CD-ROM as `FSEncrypt.java`), can decrypt a file as well as encrypt it. You create an encrypted version by typing

```
java FSEncrypt FileToEncrypt.ext EncryptedFile.ext
```

To get your original back, simply use the encrypted file as a target, like this:

```
java FSEncrypt EncryptedFile.exe DecryptedFile.ext
```

Why do you suppose this works? Remember that bytes can only hold values from 0 to 255. If you read a `byte` that has the value 65 (for instance) and then add 128 to it, it will then have the value 193, which will appear as a funny graphic character when you display it in your editor. If you then add 128 to the encrypted `byte`, it will have the value 321, which is too big to fit into a `byte`. As you remember from Chapter 3, "The Atomic Theory of Objects: Working with Object Attributes," when you overflow an integer variable, the excess is simply discarded. If you throw away the excess in this case (256), you end up with your original 65. This simple encryption technique will not thwart the efforts of federal agents to read your secret email, but it's not likely to be subject to federal export restrictions either. Take a look at Figure 14-8 to see this in action.

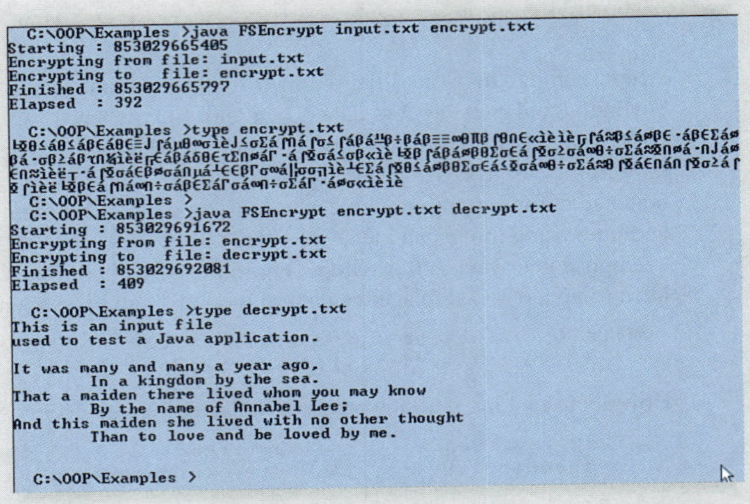

FIGURE 14-8

Encrypting and decrypting by use of
FSEncrypt

Mixing and Matching I/O Objects

By now you might be excused for suffering from some indecision. Should you use byte-at-a-time input so that you can easily process the data as it goes by, or should you use a `byte` array and go for speed? Well, fortunately, those are not your only choices. Java provides classes that let you have both. Next we'll look at some of these classes and the features they offer: *buffering*, *print formatting*, and *platform-independent formatting*.

BUFFERING: GO FOR THE SPEED

Buffering is specific to the `BufferedInputStream` and `BufferedOutputStream` classes. It attempts to speed up input and output the same way that squirrels survive the winter: by storing up data (or nuts, as the case may be) ahead of time. A buffered input stream will read as much data as possible, even before your program requests it. Then, when you *do* request it, it's already in hand and can be delivered much faster. A buffered output stream works in a similar manner. It will accept your data and notify you that everything's taken care of, without holding you up while the data is actually written to its final destination. Because CPU speeds are enormous when compared with the rate of disk output, much useful processing can be done while output data is queued up.

If you look at the hierarchy of the `java.io` package shown in Figure 14-2, it's immediately obvious that `BufferedInputStream` is only distantly related to `FileInputStream`. Does that mean that you can't use buffering when you read and write from files? Not at all. To obtain the benefits of buffering, you can simply convert your regular input or output stream to a buffered stream by using an appropriate constructor, via a technique called *wrapping*. Figure 14-9 shows how wrapping works.

Let's look at an example to see how wrapping is used to provide file buffering. The following two lines open a `FileInputStream` and then use wrapping to open a `BufferedInputStream` connected to the same file:

```
FileInputStream theInputFile = ⇐
  new FileInputStream( theFileName );
BufferedInputStream theBufferedFile = ⇐
  new BufferedInputStream( theInputFile );
```

Now you can use `theBufferedFile` rather than reading and writing from `theInputFile`, and your requests for data will automatically be buffered.

The magic that makes this possible is inheritance. The `BufferedInputStream` class expects an `InputStream` in its constructor and, because the `FileInputStream` class is a subclass of `InputStream`, the `FileInputStream` is an appropriate argument. A similar relationship holds between the `FileOutputStream` class and the `BufferedOutputStream` class. By specifying argument data types using the abstract classes `InputStream` and `OutputStream`, the `java.io` package provides great flexibility.

FIGURE 14-9

A wrapped object

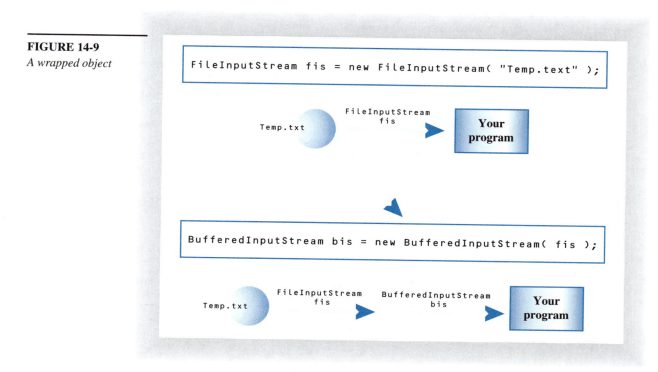

Occasionally it's important that output queued (that is, not delivered) actually *be* delivered before processing can proceed. For example, when you print a prompt on the screen asking the user to enter a number, it's usually a good idea to make sure that this request for input has actually been displayed, rather than merely queued for later output. Otherwise, the read( ) may be initiated before the prompt appears. The solution to this problem is the flush( ) message. When sent to a BufferedOutputStream, flush( ) suspends processing until the output is actually delivered. When using System.out.print( ) to debug a program, it's a good idea to call flush( ) regularly. Otherwise the program may terminate before displaying relevant information sitting in the output queue.

The application StudyBufferedStream, shown in Listing 14-3, is structured almost exactly like the StudyFileStream application, with the exception that the input and output files are both wrapped inside a buffered stream. Buffering your streams allows you to hang onto the flexibility of reading and writing a byte at a time, yet is almost as fast as reading and writing a byte array. For small files, such as input.txt, buffering doesn't offer a really dramatic speed-up, but for larger files, buffering can provide a very large improvement, as you can see in Figure 14-10.

Listing 14-3 StudyBufferedStream.java

```java
import java.io.*;
import java.util.*;

public class StudyBufferedStream
{
    public static void main(String args[]) throws IOException
    {
        // How to use command-line arguments
        StudyBufferedStream theApp = ⇐
            new StudyBufferedStream(args[0], args[1]);
    }

    // How to use BufferedInputStream and
    //BufferedOutputStream objects
    public StudyBufferedStream(String fromFile, String toFile)
    throws IOException
    {
        long start = new Date().getTime();
        System.out.println( "Starting : " + start );
        System.out.println( "Buffered copy from file: " ⇐
            + fromFile );
        System.out.println( "Buffered copy to   file: " ⇐
            + toFile );


        // How to wrap a BufferedInputStream and
        //BufferedOutputStream
        // ---------------------------------------------------
        BufferedInputStream  bufInput  = null;
        BufferedOutputStream bufOutput = null;
```

```
try
{
    FileInputStream theInput  = ⇐
      new FileInputStream( fromFile );
    FileOutputStream theOutput = ⇐
      new FileOutputStream( toFile );
    bufInput  = new BufferedInputStream( theInput );
    bufOutput = ⇐
      new BufferedOutputStream( theOutput );
}
catch ( FileNotFoundException filenotfound )
{
    System.out.println( "Could not open files." );
    System.exit( 0 );
}

// How to read and write using byte arrays
// -----------------------------------------------
int valueRead;

while ( (valueRead = bufInput.read()) != -1 )
    bufOutput.write( valueRead );

// How to close file stream objects
// -------------------------------
bufInput.close();
bufOutput.close();

long end = new Date().getTime();
System.out.println( "Finished : " + end );
System.out.println( "Elapsed  : " + (end - start) );
    }
}
```

FIGURE 14-10

Output of the StudyBufferedStream application

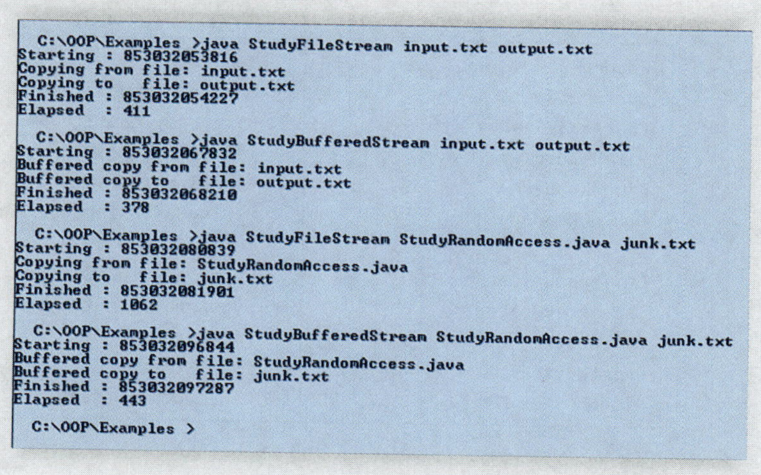

```
C:\OOP\Examples >java StudyFileStream input.txt output.txt
Starting : 853032053816
Copying from file: input.txt
Copying to   file: output.txt
Finished : 853032054227
Elapsed  : 411

C:\OOP\Examples >java StudyBufferedStream input.txt output.txt
Starting : 853032067832
Buffered copy from file: input.txt
Buffered copy to   file: output.txt
Finished : 853032068210
Elapsed  : 378

C:\OOP\Examples >java StudyFileStream StudyRandomAccess.java junk.txt
Starting : 853032080839
Copying from file: StudyRandomAccess.java
Copying to   file: junk.txt
Finished : 853032081901
Elapsed  : 1062

C:\OOP\Examples >java StudyBufferedStream StudyRandomAccess.java junk.txt
Starting : 853032096844
Buffered copy from file: StudyRandomAccess.java
Buffered copy to   file: junk.txt
Finished : 853032097287
Elapsed  : 443

C:\OOP\Examples >
```

Character-Based Input and Output

Version 1.1 of the Java Developer's Kit introduced support for character-based input and output.

Character-based input and output provide several advantages. While the classes descended from `InputStream` and `OutputStream` read and write data one 8-bit byte at a time, character-based streams read and write 16-bit Unicode characters. Basing input and output on Unicode characters makes it much easier to write programs that will function with character sets other than ASCII, which is important in software intended for international use. Also, Java's character-based stream classes buffer their data somewhat more efficiently than most of the byte-based input-output classes.

As shown in Table 14-3, the character-stream classes closely parallel the byte-stream classes. Character-stream classes descend from the abstract classes `Reader` and `Writer`, just as the byte-stream classes descend from `InputStream` and `OutputStream`. For each byte-stream class there is a corresponding character-stream class that (generally) implements the same constructors and methods.

Two handy constructors let you convert byte-streams to character-streams (that is, `Readers` and `Writers`). To convert an input byte-stream to a character-stream, you can write

```
Reader theReader = new InputStreamReader( theInputStream );
```

Similarly, to convert an output byte-stream to a character-stream, you can write

```
Writer theWriter = new OutputStreamWriter( theOutputStream );
```

TABLE 14-3
CHARACTER-STREAM AND BYTE-STREAM CLASSES

CHARACTER-STREAM CLASS	BYTE-STREAM CLASS
Reader	InputStream
BufferedReader	BufferedInputStream
CharArrayReader	ByteArrayInputStream
FileReader	FileInputStream
PipedReader	PipedInputStream
StringReader	StringBufferInputStream
Writer	OutputStream
BufferedWriter	BufferedOutputStream
CharArrayWriter	ByteArrayOutputStream
FileWriter	FileOutputStream
PrintWriter	PrintStream
PipedWriter	PipedOutputStream

READING LINES

While the byte-oriented streams you've met so far allow you to read either a single byte or an array of bytes, the character-based streams give you even more flexibility by allowing you to read lines of text. A line of text is simply a series of characters terminated by a carriage return, a carriage return and newline, or some other designated combination of characters. This useful and distinctive capability of the character-stream input-output classes is provided by the readLine( ) method of the BufferedReader class. Listing 14-4 shows the StudyReadLine application, which demonstrates the technique of reading lines from a text file. You can see the program at work in Figure 14-11.

Listing 14-4 StudyReadLine.java

```
// Reading and writing lines of text with data streams
import java.io.*;
import java.util.*;

public class StudyReadLine
{
    public static void main(String args[]) throws IOException
    {
        StudyReadLine theApp = ⇐
          new StudyReadLine(args[0], args[1]);
    }

    public StudyReadLine(⇐
      String fromFile, String toFile) throws IOException
    {
        System.out.println( ⇐
          "Copying from file: " + fromFile );
        System.out.println( ⇐
          "Copying to   file: " + toFile );

        // Wrap a BufferedReader and BufferedWriter
        // -----------------------------------------
        BufferedReader  theInput  = null;
        BufferedWriter theOutput = null;
        try
        {
            FileReader inputFS = new FileReader( fromFile );
            theInput  = new BufferedReader( inputFS );

            FileWriter outputFS = new FileWriter( toFile );
            theOutput = new BufferedWriter(outputFS);
        }
        catch (FileNotFoundException filenotfound)
        {
            System.out.println("Could not open files.");
            System.exit(0);
        }

        // Read and write the text-file line by line
```

continued on next page

continued from previous page

> **"** *Once you have the file open, reading and writing the data is simple.* **"**

```
//  ----------------------------------------
String line;
while ( (line = theInput.readLine()) != null )
{
    System.out.println( "Read: " + line );
    theOutput.write( line, 0, line.length());
    theOutput.newLine(  );

}

// Close up the file
// ----------------
theInput.close();
theOutput.close();
    }
}
```

The StudyReadLine application is very similar to StudyBufferedStream, which you saw in Listing 14-3. The major differences are

- StudyReadLine uses a `FileReader` and `FileWriter` rather than a `FileInputStream` and a `FileOutputStream`.

- Likewise, a `BufferedReader` and `BufferedWriter` replace their cousins `BufferedInputStream` and `BufferedOutputStream`, which were used in StudyBufferedStream.

- Instead of reading byte by byte, an entire line is read into the `String` variable called `line`, by use of the `BufferedReader`'s `readLine( )` method. Notice that the `readLine( )` method returns `null` upon encountering `end-of-file`, instead of returning –1 or throwing an exception, as some of the other input classes do. (Emerson wrote that "A foolish consistency is the hobgoblin of little minds." When you get frustrated with the different conventions that Java uses to signal the `end-of-file` condition, it may help to think of it as a "mind expansion" exercise.)

- When you run the StudyReadLine application, it will display each line it reads on the console, using `System.out.println( )` before writing it to a file.

- Each line that is written to the output file is terminated by calling the `BufferedWriter`'s `newLine( )` method. Because different platforms use different end-of-line characters, using the `newLine( )` method is the platform-independent way to write a line terminator to your output file.

FIGURE 14-11

*Output of the
StudyReadLine
application*

```
C:\OOP\Examples >java StudyReadLine input.txt output.txt
Copying from file: input.txt
Copying to   file: output.txt
Read: This is an input file
Read: used to test a Java application.
Read:
Read: It was many and many a year ago,
Read:   In a kingdom by the sea.
Read: That a maiden there lived whom you may know
Read:   By the name of Annabel Lee;
Read: And this maiden she lived with no other thought
Read:   Than to love and be loved by me.
Read:
Read:

C:\OOP\Examples >type input.txt
This is an input file
used to test a Java application.

It was many and many a year ago,
  In a kingdom by the sea.
That a maiden there lived whom you may know
  By the name of Annabel Lee;
And this maiden she lived with no other thought
    Than to love and be loved by me.


C:\OOP\Examples >
```

DISPLAY FORMATTING

When you use `ints`, `floats`, or `doubles` in your programs, your variables are stored in binary form. Translating this data into human-readable form is called *print formatting* and is provided by the `PrintWriter` class, which can be wrapped around a `Writer` object. The `PrintWriter` class is the character-stream class corresponding to the `PrintStream` byte-stream class, which provides you with the familiar `print( )` and `println( )` methods. Because `PrintStream` does not properly handle Unicode characters, it should only be used to generate debugging output; the `PrintWriter` class should be used to generate textual output for users.

The `print( )` and `println( )` methods of the `PrinterWriter` class, such as those of its `PrintStream` cousin, accept primitive values as well as objects. The `PrintWriter` class also provides the useful `flush( )` method, mentioned in connection with buffered streams. Handier still, specifying `true` as a second argument to the `PrinterWriter` constructor enables automatic flushing; the `flush( )` method will be automatically called after every `println( )`.

Listing 14-5, the StudyPrintWriter application, shows you how to wrap a `PrintWriter` around an output file. This gives the output file the ability to use `print( )` and `println( )` to easily generate output designed for "human consumption." Figure 14-12 shows the contents of the file produced by the application, which contains random integers. These can be compared with the values, also shown in Figure 14-12, printed to `System.out` by the application. The two sets of numbers, of course, are identical, proving that they were stored correctly.

Listing 14-5 StudyPrintWriter.java

```java
// Shows how to create a PrintWriter object
import java.io.*;

public class StudyPrintWriter
{
    public static final int MAX_NUMS = 8;

    public static void main( String args[] ) ⇐
      throws IOException
    {
        StudyPrintWriter theApp = ⇐
          new StudyPrintWriter( args[0] );
    }

    public StudyPrintWriter( String toFile ) ⇐
      throws IOException
    {
        System.out.println( "Writing to print file: " ⇐
          + toFile );

        FileWriter outputFS = new FileWriter( toFile );
        PrintWriter theOutput = new PrintWriter( outputFS,⇐
          true );

        int randomNumber;

        for (int i = 0; i < MAX_NUMS; i++)
        {
            randomNumber =   (int) (100000000.0 ⇐
              * Math.random());
            theOutput.print(   randomNumber + " " );
            System.out.print( randomNumber + " " );
        }
        theOutput.println( "" );
        System.out.println( "" );

        theOutput.close();
    }
}
```

FIGURE 14-12

Output of the StudyPrintWriter application

```
C:\OOP\Examples >java StudyPrintWriter output.txt
Writing to print file: output.txt
72138325 31864874 17901180 54584213 55755856 49964809 49888707 97397767

C:\OOP\Examples >type output.txt
72138325 31864874 17901180 54584213 55755856 49964809 49888707 97397767

C:\OOP\Examples >
```

Platform-Independent Data Formatting

Platform-independent formatting is supported by a collection of methods defined in the `DataInputStream` and `DataOutputStream` classes. These methods, which are summarized in Table 14-4, translate the internal coding of Java's primitive types into sequences of bytes that can be portably read and written. Because Java programs work unchanged on your Mac and your PC, you may—depending on your application—want to make sure that the data files you've created on your Mac work the same when moved to your PC. Without a platform-independent formatting class such as `DataInputStream`, this would not be possible.

TABLE 14-4
KEY METHODS SUPPORTING PLATFORM-INDEPENDENT FORMATTING

METHOD HEADER	FUNCTION
`boolean readBoolean( )`	Read a `boolean`
`byte readByte( )`	Read a `byte`
`char readChar( )`	Read a `char`
`double readDouble( )`	Read a `double`
`float readFloat( )`	Read a `float`
`int readInt( )`	Read an `int`
`String readLine( )`	Read a line of text (characters terminated by \n)
`long readLong( )`	Read a `long`
`short readShort( )`	Read a `short`
`String readUTF( )`	Read a Unicode string
`void writeBoolean(boolean v)`	Write a `boolean`
`void writeByte(byte v)`	Write a `byte`
`void writeChar(char v)`	Write a `char`
`void writeDouble(double v)`	Write a `double`
`void writeFloat(double v)`	Write a `float`
`void writeInt(int v)`	Write an `int`
`void writeLong(long v)`	Write a `long`
`void writeShort(short v)`	Write a `short`
`void writeUTF(String s)`	Write a Unicode string

Subclasses of `InputStream` and `OutputStream` may be wrapped within a `DataInputStream` or `DataOutputStream`. In fact, it's even possible to wrap a `BufferedInputStream` with a `DataInputStream` data stream, because the `BufferedInputStream` stream is itself an `InputStream`:

```
FileInputStream theInputFile = ⇐
    new FileInputStream( theFileName );
BufferedInputStream theBufferedFile = ⇐
    new BufferedInputStream( theInputFile );
DataInputStream theBufferedDataFile = ⇐
    new DataInputStream( theBufferedFile );
```

> *Closing a stream frees system resources that often are scarce: Prompt closing of files is one mark of a considerate and wise programmer.*

Reading and Writing Binary Numbers

Let's look at an example that puts data streams to work. The StudyReadInt application, shown in Listing 14-6, uses the `Math.random( )` method to create a series of random `floats`, which are subsequently converted to `ints`. These `ints` are written in portable form to a disk file. This file is closed and then reopened for input. Finally, the values read are displayed for comparison with the original values. The output from StudyReadInt can be seen in Figure 14-13.

Listing 14-6 StudyReadInt.java

```java
// Using DataInputStreams and DataOutputStreams
import java.io.*;

public class StudyReadInt
{
    public static final int MAX_TRIES = 8;

    public static void main(String args[]) throws IOException
    {
        StudyReadInt theApp = new StudyReadInt(args[0]);
    }

    public StudyReadInt(String toFile) throws IOException
    {
        System.out.println("Writing to temporary file: " ⇐
            + toFile);

        // Open the FileOutputStream and wrap in a
        // DataOutputStream
        // ----------------------------------------------------
        DataOutputStream theOutput = null;
        try
        {
            FileOutputStream outputFS  = ⇐
                new FileOutputStream( toFile );
            theOutput = new DataOutputStream( outputFS);
        }
        catch ( FileNotFoundException filenotfound )
        {
            System.out.println( ⇐
                "Could not open temporary file." );
            System.exit( 0 );
        }

        // Generate and write MAX_TRIES random numbers
        // -------------------------------------------
```

```
int randomNumber;
for (int i = 0; i < MAX_TRIES; i++)
{
    randomNumber =  (int) ( 100000000.0 ⇐
      * Math.random() );
    System.out.print( randomNumber + " " );
    theOutput.writeInt( randomNumber );
}
System.out.println("");

theOutput.close();

// Open the file and try to read the data back
// ------------------------------------------
DataInputStream theInput = null;
try
{
    FileInputStream inputFS = ⇐
      new FileInputStream( toFile );
    theInput = new DataInputStream( inputFS );
}
catch (FileNotFoundException filenotfound)
{
    System.out.println(⇐
      "Could not open the INPUT file.");
    System.exit(0);
}

// Read all of the data back in
// ---------------------------
while (true)
{
    try
    {
        randomNumber = theInput.readInt();
        System.out.print( randomNumber + " " );
    }
    catch ( EOFException eof )
    {
        System.out.println("\nEOF");
        break;
    }
}

theInput.close();
    }
}
```

FIGURE 14-13

*Output of the
StudyReadInt
application*

The `ints` that are written and read back from the file are stored in binary format, not in character format. This means that when you read the file using an editor, or use the MS-DOS `type` command to display the contents of the file, you will not see human-readable numbers. Stored in this binary format, each `int` requires only 4 bytes of storage on the disk. Storing the `ints` in ASCII format would require more than twice the disk space needed to store them in binary format, because the generated `ints` are up to nine digits in size. Saving this space while preserving the ability to exchange data across different platforms is the job `DataStreams` were designed to do.

You may have also noticed another difference between using a `FileInputStream` and a `DataInputStream`. While the `FileInputStream`'s `read( )` method returned the `int` value −1 when it reached end-of-file, the `DataInputStream`'s `readInt( )` method cannot use the same scheme. That is because −1 is a valid value for an `int` object which may be stored in a `DataInputStream`. By contrast, a `FileInputStream` could never hold the `int` value −1, because all `FileInputStream` values are `bytes`. With a `DataInputStream`, rather than checking for a special end-of-file value, you place your `read( )`s inside a `try-catch` block, and then catch the `EOFException`.

Random Access Files

A sibling to the `InputStream` and `OutputStream` classes, the `RandomAccessFile` class can be used for both input and output to a single file. Although not a stream class, it does provide the same platform-independent formatting methods as the `DataStream` classes. The constructor to create a `RandomAccessFile` object takes two arguments. The first argument specifies the file, either as a `String` containing the file name, or as a `File` object. (`File` objects are covered in the next section). The second argument is a `String` that should assume the value `r` if the file will be read but not written, or the value `rw` if the file will be both read and written. If the specified file does not exist, it is automatically created. To open the file `Test.txt` for both reading and writing, you would write

```
RandomAccessFile theFile = new RandomAccessFile( "Test.txt", ⇐
   "rw" );
```

Unlike `InputStreams` and `OutputStreams`, which access their data sequentially, it is possible to direct a `RandomAccessFile` to read or write beginning at any position within a file, by use of the `seek( )` method. The `seek( )` method specifies the byte-offset from the beginning of the file at which input-output is to commence. The type of its single parameter is `long`, so you needn't worry about being able to `seek( )` your way around even large files. Because the offset is a byte-offset, you multiply the number of the desired item by the size of each item stored in the file. If the file stores `ints`, for example, which are each 4 bytes long, and you want to prepare `theFile` (opened earlier) to write a new value in the sixth position, you would first use the `seek( )` method like this:

```
try
{
    theFile.seek( 4L *  5 ); // Skip past 5 ints
}
catch (IOException io)
{
    // Handle error here
}
```

This means that the next write (or read) would take place at offset 20 bytes measured from the beginning of the file. This will be the sixth record (or item), because the first record is 0 bytes offset from the beginning of the file. Notice that the seek( ) method throws an IOException if an I/O error occurs.

Listing 14-7 shows the StudyRandomAccess application, which demonstrates the use of the RandomAccessFile class. The application creates a small file holding eight random integers. The TextField labeled "File cursor" allows you to seek to a specified position inside the file. You can then read the value at that location by pressing the Read Button, or write a new value by filling in the Value TextField and then pressing the Write Button. Because there are eight integers, only seek values from 0 to 7 are accepted.

Of course, a real application using the RandomAccessFile class might store 1,000 records, 100,000 records, or more. Figure 14-14 shows the output of the application.

Listing 14-7 StudyRandomAccess.java

```
// How to use the RandomAccessFile class
import java.io.*;
import java.awt.*;
import java.awt.event.*;
```

continued on next page

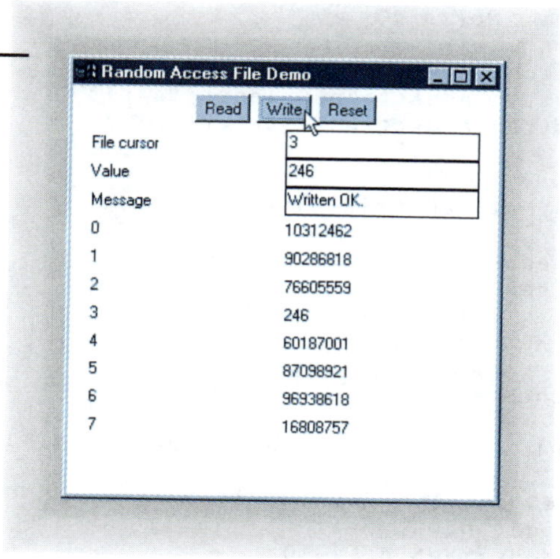

FIGURE 14-14

Output of the StudyRandomAccess application

continued from previous page

> **Reading and writing a byte at a time is not the most efficient way to copy a file.**

```java
public class StudyRandomAccess extends Frame ⇐
                              implements ActionListener,
                                         WindowListener
{
    public static final String FILENAME =
"StudyRandomAccess.dat";

    RandomAccessFile theFile;

    Button resetButton    = new Button("Reset");
    Button readButton     = new Button("Read");
    Button writeButton    = new Button("Write");

    TextField seekText    = new TextField("", 4);
    TextField theNumber   = new TextField("", 12);
    TextField theMessage  = new TextField("", 20);
    Label theSlot[]       = new Label[8];

    public static void main(String args[]) throws IOException
    {
        StudyRandomAccess theApp = new StudyRandomAccess();
    }

    public StudyRandomAccess() throws IOException
    {
        theFile = new RandomAccessFile(FILENAME, "rw");

        setTitle( "Random Access File Demo" );
        setLayout( new BorderLayout() );

        Panel p = new Panel();
        p.setLayout( new FlowLayout() );
        p.add( readButton );
        p.add( writeButton );
        p.add( resetButton );
        add( p , "North");

        readButton.addActionListener(this);
        writeButton.addActionListener(this);
        resetButton.addActionListener(this);

        p = new Panel();
        p.setLayout(new GridLayout(13, 2));

        p.add(new Label("File cursor "));
        p.add(seekText);
        p.add(new Label("Value "));
        p.add(theNumber);
        p.add(new Label("Message "));
        p.add(theMessage);

        for (int i = 0; i < theSlot.length; i++)
        {
            theSlot[i] = new Label();
            p.add( new Label("" + i) );
            p.add( theSlot[i] );
        }
```

```
        add( new Label("") , "East");
        add( new Label("") , "West");
        add( p, "Center" );

        makeNewNumbers();

        addWindowListener(this);
        pack();
        setVisible(true);
    }

    public void actionPerformed(ActionEvent theEvent)
    {
        Object target = theEvent.getSource();
        if (target == resetButton)
            makeNewNumbers();
        else if (target == readButton)
            read(Integer.parseInt(seekText.getText()));
        else if (target == writeButton)
        {
            write(Integer.parseInt(seekText.getText()),
            Integer.parseInt(theNumber.getText()));
        }
    }

    public void makeNewNumbers()
    {
        for ( int i = 0; i < theSlot.length; i++ )
        {
            Integer n = new Integer( (int) (100000000.0 ⇐
              * Math.random()));
            theSlot[i].setText( n.toString() );
            write( i, n.intValue() );
        }
        seekText.setText("");
        theNumber.setText("");
        theMessage.setText("");
        setVisible(true);
    }

    public void read( int seekTo )
    {
        if ( seek(seekTo) )
        {
            int numberRead = 0;
            try
            {
                numberRead = theFile.readInt();
                theNumber.setText( "" + numberRead );
                theMessage.setText( "Read OK." );
            }
            catch (IOException io)
            {
                theNumber.setText( "" );
                theMessage.setText( ⇐
                  "I/O exception occurred." );
                setVisible(true);
```

continued on next page

continued from previous page

> **Buffering attempts to speed up input and output the same way that squirrels survive the winter: by storing up nuts—er, data—ahead of time.**

```java
                }
            }
            setVisible(true);
            return;
    }

    public void write( int seekTo, int number )
    {
        if ( seek(seekTo) )
        {
            try
            {
                theFile.writeInt( number );
                theMessage.setText( "Written OK." );
                theSlot[seekTo].setText( "" + number );
            }
            catch (IOException io)
            {
                theMessage.setText( ⇐
                    "I/O exception occurred." );
            }
        }
        setVisible(true);
        return;
    }

    public boolean seek( int seekTo )
    {
        if ( seekTo < 0 || seekTo >= theSlot.length )
        {
            theNumber.setText( "" );
            theMessage.setText( "Invalid seek requested." );
            setVisible(true);
            return false;
        }
        try
        {
            theFile.seek( 4L * seekTo );
        }
        catch (IOException io)
        {
            theNumber.setText( "" );
            theMessage.setText( "Seek error." );
            setVisible(true);
            return false;
        }
        return true;
    }

    public void windowClosed      (WindowEvent e) { }
    public void windowClosing      (WindowEvent e) ⇐
        { quitApplication(); }
    public void windowDeiconified (WindowEvent e) { }
    public void windowIconified   (WindowEvent e) { }
    public void windowOpened      (WindowEvent e) { }
```

```
public void windowActivated   (WindowEvent e) { }
public void windowDeactivated (WindowEvent e) { }

public void quitApplication()
{
    setVisible(false );
    dispose( );
    System.exit(0);
}

public void setVislble(boolean state)
{
    invalidate( );
    validate( );
    super.setVisible(state);
}
}
```

The File Object

You can create `FileInputStreams`, `FileOutputStreams`, and `RandomAccessFiles` by use of a `String` containing the file name; but you can also create these objects by use of a `File` object. The `File` object provides a number of methods useful for manipulating files and directories, which are summarized in Table 14-5. The class also provides some `public` fields, shown in Table 14-6, that contain values useful in writing portable programs. The values of these fields vary from platform to platform, but are constant for a given platform. Constructors for the `File` class are given in Table 14-7. Note that `File` can refer to either a directory or a file, using an absolute or relative path.

TABLE 14-5
KEY public METHODS OF THE File CLASS

METHOD HEADER	FUNCTION
boolean canRead( )	Determines if the File can be read
boolean canWrite( )	Determines if the File can be written
boolean delete( )	Attempts to delete the File; returns true if successful
boolean equals(Object obj)	Determines if the File is equal to another object
boolean exists( )	Determines if the File exists
String getAbsolutePath( )	Gets the absolute path of the File
String getName( )	Gets the name component of the File (including the file-name extension)
String getParent( )	Gets the parent directory of the File
String getPath( )	Gets the path component of the File
boolean isAbsolute( )	Determines if the File is specified by an absolute path
boolean isDirectory( )	Determines if the File refers to a directory
boolean isFile( )	Determines if the File refers to a file

Table continued...

TABLE 14-5 KEY `public` METHODS OF THE `File` CLASS CONTINUED...

METHOD HEADER	FUNCTION
`long lastModified( )`	Gets the time stamp of the `File` (system dependent—use only for comparisons on a given system)
`long length( )`	Gets the length of the file represented by the `File`
`String[] list( )`	Gets an array of file names within the directory specified by the `File`
`boolean mkdir( )`	Makes the directory specified by the `File`; returns `true` if successful
`boolean mkdirs( )`	Makes the directory specified by the `File` and all necessary parent directories; returns `true` if successful
`boolean renameTo(File dest)`	Renames the `File` as specified; returns `true` if successful

TABLE 14-6
KEY `public` FIELDS OF THE `File` CLASS

FIELD	TYPE	MEANING/USE
`pathSeparator`	`String`	`String` used to separate components of path environment variable (";" on MS-DOS)
`pathSeparatorChar`	`char`	`char` used to separate components of path environment variable (';' on MS-DOS)
`separator`	`String`	`String` used to separate directory names within a path ("\" on MS-DOS)
`separatorChar`	`char`	`char` used to separate directory names within a path ('\' on MS-DOS)

TABLE 14-7
KEY `public` CONSTRUCTORS OF THE `File` CLASS

```
File(String path)
File(String path, String filename)
File(File path, String filename)
// if path is not null, filename interpreted as a relative path
```

The program ListDir, shown in Listing 14-8, uses `File` objects to print interesting information about a directory. The program will list a directory given as a command-line argument. If no command-line argument is given, it will list the current directory. The output of running the program with a command line

```
java ListDir C:\.
```

is shown in Figure 14-15.

" *Translating binary data into human-readable form is called print formatting, and is provided by the* `PrintWriter` *class.* **"**

Listing 14-8 ListDir.java

```java
// Using the File class
import java.io.*;
import java.util.*;

public class ListDir
{
    public static void main( String args[] )
    {
        String sDir;

        if ( args.length == 0 )
            sDir = ".";
        else
            sDir = args[0];

        File fDir = new File( sDir );

        if ( ! fDir.isDirectory() )
        {
            System.err.println( sDir + ⇐
              " is not a directory" );
            System.exit( 0 );
        }

        String[] dirList = fDir.list();

        System.out.println( "Directory : " + sDir );
        for ( int i = 0; i < dirList.length; i++ )
        {
            File theFile = new File( fDir, dirList[i] );

            System.out.print( "" + ⇐
              ( theFile.isDirectory() ? "d" : " " ) );
            System.out.print( "" + ⇐
              ( theFile.isFile()      ? "f" : " " ) );
            System.out.print( "" + ⇐
              ( theFile.canRead()     ? "r" : " " ) );
            System.out.print( "" + ⇐
              ( theFile.canWrite()    ? "w" : " " ) );
            System.out.print( "   " + ⇐
              new Date( theFile.lastModified()) );
            System.out.print( "   " + ⇐
              theFile.length() + " bytes" );
            System.out.println( "   " + theFile.getName() );
        }
    }
}
```

The ListDir program starts by checking to see if the user has entered any arguments on the command line. This is done by seeing if `args.length` is greater than 0. If it is not, the `String sDir` is set to "."; otherwise, it is set to the value of `args[0]`. With `sDir`, a `File` object is created by use of

```java
File fDir = new File( sDir );
```

FIGURE 14-15

Output of the ListDir program

```
C:\OOP\Examples >java ListDir c:\. > dir.txt

C:\OOP\Examples >type dir.txt
Directory : C:\.
   fr    Tue May 31  06:22:00 PDT 1994    40774 bytes    IO.DOS
   fr    Tue May 31  06:22:00 PDT 1994    38138 bytes    MSDOS.DOS
   frw   Tue May 31  06:22:00 PDT 1994    54645 bytes    COMMAND.DOS
   frw   Tue Jul 11  09:50:00 PDT 1995    92870 bytes    COMMAND.COM
 d rw    Fri Dec 27  12:19:28 PST 1996        0 bytes    DOS
 d rw    Fri Dec 27  14:35:42 PST 1996        0 bytes    WINDOWS
 d rw    Fri Dec 27  15:01:40 PST 1996        0 bytes    TEMP
   frw   Fri Dec 27  14:36:12 PST 1996      142 bytes    AUTOEXEC.DOS
   frw   Mon Jan 06  08:27:02 PST 1997      398 bytes    AUTOEXEC.BAT
   frw   Fri Dec 27  14:44:40 PST 1996       22 bytes    MSDOS.-
   frw   Tue Jan 07  10:23:38 PST 1997      197 bytes    CONFIG.SYS
   fr    Tue Jan 07  06:50:18 PST 1997     1628 bytes    MSDOS.SYS
   fr    Tue Jul 11  09:50:00 PDT 1995    71287 bytes    DBLSPACE.BIN
 d rw    Thu Jan 02  07:02:54 PST 1997        0 bytes    RECYCLED
   frw   Fri Dec 27  15:08:26 PST 1996      161 bytes    CONFIG.WIN
   fr    Tue Jul 11  09:50:00 PDT 1995    71287 bytes    DRVSPACE.BIN
   fr    Tue Jul 11  09:50:00 PDT 1995   223148 bytes    IO.SYS
 d r     Fri Dec 27  15:02:36 PST 1996        0 bytes    Program Files
 d rw    Tue Jan 07  10:13:56 PST 1997        0 bytes    OOP

C:\OOP\Examples >
```

The message `isDirectory( )` is then sent to the new `File` object. If the `File` doesn't represent a directory, the program says so and exits. If the `File fDir` is a directory, its `list( )` method is used to populate an array of `Strings` called `dirList`. This list is then processed, creating a new `File` object for each entry (by use of the two-argument constructor), and printing information about whether the entry is a directory or a regular file, along with its length, last modified date, and permissions.

FileDialogs

While the `File` class allows you to access many features of the file-system, creating interactive dialogs for opening and saving files can still be a lot of work. Many operating systems supply such dialogs. The `FileDialog` class provided with the AWT makes it possible for you to write a program that is platform-independent, while still using these operating-system–specific dialogs. The advantage of this is that the users of your Java program will see familiar screens when they perform these common tasks.

To use the `FileDialog` class, you create a `FileDialog` object, using one of the constructors listed in Table 14-8. As with other `Dialogs`, the first argument should be the `Frame` that "owns" the `Dialog`. Normally, you will pass `this`. The second argument is the title that you want to appear at the top of the `FileDialog`. The third argument is the *mode* that the `Dialog` should use. If you use the two-argument constructor, the mode defaults to `FileDialog.LOAD`. If you use the second constructor, you may also specify this same value, or the constant `FileDialog.SAVE`. Which of these two constants is specified determines whether the system-specific File Open or File Save dialog is displayed. Some examples should make this clear:

```
FileDialog fdOpen  = new FileDialog( this, ⇐
   "Open a File" ); // LOAD
FileDialog fdOpen2 = new FileDialog( this, ⇐
   "Also Open", FileDialog.LOAD );
```

```
FileDialog fdSave  = new FileDialog( this, ⇐
   "Save", FileDialog.SAVE );
```

TABLE 14-8
KEY **public** CONSTRUCTORS OF THE **FileDialog** CLASS

```
FileDialog(Frame parent, String title)
// Defaults to FileDialog.LOAD for type of dialog
FileDialog(Frame parent, String title, int mode)
// mode = FileDialog.LOAD or FileDialog.SAVE
```

Once you have created a `FileDialog` object, there are several fields you can set to change the way it works. You can use the `setDirectory( )` method to specify the file directory that should be used when the dialog pops up. But be careful: This opens the possibility for writing programs that are nonportable. For instance, UNIX machines and Macs don't have a directory called `C:\`. You might want to use the special directory name of `"."`, which means the current directory under both UNIX and MS-DOS. Also, remember that when specifying MS-DOS–style path names, you must use two backslash separators rather than one, because in a Java `String` the backslash is the escape character. Thus, to specify that the beginning directory should be the `C:\TEMP` directory, you need to write

```
fdOpen.setDirectory( "C:\\TEMP\\");
```

You can use the `setFile( )` method to specify an initial file name. The `setFilenameFilter( )` method installs a filter to display only files that match a certain naming criteria. The method's sole argument must be an object that implements the `FilenameFilter` interface, which requires only an `accept( )` method that returns `true` if a file is to be included in the dialog and `false` otherwise. The identity of each candidate file is communicated to the `accept( )` method via its two arguments, the first of which is a `File` object giving the path to the candidate file, and the second of which is a `String` giving the name of the file.

To actually use the `FileDialog` object, call the `show( )` method, followed by `hide( )`. The `FileDialog` will be displayed and then hidden only after it is dismissed. At that point you can retrieve the information that the user entered, using the methods `getDirectory( )` and `getFile( )`. These and other key methods of the `FileDialog` class can be seen in Table 14-9.

TABLE 14-9
KEY **public** METHODS OF THE **FileDialog** CLASS

METHOD HEADER	FUNCTION
`String getDirectory( )`	Returns a `String` representing the chosen directory

Table continued...

" Since Java programs work unchanged on your Mac or PC, you'll want to make sure your data files are platform independent also. "

TABLE 14-9 KEY `public` METHODS OF THE `FileDialog` CLASS CONTINUED...

METHOD HEADER	FUNCTION
`String getFile( )`	Returns a `String` representing the chosen file
`int getMode( )`	Returns either `FileDialog.SAVE` or `FileDialog.LOAD`
`void setDirectory( String dir )`	Sets the initial directory display to `dir`
`void setFile( String file )`	Sets the initial file display to `File`
`void setFilenameFilter( FilenameFilter flt )`	Installs a filter to control which files are displayed

Listing 14-9 shows the StudyFileDialog application, which demonstrates the use of the `FileDialog` class provided by the AWT. The application creates and shows a dialog that allows the user to navigate the system and choose a file. The chosen file is obtained from the dialog by use of the `getFile( )` method and displayed inside the `TextArea`. Figure 14-16 shows the application in action.

Listing 14-9 StudyFileDialog.java

```
// Illustrates using a FileDialog
import java.io.*;
import java.awt.*;
import java.awt.event.*;

public class StudyFileDialog extends Frame ⇐
                        implements FilenameFilter, ⇐
                                   ActionListener, ⇐
                                   WindowListener
{
    FileDialog theFileDialog  = new FileDialog( this,⇐
      "Open File" );
    Button    theButton       = new Button( "Open File" );
    Label     theDirectory    = new Label();
    TextArea  theDisplay       = new TextArea();

    public static void main(String args[])
    {
        StudyFileDialog theApp = new StudyFileDialog();
    }

    public StudyFileDialog()
    {
        theFileDialog.setFilenameFilter(this);
        setTitle( "Study The FileDialog Class" );
        setLayout( new BorderLayout() );
        setSize(600, 400);

        add( theButton, "South" );
        add( theDisplay, "Center" );
        add( theDirectory, "North" );
```

```
            theButton.addActionListener(this);
            addWindowListener(this);
            setVisible(true);
    }

    public void actionPerformed(ActionEvent theEvent)
    {
        theDirectory.setText("Directory: ");
        theFileDialog.setDirectory(".");
        theFileDialog.setVisible(true);
        theFileDialog.setVisible(false);
        theDirectory.setText("Directory: " + ⇐
            theFileDialog.getDirectory());
        displayFile( theFileDialog.getDirectory() + ⇐
            theFileDialog.getFile() );
            setVisible(true);
    }

    public void displayFile( String fname )
    {
        FileInputStream inFile = null;

        try
        {
            inFile = new FileInputStream( fname );

            byte[] buf = new byte[ inFile.available() ];
            inFile.read( buf );
            theDisplay.append( "" + new String( buf, 0, ⇐
                buf.length ) );
        }
        catch ( IOException e )
        {
            System.exit( 1 );
        }
    }

    public boolean accept(File dir, String name)
    {
        System.out.println("accept():");
        if (name.endsWith(".txt")) return true;
        return false;
    }

    public void windowClosed      (WindowEvent e) { }
    public void windowClosing     (WindowEvent e) ⇐
      { quitApplication(); }
    public void windowDeiconified (WindowEvent e) { }
    public void windowIconified   (WindowEvent e) { }
    public void windowOpened      (WindowEvent e) { }
    public void windowActivated   (WindowEvent e) { }
    public void windowDeactivated (WindowEvent e) { }

    public void quitApplication()
    {
        setVisible(false );
        dispose();
        System.exit(0);
    }
}
```

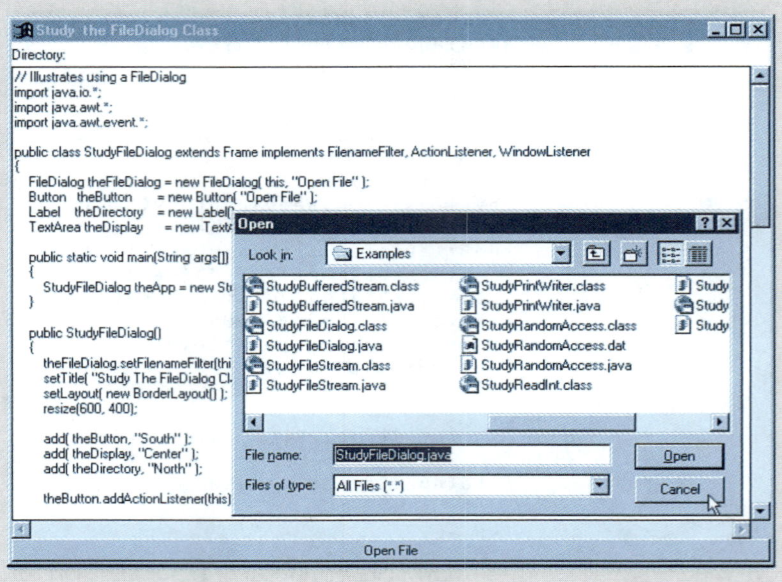

FIGURE 14-16

*Output of the
FileDialog
application*

Pipes: Reading and Writing Bytes

Before you bid farewell to streams, you'll want to visit one more interesting type, known as a *pipe*. A pipe is similar to the fresh-frozen chicken you might purchase at the market, which is neither fresh nor, at least in the view of the producer, frozen. Pipes are not files, because they don't reside on your computer's hard drive and they don't retain their data contents when the system is powered down. But they do act as channels through which data streams can flow, so they're not like ordinary program variables either. The primary use for pipes is to facilitate communication between separate program threads, a topic you'll read more about in Chapter 16, "Advanced Topics: Threads and Networking."

The program StringStream.java, shown in Listing 14-10, explores the use of pipes to convert data in a `String` into an array of `bytes`. Of course, this is a very roundabout way to accomplish such a purpose; but it is a good way to demonstrate some of the less commonly used classes in the `java.io` package. If you really need to perform this conversion, a simpler method would be to use a loop to pull off each character, convert it to a byte, and stuff it into the target array!

Listing 14-10 StringStream.java

```java
// Using pipes to convert a String to a byte array
import java.io.*;

public class StringStream
{
```

```
public static void main(String args[]) throws IOException
{
    String theString = "Jumping Java Jelly";

    StringReader inputStream = ⇐
      new StringReader(theString);

    PipedOutputStream          pipeOut       = ⇐
      new PipedOutputStream();
    PipedInputStream           pipeIn        = ⇐
      new PipedInputStream();

    pipeOut.connect(pipeIn);

    byte[] theArray = new byte[theString.length()];

    System.out.println("Input:   " + theString);

    int n;

    while (true)
    {
        n = inputStream.read();
        if (n == -1)
            break;
        pipeOut.write((byte) n);
    }

    inputStream.close();
    pipeOut.close();

    pipeIn.read(theArray, 0, theString.length());

    pipeIn.close();

    System.out.print("Output: ");
    for (int i = 0; i < theString.length(); i++)
    {
        System.out.print((char) theArray[i]);
    }
    System.out.println();
}
}
```

STRINGSTREAM'S STREAMS

The StringStream program can provide you with some interesting insights into several of Java's stream types. Let's spend a little time going through the code, searching for enlightenment.

StringStream starts by creating a String (the one whose contents will be converted into the byte array), stored in a field named theString. This String is used to construct a stream of type StringReader, which is named inputStream.

```
String theString = "Jumping Java Jelly";
StringReader inputStream = new StringReader(theString);
```

A `StringReader` is simply a stream that is connected to a `String`, which serves as the source of the stream. Rather than reading data from a file or the keyboard, when you read from a `StringReader`, you obtain characters from its associated `String`.

The program next builds a pair of pipes, one `PipedOutputStream` and one `PipedInputStream`, with the lines

```
PipedOutputStream pipeOut = new PipedOutputStream();
PipedInputStream  pipeIn  = new PipedInputStream();
```

These provide a channel through which you can move data. After creating the pipes, you join them together using the `connect( )` method, so that data written into one can be read through the other:

```
pipeOut.connect( pipeIn );
```

Your final preparation step is to create a `byte` array, named `theArray`, sized to hold the number of characters in `theString`:

```
byte[] theArray = new byte[theString.length()];
```

STRINGSTREAM AT WORK

Now comes the fun part. The program starts with a "forever" loop, which you'll note contains a `break` so it won't really run forever. The loop uses the `read( )` method to obtain a `byte` from the `StringReader`.

```
while (true)
{
    n = inputStream.read();
    if (n == -1)
        break;
    pipeOut.write((byte) n);
}
```

After reading and storing a value from `inputStream`, the program checks the value returned by `read( )` to see if `end-of-file` occurred. As previously mentioned, if this occurs, `read( )` will return a −1 and the loop will exit. Otherwise, the loop casts the `int` to a `byte` and writes it into the pipe that was constructed earlier. When `end-of-file` finally does occur, that means that all the characters from the `String` have been read. The program then closes the `StringReader` and the output pipe.

At this point, all of the characters contained in `theString` have been read and then written to the `OutputPipeStream`. All that's left is for the `InputPipeStream` to read the characters that have been written, and then do something with them. To do this, you can use a special form of the `read( )` method, provided by the `InputPipeStream` class, to read the entire contents of the pipe into a `byte` array in a single operation.

```
pipeIn.read(theArray, 0, theString.length());
```

The second argument in this form of `read( )` tells the `InputPipeStream` to fill the array beginning in its first cell (cell 0); the third parameter specifies the number of `bytes` desired. When the read has completed, you should again promptly close the now unused file.

FIGURE 14-17

Output of the StringStream application

The final step in StringStream is to loop through the array, printing the characters for comparison with the contents of `theString`, which were printed early in the program. Figure 14-17 shows that the `byte` array does indeed have exactly the same contents as the original `String`.

Summary

☞ The data moving into, and out of, a program can be thought of as a stream.

☞ Files allow data to be stored permanently.

☞ Streams and files are supported by the `java.io` package.

☞ The three main input-output classes are `InputStream`, `OutputStream`, and `RandomAccessFile`.

☞ Java extends the basic input-output classes `InputStream` and `OutputStream` to provide over a dozen more specialized types of streams.

☞ The standard program input-output streams `stdin`, `stdout`, and `stderr` are represented by `System.in`, `System.out`, and `System.err`, respectively. `System.in` is an `InputStream`, while the other two standard streams are `PrintStream`s.

☞ Many input-output methods can cause `IOExceptions`, so the `try-catch` is important when you are working with streams and files.

☞ The operating system file-redirection facilities can be used to connect a standard system input-output stream to a file. However, MS-DOS does not support redirection of `stderr`.

☞ The `read( )` method is provided by `InputStream` classes, and the `write( )` method is provided by `OutputStream` classes.

☞ `StringBufferInputStream` and `StringBufferOutputStream` can be used to read data from `String`s and to write data to `String`s.

☞ A pipe, created by use of the `PipedInputStream` or `PipedOutputStream` class, is a channel through which a stream of data can be moved.

☞ File streams, created by use of `FileInputStream` or `FileOutputStream`, can be used to read and write files stored on disk.

🐾 The `read( )` method returns an `int` value, which can assume the value −1 to indicate that `end-of-file` has been reached. This condition can also be indicated by an `EOFException`.

🐾 Files should be closed promptly when no longer needed.

🐾 Nested constructors can be used to create streams with a combination of desired properties.

🐾 `DataInputStreams` and `DataOuputStreams` provide platform-independent input and output of the Java primitive types.

🐾 `PrintWriters` support the `println( )` and `print( )` methods, which provide convenient `String` output.

🐾 `RandomAccessFiles` allow data to be read from, or written to, any desired position within a file.

🐾 The `File` class encapsulates useful attributes and methods pertaining to files and directories.

🐾 The `FileDialog` class helps make it easy to build programs that let the user navigate the file system and open or save files.

Quiz

1. "Stream" is a metaphor for _____ moving into, or out of, a program.

2. A stream that is stored on a hard disk is referred to as a _____.

3. The three main input-output classes are _____, which encapsulates stream input capabilities; _____, which encapsulates stream output capabilities; and _____, which encapsulates capabilities for random access to a file.

4. The standard program input stream `stdin` is connected to the Java object _____.

5. The standard program output stream `stdout` is connected to the Java object _____.

6. When input-output errors occur, the exception _____, or one of its subclasses, is likely to be raised.

7. The _____ method is used to get input from a stream.

8. The _____ method is used to put output to a stream.

9. A(n) _____ is similar to a channel through which data can be moved, but not saved; it can be used to connect data sources and sinks.

10. The class used to create objects that can read data files stored on disk is _____.

11. Returning –1 from a `read( )` method indicates that _____ has occurred.

12. Access to a file is terminated by use of the _____ method.

13. Platform-independent input and output of Java data types is provide by the classes _____ and _____, respectively.

14. The `println( )` method that handles Unicode character output is provided by the class _____.

15. The class used to provide access to any byte of a file, for either reading or writing, is _____.

16. The `File` class encapsulates information pertaining to files and _____.

17. Building a dialog to navigate the file structure is facilitated by the class _____.

Exercises

1. Write an application that provides an address book that you can use to keep track of email IDs of correspondents.

2. Write an application that keeps track of your valuable belongings. It should record the name of each item, its description, the date purchased, and the purchase amount. Where applicable, it should also record the date of an appraisal of the value of the item, the method of the appraisal, and the appraised value. It should be possible to delete items from the record, but it need not be possible to change them. Deletion can be accomplished by storing a `boolean` value that is set to `false` if a record is no longer to be made available.

3. Write an application that helps you balance your checking account. The application should allow you to enter both deposits and checks, which are recorded in a permanent file. The application should allow you to correct a wrong entry by calling up a transaction and editing its fields. It should also constantly update and report the current balance in the account.

4. Write an application that supports the operation of a small lending library. Your application should make it possible to register borrowers and assign them a borrower ID to facilitate transactions. The application should record charging and discharging of items to borrowers. It does not need to handle late fees, lost books, and so on.

5. Access to records of a file can be facilitated if the file is indexed on some relevant field. For example, a file used to hold credit records might be indexed by social security number. An index for such a file could be built by creating a separate file that holds the social security number for each record in the file, along with the position of the record within the file, as used by the seek( ) method. To avoid the need to update the indexed file every time a record in the indexed file is changed, records in the indexed file can be made to have a fixed length. Create an application that implements a simple credit-check file that is indexed. The file should hold social security number, name, and a number from 1 to 5 indicating the creditworthiness of the individual. It should be possible to look up a individual by social security number, to revise the information held about the individual, to add new individuals to the file, and to delete individuals from the file. Deletion can be indicated by a boolean value stored in the indexed file.

6. Based on the information in the previous exercise, create a reusable class that encapsulates the fields and methods needed to support an indexed file. Test your reusable class by using it to implement a simple application of your choice that demonstrates retrieval, addition, and deletion of records.

15
Data Structures and Utility Classes

Programmers have always been concerned about productivity. It seems that their customers are always looking for bigger and better software, and they always want it yesterday rather than today or tomorrow. While object-oriented programming helps programmers become more productive by allowing them to work at a higher, more problem-oriented level, customers are happiest when a programmer can solve the customers' problem without writing any code at all. After all, most customers don't really want software, they want solutions.

Somewhere, lost in the mists of the past, a nameless programmer first discovered how to produce programs without writing new code. Rather than "reinventing the wheel," this programmer learned to "cannibalize" programs written previously, using the "spare parts" of one system to construct the next. This programmer could cannibalize the same system repeatedly, without hampering its usability.

Seeing the advantages, other programmers quickly followed suit. Programmers soon learned that there are some components of a system that can be reused with little or no modification, and that there are other components that simply aren't worth salvaging—the effort of adapting them to a second use is too great compared with the effort of simply building an equivalent new component from scratch. Over the course of five decades of collective experience, certain kinds of reusable components have become widely known for their flexibility, finding application in everything from accounts payable systems to zoological inventory systems. These parts are known as *data structures* and *utility classes*.

In this chapter you will learn

☕ How to use Java's `Stack`, `BitSet`, and `Hashtable` classes

☕ How to use the bitwise operators to manipulate the bits within integer values

☕ How to use `Enumerations` to access all the elements of a data structure

☕ How to use `Properties` to access configuration information

☕ How to use `StringTokenizer` to parse a `String` into tokens

☕ How to create a linked-list class and use it to build novel data structures

☕ How to use `MediaTracker` to monitor the loading of images

☕ How to use `Observable-Observer` pairs to keep objects informed of the status of other objects

Meet Java's Data Structures

Java's `java.util` package contains some classes that implement a number of useful data structures, and others that provide useful utility functions. Figure 15-1 shows the family tree of key classes of the `java.util` package. The classes `BitSet`, `Dictionary`, `Hashtable`, `Vector`, and `Stack` are all data structures. You've already met the `Vector` class, which was introduced in Chapter 8, "Flocking Objects: Arrays and Exceptions."

The `java.util` package also includes several useful utility classes: `Date` and `Random`, which you've already met, along with `MediaTracker`, `Observable`, and `StringTokenizer`. Friends of the `java.util` family—not relatives but still closely associated—include `Enumeration` and `Observer`. Before you're done, you'll also learn how to create and use the linked-list data structure which, though not provided within `java.util`, can be used to build data structures of your own design. Let's begin your tour of the `java.util` package with the `Stack` class, which is one of the favorite data structures of computer scientists throughout the known universe.

Stacked and Holding: The Java Stack

Apart from the array, which is given special status by being built into most programming languages, the stack is perhaps the most-used data structure. It follows that the stack must be quite a useful data structure, which it is. Stacks are used by your programs in the same way you use a string on your finger: to help you recall things.

Exactly what is a stack? If you've ever flown cross-country, only to arrive at an airport that has been shut down, you probably know what it means to be "stacked." You and your fellow passengers, along with passengers in other planes, circled endlessly awaiting the call to land. But, to a computer scientist, this situation lacks an important property shared by all true stacks: the *last in, first out* or *LIFO* property. The LIFO

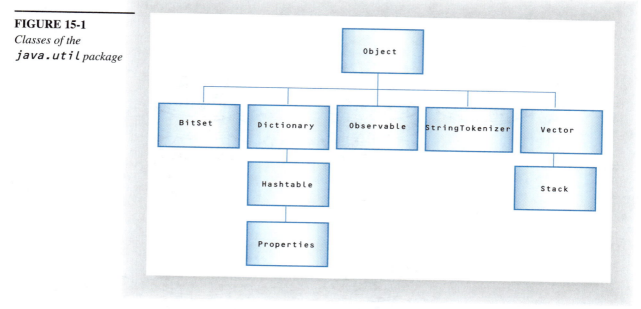

property, if applied to airport holding patterns, would dictate that the last plane to arrive in the pattern should be the first one to land once the airport reopens. You can see now that it's a good thing that airports aren't truly stacks—the wait is long enough as it is!

A good physical model of a stack is the spring-loaded device commonly used in cafeterias to hold plates or trays, as shown in Figure 15-2. There, the plate or tray loaded first will be the last to be removed, and the plate or tray loaded last will be the first to be removed. *This* is a true stack, which is sometimes referred to as a *push-down* stack, just to make sure the LIFO property is clearly understood.

The idea of a stack is simple because there are only two fundamental things you can do with a stack. You can *push* (add) a new item onto the top of the stack, or you can *pop* (remove) an item from the top of the stack. Because you can only pop the last item added—a stack has to have the LIFO property; remember—you can only pop the top-most item. The elements of the stack below the top one cannot be seen at all; they are obscured by the top element. Sometimes you may find it convenient to simply look at the top element without removing it. This so-called `peek` operation is not really a fundamental stack operation, because it can be thought of as a pop followed by a push that replaces the top element before anyone knows it's gone.

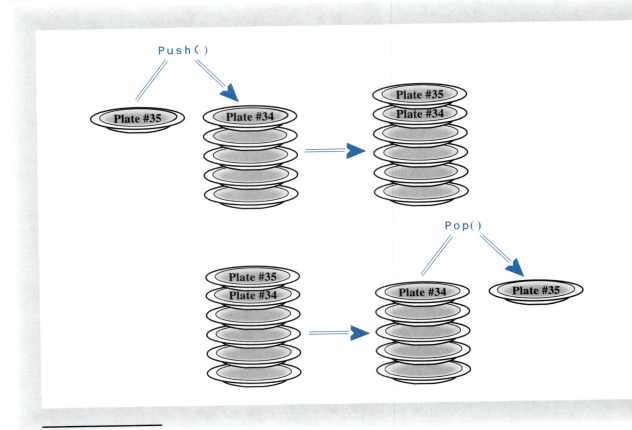

FIGURE 15-2

How a stack works

LOCAL VARIABLES AND THE STACK

Although you might not know it, you've actually been using stacks in almost every Java program you've written, because local variables are stored on a stack. Behind the scenes, Java has two areas for program variable storage: the *heap* and the stack. The heap is used to store objects when they are created. The garbage collector takes responsibility for seeing that the space they occupy is returned to the heap when the objects are no longer needed.

Java's stack is used to hold local variables. These local variables may be primitive values or references to objects. Each time a new method or block is entered, the stack grows as new local variables are added to it by pushing them onto the stack. When the method or block is exited, its local variables are no longer needed, so they are popped off the stack, which shrinks back to its original size. Of course, a given method can invoke other methods, which invoke even further methods in turn, so the push operation is not always immediately followed by the pop. But eventually the called methods must terminate, and the stack must unwind back to its starting point. Figure 15-3 shows how Java's stack of local variables works.

MAKING AND USING YOUR OWN STACKS

Java's `Stack` class makes it easy to create and use stacks within your own programs. To create a `Stack` object, you use the default (no-argument) constructor:

```
Stack myStack = new Stack( );
```

The `Stack myStack` contains no elements when first created. As you add elements by pushing them onto the stack, it grows; and as you remove elements by popping them off the stack, it shrinks. The `Stack` class has several methods that allow you to perform these and other useful operations. These methods are shown in Table 15-1.

FIGURE 15-3

Java's local variable stack

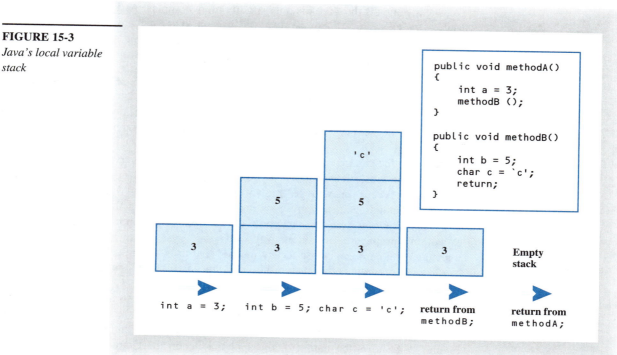

TABLE 15-1
KEY `public` METHODS OF THE `Stack` CLASS

METHOD HEADER	**FUNCTION**
`boolean empty( )`	Determine if the `Stack` is empty.
`Object peek( )`	Return the `Object` at the top of the `Stack`, without modifying the `Stack`.
`Object pop( )`	Pop the `Object` at the top of the `Stack`.
`Object push(Object obj)`	Push the `Object` onto the top of the `Stack`, returning the `Object`.
`int search(Object obj)`	Determine if the specified `Object` is on the `Stack`, returning the distance from the top of the `Stack`, or −1 if the `Object` is not on the `Stack`.

The `Stack` class in Java stores only objects. To store primitive types, you will need to "wrap" each value inside one of the special wrapper objects such as `Character`, `Double`, or `Integer`. To store an object on a `Stack`, you simply use the `Stack`'s `push( )` method, supplying an argument that references the object you wish to add:

```
Elephant theBoss = new Elephant( "Jumbo" );
myStack.push( theBoss );
```

Getting a value off the `Stack` is only slightly more complex. As you might expect, you use the `Stack`'s `pop( )` method. However, since a `Stack` can store any type of object, you have to cast the value returned by `pop( )` to the correct type:

```
Elephant theOwner = (Elephant) myStack.pop();
```

In addition to the fundamental operations implemented by `push( )` and `pop( )`, there are several other `Stack` class methods. You can use the `peek( )` method to perform a `pop( )` followed by a `push( )`; the `empty( )` method to check whether the `Stack` is empty; and the `search( )` method to "cheat" by looking through the elements below the top one.

One thing that can go wrong when you are using a `Stack` is trying to call the `pop( )` method when the `Stack` is empty. If you call `pop( )` or `peek( )` on an empty `Stack`, an `EmptyStackException` will be thrown. You can use `empty( )` to check the `Stack` before manipulating it, thereby avoiding the exception altogether, or you can use a `try-catch` block to trap the exception. Of course, another option is simply to let the exception propagate all the way up the system by adding a `throws EmptyStackException` clause to any method that uses a `Stack`, but that's considered bad form in programs other than prototypes, since it allows the unhandled exception to cause the program to terminate.

Listing 15-1 shows the `sihTesreveR` applet, which demonstrates a simple use of a `Stack`. No, the program name isn't misprinted (We hope!). You can use `sihTesreveR.html`, shown in Listing 15-2, to run the applet, and you'll see what's up. Figure 15-4 shows the output of the applet. Later in the chapter, you'll see a more ambitious example based on the `Stack` class, so remember what you've learned.

Listing 15-1 sihTesreveR.java

```
// Using the Stack class
import java.util.*;
import java.awt.*;
import java.awt.event.*;
import java.applet.*;

public class sihTesreveR extends Applet ⇐
                         implements ActionListener
{
    Stack      theStack    = new Stack();
    String     appName     = getClass().getName();
    Button[]   theButtons  = new Button[ appName.length() ];
    Button     stackMe     = new Button( "Stack Me" );
    Panel      theInput    = new Panel();
    Panel      stackPanel  = new Panel();

    public void init()
    {
        int len = theButtons.length;

        setLayout( new BorderLayout() );

        theInput.setLayout( new GridLayout( 1, len, 2, 2 ));
        for ( int i = 0; i < len; i++ )
        {
            theButtons[i] = ⇐
               new Button( ""+appName.charAt(i) );
            theInput.add( theButtons[i] );
        }

        Panel p = new Panel();
        p.setLayout( new GridLayout( 1, 3, 5, 5 ));
        p.add( new Label("")); // just a dummy placeholder
        stackPanel.setLayout( ⇐
           new GridLayout( len, 1, 2, 2 ));
        p.add( stackPanel );
        p.add( new Label("")); // another dummy
        add( theInput, "North" );
        add( p, "Center" );
        add( stackMe, "South" );
        stackMe.addActionListener(this);
    }

    public void actionPerformed( ActionEvent theEvent )
    {
        if ( theStack.empty() )
        {
            stackMe.setLabel("Unstack Me");
            stackPanel.removeAll( );
            for ( int i = 0; i < theButtons.length; i++ )
            {
                theStack.push( theButtons[i] );
                stackPanel.add( (Button) theStack.peek() );
            }
            stackPanel.invalidate();
            stackPanel.validate();
            theInput.removeAll();
```

continued on next page

continued from previous page

> **The last item added has to be the first item removed, because objects can only be added or removed from the top of the stack.**

```
        }
        else
        {
            stackMe.setLabel("Stack Me");
            theInput.removeAll();
            for ( int i = 0; i < theButtons.length; i++ )
            {
                theButtons[i] = (Button) theStack.pop();
                theInput.add( theButtons[i] );
            }
            theInput.invalidate();
            theInput.validate();
            stackPanel.removeAll();
        }
        setVisible(true);
    }
}
```

Listing 15-2 sihTesreveR.html

```html
<HTML>
<HEAD>
<TITLE>sihTesreveR.java</TITLE>
</HEAD>
<BODY>
<H1>Using a Stack</H1>
<HR>
<APPLET CODE=sihTesreveR HEIGHT=300 WIDTH=500>
</APPLET>
</BODY>
</HTML>
```

FIGURE 15-4
Output of the
sihTesreveR
applet

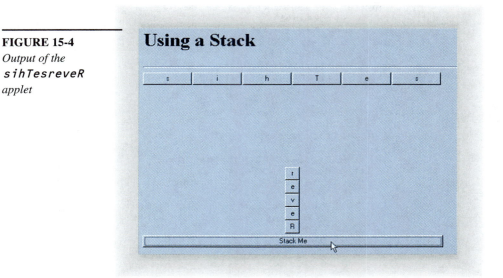

INSIDE sihTesreveR

The sihTesreveR applet takes advantage of the LIFO property of a Stack to allow you to watch as it interactively reverses a String. The applet has six fields:

- theStack is a Stack object constructed by use of the default constructor Stack( ).

- appName is a String that contains the name of the applet itself. Rather than simply hardcoding the name, sihTesreveR uses the getClass( ) method to get the applet's class, and then calls the getName( ) method to retrieve the name of the class. This is done when appName is first initialized, by use of getClass( ).getName( ). This way of setting the window title is handy if you're the sort of person who likes to change your program names, but also the type who forgets to change the window title. By retrieving the class name from the Java run-time, you ensure that the window title always displays the correct class name.

- theButtons is an array of Buttons, each of which will display a single character from the String appName.

- The Button—stackMe—is used to control the application, and the Panels—theInput and stackPanel—are used to organize the user interface.

There are only two methods inside sihTesreveR:

- The init( ) method begins by creating a new Button for every character in the String appName, and adding each Button to the Panel theInput. Next, a dummy Panel (p) is created so that the stackPanel can be nicely centered in your applet. Finally, init( ) adds both Panels and the stackMe Button to the applet.

- The second method, actionPerformed( ), does one of two things, depending on whether the Stack is full or empty. If the user presses the stackMe Button when theStack is empty, then all of the Buttons in theButtons array are pushed on the Stack. If the user presses UnstackMe when theStack is full, the Buttons are popped off the Stack and put back into theButtons array, now in reverse order.

Again, this is one of those programs you have to see to appreciate, since it's based on a simple form of animation. The figure cannot show the program's dynamic aspect. Run it yourself and watch the buttons scampering onto and off of the stack.

Looking It Up: Dictionaries and Hashtables

The `Dictionary` class is an abstract class that is fully implemented by the `Hashtable` class. Think about how a dictionary works in real life. If you know the spelling of a word, you can easily look up its meaning. In this sense the word you are trying to look up is a *key* that is associated with a particular meaning.

`Hashtables`, like arrays, store data. But because `Hashtable` entries have keys, you can go directly to a desired entry in a `Hashtable`, rather than stepping through it element by element. Searching a `Hashtable` is like looking up a word in a dictionary. Searching an array is like starting with the entry for "aardvark" and reading every word until you find the one you want. Consequently, finding an entry in a `Hashtable` is faster and easier than finding an entry in an array. Moreover, it's simple and quick to add a new element to a `Hashtable`.

CREATING AND USING Hashtables

The `Hashtable` class offers three constructors, which are shown in Table 15-2. Since `Hashtables` are dynamically sized, it's possible to create a `Hashtable` without accurate foreknowledge of its eventual size, by use of the default constructor:

```
Hashtable goodTable = new Hashtable( );
```

When using a dictionary, most of us are less concerned with how difficult it is to add items, than with how easily and quickly we can find the entry we want. The retrieval performance of a `Hashtable`—how long it takes to get back a value when you provide a key—is significantly affected by the `Hashtable`'s *loading factor*. The loading factor of a `Hashtable` is simply the ratio of the number of its current elements to its allocated current size. If the size of the `Hashtable` is 100 and you've stored 50 elements, the loading factor would be 0.5. As the loading factor moves from 0.0 to 1.0, retrieval performance drops precipitously. Thus, one quick way to improve the performance of a `Hashtable` is to start it with a size larger than you think you'll need:

```
Hashtable betterTable = new Hashtable( 200 );
```

While this works better, for best performance you can use the third form of the constructor, which lets you specify a target load factor:

```
Hashtable bestTable = new Hashtable( 200, 0.75 );
```

When the actual load factor of the `Hashtable` exceeds the specified value—in this case 0.75—it will be automatically reorganized for improved performance. Of course, the reorganization itself takes time, so there's no free ride. As a rule of thumb, performance of `Hashtables` is generally acceptable with loading factors as high as 70 percent to 80 percent, becoming noticeably impaired somewhere around 90 percent.

Table 15-3 shows methods of the `Dictionary` class inherited by `Hashtables`. Table 15-4 shows distinctive methods of the `Hashtable` class itself.

A `Hashtable` EXAMPLE

Listing 15-3 shows the `GuestBook` applet, which simulates the operation of a guest book on a Web page. Of course, this is only a simulation. As soon as the applet finishes execution, the contents of the guest book are lost. But it's possible to build a Java server application that runs continuously and keeps a copy of new guest book entries on a disk file. You should be able to transform this applet into a suitable client-server pair after mastering the information on network programming in Chapter 16, "Advanced Topics: Threads and Networking." For now, consider this a prototype of the user interface and data management functions required by a fully functional guest book.

The `GuestBook` applet presents a window that includes a `TextField` the guest can use to enter a name, a `TextArea` that can accommodate a message of indefinite size, and a pair of `Buttons` used to send the message on its way to the `Hashtable` or to retrieve those messages already saved. Figure 15-5 shows the appearance of the applet. Note in the source code how `Panels` and `LayoutManagers` are used to construct a display format that behaves well when the applet window is resized.

TABLE 15-2
KEY `public` CONSTRUCTORS OF THE `Hashtable` CLASS

```
Hashtable( )
Hashtable(int initialSize)
Hashtable(int initialSize, float loadFactor)
```

TABLE 15-3
KEY `public` METHODS OF THE `Dictionary` CLASS (IMPLEMENTED BY `Hashtable`)

METHOD HEADER	FUNCTION
`Enumeration elements( )`	Get an `Enumeration` over the elements of the `Dictionary`.
`Object get(Object key)`	Get the `Dictionary` element identified by the key.
`boolean isEmpty( )`	Determine if the `Dictionary` is empty.
`Enumeration keys( )`	Get an `Enumeration` over the keys of the `Dictionary`.
`Object put(Object key, Object value)`	Add the specified value to the `Dictionary`, associating it with the specified key.
`Object remove(Object key)`	Remove the `Dictionary` element identified by the key.
`int size( )`	Get the number of elements in the `Dictionary`.

TABLE 15-4
KEY `public` METHODS OF THE `Hashtable` CLASS

METHOD HEADER	FUNCTION
`void clear( )`	Remove all elements from the `Hashtable`.
`boolean contains(Object value)`	Determine whether the `Hashtable` contains the specified `Object`.
`boolean containsKey(Object key)`	Determine whether the `Hashtable` contains an element associated with the specified key.

Listing 15-3 GuestBook.java

```java
// Using a Hashtable
import java.applet.*;
import java.awt.*;
import java.awt.event.*;
import java.util.*;

public class GuestBook extends Applet ⇐
                    implements ActionListener
{
    Hashtable guestBook  = new Hashtable();

    Label      theLabel   = new Label⇐
      ("Guest Book", Label.CENTER);
    TextField guestName = new TextField("", 20 );
    TextArea  guestNote  = new TextArea();
    Button    sendButton = new Button("Store Messages");
    Button    getButton  = new Button("Get Messages");
    Label     visitLabel = ⇐
      new Label("This site visited 0 times.",
                Label.CENTER);

    public void init()
    {
        theLabel.setFont  ( new Font("Helvetica", ⇐
          Font.BOLD,  24) );
        guestName.setFont ( new Font("Helvetica", ⇐
          Font.PLAIN, 12) );
        guestNote.setFont ( new Font("Helvetica", ⇐
          Font.BOLD,  12) );
        visitLabel.setFont( new Font("Helvetica", ⇐
          Font.PLAIN, 10) );

        setLayout(new BorderLayout());
        add( visitLabel, "South" );
        add( theLabel, "North"  );
```

```
                    Panel p = new Panel();
                    p.setLayout( new BorderLayout(5, 5) );
                    p.add( guestNote, "Center" );

                    Panel p1 = new Panel();
                    p1.add( new Label( "Name : " ) );
                    p1.add( guestName );
                    p1.add( sendButton );
                    p1.add( getButton  );
                    p.add( p1, "North" );
                    add(p, "Center" );

                    guestName.addActionListener(this);
                    sendButton.addActionListener(this);
                    getButton.addActionListener(this);
                }

            public void actionPerformed(ActionEvent theEvent)
            {
                if (theEvent.getSource( ) == guestName
                   || theEvent.getSource( ) == getButton)
                {
                    String name = guestName.getText();
                    if (name.length() > 0)
                    {
                        String note = (String) guestBook.get(name);
                        if (note != null)
                            guestNote.setText(note);
                        else
                            guestNote.setText("");
                    }
                    guestNote.requestFocus();
                }
                if (theEvent.getSource( ) == sendButton)
                {
                    guestBook.put(⇐
                        guestName.getText(), guestNote.getText());
                    guestName.setText("");
                    guestNote.setText("");
                    visitLabel.setText(⇐
                        "Visited " + guestBook.size() + " times.");
                    guestName.requestFocus();
                }
            }
        }
    }
```

INSIDE THE GuestBook

The GuestBook applet uses a few tricks to make it easy to use—tricks that you might find handy in other programs that you write. When first loaded, the applet places its text cursor in the TextField, inviting the user to enter a name. It does this by telling the guestName field to requestFocus( ). If you press [ENTER] while the cursor is within the TextField, or if you press the Button labeled "Get Messages," the `actionPerformed( )` method will search the `Hashtable` for a previous entry under the name entered in the `TextField`. It does this by using the `Hashtable`'s `get( )` method:

```
String note = (String) guestBook.get( name );
```

If one is found, it is displayed in the `TextArea`, so that it can be modified or updated. If a match is not found in the `Hashtable`, the `String note` has the value `null`, and an empty `String` is displayed inside the `TextArea`. To make update or modification simple, the cursor is returned to the `TextArea` by use of the `requestFocus( )` method.

Pressing the Send Note `Button` causes the `Hashtable` to be updated by use of a key-value pair consisting of the contents of the `TextField` and the `TextArea`. The `Hashtable`'s `put( )` method is called to accomplish the update:

```
guestBook.put(guestName.getText( ), guestNote.getText( ));
```

Note that when you are using `put( )`, the first argument is the key, and the second argument is the value associated with that key. Once the value has been stored, the two input fields are then cleared, and a `Label` that displays the cumulative number of visits is updated.

Of course, this interface is not foolproof. You could type a message and then return to the `guestName TextField`, rather than pressing the Send Note `Button`. You could then possibly revise the name to match that of another entry in the `Hashtable` and overwrite that entry by pressing the `Button`. Your entry would then seem to have been sent by someone else. Since there's no specification for the applet, it's hard to say whether this is a bug or a feature; but a real guest book should probably have some way of authenticating the ownership of its entries, in order to avoid spurious entries by "Elvis."

FIGURE 15-5

Output of the
GuestBook applet

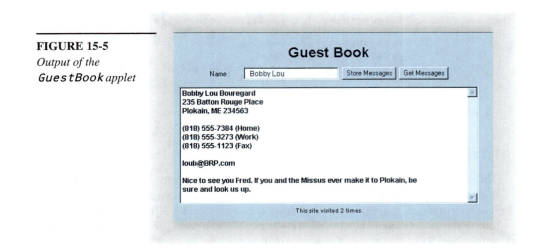

Enumerations

Using a Hashtable can present an unexpected problem. What if you want to get *all* the entries of the Hashtable? You can't use get( ) without specifying the key of each item—how do you find the values of the keys?

The answer is found in the Enumeration class. An Enumeration object contains a list of the elements of a *collection* (that is, a data structure that stores elements). Enumerations have methods that make it easy to *traverse* or *iterate* through the elements of a collection.

For example, the method Hashtable.keys( ) gets an Enumeration object that can be used to find the keys stored within a Hashtable. Here's how you might add code to the GuestBook applet that would allow you to obtain the notes from all guests. The code assumes that a new Button named allButton has been added to the applet. Pressing the new button lists all the messages left by all guests:

```
if (theEvent.getSource( ) == allButton)
{
    guestName.setText("");
    guestNote.setText("");

    Enumeration keysEnum = guestBook.keys( );

    while (keysEnum.hasMoreElements( ))
    {
        String guest = (String) keysEnum.nextElement( );
        String note  = (String) guestBook.get(guest);
        guestNote.append(guest + ":\n");
        guestNote.append(note + "\n");
    }
}
```

Once the Enumeration object is obtained, the program iterates over the keys within the Hashtable by using its hasMoreElements( ) method within a while loop. This method returns true as long as there are elements that have not yet been fetched. The Enumeration method nextElement( ) is used to actually fetch each successive key, which is then passed to Hashtable's get( ) method to get the notes stored under the key. Note that because nextElement( ) and get( ) each return an Object, it's necessary to cast the return value to the correct type (String) before using it.

There are three important things you will need to make sure you understand about this loop:

☕ You get an Enumeration object from a Hashtable object by invoking the method keys( ).

☕ You test for the end of an Enumeration range by using the method hasMoreElements( ).

☕ You retrieve an object by using the nextElement( ) method and casting the returned value to the type of object you need.

By use of `keys()` it's easy to iterate over the keys within a `Hashtable`. The `Hashtable` class also provides a similar method named `elements()`, which returns an `Enumeration` over the elements of a `Hashtable`. Other collection classes, such as `Vector`, also provide methods that return `Enumerations` over their contents.

One peculiarity of the `Enumeration` is that it's not reusable. When you use an `Enumeration` to iterate over the elements of a collection and finally reach the end, the `Enumeration` doesn't "rewind" to the beginning of the collection. If you want to start over at the beginning, you'll need to create a new `Enumeration`.

Possession Is Nine Points of Law: `Properties`

A special sort of `Hashtable`, the `Properties` class, is used in many systems to store configuration information. This is especially important in the Java world, where you often find your application running under different operating systems. A `Properties` object stores this configuration information as name-value pairs, where both the name of the configuration item and its value are represented as `Strings`. This works something like MS Windows INI files. The `Properties` class can also define a set of default values for configuration properties. If no updating entry has been made to a configuration item, the corresponding default value can be obtained.

The two constructors for the `Properties` class are shown in Table 15-5, and its key methods are shown in Table 15-6. To create a `Properties` object you can write

```
Properties myProps = new Properties( );
```

The new `Properties` object can then be updated to contain useful configuration information. For example, you can write

```
String theName  = "FavoriteLanguage";
String theValue = "Java";
myProps.put(theName, theValue);
```

to save the identity of your favorite language in the `Properties` `Hashtable`. Later, when you need to recall your favorite language, you can write

```
String myLanguage;
myLanguage = myProps.getProperty("FavoriteLanguage");
```

TABLE 15-5
KEY `public` CONSTRUCTORS OF THE `Properties` CLASS

Properties( )
Properties(Properties default)

TABLE 15-6
KEY `public` METHODS OF THE `Properties` CLASS

METHOD HEADER	FUNCTION
`String getProperty(String key)`	Get the value of the specified property.
`String getProperty` `(String key, String defaultValue)`	Get the value of the specified property; return `defaultValue` if it is not in either the `Properties` list or the default `Properties` list.
`void load(InputStream in)`	Load the `Properties` object from a stream.
`Enumeration propertyNames( )`	Get an `Enumeration` over the stored property names.
`void save` `(OutputStream out, String header)`	Store the `Properties` object to a stream, with the specified descriptive header.

The `load( )` and `save( )` methods of the `Properties` class are especially useful, because they can be used to transfer a `Properties` object to or from a stream, such as a disk file. This important ability, called *persistence,* allows the data stored in a `Properties` object to survive shutdown of computer power. To dynamically update a property value, you can use the `Hashtable.put( )` method, since the `Properties` class extends the `Hashtable` class. To save your `Properties` object, you can write

```
FileOutputStream outProp = ⇐
   new FileOutputStream("myProps.config");
myProps.save(outProp, "myprops.config: " +  new Date( ));
```

Recovering your saved data is as simple as this:

```
Properties myProps = new Properties( );
FileInputStream inProp = ⇐
   new FileInputStream("myProps.config");
myProps.load(inProp);
```

Listing 15-4 shows the Props application, which is a simple example of creating, updating, and saving a `Properties` object.

Listing 15-4 Props.java

```
// Saving and loading properties
import java.util.*;
import java.io.*;

public class Props
{
    public static void main(String args[]) throws ⇐
      FileNotFoundException, IOException
    {
        String fileName   = "props.test";
        String propName   = "FavoriteLanguage";
```

continued on next page

continued from previous page

> **"** *Hashtables,*
> *like arrays, store*
> *data. But because*
> *Hashtable*
> *entries have keys,*
> *you can go*
> *directly to a*
> *desired entry.* **"**

```
        Properties theFirstProp = new Properties( );
        theFirstProp.put(propName, "Java");

        FileOutputStream theOutputStream = ⇐
          new FileOutputStream(fileName);
        theFirstProp.save(theOutputStream, fileName + ": " ⇐
          + new Date( ));
        theOutputStream.close( );

        Properties theSecondProp = new Properties();
        FileInputStream theInputStream = ⇐
          new FileInputStream(fileName);
        theSecondProp.load(theInputStream);
        theInputStream.close( );

        System.out.println("My favorite language is: "
          + theSecondProp.getProperty(propName));

        System.exit(0);
    }
}
```

OUTPUT OF THE PROPS APPLICATION

```
C:\Ch15\Examples>java Props
My favorite language is: Java
```

THE SYSTEM PROPERTIES

Java itself makes use of the `Properties` class, as do popular Java-enabled browsers. The `System.getProperties()` method can be used to obtain the `Properties` object used by the Java interpreter. The standard system properties used by Java are described in Table 15-7. Note that certain of these properties cannot be accessed by applets. This restriction is intended to make the Java environment more secure than it might be if the related properties were easily obtainable by applets. Even in cases where applets are permitted to access a particular system property, your browser may not allow such access. For applets, access to the system properties is performed under control of the browser's security manager. The Appletviewer's security manager may allow an applet to access system properties; a given browser may even allow an applet loaded from a local file to access them. Generally, however, a browser will not allow an applet loaded over the network to access system properties, for fear this might compromise system security.

TABLE 15-7
STANDARD SYSTEM PROPERTIES

PROPERTY NAME	MEANING/USE	ACCESSIBLE BY APPLET
java.version	Version of the Java interpreter	Yes
java.vendor	Vendor identification	Yes
java.vendor.url	Vendor's URL	Yes
java.home	Directory in which Java was installed	No
java.class.version	Version of the Java API	Yes
java.class.path	Value of the CLASSPATH environment variable	No
awt.toolkit	Name of the AWT	Yes
os.name	Name of the host operating system	Yes
os.arch	Host hardware architecture	Yes
os.version	Host operating system version	Yes
file.separator	String used to separate directories within file path (usually / or \)	Yes
path.separator	String used to separate components of PATH environment variable (usually : or ;)	Yes
line.separator	String used to separate lines of text (usually \n or \n\r)	Yes
user.name	User name of the user	No
user.home	User's home directory	No
user.dir	Current working directory	No

Listing 15-5 shows the ExploreProperties application, which dumps Java's entire Properties Hashtable. The related output is shown in Figure 15-6. The application uses the propertyNames message to obtain an Enumeration over the names of all properties. The names are then used with the getProperty() method to obtain the corresponding property values.

Listing 15-5 ExploreProperties.java

```
import java.util.*;

public class ExploreProperties
{
    public static void main(String args[])
    {
        Properties system_props = System.getProperties();
```

continued on next page

continued from previous page

```
        Enumeration prop_names   = ⇐
          system_props.propertyNames();
        String prop_name;
        while (prop_names.hasMoreElements())
        {
            prop_name = (String) prop_names.nextElement();
            System.out.println(prop_name +": "
              + system_props.getProperty(prop_name));
        }
    }
}
```

It Slices, It Dices…: StringTokenizer

Another useful utility class provided by Java is the StringTokenizer class. A StringTokenizer can break a String into a series of *tokens*. In this context, a token is not something you put in a slot machine or something that allows you to ride the subway. Instead, a token is a series of characters separated by *delimiters* from surrounding tokens. In the default case, the delimiters used are spaces, tabs, and newlines—the whitespace characters. Each word in a sentence, for example, is a token, as are the operands and operators that make up an expression.

CREATING AND USING StringTokenizer

The three constructors of the StringTokenizer class are shown in Table 15-8. The simplest constructor requires only a single String as an argument:

```
static String s = ⇐
   "This sentence 'owns' fewer than 32543 separate tokens.";
StringTokenizer tok1 = new StringTokenizer( s );
```

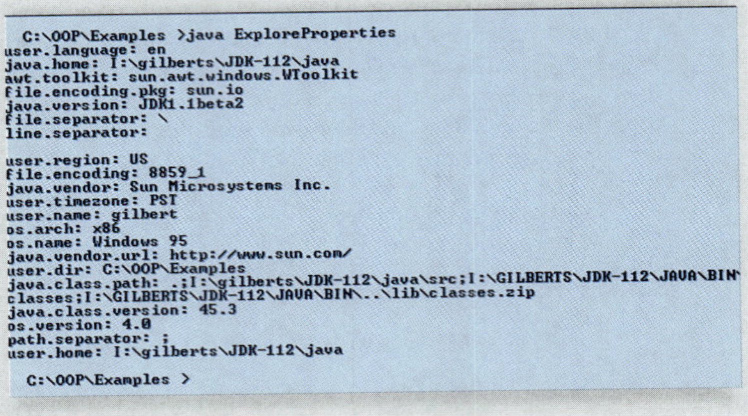

FIGURE 15-6

Output of the ExploreProperties application

```
C:\OOP\Examples >java ExploreProperties
user.language: en
java.home: I:\gilberts\JDK-112\java
awt.toolkit: sun.awt.windows.WToolkit
file.encoding.pkg: sun.io
java.version: JDK1.1beta2
file.separator: \
line.separator:

user.region: US
file.encoding: 8859_1
java.vendor: Sun Microsystems Inc.
user.timezone: PST
user.name: gilbert
os.arch: x86
os.name: Windows 95
java.vendor.url: http://www.sun.com/
user.dir: C:\OOP\Examples
java.class.path: .;I:\gilberts\JDK-112\java\src;I:\GILBERTS\JDK-112\JAVA\BIN\
classes;I:\GILBERTS\JDK-112\JAVA\BIN\..\lib\classes.zip
java.class.version: 45.3
os.version: 4.0
path.separator: ;
user.home: I:\gilberts\JDK-112\java

C:\OOP\Examples >
```

This `StringTokenizer`, `tok1`, will treat tab (\t), new line (\n), and carriage return (\r) as whitespace characters, in addition to the space character. You may want to specify a different set of token delimiters. The second and third forms allow you to include a `String`, the characters of which are considered to be delimiting characters:

```
StringTokenizer tok2 = new StringTokenizer( s, "\n\r\t \'" );
StringTokenizer tok3 = new StringTokenizer( s, "\n\r\t \'", ⇐
  true);
```

The `StringTokenizer tok2` adds the apostrophe character to the roster of delimiters, while `tok3` adds a third, `boolean`, argument, specifying that the delimiters themselves should also be returned as tokens rather than skipped.

The methods of the `StringTokenizer` class are summarized in Table 15-9. The methods `nextElement( )` and `nextToken( )` each return the next token from the `String`. The former returns an `Object`, and the latter returns a `String`; otherwise there is no difference in their function. If the third constructor form is used with its final parameter set to `true`, each delimiter encountered will also be returned, as a single-character `String`.

The application TestStringTokenizer, shown in Listing 15-6, uses the three constructors described earlier to tokenize a `String` and print the results. As you can see from Figure 15-7, each of the three `StringTokenizer`s slices and dices the `String` according to the arguments it was given.

TABLE 15-8
KEY `public` CONSTRUCTORS OF THE `StringTokenizer` CLASS

`StringTokenizer(String str)`
`StringTokenizer(String s, String white)`
`StringTokenizer(String str, String white, boolean returnTokens)`

TABLE 15-9
KEY `public` METHODS OF THE `StringTokenizer` CLASS

METHOD HEADER	FUNCTION
`int countTokens( )`	Get the number of tokens in the `String`.
`boolean hasMoreElements( )`	Determine whether there are more elements available from the `StringTokenizer`'s built-in `Enumeration`.
`boolean hasMoreTokens( )`	Determine whether there are more tokens available from the `String`.
`Object nextElement( )`	Get the next element from the built-in `Enumeration`.
`String nextToken( )`	Get the next token from the `String`.
`String nextToken(String delim)`	Switch permanently to a new set of delimiters and get the next token.

Listing 15-6 TestStringTokenizer.java

```java
// Using StringTokenizer
import java.io.*;
import java.util.*;

public class TestStringTokenizer
{
    static String s =
        "This sentence 'owns' fewer than 32543 separate ⇐
        tokens.";

    public static void main( String args[] )
    {
        StringTokenizer tok1 = new StringTokenizer( s );
        StringTokenizer tok2 = ⇐
          new StringTokenizer( s, "\n\r\t \'" );
        StringTokenizer tok3 = ⇐
          new StringTokenizer( s, "\n\r\t \'", true);

        int i = 1;
        System.out.println("Displaying tokens from tok1:");
        while ( tok1.hasMoreElements() )
        {
            System.out.println( "   " + (i++) + ". " + ⇐
              tok1.nextToken() );
        }

        i = 1;
        System.out.println("Displaying tokens from tok2:");
        while ( tok2.hasMoreElements() )
        {
            System.out.println( "   " + (i++) + ". " + ⇐
              tok2.nextToken() );
        }

        i = 1;
        System.out.println("Displaying tokens from tok3:");
        while ( tok3.hasMoreElements() )
        {
            System.out.println( "   " + (i++) + ". " + ⇐
              tok3.nextToken() );
        }
    }
}
```

FIGURE 15-7

*Running the
TestStringTokenizer
application*

```
Displaying tokens from tok1:
  1. This
  2. sentence
  3. 'owns'
  4. fewer
  5. than
  6. 32543
  7. separate
  8. tokens.
Displaying tokens from tok2:
  1. This
  2. sentence
  3. owns
  4. fewer
  5. than
  6. 32543
  7. separate
  8. tokens.
Displaying tokens from tok3:
  1. This
  2.
  3. sentence
  4.
  5. '
  6. owns
  7. '
  8.
  9. fewer
 10.
 11. than
 12.
 13. 32543
 14.
 15. separate
 16.
 17. tokens.
```

ANOTHER StringTokenizer EXAMPLE

Listing 15-7 shows the WordCount application, a program that uses StringTokenizer to count the words in a text file. Now you can find out if that 10,000-word essay was really 10,000 words! Figure 15-8 shows the output of the application. Note in the source code how the file name, passed as a command-line argument, is used to construct a FileReader, which is then used to construct a BufferedReader. Because the application needs buffering for speedy handling of large text files and because it also needs the readLine() method provided by the BufferedReader class, each of the classes must be "wrapped" around the original FileReader to provide an object with all these capabilities.

Listing 15-7 WordCount.java

```java
// Using StringTokenizer to count words
import java.io.*;
import java.util.*;

public class WordCount
{
    static BufferedReader input;
    static StringTokenizer st;
    static int count = 0;

    public static void main(String args[]) throws IOException
    {
        if ( args.length < 1 )
```

continued on next page

continued from previous page

```
    {
         System.err.println( ⇐
           "Syntax: java WordCount <filename>" );
         System.exit( 1 );
    }

    String fileName = args[0];

    input = new BufferedReader(new FileReader(fileName));

    String textLine;
    while (true)
    {
         textLine = input.readLine();
         if (textLine == null)
             break;
         st = new StringTokenizer(textLine);
         count += st.countTokens();
    }

    input.close();
    System.out.println( fileName + " contains " + ⇐
      count + " words.");
    }
  }
```

StringTokenizer AND Stack TOGETHER: THE RPN APPLET

Listings 15-8 and 15-9 show how StringTokenizer can be used with Stack to create a very sophisticated calculator applet. Figure 15-9 shows how the applet is used. Typing an RPN expression into the input TextField and pressing ENTER causes the applet to evaluate the RPN expression and display its result in the output TextField.

If you're not familiar with RPN expressions, you may nevertheless have used them, because many scientific calculators require you to enter values in RPN. Sometimes called *postfix* notation, RPN allows you to enter an operator only after you've entered both its operands. The usual algebraic way of forming expressions, sometimes called *infix* notation, places operators between operands. Thus, if you write the RPN expression

```
   1  2  +  3  *
```

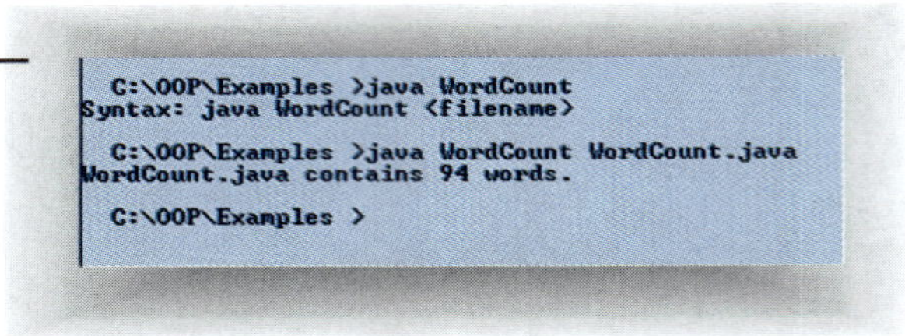

FIGURE 15-8

Output of the WordCount application

```
C:\OOP\Examples >java WordCount
Syntax: java WordCount <filename>

C:\OOP\Examples >java WordCount WordCount.java
WordCount.java contains 94 words.

C:\OOP\Examples >
```

it means take 1 and 2 and add them. Then take that result and multiply by 3. The result, of course, is 9. In regular algebraic notation you'd write

```
(1 + 2) * 3
```

Notice how the parentheses are needed to make sure that it's (1+2) that's to be multiplied by 3. Writing

```
1 + 2 * 3
```

would really mean

```
1 + (2 * 3)
```

which is 7, not 9. This capability of writing complete expressions without the need for parentheses is one of the great virtues of `RPN`. The other is that the operands are always combined in the same order they're written, from left to right. The result is that it's straightforward to use a stack to evaluate any `RPN` expression. The stack is needed to hold intermediate values as they yield the "right of way" to subexpressions involving operators of higher priority.

This approach is used within the `evaluateExpression()` method of the `RPN` applet. The method takes a single argument containing an `RPN` expression in `String` form. The method creates a `Stack` to be used in the evaluation, and a `StringTokenizer` used to break the `String` into its component operands and operators. A `while` loop is used to iterate over the tokens obtained from the method's argument. Each token retrieved from the `StringTokenizer` is examined to see if its first character indicates that it is an operator.

Let's focus for the moment on the situation that occurs when something other than an operator is found. If the token is not an operator, it must be a number. In this case, the `Double()` constructor is used to create a new `Double` that takes as its value the number contained in the token `String`. This `Double` is then simply pushed onto the stack.

If the token is an operator, its two operands should already be on the stack. The method simply pops them off the stack and obtains their numerical values by using `doubleValue()`. Then the appropriate arithmetic operation is performed, and the result is pushed onto the stack as a `Double`.

When all the tokens have been processed, the value remaining on the stack is the result. It is popped off the stack and returned so that it can be displayed.

Listing 15–8 RPN.java

```java
import java.applet.*;
import java.awt.*;
import java.awt.event.*;
import java.util.*;

public class RPN extends Applet implements ActionListener
{
    TextField theInput   = new TextField();
    TextField theOutput  = new TextField();
    Font      theFont    = new Font("Courier", Font.BOLD, 12);
```

continued on next page

continued from previous page

```
public void init( )
{
    setLayout(new GridLayout(5, 1));
    add(new Label(⇐
      "Type an RPN expression and press ENTER:"));
    add(theInput);
    theInput.setFont(theFont);
    add(new Label(""));
    add(new Label("The result is:"));
    add(theOutput);
    theOutput.setFont(theFont);
    theOutput.setEditable(false);
    theInput.addActionListener(this);
}

public void actionPerformed(ActionEvent theEvent)
{
    String s = theInput.getText( );
    double d = evaluateExpression(s);
    theOutput.setText("" + d);
}

public double evaluateExpression(String s)
{
    Stack stack = new Stack( );
    StringTokenizer tokenizer = new StringTokenizer(s);
    String token;
    Double d;
    double d1, d2;
    while (tokenizer.hasMoreTokens( ))
    {
        token = tokenizer.nextToken( );
        char c = token.charAt(0);
        switch (c)
        {
            case '+':
                d1 = ((Double) ⇐
                  stack.pop( )).doubleValue( );
                d2 = ((Double) ⇐
                  stack.pop( )).doubleValue( );
                stack.push(new Double(d2 + d1));
                break;

            case '-':
                d1 = ((Double) ⇐
                  stack.pop( )).doubleValue( );
                d2 = ((Double) ⇐
                  stack.pop( )).doubleValue( );
                stack.push(new Double(d2 - d1));
                break;
```

```
        case '*':
            d1 = ((Double) ⇐
              stack.pop( )).doubleValue( );
            d2 = ((Double) ⇐
              stack.pop( )).doubleValue( );
            stack.push(new Double(d2 * d1));
            break;

        case '/':
            d1 = ((Double) ⇐
              stack.pop( )).doubleValue( );
            d2 = ((Double) ⇐
              stack.pop( )).doubleValue( );
            stack.push(new Double(d2 / d1));
            break;

        default:
            stack.push(new Double(token));
        }
    }
    d = (Double) stack.pop( );
    return d.doubleValue( );
    }
}
```

Listing 15-9 RPN.html

```
<HTML>
<HEAD>
<TITLE>RPN.java</TITLE>
</HEAD>
<BODY>
<H1>A Reverse Polish Notation (RPN) Expression Evaluator</H1>
<HR>
<APPLET CODE=RPN HEIGHT=200 WIDTH=300 ALIGN=RIGHT>
</APPLET>
<H2>Examples
<UL>
<LI> Infix Notation
</H2>
<OL>
<LI> 2 + 2
<LI> ( 2 + 3 ) * 4
</OL>
<H2>
<LI> Postfix Notation
</H2>
<OL>
<LI> 2 2 +
<LI> 2 3 + 4 *
</OL>
</UL>
</BODY>
</HTML>
```

FIGURE 15-9
The RPN applet

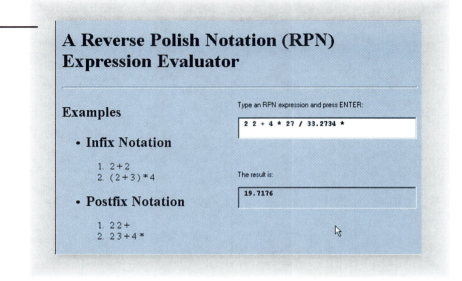

MediaTracker

Another useful member of `java.util` is `MediaTracker`, which is an important class for dealing with images. Images can be time-consuming to load, especially over a network connection. To best see why `MediaTracker` is necessary, run the applet `NoTracker`, shown in Listings 15-10 and 15-11. It's the dynamic behavior of the applet that's at issue here, so no figure can do justice to the effect. Take time now to perform this experiment.

What did you find? Unless your computer is speedier than any known Java platform at the time of writing, the applet suffered from serious flicker. While the image was loading, it was being continually redrawn on the screen and was unsteady as a result. To the user, the effect is both unpleasant and disorienting.

The applet's `paint()` method draws the same image, taken from a GIF file, at four overlapping positions on the screen. The problem occurs because it takes longer to load an image than to paint it. When an applet is told to draw an image, it attempts to do so even if the image has not been completely loaded. The `if` statement in the `paint()` method checks the value returned by `drawImage()`, which tells whether the complete image was completely loaded and therefore completely drawn. When `false` is returned, indicating the image is still incomplete, `repaint()` is called. This way, the entire image will eventually get painted; however, many partial images are also painted, resulting in flicker.

Listing 15-10 NoTracker.java

```java
import java.applet.*;
import java.awt.*;

public class NoTracker extends Applet
{
    Image theImage;

    public void init( )
    {
        theImage = getImage(getDocumentBase( ), "Jumbo.gif");
    }

    public void update(Graphics g)
    {
        paint(g);
    }

    public void paint(Graphics g)
    {
        g.drawImage(theImage,    0,    0, null);
        g.drawImage(theImage,   50,   50, null);
        g.drawImage(theImage,  100,  100, null);
        if (!g.drawImage(theImage,  150,  150, null))
            repaint( );
    }
}
```

Listing 15-11 NoTracker.html

```html
<HTML>
<HEAD>
<TITLE>NoTracker.java</TITLE>
</HEAD>
<BODY>
<H1>Loading Without MediaTracker</H1>
<HR>
<APPLET CODE=NoTracker WIDTH=500 HEIGHT=300>
</APPLET>
</BODY>
</HTML>
```

The Tracker applet, shown in Listings 15-12 and 15-13, shows how to avoid upsetting the user. With the assistance of the MediaTracker class, the output of the Tracker applet is almost as steady as that shown in Figure 15-10.

Listing 15-12 Tracker.java

```java
import java.applet.*;
import java.awt.*;

public class Tracker extends Applet
{
    final static int IMAGE_ID = 1234;
    Image theImage;
    MediaTracker theTracker = new MediaTracker(this);
```

continued on next page

continued from previous page

```
    public void init( )
    {
        theImage = getImage(getDocumentBase(), "Jumbo.gif");
        theTracker.addImage(theImage, IMAGE_ID);
    }

    public void update(Graphics g)
    {
        paint(g);
    }

    public void paint(Graphics g)
    {
        if (theTracker.checkID(IMAGE_ID, true))
        {
            g.drawImage(theImage,   0,   0, null);
            g.drawImage(theImage,  50,  50, null);
            g.drawImage(theImage, 100, 100, null);
            if (!g.drawImage(theImage, 150, 150, null))
                repaint();
        }
        else
        {
            g.drawString(⇐
              "Loading image: please be patient.", 20, 20);
            repaint( );
        }
    }
}
```

Listing 15-13 Tracker.html

```
<HTML>
<HEAD>
<TITLE>Tracker.java</TITLE>
</HEAD>
<BODY>
<H1>Loading with MediaTracker</H1>
<HR>
<APPLET CODE=Tracker WIDTH=500 HEIGHT=300>
</APPLET>
</BODY>
</HTML>
```

A `MediaTracker` is created by use of a constructor that takes, as its lone argument, a reference to the `Component` that intends to paint an image. In the `Tracker` applet, the `MediaTracker` is created by the line

```
MediaTracker theTracker = new MediaTracker(this);
```

which uses `this` to provide the `MediaTracker` with a reference to the applet itself. To use the `MediaTracker`, it must be instructed to track a particular image (or images) of interest:

```
theTracker.addImage(theImage, IMAGE_ID);
```

FIGURE 15-10
The Tracker applet

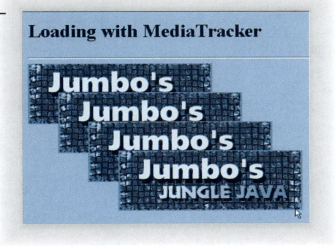

This line registers the image with the MediaTracker and assigns it an ID so that future method calls can easily reference it. Here, the field named ID is simply a static final int, which has been given the less-than-imaginative value of 1234.

The real work of the MediaTracker is done inside the paint() method. There the checkID() method is used to determine whether the image has been fully loaded. Only if this is the case does the applet execute the statements containing the drawImage() method calls. If the image has not been completely loaded, an informative message is drawn on the surface of the applet.

The result of using MediaTracker is a flicker-free, stable image. Moreover, the Tracker applet actually seems to draw its image more quickly than did the NoTracker applet. This is partly the result of certain quirks of human perception and partly the result of performing fewer repaints, since the applet doesn't struggle again and again to repaint what turns out to be only an incomplete image.

Both NoTracker and Tracker, as you may have noticed, provided overriding implementations of the update() method. The default implementation of this method would have used fillRect() to repaint the entire applet surface in its background color every time the surface was painted. Because there's no stale output to be blanked, the overriding update() simply calls paint(). By eliminating the unnecessary fillRect(), flicker is further minimized. This strategy is a good one for simple applets like Tracker, but if an applet includes animation, matters are more complex. In that case, the "old" position of a moving object *does* need to be repainted with the background color. A common solution is to keep track of the old positions of each animated object and repaint only those areas of the surface, rather than blanking it entirely.

The `MediaTracker` class includes many useful methods, summarized in Table 15-10. Several `static` constants used with methods that return status information are shown in Table 15-11.

TABLE 15-10
KEY `public` METHODS OF THE `MediaTracker` CLASS

METHOD HEADER	FUNCTION
`void addImage(Image image, int id)`	Specify an image to be tracked and the ID used to track it.
`void addImage(Image image, int id, int w, int h)`	Specify an image to be tracked and the ID used to track it, along with the width and height to which the image should be scaled for rendering.
`boolean checkAll( )`	Determine whether all tracked images have been loaded.
`boolean checkAll(boolean load)`	Determine whether all tracked images have been loaded. If `load` is `true`, initiate image loading if not previously done.
`boolean checkID(int id, boolean load)`	Determine whether all images tracked under the specified ID have been loaded. If `load` is `true`, initiate image loading if not previously done.
`Object[] getErrorsAny( )`	Get an array of images that have encountered an error.
`Object[] getErrorsID(int id)`	Get an array of images tracked under the specified ID that have encountered an error.
`boolean isErrorAny( )`	Determine whether any tracked images have encountered an error.
`boolean isErrorID(int id)`	Determine whether any images tracked under the specified ID have encountered an error.
`int statusAll(boolean load)`	Determine the combined status (a bitwise OR) of all tracked images.
`int statusID(int id, boolean load)`	Determine the combined status (a bitwise OR) of all images tracked under the specified ID.
`void waitForAll( )`	Wait for all images to be loaded (throw `InterruptedException`).
`boolean waitForAll(long ms)`	Wait for all images to be loaded, not to exceed the specified interval (throw `InterruptedException`).
`void waitForID(int id)`	Wait for all images tracked under the specified ID to be loaded (throw `InterruptedException`).
`boolean waitForID(int id, long ms)`	Wait for all images tracked under the specified ID to be loaded, not to exceed the specified interval (throw `InterruptedException`).

TABLE 15-11
KEY `public` CONSTANTS OF THE `MediaTracker` CLASS

FIELD NAME	SIGNIFICANCE
ABORTED	The image-loading process was aborted.
COMPLETE	The image-loading process completed successfully.
ERRORED	The image-loading process encountered an error.
LOADING	The image-loading process is in progress.

Linked Lists

As you're seeing, the `java.util` package provides many useful data structures. However, its repertoire is by no means complete. One useful data structure not provided by `java.util` is the *linked list*. Linked lists are workhorses of the data structure family, because many other data structures can be mimicked by the very versatile linked list. And the linked list can do a few things that members of `java.util` cannot. Figure 15-11 shows a linked list. As you can see, each element of a linked list has two parts: the data stored in the element, and a reference to the following element of the list.

Linked lists are useful primarily because they allow rapid insertion (and deletion) without the need to move many elements to make room for a new one (or fill in a hole) as in an array. Although this rapid insertion-deletion capability is of great value when you are dealing with sorted data, both lists and arrays can contain data in either sorted or unsorted order.

Even linked lists are not without their drawbacks, however. It can be time-consuming to locate an element located near the end of a linked list, because access to the elements of the list is strictly serial, just like access to the tracks recorded on a cassette tape. Moreover, linked lists lack the very handy "fast forward" button found on most cassette players. If you truly want to "visit" every element of the linked list, serial

FIGURE 15-11
A linked list

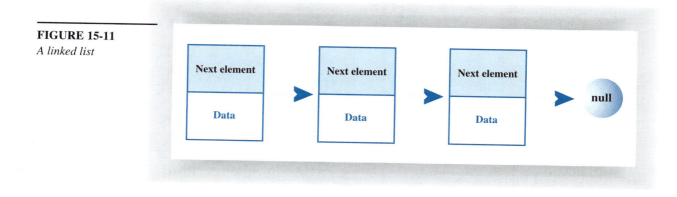

access is not a drawback; but if you simply want to access that one favorite element somewhere near the end of the list, you may have to "listen" to more than your quota of binary "blues."

Figure 15-12 shows how data is inserted into, and deleted from, a linked list. Writing methods to handle these operations is tricky because of several situations that require special handling—for example, deleting the last remaining item of a linked list.

Listings 15-14 and 15-15 show the LinkedLetters applet, which uses a linked list to store an alphabetized series of Strings. The applet allows the user to insert new Strings and delete specified Strings from the linked list. Figure 15-13 shows the output of the LinkedLetters applet.

FIGURE 15-12

Linked-list operations

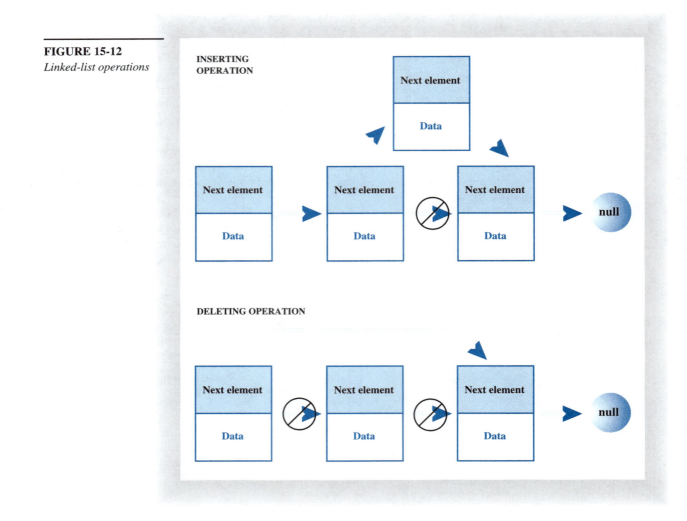

Apart from the `LinkedLetters` class itself, the applet includes two helper classes: one that represents a linked list (`LinkedList`) and one that represents an individual element of a linked list (`ListElement`). The `LinkedList` class provides three `public` methods:

☕ `addElement( )`, which is used to add a new element to the linked list

☕ `removeElement( )`, which is used to delete an element from the linked list

☕ `toString( )`, which returns a `String` representation of the contents of the linked list

As cautioned, the logic of the `addElement( )` and `removeElement( )` methods is complex and not for the faint of heart. However, if you're courageous, you should be able to verify that they work properly. Drawing diagrams like those shown in Figure 15-12 helps immensely.

Figure 15-14 shows the output of a more sophisticated application of linked lists. The `AddressList` applet, included on the CD-ROM, uses a linked list to store names and contact information. The source code from this applet is considerably more complex than that of the `LinkedLetters` applet, but a careful study can teach you much about how to program using linked lists. The applet uses a special form of linked list called a *double-ended* linked list that makes insertion of a new element at the end of the list much faster than in a regular linked list.

Listing 15-14 LinkedLetters.java

```java
import java.applet.*;
import java.awt.*;
import java.awt.event.*;
import java.util.NoSuchElementException;

public class LinkedLetters extends Applet ⇐
                          implements ActionListener
{
    LinkedList theList        = new LinkedList( );

    Panel       theButtonPanel = new Panel( );

    TextField   theInput = new TextField("", 16);

    TextArea    theOutput = new TextArea("", 1, 16);

    Button      addButton = new Button("Add");
    Button      delButton = new Button("Delete");
    Button      endButton = new Button("Quit");

    public void init()
    {
        setLayout(new BorderLayout( ));
        add(theInput, "North");
        add(theOutput, "Center");
        add(theButtonPanel, "South");
```

continued on next page

continued from previous page

```
                theButtonPanel.setLayout(new GridLayout(1, 3));
                theButtonPanel.add(addButton);
                theButtonPanel.add(delButton);
                theButtonPanel.add(endButton);

                addButton.addActionListener(this);
                delButton.addActionListener(this);
                endButton.addActionListener(this);

                theInput.requestFocus( );
        }

        public void actionPerformed(ActionEvent theEvent)
        {
            if (theEvent.getSource( ) == addButton)
            {   theList.addElement(theInput.getText( ));
                theInput.setText("");
                theInput.requestFocus( );
                theOutput.append(theList.toString( ) + "\n");
            }

            else if (theEvent.getSource() == delButton)
            {
                theList.removeElement(theInput.getText( ));
                theInput.setText("");
                theInput.requestFocus( );
                theOutput.append(theList.toString( ) + "\n");
            }

            else if (theEvent.getSource( ) == endButton)
            {
                System.out.println(theList);
                stop();
            }
        }
    }

    class LinkedList
    {
        private ListElement theHead = null;

        public void addElement(String data)
        {
            ListElement p = theHead;
            if (p == null)
            {
                theHead = new ListElement(data, null);
            }
            else
            {
                if (p.theLink == null || ⇐
                    p.theLink.theData.compareTo(data) > 0)
                {
                    if (p.theData.compareTo(data) > 0)
                    {
                        theHead = new ListElement(data, ⇐
                            theHead);
                    }
                    else
```

```
                                {
                                    theHead.theLink = new ListElement(data,⇐
                                        p.theLink);
                                }
                        }
                        else
                        {
                            while (p.theLink != null &&
                                p.theLink.theData.compareTo(data) < 0)
                            {
                                p = p.theLink;
                            }
                            p.theLink = new ListElement(data, ⇐
                                p.theLink);
                        }
                }
        }

        public void removeElement(String data)
        {
            ListElement p = theHead;
            if (p != null)
            {
                    if (p.theData.compareTo(data) == 0)
                    {
                        theHead = theHead.theLink;
                    }
                    else
                    {
                        while (p.theLink != null)
                        {
                            if (p.theLink.theData.compareTo(data) ⇐
                                == 0)
                            {
                                p.theLink = p.theLink.theLink;
                                break;
                            }
                            p = p.theLink;
                        }
                    }
            }
        }

        public String toString()
        {
            String s = "LinkedList=[";

            ListElement p = theHead;
            while (p != null)
            {
                s += p.theData.toString();
                p = p.theLink;
                if (p != null)
                {
                    s += ", ";
                }
            }
```

continued on next page

continued from previous page

```
                return s + "]";
        }
}

class ListElement
{
    public String        theData;
    public ListElement theLink;

    public ListElement(String data, ListElement link)
    {
        theData = data;
        theLink = link;
    }
}
```

> *"Linked lists are workhorses of the data structure family, because they can easily mimic many other common data structures."*

Listing 15-15 LinkedLetters.html

```
<HTML>
<HEAD>
<TITLE>LinkedLetters.html</TITLE>
</HEAD>
<BODY>
<H1>Linked Letters<BR>
How a Linked List Works</H1>
<HR>
<APPLET CODE=LinkedLetters HEIGHT=300 WIDTH=400>
</APPLET>
</BODY>
</HTML>
```

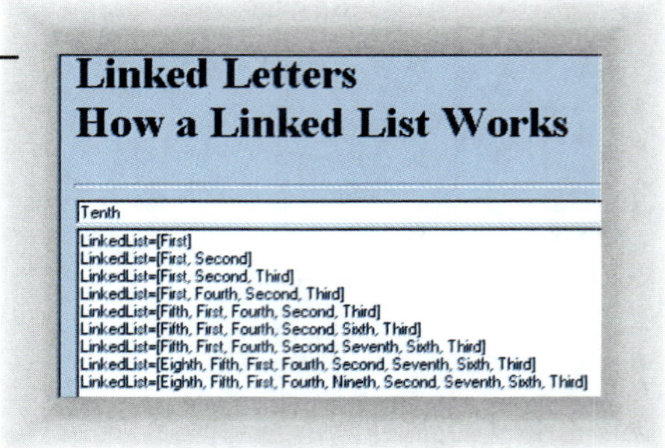

FIGURE 15-13
Output of the
LinkedLetters
applet

FIGURE 15-14
Output of the
AddressList applet

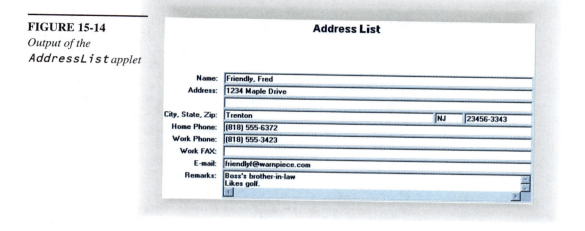

Keeping Watch: Observables and Observers

In most offices there are memos, notices, and even an office grapevine to keep people informed. But how does a community of objects keep its members up-to-date on all that's happening?

The java.util package provides a class and an interface that together address this problem. This pair is used within MediaTracker to provide its up-to-the-nanosecond information on the loading of images. The class is Observable and the related interface is Observer. The Observable class maintains a list of "interested parties" and is capable of alerting them when something important has occurred. Objects of classes that implement the Observer interface can register their interest in an Observable object by sending it the addObserver( ) message, which causes it to add them to its list. The Observer interface consists of a lone method, update( ), which is then used by the Observable to notify each registered object of important events.

CREATING AND USING ObservableS

The Observable class has a single, no-argument constructor, Observable( ). Its public methods are summarized in Table 15-12. Table 15-13 describes two protected methods of the class that are commonly used by Observable objects and objects of classes that extend the Observable class. The Observer interface looks like this:

```
public abstract interface Observer
{
    public abstract void update(Observable ob, Object arg);
}
```

Classes that want their instances to function as Observers need only declare that they implement the Observer interface and provide a suitable implementation of the update( ) method, which contains application-dependent code. The first argument of the method serves to identify the source of notification, since an Observer is free to participate in many Observer–Observable relationships. The second provides the Observer with information sent by the Observable. Its type is Object, so that any sort of data can be sent by the Observable and received by the Observer.

Observer objects invoke the addObserver( ) method on the Observable object, enabling the Observable object to maintain its list of interested parties. They then simply wait for the Observable to invoke their update( ) method and respond appropriately.

Observable objects usually extend the Observable class to add application-dependent behavior. The parent Observable class provides the important mechanisms for keeping track of interested Observers and notifying them of changes, by means of the notifyObservers( ) method.

TABLE 15-12
KEY `public` METHODS OF THE `Observable` CLASS

METHOD HEADER	FUNCTION
void addObserver(Observer o)	Add an Observer to the list.
int countObservers( )	Get the number of Observers on the list.
void deleteObserver(Observer o)	Delete the specified Observer from the list.
void deleteObservers( )	Delete every Observer from the list.
boolean hasChanged( )	Determine if the "changed" flag is set.
void notifyObservers( )	Notify all Observers of a change.
void notifyObservers(Object arg)	Notify all Observers of a change, providing them with the specified argument.

TABLE 15-13
KEY `protected` METHODS OF THE `Observable` CLASS

METHOD HEADER	FUNCTION
void clearChanged( )	Clear the "changed" flag.
void setChanged( )	Set the "changed" flag.

AN `Observer` **EXAMPLE**

Listings 15-16 and 15-17 show the `BattleStar` applet, which demonstrates the use of the `Observable` and `Observer` classes. The applet simulates the plight of a number of spaceships that have become separated from their mother ship, which is searching for them. Periodically, the mother ship emits a beacon that broadcasts its location to the spaceships. However, only about half of the spaceships are equipped with the equipment needed to receive the beacon.

The structure of the applet is simple. It consists of a top-level class (`BattleStar`) and two helper classes. One helper class, `MomShip`, represents the mother ship. This class extends the `Observable` class, giving it the capability to update `Observers` with the current position of the mother ship. The other helper class, `Ship`, represents the missing spaceships. The `Ship` class implements the `Observer` interface so that ships can home in on the mother ship's beacon. Those with the proper equipment will be quickly rescued, but the remaining ships are at peril.

To reflect the fact that some ships lack the proper equipment to receive the beacon, about half the ships omit the invocation of the `addObserver()` method that's needed to establish the `Observer`–`Observable` relationship; thus, they are unable to receive updates from the `MomShip`. These ships are red; the ships that have the receiving equipment are green.

The mother ship lacks sufficient power to broadcast the beacon continuously, so an integer variable `theClock` is used to count execution cycles and turn the beacon on and off at specified intervals. When the beacon is on, the image of the mother ship is blue; when it is off, the image is gray.

To minimize flicker as the images are drawn, the `update()` method draws them into a separate ("offscreen") `Graphics` object. Only when the image is complete does the method draw the entire image, with a single call to `drawImage()`. These technique is commonly referred to as *double buffering*.

By changing the `static final` constants, you can adjust the operation of the applet to suit your taste. You can have more or fewer ships, faster or slower ships, and random or steady movement. The latter is determined by the ratio of `MAX_DV` to `MAX_V`: A higher ratio allows the instant change in velocity (`MAX_DV`) to be larger in comparison to the current velocity (`MAX_V`). This causes motion of the ships to appear more erratic.

Another feature of the applet is that clicking the mouse on the applet surface causes the mother ship to move to the location of the click. You can make a game of this, either assisting the mother ship to rescue its offspring or thwarting the rescue. Figure 15-15 shows typical output of the program.

Listing 15–16 BattleStar.java

```java
// A Space Rescue applet
import java.applet.*;
import java.awt.*;
import java.awt.event.*;
import java.util.Observer;
import java.util.Observable;
```

continued on next page

continued from previous page

```java
public class BattleStar extends Applet ⇐
                        implements Runnable, MouseListener
{
    static final int SHIPS = 4;
    static final int NAPTIME = 100;

    Thread      theThread;
    MomShip     theMomShip;
    Ship[]      theShip             = new Ship[SHIPS];
    Dimension   bufferSize;
    Image       theBuffer;
    Graphics    bufferGraphics;

    public void init( )
    {
        theMomShip = new MomShip(getSize( ).width, ⇐
                                 getSize( ).height);

        for (int i = 0; i < SHIPS; i++)
        {
            theShip[i] = new Ship(theMomShip, ⇐
                                  getSize( ).width, ⇐
                                  getSize( ).height);
        }
        addMouseListener(this);
        setBackground(Color.gray);
    }

    public void start( )
    {
        if (theThread == null)
        {
            theThread = new Thread(this);
        }
        theThread.start( );
    }

    public void stop( )
    {
        if (theThread != null && theThread.isAlive( ))
        {
            theThread.stop( );
        }
        theThread = null;
    }

    public void run( )
    {
        while (true)
        {
            step( );
            try
            {
                Thread.sleep(NAPTIME);
            }
            catch (InterruptedException e)
            {
                // null statement
            }
```

```
        }
    }

    public void step( )
    {
        for (int i = 0; i < SHIPS; i++)
        {
            theShip[i].updatePosition( ⇐
                theMomShip.getPosition( ),
                getSize().width, getSize( ).height);
        }
        theMomShip.updatePosition( ⇐
            getSize( ).width, getSize( ).height);

        repaint( );
    }

    public void mouseClicked (MouseEvent theEvent)
    {
        theMomShip.moveTo(theEvent.getX( ), ⇐
            theEvent.getY( ));
    }

    public void mouseEntered (MouseEvent theEvent) { }
    public void mouseExited  (MouseEvent theEvent) { }
    public void mousePressed (MouseEvent theEvent) { }
    public void mouseReleased(MouseEvent theEvent) { }

    public final synchronized void update(Graphics g)
    {
        if (bufferSize == null
            || bufferSize.width  != getSize( ).width
            || bufferSize.height != getSize( ).height)
        {
            bufferSize = getSize( );
            theBuffer = createImage(bufferSize.width, ⇐
                                    bufferSize.height);
            bufferGraphics = theBuffer.getGraphics( );
        }
        paint(bufferGraphics);
        g.drawImage(theBuffer, 0, 0, null);
    }

    public void paint(Graphics g)
    {
        g.setColor(getBackground( ));
        g.fillRect(0, 0, getSize( ).width, getSize( ).height);
        for (int i = 0; i < SHIPS; i++)
        {
            theShip[i].paint(g);
        }
        theMomShip.paint(g);
    }
}
```

How does a community of objects keep its members up-to-date on all that's happening? The Observer-Observable pair can help.

continued on next page

continued from previous page

```
class Ship implements Observer
{
    static int theNumShips = 0;

    static int MAX_V  = 15;
    static int MAX_DV =  5;

    int    theX;
    int    theY;

    int    theDX;
    int    theDY;

    int    theShipType;

    int    theRadius = 20;
    Color  theColor;

    boolean isDocked = false;

    public Ship(MomShip mom, int width, int height)
    {
        theX = (int) (width  * Math.random( ));
        theY = (int) (width  * Math.random( ));
        theShipType = ++theNumShips % 2;
        if (theShipType == 0)
        {
            theColor = Color.green;
            mom.addObserver(this);
        }
        else
        {
            theColor = Color.red;
        }
    }

    public void paint(Graphics g)
    {
        if (!isDocked)
        {
            g.setColor(theColor);
            g.fillArc(
              (int) (theX - theRadius),
              (int) (theY - theRadius),
              (int) theRadius,
              (int) theRadius,
              0,
              360);
        }
    }

    public void updatePosition(Point momsPoint, int w, int h)
    {
        int dx = momsPoint.x - theX;
        int dy = momsPoint.y - theY;

        if ((Math.abs(dx) < 2 * theRadius) &&
            (Math.abs(dy) < 2 * theRadius))
```

```
            {
                isDocked = true;
            }

            theDX    = (int) (theDX + 2.0 * MAX_DV ⇐
                * Math.random( ) - MAX_DV);
            theDX    = theDX > MAX_V ? MAX_V : theDX;

            theDY    = (int) (theDY + 2.0 * MAX_DV ⇐
                * Math.random( ) - MAX_DV);
            theDY    = theDY > MAX_V ? MAX_V : theDY;

            theX = theX + theDX;
            theY = theY + theDY;

            if (theX - theRadius < 0)
            {
                theX = theRadius;
                theDX = (int) (1.5 * Math.abs(theDX));
            }

            if (theX + theRadius > w)
            {
                theX = w - theRadius;
                theDX = (int) (-1.5 * Math.abs(theDX));
            }

            if (theY - theRadius < 0)
            {
                theY = theRadius;
                theDY = (int) (1.5 * Math.abs(theDY));
            }

            if (theY + theRadius > h)
            {
                theY = h - theRadius;
                theDY = (int) (-1.5 * Math.abs(theDY));
            }
        }

    public void update(Observable observable, Object arg)
        {
            Point p = (Point) arg;

            int dx = p.x - theX;
            int dy = p.y - theY;

            theDX = theDX + dx;
            theDX = theDX > MAX_V ? MAX_V : theDX;

            theDY = theDY + dy;
            theDY = theDY > MAX_V ? MAX_V : theDY;
        }
    }

class MomShip extends Observable
{
    static int MAX_V  =  4;
    static int MAX_DV =  2;
```

continued on next page

continued from previous page

```java
int    theX;
int    theY;

int    theDX;
int    theDY;

int    theRadius = 50;

boolean isTransmitting = false;

int      theTransmitTime =   20;
int      theWaitTime     = 100;
int      theClock        =   50;

public MomShip(int width, int height)
{
    theX = (int) (width  * Math.random( ));
    theY = (int) (width  * Math.random( ));
}

public void paint(Graphics g)
{
    if (isTransmitting)
    {
        g.setColor(Color.blue);
    }
    else
    {
        g.setColor(Color.lightGray);
    }
    g.fillArc(
      (int) (theX - theRadius),
      (int) (theY - theRadius),
      (int) theRadius,
      (int) theRadius,
      0,
      360);
}

public void updatePosition(int w, int h)
{
    theDX    = (int) (theDX + 2.0 * MAX_DV ⇐
      * Math.random( ) - MAX_DV);
    theDX    = theDX > MAX_V ? MAX_V : theDX;

    theDY    = (int) (theDY + 2.0 * MAX_DV ⇐
      * Math.random( ) - MAX_DV);
    theDY    = theDY > MAX_V ? MAX_V : theDY;

    theX = theX + theDX;
    theY = theY + theDY;

    if (theX - theRadius < 0)
    {
        theX = theRadius;
        theDX = Math.abs(theDX);
    }

    if (theX + theRadius > w)
    {
```

```
            theX = w - theRadius;
            theDX = -1 * Math.abs(theDX);
        }

        if (theY - theRadius < 0)
        {
            theY = theRadius;
            theDY = Math.abs(theDY);
        }

        if (theY + theRadius > h)
        {
            theY = h - theRadius;
            theDY = -1 * Math.abs(theDY);
        }

        if (isTransmitting)
        {
            setChanged( );
            notifyObservers(getPosition( ));
        }

        theClock--;
        if (theClock <= 0)
        {
            if (isTransmitting)
            {
                isTransmitting = false;
                theClock = theWaitTime;
            }
            else
            {
                isTransmitting = true;
                theClock = theTransmitTime;
            }
        }
    }

    public void moveTo(int x, int y)
    {
        theX = x;
        theY = y;
    }

    public Point getPosition( )
    {
        return new Point(theX, theY);
    }

}
```

Listing 15-17 BattleStar.html

```
<HTML>
<HEAD>
<TITLE>The BattleStar Applet</TITLE>
<HEAD>
```

continued on next page

continued from previous page

```
<BODY>
<APPLET CODE=BattleStar WIDTH=600 HEIGHT=400>
</APPLET>
</BODY>
</HTML>
```

> " *Java's BitSet class was designed to provide a dynamically resizable compact structure for storing individual bits.* "

Two Bits and More: When You Need a Set of Bits

Although the smallest unit of data is the bit, most programs work mainly with bytes or even larger units of data. While `boolean` variables appear here and there, they certainly aren't the data type you encounter most frequently. On occasion, however, you may find yourself in a situation where you need a large number of `boolean` variables. You might try creating arrays of `boolean`s, but if you did, your program would perform quite poorly. The way that `boolean`s are stored (in most languages, not just Java) is really quite inefficient. Storing a large number of `boolean`s can quickly exhaust your system's available memory.

FIGURE 15-15
Output of the
BattleStar *applet*

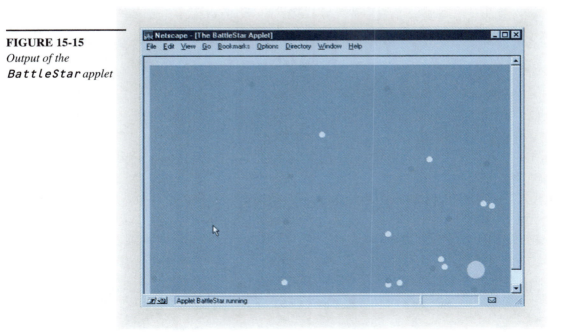

PERFORMING BITWISE OPERATIONS ON INTEGERS

One possible solution may occur to you when you recall that *all* Java's data types are stored as binary numbers. If there was some way to manipulate the individual bits within, say, an `int`, you could create an array of `int`s and escape the undesirable overhead involved with an array of `boolean`s.

The Bitwise Operators

Java provides several operators, summarized in Table 15-14, that serve precisely this function. The operators are called *bitwise* operators because they operate on all the bits of their operands "in parallel." For example, the operation of the bitwise AND operator is shown in Figure 15-16. Note how each of the 32 bits of the first operand is separately ANDed with the corresponding bit of the second operand to yield a 32-bit result.

TABLE 15-14
THE BITWISE OPERATORS

OPERATOR	MEANING
~	Bitwise complement
<<	Left shift
>>	Right shift (signed)
>>>	Right shift (unsigned)
&	Bitwise AND: result bit is set only if the corresponding bit is set in both operands
|	Bitwise OR: result bit is set if the corresponding bit is set in either operand or both operands
^	Bitwise XOR: result bit is set if the corresponding bit is set in exactly one operand

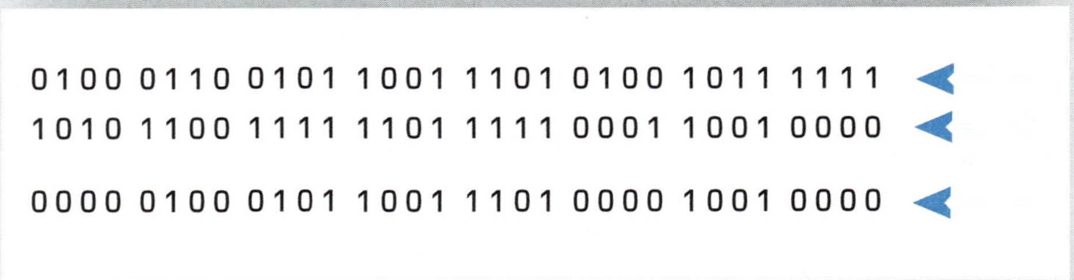

FIGURE 15-16

Operation of the bitwise AND

```
0100 0110 0101 1001 1101 0100 1011 1111  ◄

1010 1100 1111 1101 1111 0001 1001 0000  ◄


0000 0100 0101 1001 1101 0000 1001 0000  ◄
```

Because certain bitwise operators perform similar functions to those of corresponding logical operators (`&&`, `||`, and `!`), you may tend to confuse them. The distinction is this: *Bitwise* operators are used with integer operands and produce an integer result; *logical* operators are used with boolean operands and yield a boolean value as a result. You can also use the bitwise operators, `&` and `|`, on boolean operands. When used in this manner, they act like the logical operators, except that they always evaluate every part of the expression—there is no short-circuit evaluation of bitwise operations.

Testing and Setting Bits

The bitwise operators can be used to test or set individual bits within an integer. For example, the following code fragment

```
int n = theValue; // some value
if ((n & 4) != 0) // Bit 2 is "on": perform some action
```

tests whether bit 2 (bits are numbered from the right, starting with 0, as shown in Figure 15-17) is "on." If bit 2 (corresponding to 22) were the only bit set, then the value of the number would be 4. This value 4 in the test expression is commonly referred to as a *mask,* because the result of the `&` operation will include only those bits of the variable n that correspond to "on" bits in the mask. Figure 15-18 shows how this works.

Setting the value of an individual bit within an integer is done as follows:

```
int n = theValue; // some value
n = n | 2;        // Set "on" bit 2
```

Here the bitwise OR is used so that the bits turned "on" in the mask cause each corresponding bit within the result to be turned on. Figure 15-19 shows how this works.

Shift Operators

Java also provides a trio of operators than can shift the bits of an integer to the left or right. The code fragment

```
int n = theValue; // some value
n = n << 4;
```

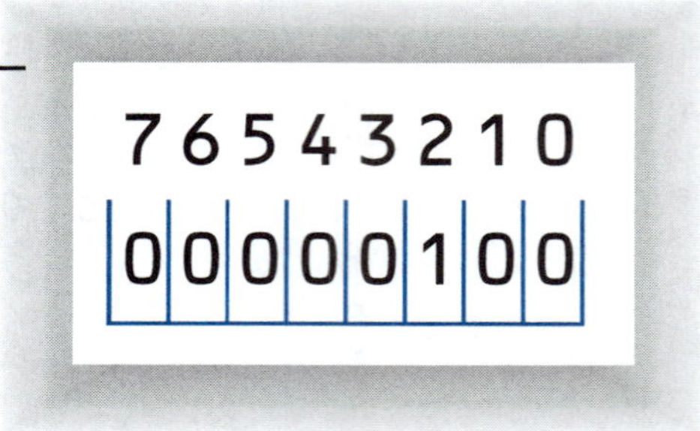

FIGURE 15-17
Numbering a bit

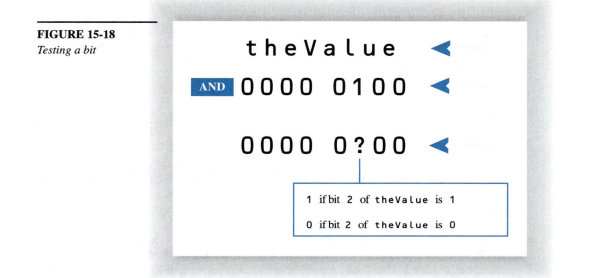

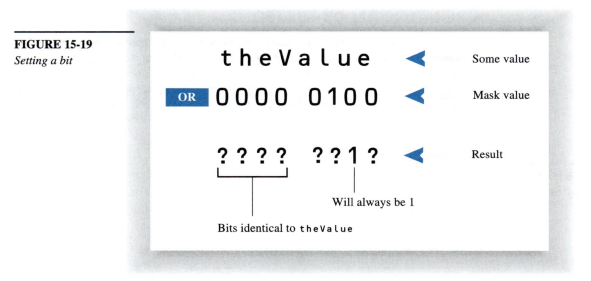

causes the bits of the integer n to be shifted four positions to the left. This is the same as multiplying n by 16 (2^4), but is much faster. Bits can also be shifted to the right, which provides rapid division:

```
int n = theValue; // some value
n = n >>> 2;
```

Here the unsigned right shift operator (>>>) is used to divide the value of n by 4 (2^2).

The unsigned right shift operator can produce some interesting results. When the bits of an integer are shifted, the vacated positions are filled with 0. Since the high-order bit of a positive integer is always 0, shifting the bits of a positive number to the right will not change the value of the high-order bit. It will be 0 both before and after the shift. However, this is not true in the case of a negative integer. The high-order bit of a negative number is always 1; shifting it to the right will bring a 0 into the vacated position, changing the *sign bit* of the integer.

To avoid this, you can use the signed right shift operator (>>). This operator obligingly notes the sign bit of its operand and replaces it with an identical bit each time the operand is shifted. Thus, the sign of the operator is preserved. Figure 15-20 illustrates how this works.

OPERATORS RECAPITULATED

You have finally met all of Java's many operators, quite an imposing assortment. This is therefore a good time to summarize them. Table 15-15 recapitulates the key properties of each operator including its precedence, operand types, associativity, and meaning. The operators in Group 1 have the highest precedence; these bind their operands most tightly and will be evaluated before operators of lower precedence.

FIGURE 15-20
Right-shifting an integer

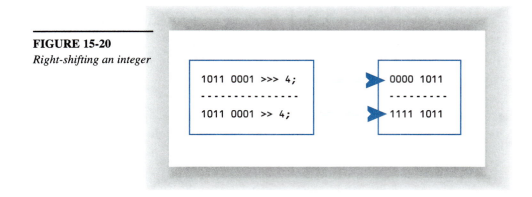

TABLE 15-15
COMPLETE TABLE OF JAVA'S OPERATORS

GROUP	OPERATOR	OPERAND TYPE(S)	ASSOC.	MEANING
1	`[ ]`	Any object, field, or	Right	Subscript
	`.`	method	Right	Membership
	`++`	Arithmetic	Right	Pre- or post-increment (unary)
	`--`	Arithmetic	Right	Pre- or post-decrement (unary)
2	`+, -`	Arithmetic	Right	Unary plus, unary minus
	`~`	Integer	Right	Bitwise complement (unary)
	`!`	Boolean	Right	Logical complement (unary)
3	`new`	Object	N/A	Object creation
	`(type)`	Any	Right	Type cast
4	`*, /, %`	Arithmetic	Left	Multiplication, division, modulus
5	`+, -`	Arithmetic	Left	Addition, subtraction
	`+`	String	Left	Concatenation
6	`<<`	Integer	Left	Left shift
	`>>`	Integer	Left	Right shift (signed)
	`>>>`	Integer	Left	Right shift (unsigned)
7	`<, <=`	Arithmetic	Left	Less than, less than or equal
	`>, >=`	Arithmetic	Left	Greater than, greater than or equal
	`instanceof`	Object, type	Left	Type comparison
8	`==`	Primitive	Left	Equal (same value)
	`!=`	Primitive	Left	Not equal (different value)
	`==`	Object	Left	Equal (same object)
	`!=`	Object	Left	Not equal (different object)
9	`&`	Integer	Left	Bitwise AND
	`&`	Boolean	Left	Boolean AND
10	`^`	Integer	Left	Bitwise XOR
	`^`	Boolean	Left	Boolean XOR

Table continued...

TABLE 15-15 COMPLETE TABLE OF JAVA'S OPERATORS CONTINUED…

GROUP	OPERATOR	OPERAND TYPE(S)	ASSOC.	MEANING
11	|	Integer	Left	Bitwise OR
	|	Boolean	Left	Boolean OR
12	&&	Boolean	Left	Logical AND
13	||	Boolean	Left	Logical OR
14	? :	Boolean, any, any	Right	Conditional operator (ternary)
15	=	Variable, any	Right	Assignment
	*=, /=, %=, +=, −=, <<=, >>=, >>>=, &=, ^=, |=	Variable, any	Right	Shorthand assignment

BUCKETS OF BITS: CREATING AND USING A
BitSet

By creating arrays of longs and manipulating their individual bits, it's possible to store large numbers of boolean values. However, you pay a price: The manipulations are rather cumbersome, requiring a combination of subscripts and bitwise operators to achieve. You might hope for something better. Java's `BitSet` class was designed to overcome this problem by providing a dynamically resizable, compact structure for storing individual bits.

The `BitSet` class has two constructors, as shown in Table 15-16. To construct a `BitSet` when you have no idea how many values you will be storing, you can use the default constructor:

```
BitSet theSet = new BitSet( );
```

If you *do* know how many values you'll need to store, or even if you have some rough idea, you can use the two-argument constructor, which supplies an initial size:

```
BitSet theBigSet = new BitSet( 10000 ); ⇐
// Store 1000 true/false values
```

This is considerably more efficient than requiring the `BitSet` to expand itself repeatedly.

Once you have a `BitSet` object in hand, you can use any of a number of methods for getting, setting, and clearing bits, as well as operating on `BitSet`s using AND, OR, and XOR. These methods are especially valuable—as is the `BitSet` class itself—when you are working with graphics and images. The key methods for the class are summarized in Table 15-17.

TABLE 15-16
KEY `public` CONSTRUCTORS OF THE `BitSet` CLASS

```
BitSet( )
BitSet(int numBits)
```

TABLE 15-17
KEY `public` METHODS OF THE `BitSet` CLASS

METHOD HEADER	FUNCTION
`void and(BitSet set)`	AND the `BitSet` with another.
`void clear(int bit)`	Clear the specified bit of the `BitSet`.
`boolean equals(Object obj)`	Determine whether the `BitSet` is the same as another.
`boolean get(int bit)`	Determine whether the specified bit is "on."
`void or(BitSet set)`	OR the `BitSet` with another.
`void set(int bit)`	Set the specified bit of the `BitSet`.
`int size( )`	Get the number of bits in the `BitSet`.
`void xor(BitSet set)`	Exclusive OR (XOR) the `BitSet` with another.

A `BitSet` EXAMPLE: INFINITE PRECISION ARITHMETIC

Listings 15-18 through 15-22 present the `BigNum` applet, which demonstrates how `BitSet`s can be used to handle storage and manipulation of a large number of boolean values. The `BigNum` applet performs addition and subtraction of 128-bit numbers, giving a precision beyond that of the primitive type `long`. Figure 15-21 shows the `BigNum` applet in operation. When you try it out, it's helpful to extend the applet to fill the entire width of your screen. Otherwise you may not see the entire 128-bit results. To perform its task, the `BigNum` applet uses two support classes, `HalfAdder` and `FullAdder`. Let's examine these two classes before explaining the applet itself.

Adding Two Binary Digits

Binary digits can have one of only two values, 0 or 1. When you add two binary digits, there are only three possible outcomes:

🐾 Both digits are 0, in which case the result is zero.

🐾 One digit is 0, and the other digit is 1, in which case the result is 1.

🐾 Both digits are 1. In this case the answer—the binary number 10—won't fit inside a binary digit, and so the result is a 0 with a carry, just like when you learned addition in grade school.

FIGURE 15-21

*The **BigNum** applet*

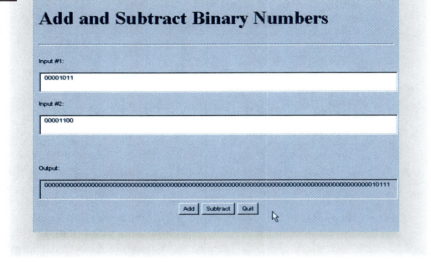

The HalfAdder class, shown in Listing 15-18, adds two binary digits, represented as booleans, yielding a sum and a carry. It is convenient to represent these single binary digits as booleans because the BitSet class uses the get(int) method to determine if a particular bit is set (that is, 1). Thus, b.get(10) would return true if the bit in the *11*th position was set (the positions are numbered relative to 0). For the purposes of the HalfAdder class, you can consider true equivalent to 1 and false equivalent to 0. The carry is needed when the inputs are both 1; in this case the single-bit sum should be 0, but a 1 should be carried forward into the higher-order position. The HalfAdder is used by calling its setInput( ) method, providing the binary digits to be added. The single-bit sum is then obtained by calling the getSum( ) method. The carry is obtained similarly, by calling the getCarry( ) method.

Figure 15-22 shows how HalfAdder works. You may find it helpful to build a truth table that proves that HalfAdder functions correctly. This is not difficult, because there are only four possible input values: Each of the two arguments must be either 0 or 1.

Listing 15-18 HalfAdder.java

```java
class HalfAdder
{
    boolean sum;
    boolean carry;

    public void setInput(boolean a, boolean b)
    {
        sum   = a ^ b;
        carry = a & b;
    }
}
```

```
    public boolean getSum( )
    {
        return sum;
    }

    public boolean getCarry( )
    {
        return carry;
    }
}
```

Considering the Carry

If all you needed to do was add single binary digits, the HalfAdder class would be sufficient. To add more than a single digit, however, you also have to take into account the carry generated by previous additions. That is where the second support class used by BigNum, the FullAdder class, comes into play.

This FullAdder class uses two HalfAdders to combine two incoming binary digits and a carry, yielding a binary digit that holds the sum, and a new carry value. The FullAdder class is shown in Listing 15-19, and Figure 15-23 illustrates its operation. Again, you may find it helpful to build a truth table proving the correct operation of the FullAdder. Its three binary arguments can assume a total of only eight values, so the table is not difficult to build.

Listing 15-19 FullAdder.java

```
public class FullAdder
{
    boolean sum;
    boolean carry_out;
    HalfAdder h1 = new HalfAdder( );
    HalfAdder h2 = new HalfAdder( );

    public void setInput(boolean a, boolean b, boolean carry)
    {
        h1.setInput(b, carry);
        h2.setInput(a, h1.getSum( ));
        sum = h2.getSum( );
        carry_out = h1.getCarry( ) | h2.getCarry( );
    }

    public boolean getSum( )
    {
        return sum;
    }

    public boolean getCarry( )
    {
        return carry_out;
    }
}
```

FIGURE 15-22

Operation of the
HalfAdder class

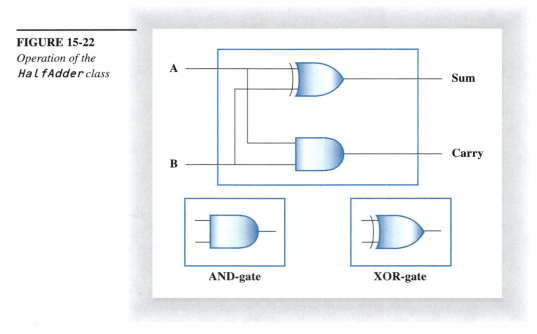

FIGURE 15-23

Operation of the
FullAdder class

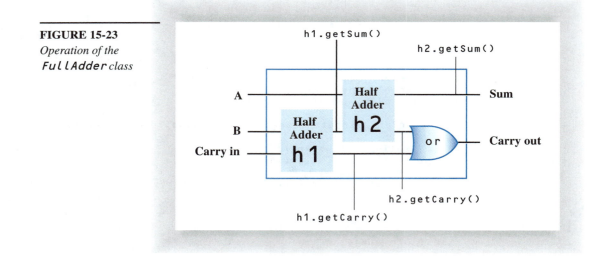

Building an Interface

Listing 15-20 shows the first part of the `BigNum` applet, including the user interface fields and methods. The applet has two input `TextFields` for getting the 128-bit values to be added or subtracted, and one output `TextField` for displaying the result.

Three buttons allow the user to add the input numbers, subtract the input numbers, or quit the applet. Within the `actionPerformed( )` method, the source of each `Event` is examined to determine which button was pressed. When the add or subtract button has been pressed, the contents of the input `TextFields` are obtained by use of the `TextField.getText( )` method. The `String` value returned by `getText( )` is converted to a `BitSet` by use of the `static` method `BigNum.toBitSet( )`. The `add( )` or `sub( )` method is called as appropriate, yielding a sum or difference `BitSet`, which is converted to a `String` by use of the `static` method `BigNum.toString( )`. The `String` is then displayed in the output `TextField` by means of the `TextField.setText( )` method.

Listing 15-20 BigNum.java (partial)

```java
import java.applet.*;
import java.awt.*;
import java.awt.event.*;
import java.util.*;

public class BigNum extends Applet implements ActionListener
{
    static final int BITS = 128;
    TextField    theFirstInput    = new TextField( );
    TextField    theSecondInput   = new TextField( );
    TextField    theOutput        = new TextField( );
    Panel        thePanel         = new Panel();
    Button       addButton        = new Button("Add");
    Button       subButton        = new Button("Subtract");
    Button       quitButton       = new Button("Quit");

    public void init( )
    {
        setLayout(new GridLayout(8, 1));
        setFont(new Font("Helvetica", Font.BOLD, 10));
        Font courier = new Font("Courier", Font.BOLD, 10);
        theFirstInput.setFont(courier);
        theSecondInput.setFont(courier);
        theOutput.setFont(courier);
        theOutput.setEditable(false);

        add(new Label("Input #1:"));
        add(theFirstInput);
        add(new Label("Input #2:"));
        add(theSecondInput);
        add(new Label(""));
        add(new Label("Output:"));
        add(theOutput);
        add(thePanel);
```

continued on next page

continued from previous page

```
            thePanel.setLayout(new FlowLayout( ));
            thePanel.add(addButton);
            thePanel.add(subButton);
            thePanel.add(quitButton);

            addButton.addActionListener(this);
            subButton.addActionListener(this);
            quitButton.addActionListener(this);
        }

        public void actionPerformed(ActionEvent theEvent)
        {
            Object theTarget = theEvent.getSource( );
            if (theTarget == addButton)
            {
                BitSet b1 = toBitSet(theFirstInput.getText( ));
                BitSet b2 = toBitSet(theSecondInput.getText( ));
                BitSet b3 = add(b1, b2);
                theOutput.setText(toString(b3));
            }
            else if (theTarget == subButton)
            {
                BitSet b1 = toBitSet(theFirstInput.getText( ));
                BitSet b2 = toBitSet(theSecondInput.getText( ));
                BitSet b3 = sub(b1, b2);
                theOutput.setText(toString(b3));
            }
            else if (theTarget == quitButton)
            {
                stop( );
                destroy( );
            }
        }
    }
```

BigNum Utility Methods

Listing 15-21 continues the BigNum applet, showing the static methods used to convert BitSets to Strings and vice versa. The toBitSet( ) method creates a new BitSet and then iterates character-by-character through its input String, setting bits within the BitSet whenever a character 1 is encountered. The BitSet is then returned.

The toString( ) method is necessary because the toString( ) method provided by the BitSet class simply lists the positions of bits that are "on." Its output format is not suitable for the purpose of BigNum. The static toString( ) method included in BigNum creates a new String and fills it with 0s and 1s according to the value of each bit within the BitSet. The resulting String is returned to the caller.

Listing 15-21 BigNum.java (continued)

```
public static BitSet toBitSet(String s)
    {
        int n = s.length( );
        BitSet b = new BitSet(BITS);
        int j = n - 1;
```

```
        for (int i = 0; i < n; i++)
        {
            if (s.charAt(j) == '1')
            {
                b.set(i);
            }
            j--;
        }
        return b;
    }

    public static String toString(BitSet b)
    {
        String s = "";
        for (int i = 0; i < b.size(); i++)
        {
            if (b.get(i))
            {
                s = '1' + s;
            }
            else
            {
                s = '0' + s;
            }
        }
        return s;
    }
```

Adding and Subtracting Big Numbers

Listing 15-22 is the final listing for the `BigNum` applet. It includes the `add()` and `sub()` methods called from within the `actionPerformed()` method. The `add()` method uses the `FullAdder` class to add each binary digit of its operands. Note how the value of `carry` is used to propagate a carry from one position to the next.

The `sub()` method is somewhat more complex, because there is no "FullSubber" or "HalfSubber" subtraction method to turn to within `BigNum`. Instead, `sub()` takes advantage of the fact that subtracting one number from another is the same as adding the twos-complement value of the number to the other number.

The `sub()` method computes the twos-complement by inverting each bit of its second argument and then adding 1. The complemented value is then added to the first argument. Their sum, which is really the difference of the original arguments, is returned.

Listing 15-22 BigNum.java (continued)

```
public static BitSet add(BitSet b1, BitSet b2)
    {
        int n = Math.max(b1.size(), b2.size());
        BitSet b = new BitSet(BITS);
        boolean sum;
        boolean carry = false;
        FullAdder f = new FullAdder();
```

continued on next page

continued from previous page

```
            for (int i = 0; i < n; i++)
            {
                f.setInput(b1.get(i), b2.get(i), carry);
                if(f.getSum( ))
                {
                    b.set(i);
                }
                carry = f.getCarry( );
            }
            return b;
        }

        public static BitSet sub(BitSet b1, BitSet b2)
        {
            // Invert the bits of b2
            int n = b1.size( );
            BitSet b = new BitSet(BITS);
            for (int i = 0; i < n; i++)
            {
                if(!b2.get(i))
                {
                    b.set(i);
                }
            }
            b2 = b;

            // Add one to the new value of b2
            b = new BitSet(BITS);
            b.set(0);
            b2 = add(b2, b);

            // Add b1 and b2
            return add(b1, b2);
        }
```

Summary

A Stack is a last-in, first-out data structure that allows access only to its most recently added (topmost) element.

The fundamental Stack operations are implemented by pop( ) and push( ).

The bitwise operators (˜, &, |, and ^) and shift operators (>>, >>, and >>>) manipulate the individual bits within integers.

A BitSet allows storage and manipulation of a large number of boolean values.

A Hashtable allows stored objects to be retrieved by use of the value of an associated key.

Enumerations allow serial access to the elements of a data structure.

A `Properties` object is a special kind of `Hashtable`, used to store configuration information, in which stored objects and keys are both `Strings`.

The `StringTokenizer` class is a special kind of `Enumeration` that can be used to parse the contents of a `String`.

Linked lists can be constructed with the aid of the `java.util` package; they provide serial access to a sorted collection of objects.

A `MediaTracker` object is used to synchronize the loading of images, which can be time-consuming, with other program operations.

The `Observable` class and the `Observer` interface can be used together to keep objects apprised of important changes to other objects.

Quiz

1. A `Stack` allows access only to its _____ element.

2. The two fundamental `Stack` operations are _____ and _____.

3. The internal Java data structure used to store fields is called the _____ and that used to store local variables is called the _____.

4. The bitwise AND operator is _____.

5. The bitwise OR operator is _____.

6. The bitwise XOR operator is _____.

7. The bitwise complement operator is _____.

8. The unsigned right shift operator is _____, and the signed right shift operator is _____.

9. The `set()` and `clear()` methods are used with _____ objects.

10. The abstract class `Dictionary` is implemented by the class _____, which stores data pairs consisting of keys and associated values.

11. The _____ class provides convenient storage of and access to configuration information.

12. By use of the `Enumeration` class it is possible to _____ over the elements of a collection.

13. The _____ method of the `Enumeration` class tests whether elements remain, and the _____ method returns the next element.

14. The _____ method is used to add elements to a `Hashtable`, and the _____ method is used to retrieve elements from a `Hashtable`.

15. When creating a `StringTokenizer` object, the programmer must identify the _____ characters that separate the tokens of the `String`.

16. Each element of a linked list has two components: one contains _____, and the other contains a _____ to the following element of the list.

17. A useful property of a linked list is that its elements can be stored and retrieved _____, unlike the elements of an `Enumeration`, `Vector`, or `Hashtable`.

18. The `addImage( )` method is used with a(n) _____ object to enable it to track the loading of an image.

19. The _____ class can notify "client" objects of changes in its status.

20. The _____ interface receives notifications of changes in the status of a "server" object.

Exercises

1. The RPN calculator shown in the chapter does not handle errors. Entering an invalid number or a mismatched combination of operators and operands can produce an incorrect result. Revise the calculator to detect, and recover from, common errors such as these.

2. Add new operators to the RPN calculator that allow it to raise numbers to specified powers (using a ^ operator), take square roots (using a `sqrt` operator), and take logarithms (using a `log` operator for base 10 logarithms and an `ln` operator for natural logarithms). Also add new operators that return the value of pi (`PI`) and e (`E`).

3. Combine the RPN calculator with a keypad, making it easier to enter numbers. Include buttons for the operators as well as the digits.

4. Add multiplication and division to the `BigNum` class. Recalling that multiplication is simply repeated addition and that division is simply repeated subtraction should help you discover a simple implementation, though one that performs far from optimally.

5. Use the `Properties` class to implement a version of the `GuestBook` applet that permanently stores its data. Use the `save( )` and `load( )` methods provided by the `Properties` class to do this.

6. Use a `Hashtable` to implement a system for keeping track of scheduled appointments, which should be stored by date and time. The system should allow the user to conveniently view the appointments for a specified day.

7. To the appointment system in the previous exercise, add the ability to store and save the appointments. You may use a `Properties` object or a `FileStream` for this purpose.

8. Use `StringTokenizer` to implement an application that measures reading difficulty of text contained within a file. The application should report the total number of words, the total number of sentences, and the average number of words per sentence. The application should also report the average number of "syllables" per word, where the number of syllables in a word is determined by counting the number of vowels, counting consecutive vowels as a single vowel.

9. Use `StringTokenizer` to implement an application that measures the complexity of the program contained within a Java source file. The application should report the number of non-comment source lines, the number of reserved words and identifiers, and the number of operators appearing in the source file.

16

Advanced Topics:

Threads and Networking

You may have heard the saying, "It is better to travel hopefully than to arrive." But, as another author has pointed out, if that were true and known to be true, none of us could ever travel hopefully. Perhaps the truth lies somewhere in between: Travel hopefully, and be thankful when you arrive. In this chapter you have arrived at the end of your journey through the wilds of Java; but in a sense, your journey has only begun. The subjects touched on here—threads and networking—are worthy of (and have been the subject of) volumes of their own. Yet while this chapter won't take you to every byway and backwater, it will give you a map to follow and a foundation to build upon as you continue your journey toward your mastery of Java.

In this chapter you will learn

- How to use threads to make your programs do several things at once

- How to avoid the thread-oriented program bugs called *races* and *deadlocks*

- How to obtain the contents of a Web document given its URL

- How to use sockets to build client-server programs that communicate between, and even among, computers

What Are Threads?

In the "stone age" of personal computing—not even as far back as the prehistory of mainframe computers—most machines ran one program at a time. In those days, if you were writing a letter with WordPerfect when your boss called frantically to ask for some year-end figures you had stored in a Lotus 1-2-3 spreadsheet, your only option was to ask him or her to wait, or to go through the process of saving your letter, shutting down WordPerfect, starting up 1-2-3, and retrieving your spreadsheet. When you were finished, you had to reverse the entire process to get back to where you left off. Thankfully, those days are gone forever.

Today, most operating systems allow you to run several programs at the same time. Depending on your machine, this can be done by using *task switching*, *multitasking*, or *threading*. Under task switching, the oldest approach, several programs are loaded into memory at one time, but only one program is active at any given time. You can switch from program to program by pressing a special hotkey or clicking the mouse. Early versions of the Windows operating system used task switching.

MULTITASKING

Task switching is useful, but it still requires you, the user, to tell your computer to stop doing one task and begin doing another. It really doesn't take full advantage of your computer's capability to do several things at once by switching between tasks very, very rapidly. Called *multitasking*, this rapid switching allows you to use your computer in a more natural way. You can have your computer print a document at the same time it recalculates your spreadsheet and downloads your email. While all this is happening in the background, you can be typing up a letter or reviewing your appointments.

In computer terms, each of these programs—your word processor, your spreadsheet, your email package, and your appointment book—is called a *process*. A process is simply a program that has been loaded from disk into memory and has started executing. The CPU rapidly switches between each process—so rapidly that it seems to humans that each process is executing simultaneously. Each program you run gets loaded into a different area of memory, and the variables and data inside your word processor are kept separate from the variables, data, and code in your spreadsheet. Each of these processes operates in a different address space and in a different *execution context*. When the CPU switches from doing "spreadsheet stuff" to working on "word processing stuff," it switches context, and the CPU finds itself looking at different data and code.

MULTITHREADING

One of the limitations of multitasking is that it is only appropriate when you want to switch between processes—different programs or different copies of the same program loaded and running at the same time. What should you do if you want a single program to perform two methods at the same time? This is useful when one method can use the partial output of another without waiting for the first to finish. You might want to begin displaying a graphic image once you have received enough bytes to complete a section, rather than waiting for the entire picture to download. In this case, you'd really prefer your image-loading method and your image-displaying method to work simultaneously, yet work on the same data. And this is just what threads provide.

The main difference between multitasking and multithreading is that threads operate inside a *single process*, not between processes. Because threads share the same address space, they also have access to the same data—at least as far as object variables (fields) are concerned. This means that in a multithreaded application your `getMyPicture( )` method can be adding bytes to the `myPicture` field at the same time your `showMyPicture()` method—executing in a different thread—is reading them. Local variables inside `getMyPicture( )` or `showMyPicture( )` are still local to each thread. If you find yourself thinking that this might lead to some coordination problems with data access, you're right. But Java, unlike most earlier computer languages, has a wide variety of tools and methods that make writing safe and secure multithreaded applications straightforward and fun.

Why Use Threads: An ABC Example

One of the best ways to learn about the need for threads is to look at a program that doesn't work correctly without them. The `ABC` applet, shown in Listing 16-1 and Listing 16-2, is a simple alphabet program that continuously cycles through the 26 letters of the alphabet, painting each in a large, red font.

A THREADLESS VERSION

ABC has a single data field, `theChar`, which holds the currently displayed character. The `init( )` method, invoked when the applet is first loaded, sets up the font and color. You'll recall that when an applet starts running, it calls the `start( )` method. Inside the `start( )` method of the `ABC` applet a loop cycles through the characters of the alphabet, first printing the character to the system console, and then calling `repaint( )` to allow the `paint( )` method to display the big, bright, red letter. A call to `Thread.sleep( 2000 )` assures that the applet will wait two seconds before displaying the next character.

You can see the result of running ABC in Figure 16-1. If you look at the system console window, you'll see that the loop is actually working, and you are cycling through each of the letters of the alphabet. The problem is that your nice red letters are not being displayed on the applet surface, only on the system console (where, of course, they're not the least bit red). Why? Because the `paint( )` method and the `start( )` method of your applet are operating in the same thread. Your loop inside the `start( )` method prevents your `paint( )` method from gaining control. To fix this, you have to move the code that controls your applet—that cycles through the letters—into its own thread.

Listing 16-1 ABC.java

```java
// Example without threads (This doesn't quite work!)
import java.applet.*;
import java.awt.*;

public class ABC extends Applet
{
    char theChar = 'A';

    public void init()
    {
        setFont( new Font( "TimesRoman", Font.BOLD, 128 ));
        setForeground( Color.red );
    }

    public void start()
    {
        while ( true )
        {
            System.out.println( theChar );
            repaint();
            try { Thread.sleep( 2000 );              }
            catch (InterruptedException e ) { ; }

            if ( theChar >= 'Z' )
                    theChar = 'A';
            else
                    theChar++;
        }
    }

    public void paint( Graphics g )
    {
        FontMetrics fm = g.getFontMetrics();
        int yPos = (getSize().height / 2) + ⇐
                    (fm.getAscent() / 2);
        int xPos = (getSize().width  / 2) - ⇐
                    (fm.charWidth( theChar ) / 2);
        g.drawString( "" + theChar, xPos, yPos );

    }
}
```

Listing 16-2 ABC.html

```html
<HTML>
<HEAD>
<TITLE>ABC.java</TITLE>
</HEAD>
<BODY>
<H1>The ABC Applet Without Threads</H1>
<HR>
<H2>(Do not adjust your computer)</H2>
<APPLET CODE=ABC HEIGHT=200 WIDTH=200>
</APPLET>
</BODY>
</HTML>
```

FIGURE 16-1
Running ABC.java

The ABC Applet Without Threads

(Do not adjust your computer)

ADDING A THREAD TO ABC

There are two ways to add threads to your applications and applets. The method that you'll use most often is to implement the `Runnable` interface. To implement the `Runnable` interface, you need only write one new method, `run()`. The steps required to hook up `run()` are very straightforward and are illustrated in the `ABCThread` applet, shown in Listings 16-3 and 16-4. Briefly, the steps required to make ABC a multi-threaded applet are

1. In your class declaration, add the phrase `implements Runnable`.

2. Add a `Thread` object as a data field. You do not need to initialize this field.

3. Put the statements you want to run concurrently inside a new method called `run()`. In the `ABCThread` applet, those are the instructions that increment the current character and that call `repaint()`. The `run()` method must return `void`. Your applet *must* include such a method, because you declared that you would implement the `Runnable` interface.

4. Inside the applet's `start()` method, initialize your `Thread` field by using the `Thread()` constructor, passing the current applet (`this`) as the argument. Once you have created your new `Thread` object, call its `start()` method, which will have the effect of invoking the method called `run()` inside your applet.

5. Add a `stop()` method to your applet. Inside your `stop()` method, you must call the `stop()` method for your new `Thread` object. If you don't do this, the thread can continue to execute even after your applet is "dead."

As you can see from Figure 16-2, the `ABCThread` applet now nicely displays each character as it cycles through the alphabet. It works because the applet's `paint()` method and `run()` method now operate in different threads, even though both of them use the same data, the field named `theChar`.

Listing 16-3 ABCThread.java

```
// Adding Threads to ABC.java
import java.applet.*;
import java.awt.*;
```

continued on next page

continued from previous page

```java
public class ABCThread extends Applet implements Runnable
{
    char    theChar = 'A';
    Thread theThread;

    public void init()
    {
        setFont( new Font( "TimesRoman", Font.BOLD, 128 ));
        setForeground( Color.red );
    }

    public void start()
    {
        if ( theThread == null )
        {
            theThread = new Thread( this );
            theThread.start();
        }
    }

    public void stop()
    {
        if ( theThread != null )
        {
            theThread.stop();
            theThread = null;
        }
    }

    public void run()
    {
        while ( true )
        {
            System.out.println( theChar );
            repaint();
            try { Thread.sleep( 1000 );           }
            catch (InterruptedException e ) { ; }

            if ( theChar >= 'Z' )
                    theChar = 'A';
            else
                    theChar++;
        }
    }

    public void paint( Graphics g )
    {
        FontMetrics fm = g.getFontMetrics();
        int yPos = (getSize().height / 2) + ⇐
                (fm.getAscent() / 2);
        int xPos = (getSize().width  / 2) - ⇐
                (fm.charWidth( theChar ) / 2);
        g.drawString( "" + theChar, xPos, yPos );

    }
}
```

Listing 16-4 ABCThread.html

```
<HTML>
<HEAD>
<TITLE>ABCThread.java</TITLE>
</HEAD>
<BODY>
<APPLET CODE=ABCThread HEIGHT=200 WIDTH=200>
</APPLET>
</BODY>
</HTML>
```

HOW THREADS ARE USEFUL

You've now seen an example program that didn't work right until it was revised to use threads. Threads are like that; they're not so much useful or interesting in their own right as they are necessary to performing, or efficiently performing, other tasks. In most programming environments, it's almost always possible to write a program to perform a given function without creating threads. Similarly, if you're content to do one thing at a time, you may be able to get along without using threads (at least until things get really busy).

Java itself, unlike most other programming environments, is built by use of threads. They're there whether you create them or not. Sometimes, as in the ABCThread example, threads intrude on your programming self-expression by compelling you to recognize their existence and to deal appropriately with them.

FIGURE 16-2
Running the ABCThread applet

" The main difference between multitasking and multithreading is that threads operate in a single process, not between processes. "

More often, you'll be drawn to use threads by the desire to create programs that respond as quickly as possible to a variety of events. This is particularly true when you write programs that use networking. As a network-capable programming language, Java aims to help you write powerful and robust software that realizes the full potential of the Internet and the Web. Threads are an important tool in this endeavor. By assigning a thread to each type of service request or to each possible requester, you make it possible for your program to handle each as expeditiously as possible and according to priorities you establish. In the section on networking, you'll see extensive use of threads. For now, let's concentrate on the fundamentals of creating them, using them, and avoiding certain common thread-related pitfalls.

Son of Thread: Creating Threads Another Way

Not only can you create a Java thread by implementing the `Runnable` interface and calling the `Thread()` constructor, you can also create a thread by extending the `Thread` class. Because of inheritance, any object created from your new class will automatically be a `Thread`. Just as you saw in the `ABCThread` applet, you still have to start the new `Thread` before it will actually run.

CREATING AN UNNAMED `Thread`

Listing 16-5, the ThreadByBirth application, shows you how to create a thread by extending the `Thread` class. Just as with `ABCThread`, this is a fairly straightforward process:

1. Create a new class and specify that it `extends Thread`.

2. To make a new thread, create an instance of your class. You do this by calling the constructor for your class, rather than the constructor for the `Thread` class.

3. Inside your application, activate your new thread by invoking the `start()` method. You don't need to supply a `start()` method; a default `start()` method will be inherited from the `Thread` class.

4. The `start()` method inside the `Thread` class automatically calls the `run()` method, which you will need to add to your application, just as you did previously. This is where you place the statements that you want the new thread to execute.

Listing 16-5 ThreadByBirth.java

```java
// Creating a simple thread by inheritance
public class ThreadByBirth extends Thread
{
    public static void main(String args[])
    {
        ThreadByBirth theApp = new ThreadByBirth();
        theApp.start();
    }

    public void run()
    {
        System.out.println
          ("No longer threadbare, but still fancy free.");
        Thread.currentThread().getThreadGroup().list();
        System.exit(0);
    }
}
```

OUTPUT OF THE THREADBYBIRTH APPLICATION

```
C:\Ch16\Examples>java ThreadByBirth
 No longer threadbare, but still fancy free.
 java.lang.ThreadGroup[name=main,maxpri=10]
     Thread[main,5,main]
     Thread[Thread-1,5,main]
```

Despite its brevity, ThreadByBirth illustrates a few interesting features. Inside the run( ) method, the currentThread( ) method (a static method of the Thread class) is used to obtain a reference to the current thread. The getThreadGroup( ) method is then used to get a reference to the *thread group* to which the current thread belongs. You'll learn more about thread groups in a moment. The thread group's list( ) method then prints a listing of the members of the thread group. You can see two distinct threads in the output, one called main and another called Thread-1. It's pretty reasonable to assume that the thread named main is the main thread started by the Java interpreter, but how do you know that Thread-1 is really the thread you created, rather than a thread related to some obscure system process, such as garbage collection?

NAMING YOUR THREADS

To address this issue, you can use the `setName()` method to change the name of your thread to a readily identifiable value. Listing 16-6 shows the result.

Listing 16-6 NamedThread.java

```
// Giving your threads a name
public class NamedThread extends Thread
{
    public static void main(String args[])
    {
        NamedThread theApp = new NamedThread();
        theApp.start();
    }

    public void run()
    {
        Thread.currentThread().setName ⇐
          ("The scarlet thread.");
        System.out.println ⇐
          ("No longer threadbare, but still fancy free.");
        Thread.currentThread().getThreadGroup().list();
        System.exit(0);
    }
}
```

OUTPUT OF THE NAMEDTHREAD.JAVA APPLICATION

```
C:\Ch16\ Examples>java NamedThread
 No longer threadbare, but still fancy free.
 java.lang.ThreadGroup[name=main,maxpri=10]
    Thread[main,5,main]
    Thread[The scarlet thread.,5,main]
```

CHOOSING YOUR APPROACH

How should you create a thread—by implementing `Runnable` or by extending the `Thread` class? Take an example: Applets are usually created by implementing `Runnable`, for a good reason. Implementing `Runnable` leaves them free to extend `Applet`, from which they inherit a great deal of useful behavior. You could create an "applet" by extending `Thread` and implementing `Applet`, but this would mean you'd have to write the code for every `Applet` method, because your class would not inherit methods from `Applet`. Some might find this fun, but it's clearly not an efficient approach.

When you implement `Runnable`, you gain access to all the behavior of a `Thread` through the static methods of the `Thread` class. Thus, there's little reason to extend `Thread` when you could inherit useful behavior by extending some other class and merely implementing `Runnable Thread`. But what about a situation where there's no useful functionality to inherit—for example, when your class would simply extend `Object`? This is a time where it makes sense to extend `Thread`, because you won't lose anything by doing so.

Threads and Applications

Because Java provides an interface called `Runnable`, as you saw in the ABCThread example, it is easy to create a class whose objects will run in their own threads. You can also easily create RunnableFrames, as Listing 16-7 shows. A RunnableFrame is a `Frame` that includes a `run()` method which runs in a distinct thread. The approach illustrated in RunnableFrame is useful whenever you want to create an application that includes threads. You'll see practical applications of this approach in the upcoming section on networking.

Listing 16-7 RunnableFrame.java

```
// Using the Runnable interface to create a Runnable Frame.
import java.awt.*;
import java.awt.event.*;

public class RunnableFrame extends Frame ⇐
                            implements Runnable, ActionListener
{
    Button quitButton = new Button("Quit");
    Thread theThread;

    public static void main(String args[])
    {
        RunnableFrame theApp = new RunnableFrame();
        try
        {
            Thread.sleep(5000);
        }
        catch (InterruptedException interrupted)
        {
            // do nothing
        }
        Thread.currentThread().getThreadGroup().list();
    }

    public RunnableFrame()
    {
        add(quitButton, "North");
        quitButton.addActionListener(this);
```

continued on next page

continued from previous page

```
            setSize(200, 200);
            setVisible(true);
            start();
    }

    public void start()
    {
        if (theThread == null)
        {
            theThread = new Thread(this);
            theThread.start();
        }
    }

    public void run()
    {
        Thread.currentThread().setName ⇐
          ("The scarlet thread.");
        System.out.println ⇐
          ("No longer threadbare, but still fancy free.");
        try
        {
            Thread.sleep(10000);
        }
        catch (InterruptedException interrupted)
        {
            // do nothing
        }
    }

    public void actionPerformed(ActionEvent theEvent)
    {
        setVisible(false);
        dispose();
        System.exit(0);
    }
}
```

> **" To implement the Runnable interface, you need only write one new method, run(). "**

INSIDE RUNNABLEFRAME

The RunnableFrame application is a little more complex than the ABCThread applet for two reasons. First, as a Frame, it has to handle closing itself, which it does in the actionPerformed() method. Second, RunnableFrame has extra Thread.sleep() calls, along with their associated try-catch blocks. These allow each thread the time it needs to carry out all of its tasks before the list() method prints the value of each thread.

Recall that threads execute concurrently. Because the Thread identified by the variable theThread is operating at the same time as the rest of the statements inside the main() method, it is entirely possible for the list() method to execute before the setName() method executes inside run(). Adding additional sleep() calls helps ensure that each thread has adequate time to complete any necessary tasks.

In the RunnableFrame application, the `start( )` method calls a `Thread` constructor, passing the `this` object as an argument. The constructor obediently creates a new thread, which is started by invoking its `start( )` method. The actual statements run by the thread are, as before, those contained in the `run( )` method, although unlike ABCThread, these statements are not contained in an endless loop. Here is the output of the RunnableFrame application:

OUTPUT OF THE RUNNABLEFRAME APPLICATION

```
C:\Ch16\Examples>java RunnableFrame
 No longer threadbare, but still fancy free.
 java.lang.ThreadGroup[name=main,maxpri=10]
     Thread[main,5,main]
     Thread[AWT-EventQueue,5,main]
     Thread[AWT-Windows,5,main]
     Thread[The scarlet thread.,5,main]
     Thread[Screen Updater,4,main]
```

Note that there are several unfamiliar threads shown in this output. These are used by the AWT to handle processing associated with GUI components. The AWT gets a thread of its own, under Windows 95 appropriately named `AWT-Windows`. The "callback" processing performed by `actionPerformed()` is handled in a thread named `AWT-EventQueue`. Finally, there is a low-priority thread whose job is to repaint the screen. This thread is named `Screen Updater`.

Starting and Stopping Threads

There are many constructors and methods associated with the `Thread` class. Important constructors are summarized in Table 16-1. The class (`static`) methods are summarized in Table 16-2, and instance (or regular) methods are summarized in Table 16-3.

The class methods of the `Thread` class work a little differently than those of most other classes. Usually class methods operate on the class itself, or on the collection of instantiated objects of the class as a whole. In the case of the `Thread` class, however, the class methods operate on the current thread—that is, the one that invokes the class method. This makes it easy to get a reference to the current thread or to put the current thread to sleep, either of which would otherwise be somewhat difficult to accomplish.

TABLE 16-1
KEY `public` CONSTRUCTORS OF THE `Thread` CLASS

```
Thread( )
Thread(Runnable task)
Thread(ThreadGroup g, Runnable task)
Thread(String name)
Thread(ThreadGroup g, String name)
Thread(Runnable task, String name)
Thread(ThreadGroup g, Runnable task, String name)
```

TABLE 16-2
KEY `public` CLASS METHODS OF THE `Thread` CLASS

METHOD HEADER	FUNCTION
`int activeCount( )`	Get the number of `Thread`s in the current `Thread`'s `ThreadGroup`.
`Thread currentThread( )`	Get the currently executing `Thread`.
`void dumpStack( )`	Print a stack trace of the current `Thread`, for debugging purposes.
`int enumerate(Thread[] threads)`	Get an `Enumeration` over the `Thread`s in the current `Thread`'s `ThreadGroup`.
`void sleep(long mills)`	Cause the `Thread` to sleep (that is, temporarily cease execution) for the specified number of milliseconds (throws `InterruptedException`).
`void yield( )`	Temporarily pause the current `Thread`, allowing other `Thread`s to execute.

TABLE 16-3
KEY `public` INSTANCE METHODS OF THE `Thread` CLASS

METHOD HEADER	FUNCTION
`String getName( )`	Get the name of the `Thread`.
`int getPriority( )`	Get the priority of the `Thread`.
`ThreadGroup getThreadGroup( )`	Get the `ThreadGroup` of the `Thread`.
`boolean isAlive( )`	Determine if the `Thread` is alive—that is, has started but has not died.
`boolean isDaemon( )`	Determine if the `Thread` is a daemon.
`void join(long mills)`	Wait at most the specified number of milliseconds for the `Thread` to die.
`void join( )`	Wait for the `Thread` to die (throws `InterruptedException`).
`void resume( )`	Resume a suspended `Thread`.

Table continued…

TABLE 16-3 KEY `public` INSTANCE METHODS OF THE `Thread` CLASS CONTINUED...

METHOD HEADER	FUNCTION
`void run( )`	If the constructor specified a `Runnable` object, call its `run( )` method; otherwise the method simply returns—normally overridden when subclassing `Thread`.
`void setDaemon(boolean daemon)`	Mark the `Thread` as a daemon (`true`) or nondaemon (`false`) `Thread`—must be called before the `Thread` is started.
`void setName(String name)`	Change the name of the `Thread` to that specified by the `String`.
`void setPriority(int priority)`	Change the priority of the `Thread`.
`void start( )`	Cause the `Thread` to begin execution—the `Thread`'s `run( )` method is called.
`void stop( )`	Force the `Thread` to cease execution.
`void suspend( )`	Suspend the `Thread`.

STOPPING WHAT'S BEEN STARTED

There's an old saying that "you shouldn't start what you can't finish." The good news, as far as threads are concerned, is that they're easy to stop once they've been started. There are two things that cause a thread to stop. A thread stops whenever the associated `run( )` method returns—as you saw in RunnableFrame—or whenever the `stop( )` method is invoked on the thread—as you saw in ABCThread.

The StoppableThread application, shown in Listing 16-8, shows how you can stop and start a thread. StoppableThread puts three `Buttons` across the top of the screen, labeled "Start," "Stop," and "Quit." In the center of the application there is a `Panel` with two lines drawn at a small angle from each other. When you press the Start button, a new thread is created and used to animate one of the lines so that it rotates around the other. Pressing the Stop button kills the action. Once the applet has been stopped, you can press Start and everything resumes from the point you left it. You can start and stop the action at will. Figure 16-3 shows the appearance of the application's screen.

Listing 16-8 StoppableThread.java

```
// Starting and stopping a thread
import java.awt.*;
import java.awt.event.*;

public class StoppableThread extends Frame ⇐
                        implements Runnable, ⇐
                            ActionListener
{
    Button startButton = new Button( "Start" );
```

continued on next page

continued from previous page

```
Button stopButton  = new Button( "Stop"  );
Button quitButton  = new Button( "Quit"  );
Panel  thePanel    = new Panel();
Thread theThread   = null;
int x1, y1, x2, y2;

public static void main( String args[] )
{
    StoppableThread theApp = new StoppableThread();
}

public StoppableThread()
{
    setTitle( "StoppableThread" );
    Panel p1 = new Panel();
    p1.add(startButton);
    p1.add(stopButton);
    p1.add(quitButton);

    startButton.addActionListener(this);
    stopButton.addActionListener(this);
    quitButton.addActionListener(this);

    add(p1, "North");
    add(thePanel, "Center");
    setSize(200, 200);

    int width  = getSize().width / 2;
    int height = getSize().height / 2;
    x1 = width / 2;
    x2 = width + x1;
    y1 = height / 2;
    y2 = y1;

    setVisible(true);
}

public void start()
{
    if (theThread == null)
    {
        theThread = new Thread(this);
        theThread.start();
    }
}

public void stop()
{
    if (theThread != null && theThread.isAlive())
    {
        theThread.stop();
    }
    theThread= null;
}

public void run()
{
    while ( true )
    {
```

```
                          try { Thread.sleep( 10 ); }
                          catch (InterruptedException e )   ⇐
                               { /* Do nothing */ }
                          repaint();
                  }
          }

          public void paint( Graphics g )
          {
              g = thePanel.getGraphics();
              g.setXORMode( Color.green );
              g.drawLine( x1, y1, x2, y2 );
              if ( y1 < y2 ) { x1++; x2--; } else { x1--; x2++; }
              if ( x1 < x2 ) { y1--; y2++; } else { y1++; y2--; }
              g.drawLine( x1, y1, x2, y2 );
          }

          public void actionPerformed(ActionEvent theEvent)
          {
              if (theEvent.getSource( ) == startButton)
                  start();
              else if (theEvent.getSource( ) == stopButton)
                  stop();
              else if (theEvent.getSource( ) == quitButton)
              {
                  setVisible(false);
                  dispose();
                  System.exit(0);
              }
          }
      }
```

CREATING AND STARTING YOUR THREAD

How does the StoppableThread application work? Because it is a multithreaded application, StoppableThread declares that it implements Runnable. As with the ABCThread applet, you also have to declare a Thread field, here named simply theThread. The constructor for StoppableThread simply puts all of the Buttons and Panels on the surface of your Frame, calculates the position of the lines that will be drawn, and then calls show( ).

FIGURE 16-3
*Output of
StoppableThread*

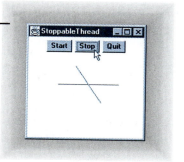

When you press the Start button, the start( ) method inside the StoppableThread application is invoked. This simply creates a new Thread—using the Frame as the argument—and then calls the new thread's start( ) method:

```
public void start()
{
    if (theThread == null)
    {
        theThread = new Thread(this);
        theThread.start();
    }
}
```

In the same way, Thread.start( ) calls the run( ) method inside StoppableThread. The run( ) method is a simple endless loop that waits for a few milliseconds (using Thread.sleep( )), and then calls repaint( ):

```
public void run()
{
    while ( true )
    {
        try { Thread.sleep( 10 ); }
        catch (InterruptedException e ) { /* Do nothing */ }
        repaint();
    }
}
```

Calling repaint( ) causes the paint( ) method to be scheduled; it will eventually be invoked by the AWT. The paint( ) method first obtains a Graphics object for the Panel so that it can draw on its surface. Next, it sets the drawing mode of the Panel to XOR mode:

```
g = thePanel.getGraphics();
g.setXORMode( Color.green );
```

When you draw using XOR mode, drawing the same figure twice in the same location has the effect of erasing the first drawing. This occurs because of a special property of the XOR operation. If you take an arbitrary value and an arbitrary mask, XOR the value with the mask, then take the result and again XOR it with the mask, what do you think the result will be? Surprisingly, it's always the original value: ((X XOR Y) XOR Y) == X.

In StoppableThread, the paint( ) method first draws a line between the coordinates x1,y1 and x2,y2. It then changes the coordinates and draws a line between the *new* points. The next time that paint( ) is called, the first call to drawLine( ) will thus erase the previously drawn line:

```
g.drawLine( x1, y1, x2, y2 );
if ( y1 < y2 ) { x1++; x2--; } else { x1--; x2++; }
if ( x1 < x2 ) { y1--; y2++; } else { y1++; y2--; }
g.drawLine( x1, y1, x2, y2 );
```

This avoids erasing the entire Panel every time you want to draw a new line.

STOPPING THE THREAD

Stopping a thread is not a gentle operation. When you send a `stop()` message to a thread, it doesn't glide smoothly to a controlled stop. Instead, the effect is similar to what happens when you throw a 500-pound anchor chained to your axle out the back window of your pickup truck as you fly down the freeway at 70 miles per hour. Most likely, the pick-up truck won't be worth a whole lot after that.

Threads act the same way. Once you stop them, they're just not of any use; you can't reuse a thread that's been stopped. On the other hand, because it's so easy to create a new one, stopping a thread doesn't do any real damage, provided you don't try to use one that's been stopped. Knowing that the `stop()` method actually does its work by throwing an error named `ThreadDeath` may help you remember not to attempt to resurrect a stopped thread.

In the StoppableThread application, the `start()` method first checks to see if `theThread` is `null` before creating a new thread. Thus, the `stop()` method needs to make sure to not only call the `Thread.stop()` method, but to also set `theThread` equal to `null` as well, allowing the garbage collector to recycle the thread's resources, and making sure that when `start()` is called, it knows to create a new thread:

```
public void stop()
{
    if (theThread != null && theThread.isAlive())
    {
        theThread.stop();
    }
    theThread= null;
}
```

Attributes and Characteristics of Threads

Despite the fact that threads are so easy to create, it still might seem overkill to sentence a thread to `ThreadDeath()` when all you really want is for it to wait for a moment. What if you *don't* want to destroy a thread, but you *do* want it to suspend execution for a time? The `suspend()` method can be used for this purpose. The `resume()` method can then be used to get the thread going again, whenever you choose. Of course, if you want to suspend the thread for a fixed length of time, you can use the `sleep()` method, which you've seen in examples throughout this book.

As do applets, threads have a life cycle, a set of predefined phases that each thread progresses through. Figure 16-4 shows the life cycle of a thread. Pay particular attention to the fact that most of the thread life-cycle methods can be called only when the thread is in a particular state. The `stop()` method is an exception, because it can be called for new threads as well as for threads that have been started and are therefore in the *runnable* state.

Figure 16-4
The life cycle of a thread

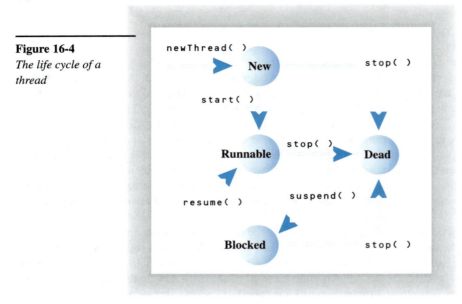

As the figure shows, threads can be in any one of four states. Table 16-4 summarizes these states. The isAlive( ) method can be used to determine the current state of a thread; it returns true if the thread has been started and not yet stopped, and false otherwise.

TABLE 16-4
THREAD STATES

STATE	DESCRIPTION
New	A newly created thread that has not yet been started via the start( ) method.
Runnable	A thread that has been started and is eligible to compete with other threads for access to the CPU. At a given point, the thread may or may not actually be running.
Blocked	A thread is blocked when it is waiting for something, for example, for its sleep( ) interval to expire, or when suspend( ) has been invoked on it.
Dead	A thread dies when its run( ) method exits or when stop( ) is invoked on it.

KEEPING PRIORITIES STRAIGHT

Most of us have priorities when we do our work. This just reflects the fact that not everything we do has exactly the same importance. Keeping a library book out past its due date has very different consequences from forgetting to pay your mortgage. Because of this, you're more likely to pay greater attention to making sure your mortgage is current than you are to getting your library books back on time—although, of course, you want to do both.

Java's `Thread` class has a similar scheme known as *thread priorities*. You can, in essence, tell your program to pay more attention to one thread than to another. Each thread has an associated number, called the priority of the thread. Priorities are needed because the CPU can run only a single thread at a time. Using priorities, threads share access to the CPU in such a way that urgent or important tasks gain access to the CPU more often and more readily. This is done by allowing threads with higher priority to run in preference to others. So, a thread with priority 7 will run before a thread with priority 3. Similarly, if a thread with priority 7 becomes runnable, it will preempt a currently running thread with priority 3, taking over the CPU.

A newly created thread inherits its priority from the thread that created it, but it's possible to change the priority of a thread by use of the `setPriority()` method. The `Thread` class includes several `public` fields that contain values useful in setting thread priorities using this method. These fields are summarized in Table 16-5.

In addition to the methods illustrated in Figure 16-4, the `yield()` and `join()` methods are useful for working with threads. The key to understanding what the `yield()` method does is to understand how Java's thread priorities work. When a thread invokes the `yield()` method, it gives up its access to the CPU. If another thread of *equal (or greater)* priority is ready to run, it will gain access to the CPU. Note that the `yield()` method does *not* yield control to threads of lesser priority; placing a `yield()` in your code will not allow the low-priority painting thread to run. If you do want to give a lower-priority thread a chance to run, you should call `sleep()` in the current thread. When you tell a thread to sleep, as long as there are no other higher-priority threads waiting to run, the lower-priority thread will gain access to the CPU.

A useful method not shown in Figure 16-4 is the `join()` method. Invoking `join()` on a thread causes the current thread to be suspended until the joined thread is dead. The `join()` method is useful for synchronizing the work of several threads.

TABLE 16-5
KEY `public` FIELDS OF THE `Thread` CLASS

FIELD	TYPE	MEANING/USE
MAX_PRIORITY	int	Maximum possible priority of a `Thread`
MIN_PRIORITY	int	Minimum possible priority of a `Thread`
NORM_PRIORITY	int	Default priority assigned to a `Thread`

DAEMON THREADS

" Once you stop a thread, it's no longer of any use; you can't reuse a thread that's been stopped. "

Java actually has two kinds of threads: *regular* threads and *daemon* threads. There is only one difference between the two types of threads. When all of the regular (user) threads inside your program have finished executing, your program will end, even if there are daemon threads still running. Daemon threads are used, therefore, for auxiliary tasks that are needed only to serve the needs of other, regular threads. The garbage collector thread, for instance, is a daemon thread. When all the regular threads are done, Java kills any remaining daemon threads and terminates the program.

As is thread priority, daemonhood is inherited by a new thread from the thread that created it. It can also be set by use of the `setDaemon()` method, but only before the thread is started, otherwise an `IllegalThreadStateException` is thrown. Daemon threads are used more by systems programmers than application programmers. Whenever you create a thread that serves no useful purpose in its own right, but simply supports other threads, you should consider making it a daemon thread. That way, when the supported threads are done, the daemon thread will be automatically killed and the program terminated. Otherwise, the program could continue indefinitely, running a thread intended to support other threads that have long since died.

Thread Groups and Thread Management

Imagine trying to bring home a dozen hamsters from the pet store without using a cage. The cage really makes things much easier. Similarly, `ThreadGroups` simplify the management of threads by making it possible to treat an entire set of threads as a unit. For example, you can kill all the threads in a `ThreadGroup` by simply calling `stop()` on the `ThreadGroup`, instead of finding each thread and calling `stop()` thread-by-thread.

You can create a `ThreadGroup` by using either of the constructors shown in Table 16-6. `Thread`s can be made part of a `ThreadGroup` when they are created, by using a `Thread` constructor that allows you to specify the `ThreadGroup` to which you want them to belong. When a `ThreadGroup` is created, Java remembers the identity of the "parent" `ThreadGroup`. Thus, `Thread`s and `ThreadGroup`s are related in an inheritance tree similar to that of classes and objects. Figure 16-5 shows such an inheritance tree.

TABLE 16-6
KEY `public` CONSTRUCTORS OF THE `ThreadGroup` CLASS

`ThreadGroup(String name)`
`ThreadGroup(ThreadGroup parent, String name)`

FIGURE 16-5
ThreadGroups and
Threads

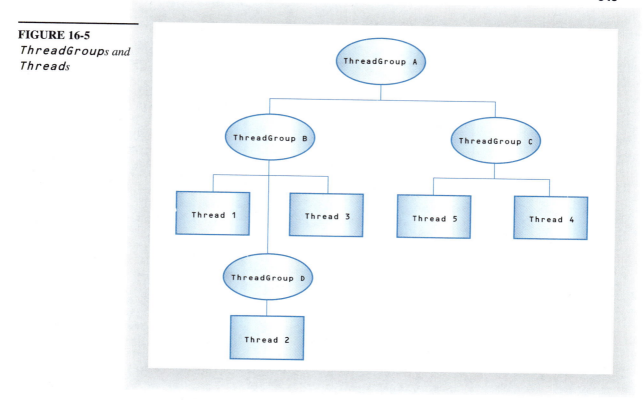

The key methods of the `ThreadGroup` class are summarized in Table 16-7. You're not that likely to need `ThreadGroups` in your own programs; they're more commonly needed in writing system programs than in writing application programs. However, it's useful to know a bit about them, because the threads that make up your program are usually part of one or more `ThreadGroups`. Many Java Integrated Development Environments (IDEs) display `Thread` and `ThreadGroup` information in their debuggers, so knowing a bit about thread groups will help you understand such displays.

TABLE 16-7
KEY `public` INSTANCE METHODS OF THE `ThreadGroup` CLASS

METHOD HEADER	FUNCTION
`int activeCount( )`	Get the number of active `Thread`s in the `ThreadGroup` and any of its children.
`int activeGroupCount( )`	Get the number of active `ThreadGroup`s with this `ThreadGroup` as an ancestor.
`void destroy( )`	Destroy the `ThreadGroup` and all of its children—the `ThreadGroup` must be empty (that is, all of its `Thread`s must have been stopped).
`int enumerate(Thread[] threads)`	Get an array containing every active `Thread` in the `ThreadGroup` and its children.
`int enumerate(Thread[] threads, boolean recurse)`	Get an array containing every active `Thread` in the `ThreadGroup` and, only if `recurse` is `true`, its children.
`int enumerate(ThreadGroup[] threads)`	Get an array containing every active `ThreadGroup` in the `ThreadGroup` and its children.
`int enumerate(ThreadGroup[] threads, boolean recurse)`	Get an array containing every active `ThreadGroup` in the `ThreadGroup` and, only if `recurse` is `true`, its children.
`int getMaxPriority( )`	Get the maximum allowable priority of a `Thread` within the `ThreadGroup`.
`String getName( )`	Get the name of the `ThreadGroup`.
`ThreadGroup getParent( )`	Get the parent of the `ThreadGroup`; return `null` if called by the top-level `ThreadGroup`.
`boolean isDaemon( )`	Determine if the `ThreadGroup` is a daemon `ThreadGroup`.
`void list( )`	Print debugging information concerning the `ThreadGroup`.
`boolean parentOf(ThreadGroup g)`	Determine if the specified `ThreadGroup` is the same as this `ThreadGroup` or a child of this `ThreadGroup`.
`void resume( )`	Resume all `Thread`s within the `ThreadGroup`.
`void setDaemon(boolean daemon)`	Set the type of the `ThreadGroup` to daemon (`true`) or non-daemon (`false`).
`void setMaxPriority(int p)`	Set the maximum priority of the `ThreadGroup`.
`void stop( )`	Stop all processes of the `ThreadGroup`.
`void suspend( )`	Suspend all processes of the `ThreadGroup`.

RACE CONDITIONS

Java makes it simple to create threads; so simple that it's possible to get into all sorts of trouble that wouldn't be likely in other languages that make threads harder to work with. One common thread-related problem is called a *race condition*, in which the result of a computation depends on which of two or more threads completes first. Such a computation has an indeterminate outcome, because it is not possible to predict the outcome. Moreover, such race conditions often result in inconsistent or corrupted objects.

Listing 16-9 shows the Race application, which demonstrates a race condition. The application includes a method called setTotal( ), which simply sets the value of the object's solitary field, an int named totalMeters. It also includes a method called getTotal( ), which returns the value of the same field.

Listing 16-9 Race.java

```java
// How race conditions work
import java.io.*;

public class Race
{
    private int totalMeters  = 0;

    public static void main(String args[])
    {
        Race theApp = new Race();
    }

    public Race()
    {
        Runner firstRunner = new Runner( this );
        firstRunner.start();
        Runner secondRunner = new Runner( this );
        secondRunner.start();

        while (firstRunner.isAlive() || secondRunner.isAlive())
        {
            try { Thread.sleep( 1000 ); }
            catch (InterruptedException e) { }
        }
        System.out.println( "Total meters run is : " + ⇐
                                 getTotal() );
    }

    public void updateTotal()
    {
        setTotal( getTotal() + 1 );
    }

    public void setTotal( int newValue )
    {
        totalMeters = newValue;
    }

    public int getTotal()
    {
        return totalMeters;
    }
}
```

continued on next page

continued from previous page

```
class Runner extends Thread
{
    Race      theRace;
    Thread    theThread;
    int       totalMeters = 0;

    public Runner( Race race )
    {
        theRace = race;
    }

    public void run()
    {
        System.out.println("Runner " + currentThread() + ⇐
                            " is starting.");
        for (int i = 0; i < 100000; i++)
        {
            totalMeters++;
            theRace.updateTotal();
        }
        System.out.println("Runner " + currentThread() + ⇐
                            " ran " + totalMeters);
    }
}
```

Looking at the Race Application

The constructor for the class `Race` creates two instances of a helper class called `Runner`. Each `Runner` object is a separate thread that runs its race by calling the `updateTotal()` method inside the `Race` class, over and over. The `updateTotal()` method works by retrieving `totalMeters` (using `getTotal()`), incrementing it by 1, and then resetting `totalMeters` by calling `setTotal()`. Each `Runner` also adds up its own "meterage" so you can compare the individual totals to the grand total at the end of the race. Can you guess what goes wrong? Figure 16-6 shows the problem.

Because each `run()` method executes 100,000 times, and there are two threads, the `totalMeters` field should have a total value of 200,000. Instead it is considerably less. The individual fields show that each thread did, indeed, execute 100,000 times, yet the total doesn't match. How can this be?

FIGURE 16-6

Running the Race application

```
C:\OOP\Examples >java race
Runner Thread[Thread-1,5,main] is starting.
Runner Thread[Thread-2,5,main] is starting.
Runner Thread[Thread-1,5,main] ran 100000
Runner Thread[Thread-2,5,main] ran 100000
Total meters run is : 160693

C:\OOP\Examples >
```

Figure 16-7 shows how, logically, the `totalMeters` field should be updated by each thread. Because `updateTotal( )` simply retrieves, increments, and sets a single value, you would expect the operations to occur in order: that is, for one thread to retrieve, increment, and update the field, and then the next thread to do the same. Updates that are applied in order in this way are said to be *serialized*. The problem, however, is that the operation of updating the field `totalMeters` is "nonatomic." It's composed of several steps, and there's no guarantee that all the steps will be finished by one thread before the other thread starts executing the same steps. Occasionally, one thread will get the value of `totalMeters` after the other thread has retrieved the value but before that thread can write back the new, corrected value. Then, when this second thread writes back its new value, the total will be one short. Over time, these discrepancies add up. When the timing is just right (or should we say "wrong"?), the new result from one thread will get stored right on top of the result stored by the other thread. The field thus ends up with an incorrect value. Figure 16-8 illustrates this schematically.

FIGURE 16-7
Serialized updates

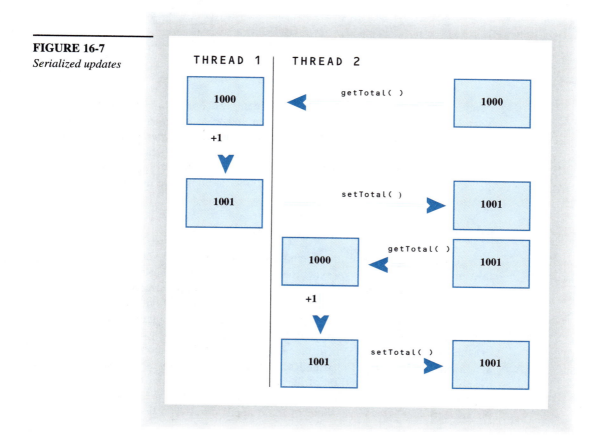

FIGURE 16-8
Nonatomic updates

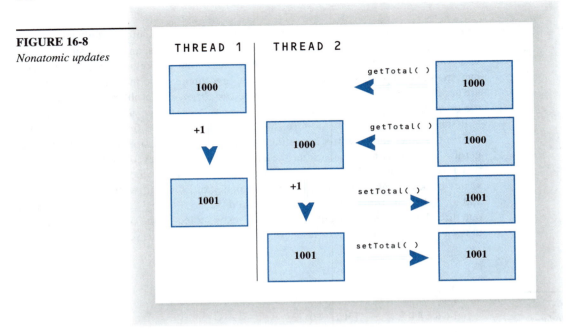

You may think that this is an artificial problem, because the update was performed in several steps. You might reason that a single update or increment would alleviate the problem. But, in this case, you'd be only partly correct. The operation of incrementing a variable is *itself* nonatomic, as are many of Java's other operations and statements. Breaking the update operation into several steps makes the problem easier to see, but the same sort of thing can happen even if you write your code in the more usual way, with fewer steps or even a single step.

Introducing synchronized Methods

How then can you prevent this potentially serious problem? Actually, it's quite easy. Java provides several sets of synchronization mechanisms that can be used to avoid race conditions. The simplest of these can be used by simply declaring a method to be synchronized. A synchronized method will be executed by only a single thread at a time; the entire method becomes atomic. If a thread is executing the method, any other thread needing to execute the method will simply wait.

Listing 16-10 shows the SynchroRace application, which demonstrates this use of the synchronized keyword. To fix the Race application, all that was necessary was to add synchronized to the definition of the updateTotal() method. Look at the output of the application shown in Figure 16-9. You'll notice that now the totalMeters field has the correct value. If you run both of these applications, you'll also notice one other side effect: The SynchroRace application runs much more slowly than the Race application. The overhead of restricting access to a single thread at a time certainly takes its toll in performance. On the other hand, no matter how fast an application is, if it gives you the wrong answer, it's not generally very useful.

Listing 16-10 SynchroRace.java

```java
// How race conditions can be avoided
import java.io.*;

public class SynchroRace
{
    private int totalMeters  = 0;

    public static void main(String args[])
    {
        SynchroRace theApp = new SynchroRace();
    }

    public SynchroRace()
    {
        SynchroRunner firstRunner = new SynchroRunner(this);
        firstRunner.start();
        SynchroRunner secondRunner = new SynchroRunner(this);
        secondRunner.start();

        while ( firstRunner.isAlive() || ⇐
                secondRunner.isAlive() )
        {
            try { Thread.sleep( 1000 ); }
            catch (InterruptedException e) { }
        }
        System.out.println( "Total meters run is : " + ⇐
                            getTotal() );
    }

    public synchronized void updateTotal()
    {
        setTotal( getTotal() + 1 );
    }

    public void setTotal( int newValue )
    {
        totalMeters = newValue;
    }

    public int getTotal()
    {
        return totalMeters;
    }
}

class SynchroRunner extends Thread
{
    SynchroRace theRace;
```

continued on next page

continued from previous page

```
Thread          theThread;
int             totalMeters = 0;

public SynchroRunner( SynchroRace race )
{
    theRace = race;
}

public void run()
{
    System.out.println("Runner " + currentThread() + ⇐
      " is starting.");
    for (int i = 0; i < 100000; i++)
    {
        totalMeters++;
        theRace.updateTotal();
    }
    System.out.println("Runner " + currentThread() + ⇐
      " ran " + totalMeters);
}
}
```

WAITING FOR GODOT: wait( ) AND notify( )

Java also provides a more sophisticated facility for synchronizing operations on an object. Each Java object has a bit known as its *monitor*. This bit is used to control access to the object; it is set whenever a synchronized method is executing. Once it is set, other synchronized methods of the object must wait until the bit has been reset before they can execute. The monitor is said to be "available" or "unavailable" depending on the state of the bit. When the monitor is "available," a thread can set it to "unavailable," execute a synchronized method, and reset the monitor to "available." When the monitor is "unavailable," a thread must wait before it can execute a synchronized method.

Several methods for working with an object's monitor are provided by the Object class. These are summarized in Table 16-8.

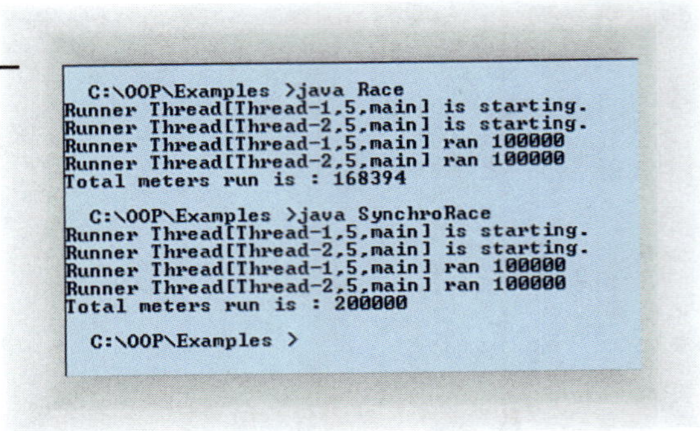

FIGURE 16-9

*Output of
SynchroRace
application*

```
C:\OOP\Examples >java Race
Runner Thread[Thread-1,5,main] is starting.
Runner Thread[Thread-2,5,main] is starting.
Runner Thread[Thread-1,5,main] ran 100000
Runner Thread[Thread-2,5,main] ran 100000
Total meters run is : 168394

C:\OOP\Examples >java SynchroRace
Runner Thread[Thread-1,5,main] is starting.
Runner Thread[Thread-2,5,main] is starting.
Runner Thread[Thread-1,5,main] ran 100000
Runner Thread[Thread-2,5,main] ran 100000
Total meters run is : 200000

C:\OOP\Examples >
```

TABLE 16-8
KEY THREAD-RELATED METHODS OF THE `Object` CLASS

METHOD HEADER	FUNCTION
`void notify( )`	Wake up a single `Thread` waiting on the `Object`'s monitor.
`void notifyAll( )`	Wake up all `Threads` waiting on the `Object`'s monitor.
`void wait(long mills)`	Wait to be notified of a change in the `Object`'s status, for not longer than the specified number of milliseconds.
`void wait( )`	Wait to be notified of a change in the `Object`'s status.

These methods are usually used with the `synchronized` statement, which has the form

```
synchronized (object-expression) protected-statement
```

where *object-expression* is an expression that references an array or object, and *protected-statement* is a statement that will be executed only if the monitor of the object identified by *object-expression* is available. The *protected-statement* usually takes the form of a compound statement. The code contained in the *protected-statement* is called *critical* code, because it is protected against simultaneous execution by multiple threads.

The `wait( )` method can be used to suspend a thread until an object's monitor changes status. It must be used inside a method or block of code that is synchronized. It operates by releasing the monitor and putting the current thread to sleep until some other thread calls `notify( )` or `notifyAll( )` on the synchronized object. Other threads can enter the synchronized method or block once `wait( )` has been called.

For this to work, the object must call `notify( )` or `notifyAll( )` at appropriate points, otherwise the sleeping thread will never be awakened. The `notify( )` method wakes the first thread that called `wait( )` on the synchronized object. The `notifyAll( )` method wakes every thread that has called `wait( )` on the object, with the CPU going to the highest priority thread among them. The methods can be used together like this:

```
synchronized (theObject)
{
    if (!somethingToDo)
    try
    {
        theObject.wait();
    }
    catch (InterruptedException interrupted)
    {
        // do nothing
    }
    // do something
    theObject.notify();
}
```

DEADLOCKS

A race condition can play havoc with your objects, leaving them in an inconsistent state. However, unless you're careful in using Java's synchronization mechanisms, you can find yourself in the hands of an equally evil enemy, the *deadlock*. A deadlock occurs when two (or more) threads are each waiting for the other. Neither proceeds, so your program is "hung," and you must terminate it and restart it.

Listing 16-11 demonstrates a deadlock condition. This application creates two threads, one called "Adam" and another called "Eve." Adam and Eve decide to spare future generations the countless hours of speculation devoted to the question of which came first, the chicken or the egg. Once he has been created, Adam goes looking for the chicken, while Eve seeks out the egg. Then each goes looking for the complementary piece of the puzzle: Adam looks for the egg and Eve for the chicken. Unfortunately, Adam can't find the egg because Eve has it. And, similarly, Eve can't find the chicken because Adam has it. The result: deadlock—the program will never finish. Figure 16-10 shows how it happens. Figure 16-11 shows the output of the Deadlock application.

Deadlocks are particularly hard to identify and track down in real programs. Careful planning is the only effective antidote. Deadlocks can occur only when a thread has one monitor and wants another. Where possible, avoid writing threads that use more than one monitor simultaneously. Carefully study any code that violates this principle for possible deadlock opportunities.

FIGURE 16-10

Looking for the chicken and the egg

Listing 16-11 Deadlock.java

```java
// Why we still don't know which came first
import java.io.*;

public class Deadlock
{

    String theFirstOne = "Chicken";
    String theOtherOne = "Egg";

    public static void main(String args[])
    {
        Deadlock theApp = new Deadlock();
    }

    public Deadlock()
    {
        User user1 = ⇐
          new User("Adam", theFirstOne, theOtherOne);
        user1.start();
        User user2 = ⇐
          new User("Eve",  theOtherOne, theFirstOne);
        user2.start();
    }
}

class User extends Thread
{

    String myName;
    String myFirstOne;
    String myOtherOne;

    public User(String name, String obj1, String obj2)
    {
        myName = name;
        myFirstOne = obj1;
        myOtherOne = obj2;
        System.out.println(myName + " has been created.");
    }

    public void run()
    {
        (Thread.currentThread()).setName(myName);
        System.out.println(myName + " has begun the quest.");
        synchronized (myFirstOne)
        {
            System.out.println(myName +  " has the " + ⇐
              myFirstOne);
            takeNap();
            synchronized (myOtherOne)
            {
                System.out.println(myName + ⇐
                  " also has the " +myOtherOne);
            }
        }
        System.out.println(myName + ⇐
          " has completed the quest.");
```

continued on next page

continued from previous page

```
            return;
    }

    public void takeNap()
    {
        System.out.println(myName + " has decided to nap.");
        try
        {
            Thread.sleep(2000);
        }
        catch(InterruptedException interrupted)
        {

        }
        System.out.println(myName + ⇐
            " is back at work, looking for the " ⇐
            + myOtherOne + ".");
    }
}
```

Networking

When you first heard about Java, you may have heard it described as "the language of the Internet." By now you realize that is not entirely correct—there is much more to Java than simply animated applets. Yet there is also some truth to the original description. Just as Java makes creating graphical user interfaces simple through the AWT, it also makes networking much easier and more straightforward than before. As with the AWT, it does this by providing a rich and easy-to-use set of classes for making network connections and exploiting the power of the World Wide Web. So, maybe what you heard was right after all: Java is the language of the Internet!

FIGURE 16-11

Output of the Deadlock application

MEET THE URLS

The simplest way to create a network-aware Java program is to use the URL class. As you recall from Chapter 1, "What's All This Java Stuff?," URLs allow you to explicitly locate and name *any* document existing *anywhere* on the World Wide Web. Creating a URL object is your key to accessing any of these Web documents, as you'll soon see. The great news (it's better than merely good) is that in Java, creating a URL object is simplicity itself. As you can see from Table 16-9, there are several constructors that can be used to make a URL object. The first constructor takes a String argument just like the one you'd type into your browser. For example

```
URL theConnection = new URL( "http://www.javasoft.com" );
```

is the URL for the Java home page.

The second constructor is useful for creating relative URLs. The first argument, a URL object, specifies a base URL, and the second gives a directory or file name relative to that base. For example, you might use

```
URL theBase = new URL("http://www.javasoft.com");
URL theDoc = new URL(theBase, "index.html");
```

if you wanted to separately specify the base and document. Either one of these constructors will throw a MalformedURLException if the form of the arguments is not acceptable. This exception needs to be caught, or specified as thrown by the enclosing method.

USING URLS

Once you've created a URL object, the URL class has a plethora of methods to get the contents of the document and to perform other useful operations. The key methods of the URL class are summarized in Table 16-10.

TABLE 16-9
KEY **public** CONSTRUCTORS OF THE **URL** CLASS

URL(String urlText)
URL(URL baseURL, String urlText)

TABLE 16-10
KEY `public` METHODS OF THE **URL** CLASS

METHOD HEADER	FUNCTION
`boolean equals(Object obj)`	Test whether the URL is equal to the specified URL.
`Object getContent( )`	Get an object representing the contents of the document addressed by the URL (throws `IOException`).
`String getFile( )`	Get the file portion of the URL.
`String getHost( )`	Get the host portion of the URL.
`String getPort( )`	Get the port-number portion of the URL.
`String getProtocol( )`	Get the protocol-specifier portion of the URL.
`String getRef( )`	Get the anchor-specifier portion of the URL.
`URLConnection openConnection( )`	Get a `URLConnection` object associated with the URL (throws `IOException`).
`InputStream openStream( )`	Open a stream representing the contents of the document addressed by the URL (throws `IOException`).
`boolean sameFile(URL doc)`	Test whether the file portion of the URL is the same as the file portion of the specified URL.

A close cousin to the URL class, the URLConnection class allows you to get information about documents that are referenced by URL objects. To get a URLConnection object, you use the openConnection( ) method of the URL class. Some useful methods of the URLConnection class are shown in Table 16-11.

TABLE 16-11
KEY `public` METHODS OF THE **URLConnection** CLASS

METHOD HEADER	FUNCTION
`void connect( )`	Open the network connection (automatically called as needed by other methods, throws `IOException`).
`Object getContent( )`	Get the contents of the document (throws `IOException, UnknownServiceException`).
`String getContentEncoding( )`	Get a `String` indicating the coding method used to store the document.
`int getContentLength( )`	Get the length of the document.
`String getContentType( )`	Get a `String` indicating the type of content stored in the document (for example, text/plain, text/html, and so on).
`long getExpiration( )`	Get the expiration date of the document, in elapsed seconds since January 1, 1970 GMT.

Table continued...

TABLE 16-11 KEY `public` METHODS OF THE `URLConnection` CLASS CONTINUED...

METHOD HEADER	FUNCTION
`String getHeaderField(String fieldname)`	Get the contents of the specified header field of the document.
`String getHeaderField(int n)`	Get the contents of the specified header field of the document.
`getInputStream( )`	Get an input stream associated with the document contents (throws `IOException`, `UnknownServiceException`).
`getLastModified( )`	Get the last modification date of the document, in elapsed seconds since January 1, 1970 GMT.
`URL getURL( )`	Get the URL associated with the document.

BUILDING A `URLConnector`

Let's take a look at an application that uses the methods of the `URLConnection` class. Listing 16-12 shows the URLConnector application, a program that allows you to connect to a URL anywhere on the Internet, and then displays information about the document that it finds there. To try it yourself, you'll need to have access to the Web, either via a direct connection or via modem. The program works the same way as your Web browser: If a standard Web browser can access a URL, so can the program. (Note that some Internet service providers supply browsers using proprietary communications protocols. The kind of connection provided by such ISPs is not adequate for the purposes of this program. If the standard version of Internet Explorer or Navigator works OK, so will this program; if they don't, it won't.) Figure 16-12 shows the result of running the application.

Listing 16-12 URLConnector.java

```java
// Using the URL class to connect to a site and read a
// document
import java.net.*;
import java.awt.*;
import java.awt.event.*;
import java.io.*;
import java.util.Date;

public class URLConnector extends Frame ⇐
                          implements ActionListener, ⇐
                                     WindowListener
{
    TextField theLocation = new TextField("", 40);
    TextArea  theDoc      = new TextArea();
    Button    fetchButton = new Button("Fetch");
    Button    quitButton  = new Button("Quit");
```

continued on next page

continued from previous page

```
public static void main(String args[])
{
    URLConnector theApp = new URLConnector();
}

public URLConnector()
{
    setTitle( "The URLConnector Example" );
    theLocation.setFont(new Font("Courier", ⇐
      Font.BOLD, 12));

    Panel p1 = new Panel();
    p1.add( new Label( "Enter a URL: " ));
    p1.add( theLocation );
    add( p1, "North" );

    add( theDoc, "Center" );

    Panel p2 = new Panel();
    p2.add( fetchButton );
    p2.add( quitButton );
    add( p2, "South" );

    theLocation.addActionListener(this);
    fetchButton.addActionListener(this);
    quitButton.addActionListener(this);
    addWindowListener(this);

    setSize( 400, 300 );
    setVisible(true);
    theLocation.requestFocus();
}

public void actionPerformed(ActionEvent theEvent)
{
    if (theEvent.getSource( ) == fetchButton
      || theEvent.getSource( ) == theLocation)
    {
        try
        {
            // Open the URL
            URL theURL = new URL(theLocation.getText());
            theDoc.setText("Fetching: " + theURL + '\n');

            // Open a URLConnection
            URLConnection con = theURL.openConnection();

            // Retrieve info about the document
            String   encoding = con.getContentEncoding();
            int      length   = con.getContentLength();
            String   type     = con.getContentType();
            long     expires  = con.getExpiration();
            Date     modified = ⇐
              new Date( con.getLastModified() );
```

```
                    // Display document info
                    theDoc.append⇐
                      ("Content encoding: " + encoding + '\n');
                    theDoc.append⇐
                      ("Content length  : " + length   + '\n');
                    theDoc.append⇐
                      ("Content type    : " + type     + '\n');
                    theDoc.append⇐
                      ("Expires         : " + expires  + '\n');
                    theDoc.append⇐
                      ("Last modified   : " + modified + '\n');

                    // Display the document if possible
                    Object urlContent = theURL.getContent();

                    String objectType =⇐
                      urlContent.getClass().getName();
                    theDoc.append( ⇐
                      "\nFetched a " + objectType + "\n\n" );
                    // Plain text
                    if ( urlContent instanceof String )
                    {
                        theDoc.append( (String) urlContent );
                    }
                    // Text/html
                    else if (urlContent instanceof InputStream)
    {
                        String s = "";
                        int b = 0;
                        while ( ⇐
                          (b =((InputStream) ⇐
                          urlContent).read()) != -1 )
                            s += (char) b;

                        theDoc.append(s);
                    }
                    else
                    {
                        theDoc.append(⇐
                          "Sorry, cannot show that type object");
                    }
                }

                // Handle badly formed URLs
                catch (MalformedURLException badURL)
                {
                    theDoc.append( ⇐
                      "Sorry, cannot interpret your URL\n" );
                    theDoc.append( badURL.toString() );
                }
                // Handle I/O errors, etc
                catch (IOException io)
                {
                    theDoc.append( ⇐
                      "Sorry, URL contents are not available\n");
                    theDoc.append( io.toString() );
                }
                catch (NullPointerException n)
                {
```

continued on next page

continued from previous page

```
                        theDoc.append(⇐
                        "Sorry, URL contents are not available\n");
            }
        }
        else if (theEvent.getSource( ) == quitButton) ⇐
            quitApplication( );
    }

    public void windowClosed       (WindowEvent e) { }
    public void windowClosing       (WindowEvent e) ⇐
        { quitApplication( ); }
    public void windowDeiconified(WindowEvent e) { }
    public void windowIconified    (WindowEvent e) { }
    public void windowOpened        (WindowEvent e) { }
    public void windowActivated    (WindowEvent e) { }
    public void windowDeactivated(WindowEvent e) { }

    public void quitApplication( )
    {
        setVisible(false);
        dispose( );
        System.exit(0);
    }
}
```

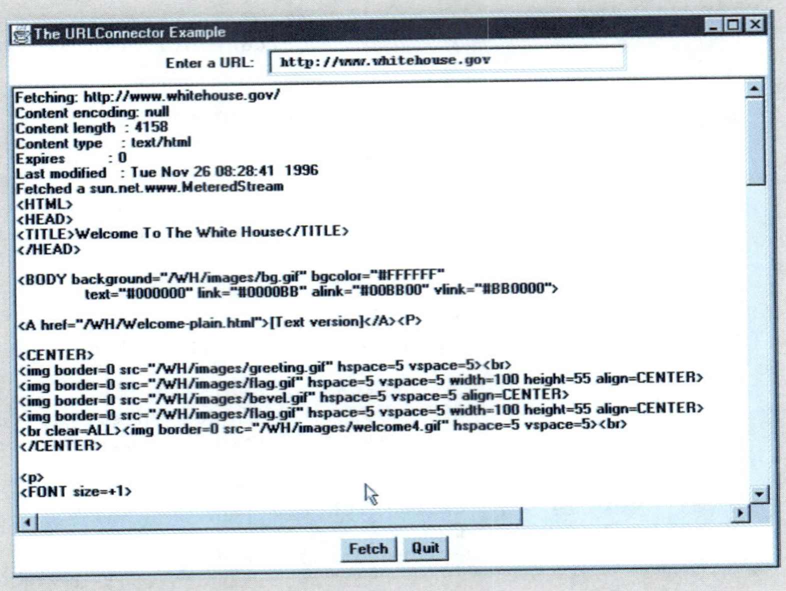

FIGURE 16-12

Using the URLConnector application

Reading the Connection Information

The URLConnector application consists of a `TextField` (named `theLocation`) at the top of the screen, into which you enter a URL. The center of the display is a `TextArea` component, which will be used to display information about your URL. The bottom area hosts two buttons, Fetch and Quit. After typing the URL to which you want to connect, you can press ENTER or click the Fetch button, which causes the application to create a URL object:

```
// Create a URL object
URL theURL = new URL( theLocation.getText() );
```

This URL object is subsequently used to obtain a `URLConnection` object.

```
// Open a URLConnection
URLConnection con = theURL.openConnection();
```

The application then obtains information about the document:

```
// Retrieve info about the document
String   encoding = con.getContentEncoding();
int      length   = con.getContentLength();
String   type     = con.getContentType();
long     expires  = con.getExpiration();
Date     modified = new Date( con.getLastModified() );
```

and then displays it in the `TextArea`:

```
// Display document info
theDoc.append("Content encoding: " + encoding + '\n');
theDoc.append("Content length  : " + length   + '\n');
theDoc.append("Content type    : " + type     + '\n');
theDoc.append("Expires         : " + expires  + '\n');
theDoc.append("Last modified   : " + modified + '\n');
```

Using Document Information

While the ability to open a document anywhere on the Web is fascinating, most of us would also want to retrieve the information *in* the document—not just the information *about* the document. The URLConnector application retrieves the specified document from a Web server. To do this, it uses the URL method, `getContent()`:

```
// Display the document if possible
Object urlContent = theURL.getContent();
```

Several types of objects can be returned by the `getContent()` method. A Web server normally provides a plain text document in a way that causes `getContent()` to return a `String`, which the application simply appends to the `TextArea`:

```
if ( urlContent instanceof String )              // Plain text
{
    theDoc.append( (String) urlContent );
}
```

Fetching an HTML document, by contrast, normally causes `getContent( )` to return an object of type `InputStream`. In this event the application reads the stream and appends its contents to the `TextArea`:

```
else if ( urlContent instanceof InputStream )   // Text/html
{
    String s = "";
    int b = 0;
    while ( (b =((InputStream) urlContent).read()) != -1 )
        s += (char) b;

    theDoc.append(s);
}
```

Other object types are possible. For example, a GIF file causes `getContent( )` to return an image. While this simple example doesn't deal with these possibilities, you can see that `getContent( )` would make it easy to construct a rudimentary Web browser.

SOCKETS: WRITING CLIENTS AND SERVERS

Although writing Web programs is both fun and useful, Java allows you to do much more. Java has built-in facilities that let you work directly with *sockets*, which are streams of data that can flow between networked computers.

When a socket is created, it has two forms of identification: a *host* and a *port number*. This allows each host to have a number of sockets in operation, each distinguished by its port number. Certain ports have been reserved for particular sorts of conversations. For example, when one host wants to send mail to another, the SMTP (Simple Mail Transfer Protocol) system will contact the destination host using port 25. The two hosts will engage in a conversation that culminates in the assignment of a new port number, specifically for private conversation concerning their exchange of mail messages. Ports numbered above 1023 are used for this purpose. Figure 16-13 illustrates this interaction.

Just as most conversations require at least two participants, communication using sockets generally involves at least two programs. One program is called a *server*, and the other is called a *client*. Deciding which should be called the server and which should be called the client is sometimes a rather arbitrary thing. The basic notion is that the client requests data and the server supplies it. It's quite possible, of course, for a server program to also request information from a client program. In the most confusing case, each is requesting information from, and providing information to, the other in about equal proportions. Flipping a coin may be the appropriate way to decide who's called what in such a situation.

FIGURE 16-13
A socket conversation

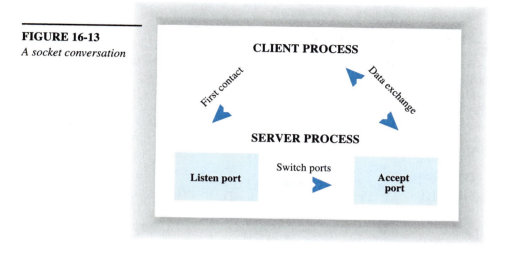

Introducing ServerSocketS

The ServerSocket class is used to create a server application that listens on a specified port for a client requesting service. To create a ServerSocket object, you use a constructor that takes the port number as an integer argument. Once you have a ServerSocket() object, the accept() method can be used to obtain a Socket object for a nice, private conversation between the server and the client. The accept() method will block (wait) until a client attaches. The ServerSocket constructor throws an IOException if an error occurs. Table 16-12 summarizes the public instance methods of the ServerSocket class.

TABLE 16-12
KEY public METHODS OF THE ServerSocket CLASS

METHOD HEADER	FUNCTION
Socket accept( )	Accept the client and return a socket that can be used for further communication (throw IOException).
void close( )	Close the ServerSocket (throw IOException).
inetAddress getInetAddress( )	Get the IP address of the client, for example, 199.184.237.201.
int getLocalPort( )	Return the local port on which the ServerSocket is listening.

The `inetAddress` Class

Recall from Chapter 1 that every machine connected to the Internet has a unique address, called its IP address. Java has a class specifically designed to represent those addresses, the `InetAddress` class. An `InetAddress` object can be retrieved by use of the `ServerSocket` class's `getInetAddress()` method. In addition, the `InetAddress` class has several class methods that allow you to retrieve an `InetAddress` object. These are shown in Table 16-13.

TABLE 16-13
KEY `public` CLASS METHODS OF THE `InetAddress` CLASS

METHOD HEADER	FUNCTION
`InetAddress[]` `getAllByName(String host)`	Return an array containing all the `InetAddress`es by which the specified host is known (throw `UnknownHostException`).
`InetAddress` `getByName(String host)`	Return an `InetAddress` by which the specified host is known (throw `UnknownHostException`).
`InetAddress` `getLocalHost( )`	Get the `InetAddress` of the local host (throw `UnknownHostException`).

Once you have an `InetAddress` object, you may use the methods shown in Table 16-14. As usual, the class also includes a `toString()` method that makes it easy to display or print an IP address, although the method is not shown in the table, because it is inherited from `Object`.

TABLE 16-14
KEY `public` METHODS OF THE `InetAddress` CLASS

METHOD HEADER	FUNCTION
`byte[] getAddress( )`	Get the four components of the IP address as elements of a byte array.
`String getHostName( )`	Get the host name.

THE `Socket` CLASS

The `Socket` class is used by the server and client to converse. Normally a `Socket` object is returned by the `accept()` method of the `ServerSocket` class, but it is also possible to manually create a `Socket` using either of the constructors shown in Table 16-15. For example, the client programs you write will need to use one of these constructors to create the `Socket` they use to contact the server. Like the other socket-related classes, these constructors throw an `IOException` in the event of an error.

TABLE 16-15
KEY public CONSTRUCTORS OF THE Socket CLASS

```
Socket(String host, int port)
Socket(InetAddress ipNumber, int port)
```

The `Socket` class also provides a number of useful methods, which are summarized in Table 16-16. Note that because a `Socket` joins two hosts, it actually has two associated port numbers: one on the local host (that is, the host on which the current thread is running) and one on the remote host.

A Socket Example

A client-server application consists of two programs that carry on a conversation with each other over the network. The EchoServer application—shown in Listing 16-13—and the `EchoClient` applet—shown in Listing 16-14—demonstrate how Java programs can carry on such a conversation via sockets.

The EchoServer program is built as a console-mode application (as are many server applications), because it does not require any user interaction. Once started, it logs all of its activity to the console window. The `EchoClient` applet presents a `TextField`, in which the user can enter characters, and a `TextArea`, which is used to display responses from the server. When the user types characters into the `TextField` and then presses ⏎ENTER⏎, the characters are sent to the server, which sends back a reply that the client displays in the `TextArea`. Figure 16-14 shows the server's activity log and the client applet's screen.

TABLE 16-16
KEY public METHODS OF THE Socket CLASS

METHOD HEADER	FUNCTION
`void close( )`	Close the socket (throw `IOException`).
`InetAddress getInetAddress( )`	Get the `InetAddress` associated with the Socket.
`InputStream getInputStream( )`	Return an `InputStream` that can be used to read data from the `Socket` (throw `IOException`).
`int getLocalPort( )`	Return the port number on the local host.
`OutputStream getOutputStream( )`	Return an `OutputStream` that can be used to write data to the `Socket` (throw `IOException`).
`int getPort( )`	Return the port number on the remote host.

Listing 16-13 EchoServer.java

```java
// A server written in Java
import java.net.*;
import java.io.*;

public class EchoServer
{
    final static int thePort = 1234;
    ServerSocket theServerSocket;

    public static void main(String args[])
    {
        EchoServer theApp = new EchoServer();
        theApp.run();
    }

    public EchoServer()
    {
        try
        {
            theServerSocket  = new ServerSocket(thePort);
        }
        catch (IOException io)
        {
            System.err.println("Socket error:  terminating");
            System.exit(1);
        }
    }

    public void run()
    {
        try
        {
            System.out.println( "Server ready." );

            Socket theSocket = theServerSocket.accept();
            System.out.println( "Client connected." );

            BufferedReader in =
                new BufferedReader(
                new InputStreamReader ⇐
                (theSocket.getInputStream()));
            PrintWriter out =
                new PrintWriter(
                new OutputStreamWriter⇐
                (theSocket.getOutputStream()),true);

            while (true)
            {
                String line = in.readLine();
                if (line == null)
                    break;
                System.out.println("Read:  " + line);
                line = line.toUpperCase() + "!";
                out.println(line);
                System.out.println("Wrote: " + line);
            }
            in.close();
            out.close();
```

```
                                    theSocket.close();
                                    theServerSocket.close();
                                    System.exit(0);
                        }
                        catch (IOException io)
                        {
                                    System.err.println("Socket error:  terminating");
                                    System.exit(1);
                        }
            }
}
```

Listing 16-14 EchoClient.java

```java
// A client applet (works with EchoServer.java)
import java.awt.*;
import java.awt.event.*;
import java.applet.*;
import java.net.*;
import java.io.*;

public class EchoClient extends Applet ⇐
                        implements ActionListener
{
      final static int thePort = 1234;

      Socket            theSocket;
      BufferedReader    in;
      PrintWriter       out;
      TextField         theField = new TextField();
      TextArea          theArea  = new TextArea();

      public void init()
      {
          try
          {
              setLayout(new BorderLayout());

              add( theField, "North" );
              add( theArea, "Center" );
              theArea.setEditable(false);

              setVisible(true);

              String host = getCodeBase().getHost();
              theSocket   = new Socket( host, thePort );

              in  = new BufferedReader(⇐
                    new InputStreamReader(⇐
                    theSocket.getInputStream()));
              out = new PrintWriter(new⇐
                    OutputStreamWriter(⇐
                    theSocket.getOutputStream()),true);

              theField.addActionListener(this);
          }
          catch (IOException io)
```

continued on next page

continued from previous page

```
        {
                System.err.println("IOException:\n" + io);
        }
    }

    public void start()
    {
        try
        {
            while (true)
            {
                String s = in.readLine();
                if ( s != null ) theArea.append( s + '\n' );
            }
        }
        catch (IOException io)
        {
                System.err.println( "IOException:\n" + io );
        }
    }

    public void actionPerformed(ActionEvent theEvent)
    {
        out.println( theField.getText() );
        theField.setText( "" );
    }
}
```

FIGURE 16-14

Output of EchoServer and `EchoClient`

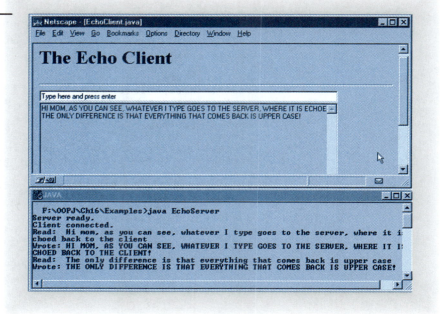

A Quick Tour Through EchoServer

The parts of each of these programs are fairly straightforward. Both the client and server programs will need to communicate on the same port. Because this is a test program, that port is "hard-coded" as the `static final int`, `thePort`. The EchoServer application has a single field, the `ServerSocket` object called `theServerSocket`. The constructor of EchoServer calls the `ServerSocket` constructor with the predefined port number, and then invokes the `run()` method. The `run()` method immediately begins listening for a client, using the `accept()` method.

The `accept()` method returns a `Socket` object that will enable the server to converse with the client. Remember from Chapter 14, "Streams and Files," that when information flows between programs, it does so by way of streams. `Socket`s are no exception to this rule. Once the server has acquired a `Socket`, it then creates a `BufferedReader` object (to receive messages from the client), and a `PrintWriter` object (to send messages to the client). These streams are acquired by calling the `Socket`'s `getInputStream()` and `getOutputStream()` methods and wrapping the result in one or more constructors that yield a `Reader` or `Writer` with the desired characteristics.

Once the server has set up the `Socket` to enable its conversation with the client, the program enters an endless loop that involves five steps:

1. Read a line of text from the client:

   ```
   String line = in.readLine();
   ```

2. Echo the line to standard output so you can see what you read:

   ```
   System.out.println("Read:  " + line);
   ```

3. Create an uppercase version of the `String` to send back to the client:

   ```
   line = line.toUpperCase() + "!";
   ```

4. Write it out to the client using the standard `println()` method:

   ```
   out.println(line);
   ```

5. Display it on the server console as well:

   ```
   System.out.println("Wrote: " + line);
   ```

A Look at EchoClient

The `EchoClient` applet begins by setting up its display. It adds the input `TextField` to the top of the screen and the output (server-response) `TextArea` to the center. The `init()` method then attempts to open a `Socket` using the host name of the computer that served the applet (retrieved by using `getCodeBase().getHost()`) and the hard-coded port number discussed earlier. If the `Socket` cannot be created—for instance, if the server is not running—an `IOException` is thrown. If the `Socket` is created, a `BufferedReader` and a `PrintWriter` object are created, just as with the server. And, as with the server, the client will receive information via the `BufferedReader` and send information out on the `PrintWriter`.

The `EchoClient` listens for input from the server by using the `start()` method, which is a simple endless loop that attempts to read a line of text from the `BufferedReader` (the server) and then display it in the `TextArea`. Of course, the server is not going to be sending any text to the client unless the client sends it some data first. In `EchoClient`, this occurs in the `actionPerformed()` method, which simply retrieves the text from the input `TextField` and then writes it to the `PrintWriter` object, which is connected to the `Socket` which, in turn, is connected to the server.

JUMBO'S LAST DANCE

"L A W Y E R S !" S A I D   J U M B O   T O   H I M S E L F

"Wouldn't you know it would have to be lawyers?" he said, as he surveyed his new clientele, the demise of the Jungle Joint still fresh in his mind.

Leaning against the bar with his elbow, his face and form obscured in the shadows thrown from the roaring oak-fueled fire by the potted tropical plants placed tastefully around the room, Jumbo surveyed his domain. In the distance, the last light of evening broke through the clouds and still illuminated the very tops of the mountains, making them seem unnaturally close. Below, across the sound and above the silent ferry making its way to the far landing, the lights of the city were clearly visible. Across the room, the tables were packed so close that there was almost no room to move between them. And, wonder of wonders, at every table sat a customer, typing away at a keyboard, ordering Brazilian Roasts and Italian Espressos, each of the screens showing a glowing logo in the upper-left corner: JT&T.

Jungle Telephone and Telegraph had really been Zenia's idea. "The vending-machine idea is all right as far as it goes," she'd said one evening, coming home after a hard day at her job as a waitress—the job she'd taken when the JavaMatic millions failed to materialize. "But what you really need to build is something that'll go to work for me," she said as Jumbo handed her a large cup of Luscious Licorice-Lime and steered her toward her favorite easy chair. And that very evening he had gotten started.

The EchoServer application is a very simple server. It handles only a single connection between a single server and client. Most real servers need to be capable of dealing with multiple simultaneous requests from several clients. Listing 16-15, the JTTServer application, shows how threads can be used together with sockets to accomplish this. The same client you used previously, `EchoClient`, can be used, but the HTML file, `JTTClient.html` (shown in Listing 16-16), attaches four clients to Jumbo's new automated ordering system. You can see the action in Figure 16-15.

Listing 16-15 JTTServer.java

```java
// A Server that can handles multiple connections
import java.net.*;
import java.io.*;

public class JTTServer
{
    final static int thePort = 1234;
    ServerSocket theServerSocket;

    public static void main(String args[])
    {
        JTTServer theApp = new JTTServer();
        theApp.run();
    }

    public JTTServer()
    {
        try
        {
            theServerSocket   = new ServerSocket(thePort);
        }
        catch (IOException io)
        {
            System.err.println("Socket error:  terminating");
            System.exit(1);
        }
    }

    public void run()
    {
        try
        {
            System.out.println("JT&T is open for business.");

            while (true)
            {
                Socket theSocket = theServerSocket.accept();
                System.out.println⇐
                  ("A customer has requested a table.");
                Connection connection = ⇐
                  new Connection(theSocket);
            }
        }
        catch (IOException io)
        {
            System.err.println("Socket error:  terminating");
            System.exit(1);
        }

    }
}

class Connection extends Thread
{
    Socket theSocket;
    BufferedReader in;
```

continued on next page

continued from previous page

```
PrintWriter out;

public Connection(Socket socket)
{
    try
    {
        theSocket = socket;
        in = new BufferedReader
            (new InputStreamReader
            (theSocket.getInputStream()));
        out = new PrintWriter
            (new OutputStreamWriter
            (theSocket.getOutputStream()), true);
        start();
    }
    catch (IOException io)
    {
        System.err.println("Socket error:  terminating");
        System.exit(1);
    }
}

public void run()
{
    int table = 0;
    try
    {
        table = theSocket.getPort();
        System.out.println
          ("Customer seated at table " + table + ".");
        out.println("Hello, table " + table +
          ", what can I get you?");
        while (true)
        {
            String line = in.readLine();
            if (line == null)
                break;
          System.out.println("Table " + table +
            " wants " + line + ".");
          out.println("I'm sorry, we're out of " +
            line + " right now.");
          out.println("Is there
            something else you'd like instead?");
        }
        in.close();
        out.close();
        theSocket.close();
    }
    catch (IOException io)
    {
        System.err.println("Table " + table +
          " has abruptly left.");
    }
}
}
```

Listing 16-16 JTTClient.html

```
<HTML>
<HEAD>
<TITLE>JTTClient.html</TITLE>
</HEAD>
<BODY>
<APPLET CODE=EchoClient HEIGHT=200 WIDTH=300>
</APPLET>
<APPLET CODE=EchoClient HEIGHT=200 WIDTH=300>
</APPLET>
<APPLET CODE=EchoClient HEIGHT=200 WIDTH=300>
</APPLET>
<APPLET CODE=EchoClient HEIGHT=200 WIDTH=300>
</APPLET>
</BODY>
</HTML>
```

FIGURE 16-15
Output of the JTT client and server

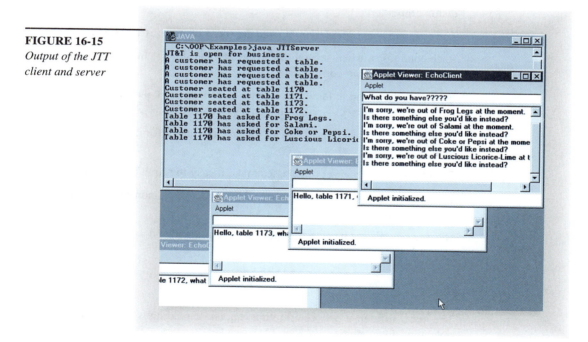

Summary

- Threads allow computers to perform multiple tasks at the same time.

- All the threads of a single program share the same address space and can therefore access the same objects.

- Each thread of a single program uses its own set of local variables.

- Threads can be stopped, in which case they cannot be restarted; they can also be suspended and resumed.

- A `Thread` can be created by an object that implements the `Runnable` interface.

- A class can extend the class `Thread`, in which case instances of the class are distinct threads.

- The statements executed by a `Thread` are those of its `run( )` method.

- Race conditions, when several threads access the same data without proper synchronization, can corrupt data.

- Java's synchronization facilities, such as `synchronized`, `wait( )`, and `notify( )`, can protect a program against race conditions.

- Deadlocks result when threads wait for one another or for other conditions that cannot occur.

- The `URL` and `URLConnection` classes make it easy to retrieve Web documents.

- The `ServerSocket` class is used in a server process, to monitor a port for incoming client requests.

- The `Socket` class is used to permit hosts to communicate with clients.

Quiz

1. The main difference between multitasking and threading is that threads operate inside a single _____.

2. All the threads of a program have access to the same _____, although they all use distinct _____ variables.

3. To implement the `Runnable` interface, a class must define the _____ method.

4. Another way of creating a `Thread`, apart from implementing the `Runnable` interface, is to create a class that extends the class _____.

5. If you want to stop a thread permanently, you can invoke the _____ method on it, but if you want to stop it temporarily, you should invoke the _____ method.

6. A `Thread` with a _____ priority number can take control of the system away from a running thread.

7. A type of `Thread` called a(n) _____ is used to perform auxiliary tasks.

8. A condition in which two threads "compete" for access to a value is called a(n) _____.

9. When two threads are each waiting for the other and cannot proceed, the program is said to be in a(n) _____.

10. Every object has an associated bit, called the _____ bit, which can be used to regulate access to the object.

11. The _____ method can be used to suspend a thread until an object is available.

12. The _____ method is used to inform waiting objects that an object has become available.

13. A(n) _____ object can be used to obtain information about a Web document or the contents of a Web document.

14. A(n) _____ object is used to represent the URLs by which Web documents are known.

15. A `ServerSocket` object is associated with a _____ number, on which the server listens for client requests.

16. A(n) _____ can be used to pass data between a client and a server running on different computers.

Exercises

1. Modify the `EchoClient` and EchoServer for use as a simple "chat" application that allows users to type messages to one another over the Internet. Your chat program should include a "login" dialog that allows the user to enter a nickname.

2. Modify the chat application described in the previous exercise so that several people can chat simultaneously. Messages should be displayed along with the nickname of the person who sent the message. You'll need to use a multithreaded server similar to that shown in the JTTServer application.

3. The game of Battleship is played by two players on a grid. Each player places a battleship on the grid, at a location known only to that player. The players then take turns attempting to locate and sink their opponent's battleship. Modify the `JTTClient` and JTTServer to allow two people to play Battleship via the Web.

4. Use the online documentation that accompanies the JDK to learn about the `StreamTokenizer` class. Use `StreamTokenizer` along with `URLConnection` to create a simple Web crawler that downloads a specified Web page and then downloads the pages referenced by the original page. Your crawler should continue to download pages until it has moved a specified distance from the original page. It should also avoid downloading the same page twice.

A

Quiz Answers

Chapter 1

1. The modern digital computer was invented in the late **1940s**.

2. Computers have three main components: **memory**, **CPU**, and **input/output**.

3. The on/off switches that make up a computer's memory are called **bits** and each can store one piece of information.

4. A byte consists of **8** bits.

5. Instructions stored in the memory of a computer are called stored **programs**.

6. The numbers that represent machine-language operations are called **op-codes**.

7. Because machine-language programs work on only a specific CPU, such programs are not **portable**.

8. Low-level languages that allow the programmer to refer to instructions and data by name are called **assembly** languages.

9. Program **interpreters** allow programmers to write instructions for an ideal machine and expand the programmer's code into machine instructions a line at a time.

10. Program interpreters were disliked by some, who felt they executed programs too **slowly**.

11. A program that translates an entire source program into machine language for efficient execution is called a **compiler**.

12. High-level languages allow programmers to focus on the **problem**, rather than on how the computer works inside.

13. The structured programming technique of attacking a problem a piece at a time is known as **divide and conquer**, **top-down design**, **stepwise refinement**, or **functional decomposition**.

14. Structured programming holds that each procedure within a program should have a(n) **single** entry and exit.

15. Structured programming recommends that programmers use only three control structures in their programs: sequence, **selection**, and **iteration**.

16. Information hiding involves the use of **local** variables.

17. Polymorphism means that different objects respond distinctively to the **same** message.

18. Inheritance allows the ability to **expand** or **extend** existing objects.

19. Encapsulation involves treating related data and instructions as a(n) **unit**.

20. The Internet began as a communications network for **military** use, known as the ARPANET.

21. The Internet is based on the use of **protocols**, standard ways of exchanging data between computers.

22. Hypertext documents allow a user to **jump** or **move** from one document or topic to another, rather than reading serially.

23. The two programs involved in Web transactions are the **server**, which runs continuously on a host, and the **client**.

24. The **client** program decides how to format a Web document for display to the user.

25. HTML is a simple language for specifying the **structure** or **form** of Web pages, not their appearance.

26. HTML embeds special structural and formatting commands known as **tags** in a text file.

27. The HTML tag used to specify an applet is the `<APPLET>` tag.

28. The device used to specify the format, location, and identity of every Web document is known as a(n) **URL**.

29. An executable Java program embedded in a Web page is called a(n) **applet**.

Chapter 2

1. In Java, programs are communities of **objects**.

2. A collection of interacting components of any sort is called a **system**.

3. Object-oriented programs are organized more like the modern **workgroup** than the old-fashioned assembly line.

4. All objects have three characteristics: identity, **state**, and **behavior**.

5. You tell one object from another using its **identity** or **name**.

6. Since an object has a(n) **state** stored by its fields, its properties can change over its lifetime.

7. Every object has **behavior** defined by its methods and knows how to respond to messages.

8. A class is a **blueprint** or **pattern** that can be used to instantiate many objects.

9. Every object is an **instance** or **member** of some class.

10. Classes give objects the ability to perform actions through **methods**.

11. Objects **invoke** or **call** methods upon receiving a **message**.

12. Classes give objects the ability to store state by defining object **attributes** or **fields**.

13. The ability to create a new class based on an old one is called **inheritance**.

14. A newly created class is called a **child class** or **sub-class**.

15. The creating class is called a **parent class** or **super-class**.

16. The created class may have new **attributes** and **methods** not found in the old class.

17. The three types of programs that can be created using Java are **applets**, **console applications**, and **GUI (graphical user interface) applications**.

18. A class definition includes a class **header** and a class body.

19. Language keywords are sometimes called **reserved words** because they cannot be used to name classes, variables, or methods.

20. Identifiers may not start with a(n) **digit** or contain **special** characters, other than the underscore (**_**) or the dollar sign (**$**).

21. In class names, every word starts with a **capital** letter.

22. Method and field names should start with a **lower-case** letter.

23. The keyword `extends` denotes **inheritance**.

24. The `import` statement is used to access library classes and packages.

25. A built-in Java object that can be used in an applet to hold text, display itself, and move around the screen is the `Label`.

26. The `new` operator is used to create a new object.

27. The `assignment` or `=` operator is used to store a value in an object.

28. The `init( )` method is run when an applet is first loaded.

29. Program readability can be improved by good use of whitespace and by **comments**, which are ignored by the compiler.

30. Methods **define** behavior and messages **trigger** the behavior.

31. When the mouse is moved over the applet window, Java sends a(n) **event** message called `mouseMoved( )` to the applet.

Chapter 3

1. Java's objects have identity, state, and **behavior**.
2. Java's values are of two types: objects and **primitives**.
3. It's possible to extend the state and behavior of **object** values.
4. Java has four integer types: `byte`, `short`, `int`, and `long`.
5. Java's family of numeric types whose members have values that include fractional parts are the **floating (point)** types, float and double.
6. Long values can store large numbers but require extra **space (to store)** and **time (to process)**.
7. Values that are unnamed and that do not change value during program execution are known as **literals**.
8. Named values that can change during program execution are known as **variables**.
9. Java stores small integers as `ints` and longer ones as `longs`.
10. Numbers specified in base 8 are called **octal** numbers and numbers specified in base **16** are called hexadecimal numbers.
11. `Char` values represent individual **characters**.
12. `Char` values use the standard encoding known as **Unicode**, rather than the more familiar ASCII.
13. Text data can be stored in `String` objects.
14. **Declaration** statements are used to create and optionally initialize variables.
15. The type of a variable and the type of its initializer need not be the same, only **compatible**.
16. Object types usually use the `new` operator to create new objects.
17. Object variables actually store the **name, address, or reference** to an object rather than the value of an object.
18. Static final variables do not change **value** during program execution.
19. Operators are used to manipulate the values stored in **literals, variables (or operands)** and **variables, literals (or operands)**.
20. Binary operators require two **operands**, while unary operators require only one.
21. Java's numeric operators include: addition, subtraction, multiplication, division, and **modulus**.
22. Expressions consist of **operators (operands)** and their **operands (operators)**.
23. An expression statement is evaluated by computing its result and then **discarding** the result.
24. Assignment operators can be used to change the **value** of variables.

25. Casts are used to change the **type** of a value.

26. The `Label` component can be used to display text.

27. The `Button` component can be used to trigger program actions.

28. The `TextField` component can be used to allow the user to enter text.

29. Fields are defined **outside** methods, while **local** variables are defined inside them.

Chapter 4

1. Objects contain methods that define their response to **messages**.

2. A method that returns no value has type **void**.

3. In addition to letters and digits, identifiers can contain the **underscore** character and the dollar sign (**$**).

4. A method **body**, which consists of a compound statement, contains statements executed when a message is received.

5. A return statement can include a(n) **expression** that specifies a value returned by the enclosing method.

6. The formal arguments of a method are sometimes called **dummy arguments**, because they are arbitrarily named.

7. While formal arguments are specified in a method, corresponding **parameters** are specified in a method call or message.

8. The values provided by a message must have types **compatible** with those of the arguments of the corresponding method.

9. Parameters passed by **value** can be altered within a method without altering the original variable.

10. It's possible to use the fact that object variables reference values, rather than contain them, to allow a method to alter the value of **fields** within the object.

11. Every method has a **compound** statement that includes one or more component statements.

12. The `this` object receives any messages that do not explicitly specify a receiver.

13. Static methods are associated with a **class** rather than an object.

14. The `drawString( )` method can be used to draw text on a(n) **applet (window) which runs inside a browser**.

15. Methods such as `init( )`, `start( )`, `stop( )`, and `destroy( )` are used to facilitate communication between a(n) **applet** and the **browser or appletviewer**.

16. The `import` statement makes it easier to refer to **library or built-in** objects.

17. Useful methods for mathematics are found in the `java.lang.Math` **class**, while the `java.util` **package** contains useful classes such as `Date` and `Random`.

18. The object-oriented design (OOD) process begins with writing a problem **description or summary**.

19. The OOD process suggests that we find the **objects** and **classes** and then find their attributes and methods.

20. The OOD process directs attention to the **events** objects must respond to and the **actions or behaviors** they must perform.

Chapter 5

1. The two Java conditional statements are the `if` and the `switch`.

2. In addition to the two conditional statements, Java has the **conditional** operator.

3. Conditional expressions are built using the **relational** operators and the **logical** operators.

4. The `==` and `!=` operators are sometimes treated as a special type of operator. They are known as **equality** operators.

5. Relational operators can be used to compare numeric values. The resulting value is a `boolean` value.

6. For strings and other object data types, the equality operators actually test **identity** rather than equality.

7. Logical operators take operands that have the `boolean` type.

8. Relational expressions joined with `&&` yield a true value if **both** expressions are true.

9. Relational expressions joined with `||` yield a true value if **either** expression is true.

10. When the first operand of an expression joined with `&&` is false, the second operand will/**will not** be evaluated.

11. When the first operand of an expression joined with `||` is false, the second operand **will**/will not be evaluated.

12. In the expression `(a || b && c)`, the first operator evaluated will be **&&**.

13. In the expression `(a && b || c)`, the first operator evaluated will be **&&**.

14. When an `if-else` has an unmatched `else`, the `else` is paired with the last preceding `if` that has no matching **else**.

15. An `if` statement **can**/cannot appear in the body of another `if` statement.

16. The `else-if` does/**does not** have a different syntax than the `if-else`.

17. While the `if` statement tests a `boolean` expression, the `switch` statement tests a(n) **integer (or `int`)** expression.

18. `Break` statements **are**/are not generally needed within `switch` statements.

19. Fall-through execution occurs within a <u>`switch`</u> unless the **case** statement ends with a <u>`break`</u> statement.

20. Most `switch` statements should generally include a <u>`default`</u> statement, to handle the possibility that the value of the test expression matches none of the `case` values.

21. The conditional operator has **three** operands, each of which is a(n) **expression**.

22. The conditional operator tends to make program code more compact but may also make it less **readable**.

Chapter 6

1. The three basic programming constructs are sequence, selection, and **iteration**.

2. The three kinds of Java loop statements are the <u>`while`</u>, the <u>`do-while`</u>, and the <u>`for`</u>.

3. The test expression of a loop has data type <u>`boolean`</u>.

4. The two main parts of a loop are the **test expression** and the **body**.

5. The body of a `do-while` loop will always execute at least **once**.

6. Two kinds of program loops are counting loops and **indeterminate** loops.

7. Given a determinate loop, it **is**/is not possible to determine the number of iterations by examining the loop.

8. The <u>`break`</u> statement can be used to exit a loop.

9. The <u>`equals( )`</u> method can be used to test strings for equality.

10. The value of a `static final` field can/**cannot** be changed during program execution.

11. One of the most common programming mistakes is the unintentional creation of a(n) **endless** loop.

12. An object's **state** is stored in variables known as fields.

13. The test expression of a loop specifies the condition under which it will **continue**, not the condition under which it will **terminate**.

14. Two types of testing loops are **sentinel** loops and **data** loops.

15. The loop that is useful for inspecting the parts of a data collection, that is, the bytes of a file, is the **data** loop.

16. The loop that is useful in searching for a specific value is the **sentinel** loop.

17. Reading a value before using it in the test expression of a loop is called **priming (the loop)**.

19. A loop placed inside the body of another loop is called a(n) **nested** loop.

20. The `continue` statement causes statements in a loop body to be skipped.

21. It is possible to exit an outer loop by using a **labeled** `break` statement.

Chapter 7

1. Syntax errors are also known as **compile-time** errors because they are discovered when the program is compiled.

2. The second major kind of errors, **run-time** errors, are found when the program is run.

3. To use the divide-and-conquer technique, you **comment out** lines of code.

4. A program **specification** describes the output and behavior of a program.

5. The goal of breaking a program during debugging is to find a way to make it fail **reliably**.

6. The most useful method in attempting to pinpoint a program bug is the `println( )`.

7. After locating and fixing a program bug, it's important to **test** the program, to find out if the original problem was really fixed and if additional problems were introduced.

8. A program should be tested using input values that are both **inside** and **outside** the valid range.

9. For even very simple programs, it is usually not possible to test **every** input value.

10. When every conditional expression within a program has been both true and false, 100% **condition** coverage has been achieved.

11. The Jdb utility can be used to set **breakpoints**, which suspend execution when a specified statement is reached.

Chapter 8

1. The `TextArea` is similar to the `TextField`, except that the `TextArea` provides **multiple lines** for input or output.

2. The `setEditable( )` method prevents a `TextField` or `TextArea` from **accepting input**.

3. The individual elements of an array are distinguished by using a number called the **subscript or index**.

4. Creating an array variable does not actually **create** the associated array unless an initializer is used.

5. Arrays in Java have a(n) **fixed** size.

6. The `target` field of the `Event` object passed to the `action( )` method identifies **the component that was the target (source) of the `ActionEvent`**.

7. A multi-dimensional array can be created by creating a(n) **array** of arrays.

8. A simple way to sort the elements of an array is to use an algorithm called the **Bubble** sort.

9. Sorting an array using the simple method used in this chapter involves testing whether pairs of array elements are in the proper order and **swapping** the contents of those that are not.

10. A `GridLayout` object can be used to establish a layout that consists of **rows** and **columns** of user-interface components.

11. When an array is passed as an argument to a method, it is passed by reference, which means the method **can**/cannot alter the values of elements of the array.

12. When an array element is passed as an argument to a method, it is passed by value, which means the method can/**cannot** alter the value of the element.

13. `String` values can be created using the `String( )` constructor or by specifying a `String` **literal**.

14. The `String` method **equals( )** can be used to test `Strings` for equality.

15. The `String` method **charAt( )** can be used to access the `char` at a given position within a `String`.

16. The `String` method **length( )** can be used to determine the length of a `String`.

17. The `String` method **compareTo( )** can be used to compare two `Strings` to determine which should be collated before the other.

18. The method **toString( )** can be used with many types of objects to convert their contents to a form suitable for printing.

19. The largest value returned by the `Random.nextFloat( )` method is just less than **1.0**.

20. A `Vector` is like an array, except that the size of a `Vector` **is fixed**.

21. A method that detects an unusual condition can throw a(n) **exception**.

22. When an exception occurs inside a `try` block, the associated `catch` statements are searched for an exception with a(n) **type** matching that of the exception that occurred.

23. The statements of a(n) **finally** are executed if any of the statements of the associated `try` is executed.

24. If a method contains statements that could cause an exception but does not contain a `try-catch` to handle the exception, the method can include the <u>throws</u> clause in its method header, which causes the exception to be re-thrown to a calling method.

Chapter 9

1. A method which provides access to the state of an object is known as a(n) <u>accessor</u> method.
2. A method that allows change to the state of an object is known as a(n) <u>mutator</u> method.
3. Fields and methods with `public` access **can**/cannot be accessed outside the enclosing class.
4. Fields and methods with `private` access can/**cannot** be accessed outside the enclosing class.
5. To implement data hiding, one generally specifies fields as having <u>private</u> access.
6. To implement data hiding, one generally specifies methods as having <u>public</u> access.
7. The `LayoutManager` that allows placement of components at the four compass points or at the center of the container is <u>BorderLayout</u>.
8. The constructor provided by Java for a class that does not explicitly define a constructor is known as a(n) **default** constructor.
9. Two constructors defined with the same name but different number of types of arguments are known as **overloaded** constructors.
10. The `this( )` method allows invoking a **constructor** method other than the one containing the call.
11. Unused memory is reclaimed by the **garbage collector**.
12. The <u>finalize( )</u> method is called on an object that is about to be reclaimed.

Chapter 10

1. In an inheritance relationship, the more general class is known as the **superclass or parent class**.
2. In an inheritance relationship, the more specific class is known as the **subclass or child class**.
3. The Java keyword that denotes inheritance is <u>extends</u>.
4. In addition to `public` and `private`, Java includes the access specifier <u>protected</u>, which is useful within the context of inheritance relationships.

5. The `this` object can be used to refer to a field of a parent class, which is shadowed by a field in the current class.

6. To prevent a class from being used as a parent class, the class can be specified as `final`.

7. Specifying a method as `final` prevents it from being overridden in a child class.

8. Casting an object to the type of its **superclass**/subclass is always safe.

9. An unsafe cast may result in a(n) **exception** event.

10. To avoid an unsafe cast, the `instanceof` operator can be used to test the type of an object.

11. Every class is a subclass of the class `Object`.

12. When a `String` expression includes a non-`String` operand, the `toString()` method is used to generate a `String` value for the non-`String` operand.

13. A package is a group of related **classes**.

14. An `import` statement allows the abbreviation of **class** names.

15. Package-level access is specified by **omitting** the keywords `public`, `private`, and `protected`.

Chapter 11

1. Colors in Java are created by using specified amounts of three colors: **red**, **green**, and **blue**.

2. Though it's possible to draw on a(n) `Canvas` component, the component has no fixed size and must be subclassed in order to be used.

3. When the AWT needs to draw a component, it invokes the component's `paint()` method.

4. When a component needs to be redrawn, a program should invoke the component's `repaint()` method.

5. The `update()` method, by default, clears the surface of a component by painting it with the proper background color.

6. Text contained in a `String` is drawn using the `drawString()` method.

7. Information about a `Font`, such as the width of a `String` drawn in the `Font`, can be obtained by using a(n) `FontMetrics` object.

8. A line can be drawn using the `drawLine()` method.

9. The outline of a rectangle can be drawn using the `drawRect()` method.

10. A filled rectangle can be drawn using the `fillRect()` method.

11. An `Image` can be drawn using the `drawImage()` method.

12. An audio clip can be played using the `loop()` method.

13. Java threads are needed to support **animation**, which is performed by rapidly displaying a sequence of static images.

14. A Java thread, when started, executes its `run( )` method.

15. A menu can be used with an application but not with a(n) **applet**.

Chapter 12

1. The widgets or controls used to create a graphical user interface (GUI) are known as **components**.

2. `Frames`, `Panels`, and objects that can contain other GUI objects are known as **containers**.

3. The screen area occupied by a component is always **rectangular** in shape.

4. A component that is **hidden** cannot be seen on the screen.

5. A component that is **disabled** does not respond to user actions.

6. A **cursor** is used to indicate the current position of the mouse.

7. `Frames` have a title **bar** while `Panels` do not.

8. `BorderLayout` allows components to be placed at the four positions of the **compass**.

9. Components added to a container using `FlowLayout` are added row-by-row, from left to right.

10. When using `GridLayout`, each component in the container is **resized** according to the size of the grid cell it occupies.

11. A `Label` is used to place text on the screen, but cannot receive input.

12. A `Button` can be clicked to generate an `Event`, but does nothing else.

13. A `Checkbox` can be clicked to toggle its state.

14. A `CheckboxGroup` can be used to combine `Checkboxes` into a set of radio buttons.

15. A `Choice` can be used to select a single item from a list but never allows selection of multiple items.

16. A `List` can be used to select multiple items from a list.

17. A `Scrollbar` has a value that can be changed by moving its **thumb**.

18. Both the `TextField` and `TextArea` extend the class `TextComponent`.

19. A `TextField` can be used to obtain a single line of input.

20. A `TextArea` can be used to obtain multiple lines of input.

21. A `Dialog` is a temporary window often used to obtain small amounts of input.

GridLook.java

```java
// Written using JDK 1.0, though compatible with JDK 1.1
// May produce warnings when compiled under JDK 1.1
import java.awt.*;

class GridLook extends Frame {
    static final int numLines = 8;
    static int frameNo = 1;

    Label      lineNo[]     = new Label      [numLines];
    Checkbox   activeLine[] = new Checkbox   [numLines];
    Choice     xPosition[]  = new Choice     [numLines];
    Choice     yPosition[]  = new Choice     [numLines];
    Choice     xSize[]      = new Choice     [numLines];
    Choice     ySize[]      = new Choice     [numLines];
    Checkbox   xFill[]      = new Checkbox   [numLines];
    Checkbox   yFill[]      = new Checkbox   [numLines];
    Choice     anchor[]     = new Choice     [numLines];
    Choice     xWeight[]    = new Choice     [numLines];
    Choice     yWeight[]    = new Choice     [numLines];

    Button update = new Button("Update");

    public static void main(String args[]) {
        GridLook g = new GridLook();
    }


    GridLook() {
        super("GridBag Workout");
        // setLayout(new FlowLayout());
        // setLayout(new GridLayout(12, 11));
        setLayout(new GridLayout(10, 1));
        Panel p = new Panel();
        p.add(new Label
            (" #   On    XPOS YPOS XSIZE YSIZE XFILL YFILL
             ANCHOR XWEIGHT YWEIGHT"));
        add(p);
        for (int i = 0; i < numLines; i++) {

            p = new Panel();
            p.setLayout(new FlowLayout());
            add(p);

            lineNo[i] = new Label("" + (i + 1));
            p.add(lineNo[i]);

            activeLine[i] = new Checkbox();
            p.add(activeLine[i]);

            xPosition[i] = new Choice();
            xPosition[i].addItem("0");
            xPosition[i].addItem("1");
            xPosition[i].addItem("2");
            xPosition[i].addItem("3");
            p.add(xPosition[i]);
```

```
yPosition[i] = new Choice();
yPosition[i].addItem("0");
yPosition[i].addItem("1");
yPosition[i].addItem("2");
yPosition[i].addItem("3");
p.add(yPosition[i]);

xSize[i] = new Choice();
xSize[i].addItem("1");
xSize[i].addItem("2");
xSize[i].addItem("3");
xSize[i].addItem("4");
p.add(xSize[i]);

ySize[i] = new Choice();
ySize[i].addItem("1");
ySize[i].addItem("2");
ySize[i].addItem("3");
ySize[i].addItem("4");
p.add(ySize[i]);

xFill[i] = new Checkbox();
p.add(xFill[i]);

yFill[i] = new Checkbox();
p.add(yFill[i]);

anchor[i] = new Choice();
anchor[i].addItem("Center");
anchor[i].addItem("North");
anchor[i].addItem("South");
anchor[i].addItem("East");
anchor[i].addItem("West");
p.add(anchor[i]);

xWeight[i] = new Choice();
xWeight[i].addItem("0");
xWeight[i].addItem("1");
xWeight[i].addItem("2");
xWeight[i].addItem("3");
xWeight[i].addItem("4");
xWeight[i].addItem("5");
xWeight[i].addItem("6");
xWeight[i].addItem("7");
xWeight[i].addItem("8");
xWeight[i].addItem("9");
xWeight[i].addItem("10");
p.add(xWeight[i]);

yWeight[i] = new Choice();
yWeight[i].addItem("0");
yWeight[i].addItem("1");
yWeight[i].addItem("2");
yWeight[i].addItem("3");
yWeight[i].addItem("4");
yWeight[i].addItem("5");
yWeight[i].addItem("6");
yWeight[i].addItem("7");
```

```
                yWeight[i].addItem("8");
                yWeight[i].addItem("9");
                yWeight[i].addItem("10");
                p.add(yWeight[i]);
            }

            add(update);
            pack();
            show();
    }

    public boolean handleEvent(Event event) {
        if (event.id == Event.WINDOW_DESTROY) {
            hide();
            dispose();
            System.exit(0);
            return true;
        }
        if (event.id == Event.ACTION_EVENT
          && event.target == update) {
            return clickedUpdate();
        }
        return false;
    }


    public boolean clickedUpdate() {
        GridBagLayout l = new GridBagLayout();
        GridBagConstraints c = new GridBagConstraints();
        CloseableFrame f;
        Button button;

        f = new CloseableFrame("Test Frame " + frameNo);
        f.setLayout(l);
        frameNo++;

        for (int i = 0; i < numLines; i++) {
            if (!activeLine[i].getState())
                continue;
            try {
                c.gridx =

Integer.parseInt(xPosition[i].getSelectedItem());
                c.gridy =

Integer.parseInt(yPosition[i].getSelectedItem());
                c.gridwidth =

Integer.parseInt(xSize[i].getSelectedItem());
                c.gridheight =

Integer.parseInt(ySize[i].getSelectedItem());
                c.fill = GridBagConstraints.NONE;
                if (xFill[i].getState()⇐
                    && !yFill[i].getState())
                    c.fill = GridBagConstraints.HORIZONTAL;
                else if (!xFill[i].getState()⇐
                    && yFill[i].getState())
                    c.fill = GridBagConstraints.VERTICAL;
```

```java
                        else if (xFill[i].getState()⇐
                          && yFill[i].getState())
                            c.fill = GridBagConstraints.BOTH;
                        switch (anchor[i].getSelectedIndex()) {
                        case 0:
                            c.anchor = GridBagConstraints.CENTER;
                            break;
                        case 1:
                            c.anchor = GridBagConstraints.NORTH;
                            break;
                        case 2:
                            c.anchor = GridBagConstraints.SOUTH;
                            break;
                        case 3:
                            c.anchor = GridBagConstraints.EAST;
                            break;
                        case 4:
                            c.anchor = GridBagConstraints.WEST;
                            break;
                        default:
                        }
                        c.weightx =
Integer.parseInt(xWeight[i].getSelectedItem());
                        c.weighty =
Integer.parseInt(yWeight[i].getSelectedItem());
                        button = new Button(" Button " + ⇐
                          (i + 1) + " ");
                        l.setConstraints(button, c);
                        f.add(button);
                }
                catch (NumberFormatException e) {
                    f.hide();
                    f.dispose();
                }
            }

        f.pack();
        f.show();
        return true;
    }
}


class CloseableFrame extends Frame {

    CloseableFrame() {
        super();
    }

    CloseableFrame(String t) {
        super(t);
    }

    public boolean handleEvent(Event event) {
```

```
        if (event.id == Event.WINDOW_DESTROY) {
            hide();
            dispose();
            return true;
        }
        return false;
    }

}
```

Chapter 13

1. An abstract class cannot be used to **instantiate** objects.

2. Any class with an abstract method is implicitly **abstract**.

3. A class that is not abstract is called a(n) **concrete** class.

4. To specify that a class satisfies the requirements of a given interface, the class is declared to **implement** the interface.

5. A mechanism that allows a programmer to associate an arbitrary action with an object is the **callback**.

6. All the fields of an interface must be declared as **static final**.

7. The primary method used to handle events in Java's original event model is the **handleEvent( )** method.

8. The **id** field of an **Event** object specifies the type of event which the **Event** describes.

9. The JDK 1.1 event model sends events directly from a(n) **source** object to a(n) **listener**.

10. Printing is performed in Java by using a special form of **Graphics** object that implements the **PrintGraphics** interface.

11. When your program has finished drawing a page of printed output, your program should call the **dispose( )** method.

12. When invoked on a **Container**, the **printAll( )** method calls **print( )** on each **Component** within the **Container**, including nested **Containers**.

13. The **forName( )** method returns a(n) **class object** for the class specified as its sole argument.

14. The **newInstance( )** method can be used to create a(n) **object**.

15. The easiest way to create a new AWT **Component** is usually to subclass the class **Canvas**.

Chapter 14

1. *Stream* is a metaphor for **data** moving into, or out of, a program.

2. A stream that is stored on a hard disk is referred to as a **file**.

3. The three main input-output classes are `InputStream`, which encapsulates stream input capabilities; `OutputStream`, which encapsulates stream output capabilities; and `RandomAccessFile`, which encapsulates capabilities for random access to a file.

4. The standard program input stream `stdin` is connected to the Java object `System.in`.

5. The standard program output stream `stdout` is connected to the Java object `System.out`.

6. When input-output errors occur the exception `IOException` or one of its subclasses is likely to be raised.

7. The `read( )` method is used to get input from a stream.

8. The `write( )` method is used to put output to a stream.

9. A **pipe** is like a channel through which data can be moved, but not saved; it can be used to connect data sources and sinks.

10. The class used to create objects that can read data files stored on disk is `FileInputStream`.

11. Returning −1 from a `read( )` method indicates that `end-of-file` has occurred.

12. Access to a file is terminated by using the `close( )` method.

13. Platform-independent input and output of Java data types are provided by the classes `DataInputStream` and `DataOutputStream`, respectively.

14. The `println( )` method that handles Unicode character output is provided by the class `PrintWriter`.

15. The class used to provide access to any byte of a file, for either reading or writing, is `RandomAccessFile`.

16. The `File` class encapsulates information pertaining to files and **directories**.

17. Building a dialog to navigate the file structure is facilitated by the class `FileDialog`.

Chapter 15

1. A `Stack` allows access only to its **topmost** element.

2. The two fundamental `Stack` operations are **push** and **pop**.

3. The internal Java data structure used to store fields is called the **heap** and that used to store local variables is called the **stack**.

4. The bitwise AND operator is <u>&</u>.

5. The bitwise OR operator is <u>|</u>.

6. The bitwise XOR operator is <u>^</u>.

7. The bitwise complement operator is <u>~</u>.

8. The unsigned right shift operator is <u>>></u> and the signed right shift operator is <u>>>></u>.

9. The `set( )` and `clear( )` methods are used with <u>`BitSet`</u> objects.

10. The abstract class `Dictionary` is implemented by the class <u>`Hashtable`</u>, which stores data pairs consisting of keys and associated values.

11. The <u>`Properties`</u> class provides convenient storage and access of configuration information.

12. Using the `Enumeration` class it is possible to **iterate** over the elements of a collection.

13. The <u>`hasMoreElements( )`</u> method of the `Enumeration` class tests whether elements remain, and the <u>`next( )`</u> method returns the next element.

14. The <u>`put( )`</u> method is used to add elements to a `Hashtable`, and the <u>`get( )`</u> method is used to retrieve elements from a `Hashtable`.

15. When creating a `StringTokenizer` object, the programmer must identify the **whitespace** characters that separate the tokens of the `String`.

16. Each element of a linked list has two components: One contains **information** and the other contains a **reference** to the following element of the list.

17. A useful property of a linked list is that its elements can be stored and retrieved **sequentially**, unlike the elements of an `Enumeration`, `Vector`, or `Hashtable`.

18. The `addImage( )` method is used with a <u>`MediaTracker`</u> object to enable it to track the loading of an image.

19. The <u>`Observable`</u> class can notify client objects of changes in its status.

20. The <u>`Observer`</u> interface receives notifications of changes in the status of a server object.

Chapter 16

1. The main difference between multitasking and threading is that threads operate inside a single **process**.

2. All the threads of a program have access to the same **fields**, though they all use distinct **local** variables.

3. To implement the `Runnable` interface, a class must define the <u>`run( )`</u> method.

4. Another way of creating a `Thread`, apart from implementing the `Runnable` interface, is to create a class that extends the class <u>`Thread`</u>.

5. If you want to stop a thread permanently, you can invoke the `stop( )` method on it, but if you want to stop it temporarily you should invoke the `suspend( )` method.

6. A `Thread` with a **higher** priority number can take control of the system away from a running thread.

7. A type of `Thread` called a(n) **daemon** is used to perform auxiliary tasks.

8. A condition in which two threads compete for access to a value is called a **race**.

9. When two threads are each waiting on the other and cannot proceed, the program is said to be in a(n) **deadlock**.

10. Every object has an associated bit, called the **monitor** bit, which can be used to regulate access to the object.

11. The `wait( )` method can be used to suspend a thread until an object is available.

12. The `notify( )` method is used to inform waiting objects that an object has become available.

13. A(n) `URLConnection` object can be used to obtain information about a Web document or the contents of a Web document.

14. A(n) `URLConnection` object is used to represent the URLs by which Web documents are known.

15. A `ServerSocket` object is associated with a **port** number, on which the server listens for client requests.

16. A(n) **socket** can be used to pass data between a client and a server running on different computers.

B

CD-ROM Contents

The contents and structure of the CD-ROM are as follows:

```
+---3RDPARTY                  Software from 3rd party vendors
|   +---JDK_1.02              Java Developer's Kit 1.02
|   +---JDK_1.1               Java Developer's Kit 1.1
|   +---WINEDIT               WinEdit from Wilson WindowWare
|   +---WINZIP                NicoMak Computing's WinZip
|   \---WORKSHOP              Java Workshop
|       +---SOLARIS           for Solaris
|       +---WIN95-NT          for Windows 95 and Windows NT
|
+---ARCHIVES                  All CD files in ZIP or TAR format
|   +---JDK_1.02              Java Developer's Kit 1.02
|   +---JDK_1.1               Java Developer's Kit 1.1
|   +---WE96Q321              ZIP file containing WinEdit 96
|   +---WORKSHOP              Solaris version of Java Workshop
|       +---INTEL             for Intel workstations
|       \---SPARC             for SPARCstations
|
\---SOURCE                    Source code for the book
    +---CHAP01                Projects for Chapter 1
    |   +---Listings          Source code
    |   \---Figures           Screen captures
    |
```

```
+---CHAP02                    Projects for Chapter 2
|   +---Listings-1.0          Code for JDK 1.02
|   +---Listings-1.1          Code for JDK 1.1
|   \---Figures              Screen captures
|
+---CHAP03                    Projects for Chapter 3
|   +---Listings-1.0          Code for JDK 1.02
|   +---Listings-1.1          Code for JDK 1.1
|   \---Figures              Screen captures
|
+---CHAP04                    Projects for Chapter 4
|   +---Listings-1.0          Code for JDK 1.02
|   +---Listings-1.1          Code for JDK 1.1
|   \---Figures              Screen captures
|
+---CHAP05                    Projects for Chapter 5
|   +---Listings-1.0          Code for JDK 1.02
|   +---Listings-1.1          Code for JDK 1.1
|   \---Figures              Screen captures
|
+---CHAP06                    Projects for Chapter 6
|   +---Listings-1.0          Code for JDK 1.02
|   +---Listings-1.1          Code for JDK 1.1
|   \---Figures              Screen captures
|
+---CHAP07                    Projects for Chapter 7
|   +---Listings-1.0          Code for JDK 1.02
|   +---Listings-1.1          Code for JDK 1.1
|   \---Figures              Screen captures
|
+---CHAP08                    Projects for Chapter 8
|   +---Listings-1.0          Code for JDK 1.02
|   +---Listings-1.1          Code for JDK 1.1
|   \---Figures              Screen captures
|
+---CHAP09                    Projects for Chapter 9
|   +---Listings-1.0          Code for JDK 1.02
|   +---Listings-1.1          Code for JDK 1.1
|   \---Figures              Screen captures
```

```
    |
    +---CHAP10                      Projects for Chapter 10
    |    +---Listings-1.0           Code for JDK 1.02
    |    +---Listings-1.1           Code for JDK 1.1
    |    \---Figures                Screen captures
    |
    +---CHAP11                      Projects for Chapter 11
    |    +---Listings-1.0           Code for JDK 1.02
    |    +---Listings-1.1           Code for JDK 1.1
    |    \---Figures                Screen captures
    |
    +---CHAP12                      Projects for Chapter 12
    |    +---Listings-1.0           Code for JDK 1.02
    |    +---Listings-1.1           Code for JDK 1.1
    |    \---Figures                Screen captures
    |
    +---CHAP13                      Projects for Chapter 13
    |    +---Listings-1.0           Code for JDK 1.02
    |    +---Listings-1.1           Code for JDK 1.1
    |    \---Figures                Screen captures
    |
    +---CHAP14                      Projects for Chapter 14
    |    +---Listings-1.0           Code for JDK 1.02
    |    +---Listings-1.1           Code for JDK 1.1
    |    \---Figures                Screen captures
    |
    +---CHAP15                      Projects for Chapter 15
    |    +---Listings-1.0           Code for JDK 1.02
    |    +---Listings-1.1           Code for JDK 1.1
    |    \---Figures                Screen captures
    |
    \---CHAP16                      Projects for Chapter 16
         +---Listings-1.0           Code for JDK 1.02
         +---Listings-1.1           Code for JDK 1.1
         \---Figures                Screen captures
```

Exhibit A
Java™ Development Kit
Version 1.1.x
Binary Code License

This binary code license ("License") contains rights and restrictions associated with use of the accompanying software and documentation ("Software"). Read the License carefully before installing the Software. By installing the Software you agree to the terms and conditions of this License.

1. Limited License Grant. Sun grants to you ("Licensee") a non-exclusive, non-transferable limited license to use the Software without fee for evaluation of the Software and for development of Java™ compatible applets and applications. Licensee may make one archival copy of the Software. Licensee may not re-distribute the Software in whole or in part, either separately or included with a product. Refer to the Java Runtime Environment Version 1.1 binary code license (http://www.javasoft.com/products/JDK/1.1/ index.html) for the availability of runtime code which may be distributed with Java compatible applets and applications.

2. Java Platform Interface. Licensee may not modify the Java Platform Interface ("JPI", identified as classes contained within the "java" package or any subpackages of the "java" package), by creating additional classes within the JPI or otherwise causing the addition to or modification of the classes in the JPI. In the event that Licensee creates any Java-related API and distributes such API to others for applet or application development, Licensee must promptly publish an accurate specification for such API for free use by all developers of Java-based software.

3. Restrictions. Software is confidential copyrighted information of Sun and title to all copies is retained by Sun and/or its licensors. Licensee shall not modify, decompile, disassemble, decrypt, extract, or otherwise reverse engineer Software. **Software may not be leased, assigned, or sublicensed, in whole or in part. Software is not designed or intended for use in on-line control of aircraft, air traffic, aircraft navigation, or aircraft communications; or in the design, construction, operation, or maintenance of any nuclear facility. Licensee warrants that it will not use or redistribute the Software for such purposes.**

4. Trademarks and Logos. This License does not authorize Licensee to use any Sun name, trademark, or logo. Licensee acknowledges that Sun owns the Java trademark and all Java-related trademarks, logos, and icons, including the Coffee Cup and Duke ("Java Marks") and agrees to: (i) comply with the Java Trademark Guidelines at http://java.com/trademarks.html; (ii) not do anything harmful to or inconsistent with Sun's rights in the Java Marks; and (iii) assist Sun in protecting those rights, including assigning to Sun any rights acquired by Licensee in any Java Mark.

5. Disclaimer of Warranty. Software is provided "AS IS," without a warranty of any kind. ALL EXPRESS OR IMPLIED REPRESENTATIONS AND WARRANTIES, INCLUDING ANY IMPLIED WARRANTY OF MER-CHANTABILITY, FITNESS FOR A PARTICULAR PURPOSE, OR NON-INFRINGEMENT, ARE HEREBY EXCLUDED.

6. Limitation of Liability. SUN AND ITS LICENSORS SHALL NOT BE LIABLE FOR ANY DAMAGES SUFFERED BY LICENSEE OR ANY THIRD PARTY AS A RESULT OF USING OR DISTRIBUTING SOFTWARE. IN NO EVENT WILL SUN OR ITS LICENSORS BE LIABLE FOR ANY LOST REVENUE, PROFIT OR DATA, OR FOR DIRECT, INDIRECT, SPECIAL, CONSEQUENTIAL, INCIDENTAL OR PUNITIVE DAMAGES, HOWEVER CAUSED AND REGARDLESS OF THE THEORY OF LIABILITY, ARISING OUT OF THE USE OF OR INABILITY TO USE SOFT-WARE, EVEN IF SUN HAS BEEN ADVISED OF THE POSSIBILITY OF SUCH DAMAGES.

7. Termination. Licensee may terminate this License at any time by destroying all copies of Software. This License will terminate immediately without notice from Sun if Licensee fails to comply with any provision of this License. Upon such termination, Licensee must destroy all copies of Software.

8. Export Regulations. Software, including technical data, is subject to U.S. export control laws, including the U.S. Export Administration Act and its associated regulations, and may be subject to export or import regulations in other countries. Licensee agrees to comply strictly with all such regulations and acknowledges that it has the respon-sibility to obtain licenses to export, re-export, or import Software. Software may not be downloaded, or otherwise exported or re-exported (i) into, or to a national or resident of, Cuba, Iraq, Iran, North Korea, Libya, Sudan, Syria, or any country to which the U.S. has embargoed goods; or (ii) to anyone on the U.S. Treasury Department's list of Specially Designated Nations or the U.S. Commerce Department's Table of Denial Orders.

9. Restricted Rights. Use, duplication, or disclosure by the United States government is subject to the restrictions as set forth in the Rights in Technical Data and Computer Software Clauses in DFARS 252.227-7013(c) (1) (ii) and FAR 52.227-19(c) (2) as applicable.

10. Governing Law. Any action related to this License will be governed by California law and controlling U.S. fed-eral law. No choice of law rules of any jurisdiction will apply.

11. Severability. If any of the above provisions are held to be in violation of applicable law, void, or unenforceable in any jurisdiction, then such provisions are herewith waived to the extent necessary for the License to be otherwise enforceable in such jurisdiction. However, if in Sun's opinion deletion of any provisions of the License by operation of this paragraph unreasonably compromises the rights or increase the liabilities of Sun or its licensors, Sun reserves the right to terminate the License and refund the fee paid by Licensee, if any, as Licensee's sole and exclusive remedy.

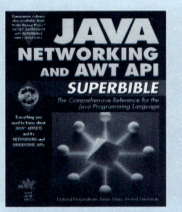

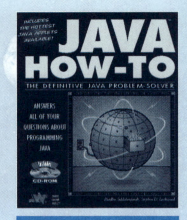

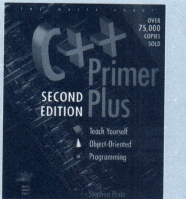

LIMITED WARRANTY

The following warranties shall be effective for 90 days from the date of purchase: (i) The Waite Group, Inc. warrants the enclosed disk to be free of defects in materials and workmanship under normal use; and (ii) The Waite Group, Inc. warrants that the programs, unless modified by the purchaser, will substantially perform the functions described in the documentation provided by The Waite Group, Inc. when operated on the designated hardware and operating system. The Waite Group, Inc. does not warrant that the programs will meet purchaser's requirements or that operation of a program will be uninterrupted or error-free. The program warranty does not cover any program that has been altered or changed in any way by anyone other than The Waite Group, Inc. The Waite Group, Inc. is not responsible for problems caused by changes in the operating characteristics of computer hardware or computer operating systems that are made after the release of the programs, nor for problems in the interaction of the programs with each other or other software.

THESE WARRANTIES ARE EXCLUSIVE AND IN LIEU OF ALL OTHER WARRANTIES OF MERCHANTABILITY OR FITNESS FOR A PARTICULAR PURPOSE OR OF ANY OTHER WARRANTY, WHETHER EXPRESS OR IMPLIED.

EXCLUSIVE REMEDY

The Waite Group, Inc. will replace any defective disk without charge if the defective disk is returned to The Waite Group, Inc. within 90 days from date of purchase.

This is Purchaser's sole and exclusive remedy for any breach of warranty or claim for contract, tort, or damages.

LIMITATION OF LIABILITY

THE WAITE GROUP, INC. AND THE AUTHORS OF THE PROGRAMS SHALL NOT IN ANY CASE BE LIABLE FOR SPECIAL, INCIDENTAL, CONSEQUENTIAL, INDIRECT, OR OTHER SIMILAR DAMAGES ARISING FROM ANY BREACH OF THESE WARRANTIES EVEN IF THE WAITE GROUP, INC. OR ITS AGENT HAS BEEN ADVISED OF THE POSSIBILITY OF SUCH DAMAGES.

THE LIABILITY FOR DAMAGES OF THE WAITE GROUP, INC. AND THE AUTHORS OF THE PROGRAMS UNDER THIS AGREEMENT SHALL IN NO EVENT EXCEED THE PURCHASE PRICE PAID.

COMPLETE AGREEMENT

This Agreement constitutes the complete agreement between The Waite Group, Inc. and the authors of the programs, and you, the purchaser.

Some states do not allow the exclusion or limitation of implied warranties or liability for incidental or consequential damages, so the above exclusions or limitations may not apply to you. This limited warranty gives you specific legal rights; you may have others, which vary from state to state.

How to Get Even More from Oracle Technology.

Apply for your free subscription to the *Oracle Alliance Journal.*

Sign Up Now!
Online: http://alliance.oracle.com
Fax: (415) 506-7255

ORACLE®

ALLIANCE

THE JOURNAL FOR ORACLE SOLUTIONS

MACMILLAN COMPUTER PUBLISHING USA

A VIACOM COMPANY

Technical Support:

If you cannot get the CD/Disk to install properly, or you need assistance with a particular situation in the book, please feel free to check out the Knowledge Base on our Web site at **http://www.superlibrary.com/general/support**. We have answers to our most Frequently Asked Questions listed there. If you do not find your specific question answered, please contact Macmillan Technical Support at **(317) 581-3833**. We can also be reached by email at **support@mcp.com**.

SATISFACTION REPORT CARD

Please fill out this card if you wish to know of future updates to *Object-Oriented Programming in Java*, or to receive our catalog.

First Name: _____ Last Name: _____

Street Address: _____

City: _____ State: _____ Zip: _____

Email Address _____

Daytime Telephone: (_____) _____

Date product was acquired: Month _____ Day _____ Year _____ Your Occupation: _____

Overall, how would you rate *Object-Oriented Programming in Java*?

☐ Excellent ☐ Very Good ☐ Good
☐ Fair ☐ Below Average ☐ Poor

What did you like MOST about this book? _____

_____

_____

What did you like LEAST about this book? _____

_____

_____

Please describe any problems you may have encountered with installing or using the disk: _____

_____

How did you use this book (problem-solver, tutorial, reference...)?

_____

What is your level of computer expertise?

☐ New ☐ Dabbler ☐ Hacker
☐ Power User ☐ Programmer ☐ Experienced Professional

What computer languages are you familiar with? _____

_____

Please describe your computer hardware:

Computer _____ Hard disk _____

5.25" disk drives _____ 3.5" disk drives _____

Video card _____ Monitor _____

Printer _____ Peripherals _____

Sound Board _____ CD-ROM _____

Where did you buy this book?

☐ Bookstore (name): _____
☐ Discount store (name): _____
☐ Computer store (name): _____
☐ Catalog (name): _____
☐ Direct from WGP ☐ Other _____

What price did you pay for this book? _____

What influenced your purchase of this book?

☐ Recommendation ☐ Advertisement
☐ Magazine review ☐ Store display
☐ Mailing ☐ Book's format
☐ Reputation of Waite Group Press ☐ Other

How many computer books do you buy each year? _____

How many other Waite Group books do you own? _____

What is your favorite Waite Group book? _____

_____

Is there any program or subject you would like to see Waite Group Press cover in a similar approach? _____

_____

Additional comments? _____

_____

_____

Please send to: Waite Group Press
200 Tamal Plaza
Corte Madera, CA 94925

☐ **Check here for a free Waite Group catalog**

SATISFACTION CARD

STOP!

BEFORE YOU OPEN THE DISK OR CD-ROM PACKAGE ON THE FACING PAGE, CAREFULLY READ THE LICENSE AGREEMENT.

Opening this package indicates that you agree to abide by the license agreement found in the back of this book. If you do not agree with it, promptly return the unopened disk package (including the related book) to the place you obtained them for a refund.

Use of this software is subject to the Binary Code License terms and conditions on pages 956 and 957. Read the license carefully. By opening this package, you are agreeing to be bound by the terms and conditions of this license from Sun Microsystems, Inc.